THE
WOODEN
HORSE

THE
WOODEN
HORSE

THE LIBERATION OF
THE WESTERN MIND
FROM
ODYSSEUS TO SOCRATES

KELD ZERUNEITH

TRANSLATED FROM THE DANISH BY
RUSSELL L. DEES

EDITED BY
W. GLYN JONES

OVERLOOK DUCKWORTH
NEW YORK · WOODSTOCK · LONDON

First published in the United States in 2007 by
Overlook Duckworth, Peter Mayer Publishers, Inc.
New York, Woodstock & London

NEW YORK:
The Overlook Press
141 Wooster Street
New York, NY 10012

WOODSTOCK:
The Overlook Press
One Overlook Drive
Woodstock, NY 12498
www.overlookpress.com
[for individual orders, bulk and special sales, contact our Woodstock office]

LONDON:
Duckworth
90-93 Cowcross Street
London EC1M 6BF
inquiries@duckworth-publishers. co.uk
www.ducknet.co.uk

This translation was financed by the Lilian and Dan Finks Foundation,
part of the Royal Danish Academy of Sciences and Letters.

Cataloging-in-Publication Data is available from the Library of Congress

Book design and type formatting by Bernard Schleifer
Manufactured in the United States of America
ISBN 978-1-58567-818-1 (h/c)
ISBN 978-1-59020-041-4 (US pb)
ISBN 978-1-7156-3731-9 (UK pb)
10 9 8 7 6 5 4 3 2 1

TO MY DAUGHTERS

CONTENTS

PART TWO: SOCRATES

ACKNOWLEDGMENTS

It would not have been possible to realize such a large and, dare I say, demanding project as writing *The Wooden Horse* without the support and critical assessment of those around me.

I would like to thank my Danish publisher Gyldendal, which backed the project from the beginning—especially my editor Birthe Melgaard who pushed the project forward with relentless, teasing and inspiring tenacity.

I am grateful to the Lilian and Dan Finks Foundation, part of the Royal Danish Academy of Sciences and Letters, for financial support for the translation—and to the Etatsraad Georg Bestle og hustrus Mindelegat, Politiken-Fonden, Højesteretssagfører Davids Legat for Slægt og Venner, Overretssagfører L. Zeuthens Mindelegat for additional financial support.

The efforts and enthusiasm of the book's translator, Russell L. Dees, have been a sine qua non. I cannot thank him enough. The same sincere thanks are due to Professor W. Glyn Jones for editorial revisions carried out with an unfailing sense of style.

In connection with the translation, Dr. Mogens Herman Hansen has been a generous sparring partner who has done his best to foster precision in certain passages in the Danish text that may have needed a little more nuance. Thank you.

I would like to thank the classical philologist Clara Elisabet Bryld who took on the difficult job of reading through the manuscript at a point when it was not entirely finished. She has corrected factual errors and provided an invaluable give and take in the formulation of my language. Anything that may be lacking is my own responsibility. Here, as well!

A special thanks to the author Judith Thurman for advice and moral support.

I reserve my greatest thanks for my wife, Suzanne, who every day for the last ten years has had to put up with Greek, misgivings and the grinding of teeth. She has been my interlocutor with a patience and passion that would be incomprehensible if she were not the person she is.

The book is dedicated to my daughters in the hope that they will in time find some of the same joy in Greek poetry and philosophy as I have experienced and that the book will be of some small assistance to them along their way. At all events, there is no spiritual heritage I would rather pass on to them—or to anyone else, since it is to a great extent through Greek culture that we have become Europeans.

TRANSLATOR'S NOTE

All quotations from the *Iliad* and the *Odyssey* are taken from Richmond Lattimore's translation of the same. The English spelling of ancient Greek names has proved to be a challenge in the translation of this text. Modern translators of Homer tend to follow Lattimore's practice of a more direct transliteration of names. Therefore, I have generally followed Lattimore's transliteration of the Greek names throughout "Part One: Odysseus." However, this practice has not been followed—or consistently followed—with respect to modern English translations of the poets and philosophers dealt with in "Part Two: Socrates." Consequently, in the latter half of this book, I follow the practice of modern translators of those works in using a more Anglicized spelling of the names. This may result in an occasional inconsistent spelling of the same name in the two halves of this book, but I believe this is peferable to the more jarring inconsisencies that would arise from the application of a strictly uniform rule. References to lines in the *Iliad* are in *Roman* and lines in the *Odyssey* in *Arabic* numerals.

FOREWORD

1

IT TOOK TEN YEARS TO TAKE TROY AND TEN YEARS FOR ODYSSEUS TO RETURN home, and it has taken ten years for me to write *The Wooden Horse*. Actually, it has taken me slightly less than a generation. Even in my school days, I read Otto Gelsted's prose translation of the *Iliad* and the *Odyssey* and became so captivated by the world it opened up that I became a student of classical languages. Later, I was also fortunate enough to study ancient Greek with one of the most important classical scholars of the day, Leo Hjortsø. He whetted my appetite for Greek poetry and philosophy. Thus, in conjunction with work on my 1970 master's thesis, it was natural for me to write a more expanded dissertation entitled "The Odyssey Motif in Homer, Virgil, Dante and Joyce."

At that time, it was my intention to investigate how it came about that our culture seems to take Odysseus and his journey as its primary myth. Through this theme, our greatest literary works—Virgil's *Aeneid*, Dante's *Divine Comedy* and James Joyce's *Ulysses*—seek to gather the entire knowledge and linguistic expression of their time. These works represent a psychological progression from Homer's epic description of his world to Dante's journey through the realms of the dead, which is both a work of imagination and an inner voyage, to Joyce's phenomenological, introspective stream of consciousness in a secularized Dublin universe of universal dimensions.

Even while I was at grammar school, classical culture was dubbed ancient rubbish, and nobody could understand why you would waste your time on something that had gathered so much dust! My teachers could apparently not conceptualize—much less legitimize the fact that for each generation it is almost a matter of life and death to preserve its historical heritage, to give it its own explanation as a part of the historical process and a continual formation of consciousness.

2

My intention with this project is to analyze and characterize the features of the origin and development of consciousness that first finds expression in a significant form in Homer's two epics. That is to say the book did not only arise from a personal fascination with and admiration for the fact that such aesthetically fully rounded works as the *Iliad* and the *Odyssey* could emerge from a past that linguistically speaking is almost unknown. It is also written from a conviction that it is necessary to acquire a deeper understanding of the past, of an epoch in which historical awareness was in the process of development. The necessity resides in determining the preconditions upon which we have been created and which we must constantly interpret anew, to understand not only the past but also ourselves. Put in the strongest terms, we might even say that we only have a future as long as we are able to see ourselves in the mirror of history.

By analyzing our embryonic Western civilisation and the almost tropical maturation over the three or four hundred years—from approximately 750 to 350 B.C.—during which it crystallises, we can determine our place in this historical sequence. We can see ourselves as historical individuals, despite all technical advances and scientific achievements—and see that we have not changed to any significant extent.

From the much broader perspective constituting the history of humanity, we must acknowledge that in a civilizational sense we find ourselves at the beginning rather than at the end. The few millennia during which our Western civilization has been in existence have changed very little in our genetic and psychological make-up, which goes back a hundred thousand years to the first homo sapiens. This makes comprehensible what is otherwise incomprehensible—for example, human conduct in war and conflict between the sexes, in which atavistic forms of behavior reveal that no great change has taken place. Mankind as mankind has not kept up. Anthropologically speaking, we live in a global world in which, despite television, computers and newspapers, many societies—and for that matter, what might be termed present-day mankind—have values and norms properly speaking more in line with Homer's world of blood feuds and its ideals of honor and prestige. From the structures of consciousness mapped out in *The Wooden Horse*, it is possible so to speak to ascertain where and why, in terms of consciousness, we now find ourselves individually and collectively.

3

A preoccupation with antiquity, therefore, is not merely a matter for philologists and archaeologists. It is also a matter of keen general and personal interest. No other writing or thinking offers such deep, qualified observational material, since the works from that period arose during the genesis of civilization and were themselves part of it, expressing and contributing to this development.

I have no desire to "blur" my analysis by introducing contemporary parallels, despite the temptation. However, it is my hope that the reader will also be able to use the book to make such parallels. For me, at any rate, the investigation has provided the basis for an overall reflection on the formation of consciousness that started some three thousand years ago and whose insights we are only beginning to understand and use for (self-) insight, and whose potential for conflict we only thereby have the possibility of resolving.

What is incredible about Greek writing and philosophy is that we are able to follow these human experiences in their genesis, to determine their character and to see how they still shape us. This is moreover an observation on the basis of which we can make assumptions concerning those times that came before and explain the process of civilization, not only as a benefit but also noting the risks and the unconscious processes relating to it. Indeed, even the utopias for a new world order that lie more or less hidden among Greek writers and thinkers from Homer to Plato contain perspectives for the future that have still not been redeemed today. On the contrary.

It is significant in this context that over this period of about three hundred years Greek literature and philosophy "invent" all the genres that have been used later: the epic (the verse story that later becomes the novel), subjective poetry, tragedy and the dialogue form of philosophical thought. These genres arise successively as evidence that they are not merely formalities as people are often inclined to believe, but arise from an existential and socio-political need to find answers to ever new forms of experience. Moreover, as will later be shown, a repertoire of narrative techniques develops that more or less embraces all the aesthetic forms of communication that later find expression in literature.

In this sense, *The Wooden Horse* is a sort of counter argument to the postmodern claim that the "great" story is a thing of the past. As the study shows, we are not merely products of a historical process, but struggle with exactly the same problems as did the Greeks. And to the extent to which we forget or deny this fact, the fundamental psychological conditions and narratives become lost to our consciousness, which is why we constantly have to look at ourselves in the light of the content of this great narrative and its consequences in order not to be its victims.

4

In my reading of the primary sources, I have tried to penetrate as deeply as I can into the mode of thinking in Greek writing. This study is fundamentally different from other works on antiquity with which I am familiar. These books, as a rule, are limited to a single work, an author or a theme. More comprehensive studies use a method in which generalizations are established through a high degree of abstraction without real textual analysis, which is why we may question their factual foundation in experience and lack any real possibility for verifying the claims and assessments proffered.

So my aim has on the contrary been to interpret the central themes on the basis of textual analysis, so that they emerge as concrete interpretations of experience— whether myth, poetry or philosophy. For insofar as the analysis is based on empirical data from the texts and not on general abstractions, I make plentiful use of quotations from the sources. This also means that the paradigmatic pattern that is gradually revealed behind the formation of consciousness is not presented as abstract categories but will be presented on a continuous basis and relating to concrete analyses.

Since the book deals with an overall theme and its variations, I have to a certain extent—in order to establish and clarify the process and overall structure—made use of summary repetitions and cross-references—with a view to fixing the reader's memory of the character of the themes and in order to show the variations they constantly undergo.

However, even though the book is conceived as a whole, the idea has been that it should be possible for the main sections to be read separately. It is hoped that the reader will get an impression of the philosophers, tragedy as a genre, the individual tragedians, and Homer, Hesiod and Socrates. And the many quotations should be able to provide a good sense of the works, so that the book as a whole can act as a sort of anthology that, in combination with the analyses, can provide a first-hand insight into the most significant Greek writers and philosophers.

5

I have benefited from the many excellent studies listed in the bibliography. However, since the work as such is based on my own analytic strategy of comparing individual works in a broader context, I only occasionally engage in critical dialogue with other scholars. In the notes, which are limited as much as possible, references are provided for my factual knowledge.

In my use of the work of other scholars, I have not confined myself to the most recent works but have also incorporated research from the first half of the last century, linked with names such as Gilbert Murray and Jane E. Harrison. I also make use of various aspects of depth and individual psychology. These theories may be uncertain by modern scientific yardsticks. Nevertheless, they have proved to be useful and, in many instances, opened up a path to knowledge that is not (any longer) accessible to modern research. I have proceeded on the basis of what has been eye-opening and verifiable (or, at least, probable) from the texts. And if I may be allowed to cite E. R. Dodds' words explaining his use of the same type of research: "*If we are trying to reach some understanding of Greek minds, and are not content with describing external behaviour or drawing up a list of recorded 'beliefs', we must work by what light we can get, and an uncertain light is better than none*" (Preface to *The Greeks and the Irrational*, p. viii).

The selection of texts is large. This is the precondition for documenting the validity of the study's overall themes and their transformations. However, it is in the nature of things that it cannot be exhaustive. I have had to use some discretion in selecting works and authors that are not only significant but also essential to my views. The most important omission is the great poet Pindar, who would have required a volume to himself—indeed, Michael Theunissen has just published a work, *Pindar: Menschenlos und Wende der Zeit*, over a thousand pages long. It is also obvious that not all texts have been read equally deeply. Here, too, I have selected texts for their intrinsic importance and their importance for my project.

6

In consideration of the scope of the project, let me sketch out its structure and some key features. The book falls into two parts: 1) "Odysseus" and 2) "Socrates." However, the chapters are sequentially numbered to emphasize that there is a comprehensive conceptual sequence in ever changing forms.

In the first part, Homer's poetic works are analyzed with the focus on Odysseus. The *Iliad* certainly deals with a dispute over a girl that breaks out between Agamemnon and Achilleus after ten years spent besieging Troy. Achilleus withdraws from battle and the Greeks come close to defeat. When Achilleus re-enters the strife—after the death of his friend Patroklos—he kills the pre-eminent hero of the Trojans, Hektor. However, he faces his own imminent death, after which Odysseus takes Troy with the help of the Wooden Horse.

This last event, which the *Iliad* leads up to and which is mentioned in the *Odyssey*, is the starting point for this study (Ch. I). My assertion is that the invention of the Wooden Horse constitutes a divide in the history of European civilization and consciousness. For the first time, we witness a human being thinking discursively—that is to say, separating action from awareness, internal and external, which until then had been a unity.

Homer's two epics are viewed as a single, unified work, while Homer himself is analyzed as a metaphor for the narrative structure (Ch. II). His guiding utopia stretches throughout both works: to achieve a lasting peace, which in a contemporary perspective corresponds to the social order or *eunomia* for which Solon becomes the spokesman (Ch. IX).

In addition, Homer intends to replace the original cult of fertility goddesses, linked to the earth and the realm of the dead, with the divine patriarchal rule of Olympus, which he more or less invents (Ch. III). The Trojan War itself is seen as a paradigm of the fundamental experience of the Greeks—that development presupposes and takes place through an unbroken rotation of strife and *eros* (Ch. IV). The philosopher Empedocles later puts this dialectic into a philosophical system.

The precondition for realizing Homer's utopia of a peaceful world order is for his hero Odysseus to prove himself in the trials that await him on his ten-year voyage home. We are given a detailed outline of his psychological character (Ch. VI). All the monsters of the voyage home emerge as deadly forces from the revolt against the mother that is a hidden theme in Homer's texts. The process of cultural development and increasing awareness presupposes that the hero liberates himself from the maternal bond as son and lover; at the same time, in her thirst for vengeance this mother, once so caring, is transformed into a destructive force in the shape of wild animals, such as boars or bears that seek to take the life of the rebellious son.

Thus, the maternal bond is the primary theme in the *Telemachy* (Ch.V) in which Telemachos' paralysis derives from his bond to his mother. His voyage away from her—to seek information on the fate of his father—describes his liberation and maturity, so that he can meet his father—and the father in himself—as an equal and take his place as his heir.

During the adventures on his voyage, Odysseus integrates the demonic, primeval maternal reality (Ch. VII) from which he freed himself as a young man. He can now return home as a more whole human being than when he left, a process that is consistently connected to death and rebirth. His final trial consists of regaining his kingdom, Ithaka, by slaying the arrogant suitors (Ch. VIII). After this, he is reunited with his wife, so they can stand together as guarantors of the new social order which will replace war and blood vengeance. Thus ends the heroic age and, at the same time, the epic has served its role as a form of cognition.

In the second main section, the whole set of problems raised in Homer is developed further—in new genres. As the first poet of whose biography we know anything, Hesiod (Ch. XI) is viewed as a transitional figure from Homer to later writing, philosophy, religiosity and science. In this connection, he unveils a misogyny that is the first but definitely not the last tangible expression of the fact that the male and, later, democracy are established on the basis of an explicit fear and oppression of women.

The individuality that the Odysseus figure partly represents is fully established in the first subject-oriented poets: Archilochus and Sappho, who each in their own way put their personal passions at the center of poetry (Ch. XII). Alongside them, the first philosophers emerge (Ch. XIII) who on the contrary seek to explain the origin, substance and impetus of the world on the basis of objective observations. Against this background, several of them (Xenophanes and Heraclitus) criticize the divine worlds of Homer and Hesiod as human projections. The key figure in this section is Heraclitus, while Parmenides is characterized as the philosopher of pure logic, who forms the transition to Plato's idealism.

In the section on the origin of tragedy (Ch. XIV), this genre is defined as an existential necessity. Myths are revived and used now to formulate the relationship between the individual subject and the gods in order to establish a basis for life in and an understanding of Athenian democracy, since tragedy is exclusively bound to Athens in the time of the city's greatness.

There are clear differences between the three great tragedians: Aeschylus, Sophocles and Euripides (Chs. XV-XVIII). In his trilogies, Aeschylus develops tragedy from its primeval form, since, as the poet of reconciliation in the *Oresteia*, he shows how the history of human development is based on a shift from a maternal right to blood revenge to a patriarchal legal system. Sophocles crystallizes tragedy around points of conflict in which human powerlessness (and elevation) in the face of the plans of the gods emerges. Contemporary political unrest (the war against Sparta) and philosophical relativism (the Sophists) are reflected in Euripides' tragedies. Human passions stand alone, faith in the gods is shaken, but behind his skepticism is Euripides' longing for a truer reality.

The study ends by showing that, in Plato's description of Socrates, we find the answer that Euripides and the crisis of the times sought (Ch. XVIII). Socrates attributes the highest value to the inner being. And Plato's utopia reflects Socrates' desire to convert his doctrine of the soul into a new form of state. Here, women would have equal status with men, which they did not have in the Athens of the day, as demonstrated, *inter alia*, in Aristophanes' comedies. My presentation ends with Socrates, because, with him, the psychic life of the soul has completely differentiated itself from the world of the body in an erotic (*eros*) quest for higher insight.

The Wooden Horse is the first mythic evidence of this development.

7

The expression "Trojan horse" does not appear in Homer, who calls it the "wooden horse"—or a "horse made of wood" (*ho hippos duorateos*, 8, 492; 512 with the adjective *mega*). The term "Trojan Horse" was apparently first used by two Latin dramatists Livius Andronicus and Naevius at the end of the 3rd century B.C., when both are supposed to have written a tragedy entitled *Equos Troianus*. The device has generally been known in English as the Trojan Horse, ever since the introduction of the term in 1574 by R. Bristow. In the course of my analysis, however, I will consistently make use of Homer's own formulation: the Wooden Horse.

PART ONE
ODYSSEUS

I

THE WOODEN HORSE—
THE MYTH OF DISCURSIVITY

1

JUST AS ODYSSEUS WAS HIDDEN INSIDE THE WOODEN HORSE, SO HOMER HAS hidden a single verse in the *Iliad* in which he in a way undermines the heroic world of war he apparently admires and praises. There is a point at which, as the Greeks are on the defensive, he has Zeus say that Troy will fall "through the designs (*boule*) of Athene" (XV, 71), a reference to the Wooden Horse. This is an indirect indication that the army's struggle over the previous ten years has been a waste of time. There has been no progress and, therefore, the Greeks are thinking of returning home empty-handed. It is only with the greatest difficulty that they are held back by Odysseus. The secret, which is never uttered, is that the city cannot be conquered by conventional heroic courage and physical strength, only by the power of the intellect.

Thus, the center of gravity has already moved from the reality of the *Iliad* to the *Odyssey*, from Achilleus' physical strength and courage—the codex of heroism that he, if anyone, personifies—to Odysseus' intellectual abilities. Odysseus certainly possesses the classical heroic virtues, but in a more ambiguous way, since despite his heroic make-up, he is particularly distinguished by his good sense and craftiness, an ability for which he is often mocked—"master of deceit (*dolos*) and guile and vulgar profit" (IV, 339), as an incensed Agamemnon says. Nevertheless, it is precisely by virtue of his intelligence, inventiveness and craftiness (*metis*) that Athene's plan may be realized and Troy can, at last, be taken—by the Wooden Horse.[1]

2

The myth[2] of the Wooden Horse, which, as Odysseus' invention, becomes the embodiment of his special intellectual abilities, is only partially accessible in the *Odyssey*. Additional information must be pieced together from other sources. In particular, I rely on Quintus Smyrnaeus' hexameters on the fall of Troy from the fourth century A.D.—not because of their great poetic quality but because, on what is in effect an abstract level, he expresses the deeper meaning of the myth of the Wooden Horse.

As Smyrnaeus tells the story, Kalchas, a soothsayer with the Greek army, has passed on an omen to the assembled leaders of the army: A falcon was pursuing a dove, which, hard pressed, took shelter in the crevice of a cliff. The falcon attacked furiously but in vain and therefore hid in some bushes, after which it could kill the unsuspecting dove when it dared to come out again. The soothsayer's interpretation is quite straightforward: We cannot take Troy by force but only by strategy and guile.[3] He uses the Greek word *bia* for physical strength and *metis* for intelligence and ingenuity. As we shall see, these two concepts cannot only be applied to Achilleus and Odysseus respectively, but also characterize the difference between the *Iliad* and the *Odyssey*, entailing a development in the complexity of human consciousness, which the *Odyssey* represents through its protagonist.

In reality, Odysseus has this potential even in the *Iliad* and in more or less open contrast to its protagonist, Achilleus. Because of the *Iliad*'s heroic predispositions, Odysseus is considered suspect for his disquieting intelligence. Not only is he called a "master of deceit" (IV, 339) but he is indirectly characterized by Achilleus as a person not to be trusted. "For as I detest the doorways of Death, I / detest that man, who hides one thing in the depths of his heart, and speaks forth another" (IX, 312-13), he says of Agamemnon, whose gifts of atonement he believes exclusively serve Agamemnon's own interests. Yet, as is apparent from the frosty reception Achilleus gives Odysseus during the embassy scene in Book IX, the statement applies just as much to him in his attempt to persuade Achilleus to return to the war. Later, however, Odysseus puts Achilleus in his place referring to the fact that, while Achilleus is certainly his physical superior, he is inferior to him in both age and experience (see quotation on page 50).

In addition, this is evidence of Odysseus' astuteness—and reveals at the same time the correlation between the two works, as even in the *Iliad* Odysseus is graced with the epithet "sacker of cities" (*ptoliporthos*, II, 278), which he gained by crushing Troy with the help of the Wooden Horse. That he, not Achilleus, became the destroyer of the city is ostensibly due to the fact that the Greeks were ultimately victorious as a result of his *metis*. It is through him that Athene's plan is brought to fruition. So in view of the virtually psychic identity existing between the goddess and her protégé, neither is it surprising that, during his later struggle with the suitors, she inspires him by making reference to the fact that it was by his "plan" (*boule*, 22, 230) that Priam's proud capital should be destroyed. Once again, the word *boule* is used, thereby creating a context and identification in the inner lines running through the *Iliad* and the *Odyssey*.

3

In Smyrnaeus, it is also Odysseus who, in an immediate extension of the soothsayer's interpretation of the omen, conceives the plan for the Wooden Horse. That the internal tension with the bankrupt heroic world, symbolized by the death of Achilleus, is not entirely a thing of the past is highlighted by the fact that his son Neoptolemos, together with Philoktetes, who cannot abide Odysseus, rejects the stratagem of the Wooden Horse with the words: "True heroes meet their enemies face to face with sword in hand."[4] However, Nestor persuades them to go along and crawl inside the horse. With this, the heroic age is fundamentally a thing of the past.

In this sense, the Wooden Horse becomes, in short, the culmination of a chain reaction of events leading not only to the fall of Troy but to the end of the heroic code itself. Not only does Odysseus inherit the arms of the fallen Achilleus as a sign that the power that once belonged to the great hero has passed to his successor— no, with his *metis* he has stepped into the position Achilleus once held in all his glory before falling without result.

With Apollodoros (circa 180 B.C.) as the primary source,[5] the events that occur prior to the Wooden Horse and likewise belong to the myth of the fall of Troy may be summarized in the following way: Kalchas prophesied that the city could only be taken with Herakles' bow, which the older hero himself had made. This required, first of all, that Philoktetes, who had been given the bow in gratitude for lighting Herakles' funeral pyre, should be brought back from Lemnos. Odysseus had left him there on the way to Troy because of his putrid wounds, the result of which was his hatred for Odysseus. Nevertheless, Odysseus together with Diomedes— in Sophocles' tragedy *Philoktetes* with Neoptolemos—fetches him back. Philoktetes is cured and brings down Prince Paris, who has shot Achilleus in his vulnerable Achilles' heel.

Secondly, Kalchas proclaims that the Trojans' prophet, Priam's son Helenos, must be taken prisoner and forced to reveal how Troy can be conquered. Odysseus also takes on this task and he persuades him to speak the truth: 1) that Pelops' skeleton (shoulder blade) is to be brought from the Peloponnesus. 2) Neoptolemos is to join the army. Odysseus brings him back from the island of Skyros, as he himself mentions in the *Odyssey*. 3) Athene's image, the so-called Palladium, which protects Troy, is to be taken out of the city. Odysseus does this by sneaking in, helped by Helen among others. 4) The walls of Troy are to be brought down. This is achieved by means of the Wooden Horse. Thus Odysseus is the driving force behind everything and with his initiative he monopolizes the course of the war to its bitter end.

4

The design of the Wooden Horse itself was the responsibility of the architect Epeios, prompted by Odysseus. In a dream Athene promises him on one occasion to assist him.[6] First, the feet are created, then the abdomen, until a colossus is raised "tall as a hill,"[7] as Virgil describes it in the *Aeneid*. According to several ancient illustrations, the horse has a flowing mane and wheels beneath its feet. It is made from planks of pine, brought from the nearby Mount Ida, and is hollow on the inside so as to contain warriors and provided with an opening at the side or a trapdoor in the belly, which it was Odysseus' job to open and close. In some versions, a rope ladder leads up to the trapdoor, although in one ancient illustration the heroes are seen climbing up on one another's shoulders.

The number of warriors varies from source to source. Homer speaks of a multitude and mentions five names (IV, 285). Others make the number twenty-three, thirty or fifty, while the epic cycle, the *Little Iliad* (*Ilias Mikra*), makes it no less than three thousand men. Among those listed in addition to the leader Odysseus were: Menelaos, Diomedes, Neoptolemos and the timorous architect of the horse, Epeios, who was the last in and pulled up the ladder.

On the horse's flank was printed an inscription in large letters: "The Greeks dedicate this offering of gratitude to Athene to ensure their safe voyage home."[8] To bolster the Trojans' faith in the illusion even more, the rest of the Greek army break camp after burning their tents. However, they hide their ships behind the nearby island of Tenedos under the command of Agamemnon but on the orders of Odysseus. For the Trojans, the question is now how to interpret and deal with the Wooden Horse, which they regard with awesome wonder. Homer relates that the assembly was divided into three: "Either to take the pitiless bronze to it and hack open the hollow/ horse, or drag it to the cliffs' edge and topple it over,/ or let it stand where it was a dedication to blandish/ the gods (. . .)" (8, 507-09)

The prophet and priest of Apollo, Laokoon, wants to burn the horse. He knows Odysseus and does not believe that the Greeks make gifts. Either warriors are hiding within it or it must be some sort of machine to smash the protective city walls, he claims, and, as Virgil describes it, casts his spear into its belly: "and the rounded hull/ Reverberated groaning at the blow."[9] But when Apollo (in Smyrnaeus, Athene) allows two serpents to coil around Laokoon and his two small sons and kill them (in some versions, it is only the sons), this is interpreted as an omen that he was mistaken and is now being punished by the gods.

The prophetic princess Kassandra has also foreseen the fate of her city and knows that the horse is filled with warriors.[10] Smyrnaeus describes how, like a roaring lioness, she attacks the horse with a torch in one hand and a double-headed axe in the other; but, from fear of retribution by the gods, the Trojans take these weapons from her.[11] Their purpose is to be reconciled with the gods. So they create a great breach in the walls of the city through which the Wooden Horse is to be pulled by means of ropes tied around its neck. But the horse is so huge that three times it strikes against the gate; the rattling of weapons is heard each time, though the doomed Trojans take no notice.

Inside the Wooden Horse, the warriors are waiting to reveal themselves. Helen, with her new husband Deiphobos, walks around the horse three times, patting his flanks, and in a distorted and enchanted voice imitating the voices of their wives. Calling each warrior by name, she arouses their desire. They all have difficulty controlling themselves and want to leap out or respond—"but Odysseus pulled us back and held us, for all our eagerness" (4, 284), in the words of Menelaos to Telemachos during the latter's visit to Sparta. Antiklos, however, cannot master his impulses; but Odysseus blocks his mouth with both hands—others claim he strangles him.

The Trojans are also fooled by the Greek warrior, Sinon, an episode not mentioned by Homer. As a part of the overall plan, he has allowed himself to be taken prisoner and makes the enemy believe on the one hand that the Greek fleet has sailed home, tired of this miserable war, and on the other that he himself has fled because Odysseus intended to sacrifice him to Apollo as atonement for Agamemnon's sacrificing his daughter Iphigenia on the way to Troy. In Smyrnaeus, he is tortured but reveals nothing.[12] He is released and, under the cover of darkness, creeps up on to Achilleus' burial mound and lights the signal fire for the Greek army.

While the ships are returning to Troy in the moonlight, the seventh moon of the tenth year, the Greek warriors steal out of the Wooden Horse. First is Echion, who falls and breaks his neck. The last to leave the inside of the horse is Epeios, timid to the end. One group makes for the city gate and opens it for the army. Accompanied by Odysseus, Menelaos immediately runs to Helen and kills her husband. Menelaos had also sworn that he would kill his unfaithful wife, but at the sight of her naked breasts, he casts aside his sword and is once again prey to her alluring power[13] (see p. 155). Troy is then overrun, annihilated to the last man— only Aeneas escapes with a group of fugitives to become the founder of Rome.

5

The myth of the Wooden Horse is intended to explain how Troy fell and to shed light on the sequence of events between the *Iliad* and the *Odyssey*. Yet, the tale has another mythical meaning, which, as suggested, sheds light on the development of civilization as such. I will further explore this meaning in connection with Odysseus as a mythical figure.

It is clear that, with the invention of the Wooden Horse, he steps out of Achilleus' shadow in the *Iliad* and takes over his position of power. As mentioned, he inherits his arms, which, like a sceptre, symbolize power. In Odysseus, however, power becomes something different from what it has been before; for despite the fact that he himself is a courageous and physically strong warrior, it is not until the Wooden Horse that his true nature steps is revealed as he moves from being a warrior to becoming a strategist. In this role, he takes over command of the Greek army with all his abilities and eventually leads to victory.

In principle, the heroic age in which the *Iliad* is played out is thus over. The focus shifts to Odysseus and the trials he and his *metis* undergo as described in the *Odyssey*—the hardships of his voyage home and battle with the suitors who have taken his kingdom and his wife. In a wider context, the slaughter of the suitors is thus anticipated by the victory over the Trojans at Odysseus' initiative, and the Wooden Horse becomes an obvious prelude to the *Odyssey*.

That the Wooden Horse and the form of consciousness that lay behind its invention—*dolos* (guile) and *metis* (shrewdness)—represent a watershed in the formation of his identity emerges from the fact that in both Homeric epics he bears the epithet "sacker of cities" (*ptoliporthos*, II, 278; 9, 504). Indeed, he uses this epithet himself, when he identifies himself to the blinded Kyklops. If anyone asks who did this, the Kyklops is to answer: "Odysseus, sacker of cities (*ptoliporthos*)./ Laertes is his father, and he makes his home in Ithaka" (9, 504-05). In other words, he specifically refers to the event in his own life that above all else is the basis for what is most important to a hero—his reputation (*kleos*) and distinction (*time*).

Even though Odysseus does not specify this, he is thinking of exactly the same event, when he at last reveals his identity to the Phaiakians; he tells of his adventures: "I am Odysseus, son of Laertes, known before all men/ for the study of crafty designs (*dolos*), and my fame (*kleos*) goes up to the heavens" (9, 19-20). No, he does not hide his light beneath a bushel, well aware that this was a stroke of genius. Just before—and as a hidden transition/preparation for the identification—he has for the same reason asked the Phaiakian singer Demodokos to sing about the Wooden Horse, which causes him, weeping with emotion, to hide his face in the corner of his cloak.

6

So Odysseus' epithet as sacker of cities refers to the Wooden Horse and is an agnomen that, in combination with a number of other epithets, reveals his intellectual ability and unique consciousness. On the one hand there is an internal connection between these epithets, and on the other he does not share them with others. They characterize him and the peculiar nature of his psyche alone. In short, the epithets are not, as is so often assumed, merely—though they are partly—formal supports for the improvising singers in the oral tale tradition, from which the Homeric epics derive and of which, in terms of epic, they represent the culmination and conclusion. The epithets have a clear substantive meaning.

Later, in a more searching examination of Odysseus' phenomenology, we shall return to his agnomena. In this context, I will merely call attention to the one most frequently used—*polymetis*, which appears in the *Odyssey* alone no less than 66 times and is also used in the *Iliad*. Like many other Greek words and concepts, it is virtually untranslatable. Its approximate meaning is knowledgeable, wily, etc., while the prefix poly—many—emphasises the multiple nature of his intellect, ranging from the practical reason to the strategic inventiveness and insight he has to display in order to return safely home.

That these intellectual skills are now the future we see described—almost caricatured—in the *Odyssey*. An instance of this is when, in his blind rage (in which he is reminiscent of the heroes of the *Iliad*), the Kyklops, an exponent of brute force, fails to resist Odysseus' tactical maneuvers. In all his naiveté, the Kyklops, to whom it was prophesied that this would happen, was expecting an enemy of the same physical format as himself: "But always I was on the lookout for a man handsome/ and tall, with great endowment of strength on him, to come here;/ but now the end of it is that a little man, niddering, feeble,/ has taken away the sight of my eye" (9, 512-16).

The epithet *polymetis* is all the more meaningful, since through it Odysseus is directly connected to Athene, the daughter of the goddess of wisdom Metis, and Zeus, the most erudite of all gods. Through his *metis*, Odysseus becomes, so to speak, his earthly counterpart, when it is said that he is "the equal of Zeus in counsel (*metis*)" (II, 169). Therefore, Athene may use him as a go-between even in the *Iliad*; and when they see each other again in the *Odyssey* she almost identifies herself with him: "You are far the best of all mortal/ men for counsel (*boule*) and stories, and I among all the divinities/ am famous for wit (*metis*) and sharpness (*dolos*)" (13, 297-99).

Once again, the words *boule*, *metis* and *dolos* are used, concepts previously contrasted with *bia*, physical power, which through Achilleus is prominent in the *Iliad*'s heroic universe. This makes Achilleus and Odysseus not only the protagonists of their respective works but antagonists in their views of life. That Odysseus ends up in the *Iliad* in opposition to Achilleus, pointing out his greater intelligence and experience, is thus an omen of an approaching fundamental change: Odysseus and his intelligence will take over, not only at the individual level but as a sign of a transformation in the entire understanding of existence itself.

7

In short, in iconographical terms the Wooden Horse signifies a shift in civilization. It not only enters the fortress of Troy with its hidden cargo, but it overturns the mythical heroic world as such with its limited ideals. It stands as a transition to a far more conscious way of relating to life, to an incipient historical reality and nascent formation of a subject in our understanding of the concept.

No, Troy did not fall to courage and physical military strength but to cunning and strategem. For as the war has surged back and forth between Greeks and the Trojans, strategic considerations have not been not prominent. The armies have clashed with one another, withdrawn or been forced back, but without a clear, calculated set of tactics. Or the prominent heroes have met in single combat.

Consequently, the prerequisite for the success of the Wooden Horse stratagem must be that enemies are defined by the same narrow view of reality as the Greeks themselves. So they fall easy prey to the Wooden Horse illusion. It is telling in this context that only the visionaries, Laokoon and Kassandra, are capable of seeing through the deception—indeed, of reading its inner life, while all the others take the horse at face value.

The *Iliad* is not, as one might immediately believe, fundamentally a work about the power of heroism but rather about its impotence. This is illustrated partly by the army's inability to take Troy and partly by the fact that in heroic anger and personal delusion the army's leaders, Agamemnon and Achilleus, paralyze its fighting ability and thereby reveal the reverse of this form of consciousness. Physical force, from which intelligence is not yet entirely differentiated, is still partly marked by the unity of subject and object in mythic thinking and in this respect constitutes a closed universe.

On the other hand, through its protagonist, the *Odyssey* becomes a work on clarity of vision, the work of a new age and a new awareness. For with the power of his spirit and understanding, Odysseus has stepped into the mythic age of heroism, experienced it fully and replaced it, even as Homer reveals its existential bankruptcy through him. Therefore, the Wooden Horse becomes a turning point not only in his own development but in that of Western civilization; for, as a strategic achievement, it represents a capacity for reflection that can distinguish subject from object and imagine what makes people act—and how.

8

More particularly, what happens is that Odysseus, by virtue of his *metis*, is able to act discursively. He establishes a duality in which the external and the internal no longer correspond to each other. He is capable of thinking his way into—and independently of—heroic reality in which there is no contrast between the internal and the external, since heroes act in accordance with and derive strength from this closed universe. For the same reason, he seems within this universe to be problematic and suspicious, which makes him a bit of an anomaly, relatively isolated from the other heroes.

Despite his courage as a warrior, he is physically different from the towering heroes. He is not so strikingly tall or ostentatious as Agamemnon or Menelaos, who boast what might be called the ordinary heroic appearance. He is described in some contexts as almost stocky (see p. 166), but is on the other hand impressive when he speaks and puts his *metis* into words. Acting alone, he brings about the fall of Troy by sheer reflection.

Furthermore, linked to this psychological mobility is his possession of a highly developed sense for making qualified decisions after inner reflection. In a given— often, critical and hard-pressed—situation, he can weigh pros and cons and determine what is the most expedient. Time and time again, this saves him and his men from the frying pan. For despite the fact that he—as well as Homer presumably— like the other heroes believes that the gods intervene in their lives by imposing blindness (*ate*), in the *Odyssey*, he accepts personal responsibility.

As a result of this understanding of his own responsibility, combined with his ability to control his passions, he, as opposed to the other heroes, is only rarely afflicted by self-destructive blindness, which also generally testifies to his insight into the world of human motivation. Inside the Wooden Horse, it is he who resists Helen's attempt to lure them out with her seductively distorted voice. He saves his men here, as he vainly tries to do on his voyage home, when they give in precisely to the blindness of temptation, to desire and to the demand of physical necessities to be satisfied here and now.

We see a similar pattern of reaction in the anger that grips Agamemnon and Achilleus, leading to such heavy losses for the army, when Achilleus in his blind rage withdraws from battle. Nevertheless, in Book XIX of the *Iliad*, Agamemnon is able to defend himself as—and create consensus around—being innocent, because he was the victim of blindness caused by the gods. In other words, the heroes of the *Iliad* lack a consciousness of the fact that the human world of action is determined by personal motives and intentions.

9

As Odysseus is described in his *metis*, there are clear tendencies toward true introspection—that is, an understanding of and ability to adapt and control his inner impulses. The most obvious passage is to be found in Book 20 of the *Odyssey*. Incensed at the sight of his faithless slave girls, he is on the verge of killing them—and thereby revealing himself. However, in an intense processing of his emotional impulses in which, as an expression of the tangibility with which they are experienced, he beats his breast and heart, he is able to bring them under control.

This passage will be interpreted in greater depth later (see p. 173), and it will be seen how Socrates quotes this very passage on several occasions as evidence of mental judgment independent of the body. In short, this means that, even though Homer has not developed a psychic spiritual life in our psychological sense of the word—*psyche* for him is the breath that leaves a person at the moment of death—his experience is such that he is aware of such a phenomenon and sees its effect in practice. So this enables Odysseus to exercise a self-control that is peculiar to him and the first example of the composure that later becomes a fundamental value in Greek thinking known as *sophrosyne*.

If the Wooden Horse is mythical evidence of how Odysseus and the civilizational progress he symbolizes with his *metis* enter the story and, so to speak, constitute the very turning point, then the extreme difficulty of his voyage home becomes an example of how, as an individual, he is tested in these qualities and thereby actually forms and develops a more differentiated self-realization of consciousness. A fundamental prerequisite for this is that he is able to draw his awareness down into the instinctive challenges of life and thereby protect himself against the blindness rooted there.

That he is able to separate himself from this world of desire with which the others are one and that he is the only one from his fleet to come safely home is in itself evidence of his superior intelligence and endurance. This makes him the true leader among the heroes of Troy, as Achilleus of course falls in the war and Agamemnon is killed by his wife on his return. It is an indication of the limits to and the surpassing of the heroic era, which is why, as we shall discover (see. p. 213), he becomes the ultimate answer to the question the Homeric narrator directs to his Muse: "Tell me, Muse, who of them all was the best and the bravest" (II, 761).[14]

10

On an individual level, Odysseus finally becomes the person he truly is by virtue of the Wooden Horse. And at the supra-individual level, he explodes the heroic world, revealing it to be too limited to serve as the basis for the future. It is Odysseus and his qualities that belong to the future and anticipate the development of Greek culture. And it will be as a (cultural) representative of this new reality that he is constituted as a mythic figure.[15] The durability and transillumination of this image is presented via the related myth, which the journey, his odyssey, is for the formation of his individuality.

Even in Achilleus' contemptuous assessment of him as a person speaking with two tongues, there is expressed an ambivalent characteristic or a human duality that will come to cost Odysseus dearly in his later reception. Depending on the emphasis placed in a given interpretations, he is portrayed alternatively as an ideal of reason, scrupulousness and patience or, by contrast, as a man greedy for power, a political animal, cynical and selfish, who acts only to achieve his own goals irrespective of their cost to other people.

He has inherited this ambiguity from his grandfather Autolykos, a son of the god Hermes, renowned for his cunning and thievish ways. The close relationship to Hermes is also revealing, because not only was he the god of thieves but also the god of transformation and interpretation—hermeneutics. Such character traits are easy to apply to Odysseus, insofar as craftiness and the ability and willingness to interpret are the basis for his inventiveness and self-control.

Moreover, Odysseus is a transformer in a wider sense of the word. Not only does he transform himself quite unheroically beyond recognition during a scouting expedition to Troy and into a beggar on his homecoming, but he primarily transforms himself from warrior into human being, as he takes possession of his own subconscious and that of his day by traveling through worlds filled with temptresses and monsters, whom he meets during his voyage home—reflections and projections of the subconscious and of repressed urges.

That Odysseus with the multiple nature of his character was not simply a mirror image of the Greeks is evident from a quick survey of the history of Western civilization.[16] His reputation has not only reached the heavens, as he himself says—no, he is a never-resting ground fire through time. He has attracted the attention of the greatest writers as the paradigm against which they have been able to measure their own time and understanding of life. In my introduction I referred to, Virgil's *Aeneid*, Dante's *Divine Comedy* and Joyce's *Ulysses*—linguistic syntheses of the cultural epochs during which these works were formed. As I say, these texts summarize the knowledge of an entire epoch. The author and the destiny of his times are realized in them, while at the same time the works contain knowledge of the destructive elements from which they seek to defend themselves as aesthetic totalities. At their center, we find Odysseus the voyager and the voyage as a mythic image of the striving and transformation of consciousness.

In their poems, Virgil and Dante tried to establish a cultural awareness linked to a utopian longing for salvation and redemption on both an individual and collective plane. This, too, resides in the figure of Odysseus, his homecoming and the re-establishment of his royal power. Indeed, it may be claimed that the Homeric epics as a whole gravitate toward an ordered world on the basis of his perseverance. In this way, the human being Odysseus realises himself on the voyage in which his realization is conditioned by the hard-fated necessity to which he is yoked.

Not only does Odysseus continue as a paradigmatic figure in our history, it may also be assumed that he had a mythic existence even before he was worked into the legend of Troy. He has features of the Year-*Daimon* but is also related to the trickster of fairy tale.[17] But no one has had his ability to survive and transform. At the same time, he becomes an example of what mythical awareness in a broader perspective is capable of, his capaciousness as a character due to his assimilation of so many representative qualities. In his shape, humanity can thus continue to work through the more or less archetypal experiences, so that telling the story of Odysseus and his myth becomes telling the story of the history of our own pre- and sub-consciousness.

Homer's epics thus become the first grand attempt in epic form to summarize in encyclopaedic fashion the received wisdom of the age in which they were conceived, and as such they later became part of Greek education, their *paideia*. How it came about that such aesthetically perfect texts emerge from the darkness of history is and will remain a mystery. The mystery bears the name of Homer. His identity is the great question with which I will undertake a further reading of the myth of the Wooden Horse to determine the character, contextual unity and, not least, the disparities in these works.

II

THE HOMERIC PROJECT

The Myth and Metaphor of "Homer"

1

N O ONE KNOWS AND NO ONE WILL EVER KNOW WHO HOMER WAS. OVER time, many have tried to provide an answer and, as yet, no one has grown much wiser. The name has a mythic etiology and tradition, which may be generally outlined in this way:

From ancient busts, he is known as a blind old wise man. This view may derive from the *Hymn to Apollo* in which he is spoken of as a blind man from the rocky Ionian island of Chios: "He is a blind man, and dwells in rocky Chios: his lays are evermore supreme."[1] The connection with Chios is based on the fact that a group of rhapsodes (i.e., reciters of epic poems) who traveled around reciting Homer came from that island, claiming to descend from Homer. They are known as the Homerids. There need not be a question of biological descent, but rather of a school of rhapsodes tracing their lineage to the original source, whether fictive or real. If—like the blind bard Demodokos in the *Odyssey*, in whom a camouflaged self-portrait has been seen—Homer is made blind, it is to show that, through the Muses, he has received his knowledge as inner clear-sightedness from the gods. It is also a part of his invocation of the Muses asking to be truly enlightened about the actual events of both the *Iliad* and the *Odyssey*.

Meanwhile, it was not only Chios that laid claim to Homer. At Smyrna, he was also venerated as a local cultural hero.[2] Five other cities have also claimed paternity. The names of the cities might differ but, for some inexplicable reason, the number remained constant. Remarkably, the two most important Ionian cities, Miletus and Ephesus, were not among them. This has led to the conclusion that the Homeric epics were not originally written in Ionic Greek but in the Aeolian dialect, which is spoken in northeastern Greece, Thessaly, and were only later translated into Ionic as a part of the cultural expansion of the area.

Another more obvious explanation might be that Miletus and Ephesus were the cradle of Ionian natural philosophy. Thales and Anaximander were among those hailing from Miletus and no less a figure than Heraclitus came from Ephesus. The latter, like his possible mentor Xenophanes, was an opponent of Homer (and Hesiod). As Xenophanes put it: All human thought originated with Homer. However, this was not only meant favorably, as Xenophanes attacks Homer for having attributed all human weaknesses to the gods: they deceive, fornicate, lie, etc. (see p. 316). Heraclitus pounces on the fact that, by linking disparate things, Homer creates a false doctrine and, therefore, according to Heraclitus, he along with Archilochus should be thrashed and turned away from literary competitions.

The most surprising thing about Heraclitus' judgment is the sense of Homer's living, personal presence that he receives by being linked with Archilochus, a poet whose biography is known. At the same time, these negative assessments provide an impression of his enormous significance for the formation of Greek culture in which his works along with those of Hesiod formed the central cultural paradigm. See, for instance, Xenophanes' assertion that all human thoughts derive from Homer. People were drilled in Homer's view of the world and the gods: of law (*nomos*) and proper behavior (*ethos*). This memorized, unreflective rote learning, together with poetry's suggestive power of seduction, also formed the background to Plato's continuation of the critique raised by Xenophanes and Heraclitus in his desire to drive the poets from his ideal city.

2

As a result of the unifying magic in Homer's name, he was credited with a whole range of works, including the epic cycle and hymns that bear his name. Indeed, the magical mythology of his name soaks up everything of significance. Not until the middle of the fourth century B.C. was he attributed with sole responsibility for the *Iliad* and the *Odyssey*.

In connection with his "dating" of the Olympian gods, Herodotus puts his peak at 400 years before his own time, which was around 435 B.C.[3] (see quotation, p. 101). A recalculation in generations of 40 years each suggests that this means a date around 750 B.C. This also corresponds to the results achieved by research on the basis of internal criteria, linguistic and factual content, where it is not possible to discover elements earlier than approximately 650 B.C.[4]

Also in genealogical terms there are many imaginative suggestions regarding Homer's origins. In an apocryphal piece on a poetry contest between Hesiod and Homer with an accompanying description of their vitae, there are various nominations for Homer's parents. From Delphi, for example, comes the following answer: "Ithaka is his country, Telemachos his father, Iokaste, Nestor's daughter, his mother."[5] That is to say that Homer was supposed to have been the fruit of a possible love relationship between Telemachos and Polykaste, Nestor's daughter, whom he meets on his voyage.

In that case, Homer would be the grandchild of Odysseus! This, too, is evidence of the authority attributed to Homer by virtue of this mythological way of thinking. He thereby becomes a first-hand recorder of his own family history. And since he and his knowledge can be derived directly from the story of Odysseus, this also underlines the fact that Odysseus was viewed as the person in whom the formation of a Greek consciousness found its decisive breakthrough. In order to emphasize the divine origin of his inspiration, another tradition makes Homer a descendent of Orpheus.

In antiquity, however, the idea already appeared that the name Homeros was not really meant to cover a single person but was almost a title, which could mean "blind," "companion" (Aristotle) or "hostage."[6] An ingenious etymological theory in recent research maintains that the name was an Indo-European compound word meaning "he who puts the songs together."[7] This points in the same direction as Pindar's description of the Homerids as "singers of woven verses."[8] And insofar as this interpretation is valid, Homer becomes a collective concept, identical with the structure of the two works, which coincides with my own analysis, now to be developed.

3

Since the contours of Homer as a biographical phenomenon are lost in the mists of mythology, I have determined to approach the question in a radically different way. His name will be used as a *metaphor* for the narrator's activity of linking or binding things together: of composing. This applies not only to the encyclopedic knowledge of the world that his texts contain but also to the comprehensive consciousness that can be extrapolated from the *Iliad* and the *Odyssey* in their compositional foundation. This metaphorical interpretative practice implies that he should not be viewed as a particular biographical individual but as a structurally formative and unifying consciousness that makes it possible to read the Homeric texts both individually and together as thematic and aesthetic units, notwithstanding all inconsistencies.

The challenge is thus to find the guiding principle behind the Homeric project that can put the works into a coherent experience and understanding.

The narrative thread of the two epics also has a clear goal, which may be summarized in a common pattern of action. The objective in each instance is indicated with amazing precision by the narrator in the very introductory verse, the initial determination of the respective work's plot and theme. Indeed, not only in the first verse but in the first word of the original Greek texts.

In the *Iliad*, that word is "wrath," *menis*. In the *Odyssey*, it is "the man," *aner*, modified by the difficult epithet *polytropos* (see p. 160). Difficult, because it means both "he who travels many (winding) paths" and "he who has an inventive and adaptable mind." With its ambiguity, this epithet perfectly covers Odysseus' character and his wanderings, including the journey to Troy. At the same time, it suggests his ample skill at extricating himself from of all sorts of difficulties—by adapting and, in the broader perspective, undergoing a transformation that brings him home to re-establish his kingdom.

The metaphor "Homer" operates so precisely right from the beginning and is only able to do so, because he is completely familiar with his works and can steer them toward their common goal, which is likewise embedded in the introductory verses. For these verses are addressed to the protagonists of the two texts and their confrontational attitudes to life. As his obsessive fury demonstrates, the wrathful Achilleus is a backward-looking hero, personifying the aristocratic-heroic culture to which Odysseus both belongs and from which he distinguishes himself with his forward-looking, rational choices and tenacity.

In addition, the two epic poems are determined in their narrative form and level of consciousness by their respective protagonists. This makes the works very different, contrasts, but—and this is a crucial factor—they are at the same time forced into the collective story they share partly on account of the earlier history that sets the stage for both works. They have the strife resulting from Helen's infidelity as a common frame of reference. It is a matter of winning a war, re-taking Helen and making their way home in safety—in Odysseus' case, to avenge himself on the suitors who have infested his house and, by bringing sexuality under control, to re-establish the social world order on peaceful values.

4

Only the later compositional analysis will be able to verify the sustainability of my claims, just as the fundamental purpose can only be fully appreciated as Homer's utopia of a well-ordered society when its entire narrative sequence, structure and range of symbols have been mapped out. However, as a way into this reading, we must in relation to the first verses—those verses which establish the theme—tentatively examine what Homer himself has to say about the direction of the narrative sequence, its *telos*.

When, upon his return and as yet unknown to anyone, Odysseus promises his faithful herdsmen that he will surely come again as the longed-for avenger, the cowherd exclaims: "How I wish, my friend, that the son of Kronos would make good/ your saying (. . .)" (*epos telesei Kronion*, 20, 236). That is to say the cowherd invokes Zeus in his quality as the fulfiller of all things, the Zeus Teleios who, in the *Oresteia* as well, controls all events and brings them to a fitting conclusion. His epithet is derived from the verb *telein*: to accomplish, which is also behind the noun *telos*: fulfillment and objective. That is to say that in invoking Zeus the Fulfiller the herdsman defines the determinative force that weaves together Homer's two texts and directs the events, since in the *Iliad* Zeus fulfils the demand of restoring to Achilleus his lost honor and, in the *Odyssey*, of bringing the hero home as an avenger and ending the war at the same time.

Zeus is present in every human life as its *telos*, as the fulfiller of life, when this life ends in death—"*thanatoio telos*" (III, 309). In this shape and function, he is right from the beginning present in the *Iliad*, which states "the will of Zeus was accomplished" (*Dios d'eteleieto boule*, I, 5).[9] This statement stands in the original text as an odd insertion, thereby generating some uncertainty as to what fulfillment Homer is really referring to.

The immediate reference is to the restoration of honor that Achilleus seeks and which his mother, the sea goddess Thetis, obtains from Zeus. This is confirmed in Book XVIII, when Thetis consoles her inconsolable son, who is bemoaning the loss of his friend Patroklos: "Why then,/ child, do you lament? What sorrow has come to your heart now?/ Speak out, do not hide it. These things are brought to accomplishment/ through Zeus" (XVIII, 73-75). At that point, the Greeks are hard pressed, driven back to their ships, and can under no circumstances manage without Achilleus. However, placed in the larger context spanned by the two Homeric epics, the will of Zeus covers the time before Troy and after it and, in reality it does not end until peace is achieved after the slaughter of the suitors at the end of the *Odyssey*.

This is to say that, through this process of conflict of which he himself is ultimately the originator and to which we shall return (see p. 121), Zeus undermines the old world of heroes and creates a new world order, new forms of life through Odysseus' slaughter of the suitors and his conclusion of peace with their families for the good of the country. For Homer, the ultimate goal of the works is to constitute this social utopia. However, it will only happen outside the framework of the action, when Odysseus has finally been reconciled with Poseidon, as he was instructed to do by the prophet Teiresias in the realm of the dead. Teiresias further prophesies that he will then return home when his *telos* is fulfilled and die in blessed circumstances as he sees that: "Your people / about you will be prosperous" (11, 136).

Thus, the action in the *Iliad* and the *Odyssey* is bound together by the same *telos*, since the claim in the first work that Zeus will accomplish his purpose is realized in the end. The format of Odysseus' destiny and character is shown by the fact that, on the part of Zeus and Homer, this whole plan is tied to him and his ability in concrete terms to implement the project. Therefore, logically enough, he is the one to invent the Wooden Horse, which is able to bring the war out of its impasse and end it in Troy; whereupon the emphasis is transferred partly to his determination on his voyage home and partly to his re-taking of Ithaka and his wife with the slaughter of the suitors.

As Odysseus approaches this goal in the *Odyssey*, the text is significantly enough filled with references to this determinative *telos*: After twenty years' absence and his trials and Zeus' gracious decision, he is once again to set foot on the soil of his homeland. This has been the intention from the very beginning, as is established by the prophecy his friend Halitherses made upon his departure: that he will return in the twentieth year, unknown—"And now all this is being accomplished"—(*nun panta teleitai*, 2, 176).

Penelope uses exactly the same expression (18, 271), when, without knowing the full implication of her words, she says that now all that Odysseus predicted when he left has come to pass: that she would marry again when their son grew a beard. She, too, is subject to and feels the law of fulfillment.

Finally, the impending fulfillment is twice confirmed by the anonymous Odysseus himself, both to the faithful swineherd Eumaios and to Penelope: "all these things are being accomplished in the way I tell them./ Sometime within this very year Odysseus will be here" (14, 160-61; 19, 305-06). The assurance with which he expresses these words, which correspond to his friend's prophecy, comes from the fact that he is now realizing what has always been intended for his destiny by Zeus Teleios: the intervention of the god in the world through his (self-) realization.

5

As the beginning of the *Iliad* has it, the will of Zeus is accomplished, though not completely until and with the end of the *Odyssey*. Although, at the *Iliad*'s narrative level, it is a matter of restoring Achilleus' honor, this does not preclude that, in a more general sense, it is a question of ending the war. This is emphasized by the fact that Zeus' plan, his *boule*, corresponds to Troy's falling by virtue of Athene's *boule* (XV, 71), i.e. the Wooden Horse and, in the longer run, Odysseus' homecoming by which peace is finally established. That this interpretation is correct is confirmed by the fact that even in Book IV of the *Iliad*, Zeus has tried to bring about peace between the Greeks and the Trojans but without success, as Hera and Athene are still in the mood for war because they feel slighted by Paris when he assigns to Aphrodite the honor of being the most beautiful goddess.

In Book 24 of the *Odyssey*, Athene asks her divine father what he intends to do now that the families of the suitors are seeking blood revenge. Is the conflict to continue—as a sort of extension of the war in Troy—or is peace to be established forever? Zeus' intention is indicated in and with his idea, his *noos*, a word that here almost means plan and corresponds to *telos*. His will is founded in reason—the organ of consciousness with which he directs and orders the world. He answers that of course she herself has already made her decision: "For was this not your own intention, as you have counseled it (*ebouleusas noon aute*)/ how Odysseus should make his way back and punish those others?" (24, 479-80). However, his counsel is to stop the war. With his advice, Zeus thus establishes that through Odysseus the course of development has at last reached a level and maturity where the new reality can be come into play. Peace is to be concluded and, at the same time, Zeus will see to it that the memory of the bloodshed is forgotten: former enemies are to live in friendship—"let them have prosperity and peace in abundance" (24, 486).

Insofar as it is the intent of both Zeus and Homer to guide the specific themes—wrath and homecoming—through the *Iliad* and the *Odyssey*, it may also be concluded that as a metaphorical entity Homer merges with the divine *telos* and does so in the composite awareness that of course belongs to the implicit narrator.

Homer as Implicit Narrative Awareness

1

In his *Poetics*, Aristotle points out that Homer stands above other later poets by *not* referring to himself:

> Homer, admirable as he is in every other respect, is especially so in this, that he alone among epic poets is not unaware of the part to be played by the poet himself in the poem. The poet should say very little *in propria persona*, as he is no imitator when doing that. Whereas the other poets are perpetually coming forward in person, and say but little, and that only here and there, as imitators, Homer after a brief preface brings in forthwith man, a woman, or some other Character—no one of them characterless, but each with distinctive characteristics.[10]

The objective, underplayed narrator whom Aristotle describes here is linked to a number of specific narrative features, including the demand for a certain degree of realism. However, the phenomena are not described for their own sake but always as a part of the description of the heroic deeds under discussion. The objectivity at which heroic poetry aims does not, however, mean that the narrator, Homer, is not subjective. He is simply hidden as *implicit* narrator or compositional awareness.

As narrator, Homer steps forth *explicitly* in the invocation of the heavenly Muses, who are to be viewed more as informants about the past than as Romanticism's sources of inspiration. They ensure his lexical knowledge, which according to Hesiod they have from their parents: their mother, the personification of the power of memory, Mnemosyne, and their omniscient father Zeus.[11] This narrative position, therefore, can be extended into the implicit narrative and compositional structure in which Zeus and Homer are united in a common *telos*—that is, the determined guidance of characters, motifs and destinies that truly make Homer an Olympian narrator.

2

Even in the *Iliad*, which otherwise contains a high degree of mythical literalness—the gods associate with human beings, the individual experiences himself through a unity of *psyche* and *soma*, etc.—Homer has explicitly inserted a narrative distance in which he several times clearly positions himself after the events narrated. The mythical heroes he describes do not exist "today", he says (V, 303; XII, 447). The men in his own time, for instance, would not be able to lift the stones that Hektor throws at the enemy, an indication that masculine strength and strength in general have been in marked decline. This emphasizes the distance between the heroic age of which he sings and the age from which he describes the events, an age that, of course, is not mentioned but is indirectly experienced as being in crisis.

What is noteworthy, however, is that Homer not only places a time distance between his works and his own epoch but incorporates a partially hidden time perspective into the *Iliad* and the *Odyssey*. For despite the fact that by its very nature the *Iliad* has heroism at its foundation, Homer nevertheless also envisions a heroic world in which the *Iliad*'s heroes surprisingly enough come to represent a period of decline. In this context, he uses Nestor as spokesman and a sort of witness to this age. Homer has Nestor's life span three generations (I, 253), so his earlier history is lost in a heroic age far older than the contingent of warriors that are on the verge of losing the war outside Troy.

When the conflict between Achilleus and Agamemnon breaks out, Nestor reproves them with reference to this earlier, nobler heroic era: "In my time I have dealt with better men than/ you are" (I, 260-61), he says, implying that the heroes in his youth were greater and more important. This he says directly with the words: "Never/ yet have I seen nor shall see again such men as these were" (I, 262), and Theseus is among those he mentions.

If we incorporate this sudden time horizon into the *Iliad*, it can only mean that the heroes are shrinking, atrophying, made as they are of lesser material than before. If this point of view is further extended to the *Odyssey* and applied to the arrogant and degenerate suitors as potential heroes, the descending curve remains extremely clear throughout Homer's heroic universe. Indeed, one can go so far as to claim that, first of all, he has summarized the entire heroic period from its origins through to its decline; secondly, he has thereby created a bridge to the crisis situation of his own day; thirdly, he has implicitly shown the necessity of the emergence of a new and different type of personality in which Odysseus is the ideal figure.

In short, the works and narrative attitude together make up a continuity that stretches from the oldest myths and heroic age to Homer's own crisis-ridden time. And this explains why his works are based on a recollection of the past, which he transformed into a forward-pointing utopian longing, while in this process moving the epic as a genre on to its culmination and ultimate purpose.

One senses here a latent counterpart to Hesiod's account of the successive ages of the world, symbolized by increasingly inferior metals: gold, silver, bronze. Hesiod himself lives in what he calls the Iron Age, a period of crisis coming chronologically straight after the heroic age, something that entirely corresponds to the progression in Homer. And just as Homer calls for a new age with the figure of Odysseus, so Hesiod does in *Works and Days* with an analysis of the decadence of his age that aims to call forth new moral values.

In other words, Homer is engaged on the same errand at an earlier time, insofar as his works are also based on the dream of a well-ordered society and thereby express a subjective assessment contrasting with what he claims is his objective portrayal and admiration of the heroic age. He certainly admires his heroes, but one can sense his negative emotional reactions. Thus, in one passage, he cannot hide his open contempt for the bloody handiwork of the war: "That man would have to be very bold-hearted/ who could be cheerful and not stricken looking on that struggle." (XIII, 343-44). In addition, he directly rejects his protagonist Achilleus' brutal treatment of Hektor's body, which he drags behind his chariot around Patroklos' burial mound: "He spoke, and thought of shameful treatment for glorious Hektor" (XXIII, 24; XXIV, 22). And of his sacrifice of 12 boys, he similarly comments: "evil were the thoughts in his heart against them" (XXIII, 176).

Other events in the *Iliad* also have a barbaric character from which Homer linguistically distances himself. For example, Zeus accuses his wife Hera of being so bloodthirsty that she would devour King Priam and his whole family raw (IV, 35). From the opposite point of view, the Trojan queen Hekuba suggests that, in retribution for her dead son Hektor, she wants, like a Fury, to devour his slayer Achilleus: "I wish I could set teeth/ in the middle of his liver and eat it" (XXIV, 212-13).

3

In this way, as an explicit narrator, Homer criticizes a warlike practice determined by raw power (*bia*), the praises of which he otherwise sings and which is incarnated above all by Achilleus. At the same time, these assessments lead into and coincide with the implicit narrator's idea of a different peaceful, human reality. This latter trait appears in the empathy Homer shows in the description of Odysseus' tribulations on his voyage home, his shipwreck and the mistreatment to which the suitors subject him. He speaks of him as a poor creature and on several occasions he applies a point of view in which his and Odysseus' thoughts merge into one, just as they have a common hatred of the suitors.

So, as narrator in the *Odyssey*, Homer is explicitly and implicitly far more in harmony with his protagonist and the norms he is developing than with the heroic code of the *Iliad*. He thereby creates greater narrative space in the *Odyssey*, which is really only natural, since the purpose of the *Odyssey* is to describe a pioneering subject.

Finally, Homer has greater power than the Bible's narrators, since he can hear and see everything Zeus has on his mind; while the biblical narrators are completely at a loss as to God's inscrutable ways. Indeed, Homer has the language of the gods at his disposal. This occurs in the so-called *dionymia*,[12] that is, the gods' own words. One of the things he tells in the *Iliad* is that the river called Skamandros by mortals is known as Xanthos by the gods—"who is called Xanthos by the gods, but by mortals Skamandros" (XX, 74). In the *Odyssey*, two *dionymia* appear: the name *moly* (10, 305) for the plant Hermes gives Odysseus as protection against Kirke, and the "clashing" rocks that the gods call *Planktai* (12, 61).

So we can say in conclusion that Homer, as a metaphoric collective figure, assumes Zeus' *telos* for his own undertaking. In a more or less implicit critique of the strife-filled values of heroic reality, the belligerent morality of the aristocracy, and the times of crisis in which he is writing, he puts forward his utopia of a flourishing, peaceful social reality. With the conclusion of peace in the *Odyssey*, he (with Zeus) allows just such a reality to arise as a long-lasting consequence of Odysseus' persistence, self-control and intelligence. So, when Telemachos maintains that the poets only sing of what Zeus wishes (1, 347-48), we must on this basis reply that Zeus and the poet can no longer be distinguished from the "Olympic point of view" which Homer has at his disposal. The poet determines what Zeus will determine.

The Oral Tradition and the Crisis Works

1

It is, of course, impossible precisely to plot either the dividing line between the conscious and the unconscious in the underlying narrative presence or the manner in which the composition has actually taken place. Milman Parry's empirical studies of the oral tradition among Serbo-Croat singers around 1930 provided a new perspective on the origins of the Homeric works. It emerged that, by virtue of a vast store of formulaic expressions, the best singers in this tradition were capable of memorizing texts of considerable length. Since a large percentage of Homer's epics are formulaic, Parry believed that he had discovered the basis of their origins; they were the result of a long tradition of singers, who each influenced, expanded and transformed the works and their formal contents.

Convincing as this theory may be, it had an unintended effect since, by isolating the formulaic expressions from their context, Parry made them more mechanical than is actually the case in Homer. The paradox is that no one has used so large a register of formulaic expressions as he, and no one has done it with such rich variation and vivacity. Certainly, formulas are important for the memory of an oral epic singer, giving him time to make choices, create rhythms and concentrate, but those in Homer are also clearly linked to the motifs and play their part in supporting the conscious unifying structure.[13]

2

Nevertheless, the revelation of the functional forms of the oral tradition did not explain how the Homeric epics came to be written down, and the problem will doubtless never be solved. The most probable explanation is that the writing down and a possible "literary" composition was undertaken by one or more highly developed poetic talents on the basis of the oral tradition. The written languages that existed in the Mycenaean culture were now lost. But through trade with the Phoenicians in the 8th century B.C., the Greeks discovered the alphabet and developed a written language for themselves—the oldest extant manuscript dates from c. 775 B.C.—which by 700 B.C. was sufficiently developed to make it possible to write down the works from dictation.[14] Hesiod's works derive from this period and, judging from the degree of their complexity, they can only have come into existence in written form.

In Homer, a single reference is found to the art of writing, in which a person makes use of "murderous symbols, which he inscribed in a folding tablet" (VI, 168-69). It is known with certainty that his works were recited by rhapsodes at the Pan-

Athenian Festival, instituted or revived by the tyrant Peisistratos in 565 B.C., and one tradition claims that the first inscription took place at his behest.[15] Yet it is possible to point to variants of these same texts among ancient authors—for instance in both Plato and Aristotle. The works were not yet fixed, either because the rhapsodes kept the oral tradition alive together with the uncertainty deriving from improvisations and interpolations, inadvertent omissions and additions, or simply not sticking to the text. It is most probable, however, that the oral and written forms went side by side for some considerable time.[16]

The final form presumably took shape at the library at Alexandria with Aristarchus (head librarian, c. 180-45 B.C.) as the driving force. After this, the works were divided into the books we now know—a division that itinerant singers might have used but which are not found in the oldest extant papyrus fragments. However, despite the presence of many apparent inconsistencies (mostly in the confusion of war in the *Iliad*, where someone may be killed in one book only to mount his chariot in the next), the works nevertheless primarily convey the impression of a structural unity of both action and themes. And this high level of artistry suggests a single creative, editorial conscious mind, which bears the name of Homer.

3

One possible explanation for the inexhaustible supply of conscious structural awareness in the Homeric epics and thereby the potential for later times to find themselves reflected in them may be explained by their being formed over a long period of time. They can be viewed as something akin to "kitchen middens," containing rudiments from the epochs during which they came into being and the full meaning of which Homer either did not have access to when they were conceived or consciously omitted to take a position on.

And the very fact that Homer on the one hand makes use of an oral narrative tradition and on the other incorporates older mythical materials from it creates a relationship between the conscious and the unconscious in his works that has almost incomprehensible consequences. It requires of the interpreter that, in order to acquire an insight into the world of meaning in his works, he or she should be compelled to extrapolate or fill in these "gaps" in his consciousness and the subtext as such—among other things, with the help of supplementary sources, without knowing exactly where the boundary for Homer's own knowledge and insight may be. We are on comparatively much more solid ground with the tragedians in which the mythic material has been thoroughly elucidated.

As Aristotle says, it is impossible to get behind Homer.[17] From this, it follows, first of all, that Homer becomes identical with the historical conception of his entire work. Secondly, he does not stop at the boundaries of his work but must be viewed through the subsequent history of its effects and the meanings that this has provoked by way of ever new interpretations of his works. This explodes the analytical view, which has seen it as its challenge to demonstrate, so to speak from verse to verse, how uneven the Homeric texts are in content and also philologically. It is research that presents itself as strictly scientific but is a victim of its own obsessions and, in its striving for objectivity, paradoxically enough ends up as pure guesswork.[18]

4

Not only are the *Iliad* and the *Odyssey* crisis works in the sense that, like virtually all literature, they are composed around crisis situations—whether subjective, collective or both at the same time. So it can be said that the *Iliad* is about the Trojan War but also that it is about the wrath of Achilleus and, ultimately, a combination of this and all the unfortunate consequences arising from it.

They are also crisis works in the deeper sense that they came into existence in a period of 500-600 years, when the highly refined Mycenaean culture that forms the historical background to the Trojan War collapsed around 1200 B.C., possibly due to the invading Dorians from the north. The Dorians are mentioned for the first time in Homer (19, 177). They settled throughout the Peloponnesus and, in the subsequent period of upheaval, the Greek population moved in great numbers to the western coast of Asia and nearby islands—among them to the Ionia where Homer's works originated; epics considered the first Pan-Hellenic works of art.

This occurred in a period in which relatively small kingdoms were being restructured on the political and social plane to form a true city-state: a *polis*.[19] The so-called "dark" centuries (approx. 1200-800 B.C.) were a time of upheaval during which innovations about which we know virtually nothing occurred and of which, as said above, we have but very few archeological traces. However, these times are discerned as linguistic and factual relics in Homer. And the very fact that his works can emerge from these dark times in such profusion is an indication of how meaningful this gestation period was in a historical sense.[20]

The traces in Homer lead back to Mycenae and no one can doubt the layering from various epochs, but it is impossible to date very many phenomena. In order to promote the heroic effect, the weapons are made archaic. Although the iron sword had been known since around 1100 B.C., the heroes fight with swords wrought of bronze while being said to have hearts of iron. And Homer does not seem familiar with the proper significance of the chariots, which were used regularly in battle in Mycenae. They act almost like taxis to carry heroes to and from the battle place. The huge, towering shield that Ajax carries also derives from Mycenaean times. Later, they became smaller and round as the swords gradually became shorter and broader. On the other hand, several battle scenes (for example, XII, 105ff; XIII, 130ff) seem to be copied from later hoplite strategy of around 700 B.C.[21] And so on.

The same uncertainty applies to the linguistic base, an artificial mixture of various dialects in which Ionian is clearly predominant, followed by Aeolian, but also including Attic and Arcadian. In addition, there are relics which, thanks to the deciphering of the Linear B tablets, can be traced back to Mycenae. The ordinary word for king, *basileus*, is sometimes replaced by the word *(w)anax*, the Mycenaean noun for (paramount) king.[22] In short, no one has ever spoken the language we find in Homer. It is an artifact, formed over the centuries and developed as a purely poetic instrument in as elastic a way as possible to correspond to the requirements of the hexameter. For example, the Aeolian dialect serves as a metric variation, and all this suppleness of the Homeric epic is striking in comparison with the peasant poet Hesiod's clumsier hexameter rhythms, documenting once again an artistic consciousness of the highest caliber.

The heroic universe of the *Iliad,* for which Homer with his dissociative criticism feels veneration, is clearly older than the *Odyssey*. For instance, there is little evidence in the *Iliad* of a realistic urban culture, which is very much present in the *Odyssey* both in the description of the polis of the Phaiakians and the urban society of Ithaka, which is described with a wealth of everyday events and people. Only exceptionally is such a reality depicted in the *Iliad*—in comparisons and in the description of images on the shield that Hephaistos forges for Achilles, images of cities at peace and at war, dancing youth, peasants plowing, etc.

On the other hand, this does not in itself preclude the possibility of the two works having been edited and written down simultaneously, as indicated by Homer's critical comments and narratory intrusions in both works. Despite this criticism on the part of Homer, the heroic virtues were later incorporated into the education of young people.

At the same time, the works became lexical textbooks and a sort of ethical-psychological enchiridion by at once showing the meaning of courage and persistence. The key concept is *arete*, which is untranslatable but indicates the highest human virtue and morality and is often translated as virtue. It is a principal concept for both Homer and Socrates, but it is also a concept that undergoes constant change and becomes more complex. Whereas Homer links *arete* with martial principles, the concept for Socrates is linked to the degree of awareness of good and evil. Yet courage and bravery are crucial characteristics, irrespective of the time.

The Homeric Heroic Complex

1

When Hippolochos sends his son Glaukos to reinforce the Trojans, he does so with an earnest injunction "to be always among the bravest, and hold [his] head above others" (VI, 209-10). Peleus also dispatched Achilleus with the same words. So succinctly can heroic *arete* can be defined.[23]

It is simply a matter of being number one, the greatest. That is how the honor (*time*) and reputation (*kleos*) that provide the hero with his identity are achieved. That is to say that identity is something acquired from without through the understanding of the surrounding world—in that the surrounding world, it should be noted, is composed of peers, other aristocrats, *aristoi*, as they are called in Greek—a word that etymologically derives from the same root as *arete*. In this way, it is confirmed that life is meaningful, worth living, since everyone shares this proud view of self, which includes being good at something (*agathos*) and brave (*esthlos*).[24] In contrast to this is the man without honor, whose anti-heroic conduct in the case of Thersites in the *Iliad* is underscored by his prattling and his repulsive exterior (II, 211 ff.).

A hero acts in a way that can serve to augment his honor. Honor as the essence of the heroic implies at the same time the inviolability and mutual assessment of the heroes take the place of the social laws of a later age. Indeed, because of the self-esteem it gives to heroes and kings to be descended directly from the gods, the hero seeks to force through his will as law. Nor is it a question of the extent to which his actions are just in the eyes of the present day, since justice does not yet exist in the form with which Hesiod provides it in the shape of the goddess Dike— and in direct contrast to those kings who ruthlessly pursue their own goals. Since Agamemnon acts as the supreme commander of the army, his injustices are themselves justified by his status. He cannot be tried before a court. So Achilleus is forced to claim his rights (*dike*) through his own will and sense of honor.

Against this background, it is no wonder that heroism can only be conceived as a warrior culture. In war and war-like situations—predatory expeditions, for example—the hero demonstrates his bravery and physical strength, which are really what is worthy of admiration and honor. For the same reason, cowardice and anything that diminishes one's honor are the worst things that can befall a hero.

From this perspective, it is not so difficult to understand Achilleus' wrath and almost senseless intransigence when Agamemnon deprives him of the widow Briseis, whom he has received as booty (*geras*) and for whom he nourishes deep feelings. He attacks Agamemnon using this extremely denigrating imagery: "You wine sack, with a dog's eyes, with a deer's heart" (I, 225). The comparison with a dog (*kyon*) is particularly insulting. Achilleus himself loudly bewails the loss of his honor when he asks his mother to seek redress from Zeus. The loss of honor is a loss of identity in the eyes of himself and other people that he is forced to restore. At the same time, the very nature of his anger provides a first-hand impression of an injured self-esteem that is unshakeable, since at the behest of Zeus things go wrong for the Greeks, and Agamemnon does everything he can to appease this wrathful man with generous gifts.

2

Just as the uncompromising nature of his anger demonstrates the hero's self-esteem, Agamemnon's violation is itself an illustration of a man who is jealous of his honor and will brutally assert himself regardless of cost. This conflict-generating situation has general brutality as its foundation, since Achilleus has received Briseis as the spoils of war and a token of honor. When Agamemnon is forced to surrender the captured woman Chryseis, by whom he is more captivated than by his wife Klytemnestra, to her father the priest of Apollo, he seeks compensation for his loss from Achilleus, whereby he cannot avoid humiliating him.

That Agamemnon has the power to do this—despite the fact that Achilleus is the foremost among the Greek heroes at Troy—is simply explained: he is in charge by virtue of the fact that he is the richest and has supplied the greatest number of warriors and ships. That is to say that wealth in itself is a power factor. As honor-based identity is acquired by following the example of one's peers and being admired by them, it is by the nature of things a question of steadily building upon one's (and one's family's) riches (*olbos*). The size of the riches palpably reflects the extent of the hero's success.

However, just as honor is diminished if one is deprived of one's property, so it is increased by generosity verging on extravagance. The Homeric epics frequently mention this liberality in the form of sumptuous gifts exchanged to seal a guest friendship.[25] In addition to demonstrating the giver's magnanimity, it has a deeper significance as such gifts bind the receiver and the giver in a mutual alliance, which is deep and binding in the life of a family as an important part of the *arete* of the aristocracy. Many gifts are accompanied by the story of "donation", a special genealogy that tells from whom one has received the gift one is passing on—as is the case, for example, with Odysseus' bow (21, 11 ff).

Guest friendship was overseen by its own god, Zeus Xenios, and a law intended to ensure one could find shelter on one's journeys. Odysseus counts on the law applying to Polyphemos, but he is mistaken because the Kyklops ignores guest friendship. So does Paris, since he not only runs away with his host's wife, Helen, but also a considerable portion of his wealth—and thereby his honor. The start of the Trojan War is thus a sort of counterpart to the strife in the *Iliad*, since Menelaos, like Achilleus, has had his honor and identity violated, quite apart from what he may feel for his wife.

If heroes never reveal any fear of death, this is ultimately due to the proximity of death characteristic of this warrior culture: it is honorable to die in battle and thereby secure an immortal reputation (*kleos*) for bravery. Thus do heroes imprint their lives on the memory of posterity—for example, in the songs Demodokos sings on "the famous actions of men" (*klea andron*, 8, 73). And this explains why Achilleus chooses an early honorable death to a long, inglorious life. In the *Iliad*, Achilleus himself sings of such heroic deeds (IX, 189).

So the great misfortune for Telemachos is not so much that his father is dead as that he has quite simply vanished and so cannot ensure his own and his son's reputation. If he had fallen in Troy like other real heroes, "he would have won great fame for himself and his son hereafter" (1, 240). Among the Phaiakians, Odysseus identifies himself as one who, by his craftiness, the Wooden Horse, has achieved a "fame (*kleos*) that goes up to the heavens" (9, 20).

3

However, it is not only male heroes who have regard for their honor and reputation. So do Homeric heroines of which Penelope is held forth as an example. Thus she says that it would be a clear advantage for her honor and reputation if Odysseus returned home to her, so she would not be forced to marry a lesser man. At the same time, Odysseus in his beggar disguise is able to praise her reputation, which like his own reaches to the heavens—"your fame goes up to the wide heaven" (19, 108)—like the reputation of an honorable and god-fearing king.

Like no other Greek female figure, she (together with Andromache, Hektor's wife, and Alkestis, who was prepared to sacrifice her own life for her husband) personifies female *arete*: chastity, domestic skill and beauty. Certainly, Penelope does not measure up to Helen in the latter. Nevertheless, she is compared to both Aphrodite and Artemis—"looking like Artemis or like golden Aphrodite" (19, 54). The comparison with Aphrodite emphasizes her dazzling beauty, which almost deprives the suitors of their senses, while the reference to Artemis indicates her chastity. In addition, her shrewdness and skill at the loom show that she has been blessed by Athene. No fewer than three of the most important goddesses are identified with her, which endows her with a fictive significance corresponding to that of her husband.

4

Self-esteem among aristocratic men (and women) also derives from the fact that they are often descended directly from the gods, that they are blood-related to them. Odysseus, for example, has Hermes as his maternal grandfather and Zeus himself on his father's side. In general, this means that they treat their subjects with the same random brutality as that with which the gods treat human beings. As far as one can judge, Odysseus is an exception also in this respect, since it is repeatedly claimed that no one has been so good to his people as he: It is said that his rule was "kind, like a father" (5, 12), which is why the swineherd Eumaios has remained faithful to him and his property.

Aristotle has defined this high-mindedness as *megalopsychia*,[26] and it is no accident that this evokes associations with *megalomania*. In the literary tradition after Homer, the *Iliad*'s greatest heroes particularly Sophocles' Ajax in the tragedy that bears his name—are used to describe the arrogance, the *hubris*, that also characterizes Agamemnon and Achilleus, which leads to blindness (*ate*), the dark side of aristocratic *arete*.

The remarkable thing is that this heroic conduct does not have features of later morality. Achilleus can thus maltreat Hektor's body apparently without it detracting from his deeds in the eyes of others. There is also consensus that the blindness (*ate*) is something imposed from without; one is struck by the gods, which is why such blindness discredits neither Achilleus nor Agamemnon. Neither reason nor sober-mindedness are attributed with any further positive significance—almost on the contrary, since these characteristics lead to a reticence that is judged unheroic.

If Odysseus is accompanied by an ambiguous reputation in the *Iliad*, the reason is primarily that he consciously follows his reason, his insight, and takes a discursive, cautious stance in his actions. Certainly, he possesses the traditional heroic virtues, but he is also the object of great suspicion on the part of the traditional heroes, who identify themselves completely with heroic *arete*. At the same time as Homer can say that Odysseus, the bearer of his utopia, is in possession of a shrewdness that is not inferior to that of Zeus, Agamemnon idiosyncratically distances himself from him as a crafty deceiver for the very same reason.

However, Agamemnon himself seems somewhat questionable. So it can be said that it is more significant when Achilleus, the true contrast to Odysseus, indirectly attacks him on the basis of the same assessment, counting him a double agent, a man who hides his true motives, saying one thing and meaning another. This applies to the crafty—i.e., strategic—conduct that, if anything, characterizes Odysseus and occasions his doubtful reputation. As Athene exclaims upon seeing Odysseus on the coast of Ithaka, one has to rise early in the morning to get the better of him: "It would be a sharp one, and a stealthy one, who would ever get past you/ in any contriving, even if it were a god against you" (13, 291-92). The long and the short of it, however, is that it is precisely the same awareness that causes the fall of Troy with the invention of the Wooden Horse.

5

In the above tragedy by Sophocles concerning Ajax and his blindness and evident *hubris* toward the gods, Odysseus is on the contrary the representative of sober-mindedness which gradually becomes subsumed under the concept of *sophrosyne*. The word means moderation and shows a spiritual healthiness based on self-awareness and self-control.[27] The worst examples of high-minded arrogance going over the top and ending in *hubris* are Paris' crime against Menelaos and the suitors' almost depraved caricature of aristocratic *arete*. As Athene says to Telemachos, it calls down nemesis, disapproval and punishment on the part of both gods and men— "A serious man who came in among them/ could well be scandalized, seeing much disgraceful behavior" (1, 228-29).

Telemachos calls the suitors "overbearing in [their] rapacity" (1, 368) and skewers the *hubris* in which they persist despite all warnings. Telemachos becomes a direct contrast to them. He possesses such great modesty (*aidos*) that Athene must prompt him in their conversation in Book 3 to get to work with Nestor—"here is no more need at all of modesty" (3, 14).

Yet, in this very modesty, we find a mode of action that portends *sophrosyne*.[28] So, even though the word appears only four times in Homer, the reality it expresses is already present and, one might add, the true foundation for the whole of the *Odyssey*. As Odysseus' heir, Telemachos carries the future within him and thus also becomes the figure to whom *sophrosyne* is most clearly applicable. This is the way his friend Peisistratos, Nestor's son, characterizes his silence and reticence upon arriving at Menelaos' palace: "he is modest (*saophron*), and his spirit would be shocked at the thought/ of coming here and beginning a show of reckless language/ in front of you" (4, 157-58).

6

If, more than anyone else, Telemachos personifies the opposition to this aristocratic arrogance and accompanying blindness, he does not get this from strangers, but as part of his inherent constitution deriving from his father. And insofar as Homer's utopian project as *telos* is to have the *Iliad*'s warrior culture replaced by a personality that certainly possesses heroic *arete*, courage and skill, he uses Odysseus' self-control to develop these very new qualities for rulers that can secure social stability (*eunomia*), based on peaceful coexistence. As said above, this complex of ideas is conceived in a time of crisis, the Iron Age, in which, in a tone of utopian longing, Hesiod creates the poem *Works and Days* for his *hubris*-infested brother and unbalanced rulers—the so-called "bribe-swallowing" kings.

The *Odyssey* ends in the same longing, after the slaughter of the arrogant suitors and the conclusion of peace with their families at the behest of Zeus and in keeping with Homer's own aims. Odysseus becomes a mediating father figure, since he possesses the same heroic qualities as an Achilleus but has a greater power of reason, all the practical intelligence that is signaled by his epithet *polymetis*. He possesses an inner authority and reason that blow apart the fundamental significance of external honor, which is mirroring yourself in your surroundings and deriving your identity from this. This is shown, among other things, by the fact that, without losing his self-esteem, he can step into and be tested in the humble role of a beggar. However, this is also one of the reasons for the suspicion among the fellow warriors he encounters in the *Iliad*.

That, for Odysseus, this is really a matter of *sophrosyne* is made obvious in his speech to Achilleus, as the man who, if anyone, embodies heroic *arete*. He is the victim of a ruinous *megalopsychia*. His wounded honor and consequent anger determine the *Iliad* as a whole and cause the loss of a great number of men, including his friend Patroklos. Odysseus tries to talk him out of the folly occasioned by his wrath by making direct reference to self-control. He tries to gain influence over Achilleus' mind by stepping into the role of a father and exploiting the fact that he is older. In support of his errand, he quite simply quotes the words of his father Peleus, admonishing him: "Be it yours to hold fast in your bosom/ the anger of the proud heart, for consideration (*philophrosyne*) is better" (IX, 256-57).

Odysseus is backed by Achilleus' old mentor, Phoinix, who tells Achilleus to swallow his anger, pointing out that even gods can be appeased (IX, 497-98). More significantly, he introduces a subversive point of view into the *Iliad*'s closed, heroic cycle by relativizing a brutally destructive war as the only way to gain glory and honor, when he asserts that fame can also be won by "debate where men are made pre-eminent" (IX, 441).

The ambassadors fail with Achilleus. He is neither to be led nor driven but, if possible, becomes even more enraged, subject to his self-esteem as the impressive character he is. He thinks only of his own good, whereas even in the *Iliad* Odysseus acts with a view to to the collective, common good. Odysseus takes the young woman Chryseis back to her father, the priest of Apollo, who has been the cause of the Greek army's being struck by the god's deadly arrows. At Athene's behest, he gathers the Greeks in parliament and puts them in their place when they want to return home, by referring to the shame it will cast on all of them. He participates in the embassy to Achilleus and, with Nestor's nod, becomes its leader. And finally he prevents Achilleus—grief-stricken—at the loss of Patroklos from sending the army on an empty stomach to an inevitable defeat.

Even though Achilleus attacks anyone who tries to talk him into reason, however, he is still rational enough to acknowledge that he is primarily a manifestation of physical force: "I, who am such as no other of the bronze-armored Achaians/ in battle, though there are others better in council" (XVIII, 105-06). He admits that others, Nestor and Odysseus, are superior to him in eloquence—as an image of craftiness and insight. And mirroring this, Odysseus concedes that Achilleus is his superior in physical strength but points out that he himself stands above Achilleus in wisdom, age and experience:

> Son of Peleus, Achilleus, far greatest of the Achaians,
> You are stronger than I am and greater by not a little
> With the spear, yet I in turn might overpass you in wisdom
> By far, since I was born before you and have learned more things.
>
> (XIX, 216-19)

The absence of Achilleus' effectiveness is also the reason why the Greeks are unable to resist the Trojan onslaught. But on the other hand, this kind of force cannot take Troy.

7

The fundamental mental difference between Achilleus and Odysseus is demonstrated in an interesting way in the emblematics of arms in the two works. It appears that while the lance (and spear) is the heroic weapon of the *Iliad*, the bow is the symbolic weapon in the *Odyssey*.

The bow is Odysseus' weapon—and it is also the weapon with which Apollo, the god of awareness, punishes the guilty. He also named his son Telemachos after this weapon, since his name ostensibly means "distant fighter."[29] The ash spear is the hallmark of Achilleus. He has inherited it from his father, who in turn received it from the wise centaur Cheiron—"which no one else of all the Achaians/ could handle" (XVI, 141-42). So Patroklos does not have it with him, when, wearing Achilleus' armor to create fear among the attacking Trojans, he replaces him in bat-tle—and falls.

The spear possesses short-lived violence as its expression and form; the bow rep-resents the long-sighted goals and mental finesse which make Odysseus the destroyer of cities and, later, bring him safely home. Moreover, the power that throws a spear at random cannot bring a person through danger demanding reflec-tion and tenacity. In other words, the bow was created from pure *metis* and, prior to the invention of the gun, was the most highly developed weapon of battle. In contrast to casting spears and throwing stones, which require pure raw physical strength and are somewhat unpredictable in accuracy, nature's own forces are exploited in the bow, the tension of the wood in combination with the strength of the human being. Shooting a bow requires a high degree of concentration and mental self-control. Plato must be thinking along the same lines when using the bow as an image of precise, targeted *metis*. He says that, if a law is properly formed, it is like an arrow aimed at its mark,[30] seeking only that which is good.

Insofar as the bow is a weapon for battling at a distance, it evokes only contempt in the eyes of the true heroes of the *Iliad* and is used to characterize the cowardly nature of Paris. When he leaps out of his hiding place in a bush and hits Diomedes in the sole of his foot, the latter mocks him:

> You archer, foul fighter, lovely in your locks, eyer of young girls,
> If you were to make trial of me in strong combat with weapons
> Your bow would do you no good at all, nor your close-showered arrows.
>
> (XI, 385-87)

Diomedes will take no more heed of his shot than if a woman had hit him. No, he adds, a spear has a completely different lethal force. The bow and the spear are here directly contrasted with one another in the form of the male-heroic as opposed to the female-insidious that have unleashed the war. But in consideration of the fact that it is Paris who kills the greatest hero of the *Iliad*, Achilleus, with his arrow, this weapon is demonstrated in a reverse mirroring to have far greater power than Diomedes will admit.

In Achilleus, we meet the classic hero, as is vouched for by his Aeolian origin in northern Greek Thessaly, whereas Odysseus is the exponent of an advancing, expansive Ionian culture of which Homer's two epics are the supreme result. In this sense, the bow is not only Odysseus' weapon but an emblem for the world of rea-son that establishes itself in the *Odyssey*.

In short, the two weapons represent the contrast between the strengths con-stituting the essential difference between the *Iliad* and the *Odyssey*: physical strength —*bia/kratos*—versus intellectual power—*metis*. Achilleus personifies martial *arete* and dies very young in this interpretation—without having taken Troy. Odysseus bears within himself a far more complex and differentiated *arete*, which masters both the cruelty of war and his own self. He has duality that Phoenix sought: acting and speaking (thinking). More than anyone else apart from Nestor, Odysseus is the master of eloquence and possesses a power of thought that takes him farther than Achilleus, indeed becoming the direct cause of the ultimate conquest of Troy.

8

It is consistent with this portrait of Odysseus that Athene uses him in the *Iliad* as a spokesman to prevent the army from returning home. As said above, it is in Book 20 of the *Odyssey* that we find the clearest evidence that, just as he entreats Achilleus, so he can tame his rebellious heart. Here, despite his furious inner spirit he declines to slay the faithless slave girls who are consorting with the suitors. In Greek, he says, "Bear up, my heart" (*kradie*, 20, 18), which expresses exactly the sort of spiritual quality he has: tenacity. For the same reason, even in the *Iliad* he is given the eponym *polytlas*—that is, "long-suffering" or "tried" (X, 248). This tenacity of his is conditional on his mental flexibility, since it enables him to resist both the humiliations of the suitors and physical necessities such as hunger and sleep.

His inner monologue is the very first example of anything resembling introspection. And, as such, it launches a style in Greek literature. Thus Socrates refers several times to this passage in the *Odyssey* to explain the *sophrosyne* of self-control. The separation of body and soul, *soma* and *psyche*, which are otherwise entwined in one another—as mutual expressions for each other—is fully underway.

The Psychological Universe

1

In Homer, we enter a world that, from a psychological point of view, is difficult for modern readers to come to grips with. It is impossible to provide a description of it in one go; but in the following I will try to sketch out some fundamental psychological aspects for which I will provide a deeper and more nuanced analysis as we proceed.

When people today think about the linked but contrasting soul and body, we see a clear distinction between the psychic and the psychogical, a distinction with which Homer is not familiar, at least not in the same form. Nor is Homeric identity derived from the soul—which is sent as a breath of spirit to Hades—but is rather linked to the body. This is apparent in the very first verse of the *Iliad* in which it is said of the fallen heroes that their souls are hurled to Hades, while they themselves (*autous*, I, 4), i.e. their bodies, become feasts for the dogs. Similarly, Homer does not conceptualize but represents his intellectual, experiential world in the epic's concrete lucidity. Certainly, experience is processed rationally, but still clad in the raiment of mythology. This means in sum that in Homer we meet a tendency toward rationality that breaks through in the philosophers and is fully revealed in Socrates/Plato in whom we can finally say that the body and soul are completely separate.

Of course, *soma* and *psyche* appear in Homer, but *soma* means the dead body, which in cremation is delivered to the flames, after the *psyche* or the *pneuma* (breath) of the soul has left its bodily sheath through the mouth, nose or the place at which the fatal wound was received and has journeyed to Hades at the moment of death. Here, the soul continues to exist as an image devoid of blood or consciousness, an *eidolon*, that has the same appearance as the person had in life. As emerges during Odysseus' trip to the realm of the dead, the dead must drink sacrificial blood before they can speak, as blood, the fluid of the life force, restores consciousness to them. Correspondingly, the body, *soma*, only achieves visibility as something essentially different from the psyche in death.

Just as human beings by and large only understand themselves in concrete action, psychological description in Homer also has a thoroughly hypostasizing character, linked to areas and functions of the body. The unity of soul and body is underlined by the functional form of limbs. They act, so to speak, as independent, energy-filled beings—as actors for the whole person, who views his limbs as friendly helpers, denoting them as close friends with the word *philos*. The person as such is sometimes identified with the head.

That the concept of the soul in our own sense and that of Plato has not yet been developed by Homer is not the same thing as saying that he and his heroes have an infantile ability to conceptualize, as has been claimed. Spiritual life is merely still partially interwoven in the spirit of myth in a subject-object relationship that is alien to us. Meanwhile, Homer's presentation has passed beyond the non-reflective stage of language in which human beings expressed themselves holophrastically without separating nouns and verbs—and, consequently, without causal relationships and differentiation between the subject and its surrounding world.[31] The earliest fertility cults belong to this stage, while—to borrow a phrase from Nietzsche—the Olympian gods and thus also Homer constitute in themselves a "*principium individuationis*,"[32] which points toward a more developed ability to reflect with accompanying development of language.

Furthermore, the Homeric Greeks established something that resembles a psycho-somatic doctrine of the soul. This must be related to the elementary observation that psychological affect triggers dramatic physical reactions in different places in the body: for instance, anger or anxiety provokes convulsive reactions in the lungs and abdomen.

The manner in which Homer describes human beings and their psychology provides exceptional insight into the form and design of mythic thinking.[33] There is no clearly recognizable boundary between inner and outer. The outside world and its phenomena penetrate the individual and motivate him to act, just as the individual extends into his surrounding with his projections. In this exchange, it is the concrete action that provides the person with life and a form of dynamic identity, as action and person work together in an enclosed whole.

But when Homer and especially his heroes have difficulty understanding the sources of human motivation, they often describe them as something deriving from the gods. They can inspire strength (*menos*), but are also the cause of human mistakes, when men are struck by blindness (*ate*). But although it looks as though people act primarily at the prompting of the gods, there are numerous examples of a subject making decisions—not least, Odysseus, who under pressure draws up several alternative possibilities for action.

This unity of subject and object also means that exterior and interior come to reflect each other. Heroes are tall and handsome, corresponding to their *arete*: courage in war, skill and loyalty. This is confirmed in negative terms in the previously mentioned portrait of the blusterer Thersites, rich in "many words but disorderly" (II, 213). He urges flight and is described in anything but heroic terms as ugliness itself: "This was the ugliest man who came beneath Ilion. He was/ bandy-legged and went lame of one foot, with shoulders/ stooped and drawn together over his chest" (II, 216-18). He is a total contrast to Achilleus, but it is Odysseus who beats him into place with his scepter.

It is striking that this problematic is turned upside down in the *Odyssey*, a sign that there has been a disruption in the relationship between the external and internal. We shall return later to Odysseus' own words on this (see p. 82), where he maintains that a handsome man may have an ugly inner self and vice versa. In the second part of the *Odyssey* he himself becomes a living illustration of this truth. Transformed into a beggar with red and watery eyes, he has an external appearance that yields nothing to Thersites. However, in the confrontation with the arrogant and handsome suitors, it is clearly revealed that beauty is an inner phenomenon, for only the beggar-like Odysseus possesses a true royal essence.

We also have a negative description of one approach to this division and contrast between external and internal in the *Iliad* when Achilleus attacks those who speak ambiguously, saying one thing and meaning another, just as all the suspicion surrounding the person of Odysseus has its source in such duality.

2

The concept of *thymos* is a dominant feature in Homer's psychology. The word has been translated as "blood-soul," an expression that clearly points to a unity of the physical and the psychological. *Thymos* is not found in a particular organ but is physically located in the bloodflow to the heart and muscles that occurs in stressful circumstances. The manifold character of the phenomenon can best be observed in action. Telemachos says to one of the suitors who throws an ox shank at

Odysseus and misses (20, 299ff.), that it would have cost him his *thymos*, his life, if he had hit him.

Thymos also appears as an inner judge, an interlocutor, with which a person can consult in situations of doubt. Or *thymos* acts as a container into which the gods blow a special spiritual power (*menos*). And as an organ of all manner of emotional affects—anger, sorrow, joy—*thymos* comes closest to representing what we understand as temperament.

That *thymos* has this sort of breadth can be seen even in the *Iliad*, where it is said: "for the Destinies (Moira) put in mortal men the heart (*thymos*) of endurance" (XXIV, 49). It is also from this psychological function that the later *feeling of self* arises, since the individual has as his existential task that of reining in his emotional impulses: of knowing himself and displaying moderation—the *sophrosyne* that is the precondition for a community's *eunomia*. In short, one steps into one's social character by taming one's *thymos*—learning to suffer and tolerate.

Other spiritual activities have a more specific connection to an organ. The lungs (*phrenes*) function with ascertainable changes in breathing and can feel anger but also, on a higher level of consciousness, receive information from the gods. The singular form *phren* designates the diaphragm (sometimes, the heart), which the Greeks considered to be the place in the body where the psychic life, the soul, was located.

However, it is the word *nous* that refers to the highest degree of consciousness. Placed within the breast, *nous* has a clear cognitive significance and is linked to the verb "to see"—that is, to understand. Thus, Zeus bears the decision on the extent to which the war is to continue or not in his *nous* (see, p. 260). The fact that *nous* also appears more frequently in the *Odyssey* than in the *Iliad* is evidence of a shift awareness between the two epics. It is also as a cognitive medium that, in later philosophy, *nous* attains its overriding significance and takes precedence over *psyche* in a conflation with *thymos*.

The heart (*kradie*) and the abdomen (*etor*), too, have emotional effects that, understandably enough, are derived from the physiological observation that organs such as the lungs and the diaphragm are highly sensitive to impressions and external stimuli. As said above, in Book 20 of the *Odyssey*, Odysseus feels that his heart (*kradie*) is about to burst at the sight of the faithless slave girls in his home.

During the archaic period, an ongoing differentiation and definition of these psycho-somatic effects take place. *Nous* and *psyche* become internal psychological facts and autonomous entities that may well be affected from the outside but also have an independent significance, which is why it becomes of crucial importance to philosophers such as Parmenides, Socrates and Plato to separate psychological life from the blind alleys of the senses in order to achieve true insight.

3

The elements of Homeric psychology and their overlappings illustrate the concrete quality characteristic of Homer's narrative universe. An increasing abstraction can be demonstrated in the language, a constant simplification that makes it easier to use—not least philosophically and conceptually. Bruno Snell has convincingly uncovered this aspect of his language.[34] Among other things, he undertakes an analysis of the verb "to see" in its many perceptual manifestations. When a tortured Odysseus is sitting on the beach with Kalypso, he stares out over the water with a gaze in which seeing means to see in a special emotional manner in a nostalgic longing for his distant homeland (5, 84). And of the eagle, it is said that it sees with such sharp eyes that in his metaphoric thinking Homer uses a visual expression and associates with it a vivid image with the same penetrating power as sunrays.

A visual literalness creates a feeling of simultaneity, corresponding to the characters' feeling of coming into existence in the moment of action and otherwise not at all. This may also be caused by the fact that at an earlier stage of development human beings did not have tense-inflected verbs but indicated the positioning of some event in time by means of a word corresponding to this. These present tense forms also gave the people of those times a sense of the presence of all things, as every single moment was charged with a vitality from the beginning of creation.[35]

As a result of the later linguistic simplification, verbs of seeing lose their concrete sensuous qualities. On the other hand, an effective breadth is achieved that makes the remaining word for "seeing" suitable for use in abstract thinking. In addition, there is the "invention" of the definite article in Greek, which Snell is convinced is the very foundation for the ability to think speculatively. The definite article exists in Homer. This implies that, despite his concrete mode of thinking, he expresses himself in a language that is ready for philosophical use. However, in Homer's conceptual world a horse is still a specific, concrete horse, not—as in Plato—a denotative concept: the idea of a horse. However, the Wooden Horse anticipates this reflection that makes it possible to think of the horse in categorical terms.[36]

Structure and Intertextuality

1

Scholars used to claim that the *Iliad* and the *Odyssey* knew nothing of each other's existence or perhaps, because of the mutual competition, in order not to weary the reader with repetitions, desisted from mutual references. However, more recent investigations have been able to ascertain the otherwise very discernible fact that they have a large repertoire of common formulas and many cross-references confirming intertextuality.[37] For instance, Books 21 and 24 of the *Odyssey* import several direct turns of phrase from the *Iliad* in order to support the martial and heroic elements in the slaughter of the suitors and the struggle with the suitors' families.

I have earlier defined this intertextuality as a determinative *telos* that is found in each work separately—and binds them together. The latter occurs in Homer's utopia of the peaceful values of which Odysseus is the herald and which can be read in Homer's more or less hidden critique of heroic-aristocratic *arete*.

First of all, this means that the radical change of conscious life, which is forming in the *Odyssey* and which—with Odysseus as the key figure—was prepared for in the *Iliad*, is also an indication that the two epics should be viewed under the same heading. For by so doing, we can appreciate not only their inter-relatedness but also the differences that are so apparent when the protagonists of the two works, Achilleus and Odysseus, are compared. Secondly, we will see that the *Iliad* and the *Odyssey* find themselves in a common, progressive field of action and meaning. They have a uniformity in composition and narrative form, an overlapping gallery of figures that also makes it possible to see these texts as forming a unity—indeed, as a magnum opus and, in reality, the first collective expression of the formation of a Pan-Hellenic consciousness and identity.

2

Although it feels as though there are major lacunae in the action between the *Iliad* and the *Odyssey*—gaps that the so-called "epic cycle" originally attributed to Homer was to fill—an unbroken montage-like narrative line can nevertheless be discerned in the two texts. Via this it is also possible to understand the antecedents to the Trojan War—i.e. the abduction and seduction of Helen.

Achilleus not only appears in the *Iliad* but also in the *Odyssey*'s description of the realm of the dead. Here his tense relationship with Odysseus is thematically maintained, about which we hear when Demodokos relates an otherwise unknown conflict between them: to Agamemnon's unvarnished delight, they start to quarrel during a festival in honor of the gods (8, 74ff.). This conflict mirrors their confrontation after the death of Patroklos, when Achilleus wants to send the army into battle at once, while Odysseus demands that the warriors should first rest and eat something.

Through Achilleus' presence in the *Odyssey*, Homer relates purely factual events that occurred after the close of the *Iliad*: his death and burial, the conflict over his weapons, the taking of Troy, the embarkation and their conflict with Athene, and the homecomings of heroes—the difficult Menelaos, the fateful one of Agamemnon—"back-story" leading right up chain of events in the *Odyssey*.

Further, it can be said that the divergence that does in fact exist between the *Iliad* and the *Odyssey* appears partly in their compositional differences, which again are defined by plot, character and the general level of consciousness and partly by teleological purposiveness. In this sense, the analysis of the compositional structure on the basis of the disposition and symbolic reflections of the narrative becomes irrefutable evidence of the implicit narrator's omniscient authority.

Of course, the division into books, for which Aristarchus is one of those given responsibility, can at times seem so arbitrary that the individual books seem at cross purposes with the action. Simply take the transition from Book 12 to Book 13 in the *Odyssey*. Book 12 coincides with Odysseus' conclusion of the story of his adventures while travelling, while Book 13 begins with the repetitive formula describing the spellbound Phaiakians. Yet, the central theme of Book 13 deals with his arrival at Ithaka.

This apparently inconsistent division can be seen as a form of narrative suspense, since the dramatic tension and the chapters do not coincide. This kind of break creates a special drive, a kind of enjambment in the presentation arising in the meter, when the syntax of the spoken language breaks the meter and drags the understanding of the contents beyond the end of the immediate line.

3

In a compositional sense, the *Iliad* is undoubtedly less closely knit than the *Odyssey*: episode is added to episode with cumulative effect. One could very well imagine more or fewer characters and battle scenes without notably disturbing the overall effect. However, in contrast to a picaresque novel, for example, where this additive effect does *not* have any ultimate goal but merely follows the hero's aimless path from one spectacular situation to another, there is clearly an inner cohesion in the *Iliad*, linked to Achilleus and the course of his wrath introduced by the first words in the work.

Certainly, Achilleus is himself absent for lengthy periods, but the battles that rage to the disadvantage of the Greeks still have his affront and refusal to participate as an underlying element. And it is a sure sign of the work's compositional flexibility that it can be read in different ways, in three or five segments of action. The following is a brief description of the tripartite structure:

Part one (Books I to IX) is linked to the vengeance Achilleus' mother, the sea goddess Thetis, obtains from Zeus for the humiliation Agamemnon has inflicted upon her son. The second part (Books X to XVI) centers on his close friend Patroklos, who persuades Achilleus to lend him his armor, whereupon he enters battle as his alter ego . . . and falls. The final part (Books XVII to XXIV) is characterized by Achilleus' grief, his intervention in the war, his killing and brutal treatment of Hektor and his ultimate reconciliation with the Trojan king, Priam, who retrieves his son's body.

The crucial point is that, behind the crowd of people and spectacle of the battles, we sense another drama—i.e., the drama inherent in the constant accumulation of force. The force originates in Achilleus' unresolved anger and his running amok after the loss of Patroklos, a psychological reaction that evolves into his sympathy for Hektor's old father in the last book and his own sense of impending death and the playful incomprehensibility of the gods. This feeling of brotherliness that he suddenly displays here clearly reaches beyond the framework of the action and reinforces the entire underlying psychological spectrum leading to the *Odyssey*.

Another compositional parameter found at all narrative levels in both epics is the ring composition. As the concept implies, it is a compositional technique in which the beginning and the ending are reflected in each other—perhaps inspired by the pictorial panels painted on vases. The phenomenon can be demonstrated in many episodes—for instance in the description of the wild boar hunt in which Odysseus receives his famous scar.

Persistent attempts have been made to demonstrate the presence of this sort of circular composition in the *Iliad* based on the observation that the first and the final books have a series of parallel features (Book I corresponds to Book XXIV, Book II to Book XXIII, etc.). However, it is not possible to maintain this ring composition. So the results of such studies have been divergent; but all nevertheless point in the same direction, suggesting that there are more or less carefully prepared moves to working out an overall compositional structure that, together with thematic links, counteracts the loose episodic form.

4

Even though Achilleus' wrath and reconciliation constitute the unifying motif in the *Iliad*, this is nevertheless veiled by the many battle scenes and large numbers of heroes. Consequently, the *Odyssey* emerges with a much clearer compositional structure, based on Odysseus as the central figure. Aristotle focuses on this unity in Chapter 17 of his *Poetics* (1455b17-24):

> The argument of the *Odyssey* is not a long one. A certain man has been abroad many years; Poseidon is ever on the watch for him, and he is all alone. Matters at home too have come to this, that his substance is being wasted and his son's death plotted by suitors to his wife. Then he arrives there himself after his grievous sufferings; reveals himself, and falls on his enemies; and the end is his salvation and their death. This being all that is proper to the *Odyssey*, everything else in it is episode.

Just as the narrative direction is more strongly pronounced in the *Odyssey* than in the *Iliad* resulting from Odysseus' homecoming and vengeance, one can with Aristotle point to a corresponding causality in the action which makes the narrative clear and adds impetus to it. Since the work works on the basis of a constant interplay between the action and the teleological goal, its consecutive presentation establishes a correlative thematic context that is far more explicit than is the case in the *Iliad*.

Thus, the *Odyssey* functions on several levels at the same time, indeed almost contrapuntally, since apparently disparate episodes become absorbed into one another so that all the narrative threads finally enter into an unbroken symbolic and creative unity. A brief review of the composition will demonstrate how precisely the sequence of action in the *Odyssey* manifests its themes and its own purposeful direction.

The *Odyssey* has an overall symmetrical structureformed of two great semicircles. The first twelve books describe Odysseus' last period before arriving home. The final twelve books deal with his retaking power in Ithaka and his reunion with his son and wife.

A subdivision of the first half also provides symmetrical results: Beyond presenting the assembly of the gods and their decision that Odysseus should escape Kalypso's island, the first four books (the *Telemachy*) deal primarily with Telemachos—his spiritual awakening by Athene and subsequent "Grand Tour." On this journey, he searches for his father and undergoes a personal maturation process, only to return home, parallel with Odysseus, to meet his father and help drive out the suitors.

In an obvious crosscut technique, the next four books (Books 5 to 8) take up the thread from the first quartet: The decision reached by the assembled gods to send Hermes to Kalypso to order her to release home-sick Odysseus. We follow the building of his ship, shipwreck, struggle with the sea—i.e. his arch-enemy Poseidon—and his arrival, naked and battered, on the Phaiakian island of Scheria.

In the next four books (Books 9 to 12), the *Apologoi*, we have a flashback description of the adventures he experiences between his departure from Troy and his reception by the Phaiakians. We are presented on the one hand with an eyewitness account, and on the other a first-person narrator in his own narrative universe, while we also gain access to a mythic reality beyond the merely realistic world of action.

The first four books of the second major section (Books 13 to 16) describe his voyage from the Phaiakians who, sympathetic after his account of his wanderings, help him to get home to Ithaka, where he meets his divine patroness Athene and the faithful swineherd. In an elegant, well-timed crosscut, Telemachos is brought home from Sparta by Athene in Book 15, and there met by his father. Everything is now ready for the decisive trial of strength with and vengeance on the arrogant suitors.

The four penultimate books (Books 17 to 20) begin and end with the seer Theoklymenos' doomladen prophecies for the suitors. Otherwise, we follow on the heels of Odysseus, who now, transformed into a beggar, enters into his own royal palace in order to see for himself the conduct of the suitors and thereby plan his strategy. His old nurse recognizes his scar, and he and experiences empathy for Penelope who, by contrast, fails to recognize him. Meanwhile, his indignation escalates at the humiliations Athene allows the suitors to heap upon him and his house in order for him to grow in strength and resoluteness.

The final four books (Books 21 to 24) deal with the actual regaining of power: Odysseus' brilliant shot with his bow, the slaughter of the suitors, his reunion with his wife and father, and his reconciliation at Athene's behest with the families of the slaughtered suitors. Thus, the work's entelechy, its purposiveness, is brought to an end: the kingdom re-established, the reborn and (self-)integrated hero now returned to his rightful place. However, as in the *Iliad*, the *Odyssey* also throws light on the concluding action, when Odysseus must once again go on a long voyage in order to become reconciled with Poseidon, before he can finally return home and attend to his kingdom until his death, in peace and full of days. Thereafter, his "individuated" son Telemachos, who has matured over the course of the *Odyssey* and demonstrates his ability in battle, will step into his father's place and secure a prosperous future for the kingdom.

5

In order completely to understand how the composition and thematic world of the *Iliad* and the *Odyssey* are connected, we must ultimately look at the temporal sequence.

Generally speaking, the works are played out against a temporal framework that takes its start with the abduction of Helen—and even more distantly in the contest among Athene, Hera and Aphrodite as to which of them is the most beautiful—a question unleashed by the goddess of strife, Eris, during the marriage of Thetis and Peleus, the parents of Achilleus (see p.121). The abduction itself takes place approximately ten years before the beginning of the war, as Helen herself says at the end of the *Iliad* (XXIV, 765–66) that it has been twenty years since she left her homeland and her husband.

The sequence of events to which the *Iliad* directly relates lasts approximately fifty days,[38] while the battle scenes—i.e., the primary content of the work—stretch over a mere four days. In addition, there are the games in connection with Patroklos' death and funeral and the presentation of Hektor's body to King Priam in the final book.

The *Odyssey* has a chronological extent of more or less the same character, if it is maintained that the work as a whole is enacted over the ten years it takes Odysseus to return home. However, as in the *Iliad*, the *Odyssey*'s plot is condensed around a relatively short time span and, as in the *Iliad*, we are placed *in medias res*. The *Iliad* greats us with the strife that breaks out between Agamemnon and Achilleus and, leading to the taking of Troy. In the *Odyssey*, events have reached a fateful point, the suitors demanding that Penelope choose a husband from among them, something she can no longer refuse, since Telemachos is now grown and Odysseus himself has charged her to marry again when his son has grown a beard. This coincides with Odysseus, at the gods' behest, finally being able to leave Kalypso and, after his visit to the Phaiakians, return home, as Fate has determined for him.

Chronologically, the *Iliad* opens into the *Odyssey* which, as mentioned, fills the lacunae in the sequence of events between the two narratives with montage-like clips. The *Odyssey*, on the other hand, reaches out beyond the framework of action by referring to how Odysseus must again go on a journey to conclude peace with Poseidon and, according to Teiresias' prophecy, return home to die after a long life as ruler in peaceful, happy surroundings.

In this respect, time is an essential factor in both composition and action, since it is in the fullness of time that the strife fundamental to the Homeric works is expiated, thereby delivering Homer's ulterior *utopian* purpose: the longing for a peaceful society which Odysseus will rule thanks to his personal qualities, tenacity, and will to return home. Similarly, within the framework of the *Odyssey*, Telemachos has developed into a man and potential ruler, able to ensure continuity in the kingdom on the basis of the same values as his father.

Compositional Reflection and Counter-reflection

1

Since Homer uses neither a conceptual nor a later psychological form of representation, he must—to be able to describe the human qualities and personal development of his characters—still resort to the way in which myth reworks (and controls) this world of experience. The artistic technique in which the narrative and the compositional aspects meet is reflection and counter-reflection. On the basis of what has already been said, we can maintain that the *Iliad* and the *Odyssey* are in themselves comprehensive mirror histories of elemental life forces: strife, the erotic, etc., and are in this sense mythic complexes with a growing ability for reflection, leading to philosophical thinking. This is based on the fact that, in the *Iliad* and the *Odyssey*, Homer not only forms his works to produce the culmination of the genre but also its conclusion.

Odysseus has been viewed by scholars as a "fixed character,"[39] that is, a figure undergoing no development, since it is maintained that he is exactly the same when he returns home as when he departed. This is both correct and incorrect. It is correct insofar as Homer does not describe a psychological process of becoming a person as in a modern *Bildungsroman*. It is incorrect, because both he and the moral interpretation linked to his tales become incomprehensible and fundamentally less interesting if this should really be the case.

This interpretation in itself shows what can happen if and when interpreters have not understood that Odysseus' personal maturation cannot be measured by contemporary psychologizing. For this is not the same as saying that Homer did not have any idea of psychology, as we have seen that he uses different expressions to describe the life of the mind and is able to describe human intentions even though there are not yet words (nouns) for them.[40]

Thus, Homer had to work out his own narrative techniques for communicating the experiences that he and the ancient Greeks obviously had to no less a degree than modern people. The narrative consequence is that he uses the surroundings: landscapes, places, vicissitudes of fortune, including the gods, as projections for what happens to Odysseus. As external clues, all these concrete references reflect what happens internally—on the basis of the literal connectedness between the external and the internal on the mythical plane on which the *Odyssey* after all is played out.

The main point of the *Iliad* and the *Odyssey* is to allow Odysseus to undergo a personal development that can make him the protagonist for Homer's underlying world view and his dream of a social *eunomia*. Since my analysis as a whole aims at investigating and demonstrating this hypothesis, I will only here give an indication of the compositional and symbolic mirroring technique he uses.

2

The war against Troy mirrors Odysseus' character as a hero. On the one hand, he converges in it with an aristocratic *arete*; on the other, he distinguishes himself by his particular intellectual quality (*metis*) and points forward to what is to come. This is especially reflected in his relationship with Athene, who is his particular ally even in the *Iliad* and who uses him for her particular purpose, when the job requires an intelligent solution. In short, in this way, she is a positive divine person-ification and a reflection of his inner self.

The journey will become the touchstone for his abilities to cope with life: determining whether he can serve the narrator's *utopian* intention. This requires him further to develop and hone his potential, which was the basis for the fall of Troy: to go from being a destroyer of cities to become a builder of cities upon his homecoming. The journey in this respect is a journey of initiation and individua-tion, as it is for his son on another level.

It is in this context that, for example, the *Apologoi* are to be interpreted: as a reflection of primal forces, temptations, in which Odysseus' tenacity, intelligence and capacity for emancipation are put under extreme pressure and he must psycho-logically integrate what these demonic figures, mirror-like, represent. For as Athene is his positive reflection, Poseidon becomes his negative, an enemy, which ultimately only makes sense as a psychological phenomenon along with all the other related chthonic forces. Thus, his wanderings, his homecoming, his transformation into a beggar, his archery skills, etc., are a part of a great unifying hall of mirrors, along with the orbit of the sun and the passing of the seasons, with landscapes, natural elements etc. Everything that is presented on the level of immediate action as an elemental folktale is revealed by this interpretative practice to be very meaningful indeed for a deeper understanding of the psychology in the works and their *telos*.

We can illustrate how everything in the *Odyssey* works together in meaningful patterns that interweave with one another to provide depth and perspective by turning to Demodokos' songs for the Phaiakians. On one level, they are apparently only sung for entertainment, but they all have a hidden thematic function.

The first song (8, 74-82), which describes the otherwise unknown conflict between Achilleus and Odysseus at a feast in honor of the gods, does not merely create a contrast between the characteristic qualities of the two heroes: force and wisdom. It also points back to their controversy in the *Iliad* and the heroic era, which came to an end with Troy, while Odysseus and the epic about him point forward. And it reveals the difference between the tradition-bound Demodokos and the subjective first-person narrator Odysseus.

The second song's story concerns infidelity (8, 266-366): on one hand, the affair between Aphrodite and Ares belongs in the *Iliad*'s panopticon of the gods, showing their human and depraved characteristics. On the other hand, it mirrors the fateful theme of faithlessness, just as the murder of Agamemnon by his wife points toward the suitors' siege of Penelope and Odysseus' slaughter of them. This theme of victory is anticipated in the third of Demodokos' songs (8, 493-520)—namely, the song about the Wooden Horse, which in a premonition of the slaughter of the suitors anticipates how Odysseus' cunning will finally end the war since, by re-establishing order in his kingdom, he makes an impact beyond the heroic age and its ideals.

3

If the mirror technique so far described is indirect in the sense that Homer does not explicitly call attention to it, it can, on the other hand—in a gradual transition—be seen that he is fully conscious of this compositional practice in his use of mirroring. For the external narrative sequence is controlled, particularly in the *Odyssey*, by the underlying thematic links that are profiled through a textual reflection or counter-story. This appears at intervals and throws light on the concrete action.

The most obvious and significant counter-story deals with Agamemnon's fateful homecoming. He is murdered by his wife Klytemnestra and her lover Aigisthos, who then rule for seven years until Agamemnon's son Orestes avenges his father. In a shocking act that inspired all the great Greek dramatists, Orestes, prompted by his sister Elektra, kills his mother (which he does not do in the *Odyssey*), calling down his mother's Erinyes as punishment.

As this dramatic sequence of events is composed as a counter-story in the *Odyssey*, it is exemplary in a dual sense. As commander and king, Agamemnon loses his honor—indeed, his entire reputation—by being murdered upon his homecoming. In a sharp contrast to Odysseus' strategic behavior with the suitors, who in principle represent the same attempt as that of Aigisthos to take his wife and power, we see the limitation of the typical hero in the tragic figure of Agamemnon.

After Odysseus learns of Agamemnon's fate from his own lips in Hades, Agamemnon becomes a cautionary figure for Odysseus. Upon his arrival at Ithaka, he directly appeals to Athene for help in avoiding "perishing by an evil/ fate in my palace, like Atreus' son Agamemnon" (13, 383-84). Athene has earlier told Telemachos that she would have preferred to return home late, like Odysseus, rather than like Agamemnon to come back and be murdered by his wife: "I myself would rather first have gone through many hardships/ than come home and be killed at my own hearth, as Agamemnon was killed, by the treacherous plot of his wife, and by Aigisthos" (3, 232-34).

Athene also praises Odysseus, because, in contrast to others returning home, he does not go straight to his family: "But it is not/ your pleasure to investigate and ask questions, not till/ you have made trial of your wife" (13, 335-36). This statement must be seen in relation to the fact that, in a mirrored perspective as the faithful, waiting wife, Penelope stands in contrast to Klytemnestra (and Helen). However, the entire assessment of Woman is influenced by the shameful behavior of these two sisters: the fact that Helen allowed herself to be seduced and became the cause of the Trojan War, while Klytemnestra killed her husband.

We will return to this judgment of the female gender and merely note that Odysseus refers to Klytemnestra as a "vile woman" (11, 384). According to Agamemnon, with her vile deeds she has "splashed the shame on herself and the rest of her sex, on women/ still to come, even on the one whose acts are virtuous" (11, 433-34), and, quite understandably, he counts Helen among these dangerous women. Against this background, he advises Odysseus not to be too forthcoming with his wife Penelope, who, by contrast, will not cost him his life. This high estimation of Penelope, which Agamemnon and the narrator of the work share, also appears in the final book, in which Agamemnon comprehends Odysseus' honor directly from her fidelity: "Surely you won for yourself a wife endowed with great virtue" (24, 193).

How determinative Agamemnon's tragedy is for the thematic sequence of events in the *Odyssey* may be deduced from the fact that it is presented in the first book by Zeus, who in a way has been affected by it. Through Hermes, Zeus has tried in vain to dissuade Aigisthos from his treacherous project and uses his refusal to justify himself as the supreme god: the gods are blamed for all the misfortunes human beings bring down on themselves. In this sense, Aigisthos and Odysseus, who is obedient to the gods, may be perceived as contrasting figures.

Finally, from the repeated description of Orestes' vengeance, we have an exemplary model for (self-)education for Telemachos, strongly inspired by Athene, who, with reference to the suitors, says: "Or have you not heard what glory was won by great Orestes/ among all mankind, when he killed the murderer of his father?" (1, 298-99).

Later, in a slightly different formulation, Agamemnon's brother Menelaos repeats these admonitory words to Telemachos: "So it is good, when a man has perished, to have a son left/ after him, since this one took vengeance on his father's killer" (3, 196). And he adds, in a passage whose authenticity has been called into doubt by others, including Aristarchus: "So you too, dear friend, for I see you are tall and splendid,/ be brave too, so that men unborn may speak well of you" (3, 199-200). Menelaos himself has heard of his brother's murder during a difficult journey home from the wise man of the sea, the shape-changer Proteus, and has raised a memorial to his brother. And with the synchronicity that links events and themes together, he returns home the very day on which Orestes is able to bury his father's murderer and co-conspirator, his mother, for whose death Orestes is not made directly responsible in Homer.

Thus, the *Odyssey* functions as a dense, finely-meshed system of references in which there are many more mirroring aspects than have been described, as we will subsequently have the occasion to observe. In sum, we may say that the individual stories and figures open up into each other and, together, create an elemental but rich world of experience and consciousness, an ever more interesting and supple narrative universe centered on the work's rugged protagonist, Odysseus.

Stages of Consciousness

1

If we maintain the idea of the *Iliad* and the *Odyssey* as a unified work governed by a single compositional drive, we can—by way of experiment to generate insight into the underlying structures of consciousness—dissolve (decompose, if you will) this progression and extrapolate vertically the layers of consciousness folded into each other.

Oldest in this hierarchy of consciousness proves to be Odysseus' travel tales, the *Apologoi*, which have clearly incorporated features not only of the folktale but also of shamanism[41] and elemental archetypal experiences. Indeed, even within the tales, we shall later see that it is possible to isolate various stages. Compare Skylla with Kalypso or the Kyklops with Phaiakians and it is clear that, even though they are all mythic figures, Kalypso and the Phaiakians have achieved a higher level of civilized development.

The next general stage of consciousness is found in the heroic era, which covers the *Iliad* and its set of norms. Here, we are still close to the world of the gods. Not only do the heroes descend directly from the gods, but the gods also participate in the battles. And although the narrator refers to a lost heroic time with giant heroes such as Herakles, here Ajax, the son of Telemon, is as big as a barn door and clearly endowed with character traits from an atavistic past. This stage corresponds to Hesiod's description of the heroic era in *Works and Days*, generational situated between the Bronze and Iron Ages.

However, even within the otherwise fixed narrative framework of the *Iliad*, a gradation can be demonstrated. Thus, we have heard Nestor, who is two generations older than the young heroes, chide them for their disputes. Compared to the heroes like Theseus he knew in his youth, he says provocatively: "Never yet have I seen nor shall see again such men as these were" (I, 262). Achilleus and Agamemnon have to swallow this slight, since they are the originators of the quarrel.

At the same time, in the heroic epoch this chronological differentiation becomes an expression of its impending doom. So, as said above, Homer ends the great age of the epic paradoxically by appearing out of thin air with a unique, fully developed work and with this culmination putting an end to the genre. With the *Odyssey* and Odysseus, he composes his way out of the heroic and into the reforms and expansive consciousness of the new age.

The third stage includes this process and constitutes the main part of the *Odyssey,* which deals with the homecoming itself and the re-establishment of the kingdom at Ithaka in a realistic and recognizable *polis* milieu, in which we meet shepherds, servants, poets, craftsmen and slaves. This occurs by virtue of and in a mirroring of Odysseus' personal traits, his dialectical gifts and ability to endure adversity, as well as the process of development he has gone through, and this makes him stand out as the ancient Greek most in line with later thought.

2

Even in antiquity, people had a notion that the concrete action in Homer's two epics held a form of consciousness that allowed for a more profound interpretation. The originator of this was Theagenes of Rhegion, who around 525 B.C. undertook an allegorical interpretation of the *Iliad* in which it is assumed that the heroes were interpreted as ideal characters embodying virtue and bravery. Similarly, we are able to ascertain that a moral interpretation of Homer took hold among certain philosophers—for example, the Cynics, who find in Odysseus (and Herakles) universal models of courage and tenacity.[42]

As I later argue, Socrates—and Plato—use Odysseus as a precursor and prefiguration of Socrates himself. This corresponds to the meaning Moses has in the Bible for the figural interpretation of Jesus. In leading mankind into the heavenly Palestine, just as Moses had led his people out of captivity in Egypt, Jesus completes what Moses began.[43]

Indeed, we can claim that the very way in which later Greeks used Homer as a paradigm for education reveals the text's potential moral universe of law (*nomos*) and custom (*ethos*). The *arete* of the heroes, despite their limitations, could serve as examples of courage, sense of duty, and—in the case of Odysseus—the discursivity and tenacity of moderation.

The *Iliad* and the *Odyssey* deal with seduction/sexuality, war, travel, homecoming and the rebuilding of a kingdom in chaos. In this combination of elemental forms of life, characterized by mythical imagery, in this concrete world of action, we will, among other things, find embedded the idea of constitutional evolution. This can be shown in the conception of succession that runs throughout the works. This is especially clear in the *Odyssey* in which, on a (depth) psychological level, the masculine heroic first person is liberated from his (primal) maternal connection, the chthonic space of consciousness in which the *Apologoi* play out—just as Telemachos also liberates himself from his mother. This expresses a profound understanding of how age and biology work together as a part of the development of personality through which an Odysseus passes—a process that is literally and symbolically linked to the theme of birth and death, as well as to the cycle of the sun and the seasons.

To the concrete, moral and typological elements is added the telos of the works, whose future-oriented goal, as said above, is the utopia of a peaceful society, liberated from the horrors of war. The foundation is built on Odysseus' character traits and journey home. Homer contrasts him with the *hubris* of the suitors, as he represents the social stability (*eunomia*) that Solon later makes the basis for his social reforms. When Antinoos throws a footstool at Odysseus, this is too much even for one of the other suitors, and he observes that the gods often transform themselves (*theoxyin*) and walk among men "watching to see which men keep the laws (*eunomia*), and which are violent (*hubris*)" (17, 487).

It is scarcely wrong to believe that Homer is here expressing his own basic view of life and finds in Odysseus the embodiment of such conduct. To Socrates, through a process of prefigurative thinking, the *arete* Odysseus displays, becomes the striving for the truth of the soul.

Unifying Narrative Elements

1

A precondition for Homer's ability to get such a comprehensive composite of consciousness to work aesthetically as a whole is that there are unifying narrative elements even in the tale's minor units, the semantic seams that support the overall composition and the general level of consciousness of the works. If such a narrative function can really be demonstrated, it would be additional documentation to suggest that a brilliant narrator has assembled and summarized the original oral material. However, it would require a separate study to provide such an exhaustive analysis. So, this section is only intended to serve as a summary demonstration of Homer's epic integrity, since he has de facto at his disposal a repertoire of narrative forms almost as comprehensive as later epic authors.

In general, as an authorial third-person narrator, Homer has the omnipotence necessary to permeate the entire universe with his consciousness. For example, he knows what the gods are thinking and is familiar with their language, as is shown in his use of *dionymia* (p. 40), and he can predict the course of events. When Poseidon teases Odysseus during the shipwreck, the narrator can call on the assistance of a sea nymph to calm us: "And yet he will not do away with you, for all his anger" (5, 341).

Despite his omnipotence, the narrator himself is subject to the absolute necessity of spellbinding his listeners, just as Odysseus keeps the Phaiakians virtually paralyzed in the iron grip of his tale. Whereas for the listeners it is a total experience in which the singers have their talents favoured by the Muses, a formal analysis can reveal the many rhetorical and artistic flourishes Homer actually uses and which determine his success as a narrator.

2

As Aristotle writes in his *Poetics*, the hexameter has proved to be the best suited for epic poetry, and so he calls it the "heroic" meter.[44] It is characterized as being "the gravest and weightiest" of the meters and that best able to assimilate dialects and metaphor. To this, we can add its power of suggestion, as it almost hypnotically allows its waves of verse to flow through the mind of the listener. And precisely through the pulse of its special rhythm, Homer avoids making his account monotonous and boring.

Formally, the hexameter uses oral diction, but Homer has developed the verse form to such an extent that, in individual verses, there is not only a break in the caesura in the middle of the verse but there are also a number of minor elisions and rhythmic groupings linked, for example, to particularly significant words. In this way, the verses scan in ever new cadences. Particularly striking is his use of enjambment.[45] For even though a particular meaning could and should stop at the end of the line, and prosody actually requires a break, he extends the meaning of its contents into the next line. As readers, we are thus bound up in a two-fold metrical movement: the verse requires a pause at the end of the line, but the need for understanding almost forces us to continue into the following line. This counters uniformity of diction and is a crucial reason why the hexameter acquires this cumulative, rolling energy in which one element is added to another either in conformity with or opposition to the fixed, basic rhythm of the versification.

3

A similar flexibility can be found in Homer's use of formulas and epithets. As already said, much has been made of them as an indication of the oral tradition behind the text. And there is no denying that they can sometimes have the effect of purely mechanical fillers, as when the villain Aigisthos is called "stately" (*amymonos* 1, 29). It is crucial to the interpretation of the Homeric epics that such fixed formulas do not stand in the way of a broader understanding of the thematic determination that is also behind the formulas. On the contrary, we can use them to establish the probable presence of a conscious authorial intent. They are not only mnemonic devices but they also serve meaningful functions by defining characters and linking the *Iliad* and the *Odyssey* together in clear overlaps that mediate the connection between the two works.

The formulas linked to Odysseus are beyond dispute the richest and most nuanced, all pointing toward the various sides of his manifold character. He is *polytropos, polymetis, polyatlas, polyphron, polymechanos*, where the prefix *poly* indicates the many-sided nature of his character. In addition, the epithetic formulas are used to emphasize the similitude governing his family. Penelope and Odysseus share the epithet *echephron*—prudent—while the son Telemachos is designated as *pepnymenos* —sensible—which says something about his personal qualities as well as his intellectual relationship to his parents. By using formulaic epithets in this way, Homer can make clear the main theme and his own utopia: restoring the divided family through the quality of intelligence and moderation that distinguishes them more than any other and makes them guarantors for the new world order.

4

Together with the formulas, the Homeric simile, *comparatio*, constitutes the most striking stylistic feature. The simile is certainly valuable as a formal phenomenon but in this context particularly on account of its semantic necessity insofar as we can give a plausible explanation for why it appears more frequently in the *Iliad* than in the *Odyssey*.

Formally, like the related metaphor, the purpose of the simile is to join together otherwise separate units of reality. Artistically, the point is to establish a greater space of experience and consciousness around the event or characters to which the simile refers. This is the case in Homer, as his similes have a particular character, which is exactly why it is designated in stylistics as the Homeric simile.

What is notable in Homer's use of *comparatio* is that the term of comparison in the formation of the image compels an independent meaning that reaches beyond the point of the comparison itself. It thus creates its own aesthetic unity and becomes, so to speak, a poem within the poem. What is interesting is that, in these "small poems," we seem to come particularly close to Homer. For they are often based upon concrete, realistic observations of nature and everyday life. There are pure descriptions of nature, similes taken from the world of hunting or tending sheep threatened by lions, or from daily tasks such as threshing, etc. (see quotation p. 269). The comparative element is most often placed first. The surprising, paradoxical feature is that peaceful images are frequently used to illustrate warriors in battle.

What does Homer accomplish with this? Two things. First, the Homeric simile is intended by means of narrative to take something unknown and strange (the *Iliad*'s distant world of heroes was to the Greeks of that time), as more comprehensible and concrete, since the simile of course is taken from ordinary, familiar reality. In short, it evens out the time distance between the lost heroic world and the situation in which the narrative occurs.

This view is confirmed by the fact that the *Odyssey*'s realistic milieu in part makes this sort of communicative tactic superfluous, since it takes place in an environment familiar to listeners. Only in the description of the slaughter of the suitors are there various similes, which shows the relationship between this episode with the heroic world of the *Iliad*.

Secondly, the high frequency of the everyday similes in the *Iliad* means that this reality or image forms a critical contrast to the aristocratic warrior culture it was otherwise intended to illustrate. In this way, just as in the formulas, Homer adds an alternative and fertile world of action to the horror of war and the heroic code of conduct. Thus, he is able to accentuate his own ideal life, which is generally expressed in the works' longing for a peaceful coexistence in which people tend their gardens and look after their animals.

5

As an omniscient narrator, Homer needs to be able to enter into his characters and understand how they make decisions for which they, and not the gods, are responsible. Summaries of thoughts occur in which the characters address their inner selves—most often in the form of *thymos*. Even though, by the nature of things, the poet does not master the sort of free indirect speech that is first developed in literary Modernism, and despite the fact that one's inner life, in principle, is a closed country, he is nevertheless able to reveal the thought process to a certain extent, so that one almost has the same angle on an event as the person experiencing it. For example, consider Odysseus' shipwreck off the island of the Phaiakians:

> But when he was as far away as a voice can carry
> He heard the thumping of the sea on the jagged rock-teeth.
> For a big surf, terribly sucked up from the main, was crashing
> On the dry land, all was mantled in salt spray, and there were
> No harbors to hold ships, no roadsteads for them to ride in,
> But promontories out-thrust and ragged rock-teeth and boulders.
>
> (5, 400-06)

The scene is realistic and told with a gentle, almost undetectable transition between what is experienced and what is narrated, which in turn promotes a sense of presence. The closest we come to a true psychological description is in the previously mentioned scene in Book 20 in which Odysseus must overcome his anger at the faithless slave girls in a long dialogue that has the embryonic character of introspection (see p. 173). Since the narrator does not master free inner monologue, he cannot create a flashback—for example, to Odysseus' youth in the recognition scene.

That characters address their hearts in direct speech is no surprise, since Homer is building on an oral tradition. Direct speech is predominant everywhere, most briefly in the form of commands, greetings, etc. As a narrative stance, its purpose is to create dramatic contemporaneity or a commonality between what is told, the narrator and the listeners, in order to achieve maximum expressive effect.

The same purpose is served by epic condensation and compression, in which a person's character is sketched in fixed outline by means of a few strokes, in indications of time, and by frequent use of quantifiers like "many"—or by the use of magical numbers such as three or nine days. Homer moreover makes use of summarizing descriptive techniques that also aim at creating an emotional identity between narrated time and narrative time, particularly in battle scenes.

In the *Iliad*, the narrator can suddenly push the listeners away and open up the huge gap in time that he otherwise tries to smooth over with similes and an oral present-tense style. This occurs when he points out the difference there is between the heroic age and the present in which he is speaking. For example, he tells how Hektor threw a stone that was so big that, even with the aid of levers, two men "today" were unable to hoist it into a wagon (XII, 447). He also moves in the opposite direction when he refers directly to "you"—"So straight for the Lykians, o lord of horses, Patroklos,/ you swept" (XVI, 584-85) and similar passages (see 14, 55; 17, 272). Such a form of address promotes a unique sense of presence, an almost cinematic close-up. On the other hand, this smoothing over of narrative distance almost destroys the epic's objective account.

As the teller of myths that he is, Homer also understands how important it is for an epic to breathe. He inserts pauses that both reduce the reader's heart and breath rates and help to build up the tension. Among other things, the similes are able to create such factors in the sequence of events by breaking up that sequence. In other cases, whole books—for example, the so-called *Catalogue of Ships* in Book II of the *Iliad*—act as a prolonged pause, digressions so long they dissolve the unity of the work.

6

A special narrative phenomenon for creating tension and unity is synchronicity, a cinematic cross cutting between contemporary events. Even Aristotle in his definition of the distinction between tragedy and epic is conscious of the dramatic significance of this effect. Here, the epic has an advantage, because it is not possible within the framework of a tragedy to present several events at one time. He writes:

> Whereas in epic poetry the narrative form makes it possible for one to describe a number of simultaneous incidents; and these, if germane to the subject, increase the body of the poem. This then is a gain to the Epic, tending to give it grandeur, and also variety of interest and room for episodes of diverse kinds.[46]

Measured against modern narrative techniques, however, we must recognize that, since Homer does not master free indirect speech, he also has his work cut out to communicate synchronous events. For example, he is forced to place the beginning of Telemachos' journey and Odysseus' final days with Kalypso, which generally coincide temporally, in extension of one another. Although this has led to the claim that the *Telemachy* is a later interpolation in the saga concerning Odysseus, it must be said with respect to narrative technique that Homer has presumably tried to achieve a logical clarity in the plot at the cost of the tension-building simultaneity of the compositional structure.

On the other hand, the epic synchronicity is rather successful in Book 15, since there is cross cutting between Odysseus' sojourn with the swineherd and Telemachos' departure from Sparta. Also embedded in this is Penelope's concern for her son and the suitors' attempt to set up an ambush. Considered as a whole, these circumstances point to the ultimate meeting of the father and son, which has been one of the deeper currents through the entire work—in preparation for the slaughter of the suitors and the re-established social order centred on the happy, erotic reunion of the separated spouses in the immovable bed.

In this sense, the time and space factor has fundamental symbolic significance not only for the external structure of the material but also for the entire Homeric project that is placed on Odysseus' shoulders through the *telos* of both works. As I have already sketched in broad outline, this time-bound thematic may be summarized in this way:

In Book 1, the optimal point of intersection is struck for the action of the entire *Odyssey*, the exact turning point at which Odysseus can return home: "But when in the circling of the years that very year came/ in which the gods had spun for him his time of homecoming" (1, 16-17). This time was prophesied by Halitherses on the departure of Odysseus twenty years earlier:

> I said that after much suffering, with all his companions
> Lost, in the twentieth year, not recognized by any,
> He would come home. And now all this is being accomplished.
>
> (2, 174-76)

To the subjective drama of this fateful turn corresponds the fact that, on the home front at Ithaka, the suitors who have besieged Penelope for three years and frittered away Odysseus' wealth have discovered the cunning with which she has kept them at bay: the shroud for Laertes, which she weaves during the day and unravels at night. So she no longer has any excuse for not choosing a new husband from among the suitors. She has her back to the wall.

At the same time, Telemachos has reached an age at which he is ready to take on the role of his father's son and with this identity to assume adult responsibility. Until the start of the *Odyssey*, he has been on the defensive, hesitant and weak, a mother's boy. Now, another woman, Athene, takes over and instills courage in him, so that, to the amazement of those around him, he appears with a masculine authority the like of which has not been seen since Odysseus' departure. Everything is at its peak and an advent-like mood of decline and re-birth predominates.

It is on the basis of an inner necessity that the *Odyssey* is woven through with time parameters. Not time in our general, airy abstraction, but as a concrete category of experience with which everyone is familiar. People clearly orient themselves and express themselves with reference to the seasons—even down to the symbolic way in which a figure such as King Laertes is described in the autumn of his decline.

The rhythm of the day is a central partner in all events. At daybreak, the heroes in the *Iliad* leave their couches and prepare for battle, culminating when the sun reaches its zenith and, at sunset, withdrawing again to their camps and spending the evening on food, song and games, before going to sleep to renew their energy in preparation for when morning once again calls on them. Peaceful everyday life, too, is defined by the rhythm of the day: Nausikaa rises early in the morning to wash, etc.

In the same way, Homer deals with the understanding of larger periods of years in clearly profiled, almost formulaic time modules. The war lasts for ten years, the voyage home takes ten years, the siege of the suitors lasts for three years, Odysseus' sojourn with Kirke lasts a year and that with Kalypso seven years. Three days, nine days, 12 and 17 days are recurring time references for Odysseus' voyages and ship-wrecks. These are time references with the same magical character as in sacred writings and fairy tales, full of mythical life from the everlastingly repeated beginnings of primal creation.

This is confirmed by Odysseus' expedition to Hades, a journey to hell of one day's duration from sunrise to sunrise. The sojourn follows the movement of the sun throughout the day and the darkness of night in the realm of the dead. These events correspond to the most significant time indication—the day on which Odysseus returns home and takes his revenge—in the transition from the nineteenth to the twentieth year. It happens in the transition from the interlunar period to the new moon—in connection with a great new-year festival for Apollo and the start of the coming year—a time of renewal and spring, in which Odysseus later mirrors his own homecoming and personality as a solar hero[47] in the slaughter of the suitors as powers of chaos and darkness.

7

Along with time, the sense of geographical space also derives significance from the cosmic-mythical act of creation. For just as time is measured by light and the movement of the sun, we can see that the dimension of space is experienced through light in its contrast to darkness. Light is personified as Eos, the dawn, clad in saffron yellow, while the sun itself, Helios, is represented as the ruler of the day, which goes down into the stream of the world, Okeanos, and thus draws pitch darkness over the world: "And now the shining light of the sun was dipped in the Ocean/ trailing black night across the grain-giving land" (VIII, 485-86).

It is experienced as though light hides behind darkness: "For now the light has gone into the darkness" (3, 335). Darkness itself is not represented as a divine figure, but rather as a substance closely connected with the realm of the dead. So the realm inhabited by the Kimmerian people—and through which Odysseus passes on his journey to Hades—borders on the underworld: "hidden in fog and cloud, nor does Helios, the radiant/ sun, ever break through the dark" (11, 15-16). A symbolic assessment of these locations will be provided below.

Seafarers as the Greeks were, surrounded by water on all sides, it is not surprising that there are accounts of the constellations by which Odysseus navigates when he sails from Kalypso's island. In general, spatial distances are experienced with the same literalness as everything else, as when it is said that the shipwrecked Odysseus is as close to the island of the Phaiakians "as far away as a voice can carry" (5, 400). Indeed, distance can even act as a measuring unit for something more abstract such as reputation (*kleos*). Odysseus reveals his identity by referring to the fact that his "fame goes up to the heavens" (9, 20), just as he says to Penelope that her reputation has reached the heavens (19, 108), like the reputation of a king who governs justly.

By utilizing time and space as supporting structural elements, Homer writes the universe and the mystery of creation into his work and thereby makes plain his position as an Olympian narrator—through several layers of other narrators.

Narrative Hierarchy, Beauty, and Enchantment

1

In the tension between Homer as explicit third-person narrator and the implicit compositional awareness, we find inserted into the *Odyssey* several narrators who may be interpreted as derivatives of the collective Homeric narrative structure. It could also be claimed that these singers incarnate stages of the oral tradition that Homer brilliantly spans—and breaks. He gives us the blind, divine singer Demodokos, the partly autodidact Phemios, and Odysseus himself as a pure first-person narrator. Of course, Homer is present in all of them, so that he and Odysseus, for example, become one in the account of Odysseus' wanderings. This is the fundamental point of view behind the problem of the narrator in Homer. We shall first look at the oral tradition, inspiration from the Muses, and the truth derived from these.

The singers in the *Odyssey*, Demodokos and Phemios, are professionals. They are connected to a particular court. Others traveled from place to place with their lyres and were considered to be the social equals of other craftsmen of whom people made use—"a prophet, or a healer of sickness, or a skilled workman,/ or inspired singer, one who can give delight by his singing" (17, 384-85). With the help of their formulas, the singers improvised before the audience, adapting themselves according to whether they were singing for kings or the people, whether they were singing in a market place or a throne room. That is to say, the songs had no invariable structure, but constantly changed form during performance to the accompaniment of stringed instruments.

Along the way, the singer might be interrupted because the audience wanted to eat. He might be asked questions, as is seen in connection with the presentations of Demodokos and Odysseus. Dance was also a part of the performance, as when the most talented young men dance to Demodokos' song. Beyond the fact that the formula provided a foundation for improvisation, the songs followed quite a fixed pattern. They contained an introduction, a poem, an expression of thanks to the

audience and the host, and an assurance that the deeds and difficulties to be related in the song were the pure and simple truth.[48]

2

Even though the singers were professional and adapted their performances to
their audience, they really claimed—to judge from Homer and Hesiod—to be
telling the truth about the past and the future. The criterion for truth was that they
had the Muses themselves as the sources of their inspiration or, rather, their information. So in the preamble to both works Homer begins by calling upon the Muse
and invoking her memory-based knowledge and visionary qualities. That the
Muses provide concrete information rather than true inspiration also clearly
appears in the *Iliad* in which, in an extended invocation, the singer calls upon the
Muses as follows:

> Tell me now, you Muses who have your homes on,
> For you, who are goddesses, are there, and you know all things,
> And we have heard only the rumor of it and know nothing.
> Who then of those were the chief men and the lords of the Danaans?
> I could not tell over the multitude of them nor name them,
> Not if I had ten tongues and ten mouths, not if I had
> A voice never to be broken and a heart of bronze within me,
> Not unless the Muses of Olympia, daughters
> Of Zeus of the aegis, remembered all those who came beneath Ilion.
>
> (II, 484-92)

In other words, the singer can say nothing himself. As a private individual, he is
as limited as anyone else. However, as the Muses enter his mind he gains the insight
that in a narrow perspective is linked to telling and communicating heroic deeds
through the images that the Muses liberate internally as visions. For as daughters of
Zeus and Mnemosyne, the Muses themselves are an expression of a cosmic consciousness and the very special recollection that, in the moment of invocation, links
the singer with the first times, as is seen from the quotation. By including the
beginning of things, even this form of world-recollection belongs together with
the original act of creation.

In his thanks to Demodokos, Odysseus also maintains that as a sacred figure the
singer stands above all others, for: "Surely the Muse, Zeus' daughter or else Apollo
has taught you" (8, 488). The metonymic connection between the god of music
and the Muses must be interpreted in the same way: an insight that no humans have
within themselves but receive from the divine—like the priestess at Delphi, who
in hexameters enounced Apollo's enigmatic replies as visions of the future. And
it must be these circumstances that make Socrates state that the poets do not
express announced themselves on the basis of their own understanding but in "a
sort of ecstasy,"[49] which like *eros* is a form of madness.[50]

In extension of this, the fact that Demodokos and Homer are blind must be interpreted as a sign that the gift of poetry is both a blessing and a curse. Blindness signals that these poets are expressing themselves via their interior vision. The insight into divine knowledge is something quite different from the experience of sight in the world, limited as it is to concretely cognizable things and experiences. On the other hand, this form of interior sight, which blindness signals in both Demodokos and Homer, fundamentally consists of the recollections from the beginning of time to which the Muses give them access.

In Hesiod, too, the Muses are the divine informants behind his poem. However, the surprising thing is that, according to Hesiod, the Muses provide false as well as true information: "we know how to speak many false things as though they were true."[51] Yet, Hesiod is in no doubt that, for his part, he possesses the truth. This has a consequence which is also present in Homer, if to a less visible degree. For as Hesiod derives his knowledge from Zeus, identifies himself with his consciousness, a hidden slip in consciousness takes place: Zeus is reduced to a figure behind the speaking figure, while the Muses themselves are help to dissolve the divine reality to which they belong. This consequence is certainly clear neither to Homer nor to Hesiod, but can already be revealed in the narrative hierarchy of the *Odyssey*, which leads straight to the poetry of the autonomous self.

<h1 style="text-align:center">3</h1>

From this perspective, we shall return to and further examine the claim that the various narrators in Homer, including himself, represent central steps in the development of the epic in the oral tradition. With respect to Homer as explicit narrator, this sort of differentiation becomes immediately visible if the invocations of the Muse in the *Iliad* and the *Odyssey* respectively are compared. It appears that, even as the theme is determined in the first lines, this is also the case with respect to the basic narrative position.

In the *Iliad*, Homer invokes the Muse in self-effacing words: "Sing, goddess, the anger of Peleus' son Achilleus" (I, 1). There is no reference to the narrator himself, who thus attributes all enlightenment to the Muse. This is in contrast to the poet's self-awareness apparent in the invocation to the *Odyssey*: "Tell *me*, Muse, of the man of many ways" (1, 1, my italics). There is in this invocation a more "modern" poet's attitude, since the subject here steps forward in a self-reference as an important part of the account.

A similar difference can be pointed out if we look at the two professional singers in the *Odyssey*, Demodokos and Phemios. In the *Iliad*, Achilleus is the only singer. However, even though he is an amateur, his songs about the fame of his heroes ("*klea andron*," IX, 189) point directly forward towards Demodokos, the singer of the Phaiakian court, who also has the "famous actions of men" ("*klea andron*," 8, 73) as his repertoire. Since Homer here uses exactly the same Greek expression as he did for Achilleus, this irrevocably places Demodokos within the retrospective tradition of the heroic epic and with it also the poetic attitude expressed in Homer's own humble invocation of the Muse in the *Iliad*.

Demodokos means "he whom the people admire."[52] And when, the day after Odysseus' arrival, King Alkinoos wants to honor his guest, the singer is brought forth with his lyre. Blind, he is led out and we learn expressly that the blindness, with which Homer was of course also attributed, is due to the Muse—"the excellent singer/ whom the Muse had loved greatly, and gave him both good and evil./ She reft him of his eyes, but she gave him the sweet singing" (8, 62-64). This is the earliest description of the artist as an initiated, stigmatized and holy man.[53] The subtext here may be Teiresias' fate, as he observed Athene bathing, upon which she blinded him but as compensation gave him the power of a seer.[54]

It is emphasized time and again that Demodokos' song is defined by the god(s). Not only is it said that his gifts as a singer come from the gods—"for to him the god gave song surpassing/ in power to please, whenever the spirit moves him to singing" (8, 44-45)—but it is directly described how the Muse stirs his desire to sing his songs of heroic deeds (8, 73). If, as Odysseus says, he can also sing of the conquest of Troy through the Wooden Horse, he will "speak of you before all mankind, and tell them/ how freely the goddess gave you the magical gift of singing" (8, 498-99). Indeed, he says, after weeping at the song, Demodokos "is like the gods in his singing" (9, 4).

It is particularly through Odysseus' reactions that we understand how powerful his songs are and how elevated Demodokos' position as a divine poet is. Odysseus weeps in torrents and must hide his face in his cloak to conceal how moved he is to hear—about himself. And as a sign of how highly he values and honors his song, he rewards Demodokos with a choice piece of meat—"For with all peoples upon the earth singers are entitled/ to be cherished" (8, 479-80). And on his own account he adds that nothing gives him greater pleasure:

> For I think there is no occasion accomplished that is more pleasant
> Than when festivity holds sway among all the populace,
> And the feasters up and down the houses are sitting in order
> And listening to the singer (. . .).
>
> (9, 5-9)

Odysseus could not give a better hidden endorsement to Homer—or, for that matter, Homer to himself, since the description of the poet's significance is linked here to his own vision of social *eunomia*.

As comparatives in the narrator's overall position, Demodokos and Phemios are almost contrasts. Certainly, Phemios' name indicates that his métier as poet has its origin in the gods, since it means "divine, poetic expression."[55] However, whereas Demodokos is employed at the Phaiakians' legendary court, Phemios serves the court at Ithaka, characterized by the transgressions of the suitors in the absence of its king. Therefore, it makes good sense that, acting in a more realistic narrative space, he appears as a more modern poet.

Moreover, Demodokos sings nostalgically of the heroic age, whereas Phemios' "modern" character is emphasized by the fact that he invents new songs (1, 352) dealing mournfully with the tribulations Athene has allowed to befall the returning Greeks. In principle, he thereby also heralds Odysseus' death. By contrast, Demodokos sings of Odysseus' greatest heroic deed: the Wooden Horse. Phemios' song makes Penelope break down: "Leave off singing this sad/ song which always afflicts the dear heart deep inside me" (1, 341-42). She weeps and asks him to stop. Almost as a command, Telemachos replies that it is not the singer but Zeus, who is the originator of Fate, concluding: "So let your heart and let your spirit be hardened to listen" (1, 353).

It is also thanks to Telemachos' intercession that, during the slaughter of the suitors, Odysseus spares Phemios' life, whereas by contrast he honors Demodokos with a chunk of meat. Yet, to save his life, Phemios asserts his divine calling as a poet to Odysseus: "The god has inspired in me the song-ways/ of every kind" (22, 347-48). However, in the same breath, he speaks the surprising words that he is self-taught, an autodidact: "I am/ taught by myself" (22, 346-47).

Suddenly, a poetic awareness is inserted, which is not found in the *Iliad*'s explicit first-person narrator, helpless without the aid of the Muses. Nor does Demodokos express such a heretical understanding of the artist. On the other hand, the statement clearly corresponds to the invocation of the Muse at the beginning of the *Odyssey*, where Homer as explicit narrator requests the Muse's help with reference to himself. In a quantum leap, we are well on the way towards the subjective first person poet that we meet in no less a figure than Odysseus. He speaks entirely on his own behalf and is the only guarantor of his truth, which is, of course, problematic when he himself is the guarantor.

4

In short, a rather flickering picture appears of the actual relationship between the narrators in Homer. Whereas in the *Iliad* an explicit narrative voice spans the entire narrative, it is much more difficult to determine immediately how much of the narrative sequence the explicit narrator really covers in the *Odyssey*. In reality, he only desires the Muse to assist him in telling about the widely-traveled Odysseus.

If the text is taken literally, this must mean in principle that he does not receive any information on the *Telemachy* or anything that occurs after the homecoming, even as Odysseus himself is inserted as the autobiographical first-person narrator in the *Apologoi*. However, there is an inner logic in the fact that this gradual becoming independent of the Muses takes place through Odysseus' boundary-crossing personality. In relating his wanderings, he quite literally establishes himself as a poet without mentioning the Muses or the gods. That is to say he is fundamentally even more radical and autonomous than the self-taught Phemios, who after all presupposes a connection with the Muses. Odysseus thus becomes literature's first true first-person narrator.

From this perspective, it seems strikingly modern that this narrative position raises a fundamental uncertainty about the truth of what he is relating. This uncertainty is further bolstered by the fact that, in the stories he relates anonymously to the swineherd and his wife in his disguise, he reveals how cunning he is in making up lies.

When King Alkinoos finally gets around to asking Odysseus to reveal his identity, it is done with the words: "So come now tell me this and give me an accurate answer" (8, 572). That is to say that there is a play on the concept of truth, which is the prerogative of the muses. By contrast, the truth now is entirely dependent on Odysseus' own account and, like the Muses, he understands how to orchestrate the truth to suit himself. For even though he later promises the faithful swineherd Eumaios to speak truly—"I will accurately answer all that you ask me" (14, 192)— he feeds him a direct lie, when, as it is said in his feigned account to Penelope, he tells "many false things that were like true sayings" (19, 204).

This fundamentally makes him into an unreliable narrator, fully aware of his own strategic mendacity. On the other hand, however, this very fact helps narratively to create an optimal ambiguity and tension in the reader. So truth only belongs to the implicit compositional awareness. In addition, Odysseus' use of language is, remarkably enough, almost identical with that Hesiod uses to describe the ambiguous inspiration of the Muses. Later, from this duality of lies and truth arises the ferocious debate on the extent to which Homer and Hesiod are reliable. For example, Pythagoras claims that he has seen the two poets punished in Hades because of their mendacious claims about the gods.

Odysseus is the master of his own words and truth. And when he reveals his identity to the Phaiakians, it occurs without the invocation of the Muses, but he reveals an odd uncertainty, when he is to tell about his wanderings, as if he must listen his way towards his own inner inspiration: "What then shall I recite to you first of all, what leave till later?" (9, 14).[56] This is in itself the description of a poet who waits for inspiration to intone properly and corresponds to the description in the *Iliad* of how Odysseus appears before he begins to speak, almost like a madman, but once he starts, everyone is enchanted:

> But when that other drove to his feet, resourceful Odysseus,
> He would just stand and stare down, eyes fixed on the ground beneath him,
> Nor would he gesture with the staff backward and forward, but hold it
> Clutched hard in front of him, like any man who knows nothing.
> Yes, you would call him a sullen man, and a fool likewise.
> But when he let the great voice go from his chest, and the words came
> Drifting down like the winter snows, then no other mortal
> Man beside could stand up against Odysseus. Then we
> Wondered less beholding Odysseus' outward appearance.
>
> (III, 216-24)

First of all, in this portrait, we meet a man of the same psychological make-up in both works. Secondly, he draws his energy from within, as if in his *metis* he has internalized the inspiration of the gods, which now streams from him, freely and self-validating. And he does not only demonstrate these abilities when he tells of his travels, but also in the lies (14, 462 ff.; 18, 138 ff.) he presents as pure truth, rife with fantasy and actual events.

In view of the talent Odysseus reveals, it is not so remarkable that the Phaiakian king characterizes him as a poet, *aoidos*—"You have a grace upon your words, and there is sound sense within them, and expertly, as a singer would do" (11, 367-68). And just as he enchanted the king of the winds, Aiolos, for a month with his stories during his voyage (10, 14), his account has dumbfounded the Phaiakians— "held in thrall by the story all through the shadowy chambers" (11, 334) long after he stopped speaking. As an enchanter, he resembles Orpheus, who made everyone around him fall silent.

Odysseus is able to evoke such a striking effect, because he is very highly aware indeed of himself as a narrator and of the tricks necessary to make listeners hold their breath. He underlines this pithily: "But come, I will tell you of my voyage home with its many/ troubles, which Zeus inflicted on me as I came from Troy land" (9, 37-38). And he does it in a way that yields nothing to Homer, as is shown by the fact that he begins with the raid on the Kikonians, a people who also appear in the *Iliad* (II, 846) allied to the Trojans. That is to say that he first takes a position relating to the knowledge and style in the *Iliad* and uses a realism that is found again in the stories with which he deceives the swineherd and his own wife. When he moves into the fabulous world of his adventures, his tale acquires its own special imprint in being his eyewitness account and his alone—with the previously mentioned uncertainty about the truth as a consequence.

The conscious wordsmith at work! He concludes with a remark that he will not retell the events he has already related—"It is hateful to me to tell a story over again, when it has been well told" (12, 452-53). He uses the Greek verb *mythologein*, which means purely and simply to tell stories and not to mythologize in our sense of the word. Odysseus demonstrates how conscious he is of his narrative effect, for instance, by interrupting himself, saying there is a time to tell and a time to sleep. He knows that such a pause increases audience expectations. Yet, he declares himself willing to continue, if Alkinoos wishes to learn of the even greater hardships he endured. Which, of course, the king does, geared up as he is by the tension Odysseus has already created with the prospect of hearing even more exciting things.

The self-esteem we must presume it gives Odysseus to enchant and seduce his listeners, however, is expressed not by himself but by Alkinoos, when he not only asks him to provide "an accurate answer" (8, 572) but in such a way that his song will abide forever: "The gods did this, and spun the destruction/ of peoples, for the sake of the singing of men hereafter" (8, 579-80). Odysseus merges here with Homer as implicit narrator, as the latter predicts that what he relates through Odysseus will be handed down to posterity.

Thus, Odysseus understands how to orchestrate his tale as a true storyteller. He pauses to create tension and, beyond giving us a vivid feeling of how spellbinding his tale is, reveals his knowledge of the role of narrator. He can reflect on it, hypnotize, economize, enchant and entice—indeed, entirely without the assistance of higher powers, he composes, brilliantly and selectively, his own narrative universe and his autobiography as eyewitness. And just as Odysseus in this way, directly or indirectly, reveals his narrative technique and his effort to captivate his listeners, this description at the implicit narrative level acts as a metapoetic presentation of the effect Homer himself intended with his work on Odysseus, the wandering storyteller.

5

The bout of weeping the singers provoke in Odysseus and Penelope is evidence in itself of how deeply they reach into their inner lives. "Odysseus melted, and from under his eyes the tears ran down, drenching his cheeks" (8, 522), are the words when he hears the account of the Wooden Horse. These attacks of tears—especially in male heroes—can seem perplexing. But the tears well up from their life experience (*aion*) and are visible evidence of how one's inner self almost melts and can no longer be kept within the container represented by the body, but must flow out through the eyes as tears—indeed, the very source of life.[57]

Thus, the beauty of the style, its *charis*, is not only external decorum but also radiant awareness. And it is on this basis that we must understand Aristotle's formal requirements for peripeties, discoveries and emotional change in epic poetry: that "the Thought and Diction in it must be good (*kalos*) in their way,"[58] of which Homer is the earliest superb example. The ultimate purpose of descriptions, digressions, etc., in the spellbinding beauty of their surface is to create space for the innermost elements of the Greek conceptual world.

At the same time, *charis* gradually becomes the boon Zeus grants mankind. As Aeschylus says, for example, in the *Oresteia*, "grace (*charis*) comes somehow violent."[59] If one adds to this the derivative concept of *charisma*, a dimension of the concept is revealed that more than hints at what a divine source of power *charis* was for the Greeks.

In Homer, it is not surprising that Odysseus provides the most qualified definition of *charis* as a psychological function. It occurs during the Phaiakian games when he is taunted by one of Alkinoos' sons, who says that he looks like a merchant. With wrinkled brow, Odysseus replies that there can be a mismatch between a beautiful exterior and an inner lack of beauty. He takes him angrily to task:

> So it is that the gods do not bestow graces in all ways
> On men, neither in stature nor yet in brains or eloquence;
> For there is a certain kind of man, less noted for beauty,
> But the god puts comeliness on his words, and they who look toward him

Are filled with joy at the sight, and he speaks to them without faltering
In winning modesty, and shines among those who are gathered,
And people look on him as on a god when he walks in the city.
Another again in his appearance is like the immortals,
But upon his words there is no grace distilled (. . .).

(8, 167–75)

Interestingly, Odysseus himself is evidence of the truth of this claim, since it is the
beauty of his speech that makes the Phaiakians believe in him and therefore help
him home. His homecoming is won by *charis*. For, as the Phaiakian king declares,
he has proved with his words that he is not a swindler of the kind of which the
world is filled: "You have a grace upon your words, and there is sound sense within them" (11, 367).

Considering that Odysseus is a master at twisting the truth so as to give it the
semblance of reality, it is a statement that sparkles with ironic narrative distance. As
mentioned earlier, the final section of the *Odyssey* is composed on the basis of the
same truth: the contrast between the beautiful but arrogant suitors with their
worm-eaten inner selves and Odysseus who, dressed as a beggar, retains his inner
regal self.

6

Beauty is a quality of life coming from within, which is manifested externally
in stylistic splendor but is rooted in moral integrity. Odysseus evokes empathy from
his listeners by the *charis* of his tale. In this way, beauty becomes a form of moral
verification and confirms what is divine and what is fortunate in the person, who
can give expression to it.

The beauty of the word exceeds all other forms of beauty and as a means for
enchantment has the power to suggest and bind the audience, as can be read in the
paralyzed reaction of the Phaiakians to Odysseus' story. But just as the Muses are
said to speak both truly and falsely, the Greeks, judging from their mythology, must
have realized that beauty contains a dangerous duality. Thus, the goddesses of
beauty, the three radiant Charites, are companions both to Apollo, the god of truth,
and to the seductive goddess Aphrodite, who is also accompanied by Peitho, the
goddess of persuasion. When Hera wants to seduce Zeus, she borrows Aphrodite's
belt: "passion of sex is there, and the whispered/ endearment that steals the heart
away even from the thoughtful" (XIV, 216-17). And the seduction of the omniscient father god is thoroughly successful.

In other words, beauty in association with enchantment has a powerful erotic
undercurrent that can make it seductive and demonic. In this context, Homer uses
the verb *thelgein*, which actually means "stroking with the hand" but otherwise
includes nuances such as to enchant, to lull to sleep, to lure and to deceive.

For example, the word can be connected to the way in which the god paralyzes heroes, as when Apollo with his resounding battle cry causes Greek warriors to forget "their furious valour" (XV, 321). However, in the *Odyssey*, the concept is used in a number of contexts to emphasize the potential danger of speech and thus poetry. The magical herbs Kirke uses to change men into animals are full of *thelgein*—"the goddess had given evil drugs and enchanted" (10, 213). With her "sweet voice" (10, 221), this goddess with such glorious hair goes around the loom, singing. Yet, most destructive, of course, is the enchanting song of the Sirens. No one can resist "the melody of their singing (12, 44).

Out of love for Odysseus, Kalypso tries to persuade him "with soft and flattering words" (1, 56) to forget going home—in exchange for the gift of immortality —a "gift," an image of death with which the Sirens also entice him. This enchantment—as a part of the erotic and demonic power game—becomes if anything even clearer, when it is told that, through alluring words (3, 264), Aigisthos was able to seduce Klytemnestra—to yield to him sexually and to kill her husband Agamemnon on his homecoming.

However, Odysseus, too, knows how to use language to deceive, as when he turns the Kyklop's head with words "full of beguilement" (9, 363). So, even though Alkinoos maintains that Odysseus has proved with his magical words that he is no rogue, this may be called a qualified truth. Having learned from earlier experiences with a liar, the swineherd Eumaios says after Odysseus' cock-and-bull story invented for the occasion that he should "not try to please me nor spell me with lying words" (14, 387). Nevertheless, he highly praises precisely this kind of speech to Penelope and uses its enchanting effect to emphasize that Odysseus is a true poet. He says, "he would charm out the dear heart within you" (17, 514), continuing:

> But as when a man looks to a singer, who has been given
> From the gods the skill with which he sings for delight of mortals,
> And they are impassioned and strain to hear it when he sings to them,
> So he enchanted me in the halls as he sat beside me.
>
> (17, 518-21)

Finally, Odysseus employs the same art of speaking when ingratiating himself to Nausikaa, addressing her "full of craft" (6, 148), just as Penelope—to Odysseus' satisfaction—"beguiled" (18, 283) the suitors with kind words to court her with more gifts.

In all these quotations, the word *thelgein* or a derivative of it is used, emphasizing the seductive power in the beauty of the spoken word. Hesiod, too—perhaps, inspired by Homer—is aware of the power of the word, when honeyed phrases issue from the poet's lips. Yet, he does not pay the same attention to the demonic aspect as Homer does, but rather concentrates on what is positive in its seductive power. As he says, the flow of words will make both the poet and the audience forget their everyday despondency and oppressive thoughts—"but the gifts of the goddesses soon turn him away from these."[60]

Yet, at the same time it is this seductive effect that makes Plato banish the poets from his republic precisely because listeners surrender to the beauty of poetry. It dissolves pain and anxiety but with its hypnotic effect stands in the way of a true recognition of the good. Homer himself in fact illuminates this risk in his description of the Phaiakians' enchantment with Odysseus' tale.

Since all later storytelling techniques in the field of composition, narration and style are largely already developed (even internal monologue is well underway) in the Homeric epics, we may conclude that they must have been composed by a highly-gifted artistic mind—with a view to being put into written form. Considered as texts, they are simply too complicated to be purely oral tales. In addition, we are able to follow their development from the more "primitive" accumulation of episodes in the *Iliad* to the sophistication of the *Odyssey*, a process that is bound up with the protagonists and the thematic world of the respective works: Achilleus' strength and wrath as opposed to Odysseus' *metis*.

However, Homer is also engaged on another, more ideological errand than "inventing" the art of poetry—namely, that of institutionalizing a new religion. He turns the heavenly Olympos of the Father God against the primeval cults of fertility and the Mother Goddess, linked to the earth, the chthonic and the realm of the dead.

III

DUAL RELIGIOSITY

Chthonic and Olympian Gods

1

IF GREEK RELIGION COULD BE DESCRIBED ON THE BASIS OF THE OLYMPIAN gods alone, it would not be nearly so complicated. First of all, however, these gods are relatively young. Secondly, they are primarily the invention of two men (or traditions): Homer and Hesiod. The existence and hierarchy of these gods belong to a period around 850-700 B.C. if dated according to their originators. Obviously, they may be older, but it may also be the case that earlier Greeks had a religious life of a different nature that influenced the structure of Olympos, which in itself led to a suppression or repression of the original fertility gods.

It must be as an acknowledgment of the human religious instinct that Plato says in *The Laws* that the Greeks and the barbarians alike believe in gods—"all mankind, Greeks and non-Greeks alike, believe in the existence of gods."[1] Elsewhere, he makes the point that the first people in Greece only believed in "the sun, moon, earth, stars and heaven, which are still the gods of many barbarians."[2] Socrates, who makes this assessment, does not further define these barbarians, let alone refer to them contemptuously. However, as the two previous quotations indicate, these alien peoples, the barbarians, find themselves at another, earlier stage of religious development, corresponding to the religious life the Greeks themselves led at the dawn of time—i.e., the worship of the primal forces in the universe.

This form of nature worship cultivated by barbarians and known among the Persians, for example, is described in Herodotus as well. He writes:

> They [the Persians] are not wont to establish images or temples or altars at all; indeed, they regard all who do so as fools, and this, in my opinion, is because they do not believe in gods of human form, as the Greeks do. (. . .) They sacrifice, too, to the sun, moon, and earth and to fire, water, and winds.[3]

If these statements are interpreted together, we can deduce a succession of religious ideas in which, in a prehistoric era, the Greeks themselves venerated anonymous nature gods. However, it is vital that these divinities are precursors in various ways to the mythology of Olympos and its gods, while the veneration of the earth and its ancillary gods and goddesses of fertility was retained side by side with the Olympian—for example, in the Eleusinian Mysteries, the festival of Thesmophoria, and other fertility cults. The primary divinities were Demeter and Dionysos. That is to say that the religiosity characterized as barbarian or atavistic had not completely disappeared from among the Greeks, as Herodotus and Plato imply in an extension of Homer's silence on these phenomena.

In short, Greek religion is not an unambiguous phenomenon. Rather, there is a duality insofar as the basis for the doctrine of the Olympian gods is a mythic religiosity that fades into the mists of prehistory. This much we know for certain, partly from archeological clues indicating that the oldest form of religiosity had collective roots in fertility rites and cults linked to the fruits of the earth, whose continuous production and nourishment were a basic necessity for the Greeks from the moment they took up agriculture.

In an analogy between the cyclic fertility of the earth and women's reproductive cycle, a link arose between the individual mother and the great maternal figure of Nature. Since the earth was created as the primal thing, as a self-reproducing female body, Gaia, religious life became linked to the maternal. This meant that even the male gods at that point were subordinate to the primal mother. With its link to the earth—in Greek, *chthon*—this cultic practice is defined as chthonic, as it is also linked to the underworld or, more particularly, the kingdom of the dead. The idea was that grain must die in order to grow, just as the dead must be laid in the earth to be regenerated through an affiliation with the family. The eternal return.

2

Since this entire section will be dealing with these forms of religiosity, I will for the moment merely make clear that the Olympian gods, living in the heavens, are a reaction—not to say a revolution—against the ruling fertility gods. If such a political terminology can be used, this is because the new gods are *de facto* an expression of a political and cultural process that can also be discerned in the statements of Herodotus and Plato. The Olympian gods are associated with aristocracy as an institution, developed as far as Homer is concerned within the framework of the Ionian enlightenment to which the early philosophers also belong.

The intention was evidently was to establish a belief system on a patriarchal foundation with clear social definitions in order to curb the fertility rites of nature religions and the maternal privilege associated with them. That this was not successful can be seen in the significance that the Eleusinian Mysteries, the cult of Demeter, retained and continued to retain. This is also evidence of the suppleness of the Athenian city-state—that it incorporated these cults into its religious life, well aware that it was vital to accommodate these religious forces that were cultivated by the population at large. It was simply a matter of integrating these cults— and thereby bringing them under control.

By their position on a high mountain, in the air, the new gods constitute an alternative to the maternal power of the earth. They are supposed to reinforce a patriarchy, which on a deeper psychological level indicates that men have liberated themselves from the bonds linking them to their (primeval) mothers—a liberation that is made difficult in the mythical realm since the Great Mother refused voluntarily to release her male offspring, which, as a fertilizing phallos, took part in her reproduction. With this liberation, the dominant maternal figure is weakened. Consequently, she is subsumed into the unknown, the unconscious, where she is divided and re-appears as the evil, all-consuming maternal figure we know from fairy tales and myths in the form of dragons, witches and wild animals. "Weak" sons, on the other hand, regress into the comforting embrace of the mother, but not heroes, who take up battle against the dragon and so become the bearers of culture.[4]

3

Since we cannot know for sure how this development took place, we must try to form a picture of it by means of plausible deduction. I presuppose that with the formation of the Olympian pantheon a transformative adaptation must have taken place in which Homer and the tradition around him took over and, to a great extent, modified existing divinities. An attempt was made to reduce the cultic characteristics of the matriarchal religion, and other features were added—upon the adoption of patriarchal gods from the Indo-European community—as a sign of a new patriarchal religion and its self-assertive consciousness. Such a development would explain why the gods often have a curious and somewhat inexplicable dual identity. They have a primitive origin but the attempt has been made to integrate them into the circle of Olympian gods with greater or lesser success.

This view is confirmed by the fact that certain gods were more adaptable than others. The most successful example is Pallas Athene, since—despite being a female divinity—she is very much at one with the patriarchal world of law and justice and, as we shall see in Aeschylus, the highest guarantor of it. But even in her case it is possible to see a chthonic emblematic representation (see p. 131), which must derive etiologically from her atavistic prehistory.

Since the names of several Olympian gods are found in the Mycenaean system of writing, Linear B, an apparent archaizing of the original nature gods has apparently taken place. While Athene seems well suited for this transformation, Hera and Aphrodite on the other hand are given very ambivalent features by Homer. Hera, for example, is described in the older Boeotian poem on the saga of the Argonauts as an especially beautiful goddess who assists Iason. That she is given the epithet "cow-eyed" in Homer may also be a sign that some of her original animistic features have survived in this view of her, just as Athene is depicted as or with an owl.

In other words, the assimilation presumes a more or less conscious reformulation and partial repression. At any rate, it can be observed that, in striving to establish the Olympic pantheon, Homer's epics do so by means of a radical retouching or subversion of the popular mother cults. It has been hypothesized that, living in a highly developed Ionian area, Homer was not familiar with the fertility gods. However, I see this as improbable, considering the thousands of years they had been part of the religious common ground. Moreover, the poet lived close to the Babylonians and the Medes for instance and must have been familiar with their nature religion, which is described hundreds of years later by Herodotus. So it is more likely that we have here yet another attempt to found a new religious view corresponding to the political and intellectual expansion taking place.

Interpretatively, this means that Homer's poems must be read with a dual aim: What he says and what does not he say. One must always remain aware of the reality, the chthonic, against which his works were composed and thus strongly determined by as a hidden precondition. It is impossible to discover how conscious he was of the objective of his strategy of repression. It can easily be imagined that the endeavor was present in the tradition he incorporates into his works. That is to say the need to make manifest a patriarchal power, combined with the development of an awareness of the self, such as occurred in this area in poets like Sappho and the early philosophers. However, the chthonic element was not so far away as to prevent it from acting as a subtext in the mythic mirroring in which Homer reflects his poetry.

There are a number of inter-related reasons why the Olympic gods are far from supreme. Their very fictionality—that they were brought into existence by means of a mental process—is obviously an important reason for their having difficulty in evoking a deeper religious feeling. They did not have the same appeal as the fertility and mother cults that arose in an agrarian population, organically linked to the cultivation of the soil, crops, grain, etc.

These divine forces were seen as present, the products of experience and, in contrast to the Olympian gods, they were also associated with specific localities with all the accompanying feeling of solidarity and cultic community. The Olympian gods on the other hand were developed intellectually, connected with a heroic aristocracy with a certain "international" stamp. They were not associated with the fundamental rhythm of life, the seasons and the cycle of growth, as the earth-linked divinities were—particularly, Demeter, on whom I will concentrate my analysis for that reason.

The Great Mother

> "Die *Mütter* sind es!"
> —GOETHE, *Faust* II

1

If, despite her enormous religious popularity and power over people—she is, as she says, the only one who can ensure the happiness of men and gods by granting fertility—Demeter is only mentioned a total of six times by Homer (five of which occur in the *Iliad*), it is eloquent evidence of the hidden but guiding intent in his works:

The formation of the patriarchal pantheon, liberated from an all-encompassing matriarchal power. The same fate befalls the cult god Dionysos, mentioned five times but more in terms of the figure of a hero and at any rate of peripheral significance in relation to his later function as the great divinity of the mysteries of fertility.

So Demeter is mentioned the greatest number of times in the *Iliad*. The field is said to be dedicated to her (II, 696). She separates the wheat from the chaff and is otherwise only mentioned together with the grain with which to make bread— "bread, the yield of Demeter" (XIII, 322).

Yet, even though Demeter's deeper meaning is partially repressed in the Homeric epics, she represents in her formulaic purpose a clear retrospective connection with that conception of fertility in which the earth is both giver and taker, like the kingdom of the dead. Of the earth, it is said that it is all-nourishing—"the prospering earth (*chthona*)" (III, 265, see VI, 213) or "bountiful earth" (III, 89), as mortals "eat what the soil yields" (VI, 142). Gaia, the earth as primeval mother, is therefore called "the earth abundant" (IX, 568). And it is claimed that the fields are devoted to Demeter (II, 696). These goddesses merge with one another and it is to this quite literally earthly power that Odysseus kneels in gratitude, kissing "the grain-giving soil" (5, 463) after landing on the Phaiakians' island.

2

Despite the economy of this formulaic information, it is nevertheless possible to form an impression of the cultic reality behind it. Most interesting is the *Odyssey*, where Demeter only appears on one occasion, but what an occasion it is! Here, there is not a shadow of a doubt about the presence of the cultic drama. The situation is this: When, on behalf of Zeus, Hermes demands that Kalypso, this splendid chthonic temptress, should release Odysseus, she sees it as the result of the gods' envy, their *phthonos*. As evidence of this, she points out that Zeus killed Iasion,[5] Demeter's lover, with a bolt of lightning, when on a thrice-turned field she lay with him, a mortal man:

> And so it was when Demeter of the lovely hair, yielding
> To her desire, lay down with Iasion and loved him
> In a thrice-turned field, it was not long before this was made known
> To Zeus, who struck him down with a cast of the shining thunderbolt.
>
> (5, 125-29)

It is beyond doubt that Homer has reached deep into the cult of fertility in this passage. That this is an archetypal story appears from the fact that in the *Theogony* Hesiod refers to the same event, with no reference to Kalypso or the lightning-wielding Zeus. On the other hand, it is related here that the act of love took place in "the rich land of Crete"[6] and the fruit of their union was the god of abundance, Pluto.

Here, under one heading, we have a stylized but nuanced complex of symbols that can be used to open up this magical and mythical cultic religiosity, which can be difficult to grasp, not only because of its foreignness but also because it appears in so many fantastic shapes. But behind them is a rather homogeneous structure of consciousness and experience, which will be sketched out in general terms below on the basis of evidence from archeology and the tradition of mythic tales.

3

In short, in the universe of Homer and Hesiod, we are in the myth of Demeter and Iasion presented with a vegetation rite to ensure the annual cycle of growth. Demeter means mother of grain.[7] She is the primary goddess responsible for the annual harvest. That she hails from Crete, where Hesiod claims she embraces Iasion, is further verified by the Homeric Hymn in praise of her.[8] It is related here that, against her will, she was abducted from her home in Crete. Of course, this is related as part of a fabrication, but the reference to Crete as the place of origin seems plausible, since it is repeated elsewhere.

This topographical affiliation is important, because it places her as a vegetation goddess in the sphere of Cretan-Minoan cults and cultures, where the maternal goddesses appeared back in the Neolithic Age five thousand years before Christ.[9] These goddesses protected wild animals, as is demonstrated by paintings of them together with lions, among other things. They inhabited the highest mountains as a sign that they ruled over the entire world, as Zeus later did from Olympos, but they were also worshipped in caves on Mount Ida and Dikte that reached far into the earth as a sign of their connection with the dark world of the realm of the dead. The Great Mother was honored with the sacrifice of bulls undertaken by the king-priest, so the potent blood flowed from the bull and through bottomless vessels, giving life to the earth from which fertility in a rebirth was to be summoned from its slumbers in the world of death.

At the same time, the rites reveal the demonic aspect of the matriarchal goddess: that, as part of her fertilization, she demands blood, slaughter, even castration (as in the cult of Kybele and Attis) or mutilation (as in the worship of Dionysos Zagreus, the god child, who every year is flensed and devoured to effect vegetative reincarnation). These are cults going infinitely far back in time, back to the Paleolithic Age, where from the period between 30,000-20,000 B.C. there is archeological evidence in the form of the so-called Venuses, which may originally derive from southern Russia,[10] then spreading across large parts of Europe as cultic phenomena.

These Venuses are, like other cult phenomena, uniform in appearance. Whether they come from Willendorf or Laussel, they are faceless but have elegant coiffures (recent studies claim that these are elaborate headdresses). All the emphasis is on the fertility of their sexual markers: bulging and over-dimensioned buttocks, breasts, hips and thighs. Remains of a brownish-red color in the porous rock testify to the paint that symbolizes the blood of the ritual sacrifice, the invocation of fertility, clearly comparing and analogizing the fertility of women and the earth to reproduce and give birth, without knowledge of the man's participation in the act of conception. This analogy is maintained through later Greek poetry and philosophy. As Plato says, "for as a woman proves her motherhood by giving milk to her young ones (. . .) so did this our land prove that she was the mother of men."[11]

4

We often see this analogical imagery in the tragedies. Here, women are compared in various ways to a plowed or sown field. The tersest expression is by King Kreon in the *Antigone*, when, at the prospect of his son losing Antigone, he cynically says: "Oh, there are other furrows for his plough."[12] In addition, the image appears in various combinations in *Oedipus the King*. Oedipus' mother and wife is compared both to a plowed field[13] and a field twice harvested,[14] namely by husband and son—that is, from this point of view, she takes the form of primal mothers who also allow themselves to be impregnated by son and lover.

All this plowing, sowing and harvesting, however, goes together with a more recent cultivation of the earth,[15] since the plow was not invented until the fourth millennium B.C. Originally, the earth lay uncultivated but provided hunters and gatherers food by reproducing itself. The earth was not sown until the introduction of agriculture. In Greece, this occurred around 6000 B.C., when true agriculture, along with domestic animals, pigs, goats and sheep, was introduced from the Middle East, where agriculture had been developed several thousand years earlier.

The comparison of plowed earth to a woman becomes an image of the patriarchalization to which women become subject during the process of civilization, as can be seen for the first time in Hesiod's misogyny (see p. 289), and the ultimate consequences of which we find in Athenian democracy—for men. In tragedy from this period, woman is seen as a wild, barbaric and animalistic force of nature that must be kept indoors in the bonds of marriage.

According to the mythical tradition, this occurred when women selected Athene instead of Poseidon as the protective deity of Athens. The myth has it that, as punishment and in order to gain control over them, King Kekrops deprived women of their franchise and, as it is put, united one man and one woman in marriage. He thereby broke down the hegemony of primal mothers, which lay partly in their promiscuous liaisons with any man who could assure their fertility, which is why no one "knew who their fathers were."[16] On the other hand, the mother (*kourotrophos*—the son-nurturing) who protected and bound her son (*kouros*) to herself—as a lover—was always known. Not until later were children named after their father with so-called patronymics: Achilleus is called Peleid after his father Peleus and so forth.

Yet, so sovereign is the Great Mother Goddess, Gaia, in her origin that, in Hesiod, she is deemed self-breeding, *autochthonios*. The world arose from her earthbody. These two things together—self-reproduction and the omnipotence derived from it—also explain why there are no pictorial representations of men from these early epochs, much less masculine divinities. These maternal goddesses are birthing maidens and basically continue to be, even when the man's role in the mystery of conception is discovered in the transition from the hunter-gatherer stage to agriculture, grain-growing and animal husbandry.

On one hand, this means that the Great Mother Goddess, in the form of a Demeter, comes to represent a higher stage of organization and, as the goddess of grain cultivation, steps into the place of the wild nature that Aphrodite represents. On the other hand, this gradually provides insight into the function of men in reproduction, since, as said above, they begin to cultivate and subjugate Mother Earth with their plows.

It is this process that figuratively becomes a fixture in the descriptions of masculine dominance and its demand for monogamy in the tragedies. For the Mother Virgin does not belong to a particular male god but to any man whose phallic power can increase her fertility. It is not until Olympos that monogamy is institutionalized and patriarchy makes incest taboo.

5

Such a sequence of events and way of thinking is concretized in the myth of the love between Demeter and Iasion on the fruitful soil of Crete—a rite whose purpose was to ensure the fertility of the seed in the Corn Mother, in the womb and in the earth, when the grain was to be sown; while the embrace in itself as a ritual happening concluded this séance with the sacred wedding, *hieros gamos*.

For even though the ritual with its mention of the thrice-plowed field contains a reference to phallic plowing, the focus is nevertheless upon the sanctification of fertilization in sacred intercourse. What this really means is described in the *Iliad*, where the act is embedded in the embrace between Hera and Zeus. Zeus wraps the loving couple in a cloud so thick and golden that not even Helios can observe them: "There/ underneath them the divine earth broke into young, fresh/ grass, and into dewy clover, crocus and hyacinth/ so thick and soft it held the hard ground deep away from them" (XIV, 347-50).

In this description, we find a luxuriant nature as yet untouched by the phallic power of the plow. The same splendor characterizes the landscape among the Kyklopes, the Phaiakians and Kalypso, who live in a pre-agricultural era in this respect. And it was as a repetition of these fertility rites that Demeter and Dionysos were later celebrated in Athens. But nature, linked to the unrestrained sexuality of fertility gods, is subjugated to the plow and transformed into private plots of land.

Blending practical and cult measures, Hesiod provides the following crystal clear recipe for assuring the grain harvest in *Works and Days*, where he also explains what the thrice-plowed field means:

When ploughing-time arrives, make haste to plough,
You and your slaves alike, on rainy days

And dry ones, while the season lasts. At dawn
Get to your fields, and one day they'll be full.
Plough, too, in springtime; if you turn the earth
In summer, too, you won't regret the work.
Sow fallow soil while it is still quite light;
Remember, fallow land defends us all,
And lulls our children with security.
Make prayers to Zeus the farmer's god and to
Holy Demeter, for her sacred grain,
To make it ripe and heavy, when you start
To plough (. . .).[17]

The quotation is remarkable in several ways. The Zeus we encounter here is completely different from the ruler of Olympos, but is his chthonic counterpart, as the Greek refers to him as Zeus Chthonios. He belongs to the world of the mother goddess, as the juxtaposition to Demeter emphasizes. Presumably, this is the same figure of Zeus we know from Minoan culture, where, protected by his mother and Gaia, he grows up as a god-child in a cave to avoid his father Kronos. He is a god-child, an initiation figure and, presumably, his mother's lover. He lives his life in the darkness of the cave, turning toward the realm of the dead as a force of creation, to which, as Homer relates, King Minos traveled every nine years—fundamentally in order to be "recharged" with the breeding energy (19, 178 ff., see p. 252) on which his kingdom depended.

In a hymn from Crete,[18] addressing Zeus as a boy or young man (*kouros*), it is described how, surrounded by his entourage of Kouretes, he heralds the new year as god of fertility. The procession of Kouretes was accompanied by percussion, which was to prevent Kronos from discovering the child through his crying. The hymn locates his cave on Mount Dikte, while elsewhere it is Mount Ida. But regardless of the exact location, the setting is Crete whence Demeter and other maternal goddesses—for example, Artemis, mistress of wild beasts (*potnia theron*)—originated.

6

If Zeus, as the father-god he has become under the influence of Indo-European rain and cloud gods, kills Iasion with a lightning bolt, it is, in a way, his own past and origins he is destroying; since in Homer he is represented as trying to control and repress the rites of the mother cults. So there also seems to be something of a misinterpretation on the part of Kalypso, since she thinks Zeus casts his thunderbolt simply out of envy (*phthonos*). Perhaps he does, but in that case the word *phthonos* has a broader meaning. For as the myth can now be interpreted, he has intervened in the sacred wedding itself by which the field is to be fertilized by the union between the corn goddess and a male corn god. It is not simply a matter of envy but, all things considered, an intervention by young gods in this cult drama, just as the Erinyes in the *Oresteia* complain that the new gods are trampling upon their ancient privileges.

In the *Hymn to Demeter*, which deals with the establishment of the Eleusinian Mysteries, it says in conclusion:

> Happy is he among men upon earth who has seen these mysteries; but he who is uninitiated and who has no part in them, never has lot of like good things once he is dead, down in the darkness and gloom.[19]

The wonder, to which the initiated, the so-called *mystes*, gained insight, was the mystery of creation, where the blessing consisted of understanding and participating in a perspective of infinity that is raised above death. On the other hand, the uninitiated must take his woeful path to Hades, without the annual redemption.

The celebration of fertility, which the mystery in Eleusis is, incarnated in Demeter and her daughter, was for the sake of the continuity of the rhythm of vegetation and the cyclical connection between life and death. The starting point in experience is the concrete reality of eternal life: the grain in the field. As said above, the link between the growth of grain and woman's fertility is based on the obvious analogy that the earth is a mother, just as a woman's uterus at the moment of conception is a field in which the seed is placed or sown.

Thus, a woman and the earth have the same form of fertility that must be ensured through the mystery. Briefly described, the great festival of the mystery took place over a week in the month of Boedromion, September-October, when the participants, the initiated, walked in procession from Athens to Eleusis, took part in ritual cleansing in the sea, sacrificed pigs (Demeter's sacred animal), displayed the sacred objects and walked in a torchlight procession as an evocation of Demeter's search for her missing daughter. The high point was the sacred wedding between the hierophant and a selected virgin, which was to ensure the grain of its growing power.[20]

In her hymn, Demeter introduces herself in this way: "I am that Demeter who has share of honour and is the greatest help and cause of joy to the undying gods and mortal men."[21] Gods as well as men derive their bliss from her, which is why she is unique. That this is not just idle talk appears in her myth from which the nature of happiness can also be defined.

In brief, the myth says that she, Demeter, with her brother (again, the chthonic incest aspect) Zeus procreated Kore—"girl," as the name actually means. Hades or Pluto fell in love with the girl and abducted her—with the approval of Zeus—from a meadow where she was picking flowers, taking her to his kingdom of darkness beneath the earth. Grieving, Demeter searched for her daughter in the moonlight of Hekate—the Eleusinian Mysteries are held at full moon presumably for that reason—until Helios, the all-seeing sun, informed her of what had happened. Angry at the gods of Olympos, Demeter wreaked her vengeance by laying waste to the earth:

Then she caused a most dreadful and cruel year for mankind over the all-nourishing earth: the ground would not make the seed sprout, for rich-crowned Demeter kept it hid. In the fields the oxen drew many a curved plough in vain, and much white barley was cast upon the land without avail.[22]

This quotation illustrates with great clarity the overwhelming power she possesses as goddess of the soil and grain, a power which not even the Olympian gods wield, since they are not able themselves to make the grain grow. And the blessing she talks about being hers alone to give must be precisely the continuing cycle of growth without which no one can live.

Only when Zeus, with Hermes as intermediary, is forced to intervene does Hades release his beloved and Demeter allow the earth to blossom, the grain to grow in the field—"And rich-crowned Demeter did not refuse but straightway made fruit to spring up from the rich lands."[23] However, Hades tricks the girl into eating a pomegranate, so that she will always be in his power. One third of the year, from winter to spring, she must reside in the realm of the dead as queen under the name of Persephone.

7

In other words, in this—the central part of the vegetation-creation drama—certain specific actors take part: Demeter and her daughter Kore/Persephone, the queen of the dead; and opposite them the King of the Dead, Hades or Pluto. Since these are fundamentally elemental figures, it is important to understand the unity and the generative idea of transformation in this parallelogram of forces.

The best way of understanding Demeter as a corn mother is to see her and her daughter as a trinity,[24] each representing a significant stage in the cycle of corn growth. In this context, Kore may be viewed as the virgin of spring, the budding ears of corn from the black soil of the fallow field. As mother goddess, Demeter is both the ripened harvest and the ur-gestalt that, in unity with the earth, ensures reproduction, i.e. the grain that—through the sacred wedding—is fertilized and placed in the newly plowed field. Persephone becomes the incarnation of grain during winter, when in a death-like hibernation in the earth it awaits germination in the mother's womb.

In Homer, Persephone appears twice as often as her mother—though only two of these occasions are in the *Iliad*, where she is called "the dread" (*epaine*, IX, 457, 569), which emphasizes the destructive aspect of her chthonic femininity. The epithet is repeated in the *Odyssey* (10, 491), but when Odysseus enters into Hades' sphere of influence, she is called "proud" (11, 226, wondrous—*agaue*). Yet he flees at the thought that she could set the gorgon, i.e. Medusa, on him from the primeval darkness.

Nevertheless, together with her consort, the King of the Dead, her task is to ensure the optimal germinating power of the seed corn. The idea behind this must be that the seed corn remains in the darkness of the kingdom of the dead during the winter months from which it germinates, just as the sun descends into the realm of the dead at night, journeying through it to rise, regenerated, the next morning and with its rays makes everything grow. In this form, paradoxically enough, Hades represents the generosity of the earth, since like Pluto he is the abundance from which the grain is revitalized year after year and sent as a gift to mankind. On earth, as the god of plenty, he is called Plutos for the sake of clarity.[25]

It is also as Pluto that, according to Apollodorus, the god of death pursues and abducts Kore, making her the queen of the underworld under the name of Persephone. Thus, Hades constitutes the locality that elsewhere is made metonymically identical with the divinity. If Pluto as king of the underworld—under the name of Plutos—is the son of Demeter and Iasion, while Persephone is really an incarnation of Demeter during the time when the grain is beneath the earth, this must logically mean that, in the shape of her daughter, she is fertilized by her son on the premise that grain acquires its high seed quality and ability to germinate through a coupling between the spouses of the underworld.

This possible connection is confirmed in several ways. At the end of the hymn to Demeter, it is said that anyone who honors Demeter and Persephone will be rewarded by Pluto: "soon they [Demeter/Persephone] do send Plutos as guest to his great house, Plutos who gives wealth to mortal men."[26] And as we heard before, the happiness and wealth that Demeter provides are equivalent to the corn harvest with great yield in which Pluto is present in the ears of corn as their potency and abundance. At any rate, Pluto must be the Zeus of the underworld (Zeus Chthonios), whom Hesiod recommends should be invoked in the same breath as Demeter to ensure the fertility of the grain.

8

In order better to understand why Homer is trying to repress the cult of the Great Mother, I will describe below how the gender polarity between the mother goddess and her lover-son is manifested.[27] As said above, it was not until the introduction of agriculture (and animal husbandry) that it became clear to people of that time that two bodies are needed. The woman is the receiving party, the man the active breeder. However, this does not mean that the primeval mother becomes subordinate. She remains—as in the cult of Demeter—dominant, and it has a crucial psychological significance for a man's developmental process that the woman is primary and he is secondary.

In her identity with the earth, the mother goddess is primary, since in the nature of things it is through her that the man comes into existence—as her son. For the same reason, the man will by his very nature be subordinate to the feminine, the mother, even though he takes part in the vegetation drama as husband and lover (brother). Beyond the differences in the relationships between Kybele and Attis, Isthar and Tammuz and many others, there is for the same reason a uniform archetypal structure.

It was not only the son's functional duty in the sequence of growth to fertilize his mother. At the same time, he must suffer death in the cycle of growth and descend beneath the earth to the realm of the dead. The Great Mother is immortal, man mortal. But whereas ordinary mortals are doomed to remain in the underworld, the goddess was able by virtue of her link with death to bring back her son and return life to him, so that through the sacred wedding he is once again able to service her with his regenerative vitality, just as the rain makes the seeds germinate. This mythos was embedded in the course of the seasons and, consequently, linked corn's cycle of growth, in which the symbolic demarcation point is the new year, when the new god, sun and spring are received to the accompaniment of great festivity. Since these rites are only described in highly fragmentary form, it is difficult to determine their content. But if this interpretation of the Eleusinian Mysteries is correct, it might indicate that the son's descent to the underworld has to do with the fact that it is here the actual fertilization takes place.

However, what is absolutely crucial is the fact that the male divinity or son in his relationship to the mother is made totally dependent on the feminine. It is actually only as a potent phallus that he is to ensure her fertilization in the *perpetuum mobile* of life. He sacrifices himself to her as a sort of phallic appendage in an eternally recurring event. This subjugation and phallic sacrifice is particularly clear in the cult of Kybele in which, like Attis, the son-lover, the priests of the goddess known as *galli* castrated themselves. They thereby gave the mother goddess their sexual power and received her care and tenderness in return, something that made difficult any attempt at rebellion.

For it will of course create conflict in such a closed circle if the son refuses to be available to his mother (and the primal feminine), but desires to become independent on the premises of his own sex. In that case, he is no longer identified with the phallos of fertility, refuses to contribute and squander his manhood, and will instead maintain a psychological course that breaks through the cycle of conception and growth. As a process of civilization, this means that he gradually breaks free, as a self, from the primal nature of the mother with its special unawareness and static character. Thus, a true incipient self begins to be formed, portending a shift from matriarchate to patriarchate.

9

In this perspective, it is not difficult to understand why the Great Mother Goddess splits off the destructive side of her chthonic nature, demonstrated in her demand for instance for blood sacrifice. For if the son no longer wishes to serve/service and fertilize the mother, she does not feel bound by her previous solicitude but in anger at his desertion tries to eliminate her rebellious son. Consequently, she demonizes herself fairy-tale figures such as witches, dragons or wild animals like bears and boars. A wild boar killed Attis—and nearly killed Odysseus.

So on the mythical plane, it is here that the struggle (with the dragon) ensues between the son, who wishes to separate himself from the all-absorbing maternal bond, and the mother, who in her re-created form as destructive force tries to stop him with fire or venom. In the cases in which the son as the fairy-tale hero, prince or knight succeeds in destroying the dragon and liberating the princess, winning the great treasure of half the kingdom, we are presented with an archetypal paradigm. With his deed, the hero has liberated himself from the maternal bond and can now meet the feminine (his anima) in the form of a woman his own age, while the treasure is a sign that he has finally taken possession of the most precious thing he possesses—his own self.

An example is Zeus' last great battle with a dragon in Hesiod: he defeats the monster Typhon,[28] whom the primal mother, Gaia, produced with Tartaros, the lowest region of hell, in an attempt to enforce her dominance—"[Zeus] lashed him with a whip and mastered him,/ And threw him down, all maimed, and great Earth [Gaia] groaned."[29] Typhon and Gaia are, in principle, one. We encounter Gaia here in a completely different role from when she lovingly took care of the newborn Zeus child in Crete and prevented his father from swallowing him.

10

If a man is to realize himself completely, he must not only differentiate himself from the primal feminine but re-conquer the feminine in a higher form by confronting and integrating what is repressed in the most frightening forms of the mother goddess.[30] Generally speaking, this process is the deeper foundation of meaning in the *Iliad* and the *Odyssey*, just as it radically separates these two works from each other.

Thus, in the *Iliad*, we encounter a thoroughly male, heroic culture, which is completely isolated in its own heroic norms from the world of women. Women are used for the sake of pleasure and breeding. Heroes really exist in a friendship and fellowship capable of resisting the Great Mother. A corresponding isolation is found in the Old English poem *Beowulf* in which the Danish heroes at Lejre live together in a great hall. However, it is revealed here how fragile this construction is in relation to the primeval feminine world. Every night, those things that have been repressed enter the hall in the form of the monster Grendel at the behest of his primal mother and massacring the defenseless warriors. Only the designated hero Beowulf can release them from this catastrophe when he battles with Grendel and later descends for the final confrontation with the demonic mother in the depths of the swamp.

With this brief discussion of *Beowulf*, it has been my intention to indicate some of the basic points of comparison with the monsters with which Odysseus must contend during his voyage home. It appears quite clearly that the reality from which people are freeing themselves, in this case the world of mothers, returns destructively until a heroic figure is ready once again to enter it, to take up the struggle and (re)integrate the values of this reality as psychological reality at a higher level of consciousness. As emerges from the myth of Beowulf, the sequence of events in the *Iliad* and the *Odyssey* is by no means unique, but is an archetypal sequence of events that does not only belong in a mythical past but from a phylo-ontogenetic perspective enters into every man's life. As son and lover. Even today!

11

This is also the case with Odysseus. During his voyage home, he faces a maternal reality that has been made unconscious by virtue of repression and now confronts him from the outside in all these demonic figures, which may just as well be ascribed to the drama of his inner life. He thus takes on the consequences of Homer's struggle to raise Olympos. This requires tremendous courage and is attended by eternal fear, as we can see when with a drawn sword in his hand Odysseus demands the sacred oath from Kirke that she will not rob him of his "manhood" (10, 301). Put in another way: she will not castrate him by transforming him into a domestic animal as she has done with the others.

That castration is the sign of powerlessness and reveals a regression to the primal maternal can also be observed in the castration cults already mentioned, in which the male priests castrated themselves in an act of self-sacrifice. The mere fact that Kirke transforms the men is clear evidence of her chthonic origin. At the same time, this is an elemental situation, since Odysseus asserts his masculine will by his sword, controls the primal power of her sex, and turns her into his compliant servant. Yet, it is a sign of her death-affiliated power that for a whole year she is able to make him forget all about his voyage home.

The *Odyssey* is thus interwoven with more or less conscious knowledge and experience of the primal force and possible destructiveness of the feminine. Agamemnon expresses the greatest anxiety in the underworld, where—from his own bloody experiences—he warns Odysseus against believing in the faithful Penelope; for by robbing him of his life, Klytemnestra has cast "the shame on herself and the rest of her sex, on women/ still to come, even on the one whose acts are virtuous" (11, 433-34). But in answer to the question of whether Homer is hostile to women, the answer will be ambiguous. On the one hand, he describes woman as a dangerous, retrogressive primal force with great insight into the destruction inherent in sexuality if it is not separated from the atavistic power of the goddess or the mother. On the other hand, he demonstrates great esteem for women such as Penelope and Arete, the queen of the Phaiakians, and Athene.

It can also be seen that women are superior to men in a number of instances. Helen appears to be stronger than her husband; Antikleia, Odysseus' mother, is superior to King Laertes, just as the Phaiakian queen Arete is clearly the dominant figure. Odysseus must go to her, not her husband, to be sailed home in safety. There is thus no doubt that women in Homer have a higher status than was later assigned to women. Hesiod is a decided misogynist, and women in Athens were subject to the control of their husbands in a way of which we gain a first impression when, as a symbol of his entry into manhood, Telemachos orders his mother to go up to her chamber.

We shall see the entire thematic and phenomenal world unfold and made more concrete in the interpretation of the *Apologoi*, for we shall make a further study of the power and might of the Olympian male gods, qualities by which, in a concealed but highly charged confrontation, they seek to take the place of the Great Mother.

The Origin and Gods of Olympos

1

That Olympos really is a more recent construct and the work of individual men emerges from Herodotus' account and dating of its genesis and of the naming and hierarchizing of the gods to which reference has already been made. Let us return to this with a more detailed quotation from Herodotus:

> I believe that Homer and Hesiod were four hundred years before my time—and no more than that. It was they who created for the Greeks their theogony; it is they who gave the gods the special names for their descent from their ancestors and divided among them their honors, their arts, and their shapes.[31]

The emphasis is on the fact that the divine powers that had previously referred to natural forces are made into the object of intellectualization, naming and division of authority. In this way, the nature gods, as described above, have been anthropomorphized and raised to an Olympian sovereignty.

Since Herodotus lived around 485–425 B.C., his dating at least for Hesiod is too early, as Hesiod was active around 700 B.C. However, Herodotus' words confirm that the Greeks viewed the Olympian gods as a relatively late invention that was due to a small number of individuals and their fantasy.

As far as we can determine, Homer must have had a profound influence on the development of the basic patriarchal attitude that is behind his invention of the Olympic gods. He seems to be more strongly opposed to the mother cults than the later Hesiod, who builds on Homer. This may be because Homer comes from an enlightened Ionia, while Hesiod lived his days in a backward, agrarian Boeotia. So in *Works and Days* we can find his advice in connection with harvest and sowing to hold sacred these respective gods: Demeter and the infernal Zeus. At the same time, however, Hesiod is more of a misogynist than Homer, which can be explained by the fact that he is younger and thus represents a more explicit rebellion against female nature.

Yet Hesiod's epistemological significance consists primarily in his systematization of the divine world on the basis of a doctrine of succession up to a higher stage of development, which Zeus represents. That this was, on the whole, a purely speculative affair is substantiated by the fact that it quickly had consequences for the reflections of the philosophers on the nature of the world and a principle of cosmic creation. The gods shrink more or less into one god, a monad, inseparable from the actual ability to imagine this by virtue of reason, *nous* or *logos*. Thus, Xenophanes postulates the idea that a unity exists and that this unity is God, whereby he argues in principle for a metaphysical monotheism in opposition to the Homeric gods.[32]

However, this duality—between the unpredictable gods and a dawning monotheism of a metaphysical nature—can already be demonstrated within the framework of the Homeric epics. The behavior of the gods leaves much to be desired, especially in the *Iliad*, where they fight and cheat one another. However, in the transition from the *Iliad* to the *Odyssey*, there is a striking difference in the interpretation of Zeus. For while in the *Iliad* he is still a young god threatened by the other gods, in the *Odyssey*, by virtue of his maturity and exaltation, he now represents a cosmic justice in which one can clearly sense the germ of a later monotheism.

2

How inclined Homer was to reflection or ideological criticism, if you will, may be read from a verse he puts in the mouth of Achilleus, containing a hidden dissociation from the carefree gods. In the final book's moving exchange with King Priam, when he comes to retrieve the corpse of his son Hektor, Achilleus, in a sudden exclamation of sympathy, cannot refrain from criticizing the way the gods mercilessly weave the web of human life with sorrows, while they themselves live without grief:

Such is the way the gods spun life for unfortunate mortals,
That we live in unhappiness, but the gods themselves have no sorrows.
There are two urns that stand on the door-sill of Zeus. They are unlike
For the gifts they bestow: an urn of evils, an urn of blessings.
If Zeus who delights in thunder mingles these and bestows them
On man, he shifts, and moves now in evil, again in good fortune.
But when Zeus bestows from the urn of sorrows, he makes a failure
Of man, and the evil hunger drives him over the shining
Earth, and he wanders respected neither of gods nor mortals.

(XXXIV, 524-34)

Untouched by death as the gods are by their very nature, they live fundamentally unaffected by human sorrow or the pain of strife. For example, Zeus amuses himself with the sight of combative gods going to war with each other—and thereby drawing heroes to their deaths (XXI, 389 ff.).

Men and gods mirror one another. Although the gods in the *Iliad* are removed from the world of human action, they participate passionately in the Trojan War, each favoring their own side. In Book IV, when Zeus wants to stop the bloodshed,

Athene and Hera oppose it furiously. They have not yet avenged themselves sufficiently for the insult of Paris' preference for Aphrodite. In addition, the gods are shown to be capricious and can at any time turn against blameless mortals, blinding or punishing them.

Although the gods can be wounded, as Ares is by Athene, they can as immortals seek to be healed, whereas doomed heroes are forced to accept their destiny. With what playful ease the gods relate to the human world may be shown, for example, by the comparison of Apollo's demolishing the Greek bastions to a boy who makes sand castles on the beach and then happily levels them (XV, 360 ff.). And even though the gods help their favorites in battle, their efforts and interventions are ultimately governed by passions that have nothing to do with human beings but their own bantering.

One explanation for the lack of concern in these playful, laughter-prone gods may be a trait inherited from their origin as forces of nature which have no moral relation to human reality. Or it may be due to a process of anthropomorphizing by which, as Xenophanes points out, they acquire far too many human faults and weaknesses. Yet, this view of the gods in Homer can only be a half truth. For in his works, it conflicts with another explanation of Olympos, in which the gods—as a part of their development—tend to represent a higher, punitive cosmic justice.

Fate and Free Will

1

The Zeus we meet at the beginning of the *Odyssey* solemnly bemoans the fact that men make the gods responsible for their sorrows, when they themselves are to blame, taking Aigisthos as a primary example. However, even at one point in the *Iliad* Zeus appears as a punitive judge—and in a comparison preserving his original role of a deity of nature and rain. It is described how, one autumn day, he had the rain hammer down like the Trojans' fleeing horses in wrath and as a punishment because powerful people on the square (*agora*) were acting against justice (*dike*): "When Zeus sends down the most violent waters/ in deep rage against mortals after they stir him to anger/ because in violent assembly they pass decrees that are crooked/ and drive righteousness from among them and care nothing for what the gods think" (XVI, 385-88).

First of all, we can ascertain here that the nature god is acting in his quality as the divinity for a burgeoning urban culture. Second, the concept of *dike* in this act of punishment is used in a unique way in the Homeric context, since Hesiod was the first to personify *dike* as the goddess of justice. Of course, Homer uses *dike* in a number of other contexts, but even in the *Odyssey* with the almost normative meaning of "in the usual way." Thus, Odysseus' mother explains to him in the underworld that he sees her in the form that usually belongs to the dead—"it is only what happens (*dike*), when they die, to all mortals" (11, 218). And Penelope shames the suitors that, in past times, it was not the *dike*, i.e. custom, of suitors to behave as they do (18, 275). Odysseus never harmed anyone, which otherwise "is a way (*dike*) divine kings have" (4, 691).[33] In being thus contrasted to evil kings, Odysseus is associated with *dike* in the same legal form the concept is given in Hesiod and in just such a contrast with corrupt rulers.

Yet, despite the fact that *dike* is not used as an explicit legal concept, it is apparent that this idea—like others for which Homer does not have a word—is present as experience and permeates the *Odyssey* in particular: What one owes the gods and what respect they demand. This aspect also appears in the *Iliad*, when Athene grasps Achilleus by the hair and he bows to her, saying: "Goddess, it is necessary that I obey the word of you two,/ angry though I am in my heart. So it will be better./ If any man obeys the gods, they listen to him also" (I, 216-18).

In other words, at the same time as Zeus rejects the projections of men at the beginning of the *Odyssey* portraying him as the model for their own flaws, he distances himself from an anthropomorphic interpretation and makes himself a metaphysical judge. As a natural consequence, the *Odyssey* becomes a demonstration of how *dike* works in practice. For whereas Odysseus is obedient to the gods and is therefore rewarded in the end, the entire behaviour of the suitors demonstrates a god-forsaking defiance, which Telemachos criticises as *hubris*. And as we understand, this arrogance is the true cause of their destruction, as expressed by Laertes upon seeing his son again: "Father Zeus, there are gods indeed upon tall Olympos,/ if truly the suitors have had to pay for their reckless violence" (24, 351-52).

The word used here is exactly *hubris*. So this human arrogance, which in later poetry, in Hesiod, Solon and the tragedies is so deeply hated by the gods and calls down their vengeance, is present even in the *Odyssey* as a violation of sacred law. With it, this work is positioned radically differently in relation to the future from the *Iliad*, where the arrogance of heroes is not punished but, to the contrary, helps increase their honor. Here we find a forward-looking sense of justice, which is reflected in the collective punishment of the suitors as well as, on an individual level, in the sight of mythical arch criminals like Sisyphos who deserve to suffer in the deepest depths of Hades as a warning to others.

It is not sufficient merely to see the gods as nonchalant, intriguing beings. Ultimately, they come to represent the norms of human behavior. Presumably for the same reason, Hesiod has Zeus marry Themis, the goddess of justice—after having first been married to the goddess of wisdom, Metis—in order to illustrate how the highest divinity takes part in and integrates justice itself, the law and order governing the world and defining the guidelines for human conduct.[34] Telemachos directs his prayer to Themis when he wants to call an assembly, for it is she "who breaks up the assemblies of men and calls them in session" (2, 69). That is, her system of justice is incarnated in lawful institutions. Not until Draco and Solon, c. 600 B.C., were the laws written down. Until then, they must have been customary law via an oral, myth-borne exemplification.

With Themis, Zeus conceived, among others, his daughter Dike, who in Hesiod seems to replace her mother as the goddess of justice. For example, Hesiod relates how, as soon someone violates justice, Dike tells her father "of men's wicked heart."[35] Then, he measures out the punishment. He is the executive power. And when the kings in the *Iliad* are called "whom the gods love," it is a sign that they represent the will of the gods on earth. So it is also a catastrophe, as apparently was the case in Hesiod's time, when corrupt rulers take bribes.

2

If you ask what sort of justice it is Themis/Dike and Zeus jointly legislate on and maintain, the shortest answer is: Fate. In Greek, Fate has several names—for example, *moira* and *aisa*. In the end, Fate is the underlying, codified plan of the world, while Zeus is the eyes and arms of that plan. As it is formulated in the *Iliad*, human life fits into this world order like the leaves on the trees:

> As is the generation of leaves, so is that of humanity,
> The wind scatters the leaves on the ground, but the live timber
> Burgeons with leaves again in the season of spring returning.
> So one generation of men will grow while another
> Dies (. . .).
>
> (VI, 146-49)

Meanwhile, the close connection between Fate and the high god is not expressed directly by Homer, but is found later exemplified in Euripides, when, for example, the dioscuros Kastor says to Orestes: "Compulsion is on us to accept this scene, on you/ to go complete the doom which Fate (Moira) and Zeus decreed."[36] The happy ending in Aeschylus' *Eumenides* similarly occurs in an action in which: "Zeus the all seeing met with Destiny to confirm,"[37] since these events were directed by Zeus in his capacity as the accomplisher of Fate: Zeus Teleios. In Homer, on the other hand, Fate is often identified with ruin or is synonymous with death. A good fate is defined negatively—Fate has not yet struck. Not yet.

That Fate weaves birth, law and death together might indicate that it has a chthonic origin and belongs to the mystery of conception, blood and death. According to Hesiod, Moira and the Fate goddesses the Moirai are also, like death, daughters of the Night, the primal darkness. Elsewhere, the Moirai are considered the daughters of Zeus and Themis, which again emphasises the link with the chthonic, since Themis is the daughter of Gaia and so herself a mother goddess. Whoever's daughters the Moirai, Klotho, Lachesis and Atropos may be, they—like the Norns in Norse mythology—spin and weave the strands of life and cut them when the time comes, just as they allot human beings their share of good and evil.

That Fate and its goddesses actively and inexorably fashion the strands of life from the moment of birth is expressed in the *Iliad* and the *Odyssey* in almost identical phrases. Fate follows a person from birth. As Hekuba complains over her fallen son, Hektor: "the way at the first strong Destiny/ spun with his life line when he was born, when I gave birth to him" (XXIV, 209-10). And similarly it is said of Odysseus and all his difficulties that "he shall endure all that his destiny and the heavy Spinners/ spun for him with the thread at his birth, when his mother bore him" (7, 196-98). In agreement with this belief in Fate, the prophecy that Halitherses advanced on his departure is also fulfilled—namelly, that he was to endure trials but return home in the twentieth year: "And now all this is being accomplished" (2, 176).

Indeed, it could be said that the assembly of gods at the beginning of the *Odyssey* and again in Book 5 takes its compositional significance from the fact that at the beginning of the epic Odysseus has reached the time fated to him when he can finally return home after twenty years abroad, ten of them spent on the home voyage—"when in the circling of the years that very year came/ in which the gods had spun for him his time of homecoming" (1, 16-17). Similarly, Hermes produces the conclusive argument to Kalypso, who is reluctant to release Odysseus: "It is not appointed for him to die here, away from his people./ It is still his fate that he shall see his people and come back" (5, 113-14). The goddess must yield and she does so, albeit under protest.

Thus Fate determines the limits, even for the gods. Even the mighty god of the sea, Poseidon, whom Odysseus has turned into a mortal enemy by blinding his Kyklops-son, must yield. He declares to Zeus that it was never his intention to annihilate Odysseus, only to make his life miserable, since Zeus promised with his nod that he would return home (13, 133). In this respect Zeus and Fate are two sides of the same coin.

Fate lies behind all actions and breaks through at some unknown point. It was thus determined by Fate that Troy should fall when the Trojans brought the Wooden Horse into the city despite all warnings: "the city was destined (*aisa*) to be destroyed when it had inside it/ the great horse made of wood" (8, 511-12). The same contradiction between characters' optimism and their devastating fate exists in the action relating to the boastful and dissipated suitors who believe they are to marry the queen, while in reality "the day of their destiny stands near them" (16, 280) with Odysseus in the guise of a beggar.

Fate, which seems unfailingly certain in its long-term goals, is just as inscrutable and indefinable for everyone subject to a given sequence of events. For whereas the gods and listeners—who share the author's compositional insight via its coincidence with Fate's underlying plan—are aware that Odysseus is on the verge of his homeward voyage, he does not know for certain, despite his journey to Hades, whether he will escape "the day without pity" (*nelees hemar*, 9, 17).

Even those who are divine or close to the gods are subject to the same uncertainty about the impact of Fate. Thus, Kirke only realizes that Odysseus is the one whose coming Hermes has foretold when he resists her magical arts—"You are then resourceful Odysseus. Argeïphontes/ of the golden staff was forever telling me you would come" (10, 330-31). The scene is a parallel to Polyphemos' experience. He has been forewarned that "I must lose the sight of my eye at the hands of Odysseus" (9, 511). But the Kyklops has expected an opponent of the same physical stature as himself and so only recognizes Odysseus when he reveals his identity.

3

So while there can be no doubt that gods and men are subject to Fate, the matter is somewhat more difficult with Zeus, since he is both the supreme god and to some extent identical with Fate, for "Zeus who rejoices in the thunder—and he well knows/ all things, the luck and the lucklessness of mortal people" (20, 75-76). It is he, for instance, who makes the fateful decisions in the cases in which the Greek heroes in the *Iliad* cast lots to decide who is to meet Hektor in single combat—"Father Zeus, let Ajax win the lot, or else Diomedes,/ Tydeus' son, or the king himself of golden Mykenai" (VII, 179-80).

The result is ascribed to Zeus at the same time as his own dependence—perhaps better to be determined as loyalty—appears in a different way. For example, he cannot change a decision once he himself has set Fate into motion with his affirmative nod of the head: "nothing I do shall be vain nor revocable/ nor a thing unfulfilled when I bend my head in assent to it" (I, 536-27).

This bond appears strongest in the *Iliad*, since he himself must decide by the weights of the scales who is to be victorious. When the battle between the Greeks and the Trojans surges back and forth, he takes "his golden scales" (VIII, 69), lifts it in the air and places "two fateful portions of death" (VIII, 70) in the scales, which on this occasion rise to the advantage of the Trojans. He uses the same procedure in the duel between Achilleus and Hektor.

In order to understand the significance of these fateful weights properly, it is necessary to go to the original text. Here it appears that the weights are not, for example, made of lead but are a form of living beings or demons known as *Kéres*.[38] Without examining in depth the mythology surrounding them, we can say that they are very ancient and belong to the underworld, where they are linked to age and death, as is indicated by the expression *ker thanatoio* (11, 399). The genitive reveals that they are related to but not identical with death. They are often described as a pair, but there is a passage in the *Iliad* providing a description of their appearance in a situation in which a *ker* acts in union with the goddess of strife, Eris—"Hate was there with confusion among them, and Death (Ker) the destructive (. . .) The clothing upon her shoulders showed strong red with men's blood" (XVIII, 535 ff.).

If these Keres as spirits of death can guide Zeus when placed on the scales, the idea must be that, by virtue of their connection to death, they show in which of the combatants death weighs heaviest, so to speak. Put differently: as powers of Fate, they must in the weighing process represent the course of a life from birth to impending death. So there is a deeper logic in the fact that in Hesiod they virtually merge with Fate, both of them being the progeny of Night: "Night bore hateful Doom (Ker) and black Fate and Death,"[39] as it is put in the *Theogony*. In addition, they are closely connected to the Erinyes, who belong to the same chthonic world of death and whose primary function in Aeschylus—more clearly than in Homer—is to avenge a murdered human being, awakened by the blood that seeps into the earth: "through too much glut of blood drunk by our fostering ground/ the vengeful gore is caked and hard, will not drain through."[40] It is also from this ancient reality that blood revenge arises as an institution.

A glance through Homer reveals, however, that the Erinyes, who in his work primarily punish perjury, are already situated in the world of blood and vengeance. Hence, a father can ask them to punish his son by making him childless (IX, 450 ff.). And his prayer is heard. A mother calls upon them to have her son killed and is heard (IX, 570 ff.). To the impatient suitors, Telemachos explains that he cannot simply marry off his mother without her consent, as in that case she would set the Erinyes upon him—"my mother will call down her furies upon me" (2, 135). Similarly, it is said that Oedipus is pursued by the Erinyes of Iokaste—"all the sorrows that are brought to pass by a mother's furies" (11, 280).

In short, death is such an ultimate fact that not even the god of all gods, Zeus, can intervene in this reality without the world order collapsing. This is most clearly expressed in the following statement by Athene relating to the murder of Agamemnon:

> But death is a thing that comes to all alike. Not even
> The gods can fend it away from a man they love, when once
> The destructive doom of leveling death has fastened upon him.
> (3, 236-38)

This is an interpretation supported by Aeschylus, who directly relates it to Zeus when Apollo says that a dead man never rises again: "This is a thing for which my father never made curative spells."[41]

There has apparently been a disagreement as to whether even the supreme god is powerless over the logic of death, and this has called for a modification. Homer, at any rate, allows him potentially to possess an omnipotent power to suspend the demands of death. This interpretation can be extracted from the story of the fate and death of Zeus' son Sarpedon. During a battle with Ajax, Zeus protects his son: "Zeus brushed the death spirits/ from his son, and would not let him be killed there beside the ships' sterns" (XII, 402-03). However, it is only possible for him because Sarpedon's fate has not yet entirely run out. When this happens a few books later, Zeus must sorrowfully watch his son being killed. But he is in such doubt as to whether he should intervene and save him from "the sorrowful battle" (XVI, 436) that his wife Hera has to talk reason and justice to him:

> Majesty, son of Kronos, what sort of thing have you spoken?
> Do you wish to bring back a man who is mortal, one long since

Doomed by his destiny, from ill-sounding death and release him?
Do it, then; but not all the rest of us gods shall approve you.

(XVI, 440-43)

If Zeus acted against death on this occasion, the other gods would demand that their favorites should be spared and thus counter their appointed destiny, something that would fatally violate the laws of birth and death.

Meanwhile, it is this unassailable law of Fate, with birth and death as the ultimate points of intersection, that endows the heroes with inner security and strength. For example, we hear of such certainty in Hektor's farewell speech to his wife Andromache, as he comforts her: "No man is going to hurl me to Hades, unless it is fated (*hyper aisan*)" (VI, 487). Thus, the heroes (and all human beings) have their measured lot in life. They die on a given and, to them, unknown day of fate (*aisimos hemar*). But heroes are different from ordinary mortals by being able through their own submission to Fate to accept the life and death they receive. For they see death not as the closure of life but rather as its culmination. And so we never hear the Homeric heroes complain that they are to die, much less show fear of death. They exist in the belief that their reputation will ensure them immortal life. Despite this apparently deterministic Fate, free will is given a certain rein.

Remarkably enough, it is Achilleus who, after Odysseus has tried to persuade him to re-enter the war, complains of the cruelty of the conflict. He does not want Agamemnon's luxuriant gifts of reconciliation but would rather return home in the certainty that his father would find a bride and land for him. Not even the treasures of Troy can make up for life, for "a man's life cannot come back again, it cannot be lifted/ nor captured again by force, once it has crossed the teeth's barrier" (IX, 408-09). His destiny seems to be to gain an immortal reputation by dying young. That, at least, is what happens. But this glimpse of Achilleus' soul is a psychological preparation for both his grief at the loss of Patroklos and his sympathy with Priam and and also his complaint in the last book at the hard lot of mankind in relation to the playful, lust-filled world of the gods.

Though difficult for us to understand, the fact is that the heroes have a predetermined Fate woven into their lifeline and a certain freedom of choice. A true deterministic view of Fate does not in fact appear until Hellenism.[42]

4

By not preventing the death of his son, Zeus avoids acting against the decision of Fate (*hyper moron/aisan*). This phenomenon of an apparent ability to change Fate appears in a number of passages in Homer. When Odysseus is struggling for his life in the sea off the Phaiakian coast, he would have been lost if Athene had not intervened and inspired him with "presence of mind" (*epiphrosynen*, 5, 437). Otherwise he would have been lost "beyond his destiny" (*hyper moron*, 5, 436).

So the formula *hyper moron* (*hyper aisan*) implies that something can happen that does not correspond to Fate's original plan. This thinking seems to open Fate to choice. In the *Iliad*, the gods intervene in a number of instances in the manner of Athene to block actions against what is determined by Fate. For example, Zeus decides to send the gods to war again when Achilleus re-enters the conflict and there is a risk that, in his grief and rage at Patroklos' death, he might take Troy, which conflicts with the higher purpose—"now, when his heart is grieved and angered for his companion's/ death, I fear against destiny (*hyper moron*) he may storm their fortress" (XX, 29-30).

The only instance in which such a contravention might take place is in Patroklos' attack on the Trojans. Here, he goes beyond Achilleus'—and the gods'?— order only to drive the enemy back from the ships. However, Patroklos becomes a victim of his heroic deeds to such an extent that, struck by psychological blindness, he forgets the words of his friend. It is here made explicitly clear that, if he had checked himself, he would have evaded death—"had he only kept the command of Peleiades/ he might have got clear away from the evil spirit of black death" (XVI, 685-87). But when he pursues the fleeing Trojans, Zeus must, after irresolutely debating with himself, allow Apollo to kill him by the hand of Hektor, for "always the mind of Zeus is a stronger thing than a man's mind" (XVI, 688), as it is written. Even before this, Zeus has decided to accept Achilleus' prayer that Patroklos should drive the Trojans back but refuses to "let him come back safe out of the fighting" (XVI, 252).

This in itself is of course an illustrative example of the uncertainty facing the reader with respect to the degree of individual freedom of choice in the *Iliad*. On the one hand, had he followed Achilleus' orders, it seems that Patroklos would have been able to avoid death; but, on the other hand, it had already been decided for him by Zeus, who in this respect is synonymous with Fate and the length of life allotted to him. That the heroes are so subject to the gods and are constantly blinded as a sign of the intervention of external forces has led to the obvious assumption that Homer's figures have no choice and act only as some kind of automatons.[43]

As has subsequently been shown, this is far from the case. Athene must grab Achilleus by the hair to prevent him from killing Agamemnon in a fit of anger; but it is ultimately his own choice that makes him refrain. Similarly, as said above, we gain many glimpses of Odysseus' considerations in and with his *thymos*.

And precisely in the *Odyssey*, this freedom of choice is made clear right from the start of the work, when Zeus bemoans the fact that men attribute their own motives to them. There is no corresponding statement on free thought in the *Iliad*, but it is supported by Athene, who says directly to Telemachos: "Some of it you will see in your own heart,/ and some the divinity will put in your mind" (3, 26-27). This statement not only demonstrates the differentiation that has taken place in the development of consciousness in the *Odyssey* but reflects a fact that is difficult to handle—the fact that the gods themselves are subject to a process of development.

5

The very fact that the Olympian gods are late arrivals means that they are not fully developed. I believe just such a process of development is an essential point in both Homer and Aeschylus. This often makes interpretation difficult, since it is necessary to adapt to the notion that a god can change and is not necessarily the same at the end as at the beginning of a work. This is simply a part of the amalgamation and transformation that takes place in the transition from the ancient and cultic to Olympos.

With respect to Zeus, we have been able to trace his genesis back to Crete, where his childhood in a cave under the protection of the Great Mother revealed that he has been subordinate to the dominance of a primal mother. We have also seen his link to life below the earth in his role as the Zeus of the underworld (Chthonios) in Hesiod. It is probably most accurate to say that in these shapes he is completely separate from the deity on Olympos. As the Olympian patriarch, however, he is the god for a wide variety of areas: he is the god of guest friendship (Xenios), of suppliants (Hikesios), the fulfiller (Teleios), the savior (Soter) and more we shall meet along the way.

If the portrait of Zeus in the *Iliad* is compared to the way he is represented in the *Odyssey*, there are, as said above, significant differences. In the *Iliad*, he clearly has a number of traits from his genesis as an Indo-European god of the sky and weather. Time and time again, he is attributed with epithets such as "of the loud thunder" (I, 353), "who gathers the clouds" (I, 511), "who handles the lightning" (I, 580), phrases clearly associated with thunder and lightning as meteorological phenomena, his origin as a nature god—and at the same time signs of his superior power, since it is with the threat of lightning that he imposes his will.

In the *Iliad*, however, he is still a young, newcomer god who has some difficulty in maintaining the position of power he has taken by force from his father Kronos. Thanks to warnings from the sea goddess Thetis, he has withstood a rebellion not long before. In return for this, she asks his help in avenging the defamation inflicted on her son, Achilleus by Agamemnon. Similarly, Zeus must warn the still potentially rebellious young gods that they will be cast out of heaven if they do not behave: "Then he will see how far I am strongest of all the immortals" (VIII, 17).

It is almost as though each Olympian god has his or her own little booth from which to run a fragmented and particularized area of life: Ares for war, Aphrodite for love, Hephaistos for fire and forge, etc. The many gods with their own competencies seem to be a contributory cause of the difficulty Zeus has in keeping order in the universe—or, for that matter, keeping control of himself.

"For the mind of Zeus is hard to soften with prayer, and every ruler is harsh whose rule is new," as Aeschylus says of the character of Zeus.[44] In the tragedy *Prometheus Bound*, Zeus maintains his brutal regime as a new ruling god with the help of his faithful followers, Kratos and Bia. They are personifications of the raw power that chains Prometheus to the rock for bringing fire to mankind—that is to say giving them capacity for invention—while Zeus was contemplating wiping out the mayfly lives of men.

Seen against this background, Zeus appears in the *Odyssey* as an absolute monarch, distant from the world of men, just as the gods as a whole have withdrawn. This is evidence of a maturation process in which Zeus is developing into a cosmic principle of justice. More than before, mortals are left to their own fate—as is witnessed in Odysseus' adventures. Odysseus must, for the most part, handle things on his own—and he chides Athene for this. He is, of course, subject to the overall determination of Fate—that he is to return home after twenty years—but he is nevertheless in uncharted territory, at any moment risking death and acting against the determination of Fate.

The *Odyssey* opens in an interesting dialogue with the close of the *Iliad*. Zeus provides an indirect answer to Achilleus' accusation that the gods give to men sorrows of which they themselves know nothing (see p. 102). The theodicy problem that is actually raised here establishes how advanced Homer is in the *Odyssey*. For it is in this context that Zeus himself provides the answer with a concrete example, when he protests at the opening of the work that men have the bad habit of attributing all their sorrows and their causes to the gods, sorrows for which they themselves are to blame. As an example, he mentions Aigisthos. This view and example are joined together with evidentiary force in this way:

> Oh for shame, how the mortals put the blame upon us
> Gods, for they say evils come from us, but it is they, rather,
> Who by their own recklessness win sorrow beyond what is given,
> As now lately, *beyond what was given*, Aigisthos married
> The wife of Atreus' son, and murdered him on his homecoming,
> Though he knew it was sheer destruction, for we ourselves had told him,
> Sending Hermes, the mighty watcher, Argeïphontes,
> Not to kill the man, nor court his lady for marriage;
> For vengeance would come on him from Orestes, son of Atreides
> Whenever he came of age and longed for his own country.
> So Hermes told him, but for all his kind intention he could not
> Persuade the mind of Aigisthos. And now he has paid for everything.
>
> (1, 32-43, my italics)

Not only is Zeus far more concerned about his own reputation and that of the gods in the *Odyssey* than in the *Iliad*, where, as Xenophanes complained, they behave like the most shameless of human beings. Through Zeus, Homer here insists on a sense of justice, the like of which is not found in his earlier work. So the *Odyssey* as a whole becomes a purposeful, compositional revelation of this justice. Aigisthos' outrage is in thematic counterpoint to Odysseus' will, determined by and resigned to Fate, to submit to his life's inexorable vicissitudes. At the same time, there is an obvious coincidence between Odysseus' psychological characteristics—wisdom, piety, level-headedness, etc.—and his Fate. The choices he makes along the way correspond to his character and the fate determined for him.

In the Greek text it is said twice in rapid succession that Aigisthos acted *hyper moron* (1, 34 and 25), against Fate. So, there was no question of inevitability as was the case with Patroklos. On the contrary, Aigisthos has been warned. He has been made fully conscious of right and wrong. So, with his criminal conduct, he not only acted against all the rules for decent human behavior but against the gods themselves. In this respect, he is a negative reflection not only of Odysseus but also Patroklos, insofar as Patroklos acts against Fate by following his heroic disposition. He acts from honor and pays with his life. In this, of course, he anticipates his friend Achilleus, who also chose a short but honorable life.

However this may be, Odysseus becomes an ideal; since, through his constant circumspection, he generally speaking acts correctly in every situation and thus—after great hardship—ultimately realizes his intended fate. He redeems his potential, while those who act wrongly become examples of what happens to people who act without moderation, struck by delusion. This notion implies that Fate always works as an organizing principle in the cosmos, punishing the rash who endanger the laws and harmony of the universe.

Delusion

1

When Patroklos goes too far, it is related that Apollo gives him such a hard blow to the back and shoulders that his head is swimming—"disaster caught his wits" (XVI, 805). The Greek expression for the delusion or mental delirium is *ate*.[45] Delusion sets in where understanding cuts out. This explains why *ate* has such a breadth of meaning, from delusion to destruction. In the experience of the Greeks, delusion and illusion lead to ruin and, ultimately, death. Since Homeric men are not yet capable of interpreting what befalls them, causes are attributed to the outside world, where delusion is most often shown as a consequence of intervention by the gods and not as the result of their personal motives and intentions, which delusion is in actual fact.

Thus, the Trojan War is from first to last determined by *ate* in a true chain reaction. It begins with a story reminiscent of the Fall of Man, when the seduced Helen abandons her husband, Menelaos, and follows Paris. This leads to the Trojan War, which in turn unleashes the calamitous events which also cover the actions in the *Iliad*, including both Agamemnon's blind attack on Achilleus and Achilleus' own blind fury, which leads to the death of his friend and of many warriors. And the war ends when the deluded Trojans drag the Wooden Horse into the city.

Delusion lurks everywhere like a deathtrap. Patroklos dies when in his blood frenzy he forgets Achilleus' orders. The Trojan warrior, the Lycian king Glaukos, is said to be struck by *ate* when he meets Diomedes and discovers that there is a guest friendship between their families and then presents Diomedes with his set of golden armor but himself only receives one of bronze. In the *Odyssey*, the most obvious example is the suitors who, despite all warnings, believe that they are to marry Penelope and gain the kingdom, when in reality they are going to meet their doom.

Helen speaks of her marital infidelity as delusion. Looking back, she says to Telemachos that in Troy she "grieved for the madness (*ate*) that Aphrodite/ bestowed when she led me there away from my own dear country" (4, 261-62). When she arrived in Troy, the delusion in which Aphrodite had ensnared her vanished. And with this, her awareness of her native land, husband and child returned to her. Her remorse is turned away in the *Iliad* by King Priam as groundless. "I am not blaming you: to me the gods are blameworthy" (III, 164), are his comforting words, though she feels no less guilty for that.

It is not surprising that, like Zeus, Aphrodite has the power to generate delusion as a consequence of obsessive power of sexuality. Even Zeus can be captivated by her belt and thereby in a metaphorical sense by the power she has at her disposal. Sexuality mingles with a feeling of honor when Agamemnon wants his lost love replaced by Achilleus' Briseis—from which flow all the misfortunes that befall the Greeks from now on.

Precisely because Homer's characters do not interpret illusions personally but as something imposed from without, Agamemnon also refuses to accept his own guilt when he at last is compelled to yield at the prospect of the defeat of the Greek army. As the cause of his offense, he refers characteristically enough to *ate*, personified as Zeus' daughter:

I shall address the son of Peleus; yet all you other
Argives listen also, and give my word careful attention.
This is the word the Achaians have spoken often against me
And found fault with me in it, yet *I am not responsible*
But Zeus is, and Destiny, and Erinyes the mist-walking
Who in assembly caught my heart in the savage delusion
On that day I myself stripped from him the prize of Achilleus.
Yet what could I do? It is the god who accomplishes all things.
Delusion (Ate) is the elder daughter of Zeus, the accursed
Who deludes all; her feet are delicate and they step not
On the firm earth, but she walks the air above men's heads
And leads them astray. She has entangled others before me.
Yes, for once Zeus even was deluded, though men say
He is the highest one of gods and mortals.

(XIX, 83-95, my italics)

Not only does Agamemnon disclaim responsibility by pointing out that even Zeus has allowed himself to be deluded—no, the remarkable thing is that his fellow warriors accept his explanation. There is a consensus with respect to his interpretation.

Everyone understands delusion and its connection to Fate in the same way Agamemnon does. So he does not lose his honor.

Delusion is always costly and destructive. With the insight he possesses, however, Odysseus is the exact opposite and understands the danger of delusion. On the voyage home, he takes every conceivable precaution. In the two instances in which he is struck by this special kind of delusion, it has catastrophic consequences. Each time, he fails to keep himself awake. His awareness is thus turned off and his men immediately yield to the temptations of delusion.

The first occasion is when they have Ithaka in sight. Odysseus has been awake for nine days, when sleep finally overcomes him. His men open the bag of winds they have received from Aiolos in the (mis)conception that it contains gold that Odysseus intends to keep for himself, after which they are blown away from Ithaka. Nevertheless, they accept responsibility for the misfortune: "for we were ruined by *our* own folly" (10, 27 my italics).

That is to say that, in contrast to Agamemnon, Odysseus takes the blame upon himself. And his entire conduct demonstrates that he has realized that a human being must take responsibility for himself as far as possible. What Fate otherwise has in mind is out of his control. This leitmotif is repeated and expanded on the island of the sun god, Thrinakia. Odysseus implores the gods for help, so that his men will not lay hands on the sun god's oxen—but only with the result that, after a sleepless watch on his men, he falls asleep with "confusion" (*ate*, 12, 372) as the result. The men eat the oxen and die at sea as punishment. Odysseus is the only survivor.

2

It shows Homer's psychological sense when he describes this blindness as swift of foot—i.e., something that develops with the same overwhelming force as the swift-footed Achilleus. Delusion throws itself upon a person with such suddenness as to make him go out of his mind. However, it does not constitute a definitive decision of fate that necessarily pins someone down once a mistake has been made. There is a way out if only you can collect yourself and put your fate on the right path again.

As it is revealed in Book IX of the *Iliad*, where Phoinix tries to talk Achilleus out of the delusion brought on by his anger, delusion can be converted and reconciliation achieved through Prayer. She is said, like Ate, to be a daughter of Zeus, but just as slow as delusion is swift. Timid, lame, she arrives late but with healing power:

> For there are also the spirits of Prayer, the daughters of great Zeus,
> And they are lame of their feet, and wrinkled, and cast their eyes sidelong,
> Who toil on their way left far behind by the spirit of Ruin:
> But she, Ruin, is strong and sound on her feet, and therefore
> Far outruns all Prayers, and wins into every country
> To force men astray; and the Prayers follow as healers after her.

(IX, 502-07)

In the *ate* of his wrath, Achilleus is unmoved by Agamemnon's offer of countless gifts to make amends. He persists in his affront, thereby becoming the direct cause of Patroklos' death in delusion, which if anything demonstrates that delusion breeds delusion. The same emotional impulse makes him desecrate Hektor's corpse. Only in the final book does he yield to Priam's prayer to deliver his dead son. Having rested in the delusion of anger, Achilleus in the *Iliad* ends in supplication and a "humanized" amenability—creating in the psychological subtext itself the transition to the *Odyssey* and its level-headed hero.

3

Odysseus' handling of human motives, the responsibility he undertakes, is a part of his development as a person and his growing understanding. For what is viewed in the *Iliad* as an intervention by divine power—from without—Odysseus is on his way to understanding from within. A confirmation of this is that, in the *Odyssey*, delusion most often directly derives from a desire for food, sleep, wine, euphoric drugs, power and sex. In this sense, the *Odyssey* tends towards an understanding of psychology and of personal morality, which is why there is a deeper justice in the fact that Odysseus, who has become conscious of this and accepted his responsibility, is the only one to return home.

He thereby builds bridges to further insight into delusion as relating to consciousness, an insight that may be described generally as follows: Psychological blindness is due to human projections that understand inner motivations for actions on the basis of external divine forces and their irresistible intervention. Logically, it follows that the way out of this stage of consciousness consists partly in the subject recognizing the nature of projection and partly his taking responsibility for his actions and motivations and partly withdrawing the projections and internalizing them. Of course, this is easier said than done, since it requires highly developed self-insight and self-control.

Sophocles' tragedy *Ajax* becomes a primary text for illuminating the anatomy of delusion. Here, it is described how Athene deludes Ajax, when—after losing the dispute over Achilleus' arms to Odysseus—he wants to kill him, but, struck by *ate*, instead kills a flock of sheep and commits suicide out of shame. In this play, *ate* is used in a number of shifting meanings, such as "yoke of blindness," "flares of ruin," "full of Ruin."[46]

Yet, at the same time as he allows delusion to occur in a Homeric manner as divine intervention, Sophocles and the play as a whole reveal that Ajax's blindness is actually due to boundless arrogance, since he rejects the necessity of help from the gods. He breaches the moderation (*sophrosyne*) that is the Greek ideal and in the drama is directly contrasted with Odysseus' gentle forebearance. In the *Oresteia*, Agamemnon is made of the same stuff as Ajax and like him pays with his life.

While the cause of Ajax's delusion is shown as being external to his consciousness, it is internalized in the love-struck Phaedra in Euripides' tragedy *Hippolytos*. Of course, she states that Aphrodite is behind her misfortune, but she is nevertheless capable of interpreting her own passions and human passions generally as internal processes when she says: "We know the good, we apprehend it clearly./ But we can't bring it to achievement. Some/ are betrayed by their own laziness, and others/ value some other pleasure above virtue."[47]

Euripides was writing at the same time as Socrates, through whom it can be said internalization is realized. In cases of doubt, Socrates listens to his inner voice, his *daimon*, as the only organ offering guidance. A force that was previously conceived as an external influence is thereby internalized and has become one with human self-understanding and conscience. Insofar as Odysseus is able to split up his consciousness and calm his agitated heart, he becomes through his self-realization and introspection the mythical figura of this process.

4

In the *Odyssey*, Athene is doubly exposed as something between an independent goddess and visualized internal energy and personality formation in the characters she supports, i.e., Telemachos and Odysseus. In them, she is internalized as an inner voice or a conscience-like court of judgement. The gods have now withdrawn. They no long move in the world of men, as they did in the *Iliad*.

This implies that the earlier direct form of association is replaced by a new communication between gods and men. Thus the *Odyssey* contains a greater number of omens, visions and dreams than the *Iliad*.[48] For while the divine was once depicted concretely and anthropomorphically, the subject now to a greater extent has acquired that reality as an intuitive field of psychological action. This changed awareness is further substantiated by the fact that presentation of psychological activity, which in the *Iliad* largely takes place on the basis of *thymos*, now also occurs with reference to *nous* (and *phrenes*)—i.e., to reason, of which *thymos* is a far more tangible spiritual component. This corresponds to the movement from the *Iliad*'s theater of war to the inner stage that the *Odyssey* is in its way—as a reflection of Odysseus' development from martial hero to cultural hero, supported by Athene.

The most decisive proof of this radical change in the world of the gods is the fact that Zeus and Athene agree at the end of the *Odyssey* to establish peace—i.e., to alter the decision made in Book IV of the *Iliad* to continue the war. Not until this point is its energy exhausted. For after concluding peace and friendship (*philoteta*, 24, 476) with the families of the slain suitors at the behest of Athene, Odysseus secures a happy future for his country. At a concrete level, this admittedly only applies to his small kingdom, but in its symbolic condensation it becomes an image of the cultural and psychological process of development reflected in the *Iliad* and the *Odyssey* together, implying the definitive end of the war with the new values of life established along the way.

We find a corresponding process in Aeschylus' *Oresteia*. As has already been said, the murder of Agamemnon is worked into the *Odyssey* as the most important parallel story. And just as the *Oresteia* ends with blood revenge being replaced by patriarchy, when the Erinyes are transformed into the Eumenides, blood revenge is also finally abolished in the *Odyssey*. That is to say that, as a state, Ithaka now represents the patriarchal social system that, with Odysseus as king and fully integrated individual, has the future before it.

Religious Duplicity

If we consider the religious development among the Greeks from the Homeric point of view, we get the impression that the Olympian gods and the patriarchal world order that was the goal triumphed over the Great Mother. But as our study will further explore, this is far from the case. Certainly, many of the annual religious festivals bear the names of the Olympian gods—but are especially directed at the divinities of the underworld.[49]

It is not possible to maintain a sharp distinction between the upper Olympian and the lower chthonic world of gods and demons (*daimones*). For example, in the hymn dedicated to her, Demeter lives on Olympos, while Zeus can be worshipped under the name of the Zeus of the underworld (Chthonios). The mysteries in honor of Demeter and Dionysos were integrated by Peisistratos into the Athenian state. There were four annual festivals in honor of Dionysos, including the great Dionysian festival in which the tragedy competitions were held. Demeter had her festivals, Zeus his, etc. If we look down the Athenian calendar, we can ascertain that every month had its own festivals in honor of the gods. Greek everyday life was in this way permeated with religiosity, something that is also confirmed by Thucydides, when he lets Pericles say: "There are various kinds of contests and sacrifices regularly throughout the year."[50]

The driving forces determining the developmental process in the worlds of both gods and men are by the Greeks attributed to *strife* (*eris*) and *love* (*eros*). In themselves, these are divine forces which act in dialectic tension, a process of interplay and counterplay, which we shall now analyze—in combination with the development of human consciousness.

IV

ATHENE AND THE APPLE OF DISCORD—ON EROS, ERIS, AND METIS

I N HIS EPIC TALE, HOMER MAKES USE OF MYTHICAL STORIES AND THEIR MODE of thinking to describe fundamental experiences of life, but he does not make them into objects of reflection, far less philosophical considerations, as was to be the case later. Rationality is interwoven with myth. I am forced once again to presuppose these facts, because in the following I intend to analyze separately the dynamic interplay between the basic life forces of which the *Iliad* and the *Odyssey* are concrete representations—that is to say, the alternation between strife (*eris*) and love (*eros*). *Eris* and *eros* are forces like gods. This will be demonstrated first in Homer's epics and verified on the basis of more conscious reflections on the phenomenology of these forces in Hesiod and Empedocles.

Eros and eris

If the Homeric works are considered as a unity from a philosophical and existential point of view, it may be said that, as a cumulative process, they contain a movement from strife in the first lines of the *Iliad* to the conclusion of peace in the last lines of the *Odyssey*. That it is actually only here that strife ceases to be a driving force can be seen from the fact that Zeus and Athene make a joint decision here to suspend blood revenge and strife. Friendship (*philoteta*, 24, 476) is enthroned. Since the *Iliad* is in the nature of things determined by strife, the gods cannot achieve this unanimity. Zeus' half-hearted attempt to stop the war in Book IV is, as said above, sabotaged by the still vengeful goddesses Hera and Athene.

This gradual change from the element of strife to the element of love is prepared for compositionally and psychologically in the last book of the *Iliad*, when the hitherto wrathful and belligerent Achilleus yields to Priam's entreaties. The feeling of tenderness and care which is thus set free is encountered again in Odysseus' relations with his crew and his attempt to bring his men home in safety despite their failings. Teiresias prophesies that the same ability to love will rule his kingdom after the conclusion of the *Odyssey*, when Odysseus will rule in peace and happiness.

It can furthermore be argued that the voyage home is also erotic in the somewhat narrow sense that it is linked to Odysseus' sexual nature—both the demonic and the elevated (demonic in his encounters with temptresses such as Kirke and Kalypso, elevated in his nuptial-like reunion with the wife who has waited so faithfully for him). His erotic ability is thus put into far greater perspective in that it is linked to his endeavor to return home, an endeavor which, as we shall see when interpreted by Plato, is related to man's highest aspiration: the development of awareness and self-realization.

It is characteristic of this dialectic between *eros* and *eris* that the *Iliad*, as a work centred on strife, is determined by the erotic—albeit in a criminal version (i.e., Helen's adultery). And conversely, as an erotic work, the *Odyssey* has war as its precondition, just as in one sense the strife is repeated in the slaughter of the suitors who have unlawfully beleaguered Odysseus' home and his wife.

There can be no doubt that the *Iliad* is a work about strife. In the first ten lines of the introduction alone, *eris* is mentioned twice. It is related retrospectively that Zeus' decision to restore Achilleus' honor is fulfilled after the fall of many warriors—"since that time when first there stood in division of conflict (*eris*)" (I, 6) between Agamemnon and Achilleus. Apollo's conflict with Agamemnon is again behind this conflict once he refuses to surrender his female booty, Chryseis. The consequence is that Apollo has unleashed disease on the Greek army, as she is the daughter of his priest. Agamemnon is forced to return the girl but then takes Achilleus' war booty (*geras*), the girl Briseis, as compensation. This is a violation of the autonomy of Achilleus' honor and of the love he actually feels for the girl. Which is to say that in a more sharply concentrated optic, the fundamental nature of the strife reflects the greater struggle with Troy that Paris' violation of guest friendship and his seduction of Helen have as their background, including the assertion of Menelaos' honor and Greek self-esteem, which have suffered a blow as a result of the Trojans' assault.

Zeus sends strife to the warriors to urge them to battle. And since strife and war are a precondition for the heroes to win honor on the battlefield, it is welcomed. "And now battle became sweeter to them than to go back/ in their hollow ships to the beloved land of their fathers" (II, 453-54) are the words when Athene has instilled fresh courage in the Greeks. At the same time, however, it shows the corrosive essence of battle and strife that even Achilleus, the hero above all heroes, would like to see it end: "I wish that strife would vanish away from among gods and mortals/ and gall, which makes a man grow angry for all his great mind" (XVIII, 107-08). But this is a wish that is only finally realized in and with the *Odyssey*.

Prehistory

1

The *Iliad* can hardly be paraphrased without bringing in the erotic element as something that is deeply interwoven in the strife. The same holds true of the prehistory leading up to the *Iliad*. The sources provide us with reasons why—by agreement with Themis[1]—Zeus initated the Trojan War: he wanted to endow the demigods with greater honor and to reduce the population of the world; or he wanted to honor his daughter Helen by setting Asia and Europe at odds for her sake.[2] In Euripides' tragedy *Elektra*, it is related that Zeus brought strife into the world with the Trojan War without explaining what the purpose was—which shows Zeus to be an aimless god and the war an absurdity (see p. 473).

On the advice of Themis, Zeus has had to give up the idea of marrying the sea nymph Thetis for it has been prophesied that her son will be greater than his father. Thetis marries King Peleus instead. Their son is Achilleus. All the gods except Eris, the goddess of strife, are invited to their wedding. In revenge, Eris rolls an apple between Athene, Hera and Aphrodite with the inscription "To the fairest." Strife immediately breaks out among the goddesses. Each demands the apple—and the honor.

Zeus refuses to make the decision. This heavy burden falls to the Trojan prince, Paris. At his birth, Hekuba has dreamt she is giving birth to a torch for the world. Even though Aisakos prophesies that he will become the cause of the fall of Troy and so should be killed, he is saved and lives as a shepherd in the mountains. Hermes guides the goddesses to Mount Ida, where, on instructions from Zeus, Paris is forced to make his choice. Hera promises to make Paris master of Asia and the richest of men. Athene promises that he will win all battles and become the wisest and most handsome of men. But Aphrodite takes the prize, when she gives him the prospect of the world's most beautiful woman, Helen, as his reward. That she is married to another is a lesser problem she has not—yet—taken into account.

2

In the second thread of the action, Helen, the daughter of Zeus and Leda and the (half-) sister of Klytemnestra, is a key figure not only because of her beauty but also on account of her mythical-social status. When she reaches marriageable age, a huge contingent of admirers turn up, among them Diomedes and Odysseus.[3] The latter is wise enough to quickly realize that he has no chance but suggests to Helen's stepfather, King Tyndareios, that he should get the suitors to swear together to defend her husband against anyone who seeks to attack his good fortune. As a reward for his advice, Odysseus asks Tyndareios to persuade his brother Ikarios to grant him his daughter, Penelope, as wife. This means that Penelope is the cousin of Helen and Klytemnestra, a point with far-reaching perspectives, as we shall see.

Helen marries the wealthiest suitor, Menelaos, the brother of Agamemnon, who is married to Klytemnestra and is king of Mycenae/Argos. After the death of Tyndareios, Menelaos takes over his throne in Sparta. On a visit to Sparta, Paris—with Aphrodite's help—seduces and abducts Helen. In addition, they make off with a great quantity of goods. Thus, the rules of guest friendship are violated and the oath is actualized. The army, which is to go to Troy to retrieve Helen and avenge the ignominious treatment of Menelaos by crushing the city, is under the command of his brother Agamemnon.

3

Despite all their differences, Achilleus and Odysseus resemble each other in one respect. They both try to avoid the military expedition, since they would rather stay home with their newborn sons. In the case of Odysseus, this is despite the fact that it was he who gave rise to the oath obliging all Helen's suitors to support Menelaos if he were to find himself in difficulties. Achilleus' mother had dressed him in women's clothing (perhaps an echo of his significance as a *kouros* bound to his mother) and sent him to Skyros, where he had a son, Neoptolemos, with one of the king's daughters, Deidameia.

To get Achilleus to reveal himself, Odysseus and his companions, Nestor and Phoinix, pose as merchants, laying out jewelry and other feminine things—but with weapons among them. The girls selected jewelry, while Achilleus seized the weapons to defend himself when the battle trumpet sounded. So even at this early stage, the tension between Odysseus and Achilleus emerged, a tension that was never to be resolved.

For his part, Odysseus, who was newly married, pretended to be mad by plowing a field with an ox and an ass harnessed to the plow and sowing salt in the furrows. Palamedes, who was almost Odysseus' equal in guile, revealed him by putting little Telemachos in front of the plow. Odysseus avoided him and had to admit his trick. But from then on, he hated Palamedes and in Troy had him condemned by placing stolen goods by his camp tent.

On the way to Troy, the expedition suffers great delays, and Agamemnon is forced to sacrifice his daughter Iphigenia in order to leave Aulis, where Artemis keeps them confined either by forcing them back or calming the wind. The myths diverge in their explanation of this point. So all of these things bode ill for the war from its very start, while during the war Hera and Athene never tire of seeking revenge for what they see as the violation of their honor:

> Their hatred for sacred Ilion as in the beginning,
> And for Priam and his people, because of the delusion of Paris
> Who insulted the goddesses when they came to him in his courtyard
> And favored her who supplied the lust that led to disaster.
>
> (XXIV, 27-30)

As a matter of course, Aphrodite protects Troy and its heroes.

If we stylize this course of events further, an interesting paradigm appears, moving from order through strife and chaos to a new, higher order. The marriage of Thetis and Peleus is certainly based on a legitimate erotic connection, but it contains the flaw that the goddess of strife is excluded. For this, payment is exacted by creating the strife leading from the judgment of Paris to the abduction of Helen and the Trojan War. This chain reaction is only halted by Odysseus, partly by taking Troy, partly on a profounder level in his wedding-like reunion with Penelope at the same time as the gods conclude peace and abolish blood revenge. The energy of strife is finally exhausted and legitimate *eros* is reinstated in the world in the superior, more secure sense implicit in Odysseus' self-realization, where power now rests on love that is not based on repression.

Division and Unification

1

The over-arching polarity is to be found in the tension between strife, which divides, and love, which unifies, binds and heals. Separation and integration. As has more or less emerged by now, however, the two areas each contain a positive and a negative side as self-validating forces in life. This is especially evident in Homer's view of *eros* but also applies to *eris*. What still appears in Homer as an epically "unconscious" treatment of an experience of the elemental forces of life acquires an increasingly philosophical character in a later age. The following summary account is merely intended to throw light on what is already present in Homer and to show the way forward from him.

2

In the *Theogony*, the work about the origin of the gods, Hesiod is the first to undertake a linking of *eros* as desire and Eros as a creative and developmental force governing the universe. First, there was Chaos, then the earth (Gaia) and the underworld arose: "Eros, fairest among the deathless gods" with power over all.[4]

Eros was spontaneously generated and so can be considered an autonomous cosmic power, which since the dawn of time has driven progress forward by the constant reproduction of new creatures, a process that also entails their demise. The conception of *eros* as the very energy sustaining life is fully developed in Plato, not least in the *Symposium*. It says here that *eros* is found "in every form of existence";[5] *eros* is shown as a creative force identical with the highest striving for goodness and beauty. As mentioned, Odysseus' journey and development can be seen as an anticipation of this aspiration.

However, Hesiod is not blind to the darker side of love, since he quite literally makes night the mother of love. In this context, he uses the word *philotes*[6]—the word Homer used about friendship (24, 476—although the word is also used about sexuality, 8, 288), but is thinking specifically of sexuality. At the same time, in the *Theogony* he puts sexuality and strife into the same formula, since he also makes Eris a daughter of Night and, thus, the sister of sensual love.

In *Works and Days*, however, he provides a far more nuanced interpretation of the essence of strife—a view that has its origin in a conflict with his brother about inheritance. He distinguishes here between good and evil strife. The latter seeks "evil war and battle;"[7] the former on the other hand seeks to stimulate life-maintining industry through healthy competition (and envy).

It is against this background that the process of creation and succession in the *Theogony* that is to be outlined in brief here is to be understood in general. One hierarchy of gods replaces another through violence, which is defined by duality or ambivalence in that it is the premise upon which the universe—and, for that matter, the individual—can develop at all. On the other hand, the process is linked to a crime against a former ruler insofar as the road to power for the new rulers goes through the overthrow of their paternal predecessors: with the help of his mother, Kronos castrates his father Uranos and is overthrown himself by his son Zeus.

3

For the Presocratics, strife was also an essential principle for understanding the dynamic in the development and transformations of the world. For Heraclitus, it is a primary metaphor, when he writes that war is the father of all things, the actual essence of Zeus, and justice itself a conflict, since all things happen through the necessity of strife. Since strife is controlled by a cosmic logos, it also follows that strife (as in Anaximander's philosophy) has a role in maintaining balance in life by ensuring that injustices are always settled and punished, an idea that has crucial consequence for Solon's philosophy of justice.

This polar tension between *eros* and *eris* is systematized in the philosophy of Empedocles. He quite simply makes strife (he uses the word *neikos*, but the meaning is the same) into part of the cosmic mechanism in collaboration with love: "And these things never cease from continual shifting, at one time all coming together, through Love, into one at another each borne apart from the others through Strife."[8] In this way, they maintain each other in a closed circuit.

Instead of *eros*, Empedocles uses the word *philotes* to designate the universal power of love. In Homer, *eros* specifically refers to desire. It may be desire for food or wine— "they had put away their desire (*eros*) for eating and drinking" (I, 469). However, it can also apply to longing for a woman and is linked to the bed and intercourse. When Hera in Book XIV of the *Iliad* has seduced him, a Zeus dazed with sex exclaims: "Hera, there will be a time afterwards when you can go there/ as well. But now let us go to bed and turn to love-making./ For never before has love (*eros*) for any goddess or woman/ so melted about the heart inside me, broken it to submission" (XIV, 314-16). This means that *philotes* (later, *philia*)[9] has a broader significance than *eros*, since the Odyssey ends with this word after the conclusion of peace with the families of the suitors—"let them be friends (*phileonton*) with each other, as in the time past,/ and let them have prosperity and peace in abundance" (24, 485-86).

Without the nature of strife, everything would stagnate in a paradisiac state. Elysium is reminiscent of Paradise, but the period in human history that is closest to the state of paradise for the Greeks is the Golden Age, described by Hesiod as the time under Kronos, a time without sorrows or aging. As Hesiod's Pandora myth shows, strife comes into the world in a departure from this paradisiacal inertia—by a violation of the prohibition on knowledge. It is this insight that Prometheus has given mankind along with fire and its accompanying skills. Awareness begins to develop, eyes begin to see, distinguish and differentiate in terms of polarities, including the gender difference. The subject gradually sees itself as something different and essentially distinct from the surrounding world: I and not-I. Left hibernating in our consciousness is a memory of this lost harmony, the Golden Age, and this memory is expressed in a utopian longing to restore what was lost—as a social *eunomia* and the awakening to consciousness of the individual and possible reunification with its divine origin, which is so to speak in one's genes, as it is described by Socrates.

Thus, we can provisionally ascertain that the development of the world as conceived by the ancient Greeks consists of an interplay between the differentiation or perhaps individualization associated with strife and the unifying and healing effects of love. It is the tension between these life forces that is also the experiential foundation for the Homeric epics and the mythical complex in which they are enmeshed.

Consequently, several steps can be traced in Homer's cultural succession, where strife is the mainspring for a process of civilization. In all its bellicosity, the heroic world is itself a breach with a "feminine" vegetative mode of being. The paternal Olympic gods represent this reaction on the teleological plane, where the *Odyssey* leads to coexistence based on friendship and peace.

If Odysseus is victorious, it is because, sober-minded as he is, he can separate the world of strife and desire, which had become mingled in the madness of delusion in the *Iliad*. It is this sober moderation that Athene awakens in him, when he is finally about to massacre the families of the suitors. She makes him put an end to the strife so that he can construct his kingdom on the values of friendship. It is also as the divine and sober personification of Odysseus' interior life, as *metis*, that we shall now look at Athene, since she herself undergoes a transformation from the pugnacious goddess of the *Iliad* to the peace-creating goddess of wisdom of the *Odyssey*.

Athene—Goddess of *metis*

1

There are several reasons to give Athene special analytical status: she is Odysseus' protectress, helps Telemachos to mature, and is behind Penelope's skill at weaving and deceiving the suitors. Thus, this family is favoured by the goddess in a very special way while at the same time, as a sort of teleological projection, she reveals the sort of intellectual capacity that binds the family together, something also confirmed by their epithets with their references to good sense.

In mythology, Athene also supports other outstanding heroes—for example Herakles and Perseus—but in the Homeric works, especially the *Odyssey*, her relationship with Odysseus is quite special, even when compared with the other heroes. This is primarily due to their spiritual identity. He shares his most frequently used epithet, *polymetis*, with Athene. He appears almost as an earthly incarnation of her wisdom.

Originally, Metis was the very name of the goddess of wisdom, Athene's mother. At times, Athene directly embodies her mother and is called Metis.[10] This means in other words that in her mirroring of Odysseus, Athene, as goddess of wisdom, points to characteristics that distinguish him from all others except Nestor. In addition, this refers to the type of intelligence forming the basis for the amazing development of Greek culture and society.

2

It is crucial to understand from the beginning that this is a form of intelligence that is practical in kind or, in other words, connects the work of the hand with that of the mind. Thus, the craftsman displays in his work a talent that is designated as *metis*, as is the case with the hunter and the fisherman in their techniques, the politician in his persuasiveness, or the soldier in his strategy and cunning. *Metis* lies in the individual's ability to consider and choose lucidly in a critical situation. In this sense, *metis* is a power of thought and a form of intelligence based on rapidity, acuteness, the ability to change one's mind, to find new paths, to be directed, precise, pensive, strategic, cunning and wise.

Since Odysseus is called *polymetis*, he must, as the epithet indicates, be master of this entire spectrum of existence to an unusual extent. He must possess the necessary skills of which the description of him, his hazardous expedition to Troy and his voyage home become a richly orchestrated illustration. He can build ships, navigate by the stars—and invent the Wooden Horse. With respect to the enemy, he can give an answer that is more complex, flexible and insightful than the reality he is up against. And it may be said that this talent for change, adaptation and transformation according to circumstances, which constitutes *metis*, is captured and amplified as far as Odysseus is concerned by his epithet *polytropos*, meaning a person who can adapt to any conceivable situation.

At the same time, he is given the epithet *polymechanos*. If we translate this as talent or a highly developed ability to get something done, then it must, in harmony with *polymetis*, imply that to a quite extraordinary degree he is able to realize the potential of his intellectual power. No one else is able to achieve his objectives as he can. And in this shape he becomes an exemplary figure for the thinking of Greek culture.

As wisdom, it is undoubtedly also this form of thinking that lies behind the development of philosophy. Yet, though I am unable to provide a definitive answer, it might be asked whether it is not at the same time the breach with this sort of intelligence that is the precondition for freeing philosophy for speculation and abstraction. For even though Socrates uses handicrafts etc. in his everyday analogies for the paths and goals of philosophy, it must be acknowledged that by confronting the sensible with the spiritual, Plato creates a definitive separation in the original concept *metis*. He creates oppositions in life—antinomies and an existential duality —whereas *metis* in the Homeric sense created unity.

3

According to Hesiod, the goddess Metis is a daughter of the Titans Thetys and Okeanos. Homer makes the latter the source of the gods (XIV, 201). It is crucial that Metis derives fundamentally from water. This explains why she can change her nature and transform herself like the waves. Since these metamorphoses contain all possible life forms, it provides her with insight into life's vicissitudes, an understanding of the beginning and cohesion in past, present and future. This is her true wisdom. And that is why she becomes such an important ally for Zeus.[11] In the struggle with his father Kronos, she gives the old Titan an emetic, so that he vomits up the children he has swallowed to avoid rivals for his throne: Demeter, Poseidon and all the others.

There is a metaphysical problem with respect to Zeus' higher *metis* in that he acquires his ability by acting in exactly the same crude way as his father. For Zeus swallowed his first wife, who was none other than Metis. After she had helped him to power, Zeus wanted to make her his wife. However, she would not allow him to embrace her. She constantly changed shape like other sea creatures—for example, Thetis, when Peleus wanted to catch her. Metis becomes in turn a lion, a bull, a fly, a fish, a bird, a flame and running water. The old man of the sea, the soothsayer Proteus, also undergoes a similar series of transformations when, as described in Book 4 of the *Odyssey*, Menelaos seeks to force information out of him. Only by being stubbornly held fast throughout their metamorphoses do these creatures finally give up and return to their original form.

In the *Theogony*, Hesiod relates that Zeus impregnated Metis "the wisest of all gods."[12] When it is prophesied by Gaia and Uranos that she will give birth to clever children who will depose him, Zeus devours the pregnant Metis. By cheating her in this way, Zeus deceives her so to speak by her own wisdom, since deceit as a category belongs under *metis*. At the same time, it is a way in which Hesiod wants to describe how, as a new ruler, Zeus literally internalizes wisdom so that it can now function from within him with Metis advising him on good and evil.

By swallowing Metis, he has achieved a dual objective. He has brought her volatile aqueous nature under control, so that her uncontrollable metamorphoses no longer threaten to burst the world asunder. And he can profit from the absolute insight she possesses by virtue of her very ability to transform herself. This makes him omnipotent and omniscient. With this wisdom, he can organize existence, determine all things and distribute to the Olympian gods their various powers and areas of responsibility. He can take in everything; his eyes are always open. No evil or foolish deed can take place in the world without his knowledge—"The eye of Zeus, seeing all and understanding all, beholds these things, too," as Hesiod puts it.[13] And just as he ensures for himself the highest wisdom by his first marriage, in his second, to Themis,[14] the goddess of justice, he gains a share of her principle of order for the universe, which is a condition for his ability to utilize his wisdom with justice. With this combination of wisdom and justice, he has created his supremacy in heaven and in earth.

4

It might have been Hephaistos or it might have been Prometheus who split open Zeus' head when it was racked with pain, allowing Athene, dressed in full armor, to spring forth, uttering the battle cry *ololy* with which she is greeted in the *Iliad*—"equal to her father in strength and in wise understanding."[15] She is, of course, a goddess of war, but, in contrast to Ares, who is the god of the raw strength of war and indeed a synonym for war as such, Athene is linked through her *metis* to the progress of war as a goddess who consciously controls and plans its course. Nevertheless, one senses a certain tension in her nature that might indicate that there were originally two goddesses who over time merged and became Pallas Athene.

As in the case of Zeus, we are able to discern a process of development. As previously mentioned, Zeus is presented in the *Iliad* as a young ruler barely in control of his own ranks, having just experienced a rebellion. In the *Odyssey*, on the other hand, he is an elevated, almost cosmically effective god of justice. He has changed, in the same way as he undergoes a development and maturing process in Aeschylus' *Prometheus Trilogy*. That is to say that, as elements in the myths of succession, the gods gradually shift mentality as reflections of the developmental process of human consciousness.

It is no wonder that a war epic such as the *Iliad* emphasizes the martial aspects of the gods. Like her father, Athene noticeably changes in psychology from the *Iliad* to the *Odyssey*. In the *Iliad*, she is primarily a strategic goddess of war, while in the *Odyssey* she figures more as a support for Odysseus, his wife and son. However, the final change takes place at the very end, after the slaughter of the suitors, when in collaboration with Zeus she establishes peace between Odysseus and the families of the slain suitors for the good of the country.

Even in the *Iliad*, Athene reveals her *metis* in connection with the war and its bloody deeds. As a goddess for practical intelligence—i.e., craft—she borders on the divine function of Hephaistos. That there is no division in her between these skills and the craft of war is seen when she lays down the veil she is about to embroider in order to fasten on a coat of mail to go to war with Ares.

Detienne and Vernant[16] have made a crucial point of the fact that her shining bronze armor is in itself evidence of *metis*; since, as a fantastic example of applied art, it is an expression of her self, indeed created by her mother Metis. Therefore, she is indistinguishable from the shining, noisy weapons that, together with her battle cry and terrifying shield, the *aegis*, are designed to terrify the enemy. The same is true of her shining eyes, which give her the epithet *glaukopis* (gleaming-eyed)—a name with which, like "the owl-eyed," she may be compared to the owl (*glaux*, derived from gleaming eye), which always accompanies her and whose eyes shine when hunting its prey. In exactly the same way, her *metis* paralyzes all opponents.

She also reveals her intellectual capacity in the way in which she controls the progress of war. It is she who seizes Achilleus by the hair to prevent him from going berserk before Agamemnon. It is she who induces a Trojan to break the truce by shooting an arrow at Menelaos because she has not yet satisfied her need for revenge for having been rejected in the beauty contest. And by the hand of Diomedes she wounds Ares himself. He wails and complains to Zeus: "It is your fault we fight, since you brought forth this maniac daughter/ accursed, whose mind is fixed forever on unjust action" (V, 875-76). Never, claims Ares, does Zeus make his daughter listen to reason—"since yourself you begot this child of perdition" (V, 880).

And Ares is right. Athene is loved by her father like no other of the gods. When he threatens to cast all the gods out of heaven if they defy his prohibition on intervening in the war, he says with a smile to Athene "my meaning toward you is kindly" (VIII, 40). In power she is the only goddess equal to the male gods—in certain instances, stronger—because she is linked so closely to Zeus. At the same time, Zeus does not hide his loathing for his son Ares: "To me you are most hateful of all gods who hold Olympos./ Forever quarrelling is dear to your heart, wars and battles" (V, 890-91). In other words, the animosity resides in the fact that Ares is war pure and simple, without *metis*, while Athene as goddess of war possesses what he lacks: shrewdness.

By virtue of her *metis*, Athene can step directly into the minds of heroes and blind them. One of the most dramatic examples is found in the *Iliad*, when the Trojans choose to follow Hektor's unwise counsel and attack, instead of following the advice of the wise Polydamos and returning to the city—"since Pallas Athene had taken away the wits from them./ They gave their applause to Hektor in his counsel of evil" (XVIII, 311-12). In the same way, it is said of the suitors that she "addled their thinking" (20, 346). The most famous example, however, is when she blinds Ajax, so that—after having lost the struggle for Achilleus' arms—he kills a flock of sheep in the belief that they are Odysseus and his men and then commits suicide out of shame.

Athene's skill at transformation must also be attributed to her *metis*, whether when, in the *Odyssey*, as an old man, she instructs Telemachos, or as a young shepherd when she meets Odysseus upon his homecoming. This is a form of cunning to which Odysseus also resorts, when he decides to spy on the enemy. In this sense, transformation and disguise are expressions of *metis*, since they reveal a highly developed ability to adapt to the surroundings and, by insight into the nature of the enemy, to fool one's opponents—as, for example, in the case of the Wooden Horse.

5

What is the relationship of Athene to the primal mothers and the fertility cults? If the question arises at all, it is primarily quite simply because she is presented as a woman—at least in the beauty contest. Secondly, so much of the iconography around her has features of the chthonic that it is difficult to pass over the topic in silence. Let me mention some of these characteristics.

Athene figures in texts as far back as Linear B[17] and so must belong to the group of primeval gods assimilated into the Olympic pantheon—in her case with particular success in that, as a woman, she is made into an exponent for the patriarchal breakthrough of intelligence.[18] Nevertheless, a heritage from more ancient times can be sensed in her iconography, as she is depicted in the company of snakes and lions and is herself sometimes represented as an owl.

Most noteworthy in Homer is her connection to Erechtheus, the chthonic earth-snake from whom Athens derived its origin and who ensured the prosperity of the city. In the mythical story, Erechtheus replaces the first king of Athens, Kekrops. Both are described as snake kings, born of the Earth as human beings with the bodies of snakes. So they belong to an earlier stage of the prosperity and were succeeded by King Theseus, who comes from outside, thereby breaking with familial blood ties. He introduces the intellectual community (see p. 444) that becomes the precondition for Athenian democracy.

Meanwhile, it is striking that, although Athene as a goddess in the *Oresteia* is made guarantor for this process of democratization, which also implies the introduction of patriarchal law, Homer in Book II of the *Iliad* makes her Erechtheus' foster mother, as his mother is claimed to be the Earth. In the *Odyssey*, she is content simply to step into his citadel. However, the myths link her even more closely to Erechtheus. The story goes that when the lustful Hephaistos pursued her, he emitted his semen on to her thigh. She wiped the blotch off with a piece of wool and tossed it to the ground, fertilizing Mother Earth, who later gave birth to Erechtheus.[19] She did not want to take on the role of mother herself, so Athene took over responsibility for the child. The oldest temple, the Erechtheion, was built above Erechtheus' dwelling in the earth. During the annual Panathenian Festival, there was a celebration of the fertility cult linking Athene to the earth-snake and thus to the chthonic.

This link to the realm of the dead is also indicated, when on the way to do battle with Ares, she puts on Hades' helmet of concealment to make herself invisible—"Athene/ put on the helm of Death, that stark Ares might not discern her" (V, 844-45). Her shield, the so-called *aegis*[20] she has borrowed from Zeus, is similarly emblematic, being encircled by (earth-)snakes "and thereon is set the head of the grim gigantic Gorgon" (V, 742-42). Not even "the bolt of Zeus' lightning" (V, 741-42) could crush the *aegis*, which together with its other accoutrements might suggest that it derives its power from the underworld.

An attempt can be made to turn the interpretation around and stress the fact that Athene has received the Medusa's head as a gift from Perseus, whose champion she is. Like another Saint George, he had slain the dragon to save the princess Andromeda, thereby breaking the crippling maternal power as a part of his own liberation and uttinghis role of hero on a par with Herakles, who also received support from Athene. In that case, the head of the Medusa must be viewed as a trophy betokening victory over the demonic power of the mother cult.[21] Athene thereby acquires the meaning she has in Aeschylus, where, as a new spiritual force, she transforms the death-linked Erinyes and places them in the patriarchal community based on law that was Athens. This corresponds to the fact that, as the goddess of *metis*, she invents the plow—man's tool for subjugating the nutritious earth, which is why she finds herself at a later stage of civilization than the fertility goddesses.[22]

If she was really a fertility goddess, linked to the earth and the realm of the dead, it must be acknowledged that this meaning, apart from the emblematics discussed, is repressed or forgotten by both Homer and Hesiod except for the connection with Erechtheus. For Athene's being born out of the head of Zeus clearly demonstrates that, as the goddess of wisdom, she is of a purely masculine origin—created by the power of thought, so to speak. It is a visualization of how, through the Olympian gods, male intelligence prevails over chthonic motherliness, whose power lay in biological birth. This interpretation is verified by the fact that, in the *Eumenides*, Apollo uses Athene's birth as an argument against the Erinyes' claim that their vengeance ensured blood rights from primeval times. Athene was not given life in the darkness of a womb but was born from her father. This proves that women are only containers for the fetus; the man procreates.

In this sense, Athene represents a way out of and insight into Mother Nature, and, together with Zeus, she becomes the epitome of the *metis* that prevails on Olympos. And as the protectress of the young heroes in their struggle to free themselves from the Great Mother, she likewise symbolically represents their masculine potential. She is also unique in neither being a real woman nor a real man but a little of each, an androgynous mediator, as the only god who can effortlessly move in and out of male and female identity. On the one hand, this demonstrates her diversity and, on the other, by virtue of her very androgyny, she becomes an exemplary figure for the human subject who, like Odysseus on his voyage home, must unite the male and the female—with Athene as his guiding star.

6

When, in Book X of the *Iliad*, Diomedes selects Odysseus as his companion on the dangerous expedition to spy on the Trojans, it is not only because of his courage but also because it will ensure Athene's favor, beloved as he is by Pallas Athene (X, 245). That he is her favorite, of course, may be explained by the fact that they have a common form of *metis*, which is superior to force in its purely physical form. And there are numerous examples of her giving him a helping hand in an emergency.

In a situation in which he is hard pressed by the Trojans, she does not allow him to be seriously wounded (XI, 438 ff.) And when, during the race in connection with Patroklos' funeral games, he is about to lag behind, she answers his prayer by making Ajax, the son of Oileus, stumble in cow dung. The other heroes rejoice, while the loser angrily cries: "That goddess made me slip on my feet, who has always/ stood over Odysseus like a mother, and taken good care of him" (XXIII, 782-83).

Odysseus is not alone, however, in attracting the goddess' attention in the *Iliad*. Achilleus and Diomedes also enjoy her favor. Nevertheless, it is clear that Odysseus has preference. She uses him in the situations where wisdom, *metis*, counts. She intervenes through him in the assembly in the *Iliad*, because he is "the equal of Zeus in counsel" (II, 169), and thus gets him to prevent the frustrated Greek fleet from sailing home before Troy has fallen.

But it goes without saying that their connection is emphasized even more in the *Odyssey*, where the spiritual identity between the goddess and her hero constitutes a primary theme. During his visit to Nestor, Telemachos expresses the hope that Athene will protect him as she protected his father: "for I never saw the gods showing such open affection/ as Pallas Athene, the way she stood beside him, openly" (3, 221-22). And when at the same time he emphasizes that no one could compare with Odysseus in cunning: "he far surpassed them/ in every kind of stratagem; your father" (3, 121-22), he has also explained why, in a sort of self-recognition, Athene "cared for him lovingly" (7, 42) and so gave him every conceivable protection.

In this way, the whole of the *Odyssey*, right from the beginning where Athene speaks in his cause in the assembly of gods, is one long proof of her care for him and his family. She sees to his homecoming and comforts and encourages his wife and son.

The actual scene where Athene and Odysseus meet again on Ithaka's stony coast demonstrates their profound psychological similarity—two masters in the art of dissimulation. As she has transformed herself into a young shepherd and the surroundings into something unrecognizable, the situation itself is a concrete example of the aspect of *metis* concerned with cunning (*dolos*) and delusion. At the same time, however, Odysseus himself provides a veritable demonstration of cunning.

Always watchful, he immediately dissembles about his identity. During his account, Athene changes into a tall, fair woman as she teasingly and kindly strokes his hand and says: "You wretch, so devious, never weary of tricks, then you would not/ even in your country give over your ways of deceiving/ and your thievish tales" (13, 293-94). Nor does he hide the fact that he derives the distinctive features of his identity from his *metis* in the sense of cunning. When he finally reveals his identity to the Phaiakians, he points out this characteristic: he is "known before all men/ for the study of crafty designs" (9, 19-20). A craftiness which, as described above, provides the basis for his greatest fame: the invention of the Wooden Horse.

Certainly, Athene teases Odysseus for his cunning fabrications but finds in them confirmation of the deep affinity existing between them. She then identifies with him, by saying:

> (. . .) for you and I both know
> sharp practice, since you are far the best of all mortal
> men for counsel and stories, and I among all the divinities
> am famous for wit and sharpness.
>
> (13, 296-99)

The distance between man and god is minimized when Odysseus takes Athene to task for not having helped him since he left Troy. She defends herself by saying that she did not want to quarrel with her uncle, Poseidon. So only now could she lend him a hand, since the objective of Fate was achieved in the sea off the Phaiakians' island.[23]

Athene has had an earlier disagreement with Poseidon when it was decided in a contest who would be the protector of Athens. He presented the city with a salt spring, she an olive tree and won, thanks to the women's votes, which, as previously pointed out, is the reason for their being deprived of the right to make their opinions known. At a political level, this supposedly reflected the transition from the old aristocracy, which had Poseidon as its god, to the new democracy with Athene as the supreme god.[24] At the same time, both gods are associated with the horse, but as far as Athene is concerned, by virtue of *metis*. For while the horse symbolizes raw, primal power in the case of Poseidon, Athene is the horse goddess, Athene Hippias, who bridles this blind power, domesticates it and makes it usable just as she provides man with the ability to cultivate the soil through the invention of the plow.

From a psychological perspective, it would also have been wrong for Athene to have assisted Odysseus during the voyage. For that is to be the touchstone of the *polymetis* he shares with Athene, who bears the same epithet in the Homeric hymns—as also do the other inventive gods Hermes and Hephaistos. He is thus forced to tackle the voyage home all alone by virtue of his own *metis*. Only in this way can he become the cultural hero he is elected to be by Athene (and Homer), since he must repeatedly demonstrate his resourcefulness, his lightning-quick ability to adapt in dangerous situations and temptations, always directed toward his homecoming.

Since he is said on several occasions in the *Iliad* to be as shrewd as Zeus (II, 169; IX, 188), we can endorse the truth of this claim by means of a syllogism deriving from Homer's own authenticating statements. For if Athene, born from the head of Zeus, is her father's equal in intelligence and if at the same time, as she herself implies, she and Odysseus are identical in their *polymetis*, then the logical consequence must be that Odysseus possesses the intelligence of Zeus and so he is the closest one can come in the archaic mind to a man who resembles the gods.

7

On this basis, it can be seen that Odysseus' person and conduct in both the Homeric epics and also in the mythological tradition surrounding him display and illustrate *metis* and the way in which it combines the practical and the intelligible. These hidden poles in the phenomenon can only be distinguished in fiction in their extreme positions. Odysseus is capable of building a ship, chopping down a tree and making precise measurements when he is to leave Kalypso's island. He can navigate according to the stars and calculate the motion of the waves on choppy seas, interpreting them as expertly as he interprets the ways of the human mind.

In his most ingenious stroke of all, the Wooden Horse, practical wisdom and true cunning—that is to say, insight into and manipulation of the mind of the enemy—work together. As we have heard, it is certainly noted that Athene is helpful to Epeios in the practical execution of the task (8, 492). On the other hand, we are not told that Athene plants the idea in Odysseus. But elsewhere, this kind of intervention is described—for example, when Penelope decides to commence the archery competition—as being put "in the mind" (21, 2) by Pallas Athene.

That Penelope, like her husband, is favored by the goddess appears from the suitors' negative description of how she has been aided by Athene in her deceptive weaving— "since she is so dowered with the wisdom bestowed by Athene,/ to be expert in beautiful work, to have good character/ and cleverness, such as we are not told of, even of the ancient/ queens, the fair-tressed Achaian women of times before us" (2, 117-19). Here, the two meanings of *metis* are clearly connected, insofar as Athene is the goddess of weaving, the practical side, but also acts as the inspiration for the guile that is conditioned by intelligence. So in her weaving Penelope combines the practical and the strategically clever, which also puts her weaving on a level with the Wooden Horse.

At the same time, her weaving has similarities to the nets used by hunters and fishermen.[25] This corresponds metaphorically to a conscious strategy, as when it is said of Odysseus' battle with the suitors that he has caught them in a net. The suitors lie dead like fish on land, when a fisherman has dragged them ashore "in their net with many holes" (22, 385). We encounter the casting net later as a collective metaphor with the same content and meaning in the *Oresteia*.

From this angle, it can be seen that Homer uses his works and stories to demonstrate how *metis* relates to physical force, not to say raw brutality, so that Zeus is superior to Kronos, Athene can outwit Ares, and Odysseus has more insight and experience than Achilleus.

This is represented most clearly in Odysseus' confrontation with the primal power of the Kyklops Polyphemos. Typical of the Kyklops in his reduced understanding of life, he imagines that the superior man it has been prophesied he is destined to meet will arrive in his own image as a physically powerful man, not like the midget that Odysseus is in his eyes (see quotation, p. 26). Thus, Odysseus' triumph is defined by the fact that he is always capable of reflecting upon the dangerous situation in which he and his men find themselves. He can control himself, deceive the Kyklops with honeyed words and wait for the right moment in order then to act rapidly—"combining all my resources and treacheries" (9, 423), he says in a formula that clearly shows that the situation as such may be determined in, with and by—*metis*.

8

Even in the *Iliad*, there is a description that anticipates this pattern. Nestor, who is the wisest of the older generation and a sort of model for Odysseus, stresses to his son Antilochos at the horse race in honor of Patroklos that he must use his understanding, since of those participating his horses are the least strong: "The woodcutter is far better for skill than he is for brute strength./ It is by skill that the sea captain holds his rapid ship/ on its course" (XXIII, 315-17). He then gives purely practical advice on how his son should steer his chariot—advice that demonstrates that cunning is based on an elementary ability to observe the motives of others, their strengths and weaknesses. Reason thus triumphs over raw strength—here symbolized by Menelaos, who, fuming with rage at his loss of honor, reaches the goal late.

Characteristic of reason, as of craftiness, is a sophisticated ability to observe one's surroundings, to consider the possibilities carefully and to act quickly and precisely when the right decision is reached. That it can be done at all is due to the fact that *metis* contains the same diversity as the ever-changing world. It is a question of being able to put yourself in your opponent's shoes and to understand his motives and modus operandi without revealing yourself. And this, as the Wooden Horse demonstrates, requires the distinction between the external and the internal to be recognised, so that your intentions *cannot* be identified. You must maintain clarity, while dissimulating to inflict delusion on the enemy, as Odysseus does with the Kyklops.

If all of this is applied to the general unity of the Homeric works, it could be said that this problem is repeated in the antagonistic contrast between Achilleus and Odysseus and, not least, in the fundamental difference between the *Iliad* and the *Odyssey*. The view of Homeric heroes that physical strength and courage are the highest form of *arete* is confronted with the forward-pointing reality, based on *metis*, that Odysseus and Athene represent. That it is actually this form of intelligence that has time on its side is demonstrated by the fact that it is not Achilleus but Odysseus, not physical strength but intellectual strength, that takes Troy.

In the following, we shall observe how Athene promotes and reflects Telemachos' maturation as he frees himself from the constricting care of his mother—with a view to becoming his father's equal and heir. At the same time, it can mythically and psychologically serve as a concrete example of a successful liberation from a constricting maternal power and the achievement of independence as a male individual.

V

THE *TELEMACHY*

NOT ONLY FOR ODYSSEUS IS THE FATEFUL HOUR ABOUT TO STRIKE. THE time for him to return home occurs just as misfortunes at home are culminating. At the beginning of the *Odyssey*, Penelope's strategy against the suitors has been played out. Telemachos has reached an age when he ought to step in as his father's heir to enforce the king's law. But he is not up to it, brooding Hamlet-like and lacking initiative. Athene's intervention in his passivity is the theme of the first four books of the *Odyssey*, which have been called the *Telemachy* after him. Athene has a dual role: she inspires him with the spiritual strength to mature and, in an extension of this, he travels abroad, at first accompanied by the goddess, to seek news of his father, to win honor for himself and, not least, to free himself from the bonds tying him to his mother.

Some analysts of Homer have seen the *Telemachy* as a clumsy attempt to tie Telemachos' story to that of his father. However, I regard his story as an unavoidable motif in the *Odyssey*'s composition. The minute account of Telemachos' development from boy to man provides a psychological account of how he acquires the characteristics necessary to assist his father and later to succeed him. In addition, from Nestor and Menelaos we obtain a considerable amount of information as to what happened to the other heroes on their voyage home—which both throws light on the homecoming theme of the work and provides a link with the *Iliad*.

The Maternal Bond

1

In his inability to act, Telemachos resembles and anticipates many a later indolent hero who, until the time comes for action, has been introverted and shown no sign of initiative, but is suddenly awakened to action and reveals a strength that perplexes those around him. The remarkable thing is that, at the beginning of the *Odyssey*, Telemachos must be something over twenty, since, according to Helen, he was an infant when Odysseus left (4, 144). So he is at an age when other prospective heroes have shown their true character. At his age,[1] Achilleus was already the foremost warrior in the *Iliad*, facing the prospect of dying at the height of his fame, while Telemachos is wandering around aimlessly like a child.

And so, like his mother, he longs for his father to return home and put things right, since he is unable to do so himself—"imagining in his mind his great father, how he might come back/ and all throughout the house might cause the suitors to scatter" (1, 115-16). A little later, a sympathetic Athene responds: "Oh, for shame. How great your need is now of the absent/ Odysseus, who would lay his hands on these shameless suitors" (1, 253-54). She wants to inspire the strength in him to think even more about his father—"she left in his spirit/ determination and courage, and he remembered his father/ even more than he had before" (1, 320-22). Indeed, his father is to be awakened in him.

Certainly, the situation in which Telemachos finds himself in the opening scene reveals how weak he is, feeling that he is up against a pressing reality that he cannot handle. At the same time, however, it is a state of mind that, in its brooding introspection, makes him particularly receptive. It opens him to the power (*menos*) with which Athene announces herself and is able to guide him toward a life of action that will also make an adult of him. However, before we look more closely at Athene's psychological intervention, the question arises of why Telemachos is so irresolute, weak and childish.

2

Despite his advanced age, Telemachos is in principle still only a child. This is confirmed by Athene herself when she tries to get him to pull himself together by saying: "You should not go on/ clinging to your childhood" (1, 296-98). He has simply not yet discovered it for himself. And when, under her influence, he finally begins to pull himself together and threaten the suitors, he refers indirectly to Athene when he exclaims: "in the time past you ruined/ my great and good possessions, while I was still in my childhood." (2, 313-14). In a very short time, through Athene's psychological intervention, he has undergone a rapid process of development, manifested externally partly by calling the assembly where he warns the suitors, and partly by traveling out into the outside world.

But this still does not explain why he has been stuck at a stage in life he should have left behind him. The answers offered by the text itself interact with each other, so that these components, which are discussed separately here, must be understood as a psychological complex that holds him back.

To begin with, it is almost too obvious that Telemachos, alone as he is, feels powerless when faced with the overpowering throng of suitors. Psychologically speaking, therefore, it is understandable that he regresses, artificially seeking to hold on to childish ways in which no one, not even himself, expects him take action.

Secondly, he has not had the best conceivable conditions for developing the masculinity required to take action. The father who more than anyone should have served as the ideal and model for him disappeared from his world when he was an infant. And no other male person has been capable of fulfilling this paternal role, not even his grandfather King Laertes, who is himself a weak figure, a subject to which I shall return.

But not only that. According to Greek thinking, by disappearing without trace, his father has lost the honor (*time*) and reputation (*kleos*) that an honorable death like that of Achilleus would have achieved for him and his son. So Telemachos can even say that he would not have taken his father's death so badly, if he had only left him a name praised by all:

But now the gods, with evil intention, have willed it otherwise,
And they have caused him to disappear, in a way no other
Man has done. I should not have sorrowed so over his dying
If he had gone down among his companions in the land of the Trojans,
Or in the arms of his friends, after he had wound up the fighting,
So all the Achaians would have heaped a grave mound over him,
But now ingloriously the storm winds have caught and carried him
Away, out of sight, out of knowledge, and he left pain and lamentation
To me. Nor is it for him alone that I grieve in my pain now.

(1, 234-42)

Through the suitors' criminal persistence, his house (*oikos*) is threatened and his property (*olbos*) depleted and in reality his honor with it. And also against this sensitive background, the allusion to the "absent father" (1, 135), whom Telemachos wants to return and re-establish the order he himself should restore but is unable to do, has a powerful effect. Another sore point is that he is in fact in doubt as to whether Odysseus really is his father—"My mother says indeed I am his. I for my part/ do not know" (1, 215-16). The problem is obviously that, in his weakness, he cannot within himself feel his father's strength, which he should have inherited and potentially had at his disposal. Transformed into a father-like figure by the name of Mentes, Athene applies her strength to this psychological vacuum—and separates him from the greatest barrier to his development: his mother.

3

No other woman in Greek literature enjoys such high regard as Penelope. For her faithfulness, she is together with Andromache and Alkestis seen as the epitome of feminine virtue (*arete*) and moderation (*sophrosyne*). So it is surprising that, though only tacitly, the blocking of her son's willpower and development into manhood is attributed to her. However, there is no doubt that this is the case, although she may not be conscious of this side of her nature.

The bond is itself determined by the fact that the boy or the son has grown up with his mother. The ritual initiation process into manhood has the character of death and resurrection—death as the son of the mother, rebirth as a man among men. This biological circumstance also explains the suffocating quality of Penelope's protection of Telemachos: she quite simply will not, cannot or dare not let him go—to which must be added the meaning he has at a personal level for her and for her future destiny.

In other words, she comes to represent the typical primal woman, including the split in the original maternal image that appears when and if the son tries to leave the primal maternal source as he becomes an independent man. For, to repeat it briefly, despite her maternal care the primal mother also exploits her sons phallically, as lovers, in her continuing process of reproduction So she cannot simply allow them to leave home, to develop their own masculine selves on their own. If sons nevertheless break away, the mother's tender care is turned into vengeance. From then on, she haunts the heroic subject as the fearsome mother dangerously transformed into dragons or ferocious animals such as wild boars and bears.

That Penelope possesses these characteristics and that they are in general crucial to a deeper interpretation of the *Odyssey* may be understood from her reactions to Telemachos' journey. These emerge when to her consternation she learns that—unbeknown to her and against her will—he has embarked on his perilous journey:

> And now again a beloved son is gone on a hollow
> ship, an innocent all unversed in fighting and speaking,
> and it is for him I grieve even more than for that other one,
> and tremble for him and fear, lest something should happen to him
> either in the country where he has gone, or on the wide sea (. . .).
>
> (4, 817-21)

Yes, but he is in his twenties and should have long ago tried to prove himself. He is not, as she says, an innocent all unversed. She has herself prevented his maturation and evidently would continue to do so if it were in her power. Or rather: if Athene had not intervened. For as Penelope states directly:

> For if I had heard that he was considering this journey,
> Then he would have had to stay, though hastening to his voyage,
> Or he would have had to leave me dead in the halls.
>
> (4, 732-34)

If she had discovered plans for the journey, she would have prevented it. And later, we learn that she incessantly laments his departure, as Telemachos himself says on his return: "since as I suppose she will never give over/ that bitter lamentation of hers and her tearful crying/ until she sees me myself" (17, 7-9).

From these passages, we can see that Penelope still regards her son merely as a child even though he is over twenty years of age. She is also ready to maintain this interpretation, insofar as—had it been in her power—she would have prevented him from going and thus effectuating his symbolic separation from her which at a deeper level permits his self-development, and she laments his departure as if he had died. Of course, it all goes completely wrong when she hears of the suitors' plot to murder him. But paradoxically, she herself constitutes the greatest danger to her son by seeking to tie him so closely to herself. Telemachos must have instinctively realized this, since, on his departure, he makes his father's nurse Eurykleia swear to say nothing to his mother until eleven days have passed (2, 372 ff.).

4

This bond between Penelope and Telemachos has its own psychological logic. Homer emphasizes that Penelope has nursed him herself (11, 448), whereas Odysseus had Eurykleia as a wet nurse. This sort of intimate contact has never been abandoned or relativized. The reason for this is that Odysseus left mother and son when the latter was still an infant. For Telemachos, this meant that he did not have a father figure to support him as he was growing up and necessarily liberating himself from the embrace of maternal power. At the same time, he became the object of the emotional (sexual) release which Penelope, in the absence of her husband, was unable to direct elsewhere. With this intimacy, therefore, she has fixed him in a regressive child-like state.

The underlying sexuality to their relationship has been further confirmed from Telemachos' seventeenth or eighteenth year, when the suitors forced their way in and began paying court, by the fact that Penelope, so to speak, placed him between herself and the suitors. So throughout the whole of his young life he has found himself in his mother's erotic field.

Penelope has not previously wanted to select a new husband from among the suitors, whom she despises. They have squandered Odysseus' wealth over the past three years and, in reality, they do not only want to marry her but also to take over his property and push her son out into the cold or actually kill him, which they do in fact attempt to do. By keeping her son in childish passivity, she has been able to postpone the day of reckoning that must otherwise take place between Telemachos and the suitors. And in order to gain time in the hope that Odysseus will nevertheless return home, she has demanded—before selecting a new husband—to be allowed to finish weaving the shroud for her father-in-law, Laertes, a garment she has worked on during the day and unravelled at night, a stratagem that has now been revealed to the suitors. And this has increased their pressure on her.

There is also the predicament in which Odysseus has put her. For on his departure, he told her to marry again when their son grew a beard: "But when you see our son grown up and bearded, then you may/ marry whatever man you please, forsaking your household" (18, 269-70). According to Eurynome, the housekeeper, she can no longer put off the wedding by keeping Telemachos in a chronic childhood, for as she says to Penelope: "Do not/ go down with a face so ravaged all over by tears, as it now is,/ since nothing is gained by indiscriminate sorrowing always./ For now your son is come of age, and you know you always/ prayed the immortals, beyond all else, to see him bearded" (18, 173-76).

Thus, Penelope is virtually forced by her own husband's words to re-marry, to leave her home and to let Telemachos take over as his successor, provided he can take possession of the kingdom. So this is the situation at the beginning of the *Odyssey*: Telemachos has been unable to free himself from his mother and as a consequence has not become an adult. Accordingly, he has not achieved the harshness demanded of him as a future ruler—and man.

Becoming Independent

1

In order to free himself from this unconscious and destructive bond, Telemachos must come to terms with his mother on his own. Athene comes to the rescue as a spiritual and masculine force, and she steps in as a goddess, where the mother has been a hindrance so far. As a woman, Athene certainly has tender feelings for Telemachos but represents even more a relationship with his father and the masculine. For, as emerges in the *Oresteia*, she, if anyone, is the goddess who breaks with the maternal principle and establishes paternal rule. And it is also as a sort of fatherly substitute that she visits Telemachos who in his brooding and powerless condition finds himself in a situation parallel that of to his weeping father on Kalypso's island.

The goddess says to him exactly "what any father would say to his son" (1, 308), when she appears in the form of King Mentes. In order to support this didactic aspect, she later accompanies him on the voyage as his mentor. And in contrast to Achilleus, who will not accept advice from his old teacher Phoinix, Telemachos is all ears and compliance. Furthermore, Athene is Odysseus' protector, which seems to be the most important reason for her coming to Telemachos' aid at all—to help Odysseus. If Athene instills strength in Telemachos by making him think more intensely about his father, this means that she is liberating his father's potential in him: "Telemachos, you are to be no thoughtless man, no coward,/ if truly the strong force of your father is instilled in you" (2, 276-77).

Put another way, the process of maturation is equivalent to taking possession of the father's strength and thereby separating oneself from symbiosis with the mother. This theme, too, is taken up by the goddess, when she says: "Are you, big as you are, the very child of Odysseus?/ Indeed, you are strangely like about the head, the fine eyes,/ as I remember" (1, 207-09). The observation is confirmed by others with respect to gesture and eloquence, the outer and inner, in which Telemachos resembles his father to a T. In this respect, he is something of a rarity, since according to Athene sons only infrequently take after excellent fathers: "For few are the children who turn out to be equals of their fathers/ and the greater number are worse; few are better than their father is" (2, 276-77). The paternity and the psychologically close connection between father and son, despite their many years of separation, are emphasized by Telemachos' name, "distant fighter," referring to Odysseus as archer or warrior in a distant land. So he bears his father in his name as a latent identity, which is why it is only a matter for him of realizing his rich paternal potential.

In other words, Athene's attempt to nudge Telemachos forward is a clear antithesis to Penelope's treating him as a child, as also emerges when Athene tells him that it is unbecoming for him to behave like a child. In the same breath, she places before him an ideal figure of his own age: Orestes, who avenged his father. Athene recommends that Telemachos should be equally courageous and attain a reputation that will last to all time. Although Homer makes no mention of the fact that Orestes actually killed his mother, the point nevertheless lurking there is that the masculine hero must slay the Great Mother in order to take possession of himself as a completely developed masculine subject.

When Athene inspires Telemachos with her divine *menos*, she tries to awaken his father within him, something he has been unable to feel before. And—like with Nestor and Menelaos later—she confirms that he is the living image of his father. In this way, it may be said that a rebirth takes place. But this is a birth on a spiritual plane, whereas in a biological sense it was the mother who originally brought her son into the world.

So on a deeper level, the voyage becomes a voyage of (re)birth under the guidance of Athene in which he becomes independent and liberates his masculinity in a configuration with his father. And as he now takes his father's identity as his own and steps into the world as a truly active being, he has in principle become his own father.[2] On this basis, he will at some time in the future, beyond the framework of the action but prepared for within it, be able to replace his father as a highly esteemed guarantor for Ithaka's monarchy and as an image of the highest world order.

2

From the moment when Athene presents herself, Telemachos begins to undergo a rapid development. Inspired by her, he does a number of things before leaving that cause surprise. He reveals himself as a young man who is about to step into character after a long period of apathy. And as a first sign that his incipient vigor lies in freeing himself from his mother, he brusquely puts Penelope in her place when she weeps at Phemios' song about the sufferings of the returning Greeks. She must learn to harden herself, he says, sending her back to her loom— i.e., showing her back to her feminine pursuits—the woman who until now had run the household as far as she has been able. He declares himself to be "the power in this household" (1, 359)—a phrase he repeats before killing the suitors (21, 490)—and thus confirms how deeply effective Athene's infusion of strength has already been.

Indeed, he commands his mother in the same tone as Hektor uses in the tender scene with his wife Andromache and their son, finally ordering her to attend to her wifely duties—"Go therefore back to our house, and take up your own work,/ the loom and the distaff, and see to it that your handmaidens/ ply their work also" (VI, 490-93). It is up to the men to take care of the world outside.

In addition, Telemachos reveals his newly acquired power when he calls an assembly, something that has not occurred in the last twenty years, since his father's departure. He thereby demonstrates his incipient rebellion against the suitors, and it is his first attempt to step into Odysseus' role as future king. He sits on his father's throne and takes his scepter, symbol of the power the gods have granted his family.

During the assembly, Telemachos tries to the best of his ability to appeal to the suitors' noble sentiments, the very sentiments they do not possess. He refers to the fact that as a gentle, fatherly and just king Odysseus allowed the suitors' families to reside in Ithaka. Hard pressed as Telemachos is, he has no option but to appeal to the suitors, which he does with ill-concealed threats: they must humble themselves, lest they call down the wrath of the gods: "Even you must be scandalized/ and ashamed before the neighboring men about us, the people/ who live around our land; fear also the gods' anger, lest they, astonished by evil actions, turn against you" (2, 64-67). It is interesting that Telemachos here introduces a way of thinking that will later become fundamental to Greek ethics as the key concept of *sophrosyne*, which may be roughly translated as self-control or moderation. At all events, the conduct of the suitors represents the direct opposite—namely, *hubris*, an arrogance that calls down the displeasure of gods and men: an avenging *nemesis*.

An upright person must surely be furious—"A serious man who came in among them/ could well be scandalized, seeing much disgraceful behavior" (1, 228-29), as Athene puts it. And now that Telemachos no longer feels himself to be a boy but an adult with power over things, he threatens personally to call down the punishment of the gods upon the presumptuous suitors—"go on, eating up one man's livelihood, without payment,/ then spoil my house. I will cry out to the gods everlasting/ in the hope that Zeus might somehow grant a reversal of fortunes./ Then you may perish in this house with no payment given" (2, 143-45). It can surely not be said more clearly.

That Telemachos' petition to the suitors to show restraint is combined with a *sophrosyne* in his own nature is documented by the text's own vocabulary. He asks the suitors to show shame—the Greek word *nemessethete* is used (2, 64). When the word turns up again, it is used of Telemachos himself by his friend Peisistratos, Nestor's son, who explains to Menelaos that it was out of shame (*nemessatai*, 4, 158) that Telemachos did not announce his arrival immediately. And this feeling of shame or rather this sense of acting with proper humility is due to his "modesty" (4, 158)—in Greek, *saophron* (*sophron*).

With this adjectival use of *sophrosyne*, Homer indicates on the one hand that Telemachos is now acting out of a sense of his own merit when he asks the suitors to show humility, and on the other that he is anticipating the future meaning of the word. It borders on a feeling of shame (*aidos*), and it also expresses the ability to exercise self-control, to be moderate. It likewise explains why he has hidden his father's strategy towards the suitors from his mother. He did it by means of self-control (*saophrosynesi*, 23, 30). So there is good reason for Telemachos' being attributed with the epithet *pepnymenos*, the thoughtful, like Nestor—and his father (8, 388).

As the deity of self-insight and thus self-control, Apollo is the god most clearly connected with *sophrosyne*, if not the god of *sophrosyne* himself. This aspect, too, is hinted at by Homer in the *Iliad*—where Apollo avoids the conflict with Poseidon about mortal men by stating that he would not, in that case, be *saophron*—"without prudence" (XXI, 462).

It throws light on Telemachos' future-orientated character formation that he is connected in this way with what finally becomes one of Socrates' cardinal virtues. At the same time, however, it shows the extent of his marginalization in the world of the Greek myths, that the idea of *sophrosyne* is not later traced back to him but to Nestor, among others, and to his own father above all. Socrates refers on several occasions to the way in which Odysseus calms his angry heart as an example of the art of self-control. We could also point to a passage in Book 18 in which Odysseus, in a phrasing strongly reminiscent of that used by Telemachos, attempts to persuade the suitors to moderation—with a general reference to the arrogant being punished by the gods: "Let no man be altogether without the sense of righteousness,/ but take in silence the gifts of the gods, whatever they give him" (18, 141-42).

Neither prayers nor warnings nor threats, however, make any noteworthy impression on the suitors. Firm in their arrogance, they seem unafraid of the gods, let alone of Odysseus' return. If he should really appear, they will kill him. Nor do they want Telemachos as king. On the contrary, they demand that he should force his mother to take as husband whichever of the suitors her father chooses. For they maintain that it is his mother's resistance to marriage and her exposed stratagem of unraveling her weaving that are the cause of their depredations. On this point, too, they violate customary law by seeking the hand of a woman whose husband is not for certain known to be dead. Telemachos will not turn his mother out of the house—partly from fear that she will set her Erinyes against him. On the other hand, the suitors threaten to eat him out of house and home.

During the assembly, Telemachos is gripped by such anger and frustration that he begins to weep. He casts aside the scepter, the symbol of rule, as a sign that he still lacks the strength to embody the dignity of royalty. However, even when Mentor censures the people, because, despite their greater numbers, they have not tried to stop the suitors with the idea of the "fatherly kindness" (2, 234) Odysseus showed them, no rebellion materializes.

Meanwhile, Telemachos' cry that *nemesis* will strike the suitors is not in vain. This is confirmed directly by Athene, who, in the guise of Mentor, says that the suitors are foolish, without understanding or a sense of righteousness, by giving no thought to death—"since they are neither thoughtful men nor just men,/ and have not realized the death and black fatality/ that stands close by, so that on a day they all must perish" (2, 282-84).

And as a warning of the suitors' impending doom, Zeus sends two eagles, which tear at each other until they draw blood. This bird portent is also interpreted by Halitherses, who is well versed in the interpretation of omens, as evidence of the fateful purposiveness at play from the first page of the *Odyssey* as an emanation of Zeus' will—and *charis*, favour—to bring Odysseus home and punish the suitors. The twenty years have now passed, since he first prophesied how long Odysseus would be absent: "I say that everything was accomplished/ in the way I said it would be at the time the Argives took ship/ for Ilion (...) ." (2, 170 ff.). The suitors, on the other hand, interpret the omen in their own favor by taking it as proof that Odysseus is dead.

The Archetype of the Journey
1

More than any other work in world literature, the *Odyssey* has created the archetypal myth of the journey. The paradigm for the developmental process throughout our cultural and literary history is an odyssey: the *Aeneid, The Divine Comedy* and *Ulysses*—they all have the *Odyssey*'s model of the journey as a sounding board.

However, there are two kinds of development attributed to the journey as portrayed by Homer—the father's and the son's. Their journeys do not have the same content or meaning. For while Odysseus is a traveler on the final leg, on the way toward himself and his final realization, the journey for Telemachos is the first step in becoming independent, which presumes primarily a breach with his mother. So it also has a deeper meaning that he should go through this stage in the development of his consciousness and maturity in a search for his father.

It is likewise understandable why traces of the original mythical initiation rituals—rites of passage—have been seen in the developmental process in the *Telemachy*. In this phase of life, young boys break with their mothers and are accepted into the world of men.[3] This can take place in a variety of rituals, but the basic ethnographical pattern seems to be similar in each case. It contains categories such as circumcision, cutting the navel cord, removal from the mother, symbolical death and rebirth as a man—after a dangerous and demanding initiation journey in which the young man must prove his talent and his courage in order to be accepted in the men's universe.

For Telemachos, the journey away from his mother also becomes a journey back to the heroic reality of men, personified by Nestor and Menelaos—and under Athene's guidance. He learns here to distinguish what does not correspond to him and accordingly to seek those things that can fulfil his longings.

However, the other journey—the one on which Odysseus is embarked—takes place in the second half of life, where it is the subject's task to integrate those sides of existence, the primal maternal and the chthonic, with which he has broken as a young man. Which is why, in the form of shadows and the subconscious, what was once repressed now threatens to swallow him like a Skylla. So it is during and through the journey that people reveal their ability. In contrast to his mediocre crew, who simply leave things alone and fall back into the unconscious, Odysseus proves here that he possesses the strength needed to meet the demonic world with a tenacity that brings him home as a complete individual, a process that is emphasized by the recurrent references to death and rebirth.

In the sagas, too, the journey is a decisive factor for maturation. Like Telemachos, young men of spirit set off from Iceland and sail to the kings of Norway, Denmark and England to gain fame from their voyage, the kind Athene speaks of in relation to Telemachos. Meetings with famous kings provide lasting honor in themselves. So it is, too, with Nestor and Menelaos who, in their high estimate of Telemachos and their insistence on his resemblance to his father, confirm him in the identity to which he was born and his future destiny as king.

Certainly, the journey will develop Telemachos primarily by liberating him from his mother's protection. However, as Athene later explains to Odysseus, she has accompanied Telemachos on his voyage also to gain glory for him and thereby, without it being said directly, to erase the shame that might attach to him on account of his inability to act at home in Ithaka: "It was I myself/ who saw him along on that journey, so he would win reputation/ by going there" (13, 421-23).

That Telemachos now actually begins to act on the basis of his father's strength as it rises in his psyche is symbolically marked by the fact that, in preparation for his journey, he descends into Odysseus' cellar, i.e., his treasure chamber, the center of his power, literally and metaphorically, to get supplies for his impending journey of initiation. That at the same time he steps out from his mother's protection and unintended weakening of him is demonstrated by the fact that in the same breath he forbids Eurykleia to inform his mother until eleven days had passed. Penelope is put out of play and, guided by Athene, the goddess of intelligence, Telemachos is finally on his way toward his true identity: liberated from his mother, reborn through his father or the patriarchal principle itself, without a mother.

2

Each in his own significant way, King Nestor in Pylos and King Menelaos in Sparta, act as a provisional father figure for Telemachos by virtue of their age, power, and heroic reputation and by their close friendship with his father. They possess the paternal authority that Telemachos has lacked while growing up. And Telemachos, who previously had only a vague feeling of the father in himself, has his striking similarity to Odysseus confirmed by these superheroes—and by Athene. At the same time, these encounters provide him with mental access to the heroic world of the *Iliad*.

This learning process is demonstrated by the fact that Telemachos, unused as he is to travelling and associating with powerful rulers, is in doubt about the decorum in his meeting with Nestor. Once again, Athene puts "courage in his heart" (3, 76).

He has "no more need at all of modesty" (3, 14), since this is why he undertook his journey—to gather information about his father's fate and to "win a good reputation" (3, 78) in the world.

Nestor, the first person he visits, is not just anybody. In the *Iliad*, we hear that he is the oldest of the Greeks, spanning three generations (I, 350 ff.; XI, 761 ff.)—i.e., he reaches back in time to the earliest and most splendid heroic epoch, when heroes such as Herakles were still at their peak—indeed, compared to this first heroic era, the heroes at Troy are only pale shadows (see p. 39). Because of his age and wisdom Nestor is the one who intervenes in all important matters during the war and puts things right. He is honored by men as Zeus is by the gods. As such, he is an archaic incarnation of *metis*, as is shown in his attempt to arbitrate in the conflict between Achilleus and Agamemnon. It is also his counsel to build the wall around the ships to protect them from the advancing Trojans.

This is to say that he exudes the highest conceivable authority and Homer is able to use this authority to elevate Telemachos' sense of his own worth in his own as well as the listener's eyes. For, as he has spoken with moderation, Nestor stresses that with his rhetoric Telemachos has demonstrated that he not only resembles his father externally but also internally. What Nestor says inseparably links father and son in the present and future of the account:

> For surely your words are like his words, nor would anyone
> Ever have thought that a younger man could speak so like him.
> For while I and the great Odysseus were there together,
> We never spoke against one another, neither in council
> Nor assembly, but forever one in mind and in thoughtful
> Planning, we worked out how things would go best for the Argives.
>
> (3, 124-29)

Significantly, Nestor not only links Telemachos with this father, but at the same time he creates a form of identity between Odysseus and himself. Odysseus likewise refers to the similarity in the realm of the dead when he tells Achilleus that his son Neoptolemos was an excellent speaker—"only godlike Nestor and I were better than he was" (11, 512). In this way, Nestor becomes a father figure and intermediary just as with his age he creates a retrospective link to the most ancient and glorious times. And this inner cohesion is supported by Telemachos being attributed with the epithet "thoughtful," *pepnymenos*,[4] (a word associated with *nous*) which is also used about Nestor —"he is too thoughtful" (3, 20) and Odysseus (8, 388), which at the overall narrative level indicates their mental brotherhood. Thus, it is indirectly revealed that the heroes of the *Iliad* represent a more violent and relatively limited phase between Nestor's age and the new rational order that Odysseus ushers in.

Nestor tells what he knows about the return of the Greek heroes, including the murder of Agamemnon. And like Athene, Nestor suggests that Telemachos should act in imitation of Orestes and take strength from his *mythos*: "So you too, dear friend, for I see you are tall and splendid,/ be brave too, so that men unborn may speak well of you" (3, 199-200). And unlike the previous occasion on which Telemachos heard tell of Orestes and thought him to be essentially different from himself, the crucial factor is that he has now matured to such an extent that he can assume this mythical identification.[5]

For on the one hand, Telemachos speaks of the immortal reputation Orestes has won with his revenge. On the other, he expresses the following desire: "If only the gods would give me such strength as he has/ to take revenge on the suitors for their overbearing oppression" (3, 205). His recurrent doubt is that he does not believe himself particularly favored by the divine powers. This both makes Nestor speak of how highly Athene esteems Odysseus—"for I never saw the gods showing such open affection/ as Pallas Athene, the way she stood beside him, openly" (3, 221-22)—and Athene herself rebukes him with the words: "Lightly a god, if he wishes, can save a man, even from far off" (3, 321). And when the goddess shortly afterwards soars into the air as an eagle, Nestor proclaims: "Dear friend, I have no thought that you will turn out mean and cowardly/ if, when you are so young, the gods go with you and guide you" (3, 375-76). This fact, that Athene now lifts herself out of his story, is the definitive sign that he has taken possession of his manhood, which he also demonstrates in his own meeting with Menelaos.

The filial bond with Nestor is made clear in the further action in that Nestor lets his son Peisistratos accompany Telemachos to Sparta, and these two young men form a bond as close as brothers. At the same time, this is a hidden parallel to the compositionally parallel series of events in which Orestes is accompanied by his close friend Pylades. This entire pattern of identification is maintained after the arrival before Menelaos, who says of Peisistratos that he resembles his father Nestor in his good sense: "why, this is the way your father is, so you too speak thoughtfully" (4, 206) in a counterpart to Nestor's comment on Telemachos' striking resemblance to Odysseus.

3

From sandy Pylos, as old and topographically modest as its ruler, Telemachos arrives in Sparta, a locality that does not correspond at all to what one connects with Spartan surroundings. The palace gleams in an aura of splendor, the like of which the two young men have never seen: "for as the shining of the sun (Helios) or the moon (Selene) was the shining/ all through this high-roofed house of glorious Menelaos" (4, 45-46). This gleaming phenomenon is due to the fact that everything in the palace is finished in beaten silver and gold. So they believe they have been dropped into the world of the gods, but Menelaos counters their astonishment and thereby demonstrates that, despite his wealth, he does not harbor the arrogance of the suitors: "there is no mortal who could rival Zeus" (4, 78). No, the gods have no reason here for envy (*phthonos*) and *nemesis*.

As a personification of the heroic era, Menelaos, like Nestor, becomes a father figure who in this spirit addresses Telemachos as his "son." However, if Nestor is a father in "spirit," Menelaos becomes so for heroic virtues (*arete*), for courage, physical strength and beauty. Since he is also Agamemnon's brother, who married Helen's murderous sister Klytemnestra, the motif of murder and revenge is again activated for Telemachos with direct and insistent authenticity. And Menelaos relates this tragic story, which weighs heavily on his mind, several times. Telemachos cannot come closer to Orestes.

Furthermore, Menelaos is already connected with Telemachos' family. He has formed such a close friendship with Odysseus that he had plans for moving him to affluent Argos and granting him that city as a reward for his efforts in the Trojan War. In addition, he can provide Telemachos with the concrete information that he has traveled to obtain. For during his own long voyage home, he extracted information about the other Greeks from the wise old man of the sea, Proteus, learning of the murder of his brother and discovering that Odysseus was with Kalypso— "That was Odysseus son of Laertes, who makes his home in/ Ithaka, whom I saw on an island, weeping big tears/ in the palace of the nymph Kalypso" (4, 555-57). Finally, Menelaos is married to Helen, and that is not the least important matter.

Upon his departure, Telemachos receives a bowl, forged by Hephaistos the god of the blacksmith's trade; it is the finest thing Menelaos owns and is a possession he himself has received as a gift. In this way, he honors Telemachos and shows him— and the listener—that he has been accepted as Odysseus' son by the world of heroic ideals of which Menelaos is the incarnation. In short, the gift indicates that he will now be able to meet his father with full honor and recreate the same order prevailing in Sparta but lost in Ithaka.

Erotic Development

1

However, one crucial aspect is missing from this initiation: the erotic. For in consideration of Telemachos' age and the fact that the *Odyssey* is woven through with sexuality and erotic insight, it can seem strange that he is apparently not associated with this motif—indeed, he seems devoid of any sex life. That is only his father's domain. However, in the story of personal maturation the *Telemachy* represents, the erotic exists as a potential for development, except that it is necessary to extract this meaning from the text through suggestions and symbolic signals.

Telemachos arrives at Pylos in the middle of a sacrificial feast in honor of Poseidon, at which Athene asks her uncle to crown Telemachos' journey with success. When he leaves Pylos again, a sacrificial feast is held in honor of Athene. Although these festivals are not immediately felt to be necessary for the action, they have an important symbolic function by delving deep into the work's religious structure. For in this way, Homer provides an impression that the country and its king are governed with great piety. For Telemachos, it has the determinative significance that he is introduced into the world of piety which has also made its mark on his father and which must have been lacking in his absence, as is emphasized by the suitors' ungodly behavior during the assemblies. Finally, the two gods, to whom Odysseus' fate is tied, Poseidon and Athene, are introduced as enemy and benefactress.

The arrival of Telemachos in Sparta takes place in the midst of no less an event than a double wedding. The bride is Hermione, daughter of Menelaos and Helen, the only child they have in common, who is marrying Achilleus' son Neoptolemos, as Menelaos had promised him at Troy. According to Euripides' tragedy *Andromache*, it was not a union leading to much happiness. That was something Hermione did not find until her marriage to her cousin Orestes. So once more one senses this shadowy figure close to Telemachos. The second wedding is between one of Menelaos' bastard sons and a girl of noble birth.

Of course, we hear no more about these weddings, which is why they might seem like addenda. But like the sacrificial feasts in Pylos, the wedding has a meaning as a mirror of Telemachos' initiation. For to the dangers connected to the voyage as an existential transition in the young man's life is added all the peril that is present in the corresponding betrothal situation. The danger here is that sexuality is awakened and acknowledged as a mortally dangerous instinct until it is bound in marriage by the social order, in the service of reproduction.

Even though it might be said that this theme is under-illuminated with respect to Telemachos, it has an overarching significance in Homer, since his whole project is founded on an erotic crime, while in the same way Odysseus' journey home is fraught with erotic minefields. The theme plays a similar vital role in the sagas, where these energetic young men leave home just after becoming betrothed, often with catastrophic consequences.[6]

If we make the experiment of imagining the wedding scene along with the description of the palace radiant in sunlight and moonlight, we have the framework for the erotic scope of the *Odyssey*. The weddings point toward the erotic destiny awaiting Telemachos, while the gleaming palace symbolically illuminates the marital happiness of the sun king and his moon queen. What their reconciliation also anticipates is the approaching reunion of Odysseus and Penelope in their sun and moon wedding. In this way, a hidden erotic subtext is assembled around Telemachos.

2

Even before Telemachos' arrival in Sparta, there is reference to the erotic. He is bathed by Nestor's youngest daughter, Polykaste, and he rises from the bath "looking like an immortal" (3, 468). That his beauty is evoked by erotic charisma is demonstrated by the fact that Athene endows Odysseus several times with a similar appearance in an erotically-charged context—for example, after his encounter with Nausikaa, he is described as "radiant in grace and good looks" (6, 237) or prior to his reunion with Penelope, when he rises from his bath "looking like an immortal" (23, 163). Thus, father and son meet in the exact same formula, something that is only made possible by a psychological intersection.

The authors of antiquity also recognize this erotic dimension with respect to Telemachos. For example, in one fragment, Hesiod has him fall in love with Nestor's daughter Polykaste, and they have a son together, Persepolis,[7] while in the cyclical poems he is married to no less than Kirke.[8]

Whether there might at the same time have been a homoerotic relationship between Telemachos and Peisistratos, who sleep in the same room (3, 399-402), has always been a problem for scholars. The question is open. The compositional system of identification is in itself good reason for their friendship. In addition, paedophilia and homosexuality in the widespread form that later characterized Greek culture is not found in Homer. The nearest we have is perhaps the relationship between Achilleus and Patroklos, which was subsequently—by Plato among others—interpreted as homosexual.[9] Perhaps one might go so far as to say that the same erotic attraction exists between Telemachos and Peisistratos as is found among boys of a presexual age, before the sexual urge towards the opposite sex becomes serious.

The Most Beautiful Woman in the World

1

Telemachos' failure to come to grips with his masculinity was due to his overprotective mother. For the same reason, his erotic life is unable to develop because his mother is there. Yet, just as the voyage liberates him from her, he meets the feminine-erotic in the form of Helen.[10] And just as the voyage makes him into a man in the heroic sense, inspired by Nestor and Menelaos (the symbols of the world of the *Iliad*), he also returns home with an awakened erotic life, spurred by no less than the most beautiful woman in the world. Only then is his personality sufficiently developed for him to be ready to meet his father.

The notion of Helen's influence on Telemachos' destiny has a deeper truth. She is actually the one who identifies him, not her husband. Just as it is Nestor who intellectually recognizes him as his father's son, so it is Helen who on an emotional level sees his resemblance to Odysseus with whom she has a special bond. Among other things, he has been her suitor and she has assisted him during his espionage mission to Troy. When she enters the hall, she cries out in amazement at the sight of the unknown youth:

> Shall I be wrong, or am I speaking the truth? My heart tells me
> To speak, for I think I never saw such a likeness, neither
> In man nor woman, and wonder takes me as I look on him,
> As this man has a likeness to the son of great-hearted Odysseus,
> Telemachos, who was left behind in his house, a young child
> By that man when, for the sake of *shameless me,* the Achaians
> Went beneath Troy, their hearts intent upon reckless warfare.
>
> (4, 140-47, my italics)

There is a somewhat piquant aspect to Telemachos' encounter with Helen—although it is not directly touched upon—that he has come to Sparta because his father has not returned home from the war of which she and her erotic goings on are the cause.

In order to understand now how she affects his erotic awakening and future—indeed, actually steps into his mother's place—it is necessary to look more closely at her own story and self-understanding in the *Iliad* and the *Odyssey*. A portrait is drawn of her as a woman filled with regret and shame over the misfortune she has occasioned. In this reaction, she is clearly distinguished from her sister Klytemnestra, who by murdering her returning spouse "splashed the shame on herself and the rest of her sex, on women/ still to come, even on the one whose acts are virtuous" (11, 433-34), as the judgment from the murdered man is put in the realm of the dead. Consequently, after her "conversion," Helen paradoxically enough comes more to resemble her cousin Penelope.

As appears from the quotation above, Helen cannot forget that she was the cause of the Trojan War and both here and many other places as well—also in the *Iliad*—she applies to herself the Greek term *kynopes*, which means dog-eyed and is translated as "slut that I am" (III, 180) or "nasty bitch" (III, 180)—she clearly believes that she is a disgrace. As she says to King Priam:

And I wish bitter death had been what I wanted, when I came hither
Following your son, forsaking my chamber, my kinsmen,
My grown child, and the loveliness of girls my own age.

(III, 173-75)

Priam has tried to comfort her as best he can by observing that she has been subject to the will of the gods (see p. 114). However, in contrast to Paris, who apologizes for his unseemly conduct by saying that one should not spurn the gifts of the gods—"do not bring up against me the sweet favours of golden Aphrodite" (III, 64)—Helen cannot reconcile herself with such an excuse and shoulders the responsibility herself, a burden she bears to her death. On the other hand, it must be noted that she never makes an active effort to change things and show her loyalty to the Greeks. On the contrary. When Paris is killed by Philoktetes' arrow, she immediately marries his brother Deiphobos. To avoid death by stoning in Euripides' *The Trojan Women*, however, she claims that, after Paris' death, she tried to steal across to the Greek camp but was taken prisoner by the guards when she lowered herself from the city wall.[11]

Helen loathes her Trojan prince consort and only takes him back under pressure from Aphrodite when the goddess with some difficulty has ensured that Menelaos does not kill him in a duel. The passage is interesting, because there is a direct confrontation between Helen and Aphrodite that reveals how tense their relationship is. Although Aphrodite has transformed herself into an old crone, she is recognized with horror by Helen: "Strange divinity! Why are you still so stubborn to beguile me?" (III, 399). Helen's fear is that the goddess will lead her even further away, into the arms of yet another of her favorites. Does she have such a scheme in mind? Aphrodite reacts furiously and threatens Helen's destruction if she does not obey her—"Wretched girl, do not tease me lest in anger I forsake you/ and grow to hate you as much as now I terribly love you" (III, 414-15).

Helen receives Paris with the scornful wish that Menelaos had killed him, this man who had bragged about his greater strength. Paris responds by demanding immediate sexual gratification. Hektor, too, mocks Paris for being weak and "woman-crazy" (III, 39). On the other hand, there is a sympathy between Hektor and Helen that makes her call herself "a nasty bitch" (VI, 344) to him and once again wish she were dead or, since the gods have given her such a terrible role, at least that she had been "the wife of a better man than this is" (VI, 350). That she in fact has Hektor in mind is verified by the fact that she bids him welcome as the one who must endure the greatest sufferings for her sake and that she grieves deeply over his death with the words: "Hektor, of all my lord's brothers dearest by far to my spirit" (XXIV, 762). At the same time, Paris becomes the model of the heroic degeneration that spreads with the suitors at Ithaka while Odysseus is away.

During her stay in Troy, Helen was still under Aphrodite's destructive influence. This is further illustrated by the fact that, as Menelaos reports, "moved by some divine spirit" (4, 274-75) and with the intention of helping the Trojans, Helen walked around the Wooden Horse imitating the voices of the Greek heroes' women in order to awaken their desire. This divinity can hardly have been any other than Aphrodite, since the attempt at seduction falls within the area of sexuality and she is on the Trojan side. And the warriors would have given themselves away had it not been for Odysseus controlling his own instinct and keeping his men in check. Whereas Helen is still subject to Aphrodite's power, Odysseus resists it because he cannot be guided by sexuality but by intelligence, personified by Athene.

2

Ambiguous as Helen's nature is, it is inevitable that opinions about her in Greek poetry should be divided—with a strong tendency to the negative. In the Oresteia, she is called "the blossom that breaks the heart with longing,"[12] while in Euripides' Orestes, after having murdered his mother, Orestes also takes the life of her sister Helen, well aware how it will please all of Hellas, where so many have lost sons and husbands because of her infidelity. However, as the daughter of Zeus, she is saved by Apollo and made immortal.

This assessment is sensed even in the Homeric epics. Yet, she is on the whole described in quite positive terms thanks to the liking that Priam and Hektor have for her. With their heroic status, they give her prestige. In grief at the loss of Patroklos, on the other hand, Achilleus rails at the madness of struggling for "the sake of accursed Helen far from his father and son" (XIX, 323). Yet he even ends up dying for her sake.

However, Menelaos, who is actually the offended party, does not reprimand Helen for her infidelity but lays the blame on Paris, who breached the rules of guest friendship. And so the cuckolded husband wants to kill him with the assistance of Zeus, the god of guest friendship—"that any one of the men to come may shudder to think of/ doing evil to a kindly host, who has given him friendship" (III, 353-54).

Unlike Priam, Nestor does not make the gods but the Trojans responsible for the violation and says that no Greek shall abandon Troy "until after he has lain in bed with the wife of a Trojan/ to avenge Helen's longing to escape and her lamentations" (II, 355-56). Telemachos, on the other hand, views her misdeed in the same light as Priam—that is, as a woe brought about "by the gods' will" (17, 119). And Penelope shares his view when she says: "It was a god who stirred her to do the shameful thing she/ did" (23, 222-23). Had she thought twice about it, Penelope seems to believe, she could have avoided being seduced by the gods—and Paris. Hence, Penelope's own chronic suspicious nature. The harshest judgment, however, comes from the shepherd Eumaios after the loss of his beloved master: "as I wish Helen's seed could all have perished,/ pitched away, for she has unstrung the knees of so many/ men" (14, 68-70).

3

That Helen's transformation really is a reality in the *Odyssey* can be interpreted from her own words. She tells Telemachos how she rejoiced when Odysseus came to Troy in disguise in order to spy on the enemy and on that occasion to kill a number of Trojans:

> The rest of the Trojan women cried out shrill, but my heart
> Was happy, my heart had changed by now and was for going back
> Home again, and I grieved for the madness that Aphrodite
> Bestowed when she led me there away from my own dear country,
> Forsaking my own daughter, my bedchamber, and my husband,
> A man who lacked no endowment either of brains or beauty.
>
> (4, 259-64)

So the madness that Helen displays in the *Iliad* under the influence of Aphrodite, has been overcome when she meets Telemachos. However, what is crucial is that her transformation and liberation from Aphrodite has been under way for almost thirty years, since by the end of the war, she has spent twenty years in Troy—"and here now is the twentieth year upon me since I came/ from the place where I was, forsaking the land of my fathers" (XXIV, 765-66).[13] A further ten years have passed before Telemachos arrives.

Menelaos had otherwise intended to kill Helen after the conquest of Troy, but, as is related in the *Little Iliad*, she only needed to bare her breast to make him change his mind. Euripides uses the same moment in the *Andromache*—"But casting sheep's eyes on her bosom, you/ Unbuckled your sword and puckered up for kisses,/ Petting that traitorous bitch, you toady of lust!"[14] In the *Lysistrata*, Aristophanes parodies the situation—"Menelaus, certainly, when he somehow caught a glimpse of Helen's two little apples bare, let his sword, I reckon, drop out of his hand."[15]

In *The Trojan Women*, however, Menelaos is determined that she should be stoned upon returning to Argos, because she has heaped shame upon him.[16] She defends herself, saying that Aphrodite lured her there, while on the other hand she saved Hellas from being attacked by the barbarians from Troy: "I,/ sold once for my body's beauty stand accused, who should/ for what has been done wear garlands on my head."[17] For Menelaos, the purpose of the expedition was to avenge himself upon those who had violated marriage and Greek friendship.[18] Hekuba, the Trojan queen, defends her son Paris by saying that it was Helen who was the most eager. For at the sight of him, she was seized by Aphrodite and madness (*aphrosyne*), and at the same time in impoverished Sparta she was fired to enjoy a share of Phrygian splendor,[19] but she treated Paris badly by constantly praising her former husband.

Helen is still as dazzlingly beautiful as a goddess, but she is not compared, as one would expect, to the goddess of love—as is, for example, her daughter Hermione "with the beauty of Aphrodite the golden" (4, 14). On the contrary, she is compared to the maiden who, if anyone, is the antithesis of Aphrodite, Artemis—"like Artemis of the golden distaff" (4, 122). This, too, may be interpreted as evidence that, after the many years she has harbored feelings of guilt, Helen has undergone a transformation, so that, in her transformed erotic essence, she corresponds to the virgin goddess Artemis. On the other hand, it is difficult to give an explanation of why she has been barren since she gave birth to her daughter before fleeing to Troy—"but the gods gave no more children to Helen/ once she had borne her first and only child" (4, 12-13).

Meanwhile, that a radical repression of Aphrodite has taken place in Helen's development emerges indirectly from the fact that, upon his return, Telemachos is greeted by Penelope, "looking like Artemis, or like golden Aphrodite" (17, 37). This dual comparison emphasizes Penelope's virtue as well as her erotic nature, waiting for Odysseus as the reward for his tenacity.

For Helen, on the other hand, the consequence may be that, in her configuration with Artemis, she no longer has a sexual relationship with Menelaos. This means, in other words, that he has a wife who betrayed him and then, to escape this aspect of her nature, avoids sexual intercourse.

Against this background, there is a hint of sadness and resignation about Menelaos in the midst of all his glory. This may have a deeper cause in that he has not been given a son by this marriage, and so there is no future for his legitimate family line. So he is highly unstable. As he himself puts it, he often sits in his home weeping and grieving (4, 100 ff.), even though he gives the thought of so many lost as the reason. However, that he is primarily thinking of Helen is supported by the fact that he has just related how his beloved brother was killed by his "cursed wife" (4, 92), that is to say his sister-in-law and Helen's sister—the two who were of one mind, as it is put in the *Oresteia*.[20] However, Helen knows how to alleviate this pain, since, like another Kirke, she has mastered the art of magic herbs, ensuring that the memory of all the evil disappears in the daze or euphoria evoked by the herbs. Even though the palace in Sparta shines like the sun and the moon, it does not seem to contain the same deep harmony (*homophrosyne*) that characterizes the reunion of Odysseus and Penelope.

4

Helen was born in Sparta, which means that, as king, Menelaos in practice rules his wife's kingdom, evidence that he is really a king in a maternal line—in the same way that it is hinted that the Phaiakian king is subordinate to his queen (see p. 223). In a patriarchal society, on the other hand, the norm is that, on marriage, a woman moves into her husband's tribe or family. In addition, it may be a sign of her chthonic heritage as a fertility goddess that, like Hekate and Medea, she can make the magic elixir. It is revealing that these herbs derive from Egypt's fertile delta, which "produces the greatest number/ of medicines, many good in mixture, many malignant" (4, 229-30). This form of fertility is associated with the primal mother stage, before the fields were cultivated by a man's plow—both in a literal and metaphorical sense. And also insofar as Helen's cult—as her erotic biography might indicate—was also linked to sexual orgies, there is a parallel to Aphrodite's cultic festivals, which link them together at a far earlier point than Homer.[21]

At any rate, Aphrodite constitutes a clear polarity to Athene—and Artemis in the Homeric universe. That Aphrodite is considered as pure sexuality, a wild, socially maladjusted natural power, is suggested by Homer when he calls her a "bitch-eyed daughter" (8, 319), the same epithet (*kynopes*) that Helen uses about her confused sexuality—and is incidentally also used about her sister Klytemnestra (11, 424). And like Aphrodite and the other primal mothers, who couple anonymously left and right, Helen does not really belong to a single man before her conversion, but in principle to all. In the myths about her, she manages to marry many times, first Theseus, who abducts her as a young girl, then Menelaos, Paris and Deiphobos, before she and Menelaos finally come together in the sign of Artemis.

As Helen appears in Homer, she seems in her aberrant state to be a weak-willed tool of Aphrodite's whims, obsessed and deluded. And although she resists, she is still constrained by the goddess' threats, as just described in Book III of the *Iliad*, where she is at first unwilling to receive Paris after Menelaos has humiliated him. Then she sees the dazzling neck of the goddess of love, "and her desirable breasts and her eyes that were full of shining" (III, 397) and addresses her as *daimonie* (III, 399). She no longer wants to be deluded. Aphrodite herself can leave the gods and serve Paris as his wife or slave. It is these words that infuriate the goddess, so she threatens to abandon Helen, which must imply that she will rob her of all the *charis* or charm with which she captivates the world. Instead, she will reap the goddess' hatred and, it is understood, die.

No explanation is provided as to how Helen, in contrast to Hippolytos, manages to liberate herself from Aphrodite and herself become a sort of Artemis. We only need to note that in the *Odyssey* she has progressed from her earlier entanglement with Aphrodite, away from the blind power of desire into a virginal *eros*. This transformation is emphasized by the fact that she is once again together with Menelaos in a marriage that is no longer threatened by blind desire but, perhaps, borne by the reconciliation of renunciation. In addition, the care and generosity she displays to Telemachos seem to be the munificence and social enterprise of transformed desire.

5

However, it is impossible completely to understand the solicitude Helen displays to Telemachos and the effect she has on his erotic future if she is not seen in a peculiar pattern of identification with Odysseus. Their mutual history goes much farther back than Troy. As said above, he was one of her many suitors and was behind the oath to support Menelaos if he were to meet with trouble.

The remarkable feature is that—like Nestor—she repeatedly demonstrates a special spiritual harmony between herself and Odysseus—indeed almost a *homophrosyne* such as exists between two spouses deeply bound to each other. Hence, it is she who identifies Odysseus to Priam in the *Iliad*, and in the *Odyssey* she tell Telemachos of the time she recognized Odysseus while he was spying in Troy even though he had beaten himself so as to be unrecognizable. "I alone recognized him in this form" (4, 250), she says, seeming to understand that she knew him thanks to their psychological similarity. She bathed and rubbed him with oil, while in return he told her of the Greek plans, which, according to the *Little Iliad*, she helped put into effect.[22]

Throughout the period during which Odysseus is away from Penelope, Helen remains the woman closest to him, which harmonizes with the fact that he courted her before he married Penelope. Yet, he brackets her and Klytemnestra together when he says to Agamemnon in Hades that the two sisters were a disaster for the Atreids, for "many of us died for the sake of Helen" (11, 437). Nevertheless, there is also a deeper bond in that Odysseus is the one who has literally and symbolically liberated Helen. By his cunning, she is liberated from Troy, the mistake of her life, which is why it is symbolically logical that he and Menelaos go directly to her when the city has fallen. No wonder she takes such care of Telemachos.

6

Just as Menelaos presents Telemachos with a valuable bowl upon departure, a rosy-cheeked Helen gives him a parting gift of a wedding dress with the words:

I too give you this gift, dear child: something to remember
From Helen's hands, for your wife to wear at the lovely occasion
Of your marriage. Until that time let it lie away in your palace,
In your dear mother's keeping (. . .).

(15, 125-28)

When Helen uses the expression "dear child"—in the original text, "my beloved son," it makes clear that she steps erotically into the very psychological position in which his biological mother had been the dominant force.

At the time when Telemachos meets her, she is still a beauty, but also an ageing woman of about forty-five if we work on the basis of the earlier calculations. From the point of view of age, she finds herself in the position of a mother, but her function is as a friend to fashion his erotic nature, releasing him from his maternal bonds and making him into an erotically mature individual. This erotic direction is not, it should be noted, linked to Aphrodite but to Artemis. It protects against the delusion of sexuality since it has, of course, Helen's own erotic transformation and identification with Artemis as a background. And the point of her bridal gown must be that Telemachos, when he meets the woman he wants to marry, can dress her in a gown from Helen and ensure for himself the same marital bliss as his father and mother.

When Penelope and Telemachos meet again after his journey, it is apparent that the feminine has acquired quite a different meaning from the maternal that kept him imprisoned in the role of a child. She greets him, not as a son, but as a blessing to her eyes or a sweet light (*glykeron phaos*, 17, 41), while, as we have already seen, he sees in her both Artemis and the golden Aphrodite. With this comparison, Penelope comes to represent a harmonious balance between the sensual and the spiritual. And since she is to keep Helen's bridal gown until Telemachos marries, she is no longer bound by maternal ties but creates the redeeming transition to a woman of her own caliber.

This means that the journey represents the final separation during which Telemachos isolates his mother and maternal suffocation from the feminine as such. This frees him to meet a woman who, like his mother, encompasses Artemis, Aphrodite, and Athene. Helen has freed him from his bonds tying him to his mother. She has shaped his erotic capacity, at the same time as Telemachos, by separating himself from Penelope, has helped her out of the role of mother, so she is ready to meet her husband as his wife when he has freed her from the suitors, as Helen suggests will happen soon.

With the assurance the gods have given Helen, she interprets a bird omen just before Telemachos' departure. An eagle comes flying from the right with a goose in its claws. She interprets this omen as meaning that Odysseus will soon return home and wreak vengeance. Thus, she not only gives a direction to Telemachos' sexuality but with her interpretation of the omen she gives him direct from the gods the information he has gone away to obtain about his father. For while Menelaos has only been able to enlighten him on the fact that he is on a remote island with Kalypso, Helen can give him the happy hope that Odysseus is on his way home to take revenge on the suitors, indeed that he might perhaps already be in his home—as, in fact, he is!

Such is the comprehensive symbolical value of the *Telemachy*. On his journey, Telemachos has undergone a transformation in his nature that encompasses all of Homer's work. From Athene herself, he has received mental strength. His intelligence, *metis*, has been identified with none other than Nestor, the wisest along with his father. As the last of the *Iliad*'s strapping heroes, Menelaos has received him in a fatherly fashion. And finally, Helen, the fairest of the fair, has awakened and directed his erotic being. He now has the personal authority he needs to meet Odysseus as a son, helper and heir. Is it any wonder that the palace in Sparta shines in his eyes like molten gold?

VI

ODYSSEUS

I

T IS NOT UNTIL BOOK 5 THAT WE FINALLY MEET THE MAN HIMSELF, THE SORELY tried Odysseus, sitting on the beach on Kalypso's island, Ogygia, and weeping with homesickness. But who is he? In the next major section of the book, we shall try to answer this question and fathom his particular psychological constitution and discover what makes him one of the most significant figures in our culture.

"The Man"

In the very first word of the first line of the *Iliad* Homer strikes the main theme of the work: "anger" (*menis*). As already said, in the *Odyssey* he leaves his listeners in no doubt that he calls on the Muse with the object of telling of "the man" (*aner*), the first word in that work and indicative of its principal motif. That the man is Odysseus is obvious. In addition, as an indication of his unique character and psychological mobility, we are immediately told that he is *polytropos*.[1]

As said above, this epithet is almost untranslatable in its wealth of nuances and ambiguities, and so it has been rendered in many different ways, depending on what dimension of his character the translator has chosen to emphasize. To Richmond Lattimore, Odysseus is the man who wanders far and wide, "the man of many ways," and to Robert Fagles, he is the man full of invention and craftiness "the man of twists and turns."[2] The only other character to bear this epithet in Greek literature is Hermes—in the hymn to that god—who may be his great-grandfather and is at all events the god of cunning and interpretation, while, by virtue of his winged sandals, he is widely-traveled as the hard-working messenger of Olympos.

That is to say that the divergent interpretations can come together in the word *polytropos* insofar as, in a series of difficult challenges, the journey can only be brought to a happy conclusion because the polytropic personality, god or man, has the insight and ability to orchestrate the dangerous situations in which he finds himself. Always to be able to adapt oneself to circumstances demands rare psychological flexibility, if not the ability to transform oneself. Throughout these vicissitudes, Odysseus retains his self-control. In other words, even in the first verse, the *Odyssey* introduces a human being of a psychological nature without parallel. And it is difficult—indeed, impossible—to consider Odysseus as a subject without a personal developmental process.

In spite of this, the custom in scholarship has been to view Odysseus as a fixed figure, an individual who does not develop (see p. 62). He is, it is claimed, exactly the same when he comes home as when he left many years before. This seems all the more paradoxical as he is presented in the Homeric epics as the most talented of all the Greek heroes, something that is of course emphasized by the many epithets surrounding his name and gestalt, all equipped with the telling prefix *poly*, such as polygon. He is *polymetis, polymechanos, polytlas, polyphron,* and *polytopos,* a man of infinite mental capacity.

However, it must be admitted that there is some justification for assessing Odysseus as an unchanging figure. It is understandable, even though it is in glaring contradiction to his psychological complexity. But if the description of Odysseus is compared with the corresponding account of his son Telemachos, it must be admitted that Odysseus is not psychologized in nearly the same way. In a way, he appears in the text as a complete, rounded personality. Not least, the very epithets listed help to convey this impression of an integrated individual. They simply establish his person as something definitive.

Nevertheless, I will maintain that he is be subject to a process of maturing and liberation in much the same way as Telemachos. Indeed, it may even be claimed that, as an embodiment of his father, Telemachos not only proves that Homer knows these human mechanisms, but that, in a psychological sense, Telemachos quite simply provides an insight into the dynamic of these developmental forms and, as described above, represents his father's background: the hero's initiation in which he is liberated from his mother and assigned his place in world of men. Odysseus now finds himself at the time of life when this reality must be confronted and reintegrated to secure self-realization.

As I have sketched out in connection with his representational technique, Homer makes use of a singular symbolic mirroring method to describe the psychological events in a human subject. He uses surroundings, events and mythical figures to mirror the stages of experience and development through which Odysseus passes in the course of a long life and under great psychic pressure. Whereas we can follow Telemachos' process of maturation into a man chronologically and in detail, it is difficult to find a corresponding sequence for Odysseus. If we examine his clearly defined personality, this symbolical developmental process through which it was formed fades out of sight and vice versa.

So in the following I will try to put the pieces forming his character together, taking them from the *Iliad* and the *Odyssey* on the basis of the stages of development into which his life seems to be divided.

The Paradigm of Development

This forms a hypothetical framework for the content and sequence of events in Odysseus' self-realization, related to his age and the localities in which his mythos plays out.

1

The first phase covers his childhood, puberty and early manhood, extending from birth to around twenty-five years of age. During this period, he grows up in Ithaka, though during his adolescence visits his maternal grandfather, Autolykos, who lives at the foot of Mount Parnassos. He was commanded to do this by Autolykos at the naming ceremony, when his grandfather even named him after his own unattractive fate. During a hunt with his uncles at Parnassos, Odysseus brings down an angry wild boar—after himself being severely wounded just above the knee. He will be recognized by that scar in the future.

As I will go into more deeply below, I view this journey, the hunt, the wound and the killing of the wild boar as a mythical-symbolical representation of how Odysseus, like Telemachos, emancipates himself from *his* (primal) mother, who loves him with the same tenderness as Penelope does her son. The wild boar he kills is an incarnation of the aspect of the divided mother figure who wants to kill her son in revenge for his becoming emancipated—the evil mother, as opposed to the good and caring mother.

Odysseus passes this first test on masculinity's path out of maternal power with flying colors and a scar, and—like the dragon slayer of fairy-tales—he receives a golden treasure as a reward from his grandfather, the symbol of his incipient and successful self-realization on the path toward becoming a cultural hero. He wins Penelope as his princess, even though it was Helen who was the first object of his attention and desire. Penelope is by far the better woman. And with her he becomes a biological father and, at a given point, takes over the throne from his not yet deceased father—something that seems baffling but can be explained. As far as it goes, then, he has fully realized what may be called a male and regal career. However, there are greater plans for him.

2

In the second phase, Odysseus realizes himself in a new role during the expedition to Troy. He becomes a warrior and emerges as an ideal heroic figure. This takes place between the ages of about twenty-five and thirty-five, the period that coincides with the *Iliad*'s heroic code. Yet, even as he embodies this reality, he clearly goes beyond it if we compare him with the protagonist of the text, the angry Achilleus. Not only does he possess a level-headed rationality, but he has also developed the shrewdness and cunning that make him beloved of Athene but suspicious to the heroes who identify completely with heroic morality. They fear his form of intelligence and he is in reality friendless.

That this heroic world fails in its self-understanding and before the demands reality places upon it is revealed by the fact that neither the Greeks nor the Trojans are capable of ending the wearying ten-year war. This requires the intelligence that Odysseus possesses—resulting in the Wooden Horse, his brilliant and acclaimed stratagem that ends the war and shows him to have passed the higher test of intelligence, which in principle makes him a world conqueror and takes him further in his quest for self-realization.

3

The third stage comes with his ten-year voyage home from the time when he is approximately thirty-five until he is around forty-five. This is the third great trial. What is interesting is that the journey comes at the time in his life, when, according to individual psychology, true self-realization takes place. He passes the midpoint of his life and from now on it is his task to integrate the world and the life he has separated himself from in the struggle to constitute himself as a male subject.

As the *Apologoi*, his travel adventures, will be read, it is not only his own repressed reality, linked to the primal feminine, that must be confronted, lived through and absorbed in order to become a complete individual. No, as the cultural figure he also is, he encounters at this stage of life the chthonic world Homer himself has denied in order to invoke and sanction the Olympic patriarch, Zeus. Everything that has been pushed aside appears in the form of the demonic and destructive, which he must face and tackle alone by virtue of his intelligence, his endurance, and his consciousness-creating capacity for memory, which never loses sight of wife and home.

So he is the only one of the company who does not die. Or, rather, he "dies" several times—for example, on his journey through Hades. However, this occurs symbolically as an image of the process of rebirth that takes place in his self-realization, in which his homecoming is also described as a death, rebirth and a resurrection.

4

The fourth developmental phase deals with Odysseus' arrival home in Ithaka, encompassing the time when he is approximately forty-five until his death; but it, too, contains a crucial test—perhaps, two. As evidence that he has passed through the trials of the journey with flying colors, he arrives in his realm with the (golden) treasure he received from the Phaiakians, a parallel to the treasure he received from his grandfather in his youth and with the same symbolic content. However, on his arrival, he is forced to hide the treasure in a sacred grotto. He cannot immediately incorporate it into his social life and property because he now faces the challenge of regaining his kingdom and his wife by driving out the suitors as the forces of chaos. To do this will demonstrate that he has truly taken possession of himself and by virtue can prevail and restore his former kingdom.

The test itself is an archery contest in which he demonstrates not only that he still retains his old strength, but that he has achieved the spiritual integrity necessary to prevail and take back his wife. He now finds himself at the highest level of consciousness as a solar hero and with the suitors' families is able to conclude the peace that was disturbed throughout the Greek world when Helen broke her marital vows. But before he can settle down and rule in happiness and contentment to the end of his days as prophesied, he has yet another journey to undertake, a fifth and final test in which he must become reconciled with Poseidon. That this development forms the basis for Homer's utopia is a point that becomes the key to reading Homer.

Character Profile

In the following, I have tried to put together a character portrait on the basis of the concrete information Homer himself has provided about Odysseus' person and characteristics.

1

Let us start with his name. He received it from his maternal grandfather Autolykos, who called him after himself, saying: "My son-in-law and daughter, give him the name I tell you;/ since I have come to this place distasteful to many, women/ and men alike on the prospering earth, so let him be given/ the name Odysseus, that is distasteful" (19, 406-09).[3]

In mythology, Autolykos is known for the exceptional cunning he inherited from his father Hermes, the god of thieves, which has made it possible for him to pull the wool over more eyes than is good for him. Consequently, his reputation is shady, and he passes on this doubtful distinction—indeed, his own character—to Odysseus by naming him after himself.[4] It is also an undeniable fact that, as a result, Odysseus is often assessed negatively in his later reception, and his problematic side is further emphasized by the fact that Sisyphos, the other great trickster in Greek mythology, is sometimes said to be his father.

Of course, Odysseus' name is not Greek—and may not even be of Indo-European origin.[5] Nevertheless, in a number of passages, Homer seems to make associations with his name—i.e., a person who, as the result of the name Autolykos has given him, comes to know what it is to hate (*odyssamenos*, 19, 407)—and thus has adopted his identity as one who does harm. For Autolykos, whose name means "the wolf himself," has brought torment and loss to those around him in the form of deception and lies. Nor is it difficult to see the same disposition in his grandson, to see the negative side of his being, which has given him such a tainted reputation —from Achilleus' renunciation of allegiance to the tragedies in which suffering always results from his appearance, with the exception of Sophocles' *Ajax*.

He, if anyone, is behind the fall of Troy, where the royal family was struck by great misfortune, as can be seen in Euripides' *Hekuba* and *The Trojan Women*. He himself relates in the *Odyssey* how he immediately left Troy for Ismaros, the capital of the Kikonians, and sacked it, cut down its inhabitants and took vast booty in the form of property and women (9, 39-42). He ensures that Philoktetes is put on the island of Lemnos, just as he is the cause of Ajax' suicide. And, albeit in self-defense, he blinds the Kyklops. Elsewhere, it is related how he takes revenge on

Palamedes, who had revealed his trickery when he refused to take part in the expedition to Troy, even though it was he himself who came up with the binding oath.

To this extent he lives up to this side of his name, which has its source in his grandfather's wolf-name. However, he is not only a person who does harm; he becomes hated himself and is persecuted and tormented. That also this disposition lay in the identity given him by his name is made clear in the introduction to the *Odyssey* when, after talking of Odysseus' many sacrifices, Athene asks her father: "Why, Zeus, are you now so harsh with him?" (1, 62). The verb translated here as being harsh—*odyssomai*—is repeated in several other contexts in which it is unambiguously related to feeling pain. For instance, it is said of his family at home in Ithaka that they were "grieving" for him (4, 111), where the verb used is *odyromai*, meaning to lament. In this sense, the associations deposited around his name and identity have a clear double meaning: he is a human being who hates and personally suffers distress at being deeply hated.

If Odysseus is the subject of suffering in the *Iliad*—that is, one who inflicts pain on others—he is himself primarily the object of suffering in the *Odyssey*. For his odyssey is an extended account of how hard he is hit, in particular because he has incurred the wrath of Poseidon after having inflicted his hatred upon his son. The sea nymph Leukothea, who saves him off the Phaiakian coast, asks why he is persecuted by the sea god with "such a harvest of evils" (5, 340). Characteristically enough, she addresses him as "poor man" (*kammore*, 5, 160; 339).

King Aiolos expels him from his realm as one suffering from the plague and hated by the gods: "Out. This arrival means you are hateful to the immortals" (10, 75). Another verb is certainly used for "to hate" (*apekhthairo*), but the feeling is the same and it is further emphasized by the fact that he is "hated" (*odysanto*, 19, 276) by Helios and Zeus because his crew have slaughtered the sun god's cattle.

From this point of view, the *Odyssey* becomes the story of one man's attempt to take possession of his name as one who inflicts and is afflicted by suffering, but he holds out and gains insight through suffering. And in this process, he lives up to the duality in his name.[6] The first evidence of the duality in Odysseus' psychology is his killing of the wild boar as a young man. He kills it but is wounded himself and receives a scar that will always be proof of his identity and is used as such by himself—and his narrator.

2

Even in the *Iliad*, Odysseus' constitutional psychology is fixed to a large extent. Although Achilleus is the main character, the effect is that Odysseus' qualities, especially his wisdom, make him the key figure in a number of important situations. It is he who motivates the Greek heroes, the army and Agamemnon, when they become discouraged and want to go home, and it is he who tries to talk Achilleus to reason. But it goes without saying that he really only steps into character, develops and becomes nuanced during his journey in the *Odyssey*, where he is the unquestioned leading figure even in the books in which he is not present. Everything is about him and his homecoming.

At the time when we meet Odysseus in the *Odyssey*, he must be in his mid-to-late forties, since he has been gone for twenty years. At the time of his departure, his son was still an infant (4, 144) and he was himself hardly a mere youth. Prior to that time, he had courted Helen and ruled Ithaka for several years, which makes an age of around twenty-five seem likely. During the games in honor of the dead Patroklos, it emerges that he is older than his opponents—indeed, he actually belongs to another generation—he is "out of another age than ours and one of the ancients./ But his, they say, is a green old age. It would be a hard thing/ for any Achaian to match his speed. Except for Achilleus" (XXIII, 790-92).

By then, ten years have gone by, and Odysseus proclaims his wisdom to Achilleus by virtue of his age "since I was born before you and have learned more things" (XIX, 219). At the same time, it would be impossible for Homer to make him a hero if he were physically decrepit, so it is a crucial point both in the *Iliad* and the *Odyssey* that he is still in possession of his former strength despite his advanced years. This is confirmed by the fact that the only one who can run faster than he is Achilleus, who bears the epithet "fleet-footed" and is described as being as fast as the wind.

Odysseus demonstrates his physical prowess when he wrestles with the tough warrior Ajax during the games for Patroklos: "Neither Odysseus/ was able to bring Ajax down or throw him to the ground, nor/ could Ajax, but the great strength of Odysseus held out against him" (XXIII, 719-20). And even though another ten years have passed in the *Odyssey*, he has not lost any of his strength. For when, challenged and insulted by the Phaiakians, he throws the discus, his throw is the longest. And none of the young suitors can bend his bow.

Paradoxically, we get the best impression of Odysseus' appearance and demeanor in the *Iliad*, when King Priam compares him to a ram wandering among the white sheep—"Truly, to some deep-fleeced ram would I liken him/ who makes his way through the great mass of the shining sheep-flocks" (III, 197-98)—an image exuding power and compact strength. Strangely enough, Priam does not know who he is. Helen informs him that it is Odysseus. He certainly seems to be less tall than Agamemnon but has a broader chest and shoulders.

This impression is supported by the Dardanian king Antenor, whom Menelaos and Odysseus visited with a view to getting Helen back. He says that Menelaos was the bigger, but when they sat down Odysseus appeared the more august. So in the *Iliad* he is viewed as stocky. The gestures he uses in important situations in which he is to speak are striking and say something interesting about his inner life. For while the taller Menelaos chatters away, Odysseus in his characteristic way sticks to the matter in hand, as quoted above (p. 80). There, it is described how he rises from his chair, stares ahead while clasping the staff in his hand, so that it might be thought he were a fool or a madman. However, once he starts speaking, no one can match his oratory. In this context, he is moreover characterized by his most frequent epithet *polymetis*, which indicates that his argumentational power has its source in his intelligence, which makes him capable of twisting and adding meanings according to all the rules of the game.

Even though this is conceived as an illustration of his intellectual capacity, it is surprising that, at the beginning of his speech, he is portrayed as a madman. In Greek, the word used is *aphrona* (III, 220), which in a literal translation means "gone out of his senses." The intention must be thus to describe the way a person looks when he not only speaks on the basis of his own reason but expresses himself under some superior inspiration, as did the prophets, sibyls and poets. We can sense he is waiting for the right words, the inspiration, just as when he is about to tell the Phaiakians about his adventures and hesitantly asks himself where he should start and finish.

There is the profounder significance here that the Greeks quite literally viewed inspiration as a form of madness. Both as a popular speaker and a storyteller, Odysseus is caught in the magical power of the word. So in the *Iliad*, his speeches are compared to a snowstorm: "the words came drifting down like the winter snows" (III, 221-22). We also hear how the Phaiakians sit flabbergasted during his tale, "all of them stayed stricken to silence,/ held in thrall by the story" (11, 333-34), while Eumaios the shepherd describes him as a poet who has received his gift of song from the gods (17, 519). And he tricks the Kyklops with honeyed words (9, 363).

If we return to Odysseus' outward appearance, he is not described in the *Odyssey* as short-legged. When he escorts Nausikaa into town, he is, to the contrary, described as a "large and handsome stranger" (6, 276). His splendid head of hair is attributed with various colors. When Athene changes him back from being a bald man (18, 355), his beard is said to be black and curly (16, 176). On the other hand, his hair is light blond (13, 429)—i.e., the color of hair the long-haired Greeks ideally had. In his long locks, Odysseus is frequently depicted in pictures wearing a so-called *pilos*, a pointed felt cap that seamen and several gods have on their heads. His skin is smooth and swarthy or sunburnt (16, 175).

Despite his ageing, his skin is still smooth and glistening and his limbs supple (13, 428) when he comes home. In order to erase his masculine appearance, Athene must consequently make him wrinkled and clothe him in rags. His shoulders are broad and strong (18, 67), his arms sinewy, as is revealed when he tucks up his rags before the eyes of the terrified beggar Iros whom he is to fight. According to Athene, both he and Telemachos have "fine eyes" (1, 208), and she makes his eyes red in order to hide their glinting beauty and strength (13, 431). When he becomes angry, he raises his eyebrows, tosses his head (9, 468) and furrows his brow, as, for example, during the slaughter of the suitors (21, 431), to send meaningful signals to his companions.

3

When the epithet *polymetis* is used to describe his speaking abilities, it is to indicate that his intelligence has a free rein in this, just as this epithet links him exclusively with Athene, which is why she uses him as her mouthpiece. On their meeting in Ithaka, she praises those aspects of his intellectual nature that point towards herself. He is, as she puts it, soft of speech, keen of wit, and prudent (13, 332).

Not only does Homer share this assessment, but he places Odysseus on a level with Zeus himself—"the equal of Zeus in counsel" (II, 169). Not as a warrior does he acquire the immortal reputation that all heroes struggle to attain, but precisely through his reason by thinking the war through strategically to its conclusion with the Wooden Horse. And it is against the background of this stroke of genius that he reveals his identity to the Phaiakians "known before men/ for the study of crafty designs (*dolos*)" (9, 19-20).

His entire being is permeated by *dolos*, a cunning that is bolstered during his voyage on account of all the dangers he encounters and must master. He is always on guard, searching, suspicious. Athene is amused by him when she meets him on his arrival at Ithaka and he immediately indulges in all manner of fabrications. She sees confirmation of their deep kinship in this: "It would be a sharp one, and a stealthy one, who would ever get past you/in any contriving; even if it were a god against you" (13, 291-92).

Odysseus does not get his cunning from strangers. Its genetic source can, as we heard, be traced back to his grandfather Autolykos. It has the result that he is always the subject of suspicion and hatred, even among his own in the *Iliad*. A master in the "ways of treachery" (IV, 339) Agamemnon called him, just as Agamemnon in the *Odyssey* characterizes his murderous wife with the same choice of words "with thoughts surpassingly grisly" (11, 432).

Seen from the viewpoint of the heroic, it is impossible not to think precisely of the feminine in relation to cunning and the negative assessment of it. It is said that female cunning is the strongest weapon in the world. And the two female characters who are supremely skilful at employing this strategy are Penelope, who uses cunning to keep her husband, and Klytemnestra, who does the same to kill hers. Women use cunning for at least two reasons. First, because they do not have a man's physique. Secondly, their insight is based on the fact that they are not at one with the male world of action. They can contemplate it from without and then devise their schemes in relation to the motives that make a man act more or less consciously— especially the latter. In this way, Klytemnestra in the *Oresteia* can manipulate Agamemnon through his vanity to his death.

The most violent reaction to Odysseus comes not surprisingly from Achilleus. From his heroic point of view, cunning, not to mention deception, is contemptible—"I detest that man, who/ hides one thing in the depths of his heart, and speaks forth another" (IX, 312-13). He himself only knows of battle, face to face with the enemy, in the front rank (*promos aner*). Yet, even though a hero like Achilleus must idiosyncratically reject cunning as a strategy, the ambush and the lie are nevertheless accepted as weapons to be employed in battle and for survival.

While spying out in Book X of the *Iliad*, for instance, Odysseus would never have been able to lure the truth out of the captured enemy Dolon, if he had not first, against his better knowledge, promised to spare his life. Nor would he have saved his own life and those of his men, if he had not tricked the Kyklops with lies and deception.

Without diminishing its dubious aspect, there is a clear consensus that it is permitted to use cunning to harm your enemy, to save yourself and your own people in an uncertain, hostile and in many ways incomprehensible world. Nor does Athene refrain from lying when in the shape of Mentes she promises Telemachos to "accurately answer all that you ask me" (1, 179), whereupon she makes him believe a direct lie. And likewise, in his stories to the swineherd and Penelope, Odysseus freely mingles fact and fiction—"false things that were like true sayings" (19, 203).

To lie is to speak in disguise, to say one thing and mean another. So disguise fits naturally into Odysseus' repertoire of stratagems. As opposed to "pure" heroes, he does not recoil from disguise and misrepresentation, with the humiliation that potentially lies in such behaviour when compared with the norms for genuinely heroic behavior. For example, he sneaks into Troy after having whipped himself into bloody unrecognizability and dressing in rags like a slave.

Of course, the clearest example of this is the transformation he undergoes with Athene's intervention. Not only is it a condition for regaining his kingdom, but these constant metamorphoses become a concrete demonstration of his polytropic capacity. Dressed up as a beggar, he can spy incognito on his enemies, the suitors, which is necessary if he is to make plans. At the same time, as part of the testing of his endurance and self-control, he must withstand humiliation at the hands of the suitors, until he has come up with a master plan and can mercilessly emerge from his rags with the radiance of a god.

4

Just as Odysseus tries to ensure his reputation by cunning, he tries like the other heroes to increase his wealth, since possessions (*olbos*), along with heroic deeds, increase one's repute. He says to the Phaiakian king that he would gladly die if only he could see his possessions again: "let life leave me when I have once more/ seen my property, my serving people, and my great high-roofed house" (7, 224-25). Not a word about his wife. To Kalypso, however, he says the reason for his homesickness is his longing to be reunited with Penelope.

Moreover, in this speech of thanks to the Phaiakians, it appears that it gives power and prestige to have great possessions: "there would be much advantage/ in coming back with a fuller hand to my own dear country,/ and I would be more respected so and be more popular/ with all people who say I make my return to Ithaka" (11, 358-61). In order to ensure that no one steals from him the gifts made to him by the Phaiakians, which far exceed what he lost during his voyage, he binds them with a magic knot he learned from Kirke. So the first thing he does on awakening in Ithaka, is check his belongings, suspicious that the Phaiakians might have stolen his treasure—"Let me count my goods and find out whether they might not/ have gone taking some of it with them in a hollow vessel" (13, 215-16), he says, beside himself at the thought of perhaps having been robbed. But he still has everything and with Athene's help he hides his precious belongings in a sacred grotto.

On his departure from Ithaka, Odysseus was already powerful with "an endlessly abundant livelihood" (14, 96), as the swineherd tells the unrecognizable Odysseus, and recites the nature of this wealth as being more than what twenty rich men own together, including various forms of cattle. Since Ithaka is a mountainous region, it is natural that wealth should be calculated in terms of heads of cattle. At the same time, this calculation reflects an economy in which value was not yet created by land. Together with cattle, slaves of both sexes were the measure of value.

In other words, owning large possessions meant power and honor: in itself, a reason why the Greeks sought—partly through piracy corresponding to the expeditions of the Vikings—to make themselves ever greater and stronger through wealth. For this also meant influence, since, through power-based wealth, people could make good marriages and acquire good guest friends—"good" in the sense of rich and powerful. As in the Nordic sagas, it was only by virtue of such alliances that it was possible to defend yourself, your family and your kingdom. Odysseus is no exception, even though his apparent greediness seems to conflict with his piety.

5

I said earlier that, by participating in sacrificial festivals on his arrival in Pylos, Telemachos is introduced to an important aspect of his father's personal character, his piety. This might seem strange in view of his cunning. Nevertheless, he is presented as a man who observes all religious ceremonies. He is also sociable—something that does not exactly characterize the other heroes, who mainly think of and seek their own honor and achievements.

With the exception of Poseidon, Odysseus also enjoys the favor of all the gods. As Zeus puts it, this is because he "beyond others/ has given sacrifice to the gods, who hold wide heaven" (1, 66-67). And as his nurse Eurykleia confirms, no one has sacrificed so many hecatombs to Zeus, although Zeus persecuted him most of all despite his "godly spirit" (19, 364). During his journey, he never neglects to thank the gods for their help. With his knowledge of the vicissitudes of life, he knows the importance of keeping on good terms with the gods and not, like the suitors, arrogantly challenging them. For the same reason, after the suitors have been killed, he charges Eurykleia to tone down her gloating and jubilation.

Homer does not himself seek to establish a psychological link between the qualities attributed to a person. However, there must be some internal connection between Odysseus' piety and the gentleness and justice he displays as king to his subjects. There is no reference to this side of his character in the *Iliad*, but throughout the *Odyssey* many very different characters stress how, as opposed to the suitors, he deals as king with those around him with unfailing fatherly concern: "a noble father, one who/ was king once over you here, and was kind to you like a father" (2, 46-47) and rules his realm "kind, like a father" (2, 234). So Telemachos cannot understand that the suitors, whom Odysseus in many instances has known since they were small and whose families he has helped, can persist in their behavior. Penelope also rebukes the suitors by stressing what Odysseus has done for their relatives:

(. . .) he did no act and spoke no word in his own country
that was unfair; and that is a way divine kings have, one
will be hateful to a certain man, and favor another,
but Odysseus was never outrageous at all to any man.

(4, 690-93)

Eumaios, the swineherd, says how merciful he is: "for never again now/ will I find again a lord as kind as he" (14, 138-39), not even if he were to return to the home of his fathers. Indeed, in her plea to the assembly of the gods for Odysseus' salvation, Athene goes so far as to make him a guarantor of royal conduct. If he is not saved, it will have consequences for gods and men: "No longer now let one who is a sceptered king be eager/ to be gentle and kind, be one whose thought is schooled in justice" (5, 8-9). The meaning of this lies in the fact that the king on earth represents the power of the gods.

Odysseus himself provides a clear piece of evidence that he possesses this piety. During his journey to Hades, he meets Ajax, whom he defeated in the contest for Achilleus' weapons. This defeat drove Ajax out of his mind so that, deluded by Athene, he killed a flock of sheep in the belief that it was Odysseus and then, out of shame, committed suicide. When Odysseus now sees him again, Ajax refuses to greet him or respond to him. Full of regret, Odysseus exclaims: "I wish I had never won in a contest like this,/ so high a head has gone under the ground for the sake of that armor" (11, 548-49). With this utterance, he expresses a hitherto unknown way of thinking that understands the necessity of placing consideration of another person higher than the code of honor on which the contest for the weapons was based. That this is a breakthrough for a different way of thinking is stressed by the fact that, by contrast, even in death Ajax has obstinately shut himself within heroism's inviolable and narrow-minded concept of honor.

This is yet further evidence that the *Odyssey* and its hero betoken a breach with the *Iliad*'s heroic universe—and point the way forward. For, as will be seen later, with this characterization of Odysseus as an alternative to a narrow code of honor as well as unaccountable rulers who are always shifting their sympathies, Homer has prepared the way for making Odysseus into an ideal king and model for his own social utopia.

6

Of course, Odysseus is not connected directly to the concept of *sophrosyne*, as was Telemachos (see p. 143), but the whole of his conduct is linked to the ideas later applied to it. When the concept really broke through as a moral guide in the 5th century's mode of thinking, not least in the tragedies, he also becomes a primary exponent of this phenomenon—for example, in Sophocles' drama on Ajax. Ajax' insane *hubris* is in stark contrast to Odysseus' *sophrosyne* and related words that have connotations of moderation and hark back to his behaviour in Homer: reason, common sense and, especially, self-control.[7]

In comparison with the *Iliad*, Odysseus' conduct also stands in glaring contrast to the blind, arrogant wrath to which Agamemnon and Achilleus are subject and which in the *Odyssey* is represented by Aigisthos and the conceited suitors' blasphemous behavior. In the following, we shall consider several examples of Odysseus' moderation and ability to make choices, combined with an incipient introspection—characteristics that are certainly present in the *Iliad* but not developed completely until the *Odyssey*—in accordance with the different forms of consciousness in the two works.

We have an example of Odysseus' reserve during the games at Patroklos' funeral, when he declines to participate in the archery contest (XXIII, 850 ff.), since he had already won a race and apparently did not want to incur the envy of the other warriors—or the gods. He certainly did not hold back from trumpeting his reputation to the Phaiakians, but he immediately objects when—after Athene's beauty treatment—they take him for a god: "I am not/ in any way like the immortals who hold wide heaven" (7, 208-09). He looks like and is a human being.

No, one must not challenge Fate or be arrogant, since experience shows that life has its ups and downs. "Of all creatures that breathe and walk on the earth there is nothing/ more helpless than a man is, of all that the earth fosters" (18, 1301-02), Odysseus warns at the sight of the suitors' uninhibited greed and senseless *hubris*. When things are going well, people never think that bad times will ever come. However, as soon as adversity arrives, people fret and bear it sullenly. So one should not cast aspersions on sacred laws, "but take in silence the gifts of the gods, whatever they give him" (18, 142). This is the pure doctrine of *sophrosyne*, even though Odysseus does not use the word.

Only once does he himself cross this boundary—when, despite the terrified warnings of his crew, he mocks Polyphemos by revealing his true identity. Here, he is clearly unable to control his offended sense of self-esteem but for years must pay the price for his self-promotion in the form of Poseidon's hatred and persecution. Otherwise, he is always awake, on his guard against the gods and, particularly, his fickle crew—in order to bring them and himself safely home.

As opposed to everyone else, he has apparently understood that delusion (*ate*) is a consequence of the subject's inability to fathom his own motives and choices. We find evidence in both the *Iliad* and the *Odyssey* of Odysseus' discursive awareness, his ability and will to consider a matter to the depths of his mind. However, since Homer has no narrative mastery of the inner monologue, the dialogues Odysseus conducts with himself take place with his *thymos*—"And troubled, he spoke then to his own great-hearted spirit" (XI, 403; 5, 464), as it is put. It is characteristic of his ability to reflect and his sense of situation that, even in great difficulty, he is capable of weigh-

ing different alternatives and making his decision on the basis of mature consideration: "Ah me, what will become of me? It will be a great evil/ if I run, fearing their
multitude, yet deadlier if I am caught/ alone" (XI, 404-06).

Since it was explained earlier how *thymos* works in Homer (see p. 54), I will
content myself here with quoting only one further example of how, in a stressful
situation, he asks himself dialectically for answers from his *thymos*. During his shipwreck off the island of the Phaiakians, he is offered help by the sea nymph
Leukothea. However, since he can never feel secure when faced with divine forces,
he is seized by his usual suspicion: "Ah me, which of the immortals is weaving
deception/ against me" (5, 356-57). A debate for and against then follows. The narrative focus is always directed inward, so as readers we feel that we know his
thoughts from the inside.

From these considerations, it may be ascertained, first of all, that he is not a
spineless tool of his emotions. Secondly, that as far as is possible within the
Homeric story, some kind of self-reflection is predominant. The highest level of this
process of development would be an introspection in which the physical manifestations of the self (*thymos, psyche, nous*) are gathered into a psychological whole.

Interestingly enough, the passage in which Odysseus is nearly carried away by
almost ungovernable indignation is also that in which, under colossal emotional
pressure, he delves most deeply into his inner life. A new mentality emerges here,
the like of which is not found in the *Iliad*. The intense agitation is caused by the
sight of the giggling maidservants, who are whoring with the suitors:

> But the spirit deep in the heart of Odysseus was stirred by this,
> And much he pondered in the division of mind and spirit,
> Whether to spring on them and kill each one, or rather
> To let them lie this one more time with the insolent suitors,
> For the last and latest time; but the heart was growling within him.
> And as a bitch, facing an unknown man, stands over
> Her callow puppies, and growls and rages to fight, so Odysseus'
> Heart was growling inside him as he looked on these wicked actions.
> He struck himself on the chest and spoke to his heart and scolded it:
> 'Bear up, my heart. You have had worse to endure before this
> on that day when the irresistible Kyklops ate up
> my strong companions, but you endured it until intelligence
> got you out of the cave, though you expected to perish.'
> So he spoke, addressing his own dear heart within him;
> And the heart in great obedience endured and stood it
> Without complaint, but the man *himself* was twisting and turning.
>
> (20, 9-24, my italics)

Despite the torrent of feelings stirred in Odysseus—which in its extensive psychosomatic register influences later writers, in Sappho among others, as a way to

portray powerful emotions—the point is that he can distinguish this from his mental processes. Of course he must beat his heart into place, but he is in control of it just as he resisted Helen's alluring voice in the Wooden Horse. And as he reprovingly says to the Phaiakian king when he flares up at Nausikaa's failure to bring Odysseus to him immediately: "For we who are people upon this earth are jealous in judgment" (7, 307).

Odysseus does not let himself be deluded or lose his self-control. On the contrary, he demonstrates that he is or has a *self*, stressed by the word *autos* in line 24. He is more than the corporal reality and physical impulses that Homer has described with immense suggestive power with the image of the heart as a growling dog. And the groundbreaking significance of the passage over the long run is marked by the fact that Socrates often returns to this quotation as a model of dialectical self-mastery.

7

As a particularly illustrative example of Odysseus' understanding of the necessity of controlling physical needs, we can take his apparent obsession with food and the importance of the stomach.

Ever since antiquity, all his talk of food has led to his being caricatured as a man with a potbelly, a glutton. This view is unsatisfactory for several reasons. Apart from their warfare, Greek heroes, generally speaking, seem to concern themselves with little other than food and drink. They meet their friends over food; they offer hospitality to strangers with food. However, if Odysseus speaks so much about food and the demands of the stomach, it is because he knows its problematic power. He has, so to speak, objectivized the stomach as an organ controlling and motivating people, seeing through it just as he has understood desire and showed himself able to control it inside the Wooden Horse.

The motif is taken up already in the *Illiad* in connection with what is to be the true test of strength between Achilleus and Odysseus, their boasting match, which at the same time contrasts a heroic self-understanding with long-term common sense. It happens after Patroklos' death when Achilleus insists on throwing the army into battle to avenge the shame, despite the fact that the warriors have had nothing to eat or drink. As he emphatically points out, he could not himself force down a bite of food: "Food and drink mean nothing to my heart/ but blood does, and slaughter" (XIX, 213-14). The army must wait to eat until the sun has gone down.

Odysseus alone opposes this on the basis of his understanding of the elemental significance of nourishment for the warriors' capacity. A hero cannot function without food and drink, is his reaction translated briefly. No one can fight from morning to night without food. The legs of a thirsty and hungry army will buckle. They will simply be massacred, whereas the warriors will be able to win if they are well fed and strengthened. He forces through this point of view as an order by referring, as we heard before, to the fact that Achilleus may be physically stronger but is dwarfed in comparison with him in terms of the sagacity deriving from the experience resulting from age (see p. 50).

It might be said that, when Achilleus yields to Odysseus' argument and command, reason has triumphed over heroic blindness. Yet, this does not only demonstrate Odysseus' intellectual force but also Homer's relativization of heroic ideals, as Achilleus impulsively, without reflection, wants to send the army to its death and thus act with the same delusion that was behind his anger and thus the cause of his friend's death.

So, whereas Odysseus gives the stomach its due in the *Iliad*, he seems in the *Odyssey* to be almost disgusted at this organ's power over human beings.[8] For he has observed that the stomach always makes demands, regardless of circumstances. Though sorrow oppresses him, he requires some time to eat before he tells the Phaiakians who he is. But he is capable of talking about these base demands in precise terms. He distinguishes them from himself as in this simultaneous revelation, admission and renunciation:

> For there is no other thing so shameless as to be set over
> The belly, but she rather uses constraint and makes me think of her,
> Even when sadly worn, when in my heart I have sorrow
> As now I have sorrow in my heart, yet still forever
> She tells me to eat and drink and forces me to forgetfulness
> Of all I have suffered, and still she is urgent that I must fill her.
>
> (7, 216-21)

Odysseus further explains how hard it is for a man to wander off, because he must suffer great evils for the sake of his "cursed stomach" (*oulomenes gastros*, 15, 343). Or perhaps it ought rather to be translated as that, a man must endure all manner of hardships for the sake of his stomach. At any rate, it is this thought that is expressed in the surprising concept of the stomach's civilizational significance. For, as he indicates elsewhere, it is ultimately to satisfy the "ravenous belly,/ a cursed thing" (17, 286-87) that men sail out on commercial expeditions and plundering raids that bring death and destruction. Nothing can stop the stomach, once it has begun to rage, he claims in his statements, which from a historical perspective seem to reflect the experience of the Greeks in their colonial expansion. In the *Kyklops*, Euripides also notices how primitive this drive emanating from the belly really is, since he has the Kyklops make his stomach and digestion his highest god—"These I sacrifice to no one but myself—never to the gods—and to my belly, the greatest of divinities."[9]

It is these alarming reflections on the demands of the stomach that have given Odysseus his reputation as a man who is inanely subject to physical needs. The question is whether this almost ideological critique of the stomach's influence may not ultimately be ascribed to the author, an influence that stretches from the instinctive behavior of the animal to human civilization.

So when, on his arrival at the island of the Phaiakians, Odysseus is compared to a lion, it is related that a lion is driven to hunt by the force of the belly—"his belly is urgent upon him" (6, 133). By its very nature, this description can only belong to a superior narrator, since the image is his. However, he lets the description merge into a corresponding observation on the human level, when Menelaos and Odysseus describe how the hunger of their men forces them to seek food—"always the hunger oppressed their bellies" (4, 369; 12, 332), as it is put formulaically. This makes Menelaos' men fish with crooked hooks, while Odysseus' crew slaughter the oxen of the sun god.

Just as we will hear later how Socrates has elevated himself above the demands of the body and the senses, we can ascertain that, as a sign of insight and mental strength, Odysseus is able to master himself. During the fateful events on the sun god's island, he can, in contrast to his men, resist the demands of his stomach and endure hunger. By taking an oath, that is to say through the most sacred action conceivable, he has tried to tether the hunger pangs of his starving men. Nevertheless, since he dare not trust them and their instinctual behavior, which revealed itself on several previous occasions (for instance, among the Lotus Eaters), he remains awake as long as he can. But as soon as he falls asleep, his crew forget all their promises and literally eat themselves to death in that, as punishment for their offense, they drown at the behest of the sun god.

Hence, Odysseus becomes the only survivor—despite his persistent attempts to bring his crew safely home, which confirms the assumption that the reality of the stomach belongs to the lowest part of the instinctual world and governs mankind if it has not become aware of this reality. From this angle, the journey becomes an image of how a human being can only survive through awareness and a will to control the senses and their desires. At the same time, this problematizes the assessment of Odysseus as food-fixated.

8

If Odysseus were to be translated into some recognizable psychological concept, it would be strength of will. It is by virtue of his strength of will that he can rise above gnawing hunger on the island of the sun god and keep himself awake for periods far in excess of what can be expected of a normal human being. And it is this very same will that gives him the epithet *polytlas*, long-suffering. This strength of will is ultimately the reason why he returns home. As a character trait, will is represented in a very visual form. When he forbids his crew to go ashore on Thrinakia, the island of the sun god, Odysseus' worst enemy Eurylochos says, "Your limbs never wear out. You must be made all of iron (*siderea*)" (12, 280).

It does not appear directly from this situation how Odysseus' strength of will is formed and that it is actually based on self-control. But this is revealed in one of the most moving scenes of the *Odyssey* when (dressed as a beggar) he is reunited with Penelope and makes her weep by relating his (mendacious) story of his encounter with Odysseus. He is deeply touched by his wife's grief: "His eyes stayed, as if they were made of horn or iron/ steady under his lids. He hid his tears and deceived her" (19, 211-12). His ability to control his emotions can hardly be described more clearly. Here he sits, after a twenty-year absence from his beloved, whom he has longed to see all those years, and he becomes the cause of her tears but controls himself, preparing himself for the impending slaughter of the suitors.

In order to show the unyielding strength of the man's will, Homer employs the wonderful new metal called iron metaphorically in several passages. For example, the dying Hektor says of the merciless Achilleus: "in your breast is a heart of iron" (XXII, 357). Likewise, it is said of Zeus that he has a heart of iron (XXIV, 295). This stands in contrast to Kalypso, who at Odysseus' suspicion exclaims that she will let him go, since "I have no spirit/ of iron inside my heart" (5, 190-92). Finally, mirroring the previous quotation, Telemachos says that nothing can save his father from death—"not even if he had a heart of iron within him" (4, 293). He has not yet grasped the extent of his father's psychological strength.

With a heart of iron, Odysseus is capable of enduring the vicissitudes of Fate, of enduring what he himself calls "strong compulsion" (*anangke*, 10, 273). Strong compulsion forces him to step naked before Nausikaa (6, 136) and after "much suffering" (6, 176) to seek protection with her mother, the Phaiakian queen. At his mother's inquiry as to why he came to the realm of the dead, he responds: "a duty brought me here" (11, 164).

Even during the siege of Troy, he understood this necessity as an existential condition. He knows the nature of homesickness from his own experience: "it is a hard thing, to be grieved with desire for going" (II, 291). The longing for his wife drives him. But at the same time he understands the burdensome necessity of the duty to successfully conduct the war to its bitter end. To return home empty-handed and without honor would be too great a shame.

To a remarkable extent, Odysseus is a person who patiently bears the trials of Fate. So like no one else he becomes a model for the philosophy expressed by Apollo in the concluding book of the *Iliad*: "for the Destinies put in mortal men the heart of endurance" (XXIV, 49).

When Kalypso tries one final time to hold Odysseus back by offering him the prospect of immortality, he is also ready to suffer shipwreck once more in order to reach his homeland: "And if some god batters me far out on the wine-blue water,/ I will endure it, keeping a stubborn spirit inside me" (5, 221-22). Similarly, he declares himself ready to withstand the humiliations of the suitors, when the swineherd warns him against searching them out; for, as he says: "The spirit in me is enduring, since I have suffered much hardship/ on the waves and in the fighting" (17, 284-85).

That Odysseus obviously bears a heavy fate, heavier than anyone else, emerges from the fact that he is attributed several times with the epithet "poor" (*kammoros*,

5, 160), where the term "poor" certainly implies someone suffering a harsh fate. In his touching encounter with his dead mother, she exclaims: "Oh my child, ill-fated beyond all other mortals" (11, 216). When Athene finally comes to rescue him upon his arrival at Ithaka, she speaks of "all the troubles you are destined to suffer" (13, 307) and says how "you must endure/ much grief in silence" (13, 310). Indeed, it must be said on Odysseus' behalf that he has already done that for twenty years. Odysseus pulls through because necessity and a will of steel are linked together in his being.

Homer does not extract a direct philosophy of life from his fate, not in the way the later Greek tragedies do from harsh human destinies. Aeschylus speaks of learning to know life through suffering, *pathei mathos*—"wisdom/ comes alone through suffering."[10] We meet this sort of figure in Sophocles' *Oedipus the King*, who in the tenacity with which he endures his misfortune is not unlike Odysseus. So if personal development and insight come through suffering, here, too, Odysseus becomes a prefiguration and model for that path of experience, not only during his journey but also when he arrives home. Reduced to the status of a beggar in his own house, spat upon like Jesus, he must rise from nothing to reassume his royal power.

9

Along with the most frequently used epithet *polymetis*, the word *polymechanos* belongs to the description of Odysseus, although it does not appear with the same frequency. These two concepts meet, as I have indicated earlier, in a zone of almost synonymous meaning as they are both connected to his unique power of spirit and intelligence, which is once again a premise for his inventiveness and cunning. But there must be a difference.

Polymetis is inclined toward the rational, corresponding to the verbal form of the word meaning to think and decide—i.e., to make a choice. On the other hand, *polymechanos* places more emphasis on the purely concrete, corresponding to the fundamental meaning of the verb (to implement ingeniously—whether applying to machines for use in war or the theater), while also conveying a sense of cunning and wiles. As a consequence of the gradations of meaning between these two words, Athene is both the deity of wisdom and weaving, while the god of the forge Hephaistos bears the epithet *polymetis* in the *Iliad* while Kirke's schemes may be called *polymechanos* (23, 321).

As *polymechanos*, Odysseus is able to apply his reason to a number of practical things that require great skill. When he is finally granted leave to sail from Kalypso's island, he knows how to build a ship. He chops down and trims twenty trees and "planed them expertly, and trued them straight to a chalkline" (5, 245). He is like "a man well skilled in carpentry" (5, 250), making the sails, fashioning the mast and finishing the ship. Then, as skipper, he is capable of navigating by the constellations Pleiades, the Bear and Orion until Poseidon has him suffer a shipwreck.

It is also a crucial point for the entire *Odyssey* that he has with his own hands and skills made his marriage bed from gold, silver and ivory, built from a tree stump on the spot, as that is the secret of its craftsmanship by which Penelope tests him. Mechanical skills are thus crucial to Odysseus' survival and make it possible for him to translate his intelligence into concrete tasks. Insofar as he is viewed as an archetypal subject who realizes his full human potential, he becomes the first example demonstrating that such activity requires both mind and hand.

Mother and Son

1

In Homer, the genealogical lineage acquires symbolic visibility in that a son is named patronymically after his father. Odysseus is often called Laertiad or "son of Laertes" after King Laertes, Achilleus Peleid after his father, King Peleus, etc. When the Greeks are to be informed of something in their war camp, it happens in the same way: "Call out wherever you go, and waken each man to give him/ your orders, naming him by descent with the name of his father" (X, 67-68). It is almost self-evident that, through the patronymic, the father insists upon his identity in the son as a sign that he is the source of his son, while in a matrilineal society sons were without fathers, conceived anonymously as the mothers' children alone. The patronymic is a countermeasure to female culture, its power and sexuality; for as the father claims his right in the naming, he stresses at the same time that he has liberated himself, which is what he wishes his son to do—in order to become a father himself.

Among the Greeks, genealogical lineage did not go nearly so far back as it did, for example, in the Bible. As a rule, it extends at most over three generations (see p. 348), where each link is calculated at an average life expectancy of thirty years. (However, the most important families from a mythical perspective, those linked to the royal houses in Mycenae and Thebes, have a longer and more convoluted genealogy).

In terms of society, genealogy determines a person's property and rank. In itself, the family is a small, closed circle, as can clearly be sensed in the case of Odysseus. The family (*oikos*) consists of the closest family members, including in-laws, which is why marital arrangements were of great importance for acquiring strong allies. In addition, guest friends were counted among the family's allies, to whom there were mutual obligations. This was also of great importance, since, as it emerges in the *Odyssey*, the power to rule was not a privilege granted automatically. As the flock of suitors shows, there was always someone waiting in the wings to take advantage when the family revealed its weakness and a power vacuum arose.

So, beyond identifying the affiliation of an individual with a family, an affiliation more important than the mere subjective sense of belonging, the patronymic must also express a magical wish for a son to inherit his father's brilliant characteristics so that he is capable of continuing the family and preferably even enhancing its possessions and destiny. But as Athene says in order to provoke Telemachos, sons can only rarely live up to their fathers: "For few are the children who turn out to be equals of their fathers" (2, 276). She says this both because it is a fundamental fact and to spur Telemachos into proving that, as the son of Odysseus, he is also capable of defending his father's realm by sustaining his identity

As in so many other things in life, Odysseus is in an unusual position, since he clearly outshines his father and has already taken power, while the latter is still alive. The reason why Laertes abdicated his throne is one of the unsolved mysteries of scholarship, especially as it must have happened while he was still in his prime. Likewise, it is impossible to understand why he was not able to rule in his son's place during his absence. The most frequent explanation is quite simply that his situation reflects the miserable state of affairs. However, this interpretation still does not explain why he stepped down in favor of his son—who, through his own father Arkeisios, is the grandchild of Zeus himself.

Nothing is known of Arkeisios. However, from what is said, we may deduce that Laertes is actually an example of a son failing to measure up to his father. At all events, it seems to be Odysseus who from some point has ensured the continuity of the family which is now threatened with annihilation if Telemachos is killed. That Telemachos must leave also reveals that Laertes has failed as a father figure.

The hidden link that seems to exist between Laertes' inadequacy and Odysseus' strength is to be found, I think, in the same place, that is to say in Antikleia, the wife of Laertes and mother of Odysseus. This hidden connection is only gradually revealed, but we may provisionally say that Laertes has been too much his wife's husband, while Odysseus has to a high degree profited from being his mother's son. On closer consideration, it appears that Odysseus' fundamental identity is determined on the basis of his matrilineal inheritance. In this, he resembles Achilleus, who is also primarily his mother's son, since he is descended from a goddess who is clearly superior to her earthly spouse.[11]

2

One of the most moving passages in the *Odyssey* is the meeting between Odysseus and his late mother in Hades. The first time she approaches the sacrificial blood that is necessary to return life and consciousness to a dead person, Odysseus has to keep her back because Teiresias must be the first to drink so as to provide him with information about the dangers awaiting him.

Then, Antikleia steps forward again and has hardly drunk "the dark-clouding blood" (11, 153) before wailing on recognizing her son. But, of course, she cannot understand what he is doing in this mournful place that is so difficult to reach. In reply, he refers to a "duty" (11, 164) to which he is subject. To his question about conditions at home, she informs him that Penelope still lives in the palace, though she is burdened with care; power has not yet slipped away from him, and

Telemachos is tilling the fields. She also tells him of Laertes' wretched state, living far from the city in a hut, where, weakened with age, he mourns the loss of his son. She herself has died, not from disease, but because of the loss of her son: "It was my longing for you, your cleverness/ and your gentle ways, that took the sweet spirit of life from me" (11, 202-03). Odysseus makes to embrace his mother; but, shade as she now is, he tries in vain three times, only to grasp a void, "nothing but an image" (11, 214), parted from life and limb as the dead are after cremation, when only the breath of the psyche is sent, unconscious, to Hades.

3

The reunion scene in Hades does itself not provide any explanation of the feelings binding mother and son. A key to their deep relationship is to be found in another reunion scene—when, on arriving home, Odysseus is recognized by his old nurse, Eurykleia.

At Penelope's command, she is to wash his feet, a ritual gesture to a welcome guest. Odysseus withdraws into the darkness, well aware that his nurse will recognise him by the scar he incurred as a young man from a wild boar during a hunt with his grandfather Autolykos. And he is right. When the nurse touches the scar, she knows whose foot she is holding in her hand. But instead of describing her feelings, the recognition evokes a flashback-like description of this event, which comes to stand as a huge parenthesis or linguistic delay before the nurse's emotions are described. At the same time, Eurykleia is used compositionally as a link between past and present.

On the basis of this scene, Erich Auerbach claims in *Mimesis* that Homer has no understanding of background depth or the creation of suspense.[12] However, instead of viewing it, like Auerbach, as a clumsily put, superficial, idyllic description, I would claim on the contrary that Homer here provides the true key to Odysseus' identity. It comes not from his paternal grandfather Arkeisios but from his maternal grandfather Autolykos. As stated above, it is he who names him, just as it is with him that Odysseus undergoes the trauma of his youth on the wild boar hunt— acquiring the scar by which he can always subsequently be recognized.

So this digression is the moment of truth, the *anagnorisis* to which Aristotle points as the dramatic turning point in a tragedy. A momentary recognition evokes a profounder understanding as this almost mythical dimension in Odysseus' identity is revealed in relation to his grandfather's dubious personality. For when Autolykos came to Ithaka on the occasion of Odysseus' birth, Eurykleia placed the child in his lap and asked him to name his grandson: "Autolykos, now find yourself that name you will bestow/ on your own child's dear child, for you have prayed much to have him" (19, 403-04).

Eurykleia hands the newborn child to Autolykos because, as she says, he has had special expectations relating to the birth of his grandson. That she wishes Odysseus to be called "the much prayed for" (*polyaretos*) may have two meanings. First, she seems to hope that the child will bear the name Polyaretos—that is, a name derived from the word for longing for something, a not unusual ancient Greek name. Secondly, one might ask why he is so strongly desired. As in so many cases, the text does not provide a direct answer. The meaning must be found in a combination of statements scattered throughout the text.

It turns out that this family has been afflicted by the peculiar fate that every generation gives birth only to a single son and heir:

> For so it is that the son of Kronos made ours a single
> Line. Arkeisios had only a single son, Laertes,
> And Laertes had only one son, Odysseus; Odysseus in turn
> Left only one son, myself, in the halls, and got no profit
> Of me (. . .).

(16, 117-120)

It emerges that the words are those of Telemachos. This makes even more understandable the burden he justly feels rests upon his shoulders. As the only son, he must carry on his father's family—or it will die out. When he leaves, the swineherd also expresses this concern, because, as indeed is their intention, the suitors may kill him and "make Arkeisios'/ stock and seed perish all away" (14, 182). This fateful circumstance means that every male child in the family is awaited with great longing. That a girl child does not have the same status is underlined by the fact that Odysseus has sisters. And so the swineherd recalls that he was brought up with the youngest sister Ktimne (15, 362).

Meanwhile, Autolykos does as he himself wishes when he names the boy after himself and his troublesome and fate-laden identity. I have already said that Autolykos exposes his grandson to great trials in life by naming him after himself, but this requires a closer account of his own history. He is described as one "who surpassed all men/ in thievery (*kleptosyne*) and the art of the oath, and the god Hermes/ himself endowed him, for he had pleased him by burning the thigh bones/ of lambs and kids" (19, 395-97). But Homer merely says that Autolykos receives this gift from Hermes. Elsewhere, however, Hermes is made his father.[13] In order better to understand Autolykos' paternal heritage and thus Odysseus' background, I will summarize briefly the mythology of Hermes.

Hermes appears in so many different forms that one must assume that he existed before the "invention" of the Olympian gods. The remarkable thing is that, in connection with Autolykos, he displays aspects of his mythology that Homer does not otherwise make use of but which on the other hand are contained in the *Homeric Hymns* in his praise, which for this reason seem older than the Homeric epics. It is related here that, on the very day he was born, he revealed his qualities as a thieving and cunning trickster. He steals Apollo's cattle and hides the theft by making the cattle walk backwards to his cradle. This is discovered nevertheless, but he reconciles Apollo's wrath by presenting him with the lyre he has also invented.

These atavistic characteristics are passed on by Autolykos. But when they are taken over by Odysseus, they are raised to a higher level of consciousness, explicitly symbolized by his relationship with Athene. Meanwhile, with their wisdom and powers of interpretation both Athene and Hermes appear as his helpers, as was the case with Perseus when he killed Medusa. Thus, a hidden parallel is made when Hermes of his own accord comes to the aid of Odysseus when he is in mortal danger from Kirke. In the *Hymn to Hermes*, he is attributed with the epithet *polytropos*,[14] an epithet otherwise only applied to Odysseus and so a sign of their power of metamorphosis and their spiritual kinship.

In further order to highlight and illuminate the background to Odysseus' cunning, various authors in the tradition after Homer have linked him to Sisyphos, the wisest of them all, as the name possibly means. In his tragedy on the struggle between Ajax and Odysseus over Achilleus' armor, Sophocles calls Odysseus a bastard, because Sisyphos is supposed to have been his father by Antikleia: "Sisyphos' shameless offspring." Ovid follows suit by calling Odysseus "the son of Sisyphos, and similar to him in fraud and trickery." In both works, these words are spoken by Ajax.[15]

The explanation for Sisyphos' supposedly being Odysseus' father is to be found in the area of crime. For just as Hermes stole Apollo's cattle, his son Autolykos succeeded in stealing Sisyphos' livestock. According to a fragment of Hesiod, Autolykos had the ability to spirit things away from between his hands.[16] Sisyphos raped Antikleia in revenge—with Odysseus as the result. However, it is not because of this misdeed that Sisyphos must slave away in Hades' lowest region of Tartaros, where he must roll his cursed stone up a mountain for all eternity—only to have it roll down again.[17]

4

So at the naming ceremony, Autolykos invites his grandson Odysseus to visit him at his magnificent house at Parnassos when he has grown up. Here, he keeps many treasures of which he will give him a generous portion. In the hope of these gifts, Odysseus goes to visit his grandfather when he is old enough and is received by him and his sons (i.e., Odysseus' maternal uncles) with kind words and hearty handshakes. He also has a grandmother, called Amphithea. She, too, takes part in the hearty welcome, embraces him and kisses his cheeks and beautiful eyes. In all haste, a sumptuous and successful welcoming party is arranged.

The next morning, Odysseus goes hunting on Parnassos with his uncles. At the sound of the hunters, a wild boar—with glistening eyes and bristling hide—charges from a thicket so impenetrable and grotto-like that "[n]either could the force of wet-blown winds penetrate here,/ nor could the shining sun ever strike through with his rays, nor yet/ could the rain pass all the way through it, so close together/

it grew, with a fall of leaves drifted in dense profusion" (19, 440-43). As the fore-most, Odysseus rushes forward with his spear:

> (. . .) but too quick for him the boar drove
> over the knee, and with his tusk gashed much of the flesh,
> tearing sidewise, and did not reach the bone of the man. Now
> Odysseus stabbed at him, and hit him in the right shoulder,
> And straight on through him passed the point of the shining spearhead.
> He screamed and dropped in the dust, and the life spirit flittered from him.
>
> (19, 449-54)

His uncles bind his wounds and stay his black blood with incantations. When his wounds have healed, his grandfather sends him home, richly burdened with the promised gifts.

The insertion of this sequence of events into the otherwise highly realistic foot-washing ceremony seems to have the same feel of myth or fairy tale as Odysseus' experiences in the *Apologoi*. So his mother, with the father and brothers she has, belongs more in the realm of the fairy tale than Penelope, whose maternal bond with Telemachos is far more psychologically based than Odysseus' initiation and emancipation. Yet there is a parallel between the development of the father and the son, which reveals the same sort of basic narrative on both a mythical and a realistic plane. But the hermetic form of narrative characterizing Odysseus' myth makes it necessary to subject the text to an interpretative and emblematic reading.[18]

We can start out from the fact that Odysseus pays a visit to the grandfather who has invited him to do this at a time when he is able to test his heroic potential. He is in his late puberty—the expression in Greek is *hebe* (19, 410), corresponding to eighteen to twenty years old—thus, at a stage in his development when sexuality is to be definitively separated from the maternal in the broadest sense of the word. He is about to establish a male ego so strong that so he does not fall back into the symbiotic and undifferentiated world of his mother, which is so tempting in its care and omnipotence.

So the hunt itself becomes the great acid test for Odysseus. Here, it will be revealed whether he can liberate himself, standing face to face with (primal) maternal power now transfigured into the shape of a vengeful, destructive wild boar. As opposed to an Adonis, who did not manage the liberation but was killed by a charging wild boar, Odysseus succeeds in asserting his masculine identity and slaying the wild beast.[19] With this, the door is opened to his continuing story as a cultural hero comfortable with his own ego. That this is a combat of archetypal scope and danger appears from the fact that from this battle to his dying day he bears the scar by which he is identified and identifies himself, as he does to his father (24, 331 ff.), the herdsmen (21, 219 f.) and Penelope (23, 74 f.).

The chthonic, primal quality of the situation is demonstrated by the cave-like dark place from which the boar charges, the thicket, a place without the life-giving light of the sun and fertilizing rain, an image of the realm of the dead and the darkness in it. This is a consistency the *Odyssey* itself stresses, as it was earlier related how Odysseus—after avoiding death in the maternal sea—lies down on the Phaiakian island to rest in a thicket, dictated by precisely the same image of a thicket that "the shining sun" (5, 479) could not penetrate. When he wakes, steps out naked into the sun and meets Nausikaa, this must be seen as a (re)birth from the all-consuming dark world of the maternal womb.

The internal link between the two episodes, the hunt and the shipwreck, might not be readily apparent. However, just as Odysseus is sent home from his grandfather, richly rewarded, so he travels from the Phaiakians with great treasure, like another Sigurd the Dragonslayer after killing the gigantic guardian dragon.

The treasure symbolizes the self he has taken possession of through his action, from the first decisive breakthrough during the hunt to the more intense formation of the ego that takes place during and in an extension of the journey.

Finally, it may be seen as intertextual evidence of this victory that, during the dangerous espionage expedition in Book X of the *Iliad*, Odysseus dresses himself in a helmet that has belonged to none other than Autolykos, a leather helmet adorned so that "the white teeth/ of a tusk-shining boar were close sewn one after another" (X, 263-64), a helmet that Autolykos has in fact stolen from someone else, Amyntor. Odysseus wears his wild boar helmet as a trophy of victory and a sign that he has adopted the power of the wild boar. There are statuettes of such a wild boar helmet going back to the 16th century B.C.[20] And, remarkably enough, Beowulf dresses in an identical wild boar helmet before his decisive battle with Grendel's mother in the marsh.

5

It is significant that Autolykos invites Odysseus to pay him a visit in the grand home of his mother's family at Parnassos. The maternal is thus stressed as a fundamental form. And even though his grandmother is barely named, it is enough to sense in the fairytale-like description the emergence behind her of a mythical figure: the attentive, caring mother. Gathered around her are her husband, Autolykos, and her grown sons, who in contrast to Odysseus have failed to escape from home, from their mother. Indirectly, this reveals that the Great Mother has a dual nature: as stated above (see p. 88), the good mother has a hidden contrasting side in the all-consuming, destructive mother figure, who turns up as a dragon or a wild animal.

Insofar as this interpretation holds good, it must also be possible to show that Autolykos fundamentally belongs to a mother-fixated universe. And this actually seems to be the case. For his being the son of Hermes only partly explains his nature, quite apart from the fact that as a *psychopomp*, that is to say the person who leads the dead to Hades, Hermes himself has a chthonic side to his nature. One crucial aspect is revealed when Autolykos' name and residence are introduced and analyzed.

As mentioned name Autolykos means "the wolf himself" or "himself a wolf," meanings that are, for the most part, synonymous. The name well suits his greediness—for example, the fact that he steals other people's cattle. At the same time, however, it is a name and an identity that place him at an atavistic stage of consciousness. The same phenomenon is met in the Nordic *Egil's Saga*, where, as evidence of Egil's grandfather's belonging to much older times, it is said that, in the evening, he turns himself into a wolf. Hence, his name is Kveldulf, Evening Wolf, a term in its turn descended from Hallbjørn Halvtrold, Half Troll, that is to say a figure that is only half transformed to be part of the human world. There is also something giant-like or troll-like in the description of Autolykos. Like the giants, he is rich in gold, intelligent, cunning and, according to tradition, experienced in magic, as is underlined by the fact the he and his sons cure Odysseus' wounds by means of incantations.

Yet another dimension appears, if the locality in which Autolykos lives and the boar hunt takes place is analyzed as a symbolical topos: Parnassos. Pausanias recites a myth in which wolves help the inhabitants of Parnassos during a storm and are honoured by the city by being called Lykoreia.[21] What is interesting here is that— until Apollo's assumption of power—Olympos is the heavenly abode of the patriarchal gods, while Parnassos and the oracle at Delphi, located on its rocky slopes was a center for a chthonic mother cult linked to Gaia and later to Themis. The oracle was guarded by a huge python, which Apollo must slay with his arrows in order to take possession of the oracle and make it a shrine to the superior male intelligence he represents, liberated from the primal maternal power.

In this context, it may be asked whether, when seen in mythical terms, Odysseus' boar hunt is not a sort of counterpart. This is confirmed in a wider perspective by the fact that, by the establishment of his own self, Odysseus not only liberates himself from his mother but brings the intelligence he has inherited from Autolykos within the higher form of intelligence and knowledge that he meets in Athene. As a goddess, she represents the transition to a world in which law is based on patrilinear descent. Development of intelligence then means transforming what comes from the wolf itself.

When Odysseus leaves Parnassos, he takes possession of his own masculine self, symbolized by the treasure of gold. And as evidence that he has passed the test, he also wins Penelope as his princess and, as his woman, she is thrust between him and his mother. However, this does not prevent him from being stigmatized with the inheritance from his maternal grandfather in his name—and in his scar.

6

Of course, due to a lack of sources and explicit statements, there is some uncertainty in the foregoing analysis of the mythical reality associated with Autolykos and the wild boar hunt. However, this reality acquires even greater clarity and documentary potential, if we introduce Odysseus' mother, Antikleia. Through his hunt and his marriage, Odysseus has liberated himself from her—as Telemachos did when sailing away from his mother—while, as we have heard, Antikleia died from longing for her son after he sailed to Troy.

In her relationship with Odysseus, Antikleia, like her mother Amphithea, is represented as radiant and caring. Antikleia thus beams with joy when her hero son returns home with treasure from Parnassos. On the mythical level, the fact that, as is obvious from her death, she herself has been unable to release him reveals how the chthonic primal mother is inextricably bound to her son. At the same time, it reveals why Laertes has not been able to free himself from her, let alone transform her. It has made him powerless against her and demonstrates her mythical power. He is only partially realized as a man and is consequently still subject to female dominance. So Odysseus, not Laertes, becomes the man in Antikleia's life. In her son, she sees not her husband but her father. It is also primarily her family and all it stands for that Odysseus will carry on.

Even her name, Antikleia, signals that she belongs to an era older than the heroic, manly world described by Homer. The name means "she who is against reputation."[22] The reputation of men, *klea andron*, which is explicitly celebrated by Demodokos and Achilleus, is above all else the justification of heroes by ensuring their immortality. If we ask about the existential function of reputation, we can say in this context that through their reputation heroes maintain and measure their masculinity and so demonstrate to themselves and to the world that they have separated themselves from the primal mother. Fundamentally, it is this process that the heroes have in common and what makes them into heroes.

So, according to her name, Antikleia is in opposition to this heroic world and is, so to speak, a denial of it, which again underlines her matrilinear foundation. In this field of meaning, we also find the explanation of Laertes' powerlessness as king and his surprising abdication. The division of power in their marriage is illustrated directly in the erotic content. In connection with Laertes' expensive purchase of Eurykleia as a slave—she cost him twenty oxen—it is told that he did not dare take her as mistress, even though he "favored her in his house as much as his own devoted/ wife, but never slept with her, for fear of his wife's anger" (1, 432-33).

That this is said at all must be a sign that Laertes actually had this desire, just as the respect he shows his wife was not common. Heroes usually slept with whomever they wanted. Indirectly, this says on the one hand that Antikleia is not to be played around with. She may well be the good mother, but her shadow or repressed side is the wild boar. And on the other hand, Laertes is at a transitional stage between a matrilinear maternal constraint and the ultimate liberation from it in patriarchy.

Antikleia here reveals an absolute power corresponding to what the Phaiakian queen Arete possesses, since she also has greater power than her husband. So Odysseus learns from Athene and Nausikaa that he must win Arete to his cause if he wants to be sure of coming home. The assent of power lies with her. The same is true in the marriage between Laertes and Antikleia.

This means that, in Antikleia and Arete, we are introduced to two women who certainly have their own idiosyncratic manifestations, but in whose origins in the mythical mother goddesses are clearly to be seen. And like Laertes, Alkinoos, the Phaiakian king, finds himself at a level of consciousness that is differentiated from the primal female to a lesser extent than that of the heroes in the *Iliad*. They are both subordinate and nowhere nearly as strong as their respective wives.

Laertes' psychological and physical dependence on his wife emerges explicitly from the fact his grief is due not only to his son's departure but especially to the death of Antikleia—"for his wedded virtuous wife, whose death has hurt him/ more than all else, and gave him to a green untimely/ old age" (15, 356-58). That is, Laertes actually derives his life from Antikleia; her strength is his weakness, while she by contrast derives life from her son and dies after his departure. In this sense, Laertes is a man who, unlike Odysseus, has been unable to free himself from the power of women. He has not been able to assert himself as a man and maintain his honor in the face of his "matrilinear" wife. This is the most obvious explanation for why he has had to hand his royal power to Odysseus, his wife's son, who himself *has* liberated himself from the power of his mother.

7

Free and strong as Odysseus has become after the boar hunt, he has assumed royal power after taking a wife, while Laertes did not go the distance in comparison to his wife and his uniquely equipped son.

This weakness may well be the reason why Laertes also failed to take care of the kingdom in his son's absence. He passes his impotent life in a hut away from the community, unable to help Telemachos. His ancient shield—"all fouled with mildew" (22, 184)—which one of the suitors' assistants takes out and vainly tries to cover himself with is significant evidence of a power he has been unable to maintain and defend, even within the family's four walls. If anything, weapons symbolize their owner's strength and honor, and in contrast to this, Odysseus' bow has retained its original strength. Since it was important to appear so powerful to the outside world that no one dared challenge the family, it was natural for his son, as the stronger, to take over after demonstrating his ability to develop.

The moving reunion between father and son, however, demonstrates that the takeover of power must have happened on the best of terms. Despite the sympathy Odysseus feels on seeing his down-at-heel father once again, he cannot resist testing him. Certainly, he still resembles a king but lacks the same careful attention that he gives his garden. Odysseus relates to him a lengthy fabrication about an encounter—with himself. Laertes is overcome by sorrow at this, so that in what is for him a rare outbreak of emotion, Odysseus lets it be known who he is and shows his scar—the token identifying him and legitimizing his power.

As yet another proof of his identity, he mentions that when he was a child he persuaded his father to give him fruit trees and vines—"We went/ among the trees and you named them all and told me what each one/ was" (24, 338-40). This scene in which the father walks with his small son in the garden produces a tenderness that transcends all time frames. We see the loving, attentive and caring father. And although as a young man Laertes conquered a city, he is seen mainly as a "gentle" man who, dominated by his wife, enjoys his garden and his son. Finally, however, his past glory is resurrected in his battle with the families of the suitors, though this is thanks to Odysseus' return and strength.

We see the succession motif, which this really is, further developed in Hesiod's *Theogony*. There, on the divine plane, the sons, supported by the primal mother, seek to usurp power from their fathers. In Odysseus' earlier history, the mother seems in the same way to have been the son's fond helper when he took over the throne from his father, but not in the same bloody manner as in the heavenly world. On a symbolical level, however, he must, as a cultural hero, necessarily overthrow his father as an element in the succession that is again the precondition for both civilizational and personal development.

On the distaff side, it could be claimed that Laertes' counterpart is Eurykleia, the now aged servant and nurse he bought along ago and, with some justification, may be said to have loved. Even in name she is the opposite of Antikleia. For while Antikleia has opposed the heroic reputations, Eurykleia's name in Greek signals that she, by contrast, supports a "widespread reputation." This means that she supports the hero in his need to assert himself through heroic deeds and so liberate himself from the mythical primal mother. In this way, she assists Telemachos, when he determines to travel in order to achieve liberation from his mother and helps Odysseus in the struggle against the suitors.

So there is also a deeper congruity in the fact that it is Eurykleia, and not Penelope, who recognizes Odysseus from his scar. It is she, along with his deceased mother, who has known him the longest. She nursed him from the time he was born and it was she who laid the newborn infant on the lap of Autolykos. And to stress the deep connection between Odysseus and Eurykleia, the recognition scene is resumed with her exclamation: "dear child!" (19, 474). Certainly, it is a figure of speech, but like the epithets it has its own deeper meaning, corresponding to the way Odysseus, Telemachos and Penelope address her: Mother (2, 349).

With this side of her nature resembling Odysseus and his family, Eurykleia appears as an old, helpful, loving woman, but, as it is seen during the slaughter, she herself has a terrifying, bloody side that reveals her links with the primal female. So loudly does she rejoice and gloat over the death of the suitors that Odysseus must quieten her down for fear of incurring the wrath of the gods: "It is not a pity to so glory over slain men" (22, 412), he says, asking her to keep her joy in her heart. However, Eurykleia has difficulty controlling herself when she reports on the bloody facts to the highly skeptical Penelope: "You would have been cheered to see him,/ spattered over with gore and battle filth, like a lion" (23, 47-48).

8

As we shall see in Sophocles' *Oedipus the King*, a subject is equipped from birth with dual parents, a psychological reality that Homer is also on the track of.[23] On the one hand, there are biological parents of an archetypical character, linked to the Great Mother, nature and the subconscious. On the other hand, there are two parents who function in daily life by caring for the child during its time of growth. While the latter couple cause no noteworthy problems for an individual liberation, it is vitally necessary for an existential development of the self to liberate oneself from the mythical parents.

It is tempting here finally to push things to their logical conclusion by claiming that it is this liberation process we witnessed during the boar hunt. When we look at the remarkable interest Autolykos shows in his grandson—indeed, as though he were his own son—and his daughter's death-bound love for this son, they appear together in the role of two mythical parents. In the reality to which they belong, such a marital connection is not taboo but the norm, since the primal mothers incestuously reproduce via their sons (and brothers). In comparison with this, Laertes as the attentive father seems along with his beloved servant, his son's nurse, Eurykleia, to constitute the supportive parents.[24]

If the slaying of the boar was Odysseus' first victory over the evil mother, a victory of which he will bear the scar as the everlasting memory, he must during the dangerous voyage home once again be confronted on a large scale with this reality as his real test of manhood.

VII

THE WANDERINGS

The Repressed and the Voyager

1

THE *Apologoi* OR *Wanderings*—ODYSSEUS' TRAVEL ADVENTURES—ARE CLEARLY the oldest stage in the Homeric epics in terms of consciousness.[1] We step directly into the world of myth, defined by a chthonic reality. As said above, in his attempt to establish an alternative masculine, patriarchal order, Homer repressed this reality from his narrative universe, which focuses on the Olympian gods. However, this had the inevitable result that what is repressed returns in the form of the demonic transformations of the subconscious, which we meet in the gallery of figures of the *Apologoi*. At the same time, it has been a crucial point that this world governs virtually everything that happens on the conscious level. So on the basis of a qualified understanding, the evident must be interpreted against the background of the hidden.

So Odysseus' voyage does not only become a journey home, but a journey backwards in chronology to a mythical past that seems to be a psychological incursion into the subconscious and its gradual appropriation, assimilation and conquest.

Indeed, from the perspective of depth psychology, it may be claimed that, now at an age of around thirty-five, half way through life, he must face up to the prospect of re-integrating those things from which he has previously separated himself.[2] And as we demonstrated in Telemachos' journey of initiation and "confirmation," this was a matter of separating the boy from his mother and the primal maternal within her. This same mode of existence characterized the heroic stage in the *Iliad*. But what is not contained within you returns to face you. So the task and challenge for Odysseus as figurant for an archetypal process of development is to return to the repressed and, so to speak, allow himself to be reborn from the primal mother, as the many allusions to death and rebirth signal. Certainly, he does so as part of his own growth but, from a broader perspective, also on behalf of Homer and mankind.

If this repressed reality in the *Apologoi* appears so evil and threatening, it is because, on separation, the maternal and chthonic on the one hand have turned into avenging figures and on the other have sunk down and become the man's subconscious, which must be illuminated and explored if he is to become a fully realized subject. In this process, he is entirely left to his own judgement and initiative. It is thus not until the final phase of his journey that Odysseus' helpful goddess friend Athene appears and supports him during the ultimate test: the slaughter of the suitors.

It is, of course, no secret that Odysseus succeeds on his own and is able to return home with the great treasure with which he is presented by the Phaiakians, a counterpart to the treasure he won during his youth by felling the wild boar. It is certainly a treasure of gold, but deep down it is an alchemical image of his redeemed self. In addition, the *Apologoi* demonstrate that the heroic courage of the *Iliad* is not sufficient for this world in which Odysseus is now travelling. This reality demands and develops a consciousness in him that belongs to the future and, ultimately, is to bear Homer's own utopia.

If the *Apologoi* are not simply a loose collection of adventure stories, tall stories and travelling legends (which they also are), it is necessary to demonstrate a form of psychological progression and coherence, regardless of the level of evolution or consciousness on which the representative figures may find themselves. So my claim is that, all inconsistencies aside, these adventures constitute a collective whole. The concrete images and stories express experiences that existed at the time when the Homeric texts came into existence and when the abstract concepts and psychologisation of a later age were not available. This ability is more highly developed in the *Odyssey* than in the *Iliad*, which is why it may be claimed that in his description of Odysseus, Homer has attempted to make the conditions for such a development a primary theme. This is reflected in the great difference between the protagonists of the two works: Achilleus with his strength-based heroic world as against Odysseus' complex intellect.

2

While it is not so easy to see a psychological process emerge in the figure of Odysseus, who seems to be fixed and complete from the start, Telemachos' journey showed perfectly clearly that the idea of a journey reflecting a personal story of development was not alien to Homer. On the contrary, Telemachos is definitely a different person on returning home than when he set out—to free himself from his mother and to meet the father without and within himself. Various parallels and synchronicities between the journeys of father and son confirm in the compositional perspective that the journey for both means self-realization, albeit on different psychological levels. Thus, Telemachos must take possession of his own self and become a mature, young man, while Odysseus must win his ultimate identity, formed through the hard trials of the journey in distress and necessity.

In the *Apologoi*, what is as yet unconscious wanders about as premonitorily alluring and frightening figures. Right from the beginning, it is indicated that, placed within this reality, Odysseus is a traveler in distress, who must withstand "many pains" (1, 4).Yet, he does not merely seek to save his own skin and reach home himself. As a responsible leader, he also strives to bring his men safely home. With his premonitory technique, Homer foreshadows that this latter project is doomed to failure. It may well be ascribed to Destiny; but, on the other hand, a contention arises between Odysseus and his men, which is why they fare so badly. The difference is simply that his crew, as Odysseus several times notes in despair, are "greatly foolish" (*mega nepioi*, 9 , 44; 10, 231), always seek pleasure and oppose his command. They are therefore condemned to destruction.

This conflict dominates right from the start. This means that Odysseus becomes increasingly isolated. He is made to look suspicious, just as he himself suspects and is on guard against his crew. That the catastrophes arise to a large degree from this mutual suspicion is seen for the first time when they reach the coast of Ithaka backed by a fine breeze from the king of the winds, Aiolos. Odysseus has remained awake on the voyage, day and night for nine days, but falls asleep shortly before they reach their goal, and his men open the bag he has received from King Aiolos in the belief that he is carrying a hoard of gold home with him. But the bag contains the winds, which with a howl blow them back to Aiolos, who turns Odysseus away as a man "hateful to the immortals" (10, 75).

Odysseus must himself have had the feeling of being cursed, since at that point he has incurred the wrath of Poseidon. In shock, he briefly considers committing suicide: contemplating whether "to throw myself over the side and die in the open water,/ or wait it out in silence and still be one of the living" (10, 51-52). Fortunately, he decides on the latter. And in this intersection between despair and the urge to survive his patience is truly formed, while at the same time he takes responsibility for the foolishness and views the misfortune as "*our* own silliness" (10, 78, my italics).

However, parallel with his choosing the way of patience, he is once and for all distinguished from his men's foolishness, as has been apparent from the outset. After plundering the Kikonians—the first people they visit after leaving Troy—they drink themselves into a stupor—"they were greatly foolish and would not listen" (9, 44), he complains. The Kikonians return and 72 of his men die. Among the Lotus Eaters, they drug themselves by eating lotus fruits and forget everything about going home, and Odysseus must force them on board, moaning as they go. When they arrive at the Laistrygones, they seek shelter in the smooth sea of the harbor—a sign of their indolence. It turns out to be a trap, because the Laistrygones attack and batter the fleet with stones. Odysseus himself is anchored outside the harbor and escapes. Only one of his twelve ships, his own, is now left, but that, too, is destined for destruction when his men finally slay the cattle of the sun god.

So Odysseus' crew is driven only by their immediate needs and urges. They are unable to think of long-term consequences, much less strategically. They are constantly ambushed by their impulses. The crew knows only the necessity determined by basic needs. They quite simply cannot keep their eyes on the ultimate goal but pursue their short-term sensual desires. And they slide, regressively and despairingly, back into the pleasurable world of the all-consuming Mother from whom Odysseus is traveling to liberate himself.

He does not travel for pleasure or to planned destinations, but into the unknown, the surprising, the dangerous, guided by what he often calls "strong compulsion" (*anangke*, 10, 273). He lets this compulsion motivate his curiosity, develop his decisiveness and cunning—that is to say the entire psychological make-up that he, unlike his men, possesses and which is ultimately the source of his endurance. And, in contrast to his crew and except during his stay with Kirke, he retains his memory as the psychological factor that, by reaching out backward, is able to bring together his personality and lead him forward and home.

All this forms Odysseus' consciousness and endurance, as he acknowledges directly when Kalypso lays out all his impending hardships before him—"But even so, what I want and all my days I pine for/ is to go back to my house and see my day of homecoming" (5, 219-20), he says, ready to face any adversity—"for already I have suffered much and done much hard work" (5, 222). And when he relates his travel adventures to the Phaiakians, he again emphasizes that no one, neither Kalypso nor Kirke, both of whom desired him for their husband, has been able to move his heart: "nothing is more sweet in the end than country and parents/ ever, even when far away one lives in a fertile/ place, when it is in alien country, far from his parents" (9, 34-36). If self-realization is linked to distress, then Odysseus, if anyone, understands even this necessity as his motivation.

3

On the surface, the *Apologoi* appear in the epic as a series of supplemental, loosely-connected episodes. Beneath the surface, however, there is a clear progression, linked to the gradual annihilation of the crew and Odysseus' determination to return home. The journey takes place in a universe many have made vain attempts to locate on a map. For despite the names provided for the destinations, the journey is not geographically recognizable. It takes place in a cosmographic space (of consciousness) corresponding to his development and symbolic death and rebirth.

This cosmography is chthonic in the sense that the no man's land through which Odysseus travels is, at a deeper level, various shades of the realm of the dead. The four directions of the compass take their symbolical meaning from this fact. He already abandons familiar seas after plundering the Kikonians. When he passes Cape Maleia (9, 80), he is blown off course[3] and then finds himself within the boundaries of the realm of the dead, as is emphasised by the fact that the first people he meets are the Lotus Eaters. He only makes an explicit statement about the inherent uncertainty of navigating the waters of the realm of the dead on arriving at Kirke's island of Aiaia:

Hear my words, my companions, in spite of your hearts' sufferings.
Dear friends, for we do not know where the darkness is nor the sunrise,
Nor where the sun who shines upon people rises, nor where
He sets (. . .).

(10, 189-93)

They now find themselves in a place so strange that he can no longer find his bearings. The location of the island is itself an illustrative example of how different laws of topography apply here from those in the ordinary, familiar world they have left behind. The island is located at the easternmost point of this world—"where Helios, the sun, makes his uprising" (12, 4). From here, Odysseus makes his journey into Hades, located in its westernmost point, where Aiolos' floating island is also located. Odysseus reaches the realm of the dead in a single day by sailing on Okeanos without crossing any continent, guided only by the navigation of the north wind. He arrives among the Kimmerian people, who live in the same misty darkness—"hidden in fog and cloud" (11, 15)—that rests on both the realm of the dead and Skylla's cave. The voyage back to Kirke takes place over a single night from west to east. He follows the course of the sun and so, in this configuration, must be viewed as a solar figure.

In contrast to Kirke's island, Kalypso's Ogygia is in the far west, that is to say the same place as Hades. However, although the place is described as a sort of Elysium,[4] the vegetation—as among the Kyklopes—consists of black poplars and alders, which also grow in Hades. In short, this demonstrates the coincidence of topography present everywhere in the *Apologoi*. Moreover, the text is consistently filled with connotations of death and the forgetfulness it brings with it.

Odysseus takes eighteen days to sail to the Phaiakian island of Scheria, sailing in an easterly direction, again following the course of the sun in its rising and setting. The localities he visits are thus scattered throughout the four corners of the world but remain within the framework of the same cosmography and are actually one and the same place, the realm of the dead, which is why normal chronology is suspended. This is further confirmed by the emblematic world of signs that applies here.

Emblematics

1

Even though the figures Odysseus encounters take on very different shapes, they, along with their localities, constitute a common reality in this universe of death. In what follows, I will set out a cross-section of some constitutional features that form what might be called a chthonic emblematic. Let us begin with the female figurants, who may well be quite different but are nevertheless so closely related that they both act as latent reflections of each other and may be placed within a hierarchy.

Most primitive is Charybdis, a daughter of Gaia and Poseidon. Her parents are thus primordial, the Earth and the Sea, and she herself is a pure elemental phenomenon, dispatched by Zeus' thunderbolt into the ocean as a raging whirlpool, a vast chasm.[5] Nevertheless, this maelstrom is viewed as a female power of nature, since three times a day she consumes all the life around her and three times disgorges the remnants of what she has digested.

Close by is Skylla, originally a beautiful girl who, according to the myths concerning Kirke or Amphitrite, was out of jealousy transformed into a monster.[6] From the darkest depths of her cave, she stretches her long tentacles out to capture passing sailors, seals and fish. Physiologically, Skylla is more highly developed than Charybdis, since she has a female form like the Sirens, who are depicted as having the torso of a woman and the lower body of a bird—although not in the *Odyssey*, where Homer seems to assume that their appearance is familiar.

The Sirens use their song to lure seafarers to their death with the call: "Over all the generous earth we know everything that happens" (12, 191). They belong to the same group of prophetic beings as the sphinx and, according to Euripides, are the offspring of Gaia.[7] As such, they are demons of fate from the underworld, which also explains why they have insight into past and future.[8] It is these soothsayings (*nekromanteia*) from dead souls that Odysseus must travel to Hades to hear. But the Sirens do not provide insight, only death, which is yet another piece of evidence that the reality in which Odysseus finds himself indeed belongs to the chthonic.

The human-like qualities in the Sirens are not merely made visible in their figures, but can also be heard in their enticing singing. Kirke, the goddess of the lovely hair, also has a human voice (10, 136). She sings wonderfully and is reminiscent of Kalypso, who also sings and is described with the same epithets as having lovely hair and speaking with mortal voice.

This enchantment (*thelgein*), which the poet and Odysseus himself as narrator weave, has its most seductive effect in these women. Kirke's ability to enchant, however, is tied to her magic herbs. On one hand, this links her to Helen, who also mastered the herbal art, and on the other to Hekate, who is the goddess of magic herbs and rules over the dead, but is either not known or passed over in silence by Homer. The Volva in Norse mythology belong to this category to whom even Odin, the universal father, must turn for knowledge about the end of the world, just as he learned to work sorcery (*sejd*) from Freya, the Norse goddess of fertility. It is true of all these women that they possess knowledge men do not have and which derives from their chthonic origin.

Kalypso's magical powers are exhibited directly in her attempt to seduce Odysseus with "soft and flattering words" (1, 56), a formulation that recalls the way in which he himself knew how to flatter Polyphemos with words "full of beguilement" (9, 364). Unlike Kirke, Kalypso lives in a cave and appears to represent an older stage of consciousness. Yet, emotionally she seems to be more human than Kirke in her love for Odysseus.

We find the highest stage of development in the Phaiakian queen Arete and her daughter Nausikaa. We feel ourselves to be back in the human world in the presence of these two women. However, this is only partially true. Like Kirke and Kalypso, Nausikaa represents an erotic temptation for Odysseus to forget his goal and his wife. And his homecoming depends on the sympathy of her mother Arete. She is described as helpful or destructive, according to Odysseus' ability to approach her, and as such represents the primordial power of women.

2

It may be said that these women are implicitly linked by the sea: Charybdis as a maelstrom, Skylla as a sea monster, Kirke as the daughter of the sea nymph Perse, a daughter of the river Okeanos, while Kalypso is the daughter of the Titan Atlas, who is said to have had great insight, since he "discovered / all the depths of the sea" (1, 52-53). Even Polyphemos belongs to this group as the son of the sea god Poseidon and the nymph Thoösa, the daughter of Phorkys, "lord of the barren salt water" (1, 72). Poseidon is also the progenitor of the Phaiakians. I will shortly explain in more detail the death-linked character of the sea in connection with this sea god.

Like the sea, the cave is a chthonic symbol. There are countless references in mythology to the far-reaching significance of the cave. Hermes, for example, was born in a womb-like grotto. And to prevent Kronos from swallowing his newborn son, Zeus, Gaia hid him, according to Hesiod, "in a remote cave beneath the secret places of the holy earth on thick-wooded Mount Aegeum."[9] In the *Odyssey*, this perspective suddenly makes it possible to see Kalypso, Skylla and Polyphemos under the same heading. Despite their differences in gender and development, they share a common reality. All three live in large caves. The caves of Polyphemos and Kalypso are surrounded by the same luxuriant, self-generating Arcadian nature that is also found among the Phaiakians.

That these caves[10] are really mental images for the realm of the dead is made clear in relation to Skylla.[11] Of her cave, it is said that it is "misty-looking/ and turned toward Erebos and the dark" (12, 80-81). So exactly the same darkness (*zophos*) rules here as rests upon and hides the realm of the dead and the realm of the Kimmerians.

This "concealing" denotes death and is a key to Kalypso's name. Derived from the verb *kalyptein*, it spans a register encompassing concealment, darkness and death. That is to say the cave in which she lives has the same associations of darkness and death as does that of Skylla. The name of the goddess of the realm of the dead in Norse mythology is Hel, which also means "the one who conceals". The Kyklops' cave is also experienced as a place of death. Once the stone is in place, there is utter darkness. Therefore, it has a deeper meaning when Odysseus calls himself "Nobody," just as, in principle, he is "nobody" for the seven years he has remained concealed with Kalypso in her grotto of death. So his liberation from there becomes a sort of rebirth.

Furthermore, Polyphemos and Kirke have obvious common features. Neither of them respects Zeus' laws of guest friendship: like Skylla, the Kyklops devours his guests; Kirke transforms them into animals. They belong to the past, when the Titans ruled and an Olympian patriarchal god like Zeus had not even been born. Related to Polyphemos are the mammoth Laistrygones: "not like men, like giants" (10, 120). The queen is "as big as a mountain peak" (10, 112). They live in a rocky place, where "the courses of night and day lie close together" (10, 86). In short, it is a locality with white nights, which might suggest that material from the North has migrated to be written down here. In their cave-like harbor, Odysseus' ships are crushed apart from his own, which narrowly escapes.

The Phaiakians once lived side by side with the Kyklopes, their kinsmen, but moved to Scheria to escape their violent conduct. They have developed something approaching a human level of civilization, as is emphasized by the fact that they live in a *polis* surrounded by a wall but still have commerce with the gods. In this sense, they become a symbol of a lost ideal society in which a certain cultural progress has taken place without the loss of divinity. That they are able to steer their ships by the power of their minds alone is another signal that they belong to the mythical universe, where no differentiation between subject and object has yet been made. They are an emblem of the lost Golden Age, also called the time of Kronos.

Thus, Odysseus' journey is one across a consistent reality, even though it is a patchwork of every imaginable kind of adventure. Figures crisscross each other in configurations and identifications and are connected to form a greater underlying whole: the primal maternal world of fertility and death, presented in its primordial demonic form, which Homer has repressed in favor of a patriarchal universe on Olympos. As a result of this repression, the chthonic reality is only expressed negatively, just as Odysseus is placed face to face with it in order to become himself in the larger sense that the word "home" also allows.

Composition

At the plot level, the compositional movement upon which the travel adventures as a whole are formed corresponds to the emblematic uniformity characterizing the subtext of the *Apologoi*. From a dramatic point of view, the sequence is partly linked to Odysseus' loss of his crew, partly to his entry into the unknown, ever more threatening and alien, together with the homeward direction maintained in his memory as a constant incentive. He makes his plans "so that things would come out the best way,/ and trying to find some release from death, for my companions/ and myself, too" (9, 420-21). Yet, even though he fails to save his stubborn crew, he develops his will and personality in the conflict with his men and the hostile forces. In the following pages, the three main phases of this sequence will be described, after which I will provide a more detailed analysis of the most important adventures in relation to this symbolic world.

The first main phase extends to his encounter with Kirke. At the center is the story of the Kyklops, the most famous story and the one that is told best. It is also the one most clearly throwing light on Odysseus' cunning and explaining why Poseidon becomes his deadly enemy—the event that is the direct cause of the ten-year delay in his homecoming. Around the blinding of Polyphemos lie other events: after the predatory expedition to the Kikonians, Odysseus is thrown off course at Cape Maleia and sails into the waters of death. The real turning point is when, after his devastating encounter with the Laistrygones, he reaches Kirke's island without being able to find his bearings.

The second principal phase begins with Kirke and ends with the time spent with Kalypso. This phase includes his journey to Hades, Skylla and Charybdis and the loss of his ship and his last men on the island of the sun god. Then, shipwrecked, he drifts ashore on Kalypso's island. When—at the behest of Zeus after the fulfil-ment of Fate—he sails from Kalypso on his self-made ship, the nymph informs him in detail about what constellations he is to follow in order to return to the world of men and time, to which the Phaiakians form the transition.

The third main phase describes the stay with the Phaiakians. Here, Odysseus tells of his adventures and thus, in the perspective of memory, begins slowly and with increasing consciousness to gather his identity around what has happened. From here, he is shepherded safely home by the Phaiakian sailors, who rule the sea as descendants of Poseidon. Since the Phaiakians' Golden Age society is a highly developed civilization, this stage in the journey constitutes a natural bridgehead to the concrete reality of Ithaka.

It is worth noting that this tripartite structure can also be set in relation to the gods whom Odysseus encounters. In the first phase, he has his falling out with Poseidon. In the second phase, he must generally speaking make do on his own, though receiving help from Hermes prior to his encounter with Kirke, while the same god arrives as a divine messenger to liberate him from Kalypso. Not until the beginning of the third phase—his shipwreck off the coast of the Phaiakians—can Athene lend a helping hand, because she no longer needs to take her uncle Poseidon into consideration now that Fate has put an end to his persecution of Odysseus.

The Substance and Meaning of the Adventures

1

Before Odysseus incurs the wrath of Poseidon, he has already had a couple of adventures that illuminate the character of his crew—or the lack thereof. The Kikonians whom he plunders at the beginning of his voyage home are not a "mythological" people but have participated on the Trojan side in the war. They hark back to the narrative universe of the *Iliad* and, from an epic point of view, form an elegant transition to the *Odyssey*. As already said, the episode also has a foreshadowing function, insofar as, even here, the crew reveals a lack of determination to reach home, coarsened and depraved by ten years of war. They do not obey orders and drink until they are incapable of fighting, so that when the Kikonians have reorganised their defence, a large number of them are killed.

The urge to become intoxicated, with concomitant loss of consciousness and memory of home, is intensified among the Lotus Eaters. This visit portends the obliviousness to home and family, a relinquishment of self, the losing of oneself in timelessness, the desire-laden enjoyment and regression into death, all of which point ahead to Kirke and Kalypso. Odysseus has to drag his men to the accompaniment of their shouts and yells away from the euphoria of the Lotus Eaters.

2

If Odysseus has been moderation itself during the earlier adventures, it is, by way of contrast, his uncontrollable curiosity when visiting the Kyklopes that costs several of his men their lives and nearly costs him his own, quite apart from the curse he calls down upon himself. It is the first and last time that he displays such provocative foolhardiness, and it is evidence that he becomes wiser along the way. There are certainly borrowings from folktales, but no other version of this adventure has such comprehensive symbolic value.[12]

It may generally be said that the story is about interpretation. We see how a new order arises from a series of misinterpretations: the small, alert man triumphs over the raw, brutal strength of a giant. Thus, a problem that implicitly reflects the shift from the display of strength in the *Iliad*, which failed to force Troy to its knees, to the protagonist of the *Odyssey*, who conquers the city with his Wooden Horse. The misinterpretation on the part of Odysseus consists of the fact that, in his blind curiosity to learn about the island, he works on the possibility that it might be inhabited by people who are "savage and violent, and without justice" (9,175). Nevertheless, he naively assumes that he will be protected by the rules of guest friendship that Zeus has provided for mankind: that strangers are to receive guest friendship and are to be safe against attack. In other words, his misinterpretation is based in his ardent desire to explore the place, to get his men with him and a pious trust in the Olympian gods whom the Kyklopes despise.

The Kyklopes live outside the rules governing ordinary lands.[13] Polyphemos calls Odysseus a fool when he asks for a visitor's gift: "The Kyklopes do not concern themselves over Zeus of the aegis,/ nor any of the rest of the blessed gods, since we are far better/ than they" (9, 275–77). Yet, the remarkable thing is that, even though the Kyklopes are described as a lawless people (*athemiston*, 9, 106), this does not mean they are godless. They are a wild people "putting all their trust in the immortal/gods" (9, 107). When Polyphemos mocks Zeus and Olympos, therefore, it must once again be a sign that the Kyklopes belong to an atavistic, chthonic stage of development, without *agora* or *polis*, which is confirmed by the self-cropping countryside. Everything "grows for them without seed planting, without cultivation" (9, 109) as evidence that this patriarchal culture has not yet subjected the maternal body of the earth to the plow. They belong to the same epoch as Kalypso, i.e. the time under Kronos, the age of the Titans, as Kronos was overthrown by his son Zeus and was himself a pre-Olympian divinity, close to his mother Gaia.

The Kyklopes' lack of a social culture is demonstrated by the fact that they live in caves, separated from each other and living from hand to mouth, as the vegetation is rich in fruits and cultivates itself. They can only weave baskets. A barbaric place, but also a place that with its tremendous fertility would to Odysseus' eye be ideal for cultivation, plowing, sowing and making into "a strong settlement" (9, 130). Homer's description of Odysseus' sense of profitable locations seems to be strongly influenced by the Greeks' expansive colonization, constantly on the lookout for fertile places to settle.

In their contempt for the gods, the Kyklopes—like the stone-throwing Laistrygones —are a primitive race that the refinements of Olympos have never reached. Therefore, the Kyklops does not understand that there is a greater force than muscular mass—that is to say, the power of interpretation (*metis*). And this determines his fate, because even though it has been foretold to him that he will be blinded by a man named Odysseus, he expects an enemy in his own image, a big, strapping brute. Not in his wildest imagination does he think it will be "a little man, niddering, feeble" (9, 514) who will extinguish the light of day for him.

Looking back, Odysseus regrets that he did not listen to his crew's misgivings but followed his impulse from his own curiosity—"I would not listen to them, it would have been better their way" (9, 228). On the other hand, from the moment they are locked within the cave, his liberation becomes a brilliant illustration of how shrewdness can overcome raw strength and demonstrates what the future demands of human intelligence. He does not follow what his heroic self-understanding otherwise prompts him to do and kill the Kyklops with his sword when he begins to eat his crew. It would be pure suicide, for "our hands could never have pushed from the lofty/ gate of the cave the ponderous boulder he had propped there" (9, 304-05).

To think is to come from darkness into the light. Not to think is, as in the case of the Kyklops, to be sent into the eternal darkness of blindness. So a long-term strategy is required, which Odysseus must work out on his own, without the help of men or gods. He is master in his own house. Or cave. After getting Polyphemos intoxicated on wine he has received from a priest of Apollo,[14] Odysseus makes himself known as "Nobody." Then, he stabs the Kyklops' eye with an olive pole, heated to a burning point in the glowing ashes. And as the well-known story goes the Kyklops calls out to his neighbors and, shrieking with pain, tells them that "Nobody" has poked his eye out, and so the neighbors go back to their own caves. Odysseus and his surviving men escape, tied to sheep—Odysseus himself tied to the ram, which, contrary to custom, is the last to walk past the staggering Kyklops. A new version of the Wooden Horse and a description of how Odysseus is victorious by virtue of the fact that he can predict and exploit his enemy's actions.

Even though Odysseus says to the Phaiakians that they must not consider him a god (7, 209), he cannot hide his arrogant delight at besting the Kyklops: "The heart within me/ laughed over how my name and my perfect planning had fooled him" (9, 413-14). He, and the Greek text, make a rhymed play on his cunning with Nobody (*Outis*) having its premise precisely in his wisdom (*metis*).[15]

Reduced as Odysseus is in the grotto, helpless against the dead weight of the stone at its entrance, becoming so much a Nobody that after liberation—despite his people's prayers to show restraint—he seeks triumphantly to resurrect his trampled self-esteem by mocking the Kyklops: Polyphemos is only getting the punishment he deserves for eating his guests—"so Zeus and the rest of the gods have punished you" (9, 479). In the next tirade, he moves it up a notch and now lets the punishment serve his own fame, linking it with his reputation as a sacker of cities, which has given his identity its greatest content. If anyone asks who has blinded him: "Tell him that you were blinded by Odysseus, sacker of cities./ Laertes is his father, and he makes his home in Ithaka" (9, 504-05).

Viewed from the whole context, the situation has a deeper function. For just as the cave is significant as a trial and a place of death, it also becomes part of the initiation ritual to a new birth, which is repeated throughout the whole of the *Odyssey*. There, he is in darkness, fundamentally as in a womb, anonymous, unborn. It is with his *metis*, his most highly developed intelligence, that he brings himself into the world, liberates himself from the womb of the cave and its deathly dark. It is not least for this reason that he shouts out his name. At the same time, he confirms the duality in his name, insofar as he demonstrates in that situation that he is both the one who has been made to suffer great pain and the one who returns it in kind (*odyssamenos*, see p. 176).

The Kyklops tries in vain to lure him back with a promise of gifts and then, in blind rage, throws such enormous boulders that cause waves upon the seas so high that they almost sink the boat. It is a portent of the shipwrecks and delays ahead, which Polyphemos' prayer to his father Poseidon helps unleash: "If truly/ I am your son, and you acknowledge yourself as my father,/ grant that Odysseus, sacker of cities, son of Laertes,/ who makes his home in Ithaka, may never reach that home" (9, 529-31). But if it is "allotted" to him, i.e. if Fate and the gods have so determined it, the Kyklops prayer is: "let him come late, in bad case, with the loss of all his companions,/ in someone else's ship, and find troubles in his household" (9, 534-35). Not only do we know, but Odysseus himself knows that Polyphemos' prayer is heard by Zeus himself, when, downhearted, he has to acknowledge that the god will not accept his thanks offering after his liberation.

3

Until the time at which the *Odyssey* begins, when he has finally endured his punishment, Odysseus is left to himself—as *polytropos*—to adapt and develop in accordance with the fate he incurred in his encounter with the Kyklopes. In this respect, the story of Polyphemos is a fine example of a story of how a chthonic primeval force in its most negative form seeks to consume humankind in its cave—just as Skylla and Kalypso each in their own way do in theirs. On the other hand, it also appears that Odysseus has the understanding necessary to avoid death in the cave's uterus-darkness. He contrives a plan to compel blind force in the shape of Polyphemos himself to move the stone from the cave's opening, thus turning brute force against itself by his own force of interpretation.

In extension of this, it may be asked just what sort of reality it is that he is at odds with as the result of Poseidon's enmity? The sea god is certainly a masculine divinity and in Homer he is even Olympian. But the very fact that he is the father of a primitive monster such as Polyphemos reveals his chthonic origin. For the same reason—at one with his element, the sea—neither does he live on Olympus but makes his home beneath the wavy depths at Aigai (possibly Aegina)—"where his glorious house was built in the waters'/depth "(XIII, 21). He is undifferentiated and maladjusted, not entirely reconciled with his brother Zeus, the god of the intellect—"I am no part of the mind of Zeus" (XV, 194), he complains, like his Kyklops son. Homer makes Zeus older than Poseidon (XIII, 357), Hesiod makes him younger.[16] That Poseidon is at all events an ancient god is confirmed by his presence on tablets from Knossos and Pylos.[17]

To understand Poseidon, we have to understand his element. As a trading and seafaring nation, the Greeks had a close relationship with the sea. It was the prerequisite for their maintaining their lives at all. Indeed, by connecting the many islands, the sea is what makes Hellas into one country. However, only a fool has no fear of the sea, for as the Phaiakians say, "There is no other thing that is worse than the sea is/for breaking a man, even though he may be a very strong one" (8, 138-39).

It is also from the sea that death stalks Odysseus. From the earliest times the sea has functioned as an image of the irrational in its oceanically fluid, contourless form, in which the waves seek to form shapes but are once again immediately leveled into the undifferentiated whole—an element without intelligence, which overwhelms and engulfs. The sea and Poseidon can be sensed behind all the figures that in one way or another try to annihilate and consume Odysseus: Skylla in her watery cave, the maelstrom Charybdis, the seductive song of the Sirens, Kirke, Kalypso, Polyphemos, and even the Phaiakians. All are linked to the sea and thereby with Poseidon.

Poseidon is called by Homer "Earthshaker of the wide strength" (*ennosigai' eurysthenes*, 13, 140) and "the Earth Encircler" (*gaieochos*, 1, 69). As sea god, he both spans the globe and shakes it with his earthquakes. This harmonizes with the mythological claim that Poseidon is Gaia's husband—his name has been interpreted as meaning the master/husband of the earth—so that, with the literalness that characterizes mythical thinking, the two divine figures may be linked together orgastically as embrace and satisfaction.

The marriage between Gaia and Poseidon is also significant because it both reveals Poseidon's place in the earliest myths and his connection to this very stage of the primal maternal. Other mythical tales also confirm this primeval relationship. For example, in the shape of a horse he impregnates the fertility goddess Demeter. Their offspring was the divine horse Arion, who participates in the race at Patroklos' funeral games (XXIII, 346 ff.), though without its origin being specified. That is why Poseidon bears the epithet Hippios and is considered to be the father of the first horse. As said above, Athene is also associated with the horse as Athene Hippias. This reveals the close and competitive relationship between the two gods, something that is given concrete form in the *Odyssey* with Odysseus as the enemy of one and the protégé of the other; see also their power struggle in Athens.

The sea and the horse may also be united to form a single idea of a demonic world of urges, related to Poseidon. On the other hand, Athene as goddess of wisdom intervenes in this imagery because of the control she exercises over these forces. Just as she invents the bridle with which the horse may be controlled, she gives sailors the skill to navigate and conquer the foaming sea.[18] When Odysseus leaves Kalypso, it is in a boat he himself has built, though thanks to the skills with which Athene has provided him, just as it is with skills he has received from her that he can steer by the constellations in the sky.

In order not to quarrel with her uncle, Athene has not provided Odysseus with assistance during the voyage, as she explains to him when he complains about her absence—ever since Troy. As he says on their reunion, "Nor did I know of your visiting my ship, to beat off some trouble/ from me" (13, 319). As said above, we may also conclude there is another reason: for if Athene had helped him on the way, the journey would not have been the personal trial and initiation that it is now. He must personally get to know the deadly forces seeking his life and learn to resist them—also as forces within his own instinctual nature. At the same time, Athene herself is dependent on the outcome, as it is through Odysseus that, on behalf of mankind, she—with Homer—seeks to gain control over the sea and all the demonic dangers it represents.

If we ask about the reason for Poseidon's aggressive attitude to Odysseus, the immediate answer will be that Odysseus has blinded his son. However, his persistent hostility in persecuting Odysseus beyond the framework of the epic reveals that the sea god is a demonic exponent for the primal maternal reality to which, despite his masculine outer form, he belongs. He is the most steadfast representative of this reality and, therefore, the greatest test of Odysseus' endurance.

As the most dangerous challenge on the voyage home at the pinnacle of Odysseus' career, Poseidon has the same initiatory purpose as the wild boar had in his puberty.[19] And as when he slew the charging boar, Odysseus now resists the attempt of this primordial power to draw him down into its watery element.

As Poseidon says to Zeus, he knows that he must yield to Fate and will never be able to prevent Odysseus' homecoming: "Since first you nodded your head and assented/to it" (13, 133–34). His power and persecution come to an end off the island of the Phaiakians, and Athene can finally take over. Yet, the sea god has not forgotten Odysseus. As was forwarned by Teiresias, after restoring order to his kingdom Odysseus must embark on new voyage to reconcile himself with the sea god. "Dear wife, we have not yet come to the limit of all our/trials. There is unmeasured labor left for the future, /both difficult and great, and all of it I must accomplish" (23, 248–49), he says to Penelope.

With an oar over his shoulder, he is to wander until he reaches a country and encounters a people who have never tasted food mixed with sea salt and who mistake the oar for a winnowing shovel. Here, he is to plant the oar into the ground and make a "ceremonious sacrifice" (11, 130) to Poseidon and to make the sea god known. Homer may associate this place with Arcadia, where, at all events, Pausanias relates that, after the fall of Troy, Odysseus erected a shrine to Athene and Poseidon.[20] Then, according to the prophesy, he will be able to return home and, as an old man, find a peaceful death, not on the sea but at the midst of his thriving kingdom. So it seems as though this is a myth of how the chthonic powers are reconciled through Odysseus and lead to growth—of which his own country stands in evidence.

4

From the island of Polyphemos, Odysseus goes to Aiolos, king of the winds, who resides on an island floating on the sea like an iceberg—"He bestowed his daughters on his sons, to be their consorts" (10, 7). This is related as the most natural thing in the world, which it may well be if the children are viewed allegorically as various wind directions. The incestuous marriages of this group of siblings are a natural consequence of the sexual code in force outside the boundaries of patrilinear descent. This type of sexual conduct was common in the world of matrilinear descent and may once again be traced back to the fertilization of primal mothers by their sons. A parallel is found in Norse mythology in the fertility god Njord's marriage to his sister, with whom he has Frey and Freya.

From Aiolos, Odysseus receives a sack full of winds, which are to ensure him a favorable voyage home. The necessity of keeping the sack closed at all costs demonstrates how important it is to be able to control the forces of nature. Because, as said above, he falls asleep off Ithaka and his envious crew set the winds free, he is blown back to King Aiolos, who drives him away as a man hated by the gods. On the seventh day, he comes to the land of the Kyklopes-like

Laistrygones, who crush his fleet, while he himself escapes—only to sail into the unfathomable world of death, where Kirke waits.

5

How radical and strong a figure Kirke is may be illustrated by the very fact that Odysseus is no match for her on his own, as he was for the Kyklops. For the first and only time—until Athene steps into the action—he receives help from the gods, from Hermes. That it is not Athene but the god of the winged feet that comes to his relief is not explained by the fact that he is Hermes' grandchild. Meanwhile, their deep spiritual kinship is emphasized by the fact that they share the epithet *polytropos*, with all that implies by way of psychological mobility and diversity. Hermes thereby appears as a projection and intensification of Odysseus' ability to transform himself—as Athene is of his *metis*.

They shake hands like comrades when Hermes meets him in the likeness of a young man with a new-grown beard. At the same time, Hermes makes no secret of the fact that Odysseus would be lost without his help—"but see I will find you a way out of your troubles, and save you" (10, 286), he says, confirming his reputation as a kindly figure. As Zeus puts it when Hermes helps Priam at the end of the *Iliad*, it is his greatest pleasure: "to be man's companion, and you listen to whom you will" (XXIV, 335).

When Odysseus meets him, Hermes is carrying his golden staff (*chrysorrapis*, 10, 273) in his hand.[21] What power this staff really holds appears in Book 24 of the *Odyssey*, when Hermes leads the souls of the slaughtered suitors into the realm of the dead. It is described here how with his staff he can lull men to sleep and awaken them, and with his staff he hurries along the souls who follow him like a swarm of hissing bats. That is to say that he who owns this staff rules over the dead, in the same way as Hades himself uses a magic wand to call souls to him from their grave.[22] In the final book, we see Hermes as *psychopompos*, the leader of souls of the dead, and as Odysseus *de facto* finds himself in the realm of the dead, it makes sense that he should receive help from Hermes, who as Hermes Chthonios belongs here.

It is interesting that the staff Hermes uses is called *rhabdos* in Greek, the same word used for the magic wand with which Kirke transforms Odysseus' men into pigs. They belong to the same reality, which explains why Hermes has insight into Kirke's supernatural arts and can tell Odysseus precisely how to deal with her. Hermes gives him the magical herb *moly* to ward off her potions. The root is black, the flower is milky white, while the name is a word used only by the gods. The flower can only be plucked from the earth by someone with divine strength. As a symbol, it is a plant that, like yin and yang, seems to unite the light of consciousness and life with the hidden cave world of the realm of the dead.[23]

When Kirke gives Odysseus the magic herbs, he rushes towards her, as Hermes has instructed him to do, with his sword drawn. Screaming, she ducks and embraces

his knees in supplication. That he can resist her makes it possible for her to identify him as *polytropos*—"You are then resourceful Odysseus. Argeïphontes/of the
golden staff was forever telling me you would come" (10, 330-31). No other mortal has been able to resist her potion before. "The wonder is on me that you drank
my drugs and have not been/enchanted, for no other man beside could have stood
up/under my drugs, once he drank" (10, 327-38). Since she now offers to share her
bed with him, he suspects her of having malicious intent and demands a sacred oath
that she will not rob him of his masculinity—"So that when I am naked you can
make me a weakling, unmanned" (10, 341). He gets his way.

Not only is this scene dramatic, it has a symbolic value that calls for a precise
interpretation to demonstrate how we are dealing with an archetypal conception.
When Odysseus attacks Kirke with raised sword, it may be read in this context as
phallic aggression, in which the male seeks to defend his masculinity against the
female will and power to turn men into animals. Consequently, the transformation
of the crew into pigs is not, as it is claimed in modern interpretations, a sign that
they are pig-like in their desires. Others, of course, have been transformed into
lions and wolves with wagging tails (10, 218). No, all these men have been made
into servants of a mother goddess, who keeps them as her sacred animals. Similarly,
it is told in Norse mythology that Freya is accompanied by sacred swine, while pigs
were part of the Greek fertility cults in the sacrifice to the mothers of the earth.[24]
For example, as protectress of animals, *potnia theron*, the Minoan Artemis also surrounded herself with wild animals.

In the mother cults, it was also a custom for male priests on castrating themselves
to sacrifice their genitals to the goddess as a sign of subjection. As an example, I have
previously mentioned Kybele's eunuch priests, the so-called *galli*, who undertook
this act in imitation of Attis. The Great Mother could thereafter dispose over the
sacrificed phallos as a part of the fertility rights.[25] This form of mutilation made a
terrified Anchises beg Aphrodite to show mercy when she fell in love with him—
"for he who lies with a deathless goddess is no hale man afterwards," are the words
he uses to express his anguish.[26]

So that is to say that through the oath he forces out of Kirke with his sword,
Odysseus will avoid castration, that is to say subjecting himself to her female dominance. He will protect the power of his manhood by binding her with the indissoluble chains of a sacred oath. In the way he conducts himself, he maintains his
male sovereignty, in contrast to Laertes and Alkinoos, who did not measure up to
their respective wives. We also see how—after being subjugated—Kirke becomes
humble and servile. She bathes him, serves him food, changes his men back, etc.,
all as a sign that the masculine has here triumphed in an image that at the time
could be held up as a model deriving from experience and as the way to a man's
making himself independent.

In this little scene, a condensed version of the great collective drama is thus
presented, a drama being enacted during this same period between the original

mother cults and the emergence of new gods such as Zeus and Apollo, the heroic gods of patriarchy and civilization.

And it turns out in reality that the greatest and most dangerous temptation for Odysseus during the entire voyage, including the war, is the exclusive comfort he receives from the subdued Kirke, as though forced back into the primal mother's smothering care for her son: "There for all our days until a year was completed/we sat there feasting on unlimited meat and sweet wine" (10, 467-68). As may be read in this description, Odysseus sinks back into the primal maternal and experiences a liberation from all the cares to which he has been subject during the voyage but which are part of the development of the individual.

As already became clear during his stay with the Lotus Eaters, the danger and temptation in these regions is that the subject may give up his memory as an identity-creating force. The poison that Kirke gives to Odysseus' men has that very aim: "To make them forgetful of their own country" (10, 236). This is what happens to Odysseus. He loses his identity, conditioned to pain and strong-willed determination to return home, sustained by memory's forward-directed light. This stands in glaring contrast to his stay with Kalypso. There, he has learned his lesson and does not make this mistake, which with Kirke could have been fateful. For there he retains the memory of his wife and home despite the goddess' attempts to seduce him.

On a deeper level, the mistake Odysseus makes with Kirke must be this: that on a mythical-psychological voyage the purpose of which is to definitively separate the woman from the maternal, he once again unconsciously reintegrates these two figures. The woman once again becomes a mother, providing for his every need. She supplies him with everything; while he on the other hand services the Great Mother sexually—and forgets the woman who is waiting.

In this state, it is those around him, his otherwise foolish men, who must sound the alarm and bring him back to his specific purpose: to return home. With a shout, they wake him from his deathlike lethargy: "What ails you now? It is time to think about our own country/if truly it is ordained that you shall survive and come back/to your strong-founded house and to the land of your fathers" (10, 472-74). In Greek, he is addressed as *Daimonios* (10, 472), a word that has many meanings: strange, favored by the gods, but in this context also demonized and unfortunate.

The voices of the men here have the task of projecting the reality that Odysseus has forgotten in Kirke's embrace. However, in contrast to Kalypso, who in her love is reluctant to release Odysseus, Kirke is immediately ready to help him. Perhaps because she is more fundamentally cold, less human, in her emotional life than Kalypso. Nevertheless, she still shows concern for him, sending him first to the realm of the dead, so that Teiresias can acquaint him with the conditions and dangers for his voyage home.

6

Book 11 about Odysseus' journey to the realm of the dead has been called the *Nekyia*, a designation emphasizing that true knowledge about the past and the future must be found in Hades. Kirke instructs Odysseus how the dead souls he allows to drink the sacrificial blood will "speak the truth" (*nemertea*, 11, 96) about the past and the future. In this way, the voyage to Hades clearly becomes a kind of initiation in which people have seen a trace of shamanism. For the shaman has this very ability to abandon his body and wander among the departed spirits in order to ask them about future life.

In Odysseus' case, Kirke gives him information about how through the river Okeanos—in the *Iliad* described as the source of everything (XIV, 201; 242)—he will reach Hades. He must follow the course of the sun and sail from east to west until he reaches Persephone's poplar grove. Here, he is to undertake the obligatory blood sacrifice, which summons up the dead.

Before he departs, Kirke instructs him exactly on how he is to conduct the sacrifice: he is to dig a pit of a cubit in length and breadth in which he is first to sacrifice milk, honey and wine, water and flour. Then, he is to take the blood of a black sheep and a black ram, with the head bowed towards Hades, and let it flow into the sacrificial pit, while he looks away. Sacrifice to Olympian gods took place in contrast on high altars, where the head of the sacrificial animal was turned towards heaven. *Escharai*, altars for the gods of the underworld, are, interestingly enough, also the name for the labia of women.

By drinking sacrificial blood, the dead souls regain consciousness, which they lost in death, and can now tell him everything he wants to know. As said above, the dead person is talked about as a soul, *psyche*, since the belief among Greeks at Homer's time was that, like a breath, the life force leaves the dying person through the nose or the mouth at the moment of death in order to travel to Hades. Here, the dead person moves about like an image, an *eidolon*, looking exactly as that person did in life.

During the séance, Odysseus stands at the sacrificial pit itself with the blood. However, from line 568, in which he sees King Minos, it seems as if, like a real shaman, he is undertaking a true *katabasis*, a descent into the world of the dead, for which reason any mention of blood sacrifice is abandoned. He now sees everything up close. His consciousness has separated itself from his body and, conversing and observing, wanders through the various regions of Hades, which seem to be organized like Dante's circles of hell. This phase extends to the close of his conversation with Herakles, when his fear of meeting Medusa makes him return to his ship.

The first person Odysseus meets in Hades is Elpenor, one of his less gifted crew members, who fell drunk from the roof at Kirke's palace. His body was left behind. So now he begs Odysseus to ensure that he is cremated and to have a grave mound built for him. Only in this way can he achieve peace and be remembered, while

Odysseus by this action will himself avoid the wrath of the gods. After his return to Kirke's island, Odysseus does indeed see to his funeral. With his drunkenness, Elpenor illustrates once again the self-destructive behavior of the crew, and it is yet another example of what will happen to those who do not return home without a lasting monument. In principle, they do not exist.

On Kirke's advice, Odysseus must first speak with Teiresias, the blind Theban prophet: "To whom alone Persephone has granted intelligence/even after death, but the rest of them are fluttering shadows" (9, 494-95). So he can recognize Odysseus without further ado. But he, too, must drink of the blood in order to utter his prophecy. Of Odysseus' later fate, he has the following to say: He must refrain from killing and eating the oxen of the sun god. If not, he will return, delayed and alone, to a house filled with suitors. After punishing them, he must set out on his final long voyage with an oar over his shoulder to reconcile himself with Poseidon, before he himself, full of days, finds peace and prosperity among his people.

Much fuss has been made over the years because Odysseus does not learn more from Teiresias. Indeed, what use is the journey to this dark place at all, when Kirke upon his return already knows and tells him everything? This is not correct. Kirke only advises him with respect to the voyage at hand up to and including the island of the sun god. Teiresias' information goes further by pointing beyond the framework of the plot toward the utopia of peace. However, with her high level of information, Kirke shows that she belongs to the realm of the dead and, for the same reason, rules over the prophecies that belong to the dead.

7

The journey to the realm of the dead also has more significance than simply acquiring knowledge about the dangers of the voyage home. After his encounter with Teiresias, the account is devoted to the primal female, the world of mothers. Antikleia, Odysseus' mother, is the first to seek him out in Hades, but he must send her away from the blood until the prophet has spoken. When the prophet has left, she returns and recognizes her son after drinking the sacrificial blood to become conscious. They speak together (see p. 180), and he finally tries in vain to embrace her immaterial shadow body.

Through Antikleia, the text opens to a gallery of primordial women in the Greek mythic world, the so-called catalogue of women.[27] The mothers appear one after another: Iokaste, Oedipus' mother and spouse; Alkmene, Herakles' mother; Leda, mother of Helen and Klytemnestra; Phaedra, who fatally fell in love with her stepson—and many more. They are sent by the female primal figure par excellence, the Queen of Hades, "proud Persephone" (11, 226). In the description of these women may be sensed the primal thrill and fascination with which Homer confronts his protagonist in order to share part in the experiences and the energy centered here. And how dangerous a place this is, we only understand at the end, when he flees in terror at the thought that Persephone might send Medusa herself:

"Green fear took hold of me/with the thought that proud Persephone might send up against me/some gorgonish head of a terrible monster up out of Hades" (11, 634-35).

Klytemnestra does not herself appear in the "catalogue of women" but is presented by Agamemnon, whom she murdered in collusion with Aigisthos. With her scandalous act, she has forever cast a shadow on women, (see p.152), he says to Odysseus, recommending him to beware of Penelope upon his homecoming, even though she is not seeking his life. In the final verses of the description of Hades, Agamemnon expands on his vision. When the slain suitors tell him the reason for their presence in the realm of the dead, Agamemnon maintains that Penelope was actually the foil to Klytemnestra and, by her fidelity, has attained an immortal reputation: "The immortals will make for the people/a thing of grace in the song for prudent Penelope" (24, 197-198). Her reputation will also increase Odyssey's own honor. We can once again maintain that, through these contrasting cousins, Homer has marked out the extremes of femininity between the chthonic and dangerous Klytemnestra and the faithful, sensible Penelope, who like her husband has Athene as protective goddess.

8

In the realm of the dead, the very essence of the homecoming motif (*nostos*) is activated, linked as it is to reputation (*kleos*). *Nostos* and *kleos* cannot be separated, because coming home is part of reputation, while a homecoming without reputation is ignominy. In Agamemnon's case the reputation he had as the commander of the army has been lost by "pitiful death" (11, 412). Klytemnestra has not only taken his life but, worse than that, she has ruined his *kleos*. This makes Achilleus say explicitly that Agamemnon's reputation would have been better served if he had fallen at Troy:

> How I wish that, enjoying that high place of your power,
> You could have met death and destiny in the land of the Trojans.
> So all the Achaians would have made a mound to cover you,
> And you would have won great glory for your son hereafter.
> In truth you were ordained to die by a death most pitiful.
>
> (24, 30-35)

This statement parallels Telemachos' complaint that his father has robbed him of his name by disappearing into thin air (see p. 138). It would have been far preferable if, like the other great heroes, he had fallen with honor and been buried at Troy. To be without *nostos*, homecoming, is thus the same as losing reputation and honor. It also emerges in the *Iliad*, when Achilleus says that Agamemnon has mocked him, "[a]s if I were some dishonoured vagabond" (IX, 648). He also asserts that, even though he wastes his *nostos* in choosing a short life of great honor, his *kleos* will last forever: "If I stay here and fight beside the city of the Trojans,/ my return home is gone, but my glory shall be everlasting" (IX, 412-13).

Homer also asks the Muse a direct question: who must be considered the greatest (*aristos*) among the Greek heroes? "Tell me then, Muse, who of them all was the best and bravest,/of the men, and the men's horses, who went with the sons of Atreus" (II, 761). And with the help of the Muse, he himself replies that, as long as Achilleus is angry Ajax is the best—"since he was far best of all of them" (II, 769)—a statement that presupposes that Achilleus is the most outstanding. And Achilleus also mocks Agamemnon when he imagines being the most important—"who now claims to be far the greatest of all the Achaians" (1, 91).[28]

However, these assessments, which are made under the aegis of the *Iliad*, must be reassessed if both Homeric epics are taken into consideration. By placing the most significant heroes from the *Iliad*—i.e., Achilleus, Agamemnon, and Ajax, who are all dead and, to put it mildly, dissatisfied in Hades—Homer provides an implicit and definitive answer. For in full context, Odysseus now appears to be the most outstanding, since he is the only one of the prominent heroes both to gain a great reputation, *kleos*, by bringing about the fall of Troy—and to reach home, *nostos*.[29]

When Odysseus meets him in Hades and speaks in praise of him, Achilleus reacts with the same ambivalence towards Odysseus as he had in the *Iliad*: as someone who speaks with a forked tongue. He rejects the praise and says he would rather be a slave on earth than a king in the underworld. Despite his great reputation, Achilleus feels that life is nothing without the homecoming he never received. For example, he has not been able take care of his old father, Peleus—as Odysseus can with his father. Sorrowfully, he asks about his son whom it was not granted him to meet. He, and Homer, seem here to take up the thread from Book 9 of the *Iliad*, in which he makes it known that he will travel home precisely in order to care for his father and to find an appropriate wife. A tribute to a long, full ordinary life versus an abrupt heroic death.

In his apparently consoling answer, Odysseus seems to reap a sort of latent vengeance for the humiliation, the mistrust and contempt to which he has been subjected by Achilleus. His answer reveals indirectly that he has, in fact, patronized Achilleus' son, Neoptolemos. Apart from Nestor and himself, says Odysseus, no one can compete with Neoptolemos in speech (i.e., intelligence). In the *Iliad*, Achilleus recognized that others were better in the assembly than he was, but no one was a greater warrior. The son's reality does not correspond to the father's. After the loss of his biological father and his heroic world Neoptolemos has in return found his spiritual father in Odysseus. They are together in the Wooden Horse when Troy is conquered, which his biological father was unable to achieve for all his raw heroic force. He died of that.

The last of the great heroes from the *Iliad* to step out of the darkness of Hades is Ajax, silent as the grave.[30] He has evidently not forgotten that Odysseus won Achilleus' armor, which Odysseus now regrets deeply: "I wish I had never won in a contest like this/so high a head has gone under the ground for the sake of that armour" (11, 548-49), he exclaims and attempts—as a sign of his human ability to feel empathy with others—to talk Ajax out of his bitterness: he, Ajax, must understand that what happened did great harm not only to him but to the Greek army, when in his delusion he killed a flock of sheep in the belief that it was Odysseus and then, from shame, took his own life (a course of events Homer assumes is well known). In his attempt to soften Ajax, Odysseus also names him as the most significant warrior after Achilleus. Nor does this do much to help. He is not able to wrest a word out of Ajax.

9

That Odysseus is really considered by Homer to be the greatest hero of his generation is confirmed, if nothing else, by his final meeting in Hades, the encounter with Herakles. Homer knew to give this meeting a special compositional weight and pregnancy. For when Odysseus has reached the nethermost region of Hades, he meets his prefiguration, the hero above all heroes: Herakles. In the mythological subtext, their relationship is shown by the fact that Herakles is also assisted by Athene during his journey through life. He greets Odysseus like a brother in spirit. The connection between them is even exemplified by Herakles, or rather his shade (as he himself has been taken up to the gods and lives there with his celestial wife Hebe) standing with his bow, the same weapon with which Odysseus is identified, the bow as a symbol of intellectual power.

Herakles recognizes Odysseus and greets him as his equal, since he himself once had to go to the realm of the dead in order to fetch the hell-hound Kerberos, one of the twelve labors he had to undertake as punishment for killing his wife Megara and his children in an attack of divine delusion, described, among others, by Euripides in the tragedy *Herakles*. Through Herakles' recognition of him, Homer places Odysseus in the greatest hierarchy imaginable, greater even than the constellation including Agamemnon and Achilleus. That this linking in thought of Herakles and Odysseus is not simply coincidence can be inferred from the fact that they are later incorporated into Cynic philosophy as exemplary figures because of their virtue, courage and endurance.[31]

On this basis, it may be plausibly concluded that Odysseus is not only the greatest figure in the Homeric opus but, together with Herakles, stands as the greatest in all Greek mythology. In a way, Herakles is simply a forerunner.

10

The prefigurative interpretation of Herakles and Odysseus not only creates a contrast with the heroes of the *Iliad* but also a qualified counter-move to the great criminals Odysseus has just seen in the lower regions of Hades, in Tartaros. There is much to suggest a later interpolation, since the vision of sin and punishment that emerges through King Minos' judgement of the dead does not correspond to traditional Homeric thinking: "I saw Minos, the glorious son of Zeus, seated,/

holding a golden sceptre and issuing judgments among the dead, who all around the great lord argued their cases,/ some sitting and some standing, by the wide-gated house of Hades" (11, 568-71).

The idea of cosmic justice, which was introduced at the start of the *Odyssey*, is exemplified in the nethermost regions of Hades by three great sinners: Tityos, who raped Leto; Tantalos, who tried to fool the gods into eating his son and from whom the curse is inherited by the house of Atreus, ultimately to strike Agamemnon, and finally Sisyphos, who enchained Death and might have been Odysseus' father.

What is new is the fact that human sinners are placed in the realm of the dead. With such a shift, the Greek people could live more securely in the knowledge that justice is exercised in the realm of the dead against those who have committed the sins and is not passed down to their descendants. As we shall see, in the time after Homer, this complex of ideas relating to inherited sin will be violently activated in tragedy with the concept of *miasma*: defilement. As opposed to Sophocles, Homer, for example, does not condemn Oedipus for incest.

11

When Odysseus' returns to Kirke's island, he does so in alignment with the rising sun, as the island is located where the sun rises (see p. 195). In this sense, Odysseus himself becomes a solar hero thanks to his journey and resurrection along with the rosy-fingered dawn. This interpretation will later be further developed against the background of the entire *Odyssey*, but is hinted at already by Kirke when she welcomes Odysseus back as an exceptional human being who is to die twice: "Unhappy men, who went alive to the house of Hades,/ so dying twice, when all the rest of mankind die only/ once" (12, 21-23).

Here, death is inseparable from birth, since, like the sun, Odysseus rises, so to speak, as newly born from the realm of the dead. He is no longer conceived only by his biological mother, but is now reborn with the insight that his journey to Hades—and in fact the entire journey—has provided and will continue to give him. However, his time of need is far from being at an end. On the contrary, the journey to Hades acts as a psychological preparation for the impending trials, where it will finally be determined whether he has now taken possession of his insight, whether he is made of the right stuff to bring himself home in complete self-rehabilitation.

First of all, he must now confront the terrifying femininity from which he fled in Hades at the thought of Medusa. Secondly, he must endure being hidden from the world for seven years with Kalypso and resist the temptation to forget his homecoming and his wife, having been made immortal in her embrace and cave. One by one, Kirke mentions the lurking dangers but cannot or will not in every case advise him on how to deal with them or what choice he is to make. She leaves that to his own judgement, because that, if anything, is the condition for his self-realization.

12

The Sirens, probably two in number, are the first danger Odysseus encounters after his departure from Kirke. Their song is enticingly sweet, says Kirke, who knows what she is talking about. But for the man who listens to them it means death, because he will never again see "his wife and little children as they stand about him in greeting" (12, 32). The Sirens tempt both with the knowledge of the achievements of the Trojans and the Greeks, that is to say the same "Iliadic" world of heroes of which Demodokos sings, and with an offer of absolute insight: "Over all the generous earth we know everything that happens" (12, 191).[32]

That they can claim this insight is evidence of their association with the realm of the dead. Kirke has instructed Odysseus how to listen to the Sirens without foundering: by having himself tied to the mast and stopping his crew's ears with wax, which he kneads and softens in the sun. He certainly tears at his bonds, but his men row deftly past.

The Sirens seem to be a link with a truly terrifying universe. Here, according to Kirke, Odysseus must choose between two evils. On the one hand, the Clashing Rocks; on the other, the two monsters Skylla and Charybdis. Odysseus must himself make the choice, but Kirke informs him on the nature of both.

Of the first rock formations, Homer uses the onomatopoeic word *Planktai*, translated by Lattimore as "Rovers" (12, 61). That, like *moly*, they are named by the gods is more than a hint that they are beyond the knowledge of mortals and are impassable and deadly. The Argonauts knew them by the name Symplegades. On his way to King Aietes to fetch the Golden Fleece, Iason was only able to force his way through them with help from Hera. Homer refers directly to this event, for which reason the epic of Iason is regarded as a source for the *Odyssey*.

Geographically, the rocks are most often placed in the Straits of Bosphorus at the entrance to the Black Sea. Regardless of location, this indicates once again an entrance to or exit from the boundless sea of death. Their mobility is generally described as a trap that shuts on those who pass by.[33] It is difficult to determine how Homer imagines them, whether they remain stationary or smash together. There are some indications that he leans towards the former view. He has made the rocks even more dangerous, if possible, by equipping them with a heavy surf that the goddess of the sea, the wife of Poseidon, Amphitrite, hurls at them: "The waves of the sea and storms of ravening fire" (12, 67).

On the opposite route to the one chosen by Odysseus, Skylla waits in her night-black grotto of death—and Charybdis by a slightly lower rock nearby, like a black hole drawing everything into the depths. Charybdis' whirlpool sinks so deep at the center that you can stare right down to the sand at the muddy bottom of the sea. "Charybdis sucks down the black water./ For three times a day she fills it up, and three times she sucks it/terribly down" (12, 104-05). Odysseus has chosen to sail past Skylla in order not to be sucked down by Charybdis. He has certainly passed on Kirke's words of warning to his crew but has omitted to mention Skylla's method. With each of her six arms, she will take that number of men from the ship without his being able to do anything to counter these elemental primal forces. It is not the slightest use that, with almost comical effect, he takes up position in the bow of the ship, armed to the teeth.

It is obvious that these phenomena of swallowing and sucking should be seen as a concretization and projection of the primal female and the fear of castration expressed by Odysseus on his meeting with Kirke. Both in the gigantic Clashing Rocks, and in Skylla's three rows of sharp tearing teeth in the cave we meet the fearful images of the vagina dentata,[34] while in Charybdis' maelstrom we find the womb of the primal mother. In the *Metamorphoses*, Ovid had Kirke turn Skylla's groin into a pack of wild dogs.[35] He thereby reveals the connection between these female monsters. For whether they are enticingly beautiful like Kirke or personified monstrosity like Skylla, they are deadly dangerous reflections of each other.

13

With a crew that has been even further reduced, Odysseus arrives at Thrinakia, the island of the sun god, which Teiresias and Kirke have strongly advised him to keep away from. The crew, however, insists on going ashore and while Odysseus at first opposes this, referring to these warnings, Eurylochos replies that he "must be made all of iron" (12, 280).

As has already been discussed (p. 176), this is an epithet that in its negativity strikes at the heart of Odysseus' personality, his iron will, which makes it possible for him to resist hunger and raise himself above the necessities of bodily life. When, deluded by the gods, Odysseus again surrenders to sleep, a lack of the same will makes the crew slaughter the cattle of the sun god in spite of their oath.

This crime cannot be hidden, as the god with his radiant eye of light is described as all-knowing and all-seeing: "Helios, who sees all things and listens to all things" (12, 323). The sun god goes to Zeus and demands vengeance for his cattle, threatening that he will otherwise remain forever in the realm of the dead. And his prayer is not in vain.

14

While his men drown, when the ship sinks after sailing away from the island, Odysseus is led directly into the embrace of Charybdis. Or more accurately, he saves himself on a rock above her maelstrom in the very moment when she sucks the water down. Clinging to a densely topped fig tree growing on the rock, he is compared to a bat, which in a wider context identifies him with a dead soul. For on their way to Hades, the dead suitors are characterized by this very metaphor: "as when bats in the depth of an awful cave flitter/and gibber" (24, 6).

At the same time, this lonely but leafy fig tree in these barren and deadly surroundings becomes a tree of life. Summoning up his last strength, Odysseus hangs here to avoid being drawn down by Charybdis, waiting for her in her fixed daily rhythm to disgorge the remains of the wreck with which he has kept himself afloat. He leaps down onto them and arrives at Kalypso's island of Ogygia, located in the directly opposite direction to Kirke's island, furthest to the west where the sun sets in the realm of the dead.

Odysseus now balances for the next seven years on this knife-edge between life and death, staying with Kalypso and with increasing disgust ever being forced to embrace the always willing goddess. It has already been described how her name, the concealer, and the cave as her dwelling place her decisively in the chthonic. Here, taken out of time, Odysseus must survive his longest endurance test, constantly exposed to the goddess' attempts to flatter and seduce him to remain with her by promising him divine immortality. As Odysseus explains to the Phaiakians, she is "a dread goddess" (7, 246).

Even when with Athene's intervention Zeus realizes that Odysseus has reached his point of destiny and sends Hermes to Kalypso, she tries to hold on to him to the very end. She objects to the gods' envy of her love; while, to Odysseus, she contrasts her own dazzling beauty with that of Penelope, subject to the ravages of age. To this, Odysseus responds:

> Goddess and queen, do not be angry with me. I myself know
> That all you say is true and that circumspect Penelope
> Can never match the impression you make for beauty and stature.
> She is mortal after all, and you are immortal and ageless.
>
> (5, 215-18)

Even if a god seeks to destroy him, he will endeavour to reach home, he maintains with a reference to his strength of will—"For already I have suffered much and done much hard work" (5, 223). She cannot persuade him into the regression that would drag him down into her all-devouring Charybdis-like femininity.

The great temptation with which Kalypso entices him is forgetfulness, just as Kirke's magic potion also led to forgetfulness. With the immortalization bestowed on him through her love, the nymph wishes to liberate Odysseus from the harsh necessity of the journey, so that "hidden" from the world, he can henceforth live completely in the light of the present moment and in paradisiac joy—a variation the euphoric fruit of forgetfulness of the Lotus Eaters, which gives release from all pain. This is the static world of the Golden Age, enticing as a dream.

On the other hand, it is an existential challenge for the individual with his memory to preserve his life in sequences of events in which meaningful choices and experiences appear like points of light as insight increases. This is where the harsh necessity that Odysseus mentions so often comes in, revealing that memory and consciousness cannot be imagined without pain. In pain, the present moment and the subconscious wrestle with each other, and we see how the past intervenes in the present, so that the subject can be redeemed in a higher self-understanding by seeing through the illusions that previously held sway. Only in this way can the past be rendered void as an evil determination and shine into the future as potential transformation.

So Odysseus preserves his memory of wife and home as a sort of antidote to Kalypso. And by virtue of this memory, he retains his identity, which by recounting his adventures to the Phaiakians he even enriches, as the journey is made into the stuff of memory which he takes into possession as consciousness by connecting paths and purposes through the power of the tale. Kalypso yields and, thanks to her good advice about the constellations he is to follow, Odysseus sails away from her amnesiac cave of death—to suffer shipwreck off the island of the Phaiakians.

The Golden Age Society—The Phaiakians

1

When Odysseus leaves Kalypso, he sails towards the east, that is to say following the path of the sun through the realm of the dead, so that it can rise the next morning in the east, the opposite direction to his Kirke-Hades return voyage. This major topographic movement implies that he is now about to leave the world of death of the *Apologoi*. The direction he takes in accordance with Kalypso's astronomical instructions[36] is described as follows:

> Nor did sleep ever descend on his eyelids
> As he kept his eye on the Pleiades and late-setting Boötes,
> And the Bear, to whom men give also the name of the Wagon,
> Who turns about in a fixed place and looks at Orion,
> And she alone is never plunged in the wash of the Ocean.
> For so Kalypso, bright among goddesses had told him
> To make his way over the sea, keeping the Bear on his left hand.
> (5, 271-77)

Since the constellations are really mythological projections of psychological states —astrological parallels to the gods—it is not surprising that we can find Odysseus' story latently retold in the heavens. In addition to being concrete guides to direction, the constellations in the firmament act as a motif parallel to his own hunt for and killing of the wild boar (the bear = the boar).[37] In fact, he takes part in a hidden identification with Orion, the famous hunter, who saw it as his life's task to hunt wild animals. So, as Homer writes, the Bear is nervous and watchful of him. Since, as we have heard, the wild animals are part of the mother cult centered on Artemis among others, we see, enormously magnified in the sky, how the male cultural hero Orion seeks to destroy the mother cult in the shape of the Bear. But as punishment, he was himself destroyed by either Artemis or Gaia. Which is to say that in his identification with Orion and in his constellation,

Odysseus succeeds in carrying out the symbolic matricide, in which the great huntsman was unsuccessful.

2

Meanwhile, things are not easy for Odysseus. On his voyage home from the Aithiopians, Poseidon learns that the gods have decided that Odysseus' time of trials is over. The sea god sees him in the boat he has built for himself on his way away from Kalypso and, although he knows he can no longer prevent destiny being fulfilled and that Odysseus will reach his country, he still wants to make his life difficult yet one last time and wrecks the ship. Odysseus' battle with the tempestuous seas and the threatening reefs seems here to be a symbolic description of how he finally wrests himself free from the demonic maelstrom of the sea and his desires. That the clothes with which Kalypso has equipped him almost pull him down, heavy with water, is also a sign that she still has power over him—"For the clothing which divine Kalypso had given him weighted him/down" (5, 321-22).

In this desperate situation, he receives assistance from the nymph Leukothea. Although she belongs to Poseidon's element, her helping hand reveals that the sea is about to change character for Odysseus. Originally, Leukothea—the white goddess, as her name means—was a princess whom Hera punished, because she looked after Dionysos as a small child. Seized by madness, Leukothea threw herself into the sea and was transformed into a sea nymph. This little myth illuminates her helpful nature. Like Odysseus, she herself has been victim of a god's anger. She knows that he will reach shore safely, if he will only remove Kalypso's clothes, which weigh him down, and dress instead in her light veil as a safety vest: "And here, take this veil, it is immortal, and fasten it under/your chest; and there is no need for you to die, nor to suffer" (5, 346-47). Afterwards, he is to throw it into the sea without looking back. Suspicious as he is towards goddesses, and not without reason, Odysseus turns over many times in his mind whether he should or dare follow her advice. However, he finally does as she recommends and can now swim without difficulty, held up by her veil.

Thus, Leukothea becomes the first woman to help him without ulterior motives. In doing so, she acts in the symbolical world of the text as a figure marking a kind of transition to Athene, who now steps in directly and instils in him a power of decision so that he shall not perish "beyond his destiny" (*hyper moron*, 5, 436). And as Poseidon departs for his sea castle, Odysseus clambers ashore, battered, exhausted, naked, but alive. And he can lie down to sleep in the iconographically same close, dark thicket, which is never reached by the rays of the sun and from which the wild boar burst forth when, as a young man, he was out hunting with his grandfather Autolykos (see p. 184). For seventeen days, he has sailed from west to east, from the world of death toward the world of life, and the next morning he rises with a new sun. Naked as a newborn child, he steps out of the cave-like thicket—only to meet the dream princess Nausikaa.

3

The question now is how the episode with the Phaiakians reflects Odysseus' journey, since they themselves take part in a series of stories he tells them. They are at the same time a mythical people and a transition to his homecoming and reunion with "normal" civilization—with all the trials that await him there.

Culturally, the Phaiakians find themselves at a stage between gods and men. The divine move quite visibly among them, take part in their sacrificial festivals, and "sit beside us and feast with us in the place where we do" (7, 203), says King Alkinoos. That they genealogically belong to the Golden Age in which gods and men consorted with each other, and where subject and object were not yet separated, is illustrated by the fact that, as a seafaring people, they have no need to row: their ships are guided by their minds:

> (. . .) their ships, straining with their own purpose, can carry you
> There, for there are no steersmen among the Phaiakians, neither
> Are there any steering oars for them, such as other ships have,
> But the ships themselves understand men's thoughts and purposes
> And they know all the cities of men.
>
> (8, 557-61)

Nor can these ships sink and, significantly enough, they sail "huddled under a mist and cloud" (8, 562). The expression clearly signals their connection to the realm of the dead, corresponding to the fact that the Kimmerians also live in a country "hidden in fog and cloud" (11, 15), just as Skylla's cave is also wrapped in a darkness (*zophos*) as black as the grave.

All this is evidence that, even though he is on his way eastward and stands on the threshold of civilization, Odysseus is still in the chthonic sphere, which now, however, has assumed a friendly appearance. This link is underlined by the Phaiakians' name, presumably deriving from *phaios*, meaning the black-grey (between light and dark), a people who in other mythological contexts worked in the realm of the dead as the ferrymen, who carried the sun in their boat, just as they sail Odysseus into the world of men like a resurrected sun hero.[38]

Odysseus' arch-enemy, Poseidon, is the progenitor of the Phaiakians. A large temple in his honor adorns the city. Originally, they were neighbors of the Kyklopes but fled to Scheria to get away these violent people. Then they founded a city with a surrounding wall and temples to ensure that no one dared to wage war against them: "We are so very dear to the immortals" (6, 203). That is to say that even though they belong to the world of the sea (and death), they are contrasted with the Kyklopes and clearly constitute a higher stage of development. (One inevitably thinks of the separation from the giants, which the Aesir establish in Norse mythology by building a wall around their castle of Asgard).

As with the Kyklopes and Kalypso, everything blossoms of itself as in the magical world of the Golden Age. At the same time, however, the hyperconscious cultivation of nature can be noted in the magnificent surroundings: the buildings making up the castle, the lavishly well-tended gardens. This, too, stands in glaring contrast to the Kyklopes' inability to exploit their rich natural resources. The ring wall and the lack of contact with other people, however, reveals xenophobia—"For they do not have very much patience with men from the outlands/nor do they lovingly entertain the men come from elsewhere" (7, 32-33), warns Athene.

In a way, the Phaiakian kingdom is an artificial paradise. Phaiakians are not nearly as talented in heroic battles as in song and dance. They are quiescent, orderly people, blessed by the gods, like the Golden Age society Hesiod describes, where "they lived like gods without sorrow of heart,/ remote and free from toil and grief: miserable age rested not on them."[39] Theirs is a dream-like utopia based on love and peace, but developmentally lacking in dynamism, without the progress that characterizes the process of civilization. But like the city-state around which the Phaiakians' kingdom is built, their society also distinguishes itself in a crucial way from the Golden Age, where everything, without any form of labor, arises and thrives of itself.

That the Phaiakians, despite the chthonic emblematics, are not unambiguously linked to the deadly element of the sea is read in the boundary-crossing significance Olympian gods such as Hephaistos and Athene have on the island, which is consonant with the fact that they are progressing towards an urban culture. Hence, the blacksmith god has created artificial dogs to guard the palace, while Athene has blessed the women with great skill at making wonderful tapestries. The men have their talent for seafaring, of course, from their progenitor, Poseidon. In an overall analysis and as an external mirror image, the Phaiakians thus come symbolically to point the way forward towards the healing and integration that is taking place in Odysseus during his storm-tossed journey.

4

This interpretation is further supported by the fact that Athene can intervene in Odysseus' fate via the Phaiakians or, more specifically, through the princess Nausikaa. Remarkably enough, this happens through her initiation to sexuality, which Odysseus comes to focus in the same way as Helen does synchronously with Telemachos—except that the relationship between Odysseus and Nausikaa is of an explicitly erotic nature.

In the form of a friend, Athene appears in Nausikaa's dream to ensure that she finds the shipwrecked Odysseus. In the dream, Athene says that, since Nausikaa has so many suitors among the finest young men, she will not much longer remain a virgin. So she should go to the beach and wash the family linen, so that, with radiantly clean raiments, she can win a reputation for her orderliness.

During the realistic and lively washing scene, in which Nausikaa and her servant girls not only wash but eat, bathe and play ball, they awaken Odysseus.

With only a branch covering his shame, he steps out from the cave-like thicket. All the girls flee, except Nausikaa. Athene inspires her with courage so that she appears as a brave girl, independent, and with a high moral self-esteem—a budding Penelope if you like.

After carefully considering how to approach Nausikaa, Odysseus instinctively links his address to the erotic motivation that Athene has awakened in her. With "words of blandishment" (6, 143), he says that the man who takes her as his bride will find happiness. After this, he expounds a social ideal with the unity of marriage, its *homophrosyne*, as its centre, reflecting his own past and anticipating his future:

> (. . .) for nothing is better than this, more steadfast
> Than when two people, a man and his wife, keep a harmonious
> Household; a thing that brings much distress to the people who hate them
> And pleasure to their well-wishers, and for them the best reputation.
>
> (6, 182-85)

When Odysseus has bathed, his appearance is embellished by Athene, so Nausikaa now sees the man before her who can fulfill the erotic longing that has germinated within her and which Odysseus, so to speak, has legitimized—"If only the man to be called my husband could be like this one" (6, 244), she exclaims for it seems to her that "he even resembles one of the gods, who hold high heaven" (6, 243). She demonstrates her wisdom, however, by refusing to accompany him to the town. She does not want to risk ruining her good reputation by giving people occasion for gossip and saying that she has herself found a husband and thus spurned her countrymen. The motif is sustained when Nausikaa's royal father, Alkinoos, later has the same idea, identifying himself with Odysseus without knowing who he is—"How I wish/that, being the man you are and thinking the way that I do,/ you could have my daughter and be called my son-in-law" (7, 311-13), he exclaims, promising Odysseus goods and gold if he will settle down with the Phaiakians.

The *eros* motif has various implications here. Through the erotic, and with their joint cunning, Athene and Odysseus have associated themselves with the strongest possible form of persuasion and seduction. At the same time, however, Odysseus has put himself in the position as a possible suitor. In some nebulous sense, he comes to resemble the suitors who are wreaking havoc in his household and harassing his wife. If the situation were to be reversed and if he were to settle there, the static society of the Phaiakians would mean renouncing the dynamic wealth of experience he has gained on the personal level and which it is his task to introduce in Ithaka in the image of the social stability he has just placed before Nausikaa.

Despite Nausikaa's sweetness and beauty, which produce great human feelings in Odysseus, she constitutes a danger to him as a representative of the society to which she belongs and its underlying regressive character. Quite surprisingly, it puts her in the same existential category as such doom-laden erotic figures as Kirke and Kalypso.

The last time Odysseus meets Nausikaa, she asks him never to forget her. To this he replies that he will forever preserve her memory and worship her. If he comes home: "So even when I am there I will pray to you, as to a goddess,/ all the days of my life. For, maiden, my life was your gift" (8, 467-68). Indeed, she has saved him in a much deeper sense than from the shipwreck. For after he has overcome the erotic temptation she potentially constitutes, she is, instead, from now on fixed in his mind as a spiritual icon. She has become a symbol of redemption, a psychological reality that indicates and ensures that he has finally clarified his relationship to the Great Mother, whom he has met in the figures of Kirke and Skylla. In this sense—as a liberated anima figure—Nausikaa becomes part of the treasure he brings home from the Phaiakians.

5

That we still find ourselves in the maternal primeval world is ultimately verified by the fact that Odysseus' salvation depends on Nausikaa's mother, Queen Arete. According to both Nausikaa and Athene, he must first seek her out and, embracing her knees, beg for help—"For if she has thoughts in her mind that are friendly to you,/ then there is hope that you can see your own people, and come back/to your strong-founded house, and to the land of your fathers" (6, 313-14), her daughter explains.

In other words, even though Alkinoos is the supreme king, a sort of Mycenaean royal deity (*wanax*) among a number of lesser kings (*basileis*) gathered around him, Arete is ultimately the real decision-maker; while the king is mainly responsible for political administration. Of course, he is also her uncle—and in Hesiod's catalogue of women he is her brother.[40] He is older but gives her "such pride of place as no other woman on earth is given/ of such women as are now alive and keep house for husbands" (7, 67-68). According to Athene, she is viewed by the people simply as "a god" (7, 71), who with her sensible advice understands how to mediate "quarrels, even among men" (7, 74). The close, incestuous relationship between the spouses—which Hesiod presupposes—confirms yet again that we find ourselves in a chthonic female universe where incest is not taboo, and the marriage actually constitutes a parallel to the marriages between King Aiolos' sons and daughters.

As is the case with Antikleia and Laertes, we are facing a female power that is stronger than her husband, who officially rules the kingdom. It is a matrilineal power that, at the archaic stage of development to which it belongs, is obviously superior to the man, a power that rules mercifully or destructively, depending on circumstances. And so it is the female will to govern the man that Odysseus must once again face and bend to his wishes.

Arete's strength is expressed in her slowness. In contrast to her husband, who is quickly ready to marry his daughter off to the as yet unknown Odysseus, his queen must, as it were, draw up her decisions from a far deeper spiritual and primordial well. She does not at once provide an answer—indeed, she hardly reacts to Odysseus' prayer for protection. And only later, when he is alone with the royal couple, does it emerge that she has noticed that he wears clothing belonging to her household and asks how this could be the case.

Odysseus responds with a long account of Kalypso and his encounter with her daughter. Alkinoos bursts out in anger because his daughter did not immediately bring him to the palace. Odysseus calms him by saying that he must not get carried away, because she acted wisely. This statement makes the king hit upon the idea of marrying him to Nausikaa—or sailing him home. The queen still does not utter a word. Her husband's energy predominates as opposed to the slow female will and, as these forces are compositionally placed in contrast to each other, we understand that it is the queen's decision that counts.

Only when Odysseus has related his earliest adventures and stops in the middle of the voyage to Hades with everyone sitting captivated does Arete break her silence and give him a positive reply, saying that she can read the anatomy and substance of his soul through what has been told:

> Phaiakians, what do you think now of this man before you
> For beauty and stature, and for the mind well balanced within him?
> And again he is *my own* guest, but each one of you has some part
> In honoring him. Do not hurry to send him off, nor cut short
> His gifts, when he is in such need, for you all have many
> Possessions, by the grace of the gods, stored up in your palaces.
>
> (11, 336-41, my italics)

Her voice clearly has greater weight and authority than her husband's, and it is significant that Arete now directly calls Odysseus *her* guest. Now the piper is playing a different tune. And the meaning of the coffer she has given him at her husband's request (as compensation for the insult one of the princes has given Odysseus) thereby acquires a new dimension. The coffer is to contain the golden treasure that Odysseus receives upon his departure. And just like the treasure he received from his grandfather after the successful wild boar hunt, this treasure is also evidence that he has withstood the trials of the voyage as a part of his own self-realization. And the enormous size of the treasure—it is infinitely greater than everything he lost with his own ship—symbolizes the great wealth of experience he has acquired for himself through his courage and endurance, which now only needs to be tested upon his homecoming.

Nevertheless, Odysseus himself is a dangerous man. As the dynamic cultural hero he is, he cannot be contained within the Phaiakians' vegetative universe. The Phaiakians seem to be aware of the necessity of protecting themselves against interference from outside, which can threaten their social and mental balance. Hence their xenophobia.

And Odysseus does interfere in this calm stability, which the people have sought after escaping the Kyklopes. This appears after his departure. The Phaiakians' ships have no problem finding Ithaka, and a sleeping Odysseus is carried ashore with his treasure. However, Poseidon finds it unforgivable that his own family has provided Odysseus this final act of support and, as punishment, he turns the ship into stone and threatens to raise the rocks around the city, as if the Phaiakians were to be sent back to a stage of living in caves. Alkinoos, who knows the prophecy of such a fate, sacrifices twelve bulls to Poseidon and in the hope of mitigating the furious sea god promises never again to help a stranger. Whether Poseidon makes good his threat is left unknown, but it shows his power to punish and to conceal with all the chthonic might, a fate from which Odysseus has now finally escaped.

VIII

THE TRIALS OF
HOMECOMING

I F, WITH RESPECT TO ODYSSEUS, THE FIRST MAIN SECTION OF THE *Odyssey* IS about how he is challenged and developed as a masculine subject or self in his struggle with the mythic primordial and maternal powers, the second main section deals with how this newly-developed self is to meet with future trials in a socially recognizable world. At Ithaka, he must regain his kingdom and wife and, by avenging himself upon the insolent suitors, reclaim his honor and thereby re-establish the stable social order, which has collapsed during his many years of absence.

Reunion
1

This transition from a mythical to an everyday, recognizable reality is clearly marked by a threshold. On the day of his departure from the Phaiakians, Odysseus looks longingly at the sunset, where the ship is to sail from Scheria, a voyage in which the ships, obeying the seamen's thoughts, steer themselves through darkness toward the light—once again, a journey corresponding to the sun's path through the underworld. With the morning star "which beyond others/ comes with announcement of the light of the young Dawn goddess" (13, 94-95), the ship anchors off Ithaka, sheltered from the huge waves and wind. Here, a sleeping Odysseus is carried ashore and placed beneath an olive tree.

Of his sleep, it is said that it was "the sweetest kind of sleep with no awakening, most like death" (13, 80-81). Sleep and death are so closely linked to each other that Homer calls them brothers in the flesh—"Sleep, the brother of death" (XIV, 231). Hesiod has them as sons of the Night,[1] a metonymic connection that makes it possible for him to say of the passing of the Golden Age: "When they died, it was as though they were overcome with sleep."[2] This means that Odysseus' awakening occurs in a symbolic gesture associated with resurrection from the dead. It is a symbolic rebirth we have seen on a regular basis, most clearly in his journey to Hades, which creates a transition from the world of the *Apologoi*, bound up with death, to a true social world of action.

In this way, Odysseus is "twice-born",[3] as Kirke calls him indirectly, when he returns from his *katabasis*. In *Birth and Rebirth*, M. Eliade has studied this death-birth motif by comparing its typology among various peoples. The patterns he demonstrates have evident similarities with the emblematics we have seen in Odysseus' travel adventures, where he, so to speak, has had to return to the womb and encounter death—in order to be born again. He here returns to the primordial basis for creation, to the maternal womb that is often symbolized by grottos and caves, such as those Polyphemos and Kalypso, the concealer, inhabit.[4]

Since this process of initiation deals with an encounter with the mother, it is often portrayed metaphorically as incest. At the same time, this journey into the maternal world of death contains all the risks we have observed: enchantment, being torn apart, descending into the realm of the dead, being swallowed up by the sea, and the threat of the Symplegades' vagina dentata. The hero withstands these trials and ultimately escapes as one newly born—as Odysseus on the coast of his own kingdom.

The primeval cosmological image of this process is the sun's daily "passing" into the darkness of the realm of the dead beneath the earth. In the same configuration, Odysseus returns home as a solar hero, reborn through the metamorphoses of his voyage through death, where he has "incestuously" confronted, withstood and integrated the feminine, which had remained in the demonic subconscious.

That this really is the theme of rebirth is further substantiated by the seasonal symbolism, which is present, though more or less hidden, throughout the second main section, linked not only to his homecoming but also to his vengeance and purging. It is several times said to be a very cold, winter: "A bad night came on, the dark of the moon, and Zeus rained/ all night long, and the West Wind blew big, always watery" (14, 457-58). And he comes home just as the old year is running out, and the new beginning, so that in his return he ushers in new life and new possibilities in the promised renewal of spring.

Secondly, it is striking that, at the moment of his awakening, he does not recognize his own kingdom. Athene has covered it in a fog. Psychologically, therefore, he seems like a newborn child, blind and blinking as he opens his eyes, unable to distinguish clearly in the foggy surroundings. He himself associates this feeling of blindness with the previous occasions when sleep came over him as a delusion: once, ten years' before, when he fell asleep off the coast of Ithaka and the crew opened the bag of winds; and once on Thrinakia, when his men slaughtered the cattle of the Sun. Suspicious and irritated, he thinks that the Phaiakians have cheated him of his treasure. He immediately counts it and notes to his satisfaction that it is intact.

2

Athene first meets Odysseus in the form of a young shepherd, then as a tall woman, and, as said above, they take great pleasure in each other's cunning (see

p. 168). Odysseus now knows he is back in Ithaka. The climate of the island and the state of its society stand in sharp contract to the sumptuous dream realm he has just left among the Phaiakians. However, Ithaka well suits Odysseus' own steely character. The island is far to the north, rocky and with a harsh climate, as he himself describes it:

(. . .) my island lies low and away, last of all on the water
toward the dark, with the rest below facing east and sunshine,
a rugged place, but a good nurse of men (. . .).

(9, 25-27)

With these characteristics, the landscape is not a suitable place for raising horses, which requires meadows. Telemachos actually had asked Menelaos not to give him horses as gifts of guest-friendship (4, 601 ff.). The main sources of nourishment are cattle, pigs, and goats, and there is good forestry: "it is good to feed goats and cattle; and timber/ is there of all sorts, and watering places good through the seasons" (13, 246-47). Grain and grapes also thrive in the place. The roads are narrow and stony, but the people have done their best to cultivate the countryside. Near the city, there is a beautiful sheltered spring, where the inhabitants fetch their water, and surrounding it is a grove of poplars. Odysseus' royal palace is called magnificent. It is separate from other structures in that it consists of several buildings and is ringed with a wall with a strong gate, making it difficult for an enemy to force, but the palace is quite modest in comparison with the glorious bastions of Menelaos and the Phaiakians.

3

After Homer has demonstrated the spiritual harmony between Athene and Odysseus, the goddess transforms him into a beggar. She makes him bald with runny eyes, adds wrinkles to his skin, and dresses him in rags. Unrecognizable as this sorry figure, he is to assess the situation and plan his strategy for bloody revenge on the suitors.

In a way, this is a new variation of the story of the Kyklops. Odysseus enters his kingdom incognito, again as Nobody. In their contempt for the gods and strangers, the suitors act in the same way as Polyphemos. Odysseus blinds the giant and reveals his identity, just as, before slaughtering the suitors, he reveals who he really is. The similarity between the episodes is also revealed when Athene helps Odysseus temporarily hide the treasure he has brought home in a sacred cave and to put an immovable boulder at the entrance. The grotto is devoted to nymphs who, along with Hermes, play a crucial role in the religious life of Ithaka. The cave has two exits—one for people, one for gods—an architectonic design that, in this case as well, symbolically suggests a link to the realm of the dead.

At the same time, the treasure corresponds to the first great treasure he received as a young man from his grandfather Autolykos after the wild boar hunt. The treasure thus becomes a symbol of the forces and experiences he has overcome and integrated. Yet, he still needs to prove that he has actually absorbed the experiences of the journey and has the necessary strength and endurance during the impending humiliations and for the vengeance itself, before he can make the treasure his permanent property, as he says to Penelope upon their reunion (23, 340-41).

The trials awaiting Odysseus from the suitors are so degrading in relation to a heroic code of honor that it is difficult to imagine an Achilleus in this sort of role. In their very radicality, these humiliations exceed all limits. Odysseus must lift himself from a social zero point, the status of a beggar, from being Nobody, to becoming once more the leader of his people, in that his personal development becomes incorporated into the life of society.

During his absence, the social order, particularly over the last three years, has been completely disrupted. The suitors have forced their way into his palace, are making free with his property and shamefully paying court to his wife. Odysseus still represents the true order in the people's memory. Pious, hospitable and merciful, "Odysseus was never outrageous at all to any man" (4, 693) and was, as proof of his hegemony, rich in cattle and slaves (14, 96). His wealth illuminates his *arete*: honor and the ability to ensure his family's continuation and to make it even more powerful than before. His absolute power is like property, amassed in his treasure chamber. That is where Telemachos equips himself for his journey and that is where Penelope finds his bow. By laying hands on his property, the suitors not only dissipate his material possessions but fundamentally his integrity and honor as well.

Since Telemachos has not been capable of defending his father's *olbos* and thus the family's *oikos*, around which everything is otherwise organized, hope still lives among all right-thinking people that Odysseus will return home and "hold his rightful place and be lord of his own possessions" (1, 117), Telemachos thinks. The suitors' ability to get away with their odious behaviour is due to the social structure. As said, every (royal) family had to defend its own property, to defend its laws. And the conduct of the suitors shows how little protection customary law provides.

Paradoxically, however, the suitors, like Odysseus, represent something new in a criminal, negative counter-reflection. Their conduct demonstrates that the heroic era is definitively past. Thus Penelope says to them that suitors once behaved differently: "the behavior of these suitors is not as it was in time past" (18, 275). Indeed, the old age is past, the time when dignified guests visited the house and were made welcome (19, 316). Even though the suitors are noblemen, sons of notable fathers, they are described right down to their actual conduct as a new, depraved generation. They appear as pure caricatures of the heroes of the *Iliad*. They are most reminiscent of Prince Paris, who broke the laws of guest-friendship and went after his host's wife. Their noble lineage helps to delude them, since they believe that they can with impunity appropriate Odysseus' possessions and his wife on the principle that you get away with what you get away with.

Their depravity is shown in the swineherd's emotional description of how for servants they make use of "young men, and well dressed in mantels and tunics, always/ with neat oiled heads and handsome faces" (15, 331-32). They whore with the young slaves and make free use of Odysseus' wealth and honor. They violate all the unwritten laws, when, ignorant of whether he is dead or alive, they pay court to his wife and try to force her to choose from among men she hates and despises. If only her husband and son would punish them. To her, "they are hateful, since all are devising evils" (17, 499), she says with their plan to murder her son in mind.

We have heard how, once Athene has inspired him with courage, Telemachos tries to speak to the suitors at an assembly: they should be "ashamed before the neighboring men about us, the people/ who live around our land; fear also the gods' anger" (2, 66). But they do not even respect the gods. Their "outrageous violence (*hubris*) goes up into the iron/ sky" (*sidereon ouranon*, 15, 329), the swineherd says to Odysseus. And when Telemachos asks for a year's respite to discover whether his father is dead—in which case he will give them his mother in marriage—they declare in their gracelessness that they will continue to consume his goods until he forces his mother to marry: "His possessions will wretchedly be eaten away, there will not/ be compensation, ever, while she makes the Achaians put off/ marriage with her" (2, 203-05).

Telemachos refuses, saying both that his mother would invoke the Erinyes (2, 135) and that it would bring him dishonor. Nor does it make any impression upon them, when—in order to prevent the murder of Telemachos—Penelope reminds Antinoos, the noblest of the suitors, that Odysseus helped his exiled father: "Oh, boisterous/ creature, why do you weave a design of death and destruction/ for Telemachos, and take no heed of suppliants, over whom/ Zeus stands witness?" (16, 420-24).

To sum up, we can establish that the suitors are guilty of *hubris*—"overbearing in your rapacity" (1, 368) Telemachos calls them, using the term *hubris*, as they are guilty of an immorality and impiety that cry to heaven. So, in Odysseus' words, their behavior will call down upon them "the day of their destiny" (*aisimon emar*, 16, 280)—that is to say the day the gods will punish this impious and vicious behavior, which has made them blind to prayers, warnings and omens. This is confirmed by a terrifying vision[5] which the seer Theoklymenos has just before the punishment:

Poor wretches, what evil has come on you? Your heads and faces
And the knees underneath you are shrouded in night and darkness;
A sound of wailing has broken out, your cheeks are covered
With tears, and the walls bleed, and the fine supporting pillars.
All the forecourt is huddled with ghosts, the yard is full of them
As they flock down to the underworld and the darkness. The sun
Has perished out of the sky, and a foul mist has come over.

(20, 351-57)

But in their callousness, they throw the seer out the gate as a lunatic.

The only sympathetic suitor, Amphinomos—and the only one of whom Penelope approves, "for he had good sense and discretion" (16, 398)—tries in vain to bring some order to his fellow suitors and tries to talk them out of killing Telemachos. Dispirited, he senses what is coming. However, he does not leave, not even when Odysseus encourages him to do so with the words: "I see the suitors, their reckless devisings,/ how they show no respect to the wife, and despoil the possessions" (18, 143-44). He, too, is appointed by the gods to die as a punishment. On this, Athene is unbending: "she would not deliver any of them from disaster" (17, 364).

When the suitors later realize that they will lose face if they cannot win the archery contest, they also admit that the purpose of their proposals is not really to marry Penelope—for there are so many other beautiful women—but to gain access to Odysseus' property. On the other hand, they refuse the strange beggar permission to make an attempt on the ground that it would mean a huge loss in honor if "some beggar man" (21, 327) knew how to string the bow. Penelope retorts that there is no honor anyway for those who consume another man's property.

His few faithful servants stand in contrast to the suitors and their followers in Odysseus' household. In order to spy, make plans and find allies, Athene advises Odysseus first to seek out the swineherd Eumaios. Eumaios passes the tests to which Odysseus puts him with flying colors. He is thoroughly loyal and, on his own initiative, has made a pig farm to preserve Odysseus' wealth more or less intact. And he praises the absent Odysseus by saying that, in contrast to the suitors, he was hospitable, merciful and known for compassion, just as he knows that Odysseus would have given him freedom from his slavery after faithful service. Moreover, he has almost been a substitute father for Telemachos, whom he greets as his "sweet light" (16, 23, *glykeron phaos*, see Penelope's similar greeting, p. 158), happy to see that Telemachos has made it through his voyage unharmed.

So it is obvious that Homer himself—like Odysseus in his dressing-down of the Phaiakian prince (see p. 82)—makes use of the contrast between the external and the internal: to appear and to be in the establishment of his universe of values. For just as Odysseus is a beggar but royal within, Eumaios is certainly a slave, though he was originally a prince and he has preserved the dignity of his noble origin. Certainly, he takes care of the swine, but the real swine are the vain young aristocrats. Social values are turned on their head. For while the suitors indulge themselves with clean-shaven, perfumed slaves, Odysseus' favorite slave is the faithful, steadfast Eurybates, simply described as an old, humpbacked black man: "He was round in the shoulders, black-complexioned, wooly-haired" (19, 209-10).[6] That is the difference.

4

The meeting between Odysseus and Telemachos is described in the dramatic crosscutting in Books 15 and 16, where we follow the simultaneous events of Telemachos' departure from Sparta, his dangerous trip home with the suitors lying in wait, Odysseus' visit to the swineherd and, finally, the long-awaited encounter between father and son.

Before Odysseus makes himself known, he first tests his son, as he tests everyone along the way. He says that, if he were the son of Odysseus, he would never have accepted the suitors' behavior but would have rather died than patiently bear their "reckless contrivings" (16, 94). Has Telemachos quietly allowed himself to be cowed, he asks, just like Nestor? Telemachos has a good answer, though he has to admit that he has not been able to handle the suitors and that his life is now in danger.

When Odysseus, whom Athene has given the aspect of a god so that he might appear almighty in the eyes of his son, finally reveals himself, Telemachos, terrified and believing that he is a victim of a delusion, exclaims: "No, you are not Odysseus my father, but some divinity/ beguiles me, so that I must grieve the more, and be sorry" (16, 195-95). Odysseus explains to him that anything is possible for Athene: "now she will make me look like a beggar, but then the next time/ like a young man, and wearing splendid clothes on my body" (16, 209-10).

Once the first emotion of the reunion has subsided, Telemachos says that his hope is now to demonstrate his true worth to his father: "Father, I think you will learn what my spirit is like, when the time comes,/ for the mood that is in my mind shows no slackening" (16, 309-10). He also demonstrates his courage in the face of the suitors, shows the strength that his journey has given him, and speaks like his father's son. Before this, they have together deliberated on their strategy towards the suitors, who number one hundred and eight men in all.[7] They must remove all weapons, and Odysseus must endure their humiliations when he arrives at his palace.

The swineherd Eumaios warns Odysseus how unpleasantly the suitors will treat him and suggests that Odysseus should remain with him. Nevertheless, the herdsman escorts him into the palace. One of the most famous scenes in the *Odyssey* is Odysseus' reunion with his old dog, Argos. It is like a token of the corruption of things that it is now lying on the midden, whereas, in the old days, he was a splendid hunting dog. As he picks up Odysseus' scent and recognizes him, he falls down dead.

Transformed into "a dismal vagabond and an old man" (17, 202), Odysseus must accept all the taunts of the suitors, even as he is planning his tactics and is tested in his ability to control his accumulating rage. Athene lets him be subjected to merciless humiliation in order to steel him for vengeance:

> And yet Athene would not altogether permit the arrogant
> Suitors to keep from heart-hurting outrage, so to make greater
> The anguish in the heart of Odysseus, son of Laertes.

> (20, 284-86)

He is mocked. They throw a beef shank and a stool at him. He must fight the beggar Iros and accept the scorn of the slave girls. This especially so fills him with anger that his heart is about to burst, and just as when he is about to kill the Kyklops, he must control himself so as not to give himself away. He goes the distance in all the trials, while the suitors are gradually shaken by his presence and seized by a sense of powerlessness, so they fall on each other and wish that the transformed Odysseus had never appeared before them. As one of the suitors says, "How I wish this stranger could have gone to perdition/ somewhere else, before he came here; he has raised such a tumult,/ and now we are fighting over beggars" (18, 401-03).

Telemachos suffers greatly during his father's trials. Yet, these insults clearly also help nurture his own daring. Violently and threateningly, he points out to the suitors that his home is not a hostelry: "This house does not belong to the people,/ but it belongs to Odysseus; he acquired it" (20, 264-65). And he asks whether it is really their intention to murder him: "if you are determined to murder me with the sharp bronze,/ then that would be my wish also, since it would be far better/ than to have to go on watching forever these shameful activities" (20, 315-17). With these words, Telemachos has clearly adopted his father's assessment, since Odysseus used the same expression that he would rather be killed than "to go on watching forever these shameful activities" (16, 107). The humiliations unite father and son in vengeance.

Nor is there a lack of omens on the part of Odysseus, when, as during his stay with the Phaiakians, he makes clear that the external does not always correspond to the internal. To the handsome but malevolent Antinoos, he exclaims: "Shame; the wits in you, it is clear, do not match your outward/ beauty" (17, 454-55). Their self-destructive arrogance is based on the mistaken view that they are great, because everyone around them is small, as he says mockingly to Eurymachos: "But now you are very insulting, and think to be short with me; also/ as I suppose, you think you are a tall man and powerful,/ because you have dealings with few men and no brave ones" (18, 381-83).

But at the same time as Odysseus provokes the suitors and gives them grave misgivings, he is himself in great doubt as to how actually to go about the slaughter. To Athene, he complains: "yet still, here is something the heart inside me is pondering,/ how, when I am alone against many, I can lay hands on/ the shameless suitors" (20, 38-40). And what about afterwards, should he succeed? Where should he turn, when the families of those killed join together and seek (blood) revenge? Athene comforts him by saying that he on whose side she stands stands well.

During all this, Penelope and Odysseus approach each other in a deep mutual empathy, which anticipates their happy reunion, but there is much more to be gone through first. Let us look at Penelope's situation.

Penelope

1

Perhaps the explanation for why there are not nearly so many pictorial representations of Penelope as, for example, of Kirke is simply that with her fidelity she does not have the same appeal to the imagination as do women with a more direct sexual fascination. She has gone down in history as the epitome of the faithful wife, one that commands respect but not portrayals; slightly boring and predictable, she just sits and waits. Hence, she has always stood in the shadow of her cousins, Helen and Klytemnestra.

And, yet, the truth is that Penelope may actually be the most vivacious woman in Greek literature, since, as said above, her nature embraces three goddesses: Aphrodite, Artemis and Athene. She is palpable and present but also in the more or less conscious way in which she binds Telemachos reveals a charcteristic akin to the original mother goddesses. She, too, has her darker side. We often hear her wailing and feel the absence of her husband, her despair that her son's life is threatened, her feeling of powerlessness at the thought of a demeaning marriage to the one of the suitors; but she smiles and laughs (18, 163) as well. We are taken into her dreams and nightmares; she portrays herself as extremely seductive to the suitors, who almost go out of their minds with desire. She scolds them and finally exhibits suspicion, self-control and cunning in her weaving that is worthy of Odysseus. White as ivory (18, 196), she is the ideal of female beauty.

In the overall picture, she reflects Odysseus' progress. First, as biological mother to his son; finally, as a beloved wife and the incarnation of his strivings, a Sophia figure and an earthly counterpart to Athene. For that reason, she does not experience clear personal growth in the same way as Odysseus and Telemachos. In this respect, she more resembles ideal women of later ages, Dante's Beatrice, Goethe's Gretchen and so on: spiritual images of a man's striving.

But even if Penelope does not seem to develop on a personal level, it is possible in relation to both son and husband to see expressed stages of female consciousness which she represents, although they are absorbed into the stories of the male figures. Bound by her biological role as mother, she is defined by the underlying Great Mother. By his own liberation and maturation to manhood, Telemachos frees her from the unconscious bond of this stage.

Like Helen, she possesses a natural sexuality, identified with Aphrodite, as she demonstrates in her erotic challenge to the suitors; but unlike Helen, she is capable of controlling her sexuality with the Artemis/Athene side of her nature. So she can be wife and lover at the same time and, as formulated by Mircea Eliade—"Woman symbolizes the transcendent intellect, wisdom."[8] On this level, there seems to be such mutual sympathy between husband and wife that he is even tested in his ability to liberate her from the chaos of carnality in the world of the suitors.

2

At the beginning of the *Odyssey*, Penelope's situation is just as painful as it is for Odysseus and Telemachos. The prospect of having to marry one of the suitors fills her with disgust. She hates it "like the plague" (18, 273) and calls the looming event the "day of evil name" (19, 571). And during her conversation with Odysseus before she has recognized him, she speaks of her "inward heart, longing for Odysseus"

(19,136) and claims that, if Odysseus came home and devoted himself to her, she would achieve an even greater and fairer reputation than that she already has, if that is possible, for as Odysseus says, her reputation has already reached the heavens (19, 108 f.). It has spread like the reputation of a king who governs his land piously and justly and makes it overflowing with prosperity.

Which is to say that Penelope reaps great honor from her fidelity. In his conversation with Odysseus in the realm of the dead, Agamemnon contrasts her with Klytemnestra, advising Odysseus from bitter experience to test her upon his homecoming and not to let his feelings run away with him. When, in the final book, Agamemnon hears of the slaughter of the suitors, he praises Penelope even more highly. She has not only increased her own reputation but also that of Odysseus, by her constancy, giving him great happiness since he has the best wife in the world (24, 193). Indeed, so great are her actions that the gods will forever grant mankind "a thing of grace in the song for prudent Penelope" (24, 198).[9]

Love spurs her to hold her ground faithfully in the face of the suitors and spurs Odysseus—despite Kalypso's offer of immortality—to choose the difficult road home to her. Love abides and provides honor. And their marriage and reunion must be seen in the light of this.

3

Regardless of what Penelope does, she will act wrongly as long as she is alone. The only thing that can cut the knot will be for Odysseus to return home. The situation is that the suitors have just exposed her strategy for delaying the choice of a suitor for husband—"I weave my own wiles" (19, 137), she says to the unrecognizable Odysseus, when she tells him how she tried to keep them at bay by weaving Laertes' shroud in the day and unraveling it at night. For three years, she has succeeded in this tactic, until she is exposed by a slave girl who sleeps with the suitors. With this, the time limit she has set for her choice and the wedding has been passed. She finds herself in constant doubt and indecision and says to Odysseus:

> Shall I stay here by my son and keep all in order,
> My property, my serving maids, and my great high-roofed house,
> Keep faith with my husband's bed and regard the voice of the people,
> Or go away at last with the best of all those Achaians.
>
> (19, 525–29)

As said above, she also has the dilemma that on his departure Odysseus himself gave her orders to re-marry if he has not returned home by the time Telemachos has grown up, the sign for which would be his beard (18, 269). And despite the fact that he does now have a beard, she has tried to keep him in a childlike state, which is why he keeps her ignorant of the journey she would try to prevent. When she discovers his departure, she is appalled, claiming that he is "an innocent all unversed in fighting and speaking" (4, 818).

This interpretation and excuse no longer hold good when he returns, full of strength after having avoided the suitors' trap. And Penelope also recognizes that her son is now grown and must want her to leave the palace, since the suitors are consuming his wealth because of her refusal to marry: "Now I cannot escape from this marriage; I can no longer/think of another plan" (19, 157-58).

Yet, before that, she had felt under pressure to marry, hoping by doing so to bring to an end the suitors' attempt to murder Telemachos. Like a lioness, she attacks the most distinguished suitor, Antinoos: "Boisterous creature, why do you weave a design of death and destruction for Telemachos" (16, 421). In vain, she makes reference to the time when Odysseus took in Antinoos' fugitive father. In short, her impossible choice consists of remaining with Telemachos (so she might be able to protect him against the suitors, although they will despoil his kingdom and honor in return), or she can marry and thereby leave him utterly alone in the face of the rejected suitors and their attempt to usurp power.

That Homeric society was clearly patriarchal is clearly seen when, even before his departure, Telemachos orders his mother up to her room, because he is "the power in this household" (1, 359). If the words startle her, it is of course because it is the first time her son has demonstrated this sense of power which Athene has infused in him. This power, meanwhile, also gives him the authority to send her home to her parents and/or marry her off. The suitors try to force his hand to do the latter by pillaging his property, but he refuses, saying that his mother would set the Erinyes upon him. The arrangement he proposes to the suitors is that, if Odysseus has not returned home within a year, he will send his mother back to her father, who may then choose her husband and provide a dowry.

In view of the fact that Telemachos and her father have such power, Penelope's apparent freedom to choose for herself when and whom she will marry creates some confusion. Nevertheless, this very freedom creates difficulties for her: if she marries, it is wrong, if she does not, it is also wrong. Her motives are mixed: on one hand there is her fidelity towards Odysseus and the fear of coming into disrepute, and on the other there is her consideration for Telemachos and the family wealth. At the same time, she loathes the suitors, precisely because they indulge and violate the usual rules of decent behavior. In addition, her self-esteem is offended. She is afraid that it will damage her reputation to marry a man of lower esteem than Odysseus, so rather die, rather go "even under the hateful/earth, and not have to please the mind of an inferior/husband" (20, 81-83).

The Skylla and Charybdis of this choice often makes Penelope weep, and Athene must soothe her with sleep. Finally, she makes a decision that she must sacrifice herself and enter into what she calls her terrible wedding. Therefore, she arranges for the archery contest, thereby bringing about the solution she cannot foresee.

4

By opposing their proposals, the suitors' claim that Penelope herself bears the guilt for their devouring Odysseus' wealth. In this context, they provide a negative description of her, which in the context of the work as a whole must be seen as a positive mark of distinction—that by her cunning with her weaving she has fooled them in a strategy worthy of Odysseus:

> (. . .) she continues to torment the sons of the Achaians,
> Since she is so dowered with the wisdom bestowed by Athene,
> To be expert in beautiful work, to have good character
> And cleverness, such as we are not told of, even of the ancient
> Queens, the fair-tressed Achaian women of times before us.
>
> (2, 115-19)

So Penelope bears the epithet "sensible" or "prudent" (*echephron/periphron*). Since Odysseus bears the same epithets, it shows that they are both spiritually profoundly linked and blessed by the same high goddess, Athene and her *metis*. And it is for this quality that Penelope wants to be judged—"For how, my friend, will you learn if I in any way/ surpass the rest of women, in mind and thoughtful good sense,/ if you must attend, badly dressed and unwashed, the feasting in the palace?" (19, 325-28), she asks Odysseus.

Athene is patroness of arts and crafts, particularly weaving. It is significant it is with her implement that Penelope spins her cunning and characterizes it herself in such a way that she says, directly translated: "I weave my own wiles" (19, 137). This corresponds to Odysseus' self-identification, "known before all men/for the study of crafty designs" (9, 19-20). Indeed, in a wider symbolical context we could compare her weaving with the Wooden Horse, in which Athene also participated. For just as it meant the fall of Troy, so Penelope's weaving has the fatal meaning that, like another goddess of fate, she spins a shroud not, as she has said, for Laertes but for the suitors, who are to be killed, when it is finished. In this sense, the shroud becomes a hunting net, like the one cunningly used by hunters—and the one Klytemnestra uses to capture and murder her husband, as will be described in the analysis of the *Oresteia*. And when all the suitors lie dead, Odysseus sees them in the light of the same metaphor: as fish caught in a net (22, 385-85).

We gain a direct insight into Penelope's cunning nature in the demonstration scene described above, in which, at the prompting of Athene and while Odysseus is present as a beggar, she presents herself as a powerful erotic attraction for the suitors. She does this to trick the suitors into making her rich gifts in their courtship of her and in this way pleases and honors Odysseus and Telemachos, since she tempts them by saying that: "she will then marry/ the man she is fated to have, and who brings her the greatest presents" (16, 392). So even though, since Odysseus left her, Penelope has lost all desire for "anointing myself with unguents" (18, 179), she beautifies herself and makes the suitors wild with desire: "Their knees gave way, and the hearts in them were bemused with passion,/and each one prayed for the privilege of lying beside her" (18, 212-13). And it is thus a seduction over which Odysseus rejoices—"Much enduring great Odysseus was happy/ because she beguiled gifts out of them, and enchanted their/ spirits—with blandishing words, while their own mind had other intentions" (18, 281-83).

Penelope achieves a triple victory in that, by using her erotic power, she wheedles out of the suitors some of the riches by which they daily reduce Odysseus' possessions. She awakens her husband's desire, when he sees her seductive talent. It must be remembered that he is used to Kalypso, and here Penelope shows that she is the equal of the nymph. Finally, the scene demonstrates that she may well be possessed of fabulous erotic attraction but, in contrast to Helen, she can contain and control the Aphrodite side of her nature—without allowing herelf to be deluded.

Before she appears, Athene has adorned Penelope's face with the same beauty with which Aphrodite anoints herself, at the same time as Penelope herself invokes Artemis. For the remarkable thing is that, in her encounter with Odysseus and Telemachos, she is compared to these two goddesses, "looking like Artemis or like golden Aphrodite" (17,37; 19,54). As she is at the same time for her link with Athene attributed with the epithet "sensible", she is the most rounded female figure we meet in Homer—or in Greek literature, since the most beautiful goddesses meet and are balanced within her. Penelope's sensuality (Aphrodite) achieves a sublimity in her that is specifically linked to wisdom (Athene) and unswerving chastity (Artemis), as she manifests when speaking to Odysseus about protecting her "husband's bed" (19, 527).

It is also in this female trinity that when Telemachos arrives home—liberated from his maternal bonds—she becomes for him the ultimate female ideal that he himself is to seek; while Penelope preserves the bridal dress he received from Helen. In this manifold figure, she constitutes a worthy answer to Odysseus.

5

After Odysseus has arrived at his royal palace dressed as a beggar, the whole text now gravitates—through the bloodbath of.revenge—towards a reunification of man and wife. Along the way, they are led to and drawn towards each other with all the psychological energy that resides in their spiritual identity and mutual longing. Their first encounter is prepared for in a carefully constructed build-up of excitement that leads to recognition, not for Penelope in the first instance, but for the nurse Eurykleia. Parallel to this, the similarity between the beggar and Odysseus becomes ever more apparent to those surrounding him.

A first, as yet unconscious, indication of their union is Penelope's dawning interest in the strange beggar and what he has to say about her missing husband, despite the fact that she has already sat through a series of hungry figures' tall stories.

Meanwhile, Odysseus puts off the meeting until after darkness has fallen to avoid attention from the suitors, a decision Penelope appreciates. With this, their psychological rapprochement is in full bloom. Like the cunning creature he is, Odysseus wants to test Penelope and raise her expectations (19, 45).

Their conversation takes place with significantly increasing intensity and intimacy: Odysseus praises Penelope's reputation, she speaks of missing her husband, the increase in her reputation that his return would mean, of her ruse of weaving the shroud, and the difficulty in which she finds herself after being exposed, as she is now forced to marry. But even in the despair she expresses, Odysseus' self-control does not desert him, despite his compassion. As on the island of the sun god, his will is iron and "his eyes staid, as if they were made of horn or iron" (19, 211); he sheds not a tear, even though he is on the point of weeping.

But it is not only that Odysseus puts Penelope to the test. The reverse is also the case. Otherwise, they would scarcely have resembled each other so much. So she demands reliable evidence that he really has met her husband, as he claims to have. He has, of course, no difficulty in providing these proofs—including a tunic and a piece of jewellery she recognizes. This makes her break down and his heart to wince with pain. But although even now he does not reveal himself, he asks her not to let her sorrow consume her. Odysseus is on his way home, he claims, only he is intent on accumulating wealth: "For Odysseus knew profitable ways beyond all other/men who are mortal, no other man could rival him at it" (19, 285-86). He will be back before the end of the year, that is to say one day very soon.

The two speakers come so close to one another in their conversation that Penelope burns with a desire to show him that she is not like other women. It seems to her Odysseus speaks with such sensitivity that no stranger has been so welcome to her before this. She also stresses that the stranger is the same age as Odysseus and must somewhat resemble him. Thus, she says to the nurse: "Circumspect Eurykleia, rise up and wash/the feet of one who is the same age as your master. Odysseus/ must by this time have just such hands and feet as you do,/ for in misfortune mortal men grow old more suddenly" (19, 358-60). So although the same rules of hospitality do not prevail as they did in Odysseus' day, as a beggar he is to be treated the same way as then. He is to be bathed, and Odysseus desires that it be by Eurykleia, well knowing that she will recognize him from his scar. He needs her as part of his tactic and so he lets her know who he is. Even before this, the nurse has spoken aloud of the striking resemblance between the beggar and Odysseus: "I say I have never seen one as like as you are/ to Odysseus, both as to your feet, and voice and appearance" (19, 380-81). Regardless of circumstances, his true identity obviously shines through.

In this identifying comparison, the nurse brings together what is still divided in Penelope's mind, despite the many signs suggesting that Odysseus is near. For example, the seer Theoklymenos has told her that he has already returned home: "Odysseus is already here in the land of his fathers,/ sitting still or advancing, learning of all his evil actions, and devising evils for all of the suitors" (17, 157-58). She has this confirmed before long. For the very moment she prays that Odysseus might soon return and put things right, Telemachos sneezes. The sneeze is in itself an sign that the gods will grant her wish that the suitors should die. Smiling, she says to Eurykleia: "Do you/ not see how my son sneezed for everything I have spoken/ may it mean that death, accomplished in full, befall the suitors/ each and all, not one avoiding death and destruction" (17, 545-46).

She seems a little slow-witted in her inability to understand who the beggar is in the light of the evident similarity that Eurykleia sees between him and Odysseus. But slowness in Penelope goes together with her wisdom and fear: "for always the spirit deep in my very heart was fearful/that someone of mortal men would come my way and deceive me/with words" (23, 215-16). She simply does not want to risk becoming the object of a seduction like Helen, to whose delusion she refers.

6

When Penelope resumes her conversation with Odysseus, she shows even greater openness and tells him of her dilemma regarding the inevitability of marriage now that she has been revealed and Telemachos is grown up. She ends by telling a dream: an eagle breaks the neck of her geese, which she has fed and enjoyed watching meanwhile. She weeps, but the eagle comforts her, saying in a human voice that the geese were the suitors and he her husband: "Now I am your own husband, come home,/ and I shall inflict shameless destruction on all the suitors" (19, 549-50).

Thus, the dream expresses in the first person what, for fear of walking into a trap, Penelope still keeps separate in her mind and who is literally sitting across from her, dressed in rags. At the same time, it is as if the dream contains a sort of slip of the tongue on the part of Penelope in that it states that she herself has fed the suitors, enjoyed the sight of them, and weeps at the loss. Does this mean that, despite her fidelity, she has nevertheless had some kind of latent satisfaction in their presence and desire?

Traditions in antiquity had it that she was seduced by Antinoos, the most distinguished of the suitors, for which reason Odysseus sent her home to her father.[10] Pausanias says that, after Odysseus had thrown her out, she first went to Sparta, then Mantineia, where her tomb was found.[11] It was also told that she had a relationship with Amphinomos, the only suitor she liked. And it was said that, with all the suitors or Hermes, she was mother to Pan.[12] In the Telegonia, one of the cyclical poems, she marries Telegonos, Odysseus' son by Kirke after he unwittingly killed his father, whom he had gone out to find. At the same time, Telemachos marries Kirke.

In Homer, the only reference to infidelity is made in the passage where Athene encourages Telemachos to go home from Sparta. The goddess makes reference to the fact that her father and brothers intend to marry the mother to Eurymachos, the suitor who has given the greatest presents, and the goddess says:

For you know what the mind is like in the breast of a woman.
She wants to build up the household of the man who marries her,
And her former children, and of her beloved and wedded husband,
She has no remembrance, when he is dead, nor does she think of him.

(15, 20-24)

The purpose of this is primarily to shock Telemachos, to hasten him on when he seems to be making things a little too comfortable with Helen. But the statement is difficult to apply to Penelope. She has precisely not forgotten her husband, but has tried in every conceivable way to keep the suitors at bay. And on all levels, the work would collapse if it really were the case. It would remove her significance as a contrast figure to Klytemnestra, who waits for her husband with a lover and an axe. And Agamemnon also praises Odysseus for his wife's fidelity. And in connection with his matricide, Euripides also has Orestes say that, in contrast to his mother, Penelope was faithful to her husband: "She refused to take a lover./ She was loyal to Odysseus."[13]

If we are to go on at all in a discussion of Penelope's dream, we could point to the regular pattern of the dream itself, its ability freely to use the remains of the day to express what was previously (sub)conscious. The geese are thus certainly her geese, in which she has taken pleasure; but, in their gross consumption, they form an associative transition in the logic of the dream to the greedy suitors. The question is how the dream can be reconciled with her pronounced contempt for the suitors. To begin with, we can interpret as meaning that it gives her a certain pleasure to be reflected in their desire, which corresponds to her erotic display to rob them of their gifts. Secondly, from this perspective, the dream might also reveal a hidden and compulsive world of desire, against which she continually sets her reason, but which constitutes an underlying threat if she gives in and slips into the suitors' world of luxury and decadence.

At all events, the eagle is an image of the avenger Odysseus, but also of Athene, for in the *Telemachy*, she suddenly disappears in the likeness of a (sea)eagle (3, 372). And before Telemachos leaves Sparta, an eagle comes flying in from the right with a goose in its claws, the omen which Helen interprets as a sign of Odysseus' impending revenge. In the eagle metaphor of the dreams and the omens, Odysseus and Athene merge, just as they constitute a common will during the slaughter of the suitors.

Odysseus also maintains that Penelope should believe the dream. In this connection, Penelope propounds a sort of dream doctrine, since she assumes that dreams have a dual nature. Some are true, proceeding through a glittering gate made of horn. The false use a gate of ivory.[14]

7

At all events, the dream about the eagle has crystallized Penelope's decision and choice. The next day, the grim wedding day, she decides to choose the suitor who is capable of bending Odysseus' bow and shooting an arrow through the twelve axe heads and with him to leave the house and transfer it to Telemachos. Odysseus is enthusiastic about this idea and promises explicitly that Odysseus himself will be present—yet still without Penelope drawing the conclusion that Odysseus and the beggar are one and the same person. In her subconscious, however, the two figures are magnetically drawn to each other. She asks him to sit with her and shorten the time until the following day (19, 589-604). Yet she immediately falls asleep, apparently because of the sense of security his presence and hidden identity give her.

In an unbelievably vivid and perceptive manner, Homer manages in Book 20 to show how the two spouses on this preconscious level are reunited through sleep. Here the boundary Penelope erected to control emotion and sexuality in her daytime consciousness is suspended. They slip together into a common sleep-determined pattern of breathing. The moment he falls asleep, she wakes with a start and wishes herself dead at the prospect of being married to a lesser man than Odysseus. But in the same breath, she also feels as though Odysseus is lying by her side—"For on this very night there was one who lay by me, like him/ as he was when he went with the army, so that my own heart/ was happy. I thought it was no dream, but a waking vision" (20, 88-90).

He wakes at her tears and feels that she has recognized him and is now standing at his head. This psychological exchange between them is a clear demonstration of their spiritual affinity on a non-linguistic level, which Odysseus in Book 6 called *homophrosyne* (see p. 222). And so they share their minds and thoughts in sleep all night before "the day of their destiny" (16, 280) dawns for the suitors, while Zeus with his thunder augurs success for Odysseus in his vengeance. To his great joy, he hears in an adjoining room a miller's wife pray to Zeus: "On this day let the suitors take, for the last and the latest/time, their desirable feasting in the halls of Odysseus" (20, 116-17). And so they do!

The Power of the Bow

1

While in Book 19, it is Penelope alone who, heavily prompted by Odysseus, decides to hold the archery contest, it is Athene in Book 21 who plants the idea in her (21, 2). In consideration of the fact that Odysseus and Athene almost merge in common intent, it may make no difference whether it is the husband or the goddess. In any event, there is a psychological process in which Penelope's final decision for choosing among the suitors follows from the intimate and spiritually-linked dialogue between her and Odysseus.

So far, the choice from among the suitors has been dictated by who had the greatest wedding gifts to offer. This criterion now falls away. After her conversation with Odysseus, her express wish not to marry a man who is not equal to him has taken its place. With the archery contest, she quite simply wants to test the suitors in a direct comparison with Odysseus. She wants to see whether they can bend his bow and shoot an arrow through the twelve axes set up to form a tunnel.

Unconsciously, she makes this arrangement because of the striking resemblance between the beggar and Odysseus, whom she still does not dare consciously to acknowledge for fear of being deceived.

That Odysseus supports her in the choice of an archery contest is, of course, due to the fact that, in this way, he can lay hands on his weapon with all the symbols associated with that and thus carry out his intention of killing the suitors and regaining his wife and kingdom.

As previously demonstrated, in comparison with the lance as a weapon (see p. 50 ff.), the bow is a recurrent theme in the Homeric epics. In the beginning of the *Odyssey*, it is stated that Odysseus uses "a poison to kill men" (1, 261) on his arrows. For the listeners of that time, this information must have immediately associated him with the greatest of all archers: Apollo, who launches his plague-infected arrows at the Greek army, and Herakles, dipping his arrows in the Hydra's poison. In the prefigurative role that Herakles has for Odysseus in Hades, the older hero is precisely introduced as an archer, "holding his bow bare with an arrow laid on the bow string" (11, 607), signalling the power that is directed from him through Odysseus into the philosophical and allegorical interpretation they later share.

In consideration of the fact that it is such a crucial aspect of Odysseus' mythology and psychology that he was one of the foremost archers of his time, it is surprising that he does not appear in this role in the *Iliad*. Of course, for his dangerous espionage incursion into the Trojan camp he borrows a bow and quiver from the Cretan King Meriones—himself a formidable shot who wins in the funeral games in honor of Patroklos—but he only uses the string as a whip (X, 500, 530). If we extend his reputation as an archer to include the *Iliad*, his failure to enroll in the archery contest may be explained by a desire not to awaken envy, as he has already won a race. However, this remains an open question. When Odysseus is mocked by the young Phaiakian princes, he meanwhile reacts in a self-assertive manner by placing himself in the tradition of mythology's most important archers (8, 215 ff.). As he claims, he is surpassed in previous generations only by Herakles and Eurytos and in his own by Philoktetes.

There is a close connection between these archers. Philoktetes has inherited his bow from Herakles, in gratitude for the fact that he lit his funeral pyre when no one else dared it is a bow that Herakles in turn had received from the god of archery himself, Apollo, and which was equipped with the excellent quality of never missing its target. During the voyage to Troy, Philoktetes is cast ashore on the island of Lemnos because of a putrid wound from a snake bite. But later, it is prophesied that Troy cannot be taken unless Philoktetes is brought back to the army with his bow.[15] Troy has already fallen once before to this bow—that is to say when Herakles himself took the city. The second time, it begins with Philoktetes shooting Prince Paris, who himself is an archer, but in a condescending way that casts a shadow on the bow as a weapon for long-range fighting.

Like Philoktetes' bow, the one that is to be used in the archery contest has a genealogy that illustrates the honor and spiritual power it contains. It once belonged to no less a man than Eurytos, who may have been Herakles' teacher but later lost in an archery contest with Herakles and was killed by him. In the *Odyssey*, the myth is told in another way. Here it is Apollo himself whom Eurytos in his blasphemous arrogance challenges to an archery duel, and the god punishes him with death. Odysseus received the bow as a gift of guest friendship from his son, Iphitos,[16] and has assumed whatever super-individual power the bow possesses.

These heroic archers seem to share the common fate of deviating from the narrow heroic code and being outcasts: Herakles who in madness killed his wife and his children; Eurytos with his blasphemous arrogance; Philoktetes, stinking from his snake bite; and finally Odysseus, who is quite simply a "polytropic" being.

2

When Penelope, planning for the impending archery contest, goes down to the chamber where Odysseus' treasure is kept, it is not to just to take any random bow but *the* bow. Since it is described as curved (21, 359, *kampyla toxa*), Homer must have had in mind the Scythian model, which had this appearance.[17] The same type is carried by his men (9, 156) and archers in the *Iliad* with an Oriental background. As a consequence of this bow's backward bending shape, it requires a special strength to string it.

In short, concentrated in the bow is the entire mythology that has come down around Odysseus, his honor gathered in the treasure chamber from which it is fetched. As it is told, he has left the bow at the palace in memory of a dear friend and guest (21, 39 ff.). However, at a deeper level it is evidence of the power he possesses, both spiritual and physical. And as a sign of his sovereignty, he always carries it when he is at home.

Viewed in this context, the nature of the fundamentally impossible task facing the suitors becomes clearly understood. In order to string the bow, they must be able to match Odysseus both on a mythical and on a personal level. Therefore, it is a bloody irony—of which there are many examples—that they mock the transformed Odysseus as a man without strength: he "does not know how to do any/ work, (. . .) has no strength" (20, 378-79), they scoff. The narrative irony comes through forcefully, when, clad in rags, he seizes the bow, and a suitor expresses the hope that he, Odysseus, will have just as much good fortune in his life as he will in stringing the bow: "How I wish his share of good fortune were of the same measure/as is the degree of his power ever to get this bow strung" (21, 402-03).

3

The decisive question is now whether Odysseus, when—to the protests of the suitors and on Telemachos' orders—he has taken the bow in his hand, possesses his former strength (his long absence taken into consideration). There has been no weakening, as is already shown by the fact that the bow, as a concrete expression of his power, is neither moth-eaten (21, 395) nor fragile. And as evidence of his undiminished capabilities, he is still able to handle it with the same ease as a poet does his lyre, since, testing its string, he produces the same sound as a musical instrument: "And it gave him back an excellent sound like the voice of a swallow" (21, 411). Again, Zeus sends his thunder to augur that the day of vengeance is at hand.

The comparison of the bow and lyre, of Odysseus as a "poet" and killer, shows that he is now permeated with the same divine power and inspiration as, for example, the poet Demodokos, Homer or, for that matter, Apollo—the archer god of poetry. Man, bow, poet, avenger and lover in one and the same figure.

This universality in the image must have been at the back of Heraclitus' mind, when he uttered his gnomic statement: "They do not comprehend how a thing agrees at variance with itself; it is an attunement turning back on itself, like that of the bow and the lyre."[18] By this, Heraclitus must mean that universal tension and harmony arises in the unity of opposites, which determine the expressive power the string gives both the bow and the lyre. The marksman is put into such universal unity when he produces the optimal tension as he draws the string towards him— by pushing the wooden bow away.

Finally, it could also be said that the bow as a weapon of intelligence, as I have interpreted it in relation to the spear and the lance, is actually used as a trap for the suitors, because it can as a matter of pure fact only be strung by its owner, as it symbolizes his identity. In this way, the bow has an implicit association with the Wooden Horse: the Wooden Horse is the reason why Helen is re-taken and, with the bow, Penelope is won back. This also brings the bow and the loom together, insofar as both "tools" are aimed at the slaughter of the suitors (*mnesterophonia*), by which Odysseus regains his honor and his property, liberates his wife and restores his kingdom.

4

A key word during the archery contest is also the word strength.[19] This is fundamentally the most important question in the archery contest: Who has the necessary strength to string the bow and thereby show himself to be Penelope's rightful husband? When the suitors speak of power, they use the word *bia* (20, 379), elemental physical force, strength of arm, if you will. On the other hand, on pulling back the string without difficulty Odysseus says—"I missed no part of the mark, nor have I made much/work of stringing the bow, the strength is still sound within me" (21, 425-26).

Odysseus does not use *bia*, but *menos*. And this is a completely different matter. *Menos*, in the sense of strength, has a greater register of meaning if we are to judge from the contexts in which the phenomenon is discussed. Homer conceived the world in concrete terms and *menos* seems quite literally to be a form of flowing energy that is breathed into the individual by the gods, often in his *thymos* (XVI,

529), chest (XIX, 202) or lungs (*phrenes*, I, 89). It provides undreamt-of strength, as *menos* cannot be "quenched" (XXII, 96) and it gathers the person's physique into a single point of strength.[20]

So Zeus, for example, instructs Apollo to fill Hektor with *menos* so that he can drive the Greeks back to their ships: "waken the huge strength in him" (XV, 232) he says—in Greek, it is even stronger: awaken his great power, *mega menos*. Athene breathes the same energy into her favorite Diomedes, so that it directly shines from him with the radiance of a corona:

> She made weariless fire blaze from his shield and helmet
> Like that star of the waning summer who beyond all stars
> Rises bathed in the ocean stream to glitter in brilliance.
> Such was the fire she made blaze from his head and his shoulders.
>
> (V, 4-7)

Athene's special blessing of divine power is depicted as such a radiance around the heroes, and so is when Achilleus finally enters into battle. Here, it is described how she places the aegis around his shoulders and places a golden cloud around his already fair hair—"and kindled from it a flame far-shining" (XVIII, 206). Indeed, she walks in front of him herself in a great light (XX, 95), which scatters the enemies, viewed as a darkness of death. The latter is recounted by Aineias, who only saves his life thanks to Zeus, who infuses him with *menos* (XX, 93).

Remarkably enough, the same signs of divine strength are repeated in relation to the effectuation of the slaughter of the suitors. For when Odysseus and Telemachos, father and son, rid the hall of weapons still hanging there from Odysseus' time—smoke-blackened and dull, as an image of their having lost their owner's magical power—Athene takes the lead and, "holding a golden lamp, gave them splendid illumination" (19, 34).

Along with the display of this light phenomenon described in the *Iliad*, we may draw these conclusions: 1) That Odysseus and Telemachos now have Athene herself alongside them as an irresistible source of power in the act of vengeance. 2) That during the slaughter Odysseus moves back into the *Iliad*'s heroic universe of battle, which is supported by the fact that the slaughter itself takes place in sequences of images including many reminiscences from it.[21]

This formative and god-given power, meanwhile, appears right from the start of the *Odyssey*, when Athene steps into Telemachos' life by filling the powerless young man with *menos*. She places "determination and courage" (1, 321) in his breast and thereby awakens his memory of his father and his family obligations. For whereas he has so far been bound to his mother, he can now feel within himself that the gods want something of him. Or put another way: he can for the first time sense his self, as it is his subject. Athene, by infusing him with power, makes him step into character. With this feeling of power, the paternal instincts begin to live within him. They take him out on his journey and lead him to the meeting with his father.

It is characteristic of this inner context in the *Odyssey* that Odysseus, upon his encounter with Athene at Ithaka, asks her to furnish him with the same *menos* he possessed when he took Troy: "Inspire me with strength and courage,/ as when together we brought down Troy's shining coronal" (13, 387-88). Once again, the situation in Troy is linked to the state of affairs in Ithaka. In both cases, he must by means of conflict (*eris*) seek to solve an erotic dispute, to liberate Helen and his own wife. And each time it happens in an amalgamation with a goddess, her *metis* and her *menos*.

Finally, it is by virtue of this power from Athene that father and son are mentally linked together. And Athene herself refers to this same force during the battle, when, in the shape of Mentor, she spurs Odysseus on by pointing out that his *menos* no longer seems to be what it once was when he fought for Helen: "No longer, Odysseus, are the strength and valour still steady/within you, as when, for the sake of the white-armed, illustrious/ Helen, you fought nine years with the Trojans" (22, 226-28). But his *menos* is what it was. He can string the bow while seated and apparently without using any notable strength, quite like a Zen master whose muscles are perfectly relaxed at the moment of shooting.[22]

5

Telemachos might be able to string the bow at his fourth attempt, but he is stopped by a discreet gesture from his father, which thus becomes evidence that he can step in his father's place when the time is right. He has qualified himself for this on his journey by following the power Athene has awakened in him, so psychologically speaking he has become himself. He can now carry on his father's work and essence. This is crucial for the family, since only one boy is born in each generation—and for the social stability the family represents in Ithaka and thereby as an example for the entire known world.

The useless attempts by the various suitors to string the bow—i.e., to measure themselves against Odysseus—are not only doomed to failure but make them appear even more clearly as a decadent generation. They try to soften the bow—made of wood and horn bound together with sinew[23] in order to achieve the maximum tension—over fire and to lubricate it, and when none of them still succeeds in stringing the bow, they decide to put off the decision, referring to the fact that it is actually a feast day for the god of archery, Apollo.

It is also their feast day in a bloody and ironic way. For it is to Apollo that Odysseus—having shot the arrow through the axes—directs his prayer, when with his first shot he kills the most prominent of the suitors, Antinoos—with a formula taken directly from the *Iliad*, where it has to do with a blow from a lance—"through the soft part of the neck the spearpoint was driven" (XVII, 49). For a short time, the *Iliad* is resurrected in the *Odyssey*.

But if, in the hour of vengeance, one's true face is revealed, then the fundamental difference between Achilleus and Odysseus also appears. Achilleus goes as it were berserk in his anger and grief, and his retrospective consciousness is made visible in his disgraceful treatment of Hektor's body, which Homer directly turns away from as "shameful treatment" (XXIII, 24).

Certainly, Odysseus is throughout merciless in carrying out his revenge with great *kratos*—a word with a similar sense to *bia*. He spares only the herald and, in reply to Telemachos' plea, the poet Phemios, but not the sacrificial priest. He commands that all the serving maids who have given themselves to the suitors be beheaded. Yet, it is Telemachos who thinks that this punishment is too gentle, and so he has them hanged instead. But even though Odysseus is described as being "like a lion" (22, 402; 23, 48), he is not mad from a blood frenzy. On the contrary, he puts a damper on the jubilant nurse, saying that it is blasphemous to gloat over slain men—"These were destroyed by the doom of the gods and their own hard actions" (22, 413). And in order not to incur the wrath of the gods, he ensures that the hall is purged with fire and sulphur.

The New Year's Festival— As Mythical Subtext

1

The dates surrounding Odysseus' homecoming and the slaughter of the suitors are so striking that there can be no doubt that they play an important role for Homer and/or the oral tradition upon which he builds. As readers, we have a clear sense throughout the *Odyssey* that there is a deeper mythical meaning to the actual times, which it is difficult to decode completely, since it is only made partially transparent. But taking my starting point in what is stated explicitly, I will make an *attempt* to analyze what is implied in this mythical subtext.

I will take as a starting point the fact that it is emphasized several times that—as prophesied by Halitherses—Odysseus "will return home (...) in the twentieth year" (2, 175; 23, 102; 23, 170). That this must be presumed to occur at the end of the nineteenth year can be read from the passages in which, after his homecoming, Odysseus restates this prophesy in unambiguous terms: "Sometime within this very year Odysseus will be here,/ either at the waning of the moon or at its onset." (19, 307-07; 14, 57-58).

Meanwhile, these dates have caused great problems in interpretation, because the word on which the meaning rests, *lykabas*, cannot be deciphered precisely. It is most probably a pre-Greek word, which has been translated as day, month, year, though not week, as the Greeks only calculated in lunar months. When Odysseus produces his prophesy for Penelope the night before the slaughter of the suitors, it could well mean the next day, but that does not fit with the fact that he uses the same formulation three days earlier to the shepherd Eumaios. It must indicate a longer period of time—that is to say from his arrival up to and including the slaughter of the suitors.

On the other hand, it is explicitly stated that the archery contest and the revenge on the suitors take place on the day on which a great religious festival is held:

"Now there is a holy feast in the community/ for the god. Who could string bows then?" (21, 258-59). The god to whom reference is made is Apollo. And since the suitors are not capable of stringing the bow, they use the festival as a pretext to put off the competition until the following day, when they will then sacrifice some goats to Apollo, noting at the same time that Apollo himself is a famous archer (*klytotoxos*, 21, 267).

In this way, a connection is established, first between *lykabas* and the Feast of Apollo and in the second place between Apollo and Odysseus, since both are archers and the vengeance killing takes place more specifically on his festival. Thirdly, it must be a New Year festival,[24] as it is held in the transition to the twentieth year, and in the interlunar phase between the disappearance of the old moon and the appearance in the sky of the new moon. *Lykabas* may in this case be applied to Apollo as the bringer of light: *Lykeios/Lykios*[25] or as the god of the new moon, Apollo Neomenios, as the Greeks celebrated the return or rebirth of the moon on the first day of each month. It is characteristic as the bringer of light that in a later tradition Apollo merges with the sun god Helios.

On this basis, it may be concluded that the Feast of Apollo must celebrate the New Year and be held at the winter solstice, when the new sun and spring are also welcomed.

A long series of phenomena support the interpretation that winter is at a close and spring is on the way. Wintry images, biting cold and storms colour the scene with the shepherd, the people are dressed in thick cloaks against the wind and the cattle sleep in caves "sheltered from the North Wind" (14, 533). The slaughter of the suitors is also surrounded by signs of spring: Penelope laments like nightingales in spring (19, 519), while the bow string, when Odysseus tests it, chirps like a swallow in his ear (21, 411), while during the battle Athene changes herself into a swallow and watches the progress of the fight from the roof beam (22, 239).

In the bloody vision Theoklymenos has had beforehand of the suitors' impending deaths, the interlunar darkness gathers around their heads—"Your heads and faces/ and the knees underneath you are shrouded in a night and darkness" (20, 351-52). He sees their deaths in the shades of the dead wandering the hallways, before descending to Hades—"The sun/has perished out of the sky, and a foul mist has come over" (20, 357). In this apocalyptic gloom, the suitors meet their end, while in the bloodbath Odysseus rises like a sun in the vault of heaven, a promise of new life.

2

In his hour of revenge, Odysseus not only receives help from Athene but is connected to the god of archery. The punishment takes place on his feast day, in his sign. Moreover, Odysseus calls directly upon Apollo in his first shot at Antinoos, praying that Apollo will grant him the "glory" (22, 8) of striking the victim's throat. This close connection to the god is also emphasized by the bow and can explain his saying that it is Apollo who has ensured that Telemachos has "grown such a man" (19, 87). This places the son within the same corps of divine assistance by which he himself is surrounded, since on the trans-personal plane Apollo and Athene become a sort of spiritual primary cause.

As the festival celebrates Apollo as divinity of the new year—indeed, as the bringer of light—Odysseus himself becomes a solar hero in his configuration with the god.[26] It is actually not surprising but it is anticipated by the description of his situation on the journey throughout the *Odyssey*. It is seen most clearly in his visit to Hades, where from evening he follows the setting sun and its route from the west through the darkness of the realm of the dead until it rises resplendent in the east, when he himself returns to Kirke's island, Aiaia—the place "where lies the house of the early Dawn, her dancing/ spaces, and where Helios, the sun, makes his uprising" (12, 3-4). And his voyage away from Kalypso's island, Ogygia, in the far west, the topos for the Kingdom of Death, takes him towards the east, where the sun rises from the realm of the dead.[27]

The same movement is repeated or extended, when, in a deathlike sleep, he is sailed eastwards by the Phaiakians. They travel between lightness and dark, in that, as said above, their boat carries the sun through the realm of the dead from its setting to its rising.[28]

So, on this new year's day, in his affinity with the deity whose festival this is, Odysseus gathers and enriches the coming year with the inner quality of his being, which he has acquired during his journey through the dark world of the realm of the dead. His arrows destroy the suitors and the nocturnally black chaos that has enveloped his house and kingdom. From his bow and its "solar energy," a new future will radiate peace, welfare and happiness when the kingdom is once again in order and he can celebrate his victory over the powers of darkness with his queen.

3

In point of fact, the new year festival with its obvious quality of renewal on every plane of life is a fertility ritual. According to Mircea Eliade, the new year ritual has both an eschatological and a cosmological meaning.[29] The old year, its sun and its moon, are destroyed; whereupon creation is recapitulated with a new moon and solstice in the cycle of the seasons, a sign of a cyclical conception of time as everything is repeated in a new beginning. The constant act of creation stretches from the chaotic forces of darkness to the light of creation; and, as the king incarnates the god, he is responsible for the course of nature, growth, and the prosperity of the community.

This implies that—as in the description of Demeter's embrace on the ploughed field—Homer is here harking back to the drama of the fertility cults. So it is also significant that the suitors make clear that the festival in honor of Apollo is celebrated by the people. Significant, because the worship of chthonic divinities such as Demeter and Dionysos took place among the ordinary peasant population, while the conduct of elevated Olympian gods is clearly the product of projections of the aristocracy. And this connection with the past via the oral tradition explains the duality that is present in Homer's description of Apollo and Odysseus, who thereby assume the character of seasonal and fertility daimons, linked to the growth of the new year, despite his favoring the Olympian deities.[30]

Like Zeus Chthonios, Apollo also has a chthonic origin that can also be traced back to the mother cults of Crete, confirmed, among other things, by the link with his sister Artemis, the goddess of wild animals. His other birthplace is Delos, as emerges from the *Hymn to Apollo*. In this context he declares himself to be the assistant of the Olympian patriarch—"I will declare to men the unfailing will of Zeus"[31]—in reference to the oracle at Delphi.

In the hymn as in many other places (for example, Euripides' *Iphigenia at Tauris*), he takes possession of the oracle by killing the chthonic Python, who guards the shrine on behalf of the mother goddesses Gaia and Themis. The appropriation is a sign of a systemic change in which Apollo as the patriarchal god of light and consciousness replaces the oracle's original mother cult. Aeschylus, on the other hand, makes use of the ancient tradition, when in the *Eumenides* he has Apollo take possession of the oracle as a gift from Phoibe, who inherited it from Gaia and Themis. In other words, this is a bloodless, matrilinear succession. This is all interpreted in connection with Apollo's role in the *Oresteia*. For the time being, it will merely be noted that Apollo appears as having a dual nature, but in Homer he is primarily linked to the Olympian world in his association with Athene.

4

As a stylized structure, three primary elements may be pointed out in the new year ritual: 1) The death and resurrection or return of the sacred king. 2) The struggle with the primordial forces of darkness, combined with a struggle to win the princess as his wife. 3) The sacred wedding, *hieros gamos*, where, in their union as sun and moon, the couple are guarantors for the fertility of the earth.

In order for the king as incarnation or bearer of divine fertility to preserve his power, he had to renew it each year or at some longer interval. There were various forms of renewal, but the content was fundamentally the same: the old king was executed and a new one stepped in his place. This could occur symbolically with the king abdicating and returning or someone else being sacrificed in his place. In addition, he was compelled to descend into the realm of the dead and to battle with the forces of death and allow himself to be humiliated, finally to conquer the hostile forces. These rituals correspond to the cult in which Dionysos

Zagreus was dismembered each year and arose again as part of the renewal of the forces of creation.[32]

A single passage in the *Odyssey* points directly to Homer's knowledge of such ritual practices centered on the renewal of the king's life energy. In the invented story that Odysseus tells Penelope, he presents himself as the grandson of King Minos of Crete about whom he also says that every ninth year he consorted with with almighty Zeus (19, 179). Plato refers to this verse in his dialogue the *Minos*,[33] which, as the name suggests, is about the famous king, who also according to Homer, became a judge in Hades. Plato's interpretation is that King Minos is taught by Zeus every ninth year and examined in what he had learned during the intervening years.[34]

The meeting took place in Zeus' cave on Mount Ida. This agrees with what we already know: that the mother goddesses were dominant on Crete and brought up Zeus in this cave. This must imply that, by visiting the cave, King Minos—like Odysseus—is in reality undertaking a symbolic death journey with a view to the resurrection that was to renew his strength as king. As a part of this sympathetic magic, in which the country's continued growth was totally dependent upon the strength of the ruling king, he must renew himself by passing through death again and again—to return in the new year with renewed life force.

To the new year's festival also belongs a drama (*dromenon*), in which a struggle or competition (*agon*) occurred. Here, the future king was to show his abilities in conflict with the forces that represented *chaos*. Familiar from fairy tales, this involved a flock of suitors struggling to win the princess.[35] The victor won the princess and the kingdom, while the unsuccessful suitors lost their lives. Through his (sacred) wedding the new king could ensure welfare and order in the country—and an heir.

The new year festival on Odysseus' return and the slaughter of the suitors has many of these mythical features. As king, he must journey through the realm of the dead and be humiliated by the suitors, but win the *agon* of the archery contest and thereby the princess or, rather, the queen. But when he wins his bride in a broader mythical sense, Penelope must in a way be considered a (virgin) princess. For just as he himself is twice-born, as Kirke says, he dies and is born twice: biologically and spiritually, he thus metaphorically twice weds Penelope.

In the mythology surrounding Odysseus, there is actually a version to the effect that he originally won her in an *agon* with several suitors—after having given up seeking to win Helene. Thus, Pausanias relates that he won a horse race.[36] Her father, Ikarios, tried to induce him to settle down in the area around Sparta-Lakonia. To do this, he would have to give up his kingdom in Ithaka and—like Menelaus in his marriage to Helen—submit to the matrilineal line. However, Odysseus refused and forced Penelope to choose.[37] Veiling her face—like the clouds that pass in front of the moon—she accompanied him back to Ithaka.

Placed within such a mythical scenario, Odysseus returns to his kingdom and demonstrates his *menos* by putting down its troublemakers, the suitors, and regaining his beloved wife. In the identification with Apollo, he becomes like the sun, bringing light and providing growth for the crops of the field, while she is his moon queen.[38]

It could be said that in his "first" wedding with Penelope, Odysseus becomes the progenitor of their son, biologically speaking a phallic wedding. With the "second" symbolic wedding, he liberates her from the imprisonment in which the suitors hold her. And this wedding becomes the guarantee for the country's future fertility. So her attraction to him, even before he has revealed his true identity, contains a latent requirement that he should prove himself as a man equal to Odysseus, which the archery contest confirms.

When Penelope is separated by her husband from the suitors' world of desire—just as Telemachos has loosed her from the maternal bond—she goes through a form of personal development. But just as the moon must borrow its light from the sun in order to shine, it is the husband's radiant consciousness that, according to mythical thinking, liberates the woman from her natural unconsciousness. In this, their sacred wedding, she is no longer merely a sexual partner but a sisterly friend, a soul mate or a Sophia figure, in which he can reflect the development of his masculine self, since they are reunited in the most significant place of all: in bed.

The Bed

1

When Eurykleia, jubilant at Odysseus' successful revenge, awakens Penelope, whom Athene had lulled to sleep during the killing, and tells her the news, Penelope reacts with her usual circumspection. With pleasure and with skepticism. For how could one man be able to take so many—no, it must be a god who killed them for their *hubris*. And, unlike all the others, she does not accept the nurse's talk about the scar as final proof. However, her conversation with Odysseus has given her peace and strength, as shown by the fact that she has not slept so well or so deeply since he left as she has during these bloody events.

While Odysseus, sitting silent and with his eyes cast down, still dressed in his bloody rags, awaits his wife's reaction, Penelope's mind alternates between hope, when she observes a likeness to her husband, and disappointment at the sight of his shabby appearance. Telemachos takes her to task because she displays such stubborn inflexibility and coldness. Odysseus is pleased that she tests him, but never before has he met such a woman—"You are so strange. The gods, who have their homes on Olympos/ have made your heart more stubborn than for the rest of womankind!" (23, 166-67). In Greek, Odysseus calls his wife here *daimonie* (strange), and she uses the same expression in her reply to him.

Yet, this obstinacy on her part is no more than a reflection of his own endurance and testing, the qualities through she has been able to maintain her fidelity throughout these many years. She is actually his own feminine mirror image, if one thinks how unmoved he was at the sight of her sorrow. And this test she now—as it were, casually and undemonstratively—puts him through is fashioned with a cunning worthy of Odysseus himself. For she says now that she will have his bed moved from their bedroom out into the hall and there have it made for him.

The essence of the test is that the bed simply cannot be moved. It is their common secret. So he puts a counter-question—who has moved it, immovable as it is, built by his own hands from the stump of an olive tree. This is the sign, he says, and after twenty years of separation Penelope can at last throw herself into her husband's arms, weeping with relief and happiness, now whole in her mind and her previously so detached feelings, as he has referred to the secret—"which no other mortal man beside has ever seen" (23, 226)—of their bed. In this sense, the bed is evidence that, despite all the trials, the marriage between Odysseus and Penelope has been unshakeable.

2

Like the bow, the bed is a profound symbol, demonstrating in concrete form the psychological identity, *homophrosyne*, that Odysseus set up as the ideal for marriage to Nausikaa: unity "in mind and thoughts" (6, 183) arises when husband and wife are deeply linked to each other to the great chagrin of their enemies. Immovable as the bed is, it corresponds to the unshakability of their relationship. And as it is built on the stump of an olive tree, their marriage is organically anchored in the same way, with its roots planted deep in the earth. From this came the strength that was previously the basis for the family's growth and the increase in its wealth, just as it will happen in the future—first through Odysseus' activities and then when Telemachos, who was conceived in the bed, succeeds him.

Now, Penelope finally explains why she has not dared to give in to her feelings. By her strength of will, she has kept her emotional and her rational sides separate. By never allowing any emotional impulse to gain the upper hand, she has sought to guard against the delusion (*ate*) that was the start of the Trojan war: that Helen allowed herself to be deceived by Aphrodite. At the same time, she does not believe that Helen would have surrendered herself to another man, had she known the price:

> It was a god who stirred her to do the shameful thing she
> Did, and never before had she had in her heart this terrible
> Wildness, out of which came suffering to us also.
>
> (23, 222-24)

Penelope does not mention her other cousin, Helen's sister Klytemnestra, but Nestor told Telemachos how she, in contrast to Penelope, allowed herself to be persuaded by Aigisthos to share her bed and be an accomplice to the murder of her returning husband (3, 264).

Both sisters have thus been seduced, fundamentally seduced, by the sexuality in their own nature, their Aphrodite quality, to which they have surrendered themselves. It acts as a chain reaction or a forest fire, as Helen's temptation is the primary cause of her sister's infidelity and her murdering Agamemnon. As can be seen from Penelope's pleasure at the dream of the geese, i.e. the suitors, she also knows the lure of sexuality, but she is able to resist it by virtue of her *metis* and self-control. And so her marriage bed, untouched by strangers, constitutes the erotic antithesis in the Homeric project.

3

There is no mistaking the symbolical mirroring. For the fact that this drama takes place around the marriage bed has a deeper cohesion in that it was here in this bed that the Greek world order was shaken by Helen's infidelity. We have heard how she constantly accused herself in the *Iliad* of being an immoral bitch. This regret has led her to the transformation we witness in the *Odyssey*. She has expelled Aphrodite from her life as a constant source of delusion, since she cannot console herself with King Priam's assurance that the gods bear the blame. Like Odysseus and Penelope, she accepts the responsibility herself, which is also the only way in which it is possible to avoid the trap of delusion.

Penelope has quite consciously lived up to her responsibility, as is made visible in her distrustfulness, her being constantly on her guard against the possibility that someone—as in Helen's case—might attempt to deceive her with false words. And Odysseus concedes that she is right in acting thus. With her fidelity and shrewdness, Penelope has healed the wounds that Helen and Klytemnestra with their all-embracing *eros* have torn in the world of Greek heroes. This has occurred with the awesome strength that belongs to the older, primal feminine stage in which the power of women is manifested in promiscuity, deadly like a female spider for whom self-reproduction is the only goal.

In contrast to Helen, who in her transformation had to eliminate Aphrodite from her nature because of the delusion the goddess has inflicted upon her, Penelope, as stated earlier, is able to unite Aphrodite with Athene and Artemis. By virtue of these divine forces and what they represent, she has been able to run Odysseus's estate for twenty years and keep the suitors at bay. On behalf of the female gender, she makes good the offense of Helen and Klytemnestra. She re-establishes and renews the power of women by also bringing an otherwise masculine form of thinking into the world of women as a potential and, in her own case, as a reality.

So it is too narrow to view Penelope as a projection of man's desire for a woman who is totally assimilated into or subordinated to male dominance. And so there is a deeper justice in Agamemnon's praise of her in the last book and his prediction that songs to her will live for ever, while his own wife will figure in "a song of loathing" (24, 200).

In brief, this means that when Odysseus and Penelope are reunited in their bed, the breach that unleashed the Trojan war is healed. Together, in the bed, the couple also constitute a positive contrast to the dangerous sexuality and female world that Odysseus himself has confronted, assimilated, and liberated himself from during his voyage. As lovers, they are bound to each other in such harmony (*homophrosyne*) that they represent the ideal sides of each other. They do not restrain, but mutually expand each other. Odysseus has liberated her from the suitors and their greedy, materialistic desires. He has plumbed the depths of the primordial, female world, so he can now be united in a lasting erotic and amicable relationship with his wife, whom he wins in the archery contest. They embrace in the solemn wedding of the new year festival, in which the sun and the moon meet in the universe and in bed.

4

Viewed overall, it is this tremendous conclusion that Homer's two epics seek to deliver. That Athene here prolongs the night, allowing the dawn to remain a bit longer in Okeanos in order to give the lovers more time with each other, demonstrates that even the cosmos is absorbed into the act. Odysseus now tells briefly the story of his voyage, not including everything about Kirke and Kalypso, but describes what might be called the instruction he has been through. He thereby determines the nature of his realization as a person and adopts it definitively as a consciousness-creating recollection: how, compelled by necessity, he has become the person he is now, resting at her side.

He has actually already begun assimilating and becoming aware of the significance of his travels while among the Phaiakians. In a narrative sense, it corresponds to the way in which the first-person narrator in the *Romantic Bildungsroman* assimilates the events in his life through a retrospective and selective point of view, in that recollection and recognition are governed by the choices that have shaped the person's destiny.

However, while a story of personal development cannot be imagined without this necessity, the union of Odysseus and Penelope deals not only with the joy they find in each other's arms but also with how costly their happiness has been and will continue to be. They have, as Odysseus expresses it, had their "full share of numerous trials" (23, 350), she as the one waiting, he suffering the hardships of the war and the voyage. The summer of their youth has been taken from them by the gods, he maintains: "The gods granted us misery,/ in jealousy over the thought that we two, always together, should enjoy our youth, and then come to the threshold of old age" (23, 210-12).

Their trials are not even over yet—"There is unmeasured labor left for the future" (23, 249), Odysseus says to his wife. And the difficulty he refers to is what was prophesied to him by Teiresias in the realm of the dead: to become reconciled with Poseidon by once again wandering through the world until he meets a people who believe that the oar he bears on his shoulder is a winnowing fan. Only then, after undertaking the necessary rituals in honor of Poseidon, may he return home and, as an old man, die in his flourishing kingdom. The prophecy stressing that his death will not come from the sea (11, 134, see quotation p. 263), must in part mean that his penitential travels have brought to an end his differences with Poseidon and, in part, confirm that he has finally liberated himself from the chthonic powers symbolized by the sea and its god.

While Odysseus is gone, Penelope must manage the household. It is apparently still too early to allow Telemachos to step into his father's place. However, through his account of his liberation from his mother and his growing into manhood, Homer has shown that Telemachos will in time be capable of taking Odysseus' place and thereby carrying on Homer's own utopian project.

IX

THE HOMERIC UTOPIA

The *telos* of Revenge

1

VEN IN ANTIQUITY, ARISTARCHUS WAS AMONG FIGURES ARGUING IN FAVOR of the notion that the *Odyssey* should more properly have ended with the reuniting embrace of Odysseus and Penelope in Book 23, verse 296. The rest—for instance, Odysseus' retelling of his adventures—was according to this view unnecessary. It must also be said that if the story had simply been about bringing a wayfaring man home to his faithful wife, and their "romantic" reunion, this ending would have been a beautiful peak experience—in the nature of a private story.

But conversely, it can also be asked what it would have meant for the *Odyssey* and the Homeric project as a whole, if the work had stopped there. In short, it would have meant that the unleashing of strife and destruction, which Eris brought into the world through Helen's treachery and the Trojan war, would in principle never have ended, as this form of energy is actually renewed by the slaying of the suitors and is not settled merely by an erotic reunion. In that case we would not have a final conclusion of peace with the assurance of Ithaka's future and well-being if there had not been reconciliation with the suitors' families, including an abolition of blood revenge. With this event, a light of liberation is cast far beyond the framework of the action and into the future. On the other hand, it would not have been possible if Odysseus and Penelope had not at the same time been united by the healing power of *eros*, which takes the place of strife. And it necessitates a unified view of the *Iliad* and the *Odyssey*.

Two things demonstrate that the element of strife is not completely exhausted with the slaying of the suitors. To begin with, as Zeus observes, Odysseus has with Athene's help returned home as an avenger—"For is not this your own intention, as you have counselled it,/ how Odysseus shall make his way back, and punish those others?" (5, 23-24; 24, 479-80). In addition, Odysseus himself is quite explicit when he explains to Penelope that, before he goes away again he will win compensation for the losses he has suffered—"many (flocks) I shall restore by raiding, others the Achaians/ shall give me, until they have filled up all of my sheepfolds" (23, 357-58).

Secondly, his dispute with the suitors' families remains. They bemoan the slaughter and, according to customary law, have only one countermeasure: blood revenge. The demand for this is also made by Antinoos' weeping father Eupeithes who, exclaims: "we shall then be ashamed forever (. . .) if we do not take revenge on the murderers of our brothers and sons" (24, 433-34). Together with Halitherses, the herald Medon tries to dissuade them from such an act of revenge. They both point out that the gods supported Odysseus and that the families themselves bear some responsibility by not having kept their sons back from their "evil recklessness" (24, 457). They deserved to die. So their successors should desist from any further persecution in order that they might not themselves be destroyed. Half of the assembly go along with the families' demand for blood revenge and prepare for battle with Odysseus—and his family.

2

As it was prophesied on his departure that Odysseus would return home in the "twentieth year" and thereby fulfill his destiny, it is not only an individual undertaking he brings to a close. His destiny is also supra-individual, bound to the will of Zeus, to his *telos* that was introduced in the first lines of the *Iliad*, linked to his function as fulfiller: Zeus Teleios (see p. 35).

In a narrow sense, the target was certainly focused with restoring Achilleus' honor, but seen in a broader perspective, this episode is really only of limited significance in the overall account. It constitutes a very limited period and does not lead to a final conclusion of the war. Whatever the reason for Zeus' sowing strife in the world, it is done with the intention of effectuating his *telos*. As Telemachos puts it, the god is capable of fulfilling (*teleseien*, 2, 34) whatever is on his mind, just as the cowherd hopes that Zeus will intervene, and he refers to him directly as Zeus Teleios (*teleseie Kronion*, 20, 236). That is to say that his epithet—which is analyzed in more detail in the section on the *Oresteia*—indicates his will and ability to realize a planned destiny and sequence of events, a theme of a work, at the same time as in this role he is fused with and becomes a divine embodiment of the compositional consciousness.

3

Through his development, endurance and personal integrity, it is placed on Odysseus' shoulders to realize this over-arching intention, which is common to the highest deity in the two Homeric epics and their narrator. For Zeus, it is a matter of using conflict as the driving force to promote his own maturation process as well as to direct the protagonist on behalf of mankind. Combined with this is Homer's idealistic dream, conceived like the works themselves at a time of crisis and change, of producing a human figure who has the necessary qualities in his personal development to become the vehicle for a new world based on peaceful values.

This *utopian* goal may be summarized as follows: Peace and the contemporaneous abolition of blood revenge are evidence that the underlying demand of the matriarchate—that blood must be paid for with blood—is now invalidated, and Homer's patriarchal objective is achieved. This view will be developed further in my interpretation of the tragedies. The bloodbath in the *Iliad* and the marital infidelity that is its cause are replaced by the love between Odysseus and Penelope. The blind rage and physical strength of Achilleus are replaced by Odysseus' perceptive *metis*, while Zeus himself is transformed from a young god, whose power is still threatened by the other gods, to a cosmic force of justice.

But first, conflict must flare up for one last time when the families of the suitors seek to avenge the avenger. However, unbeknown to them, both parties are acting in accordance with a decision made by Zeus and Athene—a decision that also finally confirms that the gods themselves have undergone a transformation.

The End of Strife
1

Against the background of the marital union of Odysseus and Penelope by which the whole universe is affected, the underlying goal—of creating lasting peace—is achieved through the deliberations between Athene and Zeus. How closely the events in the *Iliad* and the *Odyssey* are connected appears from the fact that their peace conference reflects the parallel situation in Book IV of the *Iliad*.

Even here, Zeus put the same question in almost the exact terms to Hera and Athene: whether the gods will still pick a quarrel or rather create peace between the conflicting parties (IV, 14 ff.) But at this time, the two goddesses still so thirst for vengeance because they were rejected in a beauty contest in favor of Aphrodite, that they want to see more blood. And they have no difficulty persuading Zeus, since he can thereby both keep his oath to Thetis to give Achilleus satisfaction and bring his intention behind the war to fulfilment.

During the attack by the suitors' families, Athene asks her father what he has in mind (*noos*):

> (. . .) What does your mind have hidden within it?
> Will you first inflict evil fighting upon them, and terrible
> Strife, or will you establish friendship between the two factions?
>
> (24, 474-77)

To this, Zeus replies that, since she herself desired to bring Odysseus back in the role of avenger, it must also be up to her to make the decision, but he will give her some fatherly advice to stop any further bloodshed now:

> Now that noble Odysseus has punished the suitors, let them
> Make their oaths of faith and friendship, and let him be king

Always; and let us make them forget the death of their brothers
And sons, and let them be friends with each other, as in the time past,
And let them have prosperity and peace in abundance.

(24, 482-86)

So that is to say that his reply contains a number of elements that turn out to be linked in the causal chain of his objective: when Odysseus has had his revenge, he will again be installed as king. This presupposes an agreement with his enemies, whose memory of the slaying of the suitors is wiped out in return in order that their former friendship (*philotes*) may be re-established, resulting in the kingdom's prosperity. Homer does not explain what else will happen, but judging from a similar development in Aeschylus' *Oresteia*, blood revenge will be replaced by the judicial practice of patriarchal law.

2

So the subsequent battle scene acquires a representative purpose. In general, it is to show that the war is over, as has now been determined by Zeus and Athene. At the same time, it is to show that the strength of Odysseus' lineage is intact, so the family may see to its royal duties in the future and ensure the prosperity of the country. As a sovereign sign of this strength, three generations fight side by side—the former king, Laertes, the present king, Odysseus, and the future king, Telemachos. As Laertes joyfully exclaims: "What day is this for me, dear gods? I am very happy./ My son and my son's son are contending over their courage" (24, 514-15).

During the course of the *Odyssey*, Telemachos has gained this strength through his development, his liberation from his mother, and his reunion with his father, while for a short time Laertes himself regains his former strength when Athene inspires in him so great a *menos* that he is able to incapacitate Eupeithes, the leader of the suitors' families, with his spear. The time of blood revenge as an institution is brought to an end. For as Athene separates the adversaries, she issues this challenge in the same breath: "Hold back, men of Ithaka, from the wearisome fighting,/ so that most soon, and without blood, you can settle everything" (24, 531-32).

However, Odysseus is so much in the grip of a thirst for blood that he cannot simply be stopped. In the image of Zeus' bird, the eagle, he rushes on his enemy so that Zeus himself has to cast his thunderbolt before the feet of Athene, who calls out to Odysseus: "Hold hard, stop this quarrel in closing combat (*neikos*), for fear/ Zeus of the wide brows, son of Kronos, may be angry with you" (24, 543-44).

This is in fact the only time that Odysseus is described as a warrior in the spirit of the *Iliad*, completely lost in a blood frenzy. It seems as though he is exhausting the psychological character of battle in a final blaze or spasm. "With a happy heart" (24, 545), Odysseus obeys Athene's order to stop the battle and conclude peace. On the other hand, however, this requires a final transformation in himself—that he suspends his thirst for vengeance that results from the suitors' offensive wooing of his wife, the attempted murder of his son, and the attack on his possessions.

The dynamic deriving from the war is thus exhausted in such a way that the heroic view of the world is brought to an end or rather is transformed into a new reality, forged in and with the conclusion of peace. So in reality—that is to say in relation to the gods (and Homer's) overall plan in the two works—it is only here that the Trojan war and the events leading up to it come to an end. In this sense, the war (*eris*) becomes the mainspring that brings about change and at the same time it is only concluded with the last line of the *Odyssey* in which *eros*—both in the relationship between Odysseus and Penelope and the friendship among citizens—at last takes the place of strife.

<h1 style="text-align:center">3</h1>

This all corresponds to a radical shift in the very world of the Olympian gods, since Zeus, the originator of the strife, and Athene, as the original goddess of war, the role first attributed to her in the *Iliad*, change character and become advocates of peace. This process generally reflects a movement towards the common human values that the *Odyssey* ends by adopting. Consequently, this work comes in reality to contain a contradiction to and implicit critique of the adulation of heroes and war contained in the *Iliad*, where the heroic conception of virtue, *arete*, is linked to bravery in war.

As will be seen, this conclusion corresponds to the ending of Aeschylus' *Oresteia*, in which Athene also stops the blood vengeance of the Erinyes by establishing the court at Areopagus. From now onwards, the city of Athens appears as a patriarchal *polis* in which matriarchal power has been replaced by patriarchal law. Aeschylus makes explicit in this way what was implicit in the ending of the *Odyssey*. Blood revenge, which has its origin in the violation of blood ties, is abolished in both works. According to the *Oresteia*, corresponding to external judicial practice with its inquiries and decisions, there will now be an internalized world of law in which human beings are alone with themselves and their knowledge of guilt. In addition, as a result of the reconciliation, Zeus will ensure that the survivors forget the slaying of the suitors and the demand for blood revenge.

<h2 style="text-align:center">The Royal Ideal</h2>
<h3 style="text-align:center">1</h3>

In other words, since this entire process of transformation has its premise in Odysseus, both in his personal constitution and his development and self-realization, the purpose behind Homer's work becomes that of extrapolating a royal figure who can both supersede a reality based on the maternal bond and replace the era of heroic strife which was implicitly a revolt against the maternal. It presupposes Odysseus' confrontation with and integration of this psychological and demonic reality during his voyage home.

In Teiresias' prophecy to Odysseus in Hades, we receive confirmation that this will occur when, outside the action of the work, he reconciles his dispute with Poseidon. The prediction is as follows:

(. . .) make your way home again and render holy hecatombs
to the immortal gods who hold the wide heaven, all
of them in order. Death will come to you from the sea, in
some altogether unwarlike way, and it will end you
in the ebbing time of a sleek old age. Your people
about you will be prosperous.

(11, 132-36)

His choice of words almost converges with those of the high god, which proves that his prophecy expresses the *telos* of Zeus and Fate and that this *telos* has made Odysseus into one specially chosen. It is also demonstrated by the omens connected to his homecoming in which he is described as an avenging eagle. In the form of this bird, he is one with Zeus, as eagles, which constantly portend his homecoming and revenge throughout the *Odyssey*—as can also be seen in the *Iliad*—are the surest sign of the gods' intent and favor. Thus, Priam's prayer to be well received by Achilleus is granted in this sign: "Zeus of the counsels heard him. / Straightaway he sent down the most lordly of birds, an eagle" (XXIV, 314-15).

2

As avenger, Odysseus is able in the suitors to annihilate the forces of chaos which have not only offended him and his wife but, in their *hubris*, have mocked the gods. That he is fully conscious of the king's significance for his country becomes apparent, when he compares Penelope's fidelity with the reputation of a good king:

(. . .) your fame goes up into the wide heaven,
as of some king who, as a blameless man and god-fearing
and ruling as lord over many powerful people,
[builds the land with law and right]*, and the black earth yields him
barley and wheat, his trees are heavy with fruit, his sheepflocks
continue to bear young, the sea gives him fish, because of
his good leadership, and his people prosper under him.

(19, 108-14)

As may be understood from the quotation, justice, law and right simply become a cosmic tribunal in which heaven is again on earth—or almost—thanks to the unique character and *charisma* of this type of king. Not only is he able to secure order in his kingdom but even organic life unfolds as a force from his character and

---

* Trans. note: the bracketed text deviates from Lattimore to reflect the Danish translation, echoing a familiar Danish adage and helping to clarify remarks in the text below.

form of government: cattle breed, fruit trees are weighed down with fruit, etc. And, in a sign of the strength and magnitude of the idea, Socrates refers to this passage in the *Odyssey* to illustrate how the gods reward the just.[1]

That the just king is an emanation and incarnation of the divine is an idea that makes itself felt throughout the history of early European culture. Kings were significant as representatives of the gods or of God, after human beings severed their immediate ties with the gods—whether in Paradise or the Golden Age, as the Greeks described the age under Kronos.

In the Golden Age, they find a utopian precursor to an ideal form of state. In the *Odyssey*, the state of the Phaiakians is just such an anticipation, a Golden Age society in which gods and men still consorted and in which all things are overflowing with paradisiacal abundance because the kingdom is governed on the basis of peaceful values. And although the Phaiakian realm is seen as a regressive society, it forms a model in the sense that, as a forward-looking urban culture, it represents the utopia for which Homer makes himself spokesman.

3

As in so many areas, Homer agrees with Hesiod here. For the sake of perspective, I will briefly discuss how, in the *Theogony*, Hesiod expresses the same idea that Zeus is the "source of kings."[2] This requires kings and rulers with the right disposition. For as Hesiod, in almost the same words as Homer, says in *Works and Days*:

> But when the judges of a town are fair
> To foreigner and citizen alike,
> Their city prospers and her people bloom.[3]

This is contrasted with the so-called "bribe-swallowing" kings—that is to say rulers who, like the aristocracy in the times of crisis during which Homer and Hesiod created their works, look only after themselves, rule without regard for the people, pronounce false judgements and are open to bribes. And as this was the immediate situation for him, Hesiod feels that he is living in the worst of all ages, which, using a metallurgical term, he calls an Iron Age, which in a declining succession has followed the Golden, Silver and Bronze Ages. His utopia heralds a new Golden Age, but this requires a sense of justice to prevail and life to be based on good order and tranquillity.

How fundamental this mode of thinking becomes for future Greeks is demonstrated by the fact that in the *Republic* Plato refers to Homer and Hesiod in his account of the optimal legal principles.[4] If prosperity and fertility flow from a good king, this must mean that he has taken over the role that previously belonged to the goddess of fertility. This stage of development, too, is a consequence of Odysseus' self-realization, expressed in his regained patriarchal power and happiness in love.

Odysseus as an Ideal Figure

1

In a recapitulation of Odysseus' *mythos*, the rhetorical question may be raised: Why does he of all people become the ideal figure of a ruler, the elect of the gods and Homer? The answer lies in the earlier account of his psychological profile.

As one who still offered sacrifices, showed piety, and was mild and just as king, he is placed in glaring contrast to Aigisthos, who ignored all Zeus' warnings, seduced Klytemnestra and murdered her husband, his cousin. So like the suitors, he gets what he deserves. Without hiding his own tumultuous experiences, Odysseus also recommends the suitors "to take in silence the gifts of the gods" (18, 142). This self-help, which he here defends by referring to the gods, can be summed up with the word for moderation, *sophrosyne*, which also makes him restrain the nurse as she gloats after the slaughter.

As quoted above (p. 171), Penelope also emphasizes to the suitors Odysseus' excellent qualities as king. In contrast to other rulers, he did not have the despicable habit of alternatively showing hatred and favor to his people. On the contrary, Odysseus inflicted no injustice on anyone. Once again, tyrannical caprice seems to reflect the same contemporary, insecure situation that finds expression in Hesiod, which once again confirms Homer's character as a "witness to the times," over a succession of crisis-ridden years.

Odysseus already displays these character traits in the *Iliad*, when he tries to persuade Achilleus—by referring to his aged father—to moderate his belligerent personality: "be it yours to hold fast in your bosom/ the anger of the proud heart, for consideration is better" (IX, 255-56). His words fall on barren ground, however, imprisoned in self-reinforcing demony and delusion as Achilleus is. Moreover, it is evidence of Odysseus' future significance that, unlike Achilleus, he uses his intelligence to understand and interpret his choices, a continual discursive practice in which he exercises his ability to reflect, his patience and his self-control.

Heroic *arete*, I will repeat briefly, is external in the sense that a hero relates solely to his reflection in those surrounding him and their estimation of him. It is in being seen and admired that he feels himself, not by virtue of some inner life. For the same reason, heroic *arete* has no real moral categories, nor is it connected to justice, let alone to wisdom. The *arete* of wisdom can only be conceived in a warrior's conduct. The hero must necessarily create war in order constantly to confirm himself in the eyes of those around him and thereby continually to enhance his reputation (*kleos*). He who shrinks from battle or loses his property is shamed.

It is these demands for moderation that Odysseus true to his nature makes, and this answer he gives. On his homecoming, in the light of his previous violent conduct, he succeeds in formulating a morality that contains humility as a virtue. As this person who has come so far by virtue of his own development and will, Odysseus becomes the embodiment of a new *arete*.

He himself emphasizes this contradiction between external and internal values, when he berates the Phaiakian prince for mocking him. As he says (p. 82), being beautiful, a heroic quality, counts for nothing, if one speaks and acts unwisely; whereas, an ugly person may be favored by the gods with the ability to speak well and thus a spiritual strength that arouses the admiration of the world, so that when he walks through town, "people look upon him as on a god" (8, 173). It is on the basis of exactly this same contrast, taken to its furthest extreme, that Homer creates the appalling tension between Odysseus, transformed into a beggar but with a kingly heart, and the suitors who strut like peacocks in their decadent finery but are rotten at heart.

2

Since Odysseus is able to infer the functions of a good king from his wife's fidelity, it must also be possible to turn his conclusion around and say that the orderly foundation of a country and a kingdom—its *eunomia*—very much depends on the stability of marriage. This is also the basis for Odysseus' words to Nausikaa (see p. 222) in which he holds marriage up as an ideal on the basis of his own past—and future: nothing is so joyful, so splendid as two who love each other in the perfect *homophrosyne* of harmony.

Of course, this statement must be seen against the background of the *Iliad*: Helen's marital infidelity and the war it unleashes. Marital fidelity thus becomes the means by which sexuality as a demonic, blinding life force can and must be fettered. And, so, in the last book, having learned from his own harsh experience, Agamemnon is able to say that Penelope waited faithfully for Odysseus to his great joy, for "surely you won yourself a wife endowed with great virtue" (24, 193).

In addition, he gains an even greater spiritual accord in his reunion with Penelope. Their common *metis*, psychological and erotic unity become the foundation for the stability of Ithaka's future government. And the depth of their union is demonstrated by the fact that the cosmos enters into their erotic union, while as their gravitational pull, the Homeric epics ultimately have Penelope's embrace as their final goal. In her acceptance, Odysseus becomes the restored husband and king—only now do all his experiences become real; only now does he become whole.

In this, Odysseus and Penelope are not only contrasts to Helen and her criminal *eros* but also to Agamemnon and Klytemnestra, who throughout the *Odyssey* act as negative mirror images in which a one-dimensional hero loses his life to his chthonic woman. In the *homophrosyne* of Odysseus and Penelope, a new era of new moral values, of peace and love, arises in which the primal mother is resolved and integrated into the patriarchal society.

In this sense, the *Odyssey* has two related compositional goals: as elements in his self-realization, Odysseus' voyage and *eros* become the first objective, the condition for the conclusion of war. Secondly, during this process, the Olympian character is changed from the *Iliad*'s young gods of war to the *Odyssey*'s responsible, mature gods of peace, personified by Athene, Apollo and Zeus, who together symbolize the social practices of patrilinear descent.

3

It is from this same perspective that Telemachos and his development become fully comprehensible; it highlights why the *Odyssey* can under no circumstances do without the *Telemachy*. Homer has Telemachos go through a voyage to maturity, which admittedly cannot be compared with that of his father but nevertheless has such content combined with the personal qualities he has inherited from Odysseus, that one can be confident that he will be able to take over and secure the continuity after his father. When, together with his father and grandfather, he faces the families of the suitors, he proves his right to inherit, for, as he says to Odysseus: "You will see, dear father, if you wish, that as far as my will goes,/ I will not shame my blood that comes from you, which you speak of" (24, 511-12).

From now on, Telemachos as the rightful heir is ready to take his place on the throne, which he could not do at the beginning of the work when he tried to call a popular assembly. As Nestor pointed out, he not only looks like his father, but he has inherited his ability to speak, a sign that the internal corresponds to the external. So Telemachos is also finally able to live up to the model held up to him as an ideal by both Athene and Nestor: Orestes. And with this, he becomes a young man with a stake in the future of the next generation.

Homer the Utopian

1

With the Wooden Horse, Odysseus became *a sacker of cities*, the event, if any, to which his reputation is linked. As a *builder of cities*, he ensures his country's future, peace and stability by killing the suitors. The ten-year long voyage between Troy and Ithaka contains this self-realization, which is the true source of power behind the rebuilding of the kingdom. And on this basis it can be claimed that Homer himself uses Odysseus' development to express his own utopian longing for *eunomia*.

So that, although it might seem curious, when the originator of the poetry contest between Homer and Hesiod (see p. 33) makes Homer into the son of Telemachos and Polykaste, Nestor's daughter, whom he meets during his voyage (thus making him into Odysseus' grandson), it has a deeper logic of symbolically showing Homer's close spiritual kinship to this family. Homer simply uses Odysseus' personal character and development to project the general plan, which at the narrative level is attributed to Zeus and on the compositional level coincides with his own concept of society and life.

For, as said above, the objectivity for which the narrator strives does not mean that Homer is not subjective. A clear example of this was his disgust at Achilleus' shameful treatment of Hektor's body and his pronounced loathing for the war (see p. 39). Likewise, his contempt shines through his description of the suitors' *hubris* and their degenerate lifestyle. On the other hand, he empathizes with Odysseus in his battle against harsh necessity, admiring his endurance, his multifaceted cunning, and his ability to control himself.

Thus, in actual fact, the Homer of the *Odyssey* is closer to an author such as Aeschylus and a legislator such as Solon than to the heroes he describes in the *Iliad*. This is immediately apparent in the *Odyssey*, when the narrator places crucial importance on the fact that, during his voyage home, Odysseus thought about more than himself, something that heroes are otherwise not in the habit of doing. He displayed concern and did what was in his power to save his crew, but, as the foolish creatures they were, they were destroyed—and all because they possessed neither temperance nor the strength to resist the temptations that were forced on them. They slid regressively back into thoughtless sensual pleasures.

2

So we are presented with the evolutionary paradox that the *Iliad*'s militant heroism forms a transition to and precondition for the peaceful coexistence with which the *Odyssey* concludes. The internal structure deals with the fact that the heroes and the closing of their era represent an implicit rebellion against the dominant mother cults. They liberate themselves by virtue of their heroic code but are still really defined by the reality from which they have marginalized themselves.

Homer is silent about the fertility goddesses and their positive effects, not because, as it has been claimed, he does not recognize their primordial existence, but because his objective is to replace them with an Olympian patriarchy. For that reason, too, he can only describe the chthonic as demonic forces in the *Apologoi*. And at the same time he has in Odysseus developed a figure whose *metis* permits him to transcend the heroic universe of the *Iliad* as well as the Great Mother; just as, on his last voyage, he settles his final account and reconciles himself once and for all with Poseidon, the atavistic god of the seas.

Since Homer's narrative awareness is suspended between these internal contrasts, the vehicles of his forward-looking search for redemption, he makes use of a large number of contrasts in his composition. Most important, of course, is the divergence between the warlike world (*bia/kratos*) of the *Iliad* and the more human and rational reality of the *Odyssey*. From this point of view, in other words, the *Odyssey* acts as a critical disavowel of the *Iliad*. This is seen again in the contrast between Achilleus' wrath and Odysseus' will to return home by virtue of his intellect. It is also possible to add other apparent compositional contradictions: Aigisthos v. Odysseus, Penelope v. Klytemnestra/Helen, Penelope/Odysseus v. Klytemnestra/Agamemnon, Odysseus v. Achilleus, Odysseus v. the suitors, and Antikleia v. Eurykleia, while the latter also figures in a contrast with the faithless servant girl Melantho, but correspond to the faithful shepherd

Eumaios, etc. From this field of tension, it is possible to extrapolate Homer's underlying philosophy.

3

Even in the *Iliad*, it is possible to read a critical counter movement to the heroic cultivation of bravery and exclusivity of war—directly when Homer denounces Achilleus' atrocities against Hektor's body and war as such, more implicitly in the similes he uses. As said above, he takes these largely from ordinary, everyday life or the natural scenery he seems to know intimately. As an example, let us take the battle scene in the cloud of dust kicked up by the horses:

> As when along the hallowed threshing floors the wind scatters
> Chaff, among men winnowing, and the fair haired Demeter
> In the leaning wind discriminates the chaff and the true grain
> And the piling chaff whitens beneath it, so now the Achaians
> Turned white underneath the dust the feet of the horses
> Drove far into the brazen sky across their faces.
>
> (V, 499–504)

War and the everyday are interwoven as in the frieze of images on Achilleus' shield, forged by Hephaistos himself.[5] The world of farmers, the scene with chain dancing, vineyards, waving fields of corn are contrasted here with the siege of a city and the merciless slaughter of the inhabitants with a view to material gain. An illustration of how heroism, as exercised by the owner of the shield, contains within it a brutality which Homer fundamentally wishes to be replaced by the peaceful values of ordinary life.

Homer's sympathy for the ordinariness of everyday life and for ordinary people is expressed in the *Odyssey* through his description of the shepherds and a servant girl such as Eurykleia. In the case of Eumaios, his human qualities are symbolically indicated by a discrepancy between his distinguished origin and his poor position as a shepherd. These humble folk have remained faithful. And it is a crucial point that Odysseus can only regain his kingdom in an alliance with these people who have the humble view of life of which he speaks to the suitors. Not to seem, but to be.

4

So in Homer's work there is a clear longing for the orderly peaceful conditions that are the final answer in the *Odyssey*. Through Odysseus and his wife and son, Homer has directly formulated the demand for justice in the exercise of power— ironically enough, most explicitly through one of the suitors, who, in fear of the increasingly threatening attitude adopted by Odysseus as a beggar, puts forward the hypothesis that one must be on guard against the gods, because they travel the country incognito, "watching to see which men keep the laws (*eunomia*), and which are violent (*hubris*)" (17, 487). The implication is that Odysseus could be a god.

From this, the moral may be derived that order requires a pious and righteous king, as Odysseus is described. For if "law and order" reign, the people and the crops will thrive "because of/ his good leadership" (19, 113–114).

With this we are back with the claim that an essential part of the *Odyssey* was conceived at the same time as Hesiod was writing his works and feeling that he was living in the decadent age of iron. In *Works and Days*, he warns his greedy brother against *hubris* but equally seeks to bring corrupt rulers to reason. And in the *Theogony*, he has Zeus conceive with Themis, the goddess of justice, the daughters known as the Horai,[6] who can ensure such a world of law and order and who on a cosmic plane ensure the proper balance of nature: Eirene = peace, Dike = justice, and Eunomia = justice, which Solon makes the foundation for his constitution.[7]

5

Solon, if anyone, is the statesman who tried to realize these ideas in a written legal code. Mention of him here is to make visible what is more or less latent in Homer's and Hesiod's dream of a peaceful and just social *eunomia*. In difficult political times, during which rich landowners and oppressed and debt-ridden peasants found themselves in a tense situation that threatened civil war, Solon was named as *archon* in 594/93 B.C. *Eunomia* is the collective goal for the citizens of the state, which on an individual level requires that people should be capable of exhibiting self-control, as is witnessed by the maxims attributed to Solon (and the oracle at Delphi): "Everything in moderation" and "Know thyself."[8]

He expresses this, his primary message, in one of his philosophical poems[9] which can be paraphrased as follows: The gods will not allow Athens to be destroyed, since Pallas Athene holds her protective hand over the city. But at the same time its social order is threatened by the citizens' lack of moderation. Because of injustice, their craving for money and their scandalous *hubris* will inevitably lead to multiple conflicts (*eris*). However, justice in the form of Dike will intervene in the disorder (*dysnomia*), and Eunomia will chain injustice and put an end to the unrestrained arrogance. And the poem ends: "Under her regime (Eunomia), all things are proper and prudence rules human affairs."[10]

Solon can only imagine a supra-individual intervention, as he assumes an immanent, just law in life that does not allow human beings to lift the world order off its hinges. We shall also see this sort of universally effective representative of justice, Dike, philosophically justified at about the same time in Anaximander's cosmological thinking (see p. 315). Zeus does not sit silently by as human beings commit *hubris*. And even though it may happen that the punishment is not meted out with immediate effect, experience shows that the sin is always punished at some time or other, since, if appropriate, it can be passed down to a member of the family. In this way, justice maintains a steady balance between sin and punishment.

Not only does this explain for the Greeks of the 6th century B.C. and thereafter why apparently innocent people are suddenly struck down by misfortune, but it is also a way of thinking that on the one hand demands constant awareness of personal responsibility and on the other hand leads to a fear of *miasma*, of defilement—for which almost panic-stricken cleansing rituals are developed to anticipate and prevent.[11] Nothing corresponding is found in either Homer or Hesiod. Ritual cleansing is here connected to sacrifice, the washing of hands before eating or the "sulphuring" of the hall in which the bloody slaughter of the suitors has taken place.

What Solon does more particularly as lawgiver is, as *archon*, quite simply to transfer the physical power (*kratos*), which distinguishes heroes such as Achilleus, to the justice inherent in the world. As he writes: "This I achieved by the might of law, combining force (*bia*) and justice (*dike*)."[12] He writes down his laws, conscious that human beings only follow their leaders by neither having too much freedom nor being too restricted, since any form of exaggeration leads to *hubris*.[13]

In order to achieve social order (*eunomia*), he must find the middle road, *sophrosyne*, at the same time as seeking to secure a legal process for each individual person, "the lower class as well as the higher." By higher or richer, he is thinking of the nobility and the group of affluent citizens in possession of a great deal of landed property, who were trying to maintain their privileges on the basis of the new wealth created by colonization and the introduction of Attic coinage.

The cause of the period of colonization from approximately 750–600 B.C. was presumably overpopulation, which reduced the plots of land on which people made a living. And the peasants were not able to switch their agricultural methods to the cultivation of wine and olives when grain from overseas possessions began to pour into Hellas, as a result of which those with debts had to submit to forced labor. At the same time, by virtue of their wealth, merchants began to demand political influence. Power was no longer to be an inherited privilege but determined by financial strength.

Moreover, the aristocracy also changed their way of life and, inspired by the Orient, adopted a luxurious way of life (*habrosyne*).[14] Previously, it was the aristocrats, the best (*aristoi*) as the name states, that had led the armies—like the heroes of Troy. They developed into a corrupt power elite that no longer went to war but, instead, cultivated singing games and sports; homosexuality was a common erotic preference, and a life of indolence was sweetened by luxuries from the colonies.

This all occurred at the cost of the debt-ridden lower classes. Consequently, Solon's recipe was a law requiring debt restructuring, and he forbade any form of security that would threaten personal liberty. He also purchased the freedom of those who, on this basis, had already been sold into slavery. *Seisachtheia* is the term used of this process: to cast off a burden. Meanwhile, his reforms did not lead to a redistribution of land, since, as he writes, "it does not please me to act with the violence of a tyrant nor to give equal shares of our rich country to worthless and noble alike."[15]

Solon's statement indicates how far we still are from true democracy. At the same time, he warns against tyranny in which, because of ignorance, the people will be bound in slavery. However, it is not until Cleisthenes' division into 139 *demes* ("municipalities") more than one hundred years later in 507 B.C. that the aristocracy's monopoly on power was finally broken. According to tradition, Solon accepted the consequence of his warning against tyranny, because when he received the offer to become a tyrant, he replied by leaving Greece for ten years.

6

That Homer as a poet has the same intentions as Solon, even though there is not the same degree of reflection in the epic form, seems to be confirmed by the fact that he not only points towards Solon and touches on a number of related themes, but his works later become a cornerstone of the education (*paideia*) of young Greek men.

Politically speaking, using the same approach and the same arguments as Solon, Odysseus founds his future peaceful, political rule on the same co-operation between royal power, the nobility (including the families of the suitors), and the working people: shepherds, craftsmen, etc. As a fictitious figure, he spans a vast historical continuum. His origins reach back into a mythical context in which he may have acted as a year-*Daimon* or sun god; he then finds his warrior and heroic identity in the *Iliad* and in the *Odyssey* becomes a political model for a democratically minded *tyrannos*.

Of course, we look in vain for the word tyrant, *tyrannos*, in Homer's vocabulary. Nevertheless, it can be wondered whether, with Odysseus as ruler, he did not direct his political utopia towards an absolute, powerful and just ruler, a king in the style of the first tyrants. It is crucial to understand here that the concept of tyranny did not originally have quite the same negative connotation as it does today. The tyrant as a concept of an evil ruler did not truly appear until the 4th century B.C., particularly in connection with the dictatorship in Sicily.

The first tyrants appeared in the sixth century B.C. in the flourishing city of Corinth and somewhat later in Athens, while Homer himself may have known the phenomenon from the Greek colonies in Asia Minor. They were most often recruited from the nobility, but—like Odysseus—achieved their power by associating themselves with the people, the farmers, and a new power factor that had recently appeared, the so-called *hoplites*: an army consisting of the city's own citizens, who could afford to equip themselves with battle equipment which was easy to move about in since it was primarily made of leather. Marching in phalanxes, this type of force appeared to possess a different kind of mobility and effectiveness from the earlier bronze-clad warriors.

Historically speaking, it is not entirely clear what brought the tyrants to power, apart from the ordinary turbulence of the time. However, what seems certain is that the aristocracy that replaced the original kings had with their life of luxury and through financial exploitation seriously put themselves at odds with the people:

these are Hesiod's "bribe-swallowing" kings and Homer's suitors.

All in all, this meant that there were great political tensions during the period, and tyranny became the answer to them. And by allying themselves with the people, the earliest tyrants saw the emergence of an incipient democracy, although the nobility remained a decisive political power factor.

Solon had warned against tyranny, but this did not prevent the political developments. Peisistratos took over in Athens and with a few brief interruptions ruled as a tyrant from 560 B.C. until his death in 527 B.C. He was succeeded by his sons, until the tyranny fell in 510 B.C. The hypothetical question now is whether Homer may have had this sort of tyranny in mind as a role model and political successor if the Homeric epics—as one scholarly tradition believes[16]—were actually written at Peisistratos' request in connection with the great Panathenian festivals every fourth year at Athens.

The story of Peisistratos is not to be told here, but his three periods of rule involved a huge cultural and religious expansion. He raised temples and, among other things, built a great hall to be used for the Eleusinian Mysteries. Likewise, he incorporated Dionysos into Athens' religious life along with the accompanying drama competitions. In this sense, he became the ruler who more than anyone absorbed the chthonic cults into the life of the state—to control them, if for no other reason. In addition, he implemented a number of political initiatives that had been devised by Solon but not brought to fruition—for example, subsidies to financially hard-pressed peasants, thus paving the way for a true process of democratization under C leisthenes.

Herodotus relates that Peisistratos was named after Nestor's son, who accompanied Telemachos on his journey.[17] Others were of the opinion that the opposite is the case: that Nestor's son was named after the tyrant as a mark of respect. Regardless of what is the truth, if we concede to Peisistratos the honour of having occasioned the writing down of Homer's poems, we could in this context say that Odysseus is his mythical prefiguration, to which he has given immortality by allowing his odyssey to be written down.

All the uncertainty that is linked to Homer's name and the origin of his texts falls away when we move into the reflective breakthrough made by poets and philosophers whose biographical data are verifiable. It is a movement from mythical to historical thinking. We journey from the *Iliad*'s cultivation of external beauty and honor to the *Odyssey*'s emphasis on inner values such as consciousness and self-control, values which are given their fullest expression in Socrates.

PART TWO
SOCRATES

THE SUBJECTIVE
AND REFLECTIVE
BREAKTHROUGH IN
POETRY AND
PHILOSOPHY

1

WHEN THE *Iliad* AND THE *Odyssey* BURST FORTH FROM THE SO-CALLED dark centuries as the masterpieces they almost incomprehensibly are, it clearly looks as though Greek culture came into existence out of the blue in some incredible process of condensation. Pre-conscious impulses are crystallized and made aware of themselves in the incipient subjectivity and rational thinking that are centered especially on the figure of Odysseus. The epic achieves its highest flowering here and at the same time, paradoxically, eradicates its own genre, as the heroic and aristocratic view of the world on which Homer builds does not exist in the transition to the archaic age.

As a collective event, this process becomes clearer if we introduce the literature and philosophy from the time when the Homeric epics presumably find their definitive form around 700-500 B.C. The reasons for this great social, cultural and mental leap forward socially are due to many interacting factors. It cannot have occurred within some closed area of consciousness. For despite the sparse information about what actually happened in the dark ages around 1200-800 B.C., it must have been tumultuous time of trouble and upheaval in which powerful social, political and economic forces as well as a vast store of knowledge accumulated through the previous centuries played a role.

Greek culture absorbed impulses from highly developed civilizations in the East and from Babylon and Egypt, etc. These acupunctural points of consciousness gave sustenance to the Greek religion and furnished it with a brilliant array of gods. The link was trade and, especially, the great waves of colonization toward the east, whether occasioned by invading Dorians in the 12th century B.C., or overpopulation, or both, culminating in the final wave of colonization around 750-500 B.C.

An analysis of influences from the East falls outside the purview of this study. Yet, as a general comment, it is possible to say that the encounter with the Orient meant a liberation of forms of life and expression. The highly stylized patterns on vases, for example, are replaced by sophisticated mythological scenes. New forms of verse closer to the spoken language loosen up metrical schemes, so that the rhythm of the language can convey the passion of a personal statement. In logical thinking, the early philosophers seek to understand the origin and substance of the world rationally and to separate this understanding from a mythological way of thinking.

2

Know thyself, *gnothi se auton*, was the maxim of Solon and the oracle at Delphi. Consciousness is placed within psychological processes, which for the Homeric figures were unconscious and were viewed as coming from without as an intervention of the gods, as an increase of energy (*menos*) or as delusion (*ate*). And if the human world of motivation can no longer be attributed to the gods but to men themselves, moral conduct ultimately becomes a question of self-knowledge. True personal responsibility was alien to Homer's heroes. Cognition can only be developed through self-insight. Through his dialogues, Socrates strives more than anyone to achieve a self-understanding that punctures the illusions men harbor and for which they had hitherto given the gods responsibility. In this, Socrates completes what Odysseus begins: ensuring that men learn to know themselves and to take responsibility for their actions.

The poets and thinkers who will be brought into the remainder of this book will be placed in a chronological sequence, which, it is to be hoped, will be able to demonstrate and prove that the period's own dynamic awakens ever new human abilities and the resultant need for interpretation and expression. To this end, new genres arise, such as poetry written in the first person, tragedy and philosophical discourses. Perhaps the most important inspiration from the East to promote these challenges came from the Phoenicians—that is to say the alphabet, which to judge from all the evidence was "imported" to Hellas in the 8th century B.C. The linear scripts that were used in the Minoan and Mycenaean cultures four hundred years previously had apparently been forgotten, but a number of words from this period of their greatness survived in the later Greek language.

3

Writing was a hugely contributory factor in the epochal step we now witness. As a result, letters actually become a political necessity for the incipient democratization and parallel relativization of the power of aristocracy. When a law is published, it becomes accessible to all, as with Solon, and people are no longer dependent on a ruler's more or less perfunctory dealings with *nomos*. In this sense, writing lays the foundation for the institutionalization of the city-state. In addition, the written language occasioned long-term deep social changes but brought about no less radical transformations in intellectual life—namely, in a further development of poetry and the establishment of philosophy.

In *The Muse Learns to Write*, Eric A. Havelock summarizes his lifelong study of the transformation of an oral culture into a written one. The main point is that the oral tradition from Homer and Hesiod only slowly relaxed its hold on successive authors and philosophers. Both the Presocratics and tragedians such as Aeschylus and Sophocles still display powerful oral elements in their works. The final transformation he dates to around the time of Euripides' death in 406 B.C. So the Muse certainly learns to write, but she continues to sing for a while yet.

Havelock describes this process as a movement from ear to eye, which on a mental plane may be sketched out as follows: Orality is based on a retrospective memorization of laws and customs, a form of knowledge upon which didactic memorizing is based, something, however, that at the same time ties the intellect down in to a sort of encyclopaedic conservatism. All mental energy is fixed and conserved. There is no room for critical awareness or personal development. Gradually, as this constrained energy is liberated through the written word, the liberated psychological energy is invested in the ability of writing to operate in an analytical, critical, forward-looking reflection in which the perceiving subject, the self, is projected in a clear separation of knowledge and experience. Havelock has explored this phenomenology in his analysis of Plato, where we shall return to this problem.

Whereas oral culture makes use of the epic, a narrative form with active individuals and an express anthropomorphization of natural phenomena, the written word tries to put conceptualization in its stead and to raise topics that can be made the object of logical, abstract discussion. Man is set up as a general category as opposed to the specific characters of a story. Epic action is replaced with logical discussion. And as Bruno Snell has shown (see p. 56), a significant simplification takes place in the development of the verb in an interplay with the definite article.

Only when something is written down do we have the opportunity to reflect upon it, to discuss it and distinguish it from the person responsible for the written proposition. This is clearly different from an oral presentation in which speech and message merge and allow no opportunity for reflection, as we cannot go back and reflect on what has been said. In addition, the oral presentations deriving from song and dance had a hypnotic effect—as emerges from statements of Homer and Hesiod to the effect that we forget our sorrows when we listen to poetry. And this suggestion is precisely what Plato is aiming at when he banishes poets from his *Republic*.

4

As the person writing something down is distinguished from what is written, the writer himself steps forth as a person, making himself visible as a subject. Thus, it is in subjective poetry that we can most clearly follow a development—a development not merely in style, but in fundamental values. In what we might call a gradual secularization, emphasis shifts away from the divine inspiration of the Muses, corresponding to an orientation in the world on the self's own premises, a movement from mythical awareness, which still plays a part in Homer, to a form of knowledge and experience in which the perceiving individual starts out from his own feelings and passions.

Admittedly, the cosmology Hesiod presents in the *Theogony* is still mythological, but it nevertheless represents an initial, rational attempt to place things in some systematized causality. In addition, he distinguishes himself as an independent authorial personality, while devoting space in *Works and Days* to his personal life story and daily life as such.

Over the next centuries, this individual approach to life is extended and intensified in poetry. The first true subjective poets, Archilochus and Sappho, take their bearings in the world from their personal passions. Their poetry is clearly an instrumentation and manifestation of pure subjective feeling in a more or less charged and critical relationship with their surroundings and the opinions obtaining there. A clear separation takes place between the subjective and the objective, which were unified in the Homeric mind, although, with the figure of Odysseus, Homer created the foundation for this process.

However, it is appropriate to point out that this poetry appears in such finished form that, in *Arkaisk Græsk Lyrik*, Holger Friis Johansen proposes the hypothesis that its genesis, like that of the Homeric epics, has far deeper, unknown roots. In response to this: 1) There were no water-tight partitions between the epic and such poetry, as emerges in Homer's unmistakable presence in the stylistic figures and assessments of later poetry. These poets were thoroughly familiar with his works, presumably in oral form, and may have developed in interplay with them. 2) Even in Antiquity, Archilochus was already viewed as the person who created the iambic form (see p. 299). 3) We can say nothing for certain about any earlier subjective poetry and are forced to place Archilochus as the oldest known subjective poet, followed by Sappho, who has clearly learned from him—and from Homer.

Whether this subjective poetry had an earlier source or not, it is a certain that in its contents it belongs to a different intellectual level from Homer. If by nothing else, this is confirmed by the parallel establishment of philosophical reflection. For at the same time as the subjective lyrical poets separate consciousness from its surroundings and invest it in their inner life, a contrary movement takes place in the philosophy that arises in this period. Like the poetry, it also emerges in Ionia and is a central element in its explosive culture, but these philosophers, by contrast, seek to fit the world into an objective observation of nature.

If drama is also introduced into this context, we can see that virtually every genre arises in Greek culture over the course of a little more than 350 years, in the period from 750-400 B.C.: epic, choral and lyric poetry (including philosophical poetry), philosophical prose and dialogue as well as tragedy and comedy. It is crucial to realize that these genres do not come into existence as formal experiments but arise from an existential necessity. They are produced successively by the human need to understand and express the world and life—through the intellect.

XI

HESIOD AS TRANSITIONAL POET

The Calling of the Poet

1

WHILE BIOGRAPHICAL DATA ABOUT HOMER FADES INTO THE MYTHICAL tradition of oral poetry, which obliterates his identity as a concrete person, we meet Hesiod in his works as a living figure. Chronologically, we find ourselves around the year 700 B.C. So there is a rough chronological coincidence between Homer and Hesiod. According to some traditions, they were cousins, and a text has come down telling of their origins and of a competition between them at Euboea. The king awards the prize to Hesiod because he encourages people to keep the peace, whereas Homer is the poet of war and slaughter.[1]

In brief, this means that Hesiod is a strange and remarkable transitional figure in cultural development. Partly inspired by Homer, he continued the oral tradition in epic hexameters; on the other hand, he investigates reflectively the origin and progression of life in the *Theogony*.* At the same time, in *Works and Days*, he delivers an ideological attack on the norms and political chaos of his time in a deeply personal dispute over inheritance with his brother.

2

There is an immediate world of difference when we move from Homer's aristocratic values to Hesiod's agrarian Boeotia: the plough has replaced the sword, labor the heroic deed. The distance is, of course, greatest in comparison to the *Iliad*'s universe of battle. The *Odyssey* provides an empathetic description of the common people—for example, the herdsmen who help Odysseus. Homer thus acts as a mediating figure between the heroic age and its great epic and the reality of the world in which Hesiod's *Works and Days* is played out, described as a period of decay after the heroic age.

*Tramslator's note: Throughout, "Th." indicates the *Theogony*; "WD" *Works and Days*.

From this perspective, Homer is at the threshold of the age in which Hesiod lives and writes his works. They have a sort of utopianism in common, since their goal is to "invent" works that ultimately testify to a world ruled by divine justice. Despite their differences, they have a number of features in common, indicating continuity and coherence. That, in his own environment, Hesiod is Homer's poetic heir is verified by the fact that he continues Homer's language and style, often borrowing directly, which indicates that he became familiar with him at an early age. His command of meter, however, cannot bear comparison with Homer's stylistic splendor and plasticity. This is poetry with lumps of soil beneath.

Hesiod tries to conceptualize what is still latent in the Homeric epics. Homer's epics are themselves guided by a need to process reality to provide an assessment of the world that has the conceptual as potential. Let me merely point out that the whole of the *Odyssey* demonstrates the presence of an ultimately prevailing divine justice. Hesiod's two works also aim to describe this same world order at a higher reflective level. Yet he cannot present his ideas purely conceptually but, as a poet, still needs to use allegory to support his analysis. He does so in the *Theogony* by showing how the world arose, while in *Works and Days*, via the conflict over inheritance with his brother, this event is introduced into the world of men as a personal matter reflecting the moral decay of his contemporaries.

3

It may be surprising that, coming from rural and intellectually backward Boeotia, Hesiod could become Homer's heir and thus in reality continue the expansive age of enlightenment coming from Asia Minor. Nevertheless, by linking the little biographical information that Hesiod provides in his description of his poetic calling, we can establish a reasonable psychological basis for this fact.

He writes that his father came from Cyme (WD 635), an Aeolian city on the coast of Asia Minor. Due to declining fortune as a tradesman, he moved to the village of Askra, located at the foot of Mount Helicon, sacred to the Muses. As Hesiod puts it with his understated humor: "He did not flee from riches or success" (WD 637). However, we can deduce from the conflict over inheritance that his father must have accumulated some earthly goods—otherwise, there would have been nothing to fight about.

Hesiod was born and raised in this rural society, where the population consisted of peasants and cattle owners. A free and industrious people, tied to the soil. Hesiod was himself a farmer and herdsman, but must have had a different psychological constitution as well, a key to which can be provided by the topography. He speaks of his birthplace Askra in negative tones, as a place that is "harsh/ in winter, miserable in summertime,/ not really good at any time of year" (WD 640-41). If this is his assessment of the village and its potential, we can understand his inner discord, as he must have gained knowledge of his father's rich cultural heritage from Asia Minor, including Homer.

In the proem to the *Theogony*, Hesiod describes his calling to poetry while he was tending sheep at Mount Helicon. It was an awakening that corresponds psychologically to the side of him that through his father goes back to the Asia Minor enlightenment and separates him from this narrow rural society. Yet he must have continued to live there, as he writes that only once in his life has he been to sea— when he won a poetry contest at a funeral ceremony at Euboea: "I conquered with a song/ and carried home a two-eared tripod" (WD 657).

This must mean that from the moment the Muses awoke him to poetry, he no longer viewed his surroundings as a farmer or a shepherd but as a poet and ultimately as a didactic prophet, as he asserts that the Muses proclaim the truth through him. This is the way in which the Muses speak to him in an introductory hymn-like encomium:

> You rustic shepherds, shame: bellies you are,
> Not men! We know enough to make up lies
> Which are convincing, but we also have
> The skill, when we have a mind, to speak the truth.
>
> (Th. 26-29)

If we dissect these lines, they show the development Hesiod has undergone from country bumpkin to no mean self-assuredness as a poet. The first line contains an echo of Odysseus' attack on the stomach as an irksome source of error, when instinctual life governs Man's choices. But then the Muses enable Hesiod to become intellectually active, making him the thinker of his generation, since in his two poems he explicitly formulates the initial guidelines for religious life and a moral and political value system.

At the same time, it is surprising that the Muses report that they cannot always be trusted. The inspiration (*logos*) with which they provide men may be illusory or mendacious. But when? In the historical context, the answer may be that what they say is unreliable when in a invented form such as fairytale or fiction. If this is correct, it may indicate that Hesiod implicitly turns against the Homeric universe, from which he otherwise derives so much in terms of style and language, to claim that *he*, Hesiod, speaks the truth. The truth must be based on his not being interested in illusions but in facts: the factual element in the *Theogony*, described on the basis of the creation of the universe, and the justice which, in *Works and Days*, is translated into relations between human beings.

4

The basis for Hesiod's claim that he prophetically passes on the Muses' truth is that on the one hand they select him and on the other that the truth in the

Theogony encompasses existence right from its beginning (*ex arches*), or, as Hesiod puts it in his own words: "Tell me these things, Olympian Muses, tell/ from the beginning, which first came to be?" (Th. 114-15)

Then follows the splendidly presented cosmogony, going back to Chaos and gradually setting the universe in motion to produce a true cosmology. The Muses are obviously not merely the sources of inspiration, but, as in Homer, they are providers of information. In Homer, they provide information on events at Troy and on Odysseus' journey, while in the case of Hesiod they tell of the origin of the world through the divine forces that are invested in it in mutual division.

If the Muses are able with certainty to provide the information that Hesiod incorporates into his poetic systematization, it is because of their origins. For they were born of the goddess of memory, Mnemosyne, and have Zeus as their father. In *Works and Days*, which also begins with an invocation to the Muses—"Pierian Muses, bringers of fame: come/tell of your father, Zeus" (WD 1)—Hesiod explains to his slow-witted brother that in his teaching, he, Hesiod, derives his knowledge from the mental world of Zeus: "I can/ tell you the will of aegis-bearing Zeus, for I have inspiration in my songs,/ because the Muses taught me how to sing" (WD 661-62). And since the Muses in Hesiod's inner self make clear their father's ideas, he can provide information about everything in the world—even voyages by sea of which that he otherwise has no understanding whatever.

So the Muses equip Hesiod's poetry with the encyclopedic power of memory on which its truth value is based, going back to the beginning of time and containing all the knowledge the Muses have inherited from their father. And they give to Hesiod the same abilities they themselves possess, to sing of "the things to come/and the things which were before" (Th. 33, 38) and of "the glorious deeds the men of old performed,/ and hymns the blessed ones, Olympian gods" (Th. 100-101). And just as the Muses' beautiful voices are described as delicious flowing sounds, so it is said of this poet so blessed by the gods: "His voice flows sweetly from his mouth" (Th. 97). Moreover, he resembles the sagacious king, for when he pronounces his judgment "from his lips/ flow honeyed words" (Th. 84).

The interesting thing is that with this formulation Hesiod recalls the verse from the *Odyssey* in which Odysseus fools the Kyklops with sweet words (9, 363). In other words, Hesiod must link up with the tradition in Homer that is based upon the narrator's power of fascination if not seduction (*thelgein*, see p. 83). This is all the more surprising, as the memory which the Muses and the poet release as truth in their song also contains forgetfulness. Indeed, the Muses are actually born to "bring/ forgetfulness of evil, rest from pain" (Th. 55). Exactly the same effect is achieved aesthetically when in his sweet voice the poet sings his songs of the past and the future for then the suffering being whose heart is withering with sorrow "(. . .) forgets his heavy heart,/ and has no memory of any grief" (Th. 103-104).

An understanding of this paradox concerning forgetting and remembering seems to point in two directions. On the one hand, with reference to Plato, we can claim that Hesiod indirectly reveals that poetry consists of illusion. Through words, rhythm, dance and song, suggestion and hypnosis are evoked, standing in glaring contrast to rational thought, which is why Plato wants to banish the poets from his ideal state.

Or, on the other hand, it can be said, as I have already done in my interpretation of the *charis* phenomenon in Homer's poetry (see p. 82), that the forgetfulness and ease of pain embedded in poetry are due to a cathartic effect, of which tragedy later becomes the supreme exponent. In this case, the effect consists of freeing the suffering individual—by entering into the poem's memory of the history of the universe—from his own private pain, that grain of corn that fills nothing in the great meaningful, portentous story that embraces both man and cosmos. It is this reality in which the poet's sweet words place the subject, just as the righteous kings can soothe the contesting parties with sweet words and lead them to a superior social order.

5

Although it proved possible to discern a targeted *utopian* project in the Homeric works, it was not possible exactly to ascertain Homer's self-understanding as a poet. Of course, he invokes the Muses, but he does not appropriate them to the same extent as Hesiod. This process of appropriation in itself may indicate that Hesiod is well on the way towards having the poet step forth as his own creator, whereas Homer was ultimately a mouthpiece of the oral tradition.

The Muses may well be behind Hesiod's true knowledge. But from the point of view of textual history, we must assume that he is disposed toward material coming from myths, local popular superstitions and other epics, particularly Homer. He has reworked this source material in his own way. This sort of amalgamation and transformation of material is difficult to imagine if it was not done in writing—an assumption further supported by the fact that in the conceptualization at which he is aiming, Hesiod reduces the epic element. And although he must cling to allegory, the formulas familiar in oral poetry are entirely gone. With this, his works become the first truly "subjective" poems, and he himself the first true autonomous poet. The sermonizing ambitions imbued in his work are also seen from the fact that—like Socrates later—he specifically claims to be speaking the truth.

He certainly ascribes the finished result to the Muses, but this form is experience leads to a self-awareness in the poet that is expressed by the fact that with his words he systematizes the gods and the world.

As a creator of awareness, he is not only parallel to the sagacious kings who speak sweetly and truly but, as a creative interpreter and mediator he is on a par with Zeus himself, whose thoughts and intentions he shares and can translate into religion, law and science.

Since Hesiod derives his knowledge from Zeus and makes himself one with his mind, he is not far from turning Zeus into a mere figure behind the speaker. And on this basis he is able to finish *Works and Days* with the following salutation to his brother: "Follow all this" (WD 760); "he is truly blest/ and rich who knows these things and does his work,/ guiltless before the gods, and scrupulous,/ observing omens and avoiding wrong" (WD 826-27). Not only has Hesiod here put himself in the place of the god whose voice he is, but, as a source of inspiration for the poets the Muses paradoxically also play their part in dissolving the divine reality which it is otherwise their task to mediate and confirm.

Family Tree and Succession

1

The *Theogony* is conceived as a grand attempt to introduce a rational and systematic understanding into the urgent question of how the world and the gods arose. But since Hesiod has not yet developed a logical conceptualization, he has recourse to an allegorical form. He combines two analogical modules of representation: on the one hand, a monarchical hierarchization, and, on the other and inseparable from it, a family tree. This automatically introduces the idea of succession: sons replace fathers in the shifting (divine) hierarchies whose mutual conflicts result in further development towards ever more complex forms of consciousness and organization.

His use of these analogies is in itself an indication that he has not yet developed the conceptual apparatus that leads from myth to the logos of abstraction. Nevertheless, he is well on the way, and his idea of succession is evidence that a notion of progress is present in his view of development, even though the word for this does not yet exist.[2]

2

However, Hesiod's description is not limited to the origin of the gods but, quite simply, the formation of the entire world, including forces such as strife, deceit and desire. The only things he fails to mention are human beings, animals and plants. The creative principle is feminine in nature in that both gods and the world come into existence through a birth in which primordial mothers are able to conceive through self-fertilization, *autochthonios*. Gaia appeared immediately after Chaos, which was the first of all things (*ex arches*), since Hesiod apparently could not imagine pure nothingness.

Gaia, the earth mother, then brings Uranos, heaven, into the world, and together they breed the mountains, valleys, seas and rivers, and also intelligent children such as Rhea, Themis and Kronos. However, Uranos felt such fear and anger in the face of his offspring that fear made him stuff the children back into their mother. While, in other mythologies, there is a clear idea that Heaven and Earth, as the first cosmic parents, are a procreative unit that gradually separate from each other, this process of separation is not clear in Hesiod's presentation, although it is presumably taken for granted.[3]

In collusion with his mother, Gaia, Kronos castrates his father and takes power.

But it has been prophesied by his parents that he will be overthrown. So he eats his own children as they come into the world. However, he is fooled by his wife, Rhea, who gives him a stone and, in the belief that it is Zeus, he swallows it. Zeus is brought up in a cave on Crete (see p. 94), cared for by Gaia until he is big and strong enough to subdue his father after having forced him to regurgitate his siblings: Hades, Hera, Poseidon and Demeter.

3

In this stylized presentation of a succession that is described at length, we can again note that it is the mothers who secure power for their sons, at the same time as the rulers gradually become physically weaker but mentally more mature. By virtue of his "crooked-scheming" (*agkylonetes*, Th. 137), i.e. his cunning, Kronos is able to overthrow his father Uranos. Yet, although he possesses some part of *metis*, wisdom, he continues his father's rule of terror by swallowing his children and showing no moderation in his rule.

In spite of this violent nature, however, Kronos is not viewed as a supreme patriarchal god. He is helped to power by his mother, Gaia, and is not addressed as father but as king (*tyrannos*). And if the Golden Age—the time under Kronos—is included under his regime, this is because he is an exponent of the matrilinear principle, in which all creatures—including the Kyklopes and Kalypso—grow of themselves. Private ownership does not exist, just as children at this stage of development do not know their fathers, conceived as they are in the universal promiscuity of the mothers. Like Laertes and Alkinoos, Kronos is thus rather at a transitional or intermediate stage on the way to the patriarchal form of government which Zeus succeeds in imposing.

As long as Zeus himself stays in the cave on Crete under the protection of the Great Mother, he remains at the same level of development. The crucial point is, however, that—as in Homer and later Aeschylus—he is developing and being transformed. His conflict with primordial forces such as giants and titans is the first sign of his departure from and revolt against this world. Likewise, it is proof of the order obtaining there that Gaia through Tartaros gives birth to a fearsome dragon (*drakon*) Typhon in order to destroy the rebellious son (and lover). That the dragon in reality is an extension and incarnation of the primordial mother's chthonic destructive power is demonstrated by the pain she suffers on its death: "He lashed him with a whip and mastered him,/and threw him down, all maimed, and great Earth groaned" (Th. 857-58).

4

With this, the evil strife that has been part of the development of the world and Zeus' elevation to patriarchal god has been brought to an end. From the point of view of composition, this cosmological level in Hesiod's work has from the beginning of the text acted as a purposive force, though hidden from those involved and from the reader until this force appears in the order and peace that now rules in heaven. It represents a sort of cosmic *eunomia*, sung by the Muses as "the laws and the courteous ways of all/ the immortals" (Th. 66-67), *nomos* and *ethea*—that is to say the general rule of law and personal morality. Hesiod enumerates requirements of this sort for his brother and for rulers generally in *Works and Days*.

In his phase of revolt and liberation, Zeus acts exactly like the heroes of the *Iliad*, with power and with strife. When he takes over the Olympian throne, he promotes himself by violence, always accompanied by the two bullies: Kratos and Bia (Th. 385). In this sense, the *Theogony* is based on the archetypal tale in which male gods, as well as heroes, must liberate themselves from their maternal bond in order to take culture further. As a patriarchal god, Zeus also founds his heavenly kingdom on the very quality that primarily characterizes Odysseus, his wisdom, *(poly)metis*. As a total contrast to his father, he thus possesses a truer power of thought (*metieta*, Th. 57, 658) and, as he gradually develops, becomes wise in counsel, mild and thoughtful, respecting the rights of others and capable of mercy.

In this way, Zeus concluded peace by generously apportioning an area to each god, not by assuming absolute power like his father—"Thus/ he gave out rank and privilege to each" (Th. 885-86). So his wisdom is different from Kronos' "crooked thoughts," which have the same sort of cunning as that used by the mother goddesses, Gaia and Rhea, when they help their sons to kill the obstructive father figure. Their shrewdness is linked to the evil strife, whereas, when transformed and made wise, Zeus becomes the god of justice and reconciliation, as was also the theme in Aeschylus' trilogy on the conflict between Prometheus and Zeus.

In order to represent this transformation visually, Hesiod first has Zeus marry Metis, the goddess of wisdom, who on being swallowed by him is internalized and now from within, from his stomach, imparts his universal wisdom to him. Then he marries Themis, the ordering principal of heaven and earth, whom he can govern with the wisdom he has already acquired. As said earlier, they conceive the Horai together: Dike, Eunomia, Eirene (Th. 902). As incarnations of their father, these daughters are anthropomorphic visualizations of the contents of the present order: Dike as executor of justice, Eunomia the social order, and Eirene the goddess of peace. This trinity—as is also implicit in Homer's utopia—constitutes the foundation of both the cosmic and human order of justice.

Although Hesiod does not use the term for moderation, *sophrosyne*,[4] it may be said that this interplay between *eunomia* and *dike* must be viewed as the precursor of the demand for self-control of which Solon, as said above, becomes the primary exponent in his call for everything to be done in moderation and for each person to learn to know himself.

So the *Theogony* shows the genesis and codification of Zeus' being and essence, while *Works and Days* illustrates how these principles ought also to be translated into earthly existence. Hesiod meanwhile uses his personal conflict over an inheritance to throw light not only on his brother's greed but also on that of current rulers. And since evil strife and evil as such, which have determined the origin and evolution of the universe, have now entered into the world of man, Hesiod makes his ethical demands.

Misogyny

1

Like the Homeric epics, the process of development that Hesiod presents in his texts and of which he is himself forms part as a person illustrates on a (depth) psychological level the struggle between the sexes and the transition from matriarchate to patriarchate. And let it straightaway be said that, with his pronounced misogyny, Hesiod is far more radical than Homer—and perhaps for that very reason represents a younger stage forming the transition to the oppression of women in Athenian democracy. At any rate, this course of development makes clear that the process of civilization is intimately connected with the revolt of the sons against the Great Mother figure and her cult world.

However, the case is not quite so simple. For while Homer apparently sought to repress the fertility cults by establishing Olympus, Hesiod, as quoted above, emphasizes that people must at all costs remember to implore the powers of the earth: "Make prayers to Zeus the farmers' god and to/ holy Demeter, for her sacred grain,/ to make it ripe and heavy, when you start to plough" (WD 465-68). With his agrarian roots, he apparently does not harbor the same aversion towards the underworld as the Ionian Homer.

And yet it is apparent that Hesiod feels it important to pass on his knowledge of the Great Mother's demonic ambiguity. He does this in a dual exposition. Gaia is introduced at first as the good mother, while all the negative forms of life are born by Night "although she slept with none of the gods" (Th. 213). She is the mother of Death, the goddesses of Fate, deceit, sexuality, misery, age, and "strong willed Strife" (Th. 226).

But neither does Hesiod allow Gaia to escape. He latently cuts a section through the primordial mother herself to reveal that she is both a good and an evil mother figure. She takes the new-born Zeus to be cared for in the maternal cave on Crete. Yet, as we heard before, she brings Typhon into the world to punish him when he emancipates himself from her earthly womb. The dragon—even more clearly than the wild boar that Odysseus kills in his puberty—is evidence of the challenge awaiting rebellious sons and heroes from the offended primordial mother.

2

Hesiod's loathing for women, however, is most tangible in *Works and Days* when he moves this cosmological perspective down into recognizable everyday life. Here, he links woman and sexuality together, so that, in league with this mighty power, she becomes a great danger and does great harm to man. Hence, he cannot advise his irresponsible brother enough on this topic—indeed, in his negative view of women, he seems to be directly echoing Agamemnon's words when in the *Odyssey* he says of his murderous wife that "a song of loathing/ will be hers among men, to make evil the reputation/of women, even for one whose acts are virtuous" (24, 200-202).

So his brother Perses must be extremely careful: "Don't let a woman, wiggling her behind,/and flattering and coaxing, take you in" (WD 373-74), Hesiod warns. "She wants your barn: woman is just a cheat" (WD 375), he admonishes, applying the same lesson as Homer applies to the sisters Helen and Klytemnestra. Similarly, the underlying threat and fear of castration in Kirke, against which Odysseus secures himself with an oath to prevent her from robbing him of his manhood, is clearly emphasized in Hesiod, when he says several times to his brother that woman with her barren desire makes a man old before his time—"The greedy wife will roast her man alive/without the aid of fire, and though he is/quite tough, she will bring him to a raw old age" (WD 704-05). And as in the Law of Moses, he warns against bathing in the same water as a woman— "The punishment is awful, for a time" (WD 754), he claims, presumably thinking that the man in such a case will be struck by the *miasma* of blood from her menstruation.

Despite his hatred or fear of women, Hesiod knows that women cannot be avoided for reproduction. If man avoids marriage and the troublesome dealings with women, "at last he comes/ to a miserable old age, and does not have/ anyone who will care for the old man" (Th. 605-07). Consequently, it is a matter of finding a woman, a virgin of fifteen or sixteen, on whom the man can imprint "sober ways" (WD 699). For in order not to be made a fool of or oppressed by his wife, he must in fact, like Odysseus in relation to Kirke, force the woman with his "sword". Otherwise, he will be victim to "one of the deadly sort (. . .) with never ending pain inside his heart/ and on his mind" (Th. 610-11).

In short, Hesiod is more explicit than Homer, since he lets the struggle of the sexes play itself out in a familiar reality and does so with a view to establishing male dominance over women. There seem to be two reasons for this clarity in comparison with Homer. There is in the first place the very fact that Homer's two epics take place in a distant mythical world. And secondly, this primordial conflict seems only to be intuited by Homer and not yet made into the social and political reality that we find in Hesiod as part of man's self-realization and his patronization of the sphere of power.

We can in this context refer to the poet Semonides as possibly being under the influence of Hesiod when he wrote a quite long, idiosyncratic pasquinade about women. As he says there, they have from the hand of god a mind quite different from a man's. They are then represented in every conceivable derogatory comparison with animals: donkeys, cats, etc., with accompanying negative characteristics, and he concludes: "Women are the greatest evil Zeus has created."[5]

3

As said above, the *Theogony* and *Works and Days* are bound together by an underlying notion of justice, the teleological guidance that is the basis of the compositional intent in both works. However, the clearest example of this overlapping may be found in the use they make of the myth of Pandora, the woman who brings evil into the world of men. In fact, it may be said that Hesiod's texts are linked by a common hatred of women.

The myth has two clear functions: 1) It is to clarify generally the nagging theodicy problem of how and why Zeus created evil and, with the shift in power in heaven, moved it to earth. 2) The myth is to demonstrate that evil is due to woman, and it acts as a kind of theodicean explanation of the existence of evil.

With Pandora, Hesiod thus creates a female figure who acts as the archetypal evil-minded woman, a parallel to the Biblical Eve. Pandora is also the cause of a fall from mankind's divine co-existence with the gods under Kronos. For, as he says of Pandora, "from her comes all the race of womankind,/ the deadly female race and tribe of wives/ who will live with mortal men and bring them harm" (Th. 591-93). Zeus put women and Pandora into the world of men as a curse: "women are bad for men, and they conspire/ in wrong" (Th. 601-02).

The idea seems to be that, before Pandora came into the world, human beings were exclusively male (WD 90 ff.). They lived in a Golden Age, were never sick, did not need to work, and remained forever young. Yet, it is difficult to imagine that Hesiod really means that the earth was at first only inhabited by men, as in that case he does not take procreation into consideration. So it is more likely that he allows Pandora to represent the evil-minded woman, as he may have built on an older myth, according to which Pandora was the Earth itself as a young girl.[6]

To relate his myth, which resembles the story of the Fall of Man, Hesiod ties the myths of Prometheus and Pandora together. They are told a little differently in the *Theogony* and *Works and Days,* but are interpreted here together to illuminate their full extent and meaning. The starting point is that in a struggle against his fellow Titans, Prometheus had helped Zeus to power. Later, they compete in sagacity (Th. 534). Prometheus succeeds in deceiving Zeus with a meal in which Zeus receives the poorer part, the intestines, instead of the meat. Zeus takes it out on mankind, depriving them of fire. But Prometheus brings it to them, hidden in a fennel stalk. And it is as a punishment for this offence that Zeus invents and dispatches the woman Pandora.

In both versions, Hephaistos creates her from water and earth. In the *Theogony*, however, it is only Athene who equips her with the incomparable charms that make her so irresistible and fatal to man. The description in *Works and Days* is far more detailed: Athene makes her skilled at weaving, Aphrodite makes her desire irresistible, and Hermes endows her with the ways of thieves. Even though Prometheus warns his brother, the backwards-looking Epimetheus, he cannot keep his fingers away from this female phantasm. She opens her box and misfortunes tumble out upon men. At the last moment, she shuts the lid so that hope remains in the box, hope that would make it possible for mankind to withstand its torments. She gets her name Pandora—*all gifts*—from these qualities she has received from the gods, which have contributed to her seductive power of illusion. With her, the carefree, vegetative peace of the Golden Age, which corresponds to the biblical state of Paradise, is broken.

Like the story of the Fall in the Bible, Hesiod has clearly combined dawning knowledge and sexuality. With her seduction of Epimetheus, Pandora unleashes her evils into the world. This occurs in an extension of the knowledge that fire symbolizes as the source of civilization, technical ingenuity etc., as it is also described by Aeschylus in *Prometheus Bound*. Human beings are not themselves particularly active in this process, which must be due to the fact that they are at a preconscious stage of development. The initiative comes from Prometheus' rebellious defiance and his attempt to make himself wiser than Zeus. So he becomes a Greek parallel to Lucifer, who with his *non serviam* also refused to serve.

4

Like the unfortunate copy of the divine that Pandora is, she has an intertextual connection with Helen, thereby becoming an example of how Hesiod uses his great predecessor. He says Pandora has "a face/ like an immortal goddess" (WD 63-64), just as Homer says of Helen, "terrible is the likeness of her face to immortal goddesses" (III, 158). In the original language, the two formulations are quite identical, emphasizing that Hesiod has taken his description of Pandora from Homer's Helen.[7] In this way, Helen has the same function for Homer as Pandora has for Hesiod. And it explains why Helen's birth in the cyclical poem *Cypria* is described as an event that is to bring great misfortune.

One thing Pandora and Helen have in common is that they are both deceptions. Their wonderful external beauty, copied from the appearance of goddesses, is accompanied by an inner quality that destroys all around it. With it, they bring down catastrophe on men/mankind. This aspect of sexuality is not so clear with respect to Helen as it is for Pandora. As in the Bible, she is associated with knowledge brought about by the Fall, being the punishment for Prometheus cheating Zeus and giving fire to mankind, the awareness that is a condition for their cultural development.

In Homer, Penelope becomes the counterpart to Helen and her sister, Klytemnestra. And as the liberated, undemonized woman, she becomes the wifely ideal that Hesiod envisions but cannot quite portray, which may be the reason for his despondency.

Eros and Conflict

1

In other words, the Fall has the paradoxical effect of certainly placing mankind in the category of evil, but at the same time—by removing man from his unity with the gods—becoming a precondition for civilization. Subject is separated from object, and this sets in motion the cultural development that, according to Hesiod, leads to the formation of the family and work and the development of technical skills. In the same way, it must be said that the universe as described in the *Theogony* has successively individuated itself through the intervention of strife, insofar as the underlying objective is the world of justice that Zeus finally succeeds in establishing. As we have seen, strife is here able to function in close co-operation with wisdom, as in the case of Kronos, who castrated his father with crooked ideas, while Zeus' world plan is based on *metis*.

"Strong-willed Strife" (Th. 226) is Hesiod's term for the phenomenon, which he sees as a necessary ferment. That is to say that, like Homer but more consciously and more articulately, he finds in conflict the principle that moves the universe forward towards an ever higher awareness, incarnated in Zeus. The same insight must be the basis for Heraclitus' statement: "War (*polemos*) is father of all and king of all."[8]

2

The plan or direction sensed behind the dynamic necessity of strife must logically presume a purpose to the universe. It seems as if Hesiod had this insight, but was not able to work it into the evolution of his world system, just as he does not directly relate this force to strife. However, it is indicative of the strength of his reflective power that he invents Eros as the hidden, governing, formative power he makes emerge shortly after Gaia:

> (. . .) [then] Love, the most beautiful
> Of all the deathless gods. He makes men weak,
> He overpowers the clever minds, and tames
> The spirit in the breast of men and gods.
> (Th. 120-23)

He does not say any more, but it can be understood that Eros is the very creative force from which all things arise and which heals what strife puts asunder. Although Hesiod says no more about Eros, it can be assumed that in its origin and differentiation the entire universe is an emanation of Eros. And in some way, this creative force, Eros, is kept apart from sexuality, which is born together with strife and deceit. That sexuality is viewed so negatively must for its part be due to the fact that it is linked to woman and the fear of castration, a fear Odysseus also harbored in his encounter with Kirke.

In sum, it may be said that Hesiod relates more reflectively to the forces in life, *eros* and *eris*, that Homer also includes in his works, but in the case of the latter as pure narrative. As we shall see, it is not until Empedocles that a philosophical doctrine in which these fundamental figures work together as a universal force is established.

Yet another proof of Hesiod's inexhaustible ability for reflection is the fact that, in *Works and Days*, he once again considers the nature of strife, as he must have realized—if *Works and Days* chronologically follows the *Theogony*—that strife is not only a necessary evil but a necessary good. Thus, he emphasizes to his lazy brother that conflict has two natures which are essentially dissimilar. One is evil, leading to war and conflict between people. Implicitly, this is this road of strife that his brother Perses follows and should abandon. Instead, he should follow the other, benevolent form of conflict, which arouses striving and enterprise partly as a consequence of envy! In short, Hesiod describes something for which he has no words: the competitive mentality, in which he finds a foundation for life. He states quite plainly: "A man grows eager, seeing another rich/ from ploughing, planting, ordering his house; so neighbour vies with neighbour in the rush for wealth: this strife is good for mortal men" (WD 23-24).

Justice and Utopia

1

Evidence that the strife between the brothers is not pure fiction on Hesiod's part may be found in the fact that it is possible in his plethora of didactic words to find the private background history, which is his motivation for writing his poem, resolved. But at the same time his aim is higher, as his own private conflict serves as a paradigm for mankind in the rules for life he sets up for his troublesoome brother.

Pieced together, the conflict may be paraphrased in this way. After their father's death, the brothers shared the inheritance. Perses seems to have squandered his quickly, whereupon, saddled with debt, he has gone into trade and, shortly before the writing of the poem, has visited Hesiod to ask for a larger share of the inheritance, though without being able to press more out of him. On the other hand, he is now given a lesson in the poem on how to become a decent person, that is to say a kind of mental inheritance and fraternal assistance:

> And I will neither give nor lend to you.
> You foolish Perses, go to work! The gods
> Have given work to men; don't let it be
> That you should take your children and your wife
> And beg, with downcast spirit, for your food
> From neighbours who refuse to care.
> (WD 396-401)

These rules may be derived from the title *Works and Days*, where the Greek word for works is erga—i.e., deeds or works. This certainly refers to the practical aspects of work in the fields, shipping, etc., and to the good and bad days for these jobs. But work as such has a fundamental moral dimension, since it is work that accumulates and provides a human being with his identity and dignity.

So work becomes the greatest conceivable virtue (*arete*), the supreme good: "Good habits are man's finest friend, and bad/are his worst enemy" (WD 471-72). One can scarcely imagine a train of thought further from Homer's heroic ideal, particularly in the *Iliad*, where virtue is primarily identical to martial courage. As "divinely conceived" kings, the heroes had everything given to them from above, while the everyday work was undertaken by slaves. They themselves barely lifted a finger.

If Hesiod goes to all the trouble of setting his brother straight, it must be his view that morality, in the sense of *arete*, can and must be learned. He describes it in an image that would later become common in moral and didactic literature, the difficult path of virtue:

> Oh foolish Perses: Badness can be caught
> In great abundance, easily; the road
> To her is level, and she lives nearby.
> But good is harder, for the gods have placed
> In front of her much sweat; the road is steep
> And long and rocky at the first (. . .)
> (WD 287-90)

The person or, more specifically, the man is perfect who of himself understands what is best. A person who is willing to learn is also valuable, whereas the person with deaf ears is a complete fool. So work can never be a disgrace, although laziness is, provoking the hatred of gods and men—"Both gods and men despise him, for he is/ much like the stingless drone, who does not work/ but eats, and wastes the effort of the bees" (WD 304-05). Thus, Hesiod uses the first part of *Works and Days* to establish work as a moral category. In the second part, he translates it into practice—and stresses to his brother and everyone else: "Preserve a sense of right proportion, for/ fitness is all important, in all things" (WD 694-95).

2

Behind the idea of work as man's ennobling goal there is a deeper representational pattern, linked to the idea of justice developed in the *Theogony*, which can be applied in the concrete world of action in *Works and Days* via the interconnection of law and personal morality. For, just as the Muses praise "the laws (*nomos*) and courteous ways (*ethea*)" (Th. 66), Hesiod, as the Muses' witness to truth, sees it as his task to describe the same world of laws in life on earth.

Because Perses tried to press his inheritance case with the ruling and, it may be imagined, venal aristocrats, Hesiod has occasion to attack this tarnished form of government: "The lords who love to try a case like that,/ eaters of bribes" (WD 38-39). The phenomenon was not unknown to Homer, since even in the *Iliad* he speaks of Zeus' anger with mankind: "After they stir him to anger/ because in violent assembly they pass decrees that are crooked,/ and drive righteousness from among them and care nothing for what the gods think" (XVI, 386-88).

The judicial royal power, to which in the *Theogony* Hesiod ascribed the same inspiration from the gods—"lords are from Zeus" (Th. 96)—as that in which he himself participated as a poet, is now indicated as being corrupt. Even as he seeks to persuade his brother to tread the path of righteousness, he directs a general warning to these kings and their followers on behalf of the highest court of justice, the goddess Dike—whom, like Eros, Hesiod invented, presumably to create a more active judge than Themis. Dike speaks to Zeus, telling him of the unjust hearts of men, that "the city suffers for its lords/ who recklessly, with mischief in their minds,/ pervert their judgements crookedly" (WD 260-62). The word *dike* appears of course in Homer in the quotation above, but it does not have the same moral content, since the word is almost identical to custom and what is normal (see p. 103).⁹

Hesiod's intense feeling of a genuine morality, linked to *dike*, is displayed when he praises the judge-king who dispenses justice. Through him, a divine blessing flows to the city and country, so that justice is experienced as pure welfare and social order. As he puts it,

> But when the judges of a town are fair
> To foreigner and citizen alike,
> Their city prospers and her people bloom;
> Since peace is in the land, her children thrive;
> Zeus never marks them out for cruel war.
>
> (WD 225-29)

So justice expresses itself in this way: as a cosmic force guaranteed by kings in their representative capacity. This is a way of thinking that corresponds to Homer's purpose in the *Odyssey*: to produce a royal figure who, through his own personal development, has achieved such a degree of wisdom and a sense of justice as to be able to ensure his land and his people strength, freedom and wealth.

3

Since "the eye of Zeus sees all" (WD 267), Hesiod concludes that, as the personification of justice, he will prevent the lawless from attaining rights over those who obey the law. Otherwise, it makes no sense to obey the law (WD 270 ff.). Once again, Hesiod is thinking of his own controversy with his brother. However, he is clearly unsure of the outcome of his case. This is because the ways of Zeus are inscrutable, as they were in Homer. Regardless of how much you may exert yourself and work, there is a chance he will turn his back on you: "But Zeus who holds the aegis has a mind/ unknowable for men and changeable" (WD 483-84). So man's free will is more or less the same as in Homer. People are free and may qualify, but they cannot understand the whole context and so they are subject to the divine will.

However, one thing is certain: a person calls down judgment upon himself if he ignores appropriate moderation but persists in *hubris*: "Oh Perses, follow right; control your pride" (WD 213). He is not only speaking to his quite uncomprehending brother (WD 286), but also to the kings. If they do not listen to him they are foolish, as they will call down upon themselves punishment from Zeus, who "made this law for men" (WD 279-80). In this sense, Hesiod is the proponent of a personal sense of responsibility that is still only in its infancy in Homer and only becomes completely politically fully developed by Solon.

4

The myth of Prometheus/Pandora is certainly told with a different emphasis in *Works and Days* from that in the *Theogony*. And yet we are in no doubt that it is in this context we can find the reason for the decline in standards in the history of mankind, which at the same time paradoxically also produces culture and raises awareness. In contrast to the *Theogony*, which from first to last is an extended allegory, *Works and Days* lack a basic allegorical form around which Hesiod could concentrate his ideas. Nevertheless, in the first main section of the text, he makes use of a series of related symbols to support and clarify his ideas. In an extension of the myth of Pandora resembling the biblical Fall, he describes decadence extending over five ages that are called after metals of decreasing value.[10]

The generation from the god-like Golden Age is followed by the far inferior Silver and Bronze Ages. Then comes the Age of Heroes, which with its Homeric god-like heroes resembles the Golden Age. Hesiod's own age is characterized by the poorest metal, iron. Children no longer obey their parents and, with a scarcely hidden reference to Perses, Hesiod says that the lesser man will harm the better. This generation, too, will be destroyed according to this notion and law of succession, which—since the gods' own successive generations—has come down into the world of men.

On this basis, in the shape of a fable, Hesiod can attack the ruling kings in a Homeric simile, which he claims that they must surely able to understand without interpretation: a hawk seizes a songbird, which screams in pain but learns from the hawk that he who opposes the strong will lose. At the same time as Hesiod once more aims at the current rulers with this image, he can, in the light of it, focus on his personal conflict with his brother and assert that *hubris* is evil and righteousness good, and ultimately justice will be done—"Justice in the end will win the race/ and Pride will lose" (WD 217-18).

5

So we can conclude that Homer and Hesiod converge in their views of the world. Both poets create a vision of justice victorious that is *utopian* in its scope. In the *Odyssey*, the arrogant suitors, who correspond to Hesiod's "bribe-swallowing" kings, reap their punishment; whereupon Odysseus rebuilds his kingdom on the same triad of justice (Dike), social order (Eunomia) and peace (Eirene), which is a utopian *telos* for Hesiod.

Homer presents a message, embedded in the epic presentation, corresponding to his poetic presuppositions and level of awareness. Hesiod represents a further step. He emerges as a personal poet, subjective and reflective, with clear didactic and prophetic aspirations, based on the fact that the truth is revealed through him from the Muses, a truth determined by and preserving memory and which comes from Zeus. So although he expresses an eschatological mood of destruction in his description of the *dysnomia* of the Iron Age, his will is ultimately governed by a dream of salvation, where the supreme god disappears in part behind the motives of his passionate spokesman.

It can be extrapolated that Hesiod's utopia is linked with the idea of the return of the Golden Age in which may appear the transformation of strife from which *Works and Days* actually derives. Evil strife must be replaced by good strife, which provides personality with an objective through circumspection, moderation and, first and foremost, hard work. In general, political leaders are required who have as their ideal a sense of justice that can provide a country with fertility in the broadest sense of the word. Again, we must point to Solon as the answer to this expectation. With his idea of *sophrosyne*, he argued against the increase of wealth that leads to *hubris* and calls down the judgment of the gods.

From this perspective, *Works and Days* becomes a Boeotian peasant poet's amazing and visionary attempt to save mankind by providing a mythological explanation for its Fall and a number of practical and moral instructions for its salvation, all on the basis of personal experience. In this sense, his work is also a piece of subjective poetry anticipating a true individual lyric poetry in the work of Archilochus and Sappho, just as in his poetry on the origin of the world and its moral demands he forms the basis for the earliest Presocratic philosophy and its conceptualization—from the beginning.

XII

THE LYRICAL SENSE
OF SELF

Archilochus—Warrior Poet⋆

1

W ITH *Works and Days*, POETRY BEGINS IN EARNEST TO EXPRESS EXPERI-
ence on a subjective basis, and in this area Hesiod points forward to
Archilochus. He came from the island of Paros, located in the Ionian
language area, which is to say that, in a quite different way from Hesiod, he had
direct access to the progressive cultural development in the Greek colonies on the
west coast of Asia Minor. He wrote his poetry in the middle of the 7th century B.C.,
as, among other things, can be understood from a fragment (71) that describes an
eclipse of the sun that can be dated to 4 April 648 B.C.[1] According to tradition, he
was a bastard, the progeny of a distinguished father and a Thracian slave girl, and he
died in a battle between Paros and Naxos, ostensibly killed by an enemy soldier by
the name of Korax, who was later driven from the temple of Apollo for killing a servant of the Muses.[2] Archilochus is "the first 'subjective' artist," says Nietzsche, referring to the fact that in his poetry we can hear the cry of hatred, mockery and desire.[3]

Like Hesiod, he had a dual social role: Hesiod as peasant and poet, Archilochus
as poet and warrior. But, whereas we do not know whether Hesiod continued his
life as a shepherd and peasant after receiving his calling as a poet, Archilochus
remained a professional soldier. He himself says that he is the servant of Ares, but
that he is "skilled in the lovely gift of the Muses" (1). It was claimed even in antiquity that he was the inventor of many poetic metres. Clement of Alexandria writes
for instance that the iamb was invented by Archilochus of Paros.[4] And as Aristotle
points out, this meter, which is later used in dramatic dialogues, is the best for

⋆ Translator's note: The fragment numbers refer to Archilochus' poems as collected in *Greek Elegy and
Iambus* II (ed. by J. M. Edmonds, Loeb Class. Lib. 259). Unless otherwise indicated, translations of the
poems are from Guy Davenport, *Carmina Archilochi: The Fragments of Archilochos* (1964), which are numbered differently and indicated as the second parenthetical number. Fragment numbers referring to
Sappho's poems are from *Greek Lyric I* (ed. by David A. Campbell, Loeb Class. Lib. 142). Unless otherwise
indicated, all translations of Sappho's poems are from Mary Barnard, *Sappho: A New Translation* (1975).

rendering everyday language. Or, put in another way: this meter can express human experiences and feelings even better than other verse forms. So, the subjective breakthrough in Archilochus gives birth to this metrical invention almost as a virtual inner necessity.

He certainly takes Homer as his model (as do all Greek poets)—in some passages quite openly—but his focus is on himself and his own highly personal views. Indeed, it might really be said that, given the notion of subjectivity, he negates Homeric poetics by *not* invoking the Muses. Everything he does is his own. He bases his poetry neither on family relationships nor on cycles of legends. He ridicules external signs of honor and despite his métier as a soldier he is antiheroic in attitude.

In his realism, he is moreover an extension of Hesiod but he takes it further artistically. Without embarking on a more profound stylistic analysis, we can observe how he develops a lapidary, biting, often satirical form of poetry in which this iambic meter, so close to spoken language, dissolves the objectifying, epic metrical patterns to make space for his personal register of emotions. The images in his texts are uncompromisingly drawn with a chiselled clarity that liberates his poetry from the past.

2

If a given metrical pattern is not simply a formal arrangement but carries within it a particular view of the world, it may be concluded that, with the development of his short form and iambic verse, Archilochus mounts a covert countermovement to the heroic-aristocratic view of the world residing in the grand epic of the hexameter. However, the hexameter is preserved in the elegiac distich of which Archilochus is also a master. Regardless of his choice of verse, however, he is predominantly satirical in his poetic approach, whereas Hesiod was didactic. Hesiod raised pastoral life to universal significance, while Archilochus approaches the world pragmatically with his satire, which is founded on the norms of the city-state.

As a genre, satire in itself presupposes an audience. This must mean that, in his poetry, Archilochus does not only express his own opinions but does so in consensus with a new population group. To a certain extent that is. For just as Hesiod with the beautiful voices of the Muses attacked the country folk as "bellies," as instinctual, lower beings, Archilochus has no less sharp an eye for the pettiness of city folk, as for instance he does not expect to achieve any recognition as a poet from his fellow citizens.

His tongue was no less sharp than his sword. His acerbic nature is also noted in a comment from antiquity: "The tomb by the sea is the grave of Archilochus, who first dipped a bitter muse in snake-venom and stained gentle Helicon with blood."[5]

On the one hand, Archilochus like Hesiod, uses his own experiences to objectify his ideological criticism of aristocratic values. On the other, he expresses a gradual transition to a world of passion, full of hatred and desire, that is distinctly his own and, in a negative reflection, points the way forward to Sappho's radical internalization of emotional life.

3

Although Archilochus distances himself from aristocratic morality, this is not the same as looking down on his calling as a soldier as such. Almost in the style of a Homeric warrior, he describes how he leans on his spear, eats the bread and drinks the wine that his bloody handiwork has procured for him. Not without pride, he tells in his poetry of a battle with the warriors of Euboea, famed for their spears (3).

And yet this virtual heroization of the harsh life of the professional soldier is exceptional. For just as life as a mercenary has sharpened his eye to the weaknesses of urban dwellers, so he developed a clear vision of the heroic *arete* found in Homer, particularly in the *Iliad*, so that his poems almost express a denial of the heroic concept of honor. To the Homeric hero, his honor (*time*) and resultant reputation (*kleos*) were a matter of life and death, whereas the new and groundbreaking feature in Archilochus is that he will not risk his life for external honor.

He makes this clear in a presumably autobiographical elegy in which, during a clash with the Thracians, the first-person narrator is forced to flee and leave his shield hidden in a thicket. A Thracian warrior then boasts of having taken it into his possession, but what does that matter, for, as the poem freely translated concludes: "Life seemed somehow more precious./ It was a beautiful shield./ I know where I can buy another/ Exactly like it, just as round." (6; 79).

It is difficult to imagine anything further from the Homeric hero. In Homer, arms and armor are an inseparable part of the hero's identity—just think of how Patroklos practically acquires Achilleus' identity when he dresses in his armor. So the loss of weapons is the same as tarnishing one's honor and vice versa: capturing an enemy's arms meant an enhancement of reputation. There was no greater shame than to lose one's arms.

In short, Archilochus' assertion that he can simply obtain a new shield must, as said above, be interpreted as evidence that the notion of what is of value has moved from external honor to an internal assessment, that it is now a thing in the mind. It is a shift that on a psychological level corresponds to the gradual movement from shame and the fear of losing face to true sense of guilt. It cannot be claimed that Archilochus gives explicit expression to this form of consciousness. Yet, as such a conceptual ability requires a person to be capable of considering his own motives, we have the premise for this partly in Odysseus' incipient introspection (see p. 173) and partly in Archilochus' breach with inherited conventions, in which the ability to assess people individually is being developed.

From this newly-established element within the human being originates the rational doctrine that life is more valuable than external honor, while the Homeric heroes are ready to sacrifice their lives for honor and, with head held high, accept death if it is linked to an immortal reputation. On this basis, it can actually be claimed that Archilochus wrote his poems as counter-texts to the *Iliad*'s basic notion that with his early, heroic death Achilleus secures an eternal life for his reputation.

4

In Homer, heroic status could also be seen in purely external qualities, in height and in splendor. One should look good. We found the starkest conceivable contrast between Achilleus and the ugly Thersites. However, in the *Odyssey*, we could as a new theme see that a person could have a handsome exterior but be disgusting inside and vice versa (the suitors vs. Odysseus). On this point, too, Archilochus introduces his criticism and satire by again indirectly emphasizing the value of inner human qualities. It is not a matter of seeming but being. He writes:

> I do despise a tall general,
> One of those swaggerers,
> A curly-haired, cheek-frilled
> Whisker dandy.
>
> For me a proper officer's
> Short and bow-legged,
> Both feet planted well apart
> Touch in the guts
>   (58; 282)

In this tall commander, we recognize an Agamemnon as described in the *Iliad*— "this Achaian man of power and stature" (III, 167), but here in caricature, an idler strutting like a peacock. In contrast is the stolid little man with bow legs, whose strength is based on inner courage, a man resembling Odysseus insofar as he was seen as stocky and a contrast to Menelaos (see p. 166). Of course, Archilochus undermines the heroic external aspect, but he maintains the high morality of martial courage.

Nevertheless, it must be acknowledged that Archilochus is so constitutionally unheroic in voice and deed that we can well understand why the Spartans were forbidden to read him and why his books were removed from that state as unseemly, since they would harm their children and inhibit their intelligence.[6] In this assessment, we find the difference between Sparta and the other Greek city-states. The Spartans repressed the criticism Archilochus expressed and tried instead to live up to the heroic ideals, as can clearly be seen in the Spartan court poet Tyrtaeus, who places struggle and courage above all other human characteristics: "For the man is not *agathos* (brave) in war, unless he endure seeing the bloody slaughter."[7]

5

If it can be said on the one hand that Archilochus confronts the heroic legacy as a form of social acceptance from within, it can be maintained on the other that he likewise liberates himself from the norms of his time by virtue of his inner life. Like Heraclitus later, he expresses no small contempt for the mass of mankind. For example, he writes to a friend that no one could count on any enjoyment in life "who heeded the censure of the people" (8).[8]

He says no more, but he must be implying that people are always gossiping, judgmental and prudish. So it does not pay to protect one's reputation. In a longer perspective, it can be seen that, just as he distanced himself from the notion of honor, so he dissociates himself from the value of fame, that thing which, if anything, secures one's reputation, as when Odysseus says to Penelope that her fame has reached the skies. If you adjust what you do for the sake of fame, it interferes with your self-realization, and you will ultimately lose your life. This is pure sabotage of the fundamental conception of heroism.

That this is really what Archilochus believes is confirmed by a few iambic phrases on the unreliability of public opinion. For, as he says, it is a matter of living as long as you are alive, for no one can count on honor from one's countrymen after death (63). The dead will always come off worst, so it is ridiculous to sacrifice your life for external honor. Insight without illusions tells him that he can only count on himself, his own inner self, as valuable; all externalities are beyond one's control. For the same reason, he is totally indifferent to wealth and power—nor is he jealous of the "works of the gods" (25), just as it is beyond him to strive to become a tyrant.

6

Regardless of whether it is due to Archilochus' position as warrior and poet or his own peculiar constitution—or both together—on an existential level in his hard-chiselled, matter-of-fact short verse he derides heroism as an outdated, external life form. In addition, he repudiates the norms of his time on which he otherwise bases his critique of aristocratic values as a hindrance to a true life. In principle, he is thrown back on himself, forced to "invent," to reveal the inner life as the true vehicle of meaning in existence.

He also makes this internalization a general doctrine of life. For by observing the fundamental rhythm of life, its shifting upturns and downturns, he understands that life consists of a basic, fixed rhythm. Therefore, it is up to the individual to learn to know himself and to act in consonance with life's inevitable vicissitudes, neither rejoicing in victory nor weeping in defeat, but enduring:

Soul, soul,
Torn by perplexity,
On your feet now!
Throw forward your chest
To the enemy;
Keep close in the attack;
Move back not an inch.
But never crow in victory,

Nor mope hang-dog in loss.
Overdo neither sorrow or joy;
A measured motion governs man.[9]

(66; 72)

Whereas he otherwise dissociates himself from Homer's heroism, it is possible to hear the voice of Odysseus in these lines. First, in the invocation to his soul, which is a clear echo of Odysseus' speech to his vehement heart at the sight of the faithless servant girls (20, 9 ff. see p. 173). In both, the rebellious inner self is invoked with the word *thymos*. But since the world, as was later to be the case in Sappho, arises through the subjective temperament, he uses *thymos* in a different way from Homer and describes a true endogenous reality, which is itself the basis for the lyric drive in his poetry.

Then there is a clear parallel to Odysseus' reprimand to the suitors telling them to show humility towards life, which raises a man up one moment only to cast him down the next. In this sense, Odysseus becomes a sort of prefiguration of Archilochus himself: two men of the same stuff, with the same endurance and flexibility when it comes to adapting themselves to the rhythm of life. Both master the difficult art of self-control under the pressure of life.

How important this latter psychological feature is in the eyes of Archilochus can be seen in a poem he writes on the occasion of a catastrophe in which many fellow townsmen are drowned. He demands that those who grieve should maintain their self-control, for in that alone resides the buffer the gods provide for the ups and downs of life: "Grit your teeth,/ not all of us need be women." (9; 121). In this, we can hear Apollo's words to the other gods: "for the Destinies put in mortal men the heart (*thymos*) of endurance" (XXIV, 49). Or as Archilochus says elsewhere: "Attribute all to the gods,/ They pick a man up,/ Stretched on the black loam,/ And set him on his two feet,/ Firm, and then again/ Shake solid men until/ They fall backward" (56; 23). From this, we can assume that he shares Hesiod's view that the ways of the gods are inscrutable as they rule and intervene in the world of man.

The similarity to Odysseus is there, but there is also a clear difference. In his endurance, Odysseus is able to look forward to a definitive victory and happy ending to events if he is sufficiently strong-willed. But there is no happy ending for Archilochus; only the relentless rotation of good and bad times. Life demands patience, adaptability and an understanding that says that one should not put too much emphasis on either success or failure. Keep cool!

7

Insofar as a man is seen at his most naked and unaffected in his passions, this is true of Archilochus. For whereas in the poems so far discussed, he has after all had an ideological and satirical filter between himself and the surrounding world, this distance is broken down in some texts driven by profound personal scruples. So there is a question of payment in kind in his vengeful desire to see a friend who has let him down lie shipwrecked on the shore—"spitting brine,/ At the edge of the cold sea, like a dog."[10] The emphasis he here attaches to friendship and his fury when it is betrayed again show how important human values are to him at the same time as his own inner self becomes remarkably visible in the destructive distortion occasioned by hatred.

It appears that, despite his praise for self-control, there is at least one area of life it in which it is extremely difficult for him to control himself—namely, love when experienced as desire and loss. According to tradition, he loved Neoboule, whose name figures in the following fragment: "O that/ I might but touch/ Neoboule's hand" (71; 232). Her father, Lykambes, at first approved their marriage but then changed his mind. Archilochus then attacked him with such a hate-filled and mocking poem that, according to tradition, he took his own life.[11] Once again, we see in his poetry the interplay between a poem and its surroundings, as the point must be that it was not the words of the satire as such that killed the father-in-law to be, but the shame and ridicule it brought down on him. And as in the case of his false friend, we see again how Archilochus' true nature breaks through and is individualized when his feelings are hurt. Love is inverted into hate.

A number of fragments reveal just how strongly he is really gripped by desire. One of them corresponds to Hesiod's view of Eros as a force that leaves human beings weak in the knees (p. 293). Similarly, Archilochus says that desire, which makes people weak, has overwhelmed him (85): "Miserable with desire (*pothos*)/ I lie lifeless,/ My bones shot through/ With thorny anguish/ sent by the gods" (84; 29). Or he describes how he physically experiences the hold desire takes of him: "And under your love of lust (*philotetos eres*),/ Seeing nothing else for this mist,/ Dark of heart, dark of mind" (103; 11).

Behind the image of the dark mist descending upon his eyes we sense Homer's description of how the soul leaves the warrior at the moment of death. If Archilochus makes use of this image, it is obviously because he experiences unsatisfied sexuality as a sort of death. And surprisingly, the self steps forward at the moment when the world denies him erotic fulfilment. In the negation of desire, by its being dammed up, the individual emotion forces its way through with an all-encompassing intensity. The subject is manifested in the pain of love, for here there is neither the pleasurable *eros* found in Homer nor Hesiod's sexual union for the purpose of propagation and future support.

At the same time, it is an experience of love that points forward towards Sappho, whose whole existence becomes a question of erotic climax or loss: hero or zero. Like Archilochus, she links her life story to an existential feeling of upturns and downturns. But whereas Archilochus allows this experience to encompass life as a whole, Sappho gathers it exclusively around love. In contrast to Archilochus, for whom the erotic world is something which in his frustration and loss he fights tooth and nail, Sappho internalizes love in an abandonment to death.

Sappho—The Tenth Muse

1

Antiquity had no doubt that Archilochus was Sappho's teacher. As Horace writes, the "masculine Sappho"[12] created his muse with the help of Archilochus' meter. Indeed, the comic poet Diphilos makes him into her lover.[13] No more should be read into these statements than an attempt to express a spiritual kinship between the two poets. The poetry of their contemporary Alkaeus is also a blend of sharp political insight and the pain of love. Like Sappho, he also came from Lesbos.

At any rate, it is Sappho who is most consistent in developing a pure poetry of feeling. In this, her temperament cannot be more different from Archilochus and his (hate) poetry. She herself says that her heart cannot hate, gentle and kind as it is (120). Her sweetness is perhaps most strongly felt in a little poem to her daughter Kleis, who must have been fair-haired, as the mother compares her to a golden flower. She would not exchange that flower for all the splendors of Lydia (132), which is saying something, since Lydia at that time was the quintessence of extravagance and refined elegance.

As is the case with the other poets of this time, what biographical knowledge we otherwise have of Sappho is based on a mythologizing tradition. It is claimed that she was born during the 42nd Olympiad—that is in 612 B.C.—on Lesbos. She had three brothers. As a young girl, she had to flee to Sicily, presumably because of political unrest, but returned to Mytilene, made a good marriage and then had her daughter Kleis, so called after Sappho's mother. There is a tradition to the effect that she committed suicide by leaping from a cliff because of unrequited love for the exquisitely handsome ferryman Phaon.

She was supposed to have been very small, dark-skinned and extremely ugly.[14] So, when Socrates calls her "beautiful Sappho,"[15] it must be on account of her inner beauty, the supreme beauty of her poetry, which also makes Plato refer to her as the tenth muse.[16] As one fragment has her say, she surpasses all other female poets by as much as Homer does the male.[17] Her fame in antiquity was already great. So was her oeuvre, collected in ten books, just as—presumably to emphasize her genius—it was claimed that she had invented the plectrum[18] and a special lyre (*pektis*).[19]

Of course, it was the question of her love life that most absorbed people. She is called a "woman-lover" (*gynaikerastria*[20]) and is said to have acquired a bad name because of "unclean friendships" (*aischras philias*[21]) with young girls. "Did not girls learn to love?"[22] asks Ovid, while she remarkably enough addresses her friends as hetaerae—"Now, today, I shall sing beautifully for my friends' (*het-*

airais) pleasure" (160). Such words may have been the reason why she was considered a prostitute.

However, as there are no concrete references to sexual activity but plenty of connotations pointing in that direction—from lesbian love to group sex[23]—there is plenty of scope for interpreting the erotic content of her manners and poetry. This much, however, is certain: her poetry contains the same forms of address that homosexual men used with their boy lovers.[24] So on the one hand her poetry has a clear sexual subtext. On the other hand, her *eros* has also been elevated to a spiritual endeavor, corresponding to the way Socrates adored young men. Thus, Maximus of Tyros exclaims: "What else is one to call the love of the woman from Lesbos except the Socratic art of love?"[25] And as he points out, both loved many and emphasized the beauty of all things—surely basing his words on the *Symposium* in which Diotima explains to Socrates the ways of love from a sensual and particular *eros* to its ever-higher purification.

2

But let us look more closely at Sappho's poetry with a view to a more precise definition of her instrumentation of personal passion and thereby, in a literal sense, subjective poetry. By comparing information from many fragments, we can form an impression of the elegant milieu on Lesbos, where, in good times and bad, Sappho thrived with her friends. It was a milieu that could not have been more different from the military life of Archilochus. And just as this left its traces on the stark realism of his poetry, so Sappho's poetry bears traces of the sensual, luxurious and cult-like reality in which she lived and breathed with Anaktoria, Atthis or whatever the girls happened to be called.

Thus, she invokes Aphrodite in order that the goddess of love from Crete (2) might be present in the temple, located in a beautiful orchard of apple trees (the apple is a symbol of love), where cool water babbles between branches sheltered by roses. Here, the goddess will pour nectar into golden goblets for the festival. Sappho herself wants to entertain with her beautiful singing, since, as she says, there must be no tears in the house of the Muses (150), and she surrenders to inspiration, addressing her lyre with the words: "Come now, my heavenly tortoise shell: become a speaking instrument" (118).

The girls have wound garlands of flowers around their necks and in their hair (81), as Aphrodite does not care to see them ungarlanded. They put colorful sandals from Lydia on their feet (39), rest on soft cushions (46) and dry their limbs on purple, perfumed towels (101). In the garden, nightingales herald spring with their infinitely gentle voices. There is dancing in circles around the altar beneath the full moon (154), where Zeus, Hera, Dionysos and not least Aphrodite's dead lover Adonis are also celebrated. Of Adonis, she writes: "Young Adonis is dying! O Cytherea, what shall we do now? Beat your breasts, girls—tear your dresses asunder!" (140).

The poetry conjures a truly lesbian Arcadia, a self-validating female universe, where erotic enjoyment is united with cultic festivity and where men in the nature of things are forbidden access—a fertile, sensual world full of enjoyment, untouched by masculinity's ploughing.[26]

3

So it is crucial to understand how Sappho's cultivation of *eros* makes her into a poet and an independent individual. We see this process of becoming independent through the ability to love unfolded for instance in a poem in which—like Archilochus—she dissociates herself from heroic aesthetics. She describes what to her is the most beautiful thing on earth and gives expression to her wholly personal assessment. For many, the most wonderful thing is the sight of armies and horsemen—that is to say the heroic. Each to his or her own. She is herself not in doubt: "I say that [the finest sight is] whatever one loves" (16). Note the subjective choice, the words perhaps a covert allusion to Odysseus' words on the relative nature of choice: "for different men take joy in different actions" (14, 228). At any rate, Sappho herself refers to personal reflection and doubt when in a given situation (about which we are not informed), she writes: "I do not know what to do; I am of two minds" (51).

In other words, like Archilochus, she puts her inner emotional life above her external posture, choosing love, the irresistibility of which is exemplified by a reference to Helen (16). This, the most wonderful woman on earth, who is otherwise encompassed by so much censure in the literature of antiquity, becomes a heroine to Sappho. Why? Because Helen alone followed her passion and put aside any concern for those close to her, led astray by Aphrodite.

By identifying herself with Helen in this way, Sappho has brought herself into the erotic minefield behind the Homeric epics. However, if this were about making sexuality conscious in order to avoid Aphrodite's trap, it might conversely be said that, in a contrary movement, Sappho makes absolute Helen's form of passion. On this point, she is also far away from Archilochus, who, as we heard, like Homer, saw in the *eros* of desire the power of delusion that robs even the wisest of reason and causes great suffering. Sappho embraces this love as a personal, meaningful destiny. Consequently, she experiences *eros* as a vast, supernatural source of power. What she seeks in life is passion as pleasure but also as pain in loss, separation or jealousy, and lack of contact with one's lover.

In the poem on Helen it is precisely separation that evokes a special form of dual recollection, sweet and tormented, as she remembers a distant, beloved girl:

> the dear sound of your footstep
> and light glancing in your eyes
> would move me more than glitter
> of Lydian horse or armored
> tread of mainland infantry.

To be parted is like dying, as is seen from the following words: "When she left, she wept/ a great deal; she said to/ me, 'This parting must be/ endured, Sappho. I go unwillingly'" (94). A similar feeling of love, persisting until death, leads to jealousy, especially directed against Atthis, who apparently deserted her for Andromeda, who may have been leader of a rival *thiasos*. Plaintively, she writes: "Atthis, you hate even the thought of me. You dart off to Andromeda" (131). Of course, this fragment may be linked to another, more general expression of Sappho's love, an expression that in its phrasing can be traced back to the description of love in Hesiod and Archilochus as a power that causes powerlessness: "Irresistible and bittersweet that loosener of limbs, Love reptile-like strikes me down" (130).

These two lines provide Sappho's experience of *eros* in brief form. Eros is described as a worm or a snake with a double effect: sweet and painful. The actual compound she uses to describe the duality of her feeling (*glykypikron*: sweet-bitter) denotes a leap in the ability sensitively to experience and understand. Homer has no corresponding spiritual gradation, only a quantification with the prefix *poly*, which indicates a great amount of a single quality: *polymetis*, etc. The world has become deeper, more manifold and complex.

4

In order to give her choice of *eros* authenticity, Sappho was compelled to create a special metrical unit, the so-called Sapphic strophe. Indeed, she had to renew herself right down to the formation of individual words—and recreate the language. In a lengthy poem, she similarly describes erotic conflict and crisis in purely psychosomatic terms. The background appears to be that one of her female friends is to be married and the groom—or at least a young man—is sitting between her and the one she loves. She calls him the equal of the gods. Why? Perhaps because he is as beautiful as a god. Perhaps because he sits near her beloved and yet can endure this closeness or perhaps because he has won her lover's heart. It could also be a combination of all these reasons.

At any rate, at a distance from the object of her emotions she must suffer the entire gamut of passions, as passion is intensified by the force of jealousy, in that they are separated by a third person. The final strophe says:

I drip with sweat;
trembling shakes my body
and I turn paler than
dry grass. At such times
death isn't far from me.
[All this I would dare endure, if only . . .]*

* Translator's note: deviates from the Barnard translation.

Brought to the edge of the grave by her emotions, the experience, as we also observed in Archilochus, opens up to a complex understanding of the vicissitudes of life that are exclusively linked to the power of *eros* or sexuality, as again and again it seizes her, lifts her up and dashes her down. Like another Odysseus, however, she learns in this way to bear this sweet, self-created pain. The ego is thrown back on itself by this erotic obstacle (journey, desertion, etc.) and is individualized as this mixture of distress and joy is transformed into a category of cognition.

And, interestingly enough in this context, in the only fully-preserved poem by her, a poem to Aphrodite (1), Sappho defines her erotic lot in life as "harsh affliction" (*chalepan merimnan* = heavy sorrow, worry—The very same harsh affliction that became a driving force in Odysseus and developed his patience. Of course, in her poem, Sappho prays to Aphrodite to take this unbearable fate from her, but only to have it imposed on her once more. For, as so many times before, the goddess is to assist her. Driving from her father's palace in a chariot drawn by beautiful sparrows, she meets Sappho with a speech that, as a projection, corresponds to her own burning desires as the goddess says: "Whom has Persuasion to bring round now to your love?"

Aphrodite is to make Sappho's beloved turn to her, no matter how. For as the previous poem put it, she can endure anything "if only . . ." The lacuna in the text could appropriately be filled in with the formula: If only I love. In this position and in her identification with Helen and Aphrodite, Sappho has made her bitter-sweet choice, pledged herself, if you will, but a new, individual understanding and feeling of life arises with a shocking effect in the poem's linguistic comparison of the intensity of this passion: "As a whirlwind swoops on an oak Love shakes my heart" (47).

While Sappho thus—by channelling the desire and pain brought about by passion—looks into herself in an extreme subjectivization of emotional life, there arises in the same area and at the same time—in an attempt to interpret the origin, development and essence of life—a diametrically-opposed, philosophically-oriented science, which aims empirically at objectivizing human cognitive ability.

XIII

PRESOCRATIC THOUGHT*

A Common Field of Meaning

1

IN THE *Theogony*, HESIOD PRAYS TO THE MUSES TO ENLIGHTEN HIM ON THE beginnings of things (*ex arches*)[1]—after which, in a mythological allegory, he creates an account of the origin and construction of the universe. This is clearly an attempt to place the world within a system, to create a comprehensible and at least partially exhaustive cosmology. But despite the rational intent in this, a truly philosophical and scientifically-based way of thinking arose in Ionia, more specifically in the city of Miletus, around 600 B.C., with Thales as its originator. Thales believed that water was the basic element, which may in itself reveal a continuing link to the Homeric world, in which water, Okeanos, the river encircling the globe, is presented as the source of all things, "whence the gods have arisen" (XIV, 201).

However, although this connection may go back to Homer and Hesiod, the decisive element in this incipient natural philosophy as a whole is that it refuses to be satisfied with the mythological rationality found in Hesiod. It seeks to understand natural phenomena in themselves on the basis of an attempt at empirical observation. However, it is by the nature of things impossible to avoid speculation in seeking to understand what is hidden behind our immediate sense observations, just as the old gods and their mythology every so often raise their heads as explanatory models.[2]

It is not certain that, as tradition has it, Thales studied in Egypt.[3] However, this suggestion testifies to the influence of the Orient, which is generally behind Greek philosophy and explains why Presocratic philosophy does not emerge out of thin air.[4]

Interpretation is made more difficult, moreover, by the fact that the earliest philosophy is only known through fragments and notes to textbook-like compendia and in later philosophers such as Plato and Aristotle. This creates significant uncertainty in the understanding of a particular philosopher's thought, as is underlined by the often divergent traditions. They may be colored by misunderstanding and mis-

---

* Translator's note: References to Presocratic philosophers will provide a cross-reference to the fragment numbers in Diels-Kranz (DK), *Die Fragmente der Vorsokratiker* (1964). Unless otherwise indicated, translations of the Greek texts are from G.S. Kirk & J.E. Raven (KR), *The Presocratic Philosophers* (1957), except that translations of Heraclitus are from Charles H. Kahn (CK), *The Art and Thought of Heraclitus* (1979).

interpretations, for example, due to the inclusion of later philosophers' own views. But despite lacunae and deficiencies, I believe it is possible to provide a bird's-eye view of the questions under debate. Indeed, I believe the questions are more interesting and revealing than the answers when, as here, it is a matter of defining the form of consciousness and level of development of Presocratic philosophy. This can be done more especially since the individual philosophers are inspired by each other, even though the inspiration is often formulated as polemical criticism and masks mutual competition.

On the one hand, they are agreed in rejecting Homer and Hesiod as some kind of illusionists. We see this in Xenophanes and Heraclitus. On the other hand, Heraclitus is also just as blunt, when he calls Pythagoras' teachings "artful knavery" (CK XXV; DK 129), whereas Parmenides is more circumspect in his critique of Heraclitus. The intention with such a critique is apparently to represent a predecessor as false and deluded, so that the individual philosopher can use his point of view as a springboard to claim the ultimate truth for himself. Like Hesiod, Parmenides does so by claiming that he has received the doctrine of the true way from a celestial goddess.

2

In this way, a wide area of meaning with mutual references and reactions is established, which is why we are not as dependent on the differences in meaning among the various fragments. It is possible to establish a search and an inquiry that through a common lens enable us to put together a paradigm, which will be further developed and concretized in our discussion of the respective philosophers. I will tentatively separate the following areas as the most important:

1) *Genesis* is the cosmological question with which Hesiod also wrestled: How and from what did the universe and the world arise? 2) *Physis* relates to the substance of nature, the elemental—earth, water, air, fire—of which everything is formed. 3) *Metamorphosis*: all the natural philosophers seem to have been struck by the transformations that take place in the world and the transitions there are between opposites such as heat and cold, day and night. 4) *Causality*: this might also be called the driving force or guidance in the processes and transformations of life. In brief: what are the forces that direct events in the broader development of the world? 5) *Monotheism*. Several Presocratics derive the prime cause, the prime mover, from a divine principle of a monotheistic and metaphysical character in spite of their scientific predisposition. And Xenophanes simply presumes that there is one and only one god. 6) *Hermeneutics*: a reflection upon the requirements and conditions appertaining to philosophical knowledge itself. 7) *Subjectivity* or the psychological includes the inner world and, for the first time in developmental history, is clearly occupied with the psyche as a spiritual arbiter that is the precondition for cognition and may form part of a karma-like process of reincarnation.

This typology can also be attributed with a topological localization, as there are two primary philosophical lines of thought or schools, each with its geographical center of gravity. As has already been said, the oldest is linked to the Ionian region, in particular to the cities of Miletus and Ephesus, where it is primarily defined by scientific thinking. The other, somewhat later school is located in southern Italy and Sicily and was created by Greeks who migrated from Ionia.

Thus, Parmenides came from Elea, located on the west coast of southern Italy. Rejecting the external world of the senses as a sham reality, he established the basic rules for logical thinking. Not only are reason and reality opposed, but even the logical process of deduction is contrasted with the demands of natural philosophy for inductive investigation. This becomes a dichotomy that can be traced through the whole of Western philosophy's distinction between idealism (deduction) and realism (induction), just as the problems of epistemology that the Presocratics generally raise can also be traced in all later philosophical work in our culture.

The following account will be very selective indeed, since its purpose is primarily to explain the positions set forth in Presocratic phenomenology. This means that I cannot discuss all the Presocratics, and I will not provide a complete portrayal of those to be considered, limiting myself merely to what to my mind is typologically most interesting. I will make Heraclitus the subject of the most thorough analysis. This is undoubtedly on account of a personal fascination with him, but especially due to the fact that, in a particularly urgent and original way, he introduces the subject, the self, into his empiricism and in this way forms a philosophically vital connection between Odysseus and Socrates.

Anaximander's *apeiron*

1

Although the natural philosophers themselves searched for rational principles, the tradition concerning them is fraught with myth-making. It was obviously the intention to present them as something extraordinary and unique. That this was not entirely without a basis in reality is confirmed by Heraclitus' life story, by Diogenes, who lived in a barrel, and by Empedocles, who parades his megalomania: "I go about among you all an immortal god" (KR 478; DK 112).

Moreover, the mythologizing by tradition was intended to create order and a comprehensible sequence in the philosophical ranks. Thus, Anaximander is made into a relative and student of Thales, who was approximately his age and died about 545 B.C. during the 58th Olympiad at the age of sixty-four. Posterity seems to want to make Anaximander the primary exponent of the entire breakthrough of a new exact world of science. As a sign of this, alongside his philosophy, he was supposed to have produced the sundial, a celestial globe and the first map of the world.

It was also new that the book he wrote on nature (*Peri physeos*[5]) was in prose. Since Homer and Hesiod were considered to be the great educators—and continued to be for a lengthy period—poetry was otherwise the most authoritative genre. It is impossible to say whether Anaximander's use of prose was a reaction to this, an attempt to liberate thought from its encapsulation in poetry and thus myth. It can only be observed that Parmenides and Empedocles—even Xenophanes, who was so critical of Homer and Hesiod—versified their philosophies and used mythical analogies to formulate their ideas.

2

Although Thales may have been his teacher, Anaximander rejected the doctrine of water as the fundamental material of creation and replaced it with the concept and function of *apeiron*. This phenomenon can be found in Homer, though only to indicate something of infinite extent. As a ferment of creation and development, *apeiron* to Anaximander means the boundless, the undetermined, the undifferentiated or that which no one can evade. If we cut through the various definitions, we can say that he made *apeiron* synonymous with *arche*, i.e. the very first thing, as Chaos was for Hesiod before there was anything else: Everything is either a beginning (*arche*) or comes from a beginning (DK A 15).

Yet logically, *apeiron* must itself be without a beginning, as it would be limited if the opposite were the case. So *apeiron* has "no beginning (. . .) but this seems to be the beginning of the other things, and to surround all things and steer all" (KR 110; DK A 15). As the creative and governing principle *apeiron* is, Anaximander not surprisingly gives the phenomenon the same status as the gods. He calls it "divine" (*to theion*, KR 110; DK A 15) and consequently considers it "immortal and indestructible" (KR 110; DK A 15). Seen in relation to the profusion of gods in mythology, the concept of *apeiron* is not only a bold intellectual construct but it shows a tendency towards a monotheistic view at the same time as—in a scientifically valid manner—solving the question of the genesis and causality of things.

If we take a further step and ask what it is that *apeiron* as a concept of the divine creates and directs, the answer is the fundamental elements of the material world. *Apeiron* "is the sole cause of all generation and destruction, and from it the heavens were separated, and similarly all the worlds, which are infinite in number. And he declared that destruction and, far earlier, generation have taken place since an indefinite time, since all things are involved in a cycle." (DK A 10).[6]

This is to say that our world must have arisen in a hypostatization by being separated from the undifferentiated in which all things exist as potentials, blended into each other, to be defined in creation in the countless forms of polar oppositions: "for the elements are opposed to each other (for example, air is cold, water moist, and fire hot)" (KR 107; DK A 16). When their time comes to an end, they will return to the limitlessness from which they arose and so forth.

3

Heraclitus in particular was supposed to have made the transformation of oppositions into the core of his philosophy and, like Anaximander, was supposed to find in strife the hidden mainspring of this process. Anaximander puts it this way: "And the source of coming-to-be for existing things is that into which destruction, too, happens 'according to necessity; for they pay penalty and retribution to each other for their injustice according to the assessment of Time" (KR 103; DK A 9 + B 1).

In Greek, the word *dike*, justice, is used. Thus, he analogizes from legal usage a law with respect to wrongs and punishment, thereby applying the human legal world and morality of the polis to the works of nature. The idea seems to correspond to Solon's idea of justice, according to which justice is something immanent in life, which at a given time will always redress all wrongs.[7] Or put in a different way: A crime will always be punished and he who has suffered harm will receive recompense.

Since political and philosophical thinking weave in and out of each other, as can also be observed in most other philosophers, most clearly in Plato's *Republic*, it is obvious that the rise of the city-state is the vehicle of philosophy.[8] The conception of cosmic justice in combination with the city-state may possibly also have left its mark in Anaximander's view of the place of the earth in the universe, when he says: "The earth is on high, held up by nothing, but remaining on account of its similar distance from all things" (KR 126; DK A 11).

Insofar as the earth constitutes a fixed point of balance, it corresponds to the goal of the democratic process—to dissolve the hierarchy that still exists in Hesiod. That is to say that the earth as the center of the cosmos is a guide for how the political cosmopolis should be governed by a sort of geometric equality and justice, just as Solon's middle class was given the task of balancing society's polarization of rich and poor.[9]

4

From a cosmological perspective, strife, which leads to some offense with subsequent punishment, has its source in the transformation of oppositions. It conveys causality, while inherent justice ensures universal harmony. Since Anaximander claims that "an infinite number of worlds" derive from the governing *apeiron*, the question is whether these worlds are synchronous or consecutive. If it is assumed that the idea of many chronologically contemporary worlds is first formulated by the atomists, the most obvious thing is to imagine that Anaximander follows the notion of succession behind Hesiod's cosmology, corresponding best to his own view that oppositions arise consecutively from *apeiron*, come into conflict, and disappear back into the undifferentiated mass from which they originated.

It is true that the Ionian natural philosophers are said not to have concerned themselves with spiritual matters but left them to the poets. Nevertheless, we can see that the laws of human life are an underlying precondition for Anaximander's recognition of the universality of justice. His thinking moreover expresses a deep understanding of how the human psyche forms images in the surrounding world, which may have been an inspiration for Xenophanes' critique of mythological religiosity.

Projections and Monotheism—
Xenophanes

If Xenophanes is brought into this context, it is not only because he belongs here chronologically but because he represents an essential step forward toward the recognition of the meaning of inner experience of the world. Born around 570 B.C. in the Asia Minor city of Colophon, he emigrated to southern Italy and is said to have founded the important school of philosophy at Elea. He may be the best example—at any rate, the first—of a radical consciousness that made a stand against mythological thinking. Paradoxically enough, it was expressed in didactic poetry—paradoxically, because, as said above, this was the most important educational paradigm at the time as it is precisely on Homer and Hesiod that he makes his sharpest attacks.

He quite simply rejects any anthropomorphic conception of the gods and makes himself a spokesman for the view that the gods are human projections. Homer and Hesiod, he says, show the gods acting in petty and dishonorable ways, stealing and acting immorally. This is because they are created on the basis of the world of human motives: "But mortals consider that the gods are born, and that they have clothes and speech and bodies like their own."[10] He supports this by pointing out that the Ethiopians think of the gods in their own image—as black with snub noses, while the Thracians made them red-haired and blue-eyed.

For Xenophanes, on the other hand, the god becomes a metaphysical phenomenon around whose consciousness all things revolve without itself being concerned: "Always he remains in the same place, moving not at all; nor is it fitting for him to go to different places at different times, but without toil he shakes all things by the thought of his mind."[11] So God is separate from the world by being the moving, determining force behind everything, at the same time possessing a perfection that is found nowhere else: "One god, greatest among gods and men, in no way similar to mortals either in body or in thought."[12]

If the god is not like man in form or thought, it must follow by logical necessity that man can never fully comprehend much less understand his world. Homer already expressed something like this in his invocation of the Muse (see p. 76). And Hesiod continued in this vein in his prayer to the Muses asking them to inform him of everything from the beginning of life. And Xenophanes draws the same epistemological conclusion: "No man knows, or ever will know, the truth about the gods and about everything I speak of: for even if one chanced to say the complete truth, yet oneself knows it not; but seeming is wrought over all things."[13] But he believes that, despite the fact that the gods from the beginning have hidden the essence of things from man, it will be possible over time to achieve a better understanding.

Against this epistemological background, I want to turn to Heraclitus, since the very premise for human knowledge, the self, is such a central motif in his philosophy at the same time as his vision of the construction of the universe distinguishes itself from and corresponds to Anaximander's thoughts on *apeiron* and the polar tension in existence.

Heraclitus—The Man Who Would Be Obscure

1

Tradition has it that Heraclitus had heard Xenophanes with his own ears and might have been a student of his. Nevertheless, he develops his own quite personal philosophical ideas, corresponding to his statement: "I went in search of myself." (CK XXVIII; DK 101). In this fragment, he points toward what is peculiar to him—that is to say he makes himself, the subject, into an object for the cosmos, as he has everything occur from within. Starting out from the view that there is a fundamental correspondence between psyche and cosmos, self-insight also becomes an investigation into universal laws.[14]

From the biographical information we have on Heraclitus, however true it might be, we understand that he lived his life away from the city in order to ensure that his knowledge was not limited by accepted norms. That would prevent him from gaining insight into the underlying context that is hidden from immediate habitual thinking—"nature loves to hide" (CK X; DK 123).

So it is necessary to jettison everything that seems distracting. Like a disciple of Jesus or the Gnostics, the individual seeking insight must break away from his parents, i.e. from the entrenched prejudices of tradition: "We should not listen like children to their parents" (CK XIII; DK 74), he stresses. In short, it takes a tremendous amount of work to gain insight, an Odysseus-like endurance—indeed, more than that. It requires trust and faith, since you must be prepared to resign yourself to hopelessness: "He who does not expect will not find out the unexpected, for it is trackless and unexplored" (DK 18). We have to be as cautious as a gold miner, who digs up a huge amount of earth, but only finds a small amount of the precious metal (CK VIII; DK 22).

Heraclitus himself lived in accordance with this requirement of exile. He was born in the Ionian area, in Ephesus. On the basis of information that he flourished at the time of the 69th Olympiad (504-01 B.C.)—people estimated that the culmination (floruit) of a human being took place around the age of 40—he must have been born around 545 B.C., the heir to a royal title to boot. This title he passed to his brother and then withdrew to the mountains into lonely contemplation. And it is told that he became such a misanthrope that he left the book he is supposed to have written to the city's protectoress Artemis in order that no unworthy hands should touch it.

He is called obscure. Posterity found it difficult to understand him because he did not leave behind any clear philosophical system but has come down to us in a set of aphoristic, somewhat hermetic fragments, gnomes, which can nevertheless be united into something resembling a coherent conceptual construction. He indirectly characterized his method in a description of the answers of the oracle at Delphi: "The lord whose oracle is in Delphi neither declares nor conceals, but gives a sign" (CK XXXIII; DK 93). This art of intimation has something of the same interpretative quality as the maieutic questioning to which Socrates subjects his students. The obscure appeals to the searcher, awakening, making uneasy and demanding that one find an answer from one's inner grappling with oneself, as the Delphic motto—and Solon—anticipated: Know thyself!

2

Heraclitus obviously not only felt the necessity to leave his family but, like Xenophanes, to dismiss the great poets and creation paradigms of the past, again represented by Homer and Hesiod.

The first of these, he believes along with Archilochus, should be driven with a stick from literary competitions (CK XXI; DK 42). And of Hesiod, he says that he claimed in the *Theogony* to know a great deal, for which reason his work became a textbook, but according to Heraclitus, he "did not recognize day and night: they are one" (CK XIX; DK 57).

Heraclitus refers to the passage in the *Theogony* in which Hesiod claims that day and night pass each other in "the great bronze threshold,"[15] i.e. the entrance to Hades, which is why they are never there at the same time. Heraclitus argues the opposite—that day and night constitute a unity, because they are part of one and the same universal process, of which human beings are also a part. Socrates is the first to see in the natural world something essentially different from human nature, which is why he is not particularly interested in natural laws.

Heraclitus is also hostile to the mythological view of the world and dissociates himself from the mystery cults: "The mysteries current among men initiate them into impiety" (CK CXV; DK 14), he says, referring, among other things, to the Bacchantes. It is especially the cult of Dionysos he turns against: "Hades and Dionysos are the same, him for whom they rave and celebrate the festival of Lenaia" (CK CXVI; DK 15). That Hades and Dionysos could be the same is viewed by some scholars as an enigma. However, since both are chthonic divinities, Heraclitus' identification makes sense.

3

As a philosopher, Heraclitus is an elitist; for when he says, "One man is ten thousand, if he is best" (CK LXIII; DK 49), he must, of course, be thinking of the philosopher, whose life is guided by the love of knowledge: "Men who love wisdom must be good inquirers into many things indeed" (CK IX; DK 35).

In several of his gnomes, he also operates with a contrast between the many and the individual and is very explicit indeed when he writes of the many that they are unconscious: "Most men do not think about things in the way they encounter them, nor do they recognize what they experience, but believe their own opinions" (CK IV; DK 17). Instead, people believe "the poets of the people" (CK LIX;

DK 104, yet another denunciation of poetry) and even though the mass of men hear, they seem to be deaf: "absent while present" (DK 34).

To stress even more the difference between the lover of wisdom and the obdurate mass, he himself—despite his attack on the poets—uses a metaphorical pairing, namely, the opposition between figuratively being awake and sleeping. Heraclitus says that "the world of the waking is one and shared, but the sleeping turn aside each into his private world" (CK VI; DK 89). For when people are asleep, their sense channels are closed through which reason as a cognitive organ is divided from its surroundings, while in the waking state, it can once again—as through a window—perceive the world. The cognitive act itself is based on and dependent on a close exchange between consciousness and the world, where the senses serve as the links. This otherwise hidden reality is intimated through signs in the surroundings and is interpreted by the subject, where "the wise is one, knowing the plan (*gnome*) by which it steers all things" (CK LIV; DK 41).

4

We may use this statement as a transition to describe what sort of plan or insight the wise man assumes by virtue of his own inner conscious order. It is called *logos* by Heraclitus. From the fragment that apparently introduced his book, it appears that *logos* is recognized through analysis, as "I set forth, distinguishing each according to its nature and telling how it is" (CK I; DK 1). In the same fragment, he says that "all things come to pass in accordance with [*logos*]" (CK I; DK 1).

The concept has a rather open meaning: word, language; but in its general function it must almost be understood as goal, intent, plan (*gnome*). That is to say that in Heraclitus' *logos*, we find virtually the same governing mechanism that Anaximander found in *apeiron*. The person of understanding will be distinguished from people who are not conscious of what they do. The consequence of this is that they do not share in the community found in an all-comprehending *logos* but are cut off in their individuality—"Although [*logos*] is shared, most men live as though their thinking were a private possession" (CK III; DK 2).

So this reason-based analysis leads to *logos*, which, as we just heard, may be characterized as "the common." Like Anaximander, Heraclitus here uses an analogy to the legal form of the city-state. For a city is governed by what is shared by all, and in this is reflected "divine law" (CK XXX; DK 114) as the system of the cosmos corresponds to and maintains the soul. So it is paradoxical that each person who searches his inner self invariably cuts himself off from the cosmic community in *logos* and separates himself into his own private realm. On the other hand, for the lover of wisdom who takes his understanding from what is common, insight into *logos* will appear in a homology in which "all things [are] one" (CK XXXVI; DK 50). This means in a sort of hermeneutic circle that, by exploring oneself, the subject finds the cosmic and through the cosmic his true self.

5

Against this background, if we raise the question of what knowledge of the common actually contains, the answer is: it contains the element in the universe in which all oppositions are transformed and united. And insofar as this process of transformation takes its character from the element of fire, it must mean that fire can be interpreted as a concretization of the dynamic effect of *logos*. The world is produced neither by men nor by gods—"but it ever was and will be: fire ever-living, kindled in measures and in measures going out" (CK XXXVII; DK 30).

Or put in another way: since fire and *logos* are connected, fire becomes a constantly acting dynamic, while *logos* is the plan behind the effectiveness of the fire in the process of transformation. Fire is thereby both inside and outside the world. In this respect, earthly fire merely constitutes an insignificant part of the divine fire that is God himself or the only wise one.

By exploiting these characteristics of fire, Heraclitus is able to illustrate his idea that the world is in constant flux. By its nature, fire unites the oppositions that rule everything. For example, day and night are opposite principles but combined in a cosmic unity as two sides of the same coin. Everything is one and yet in motion. As a result of the unity of opposites, the road up and down is the same (CK CIII; DK 60), but Heraclitus notes the infinite process of change that results in everything being in motion, never at rest. So existence may be compared to the currents in a river: always the same and always different, which is why you cannot bathe in the same river twice (CK LI; DK A 6). Fire creates and destroys in an unending process that ensures life the necessary power to exist, just as day and night are ever shifting: "All things are requital for fire, and fire for all things, as goods for gold and gold for goods" (CK XL; DK 90).

As Anaximander also conceived it, the inner balance of the oppositions must be defined as an "attunement" or "how a thing agrees at variance with itself" (CK LXXVIII; DK 51). Figuratively, this state is comparable to the tension that makes the bow and the lyre function—the bow as it takes its strength from the pull, when the string is tightened and the wood is pushed in the opposite direction.

6

In consideration of the great significance strife and love had for Homer and Hesiod in their epic understanding of the expansive development of the world, it is to be expected though still remarkable that we find the same conception and experience again in others of the Presocratics. We heard about Anaximander's view of transformation as a continuous legal process. And when Heraclitus is to explain what sort of power is behind the dialectic of oppositions, he refers to an eternal condition of war or strife as he writes: "One must realize that war is shared and conflict is justice, and that all things come to pass in accordance with conflict" (CK LXXXII; DK 80).

That strife is as necessary as justice demonstrates that strife, like *logos*, is an existential condition. At the same time, Heraclitus clearly annuls Hesiod's distinction between good and evil strife, since he elevates the principle of tension and opposition through his notion of unity to an all-embracing structure: "War is father of all and king of all; and some he has shown as gods, others men; some he has made slaves, others free" (CK LXXXIII; DK 53).

In short, like the Olympian father, strife becomes a sort of executor of fate. And since war acts in harmony with justice, it becomes fundamentally identical with *logos*, for which reason Heraclitus does not need love as reconciliation. However, it might be said that fire has something of the character of *eros*, since its transformational power is both destructive and creative.

7

With the metaphysical concept that *apeiron* is for creation, Anaximander laid the foundation for a monotheistic religiosity, i.e. the conception of a cosmic god who rules an ordered universe. This notion of a god was directly underlined by Xenophanes. And it is hardly incorrect to assume that Heraclitus also fundamentally views *logos* and fire in their common effect as a divine, metaphysical plan.

He often speaks of the god (*theos*) as corresponding to his description of *logos*— "For god, all things are fair and good and just" (CK LXVIII; DK 102)—"The god: day and night, winter and summer, war and peace," etc. (CK CXXIII; DK 67). It is this divinity he contrasts to what he considers to be the unholy mysteries, at the same time raising the holy up into metaphysics, far beyond the ability of men to grasp: "A man is found foolish by a god, as a child by a man" (CK LVII; DK 79).

And he maintains, "The wise is one alone, unwilling and willing to be spoken of by the name of Zeus" (CK CXVIII; DK 32). The fragment is clearly based on a contradiction, but the underlying meaning must be that the ultimate and only truth does not correspond to the "usual" Zeus but to a supreme deity that nevertheless allows himself to be called Zeus because this god is the source of everything. In this sense, the name denotes a radical breach with an anthropomorphic view of god, as Zeus forms a sacred unity that, like the monotheistic God of the Jews, has many names—but yet is one.

Likewise, Heraclitus seems to share Xenophanes' view of the limits of human knowledge: "Human nature has no set purpose, but the divine has" (CK LV; DK 78). Yet, although *logos* in its full glory is beyond the grasp of human understanding, this does not imply a total epistemological impotence. It is a question of objectively observing the universality in what is known as "common". On this point, Heraclitus extends the Ionian natural philosophy by maintaining that empirical analysis must necessarily be based on sense observations.

"Whatever comes from sight, hearing, learning from experience: this I prefer" (CK XIV; DK 55), he says. Hence, he believes that the precondition for acquiring knowledge is observation of the concrete world. Here, *logos* is hypostatized and allowed to reveal itself through the soul's homology with *logos*, but without any hope of being able to achieve the same insight as God. "Eyes and ears are poor witnesses for men if their souls do not understand the language" (CK XVI; DK 107), he says, using the concept of *psyche*, soul, in the same sense we have for the word, a special rational arbiter which the individual must have at his disposal in order to achieve true knowledge.

So neither is it experienced as a paradox when Heraclitus imagines that the road to the common element in *logos* goes through the self, when he writes, "I went in search of myself" (CK XXVIII; DK 101). In addition to hereby introducing an introspective cognitive practice, he presumes that the self can act as a cognitive organ for *logos*. And this is only possible if, as a created phenomenon, the self converges with the created universe.

Such a nexus between subject and cosmos implies that the external can be known through the internal. By looking inward, we can examine the hidden reality behind the external forms of appearance. That the internal has this authority can be seen from the fragments in which Heraclitus deals directly with the activities of the soul, which appear as a self-validating reality, differentiated from its unity with the object, which was so characteristic of mythical thinking. In its homology with the *logos* of the universe, the soul simply appears as an internal, infinite space: "You will not find out the limits of soul by going about, even if you traveled over every way; so deep is its [*logos*]" (DK 45).

But at the same time he also says, "To the soul belongs a [*logos*] that increases itself" (CK CI; DK 115). If these statements are coupled together, it must mean that, by virtue of his knowledge, man can share in the infinity of the soul, though without ever being able to reach the end of the road, since the universality of *logos* is always increasing. The soul is enriched by penetrating *logos* analytically at the same time as the almost metonymic connection between *logos* and fire has the effect that the soul or the self share in fire's power of transformation: "A gleam of light is the dry soul, wisest and best" (CK CIX; DK 118).

The idea behind this impenetrable expression must be that the dry soul is filled by the *logos* of the world, since, elementally, fire is *logos*. A dry soul thus contains goodness and wisdom as opposed to the wet, i.e. the drunken, stupid soul, that in its drunkenness has metaphorically quenched the fire/*logos* of knowledge: "A man when drunk is led by a beardless boy, stumbling, not perceiving where he is going, having his soul moist" (CK CVI; DK 117).

The soul can be one with *logos*, but also immersed in water like the drunkard, who corresponds to those stupid, lazy and absent-minded individuals whom Heraclitus continually attacks. Consequently, it is a matter of discovering the *logos* burning within us and of keeping it clean and dry, so it will continue to expand, as the soul contains the greatest conceivable reality, unlimited as it is, by bearing the world's *logos* in itself as an inner light. If this light is extinguished in a person, he will remain in the dark, regardless of his other qualities.

Since Heraclitus assumes that the soul consists of fire (CK CXIIIA; DK A 15), we must ultimately be able to conclude that it possesses eternal life, even though he makes no clear statement on this. But this idea was common at the time of

Pythagoras, with whom he was familiar, and it was expressed later by Plato, where immortality encompasses the select wise men.

As long as the gods—as in the Homeric universe—walk among men and interfere in their affairs, the extent to which the individual may take personal responsibility is limited, except with respect to honor. In the same process in which the soul separates from the body, the temporal from the hereafter, it is up to the individual to take responsibility for himself and his soul. It is this obligation that is expressed through Heraclitus' fragments, distinguishing the wise from the foolish: "Man's character is his fate" (CK CXIV; DK 119), he says, using the word *daimon* about this destiny.

In Homer, god(s) and *daimones* are partly synonymous, although *daimones* function on a lower, more anonymous level. Here, however, Heraclitus obviously imagines that it is the character of a person, his ability to choose rightly or wrongly, that determines his destiny, an idea that is continued in Plato in connection with Socrates' own *daimonion*.

Metempsychosis—Pythagoras

Heraclitus was not only critical of Homer and Hesiod, but his slightly older colleague Pythagoras also attracted his disapproval. As Heraclitus says, he pursued inquiry further than any other person but created "artful knavery" (DK 129). Despite this condemnation, they have much in common. Both were brought up on Ionian natural philosophy, although Pythagoras settled in southern Italy. And each in his own way, they were the first to stress the significance of the soul.

Under his otherwise indeterminate influence from Orphism, with its roots in the Orient, Pythagoras developed a doctrine of the soul that later influenced Empedocles and not least Socrates' account of the soul in the *Phaedrus* and the *Phaedo*. The greatest difference between Heraclitus' and Pythagoras' view of the soul is that, while Heraclitus clearly sees the soul in its psychic dialectic with the world of the senses and cosmic space, to Pythagoras the soul is almost in contrast to the physical body. For as, according to his view, the soul originates in the divine, it must—as Heraclitus probably also believed—be immortal, but, due to some Fall, has unfortunately become incarnated in an evil, earthly body.

Consequently, the notion of a fallen soul—in its opposition to the body—is accompanied by a longing to be reunited with the lost ideal world. A condition for this is to keep the soul free from the sensual. Like the almost contemporary Buddhist doctrine of karma, the soul is subject to a constant *metempsychosis*, the transmigration of the soul, to achieve a higher level. Pythagoras' doctrine, according to tradition, is: "first, that he maintains that the soul is immortal; next that it changes into other kinds of living things; also that events recur in certain cycles, and that nothing is ever absolutely new; and finally, that all living things should be regarded as kin" (KR 271; DK 14 A 8a).

Whereas, as we have heard, *psyche* in the Homeric epics was the life or breath that, at the moment of death, leaves the person through the mouth and migrates to the realm of the dead, *psyche* now means soul, and the soul thus established the body as its opposite, as *soma*. Indeed, bodily existence is now viewed as a prison around the soul's activity and migration, as is also very much the case in Socrates. The notion of *metempsychosis* is again found in Empedocles, as we shall see.

To Anaximander's *apeiron* and Heraclitus' *logos* corresponds a cosmology in Pythagoras that is based on the harmony of numbers reaching into the world of the soul—"All the properties of numbers and scales which they could show to agree with the attributes and parts and the whole arrangement of the heavens, they collected and fitted into their scheme" (DK 58 B 4 + 5).[16] We shall leave it with this account from Aristotle and direct our eyes toward the great breakthrough for the deductive logic of human thought in Parmenides.

The Logical Necessity of Thought— Parmenides

1

Despite the differences among the philosophers presented so far, they have one thing in common: their aim of (so far as possible) making the world of the senses into the object of empirical analysis. Parmenides, born around 515 B.C., may have been a student of Xenophanes and may have had conversations with the young Socrates, as Plato claims. At any event, he draws the opposite logical conclusion, arguing that the external, objective world is illusory. Therefore, the true world of light and *logos* is to be sought behind the surface of things, where it is to be found as something existing in itself. In the philosophical, hexameter poem that has come down to us, an experience of revelation is described, reminiscent of Hesiod's encounter with the Muses at Helicon. Presumably Parmenides must use this ploy, because he alone with his "vision", and a poetic transformation into allegory, can capture the invisible principle of the immanent and, through the lyrical form itself, provide his view with authoritative status.

Parmenides says how he is guided by the "daughters of the Sun" (KR 342; DK 1) who, from the symbolic level in the text may almost be viewed as an inner clairvoyance, from the abode of Night, which is identical with the dark kingdom of death of human illusions. After passing through the gate between night and day up in the sky—the gate to which Dike, justice or perhaps in this context truth, has the key—he comes before the goddess herself.

She reveals the deeper, hidden truth to Parmenides, a doctrine that is far from the beaten track and ordinary beliefs (*doxa*) of mortals, veiled by the stunted experience of convention. True knowledge is about being, that which "is," as opposed to that which "is not." Only *logos*, in the sense of reason, can come to this insight. The world of the senses and ordinary experience are deceit, while understanding follows an exclusive inner voice.

2

That is to say that, in a polemic with his predecessors who sought to explain the origin, structure and substance of the world, Parmenides denies the reality of the senses and in its stead places logical deduction and the consistency of pure thought, based on the syllogistic contradiction of being and not being. From this contrast, it also follows that being has always existed, since—as with *apeiron* and *logos*—it is impossible to imagine anything preceding, while not being has never had any real existence. So Parmenides must also reject the notion of transformation, which claims that things come into being and disappear again. On the basis of stringent logic, this is an impossible conclusion. It is either/or.

However, it is just this kind of thinking that characterizes "mortals (. . .) knowing nothing" (KR 345; DK 6-7), conventional thinking that—as he puts it in words resembling Heraclitus' critique of public opinion—makes people "deaf and blind" (KR 345; DK 6-7). They combine being and non-being together in a jumble, which is why Parmenides warns: "nor let custom, born of much experience, force thee to let wander along this road thy aimless eye" (KR 346; DK 6-7).

At the same time, he provides an account of the ontology of being, to which, as with the other philosophers, is attributed a metaphysical status, insofar as being can neither arise nor perish, but—like a sphere—is "without end" (KR 347; DK 8). Divinity is based on the fact that being is defined by *dike*, justice, as we first saw in Anaximander. As Parminides sees it, it is *dike* that ensures the harmony of existence by maintaining being in its basic form and keeping a tight rein on it, whether by the force of necessity, *anangke* or Fate itself, Moira.

While the first main section of the poem describes Parmenides' access to the truth about the logic of thought, the second part contains a cosmology. This is paradoxical, since Parmenides apparently inserts into his pure world of thought a comparison with natural philosophy's doctrine of the senses, operating primarily on the basis of the opposition of light and dark. There has been an intense debate over the years as to how this apparent inconsistency is to be explained, whether the poem's two halves really preclude each other, etc. In this context, the central point has been to show how radically Parmenides absolutizes thought as deductive necessity in a disavowal of the world of the senses as sham and deceit.

With this doctrine, he anticipates Plato's doctrine of the illusory shadow and cave world from which men must turn their eyes in order to gain a personal insight into the elevated reality of the ideas.

Strife and Love as Philosophical Principles—Empedocles

1

The last stage in this selective presentation of Presocratic philosophy is represented by Empedocles. As a compiler and epitomizer, he unites a number of ideas we have already encountered and explains them with exemplary clarity. His biographical data are extremely unclear, but the culmination of his comprehensive work as rhetorician, physician and philosopher was presumably around 450 B.C.

It is said in the tradition surrounding him that he admired and was closely connected to Parmenides. The claim looks reasonable insofar as, like Parmenides, he wrote a didactic poem in hexameters to an otherwise unknown student named Pausanias. Like Parmenides, he invokes an initiating goddess—"much-wooed white-armed maiden Muse"[17] (DK 3). The remarkable feature, however, is that the goddess is to help him to deny the very truth into which the goddess initiated Parmenides. Empedocles wants the world of the senses back as an object of cognition and commands his disciple to investigate "each thing in the way by which it is manifest" (KR 419; DK 3). Yet, he does not fail to notice the uncertainty with which perception in principle is encumbered, the limitations and sources of error, as he points out that one should not put more faith in sight than in hearing (DK 3).

2

It is to Empedocles' cognitive credit that he summarizes and formalizes the concrete objective world and its origins. As far back as Thales, one single element, water, was made the source of everything; it was fire in Heraclitus and air in Anaximenes (the third of the great early Ionian natural philosophers). However, Empedocles is the first to put the four elements into a single coherent, consistent system, also including earth. He considers these four elements to be the cause of the world's beginning, for which reason they are given the same ontological status as *apeiron*, *logos* and being in Parmenides.

Since each element is complete in itself, it means that the substances are not, as in Heraclitus' doctrine of metamorphosis, transformed into one another. Even when they establish close connections, they are not transformed, according to Empedocles, but in the amalgamation preserve their peculiar qualities, which acquire concrete visibility when they are once again separated from their union. This process is the basis for life's eternal circle, the energy for which derives from the elements' ceaseless merging and separating.

3

However, Empedocles is not satisfied with this theory but—in an extension of Anaximander's ideas of punishment and reward and Heraclitus' idea of war as the father of all things—he tries to capture the inner causal dynamic in the cycle of the elements. He distinguishes two basic driving forces: love and strife. In short, he bases his philosophical system on the same forces we could observe as the latent experiential foundation in the developmental tension in the Homeric epics, just as Eros was for Hesiod the central principle of creation, with which strife could interfere, destructively or creatively.

Empedocles anthropomorphizes these dynamic and mutually effective forces as Aphrodite and Ares respectively. This demonstrates that mythical thinking still had a hold on philosophical conceptions in spite of its scientific character, just as the gods could conversely be viewed as conceptualized principles.

These two opposites are conceptualized as love (*philotes*) and strife (*neikos*), and like *apeiron* they seem almost to have a self-validating elemental existence alongside the other elements. Of course, Empedocles says that these guiding forces are invisible, but the philosophical work in itself must consist of the ability to acquire an insight into this dynamic via meditation, so to speak—indeed to allow it to open up in the mind like some inner movement. He describes the process as the four elements being blended, "loved by each other and made alike by Aphrodite" (DK 22). On the other hand, hostility or strife (*neikos*) is predominant where things are distant from one another. They are "absolutely unwonted to unite and very baneful."[18]

Love and strife alternate in occupying a dominant position in the world cycle: "There are these alone, but running thorough one another they become men and the tribes of beasts, at one time coming together through Love into one order, at another each borne apart from the others by the enmity of Strife, till they have grown into one and are utterly subdued (KR 460) (. . .) inasmuch as they [the elements] never cease changing place continually, so they always exist within an immovable circle" (DK 26).[19]

4

Although the cyclical nature of this process makes it in principle unending, Empedocles seems nevertheless to have imagined a constant starting point—the place where love reigns supreme and all the elements are gathered into a ball-shaped sphere of unity called *sphairos* (DK 27, 30, 31). In this state, there is perfect stillness under the "hegemony of Love," where "queen Kypris" (KR 466; DK 128), alias Aphrodite, rules. This inertia only lasts until strife, Ares, once again disrupts this restful tranquility with his trouble-making: "When strife again begins to dominate, movement again arises in the *sphairos*" (DK 27, 30, 31). However, Empedocles fails to draw the obvious conclusion that, if strife did not take this initiative, everything in the universe would stagnate, the cycle would be brought to a standstill, and all further development cease.

The actual circular movement itself goes through four stages: 1. The perfect state of love, no strife. 2. Strife enters into the picture, splitting and cleaving. 3. Strife gains the upper hand. 4. Love intervenes and the elements begin once again to gather and move towards the initial stage's point of rest. And so on. Insofar as the initial stage is the original starting point, *sphairos*, this implies that the universe and mankind originally rested in a state of innocence, corresponding to the Golden Age. In other words, strife intrudes and brings about a Fall, which he describes as a sort of murderous cannibalism: "And likewise son seizes father, and children their mother, and, tearing out the life, eat the flesh of their dear ones" (KR 469; DK 137).

The inspiration for this view may come from Pythagoras, not least from his underlying Orphism, as the Fall in Orphism is linked to a form of cannibalistic behavior in which the Titans tear apart and devour the Dionysos child. Transferred to human history, the same thing happens as a consequence of the growing evil of strife. So, as with the Pythagoreans it becomes the purpose and task of the soul to cleanse itself so that, once more transformed, it can find its way back to divine love.

The fall of man leads to an earthly incarnation lasting the equivalent of 30,000 earth years. In this period, the soul must endure punishment for its original sin before it can escape the cruel cycle of birth. As Empedocles puts it, remembering his own arrival on earth: "I wept and wailed, when I saw this unfamiliar place" (KR 473)—"this joyless place" (KR 473). In his own history of reincarnation, he has already been "a boy and a maiden, a bush and a bird and a dumb fish" (KR 476; DK 117). But in the end, the miracle will occur, when souls are redeemed in all their divinity, for "they arise as gods mighty in honour, sharing with the other immortals their hearth and their table, without part in human sorrows or weariness" (KR 477; DK 146-7). Socrates expresses a related idea at the hour of his death.

Conclusion

It may be surprising that Empedocles was the first of the Presocratic philosophers to include the earth as an element, particularly as both Homer and Hesiod have thoughts pointing in that direction. Or perhaps that is the reason. For it could be said that by subjugating creation to Gaia, Hesiod brought gods and men under the chthonic. For just as Homer sought in his works to suppress or repress the chthonic forces, it might seem as though the Ionian philosophers in their intellectuality seek to establish an empirical understanding of nature representing a purely masculine form of intellect. This is only a hypothesis, but Presocratic philosophy is at all events a triumph for a new form of intellectuality.

All in all, the most important result of the Presocratic attempt to understand the origins, substance and mechanics of the world may be the revelation of the organ by which human beings comes to apprehend. So, even though they began as natural philosophers without any interest in spiritual life, they end up presenting the soul and the subject as a source of knowledge, exactly as we see it expressed in the contemporary poetry of Archilochus and Sappho.

Even in Anaximander, it could be observed that the soul as a source of insight, of consciousness, was implicitly present. In Pythagoras, the soul develops through *metempsychosis*. And Heraclitus makes the subject an object of the cosmic reality with which the soul is identical.

In Parmenides, being has existence solely by virtue of the logic of thought. Empedocles further develops these conceptions, which, however, only acquire their full strength in Socrates' doctrine, as his pedagogy aims at knowledge of the soul and truth, at the same time as he rejects the preceding natural philosophy as nebulous.

However, with philosophy, we have moved far away from the world of the myth, despite its touch of allegory. In a chronological overlap, myth returns with renewed force as an essential vehicle for ideas. It happens in the new genre: tragedy.

XIV

THE LIFE AND FORM OF TRAGEDY

I T MAY BE SAID THAT ATHENS' GREATEST CONTRIBUTION TO WORLD LITERATURE was surely to bring tragedy to perfection. As we have seen in the foregoing, a new genre will arise from an existential and social need at a given historical point to work through and interpret existing reality. So what is the need from which tragedy arises? What invokes it as an answer and form of experience.

The Return of Myth— Dithyramb and Genesis

1

At the same time as Greek drama emerges as the pinnacle of poetic practice, it makes a remarkable return to myth as earlier presented, for instance, in Homer's epic poetry. Thus, Aeschylus was quoted in antiquity as saying that his tragedies were nothing but scraps from Homer's banquet,[1] and Socrates says that Homer seems to have been "the first teacher and beginner of all these beauties of tragedy."[2] Like some continental shelf, the genres of epic and tragedy connect with each other beneath the other forms of literature that had arisen in the meantime. But whereas with his use of myth Homer sought to convert aristocratic and heroic ideals into peaceful values, the myth redivivus was to formulate a new set of rules for democratic citizens of Athens.[3]

In the intervening period, the significance of myth as the great story and essence of human life had been severely reduced. It was without significance for Archilochus' anti-heroic poetry, and it was not used by Solon or other "existential" poets such as Semonides and Mimnermus. Hesiod certainly used myths in *Works and Days*, but only to illustrate his everyday morality; while Sappho introduced the mythical as a lyrical accompaniment to a mood in order to reflect her erotic despair and longing. In addition, it is clear that mythical thinking was generally toned down in the Presocratic philosophers as they attempted to distance their perception from myth and make it scientific.

2

It seems to be beyond doubt that Dionysos and tragedy are inextricably linked. He was the deity of the Great Dionysia in Athens, where the competitions in tragedy were held in his honor. On the other hand, it is difficult to explain the reason for this link and its origin, in that—apart from a few exceptions—the god never appears in the tragedies.

In the following, I will offer a theory that has as its premise—as is the case with all other gods—that Dionysos appears in different forms, depending on the function attributed to him. Different but the same. The infant god Dionysos Zagreus, worshiped by the Orphics, is not entirely identical to the Dionysos we meet at the head of a parade of orgiastic satyrs and bacchantes as the god of wine or of tragedy. And yet, there is an area common to them all, concerned with his significance as a chthonic divinity for the fertility mysteries, the ecstasy and the renewal of life.

Let us take our starting point in Aristotle's description of the origin of tragedy and comedy as improvisation: "the one originating with the authors of the *dithyramb*, the other with those of the phallic songs, which still survive as institutions in many of our cities."[4] Tragedy obviously developed according to its own laws, as writers concentrated on it in the *dithyramb*, which formed part of the essence of the genre—"only after a long series of changes that the movement of Tragedy stopped on its attaining to its natural form," as Aristotle maintains.

In other words, the *dithyramb* had a potential that separated it from the phallic songs that for their part developed into satyric drama and comedy. In *The Laws*, Plato agrees that there was a clearer division of genres in more ancient times: "One kind of song, which went by the name of a hymn, consisted of prayers to the gods; there was a second and contrasting kind which might well have been called a lament; paeans were a third kind, and there was a fourth, the *dithyramb*, as it was called, dealing, if I am not mistaken, with the birth of Dionysos."[5]

The question of whether Plato has committed an etymological blunder and seen the *dithyramb* as meaning "double doors" (*di thyrai*) is of less importance in relation to the fact that he connects the *dithyramb* with the birth of Dionysos, i.e. indirectly makes it a song of birth and initiation.

We may find a link to the understanding of what this has to do with tragedy in Euripides, whose *The Bacchae* is the only extant tragedy about the god and his distinctive features. Dionysos is attributed with the byname of Dithyrambos in view of the myth that he has been twice born—by his mother Semele and by his father Zeus, who utters the peculiar words: "Dithyrambos, come!/ Enter my male womb."[6]

In brief, the myth tells how, in her jealousy, Hera lured Dionysos' mother, the Theban princess Semele, to ask Zeus to display himself in all his glory. He revealed himself with thunder and a bolt of lightning which destroyed the mother; but he saved the son from the flames and sewed him into his thigh, from which he gave second birth to him from the "womb" of the thigh.

Not only is it remarkable that a man can give birth but also that this birth is parallel to that of Athene, who was born from the head of Zeus. Dionysos, on the other hand, is born from the supreme god's lower parts. Is the mythical meaning that, just as Athene came to represent masculine consciousness, so the birth of Dionysos is evidence of how the sensual, chthonic world to which he is appointed fertility god is quite literally brought under the principle or control of the father? It could be interpreted in this way, when Zeus says to his son: "I name you Bacchus and to Thebes/ proclaim you by that name."[7]

Tragedy seriously began to develop as an independent genre on the basis of the *dithyrambic* choral lyric during the rule of the tyrant Peisistratos, who, along with the Eleusinian Mysteries, incorporated Dionysos into the religious life of the state. In this way, he could accommodate the general public's worship of the god and bring the Dionysian intoxication, which washed over Hellas like a wave, under control. In practice, this means that he patriarchalizes Dionysos as Dithyrambos and provides him with all the liberty of action that Euripides shows Zeus as promising his son.

He links the god to the Great Dionysia, which is a tacit admission that tragedy has its origin in his birth song and the choral form that reappears in tragedy. At the same time this is clear proof that Dionysos, as the chthonic divinity he was, is brought within patriarchy—as the Erinyes are in the *Oresteia*. Peisistratos is thus able to link the intense religious mood that Dionysos had created in people with Athens' self-consciousness and incipient democracy. In addition, the tyrant and the god correspond to each other in the latent sense in that, politically, both represented an opposition to torpid aristocratic norms.

3

While the basic form of tragedy developed from the Dionysian *dithyramb*, its content derives from myth, especially as it is known in Homer. Aristotle lived around 150 years after the rise of tragedy, which is why his description is encumbered with the same uncertainty that surrounded the rise of the epic. Nevertheless, he describes the process of development as follows: "Tragedy acquired also its magnitude. Discarding short stories and a ludicrous diction, through its passing out of its satiric stage."[8]

This must mean that, in its primordial form, tragedy only made use of the myths as loosely connected short stories. In the word "magnitude" is hidden the reawakening of myth in its grand form, in which it was to gather and interpret a dramatic sequence, ensure its unity, and provide a comprehensive view of life. Tragedy is thus condensed in a unifying mythical plot in which music and dance represented an integral choreographic and dramatic constituent element.

Beyond the brief accounts in the satyric dramas, Aristotle says that the Dorians in the Peloponnesus claimed to be the originators of tragedy, referring to the fact that the word "comedian" comes from the word for outlying hamlets (*komai*, which the Athenians called *demes*), where such figures used to wander about. Remarkably enough, on the other hand, Aristotle makes no mention of the poet Arion, who settled in this area and is mentioned elsewhere as the poet who in the 7th century B.C. first endowed the *dithyrambic* choruses with the character of tragedy. Herodotus relates that the first dithyrambic chorus was first arranged by the tyrant Periandros in Corinth,[9] while the connection with the cult of Dionysos arose when the tyrant of Sicyon transferred the tragic chorus of the hero cults to the worship of Dionysos.[10] In Athens, tradition has it that the first named tragedian Thespis won a prize for a tragedy around 534 B.C. under Peisistratos.

4

It is also the birth of tragedy that Nietzsche tries to establish in his first work from 1872, *Geburt der Tragödie*. He, too, assigns its origins to the Dionysian dithrambs and the orgiastic life he imagines existed in connection with it. This is not the place to consider his views in detail, so I will merely note certain important ideas as a kind of explanatory prehistory to the definition of the genre of tragedy that Aristotle establishes in his poetics.

According to Nietzsche, tragedy in its primordial form was played by a chorus of satyrs, acting as "the mirror image in which the Dionysian man contemplates himself."[11] The audience went into an ecstasy of the fellowship as an organic part of the collective body. People did not simply watch, listening as though it was a rhapsodist declaiming the works of Homer for instance. Rather, the cultic rite released them from their cultural straightjacket: "The Dionysian Greek wants the truth and nature in their most forceful form—sees himself changed, as by magic, into a satyr."[12]

As we shall see later, it is also as such a figure rebelling against values that Euripides portrays Dionysos in *The Bacchae*, describing the tension between the new Dionysian divinity and a rigid social system. Nevertheless, in Nietzsche's interpretation Euripides is made responsible for the end of tragedy. For, as Nietzsche maintains, his predecessors conceived their dramas on the basis of mythical greatness and primordial power. Euripides, on the other hand, draws on civic mediocrity and intellectualizes the orgiastic: "Euripides brought the *spectator* onto the stage."[13] So the divinity speaking out of Dionysos in *The Bacchae* is neither the god of wine nor Apollo, "but an altogether newborn demon, called Socrates."[14] Consequently, knowledge and insight do not come from the divinity of darkness, are not lifted up into the light of ecstasy, but express intelligible cognition. Nietzsche believes that this can be demonstrated in the function of the chorus, since in his interpretation the chorus is the dramatic arbiter in which the mystery of Dionysos has hibernated. But in Euripides, the chorus is superimposed and theatrical—"a dispensable vestige of the origin of tragedy."[15]

In addition, Nietzsche complains that another new divinity, Apollo as the god of light and consciousness, pushed the Dionysian chorus into the background. He is irked to see Apollo with his enlightenment smothering the titanic forces of existence; but Nietzsche here overlooks the fact that the real accomplishment of tragedy was to unite Dionysos and Apollo. For even as it draws force from the Dionysian, it raises itself to insight into this reality, insofar as Apollo acts as the word that creates a dialogue and action through which tragedy comes to consciousness of itself and the meaning of its myths.

Of course, this pushes things to extremes. Nevertheless, it seems as if, in his own rebellion against his father, Nietzsche is unconsciously obsessed by a regressive dream of slipping back into the chthonic primordial mother. In that case, he is acting against Dionysos as Dithyrambos, who, born of Zeus, in configuration with the patriarchal god, acquires power over the world. As Dionysos and Apollo are united in tragedy— like consciousness and sensuality under the aegis of paternal right—they also shared power between themselves at Delphi. When Apollo left during the winter months, Dionysos moved in and was praised with *dithyrambs*. His statue was placed in the west gable of the temple, where the sun sets, while Apollo with his sister stood in the east gable, where the sun rises. In this union, they could act together; whereas Nietzsche ended his days insane in the arms of his mother and sister, but that is another story.

Dramaturgy

1

We may cautiously propose the following hypothesis on the development of tragedy: In the *dithyramb*'s original encomium of Dionysos, his life and deeds are recounted by the chorus leader in an exchange of song and dance with the chorus. In the middle of the 7th century B.C., the chorus leader began to fill in his role in dialogue with the chorus and developed into the first actor. A dramatic space for action arose, where a single myth was to condense the sequence of events.

This scenario is confirmed by later developments. As Aristotle maintains, it was Aeschylus who went from one to two actors. Sophocles introduced the third. At the same time, the chorus recedes ever more into the background as the spokesman for the poet. In Aeschylus' *The Suppliant Maidens*, the chorus even plays the leading role; while in Euripides its role is reduced to providing a mood-setting lyrical element, a development of which the tragedian Agathon (whose victory in 416 B.C. at the Lenaean festival is celebrated in Plato's *Symposium*) was supposed to have been the originator.

Parallel to this, the formal structure of tragedy—perhaps deriving from the ritual sequence (*dromenon*[16]) in the dithyramb—was formed by a prologue, the chorus' entrance song (*parados*), the plot-driven episodes in which the actors appear, the chorus' song from the orchestra (*stasima*) and the closing song (*exodus*). In addition comes the construction of the stage, the introduction of scenery, a hoist for the deus ex machina—in short, the whole theatrical apparatus that appears in later theater but was formed already in Greek tragedy—not forgetting comedy.

2

Tragedy most likely means "goat song," derived from the word *tragos*, goat, though the reason for this is unclear. Several explanations have been offered: that the chorus was originally dressed in goat skins and/or danced about like he-goats, that the sacrifice of a goat may have been performed, that a goat was the prize for the victor, that it was due to the original *dithyrambic* context between tragedy and the satyric drama. Only one thing is certain: tragedy's link to Dionysos as the god of fertility. The oldest Dionysian festival was held in Anthesteria, at the beginning of February, during which the coming spring was celebrated for three days—among other things with sacrifices to the chthonic Hermes to placate the powers of the underworld.

The tragedy competitions were held twice a year. First, at the Lenaian festival (January/February), in which the term *lenaia* refers to Dionysos as Lenaios, the god of the wine press. This festival forms the background to Aristophanes' *The Frogs,* and everything indicates that it was especially comedies that were performed on this occasion, though from around 440 B.C. there were tragedies as well—it was for instance at this festival that, as said above, Agathon won the prize for tragedy.

The greatest event was the Great Dionysia for Dionysos Eleuthereus, who in his connection to Athens differs from the Rural Dionysia in December. The Great Dionysia of Athens began on the tenth day in the month of Elaphebolion (March/April) and lasted seven days. Unlike the Lenaian festival—where the plays were performed at another theater—everyone could participate, even visitors, so the city was teeming with people from near and far. They took their places on the wooden benches and, later, stone seats of the semi-circular Theater of Dionysos, which is almost glued to a slope at the Acropolis.[17]

The participating poets, three in number, were designated by the eponymous *archon*, who, among other things, supervised the Dionysia and after whom the year was called. Each tragedian was to compete with three tragedies and a satyric drama. The (12) 15 members of the chorus—(15) 18 in Sophocles and Euripides—were appointed from among the city's residents.[18] The *archon* also chose the wealthy patron who, as *choregos* (producer), was to pay for the equipment for the chorus and probably acted as chorus leader himself. The fact that citizens were appointed as members of the chorus—as they were to political councils—confirmed the close emotional bond between the state and its inhabitants cutting across social boundaries.

The festival itself began when the small statue or wooden sculpture of Dionysos, which according to tradition originated in the Boeotian city of Eleutherai (hence, the epithet for Dionysos), was brought out of his temple near the theater. It was taken to the Academy, from which it was again taken back in a torchlight procession led by young boys (armed with spears and shields—presumably as symbols of the city's strength) and young girls (carrying baskets on their heads, symbolizing the city's fertility), followed by actors, chorus members and, finally, the audience, all in remembrance of Dionysos' arrival to the city.

The statue of the god was present at all the performances, and its high priest sat on the marble throne in the front row. On the stage itself (the orchestra), an altar was dedicated to the god. The festival lasted from dawn until late evening. The first days were devoted to competitions for *dithyrambic* poetry between boys' and men's choruses in which five hundred chorus members participated. On the third day, five comedies by various poets were performed. Over the next three days, the tragedy competition was held between the selected three authors, each of whom contributed three tragedies and a satirical drama (of which only Euripides' *Kyklops* has survived). Then the victors were named through an ingenious procedure. There were prizes for the winning poet and the best leading actor, and the victorious *choregos* was honored. Perhaps as an expression of the sacred background, the plays were only performed once—though from *The Frogs* it can be understood that an exception was made for Aeschylus, whose tragedies at some time began to be performed again.

3

The above description is surrounded by considerable uncertainty. The same is true of the actual framework surrounding the performance of tragedy, as we have to base ourselves on sparse evidence and archaeological finds. Nevertheless, on this basis, Arthur Picard-Cambridge in *The Dramatic Festivals of Athens* puts together an interesting picture of all conceivable circumstances surrounding the tragedies: the competitions, festivals, staging, actors and their equipment, etc. And although he does not try to interpret the meaning of these various functions but primarily notes the actual situation, a dramaturgical unity is created of what to our eyes, accustomed as they after all are to stage realism, is a distinctive scenario.

We can imagine the chorus marching in, accompanied by flautists. The chorus probably performed in shifting formations, dancing, but in a stationary dance, in which hands and bodily gestures in rhythmic movements articulated the emotions of the chorus to the fateful events of the story.

The relatively small number of actors, *hypokrites*, had to play different roles, which the use of face masks made possible. Through a systematic reading of all the tragedies, Picard-Cambridge calculates that it could be done with only three leading actors, all men, who of course also played the women's roles. The masks were affixed with an elasticated band and were individualized by hair glued on (Helen had beautiful, golden hair to emphasize her beauty). Eyebrows, noses, etc. made the respective characters easily recognizable.

With respect to the stiffness that some of the masks must have inflicted on the actors, Picard-Cambridge raises an obvious question: how did they perform a kissing scene or show a stream of tears or other emotional outbursts? He concludes that it must have been done through a highly stylized staged choreography. Not only did the actors have to master their dialogue but they had to recite lyrical song parts. Since the great Theater of Dionysos in Athens held around 15,000 noisy spectators who expressed their satisfaction and dissatisfaction vociferously, this along with the musical accompaniment of the actors required formidable intonation and accentuation. So resonance must have been an important criterion for the ability of an actor.

The audience was very mixed. The distinguished priests, *archons*, etc. sat on the foremost benches. Prisoners were freed to be able to participate; there were children and presumably also women present - note the tradition that women fainted at the sight of the Erinyes in the *Oresteia*.

It is usually assumed that the myths on which the tragedies were based were well known, so that part of the excitement was seeing how a poet had made innovations in the material. For as Aristotle writes in his *Poetics*, the poets themselves must invent subjects, but also "devise the right way of treating them."[19] He also indicates elsewhere that such prior knowledge belonged to the elite: "Even though the known stories are only known to a few, they are a delight none the less to all."[20] This is confirmed by the fact that, in certain tragedies—especially those of Euripides—a summary of the myth can be found to fill in the missing background for the general audience. Aristotle believes that tragedy can be a pleasure for all regardless of educational background because he attributes a universal validity to it. This is an oblique indication of why tragedy was to become the genre that the political and cultural situation in Athens called forth.

Tragedy's Athens

1

Regardless of the roots and earliest forms of tragedy, the decisive thing is that it is only known from Athens. It is here the genre was finally created, closely connected to the establishment of the city as a power center in the Hellenic world. Tragedy is not merely coincidental with this historic occurrence but reflects and supports the process in the political and social spectrum of action in domestic and foreign policy.

The turning point in the emergence of Athens as a great power was the victory over the Persians at Salamis in 480 B.C., where, against all odds, the Athenians crushed the Persian fleet—"the sea no longer was visible,/ Filled as it was with shipwrecks and the slaughter of men,"[21] as Aeschylus recounts in his tragedy *The Persians*. It is from this time that it is possible to date Athens' political dominance as well as the city's cultural flowering, which took place over the next fifty years of peace—until the outbreak of the Peloponnesian War and the plague that took Pericles, the dominant politician of the age and the guarantor of stability and growth. From then on, crisis followed crisis, and values broke down.

Salamis' emblematic significance for the consciousness of the Athenian people is emphasized by the fact that the three tragedians are given mythological significance in relation to this victory. It also illustrated the significance attributed to tragedy. Aeschylus was supposed to have participated in the battle himself, as he had done ten years earlier at Marathon. Sophocles took part in the victory parade, and Euripides was born at Salamis on that very day. In addition, it has a symbolic significance that the oldest preserved tragedy is precisely *The Persians*, which describes the defeat through the eyes of the losers, just as it is symbolic that the *choregos* of the piece was Pericles.

In domestic politics during these years, a radical change took place in the political life of Athens. After the fall of the tyranny of Peisistratos and his sons, the aristocracy had tried in vain to regain their old feudal privileges. But Cleisthenes and successive democrats such as Ephialtes and Pericles (who, as Thucydides describes him, was actually an autocrat) introduced reforms with roots going back to Solon, breaking down the original tribal system of blood kinship. The four *phylai* (tribes) were expanded to ten, cutting across geographic boundaries, mixing citizens with each other. The number of council members was increased to 500 and the financially poorest social group, the thetes, received the franchise.

2

This and many other political measures too numerous to go into demanded a shift in the minds of the people, since the core of the understanding of the individual's place now moved from the family to the *polis*. This required not only new institutions but also new interpretations of human conduct and self-understanding.

It was in this socio-political context that tragedy offered its interpretation of life. The three great tragedians, each in their own way, saw it as their calling on the foundation of myth to develop a view of life for the new Athenian citizen. So the myths acquireed a dual purpose. They were supposed to reach back to the lofty values found there (just as the ten *phylai* were named after Attic heroes) and, at the same time, give space to a new interpretative practice corresponding to life in Athens.

In the case of Aeschylus, for example, this was done by dramatically interpreting and constructing Solon's view of *hubris*. In addition, he is the tragedian who most explicitly articulated the point of view that may be said to be the fundamental formula of tragedy: In myth, a story of suffering is played out, the *pathos* of which the audience can identify with and learn from—a doctrine known as *mathos*. The formulation is crystallized as *pathei mathos*—"you can learn from suffering,"[22] as it is put with an emphasis that resonates in every Greek tragedy.

Through the story of suffering that tragedy was played out before one's eyes, one was to learn respect and obedience to the gods, piety, and to realize the necessity of a self-controlled life, without arrogance and greediness, but guided by *sophrosyne*. Only in this way could a citizen ensure the health of his soul, which Aeschylus calls "*hygieia phrenon*."[23] This soul—from the virtually complete coincidence between individual and political life—was an unavoidable factor in the strength of the city. For even though the aristocracy still had significant political power, it was now the new collective democratic community that constituted the backbone of the state, a unity of gods, *polis* and individual—something that was all the more important because Athens did not have a true dogma of state religion on which to support itself.

Here, tragedy intervenes and displays the power of the gods and the powerlessness of men. That is to say that as a genre it fulfills a religious function in principle, concretely exemplified through the mythical plot's realization of the intervention of the gods in human life. From this perspective, it is clear why the tragedy competitions, attended by the *eidolon* of Dionysos himself, would have been the state's annual spiritual climax. The stage was not a casual entertainment but demonstrated its origin in the cults. Not only did the actors identify themselves with their mythical

roles but the audience, too, entered into the universe of conflict, full of the empathetic compassion and fear that Aristotle demands of tragedy to promote the *katharsis*
at the heart of the doctrine of cleansing suffering: the explanation of the ways of
the gods and vital self-insight, also heard in the command of the oracle of Delphi
to know oneself.

Tragedy According to Aristotle

1

It is not my intention to provide an exhaustive interpretation of Aristotle's
Poetics, as his purpose is to present a general theory of poetry. However, since he
uses tragedy as a paradigm, we can turn to his observations to establish a number
of its general constituent forms. For the important thing is not that, via the nature
of the poetics, he establishes a set of normative rules for tragedy but that they are
based on experience and a still usable empiricism, written relatively close to the
rise of the genre. This presentation of the fundamental Aristotelian views on
tragedy will also serve as a foundation for my analytical reading of the tragedies.

It speaks for the inherent and unique meaning of tragedy that Aristotle makes it
his chief paradigm, linking it to Homer, as tragedy, like the Homeric epics, is based
on the fable, *mythos*, which he calls the "soul" (*psyche*) of tragedy.[24] So characterization is not at the center as we might expect. On the contrary, the psychology of
the characters is "secondary" to the dramatic development, on a level with the associated reflections, "the element of thought."[25] As he puts it in a key passage: "In the
play accordingly they do not act in order to portray the Characters; they include
the Characters for the sake of the action. So that it is the action in it, i.e. its Fable
or Plot [*mythos*], that is the end and purpose of the tragedy; and the end is everywhere the chief thing."[26]

The end in Greek is defined as *telos*, the purpose, which we have also analyzed
as a central category of understanding in Homer's works, linked as the purpose is
to the juncture at which the will of the gods and the compositional intent meet
and resolve each other.

2

Even Homer and Hesiod spoke of the power of the fable or poetry over the
listener. The Phaiakians were struck dumb during Odysseus's description of his
travel adventures, while Hesiod notes the relief from pain that the Muse-inspired
poet produces. This effect is if possible even more strongly present in tragedy (and
comedy), due to the *mimesis* of the action, its imitative nature. Aristotle is clearly
strongly influenced by Plato's description of art as mimetic in Book 3 of the
Republic. Here, Plato explains that the effect of *mimesis* lies in the fact that the tragedian does not mediate between characters and action—"when someone takes out
the poet's connections between the speeches and leaves the exchanges."[27]

In this sense, *mimesis* becomes a direct imitation of life in action, what might be called *mythos* in a pure form. As spectators, we are, according to Aristotle, witnesses to "what might happen."[28] In the mimetic as action, in other words, there is an inner necessity to what happens, not simply as a one-time event but through its mythic potential as something that has happened and can always happen again. It is the very possibility of repetition that is the premise for the *mythos* of an action to be what is called "gripping."

At the same time, there is a deeper reason why tragedy as a universal statement of life is superior to history. As Aristotle says, tragedy is more "philosophical" and "of graver import" (*spoudaioteron*).[29] History, on the other hand, is characterized by particularity: the events are self-enclosed. The individual events are set out in a sequence of cumulative, conjoined factors; whereas tragedy is *mimesis* of what happened in a composed, eternally valid context, whose dramatic effect consists of unfolding in a drama, since the word drama derives from the verb to act (*drao*).

The audience witnesses a plot that shows "what such or such a kind of man will probably [*eikos*] or necessarily [*anangkaion*] say or do."[30] Consequently, the purpose of myth, its *telos*, becomes to describe this generalized form of existence mimetically. And the very requirement of necessity limits the number of themes and persons. It explains why most tragedies are set in the cycle of myths surrounding Troy and particularly linked to the great royal families in Thebes (the Labdakid: Laios, Oedipus, Dionysos) and Argos/Mycenae (the Atreid: Agamemnon, Orestes, Elektra).

Concerning this use of myths, the following general rule applies, formulated by Aristotle as: "At the same time, even with these there is something left to the poet himself; it is for him to devise the right way of treating them."[31] As has already been said, it is a point of view he modifies elsewhere with reference to the fact that only a few of the spectators are familiar with the myths, but all are gripped by the universal element in tragedy.

3

Common to these tragedies, which developed according to moral necessity, is their *telos*: to describe human suffering, *pathos*. For without *pathos*, the audience cannot experience what is gripping about the *mimesis* in the play, as the characters elicit "pity (*eleos*) and fear (*phobos*) in their fateful deeds wherewith to accomplish [the play's] *katharsis* of such emotions."[32]

Aristotle does not himself provide any definitive explanation of *katharsis*. This has led to all manner of explanations over the course of time. However, if we remain with Aeschylus, he speaks of suffering as a teacher—"the wisdom won from pain,"[33] as he puts it in the *Oresteia*, referring not only to pain but everything that happens to a person. In the spectator's mind, suffering (*pathos*) must be transformed into insight (*mathos*), and this happens through a sympathetic identification with the suffering we witness and may at any moment be subject to—hence we are gripped by both pity for the characters and fear for them and ourselves.

Or put another way: suffering is *eo ipso* assured with the failure of interpretation upon which the tragedies are based, no matter what unleashes the catastrophe: the gods' more or less comprehensible intervention in human life, the psychological constitution of the characters, etc. *Katharsis* must appear just at the point where empathetic identification is accompanied by the characters' and/or the tragedy's interpretative will to understand and bear these failures as an unavoidable characteristic of life: that fortune can suddenly turn to misfortune. This insight into what happens of necessity can as exaltation promote the health of the soul. The individual is constructed through his or her understanding of the forces of life and the subject's own fragile place in this immense field of tension which the characters act out and the audience in pity and fear embraces from personal knowledge and personal insight.

Strangely enough, Aristotle seems not to have noticed that in many tragedies there is in fact a mediator between the audience and the characters' stories of suffering. I am thinking here of the chorus, which with a mixture of pity and horror follows the fateful course of events, be it an Orestes, an Antigone or an Oedipus. The examples are legion. And in a formula using Greek terms we could summarize Aristotle's thought process in this way: The *mythos* (story) of tragedy has as its *telos* (goal) a *pathos* (suffering) that reaches beyond the framework of the action as *mathos* (learning and insight), since the audience experiences an *anamneusis* of the plot through fear (*phobos*) and pity (*eleos*) and thus effects a cure of its soul (*hygieia phrenon*) in a psychological elevation (*spoudaioteros*) and cleansing (*katharsis*).

4

The philosophical generalization of tragedy, its elevation to universality, confirms that its *telos* has a moral aim. This is put directly, if somewhat satirically, by Aristophanes in *The Frogs*, where he has Euripides say of poets that they are admired: "For skillfulness and for good counsel, and because we make people better members of their communities."[34] Aristotle formulates it in more general terms: "Tragedy is an imitation of personages better than the ordinary man."[35]

The purpose of tragedy is to describe human beings in a better way, as opposed to comedy—claimed to originate in Sicily—which makes them worse. Thus, in reality, only a small number of mythical figures can be used in drama. On the one hand, the characters that stand above the ordinary and average must not be infallible, or the misfortunes to which they are subjected will not arouse fear and pity but only incense the audience. On the other hand, they cannot be so bad that the spectators will merely gloat over the punishment they bring down on their sinful heads.

No, the dramatically suitable figures must be given some sort of "flaw" (*hamartia*),[36] which makes it reasonable for the person in question to suffer misfortune but can, at the same time, act as an object of identification. Of what this pronominal *hamartia* consists, Aristotle does not explore in depth. He mentions Oedipus as an example, and this could indicate that the flaw lay in his ignorance. If we compare Oedipus' psychological constitution with other heroes for whom things go cruelly wrong, we must conclude from the empirical evidence that the flaws have a far greater reach and are linked, for example, to the psychological life of the characters—i.e., *hubris*, such as the impious arrogance (*megalopsychia*) of Ajax, the *hubris* of vanity in Agamemnon, anger (Oedipus), desire, etc. So *hamartia* almost seems to be synonymous with *ate*, delusion, which arises from a person's misinterpretations. In this sense, tragedy functions as a description of the consequences of the subconscious, in which the sequence of events follows the mind's gradual enlightenment.

5

However that may be, suffering is brought about in a uniform way—by the transition (*metabasis*) from fortune to misfortune.[37] What is dramatic in suffering is to be found here. To imprint this *metabasis* on the mind of the audience, a single issue is required, Aristotle claims. It must not be dual, as is the case in the *Odyssey*, where the good and the evil ultimately suffer different fates. In the *telos* of the action, tragedy must ultimately end in the unambiguous and inescapable, as when Oedipus blinds himself.

Unity is naturally also a precondition for tragedy's ability to move towards its goal along a dramatic curve, as "*mythos* is a unity."[38] Unlike the epic's expansive episodic construction, its cumulative interlinking of events, tragedy must have a certain extent, but it must also be compressed: "In plays, the episodes are short; in epic poetry they serve to lengthen out the poem."[39] As Aristotle puts it later, "consider the *Oedipus* of Sophocles, for instance, and the effect of expanding it into the number of lines of the *Iliad*."[40] This means that unity of time and place must be observed and the action developed within a single, continuous "cycle of the sun," clearly structured and directed.

On the other hand, the action itself, if it were up to Aristotle, must have a complicated structure in order to capture the necessity in the tragedy's failure to interpret and comprehend. The course taken by this necessity often has two related forms: 1) *Peripeteia*'s sudden change from fortune to misfortune. 2) The achievement of undertanding, *anagnorisis*, the moment of truth. In *Oedipus the King*, Aristotle's paradigmatic tragedy, there is a coincidence between these two dramatic factors when Oedipus finally understands who he is.

As the chorus says to Oedipus, "Time who sees all has found you out."[41] Again and again in our concrete analyses we shall meet time as a leading actor, who finds the guilty party and punishes. It may be a long time or short, but justice will be done in the fullness of time. This is not something Aristotle accounts for, but, if we compare it with Homer's view of time, we can see that the concept of time has taken on a remarkable precision. In Homer, time was a concrete thing, bound for instance to the duration of the war; but in the *Odyssey*, it clearly appeared as the category of fate and understanding in which Zeus' intention was fulfilled, bringing about Odysseus' homecoming and vengeance after twenty years, as had been fore-told to him.

In the tragedies, the whole plot is bound to precisely this way of thinking about time, the catastrophic moment itself in which the fateful sudden change divides the time before and the time after. The greater the contrast there is between the before and the after, the greater the tragedy, of which Oedipus, if anyone, is an example. In this sense, time as a causal factor is a co-creator of the drama. Tragedy actually depends on this general development of a true consciousness of time, as is supported by the fact that history arises as a prose genre during the same period with such names as Herodotus and Thucydides.

In Oedipus' case, the fateful complication or knot (*desis*) is linked to a shift in time—outside the framework of the tragedy. But when his past catches up with him, his identity is illuminated in the dissolution of the complication, which Aristotle calls *lysis*. The unconscious is illuminated through this form of suffering, *pathos*, which brings insight to the characters and spectators. The riddle of Oedipus is hidden in time, and his detective work to discover his true identity demonstrates in itself that the *mythos* of the tragedy lies in the interpretative initiative for which the protagonist, here as king, makes himself responsible. This initiative also includes the audience through its empathy in such a way that Oedipus' *anagnorisis* also becomes the moment of truth for the audience. Thus, *katharsis* is synonymous with having participated in the interpretation of the subconscious, which by time, through the action, is brought into the daylight.

The audience itself thereby becomes enlightened and permeated by the truth, by the insight implied by the requirement to know oneself, which is the precon-dition for the health of the soul. In a circular argument, this implies that tragedy as *mythos* creates insight by illuminating the necessity of life in order to improve peo-ple. Thus, tragedy's existential intent comes in a philosophical sense to resemble Socrates' lifelong effort.

6

Oedipus the King is the crowning example in Aristotle and in a way becomes the tragedy to end all tragedies. Nevertheless, it is peculiar that Aeschylus is rarely men-tioned by Aristotle, since it was he who brought tragedy to the point of becoming, so to speak, the state poetry of Athens. Nor does he mention Aeschylus' use of the trilogy, presumably because it still bears too clear a mark of the expansive action and plot of epic poetry and so cannot serve as the ideal type. In this context, Sophocles becomes the figure who best fulfils his ideal requirements, but he also defends Euripides. Although, according to Aristotle, Euripides does not honor the structural requirements of drama and breaks a golden rule by not making the chorus an active character, he seems "the most tragic certainly of the dramatists,"[42] particularly by making use of the single issue.

However, we can ascertain in our reading of the respective tragedians that

Aeschylus does not only develop tragedy but, in his *mythos*, allows it to reflect contemporary political and social conditions and, in the *Oresteia*, to insert myth directly into the formation of the Athenian state. He binds the individual to the state through an awe in which he warns against anarchy as well as despotism—and on the mythical plane he replaces the blood revenge of the maternal system with the judicial practice of the paternal system.

In Aeschylus, action and reflection are not yet clearly separated, while a character such as Sophocles' Oedipus becomes psychologically conscious of his identity through an unraveling of his earlier history. Sophocles has preserved awe, but in a clearer demonstration of the powerlessness of people with respect to the gods. Euripides, on the other hand, shows how the values formulated by his two predecessors are broken down *from without* by the degeneration of the political state and *from within* by the irrational, in which the very the existence and justice of the gods are put to question.

As a triad, the three great tragedians come to represent distinctive stages of consciousness during this period. Aeschylus is the one who shapes tragedy and establishes the fundamental norms around *sophrosyne* and piety necessary for citizens to display, a thought process in which he is a direct extension of Solon, seeking to reconcile conflicting forces. Sophocles, if anyone, becomes the poet of piety, as he attributes to gods and Fate an inscrutable will to which men are subject. And Euripides is the poet of negative values, revealing the consequences of the dissolution of the state for human life with a deep-seated longing for resolution.

A singular mark of the rich cultural flowering in which these tragedians worked is that the process takes place in a series of overlappings in that they are an inspiration to each other. A chronological reading might give the impression of a simple successive development in which one poet is replaced by the next, but this is not the case. On the contrary, they exert a great influence upon each other. For example, Aeschylus learns to use the third actor from Sophocles, and Sophocles adopts a series of technical concepts from the younger Euripides, who in turn, by relating his pieces to contemporary social conditions, resembles Aeschylus more than Sophocles. We are presented with evidence of this inter- and counterplay in the conflict between Aeschylus and Euripides in Aristophanes' *The Frogs*, in which they come to blows over who is the more important; while Sophocles wisely withdraws from this competition. These similarities and differences will be looked at in more detail in the concrete analyses to follow.

XV

AESCHYLUS

The Poet from Eleusis

1

THE TRAGEDIES TURNED TO MYTH ONCE AGAIN AS THE MATERIAL THROUGH which poets could present their insight and view of life. The experience contained within the old fables could be used both to interpret the fundamental human condition and the contemporary situation. Tragedy created memory and continuity with its mythical past in which people had their roots, and which in reality was not so terribly far away. Pindar, the writer of odes, also used mythical prehistory, though for a more nostalgic purpose, to express a longing back to the days before tyranny and to the days of the fundamental heroic values he praised in his grand odes to Olympic heroes. Aeschylus, on the other hand, tries in drama to formulate a vision of life for the new age, which dawned in Athens when the city was constituted as a democratic state.

Meanwhile, it is surprising that Aeschylus—in comparison with Homer, upon whom he draws quite considerably—appears as both an older and a younger poet. He seems older in penetrating and thinking via the mythical reality relating to the maternal cult. In the *Oresteia*, he thus creates a world connected to the life of the underworld, to blood revenge and the Erinyes of the Night, which clearly feels older than the Olympian gods and heroic world of Homer. It might even be said that Aeschylus thereby extrapolates the night or shadow side of the Homeric universe. Not only does he bring to light the effects of the maternal nature upon human life but he also reveals how in its tyrannical arrogance the aristocracy of the heroic age unleashes the primordial female forces that the age tried to limit. Due to gross injustice (*hubris*), the false steps (*hamartia*) of blood guilt are inherited in the family as *daimonia*, delusion (*ate*) and pollution (*miasma*).

In my analysis of his works, my conclusion that Homer did not have or did not use the same knowledge is based on the fact that he conceived his works in the enlightened region of Ionia with a view to establishing a patriarchal form of government—by repressing fertility cults such as that of Demeter.

2

If we dare lend credence to the information we have about Aeschylus' life and work, we may find an explanation for why he had this special insight into the mythical and cultic. He is supposed to have been born in 525 B.C. in the *deme* of Eleusis, where his father, Euphorion, was a member of the nobility. The family belonged to the cult surrounding the Mysteries. It is not known whether Aeschylus himself was initiated, but if we adhere to Aristophanes, there are things that point in that direction, since in Aristophanes' *The Frogs*, written fifty years after his death, Aeschylus calls upon Demeter for help in his competition with Euripides: "Demeter, who didst nurture my mind, grant that I be worthy of thy Mysteries!"[1] According to Aristarchus, Aeschylus was condemned to death for revealing secrets of the mysteries and pardoned only because of his heroic effort during the battle of Marathon.[2]

This biographical data is not sufficient to explain the groundbreaking quality of his poetry and the sudden, almost tropical flowering of tragedy in his hands. Aeschylus is the right man in the right place—also in relation to external factors that crystallized politically and intellectually during his time. This explains why, within such a short time, he is joined by two equally significant dramatists, after which grand drama dies out. As in other transitional periods, for instance the Renaissance or the Golden Age of Painting in Copenhagen, the spirit of the times and its ripening provide the underlying explanation for an otherwise incomprehensible concentration of groundbreaking artists and thinkers.

3

From a political point of view, Aeschylus grew up during the decline of tyranny and the succeeding development of democracy, in which Cleisthenes continued what Solon had begun with reforms completed by Ephialtes and Pericles. Aeschylus seems to have been an opponent of the radical changes of 462 B.C. that, among other things, diminished the power of the Areopagus Council. In his description of the council's sacred origin in the *Oresteia,* he provides a possible defense for its authority. The long and short of it is that he personally witnessed and to a significan extent took part in the upheavals that occurred during his lifetime, including the war with the Persians.

As described above, artistically, the development of tragedy had been on a parallel track during these years. Aeschylus himself probably made his first appearance in 499 B.C. *The Persians*, the oldest extant tragedy, is from 472 B.C. It was once believed that *The Suppliant Maidens* was the oldest because the chorus here has such a dominant role—indeed, it is in reality the main character. This was taken as evidence that Aeschylus was still under the influence of the original form of tragedy, which had not yet revolutionized drama with the introduction of the second actor. Aristotle describes this course of development: "The number of actors was first increased to two by Aeschylus, who curtailed the business of the Chorus, and made the dialogue, or spoken portion, take the leading part in the play."[3]

This "expansion" contributed, of course, to a significant increase in the dramatic effect as, in their dialogue with the chorus and the chorus leader, the characters could establish a whole range of struggling wills and intentions. As G. F. Else has demonstrated,[4] judging from his surviving tragedies, Aeschylus only gradually—and basing himself on Thespis—develops a true dramatic conflict. So the violent events of the tragedy are already a thing of the past in *The Persians*; in *Seven Against Thebes*, they take place off stage; while the conflict comes to a head in *The Suppliant Maidens* in the encounter between the Danaids and King Pelasges, when they demand refuge and the king has to take both the gods and his people into consideration. Not until the *Agamemnon* and the *Oresteia* as a whole is a true conflict played out against a background of earlier catastrophes: Helen's desertion, Agamemnon's sacrifice of his daughter, and the bloody taking of Troy. In addition, there is high drama in the encounters between Agamemnon and Klytemnestra, Klytemnestra and Kassandra, Orestes and Klytemnestra, Apollo and the Erinyes.

In this context, G. F. Else claims that Aeschylus is the true inventor of the third actor, since three actors appear in most of the scenes of the *Oresteia*. Yet Aristotle maintains that the third actor is Sophocles' "invention". In this case, Aeschylus adopted his younger colleague's dramatic technique, and tradition has it that he said: "It is a pleasure for an older man to learn from a younger."[5]

4

Aristophanes' comedy *The Frogs* is an important source for throwing light on Aeschylus' position as a tragedian, even though the information comes through a fictitious device—Euripides' parody of and sarcasm at the expense of his great predecessor. It happens in the competition that Aristophanes sets up in the realm of the dead to determine which of the great tragedians is the greatest. In brief, Dionysos has descended to Hades to fetch Euripides, because the god misses a proper tragedian after the death of Euripides in 406 B.C., the year the play was written. Upon his arrival in Hades, Euripides has immediately sought to take the poet's throne from Aeschylus. A contest arises between them to find out who is the better and thus to determine whom Dionysos is to bring back to earth—and to the theater.

As the chorus leader announces, Aeschylus was the first Greek to erect "towering structures of majestic words and to give elegance to tragic balderdash."[6] Euripides, with his fluency and his interest in everyday things, mocks Aeschylus' pomposity, all his talk about war, that is to say the heroic disposition and especially Aeschylus' heavy, baroque style, which Euripides characterizes as "swollen as it was from bombast and overweight vocabulary."[7] Euripides is particularly hard on his metaphorical mannerism—"tawny horsecocks," etc.—of which no one in the audience understood a word. And as we shall see in our reading of the *Oresteia*, Aeschylus certainly works in a passionate, linguistic, metaphorical and thoroughly structured symbolical universe in which there can certainly be doubt as to how the images are to be interpreted.

In the face of Euripides' biting attack, Aeschylus claims that his poetry has sprung from "a good source"[8] and mentions Orpheus and Homer. He claims that with his blasphemous and degenerate descriptions of illegitimate passions such as Phaedra's and by dressing his characters in rags corresponding to their inner worth, and much more in the same tone, Euripides has torn down the moral and respectable models that he, Aeschylus, has set up.

It may well be that Aristophanes has hidden behind his characters, the parody. But when, to Euripides' great annoyance, he has Dionysos award the victory to Aeschylus and take him up to Athens again, it is ultimately an indication that Aristophanes, as the conservative and social critical poet he was, preferred the older tragedian's moral universe and *arete*.

The Trilogy as Dramatic Necessity

1

There is something in Euripides' negative talk of the heaviness of Aeschylus' dramatic expression, as he uses no fewer than three tragedies to unfold and create a resolution in his thematic world: the trilogy—which is actually abandoned by Sophocles and Euripides. This happens not only because the trilogy is a cumbersome form, but for a number of internal reasons and is evidence of some crucial shifts in interest, including an increase of dramatic tension. By the very nature of things, the trilogy has an epic quality that harks back to the Homeric narrative tradition. But for Aeschylus it is necessary to communicate his view of life in a triptych: to suffer is to learn.

Through the sufferings inflicted upon the characters (or upon themselves), both they and the audience can gain an insight into Aeschylus' goal, his *telos*, in the trilogies: to show human illusions and explain the justice of the gods. *Telos* converges with theodicy. But not only are the ways of the gods inscrutable—no, because of their personalities, the characters are to a great extent themselves responsible for the catastrophes they bring down on themselves. A primary motif is *hubris*, to which reference has already been made—the desire to accumulate power and wealth.

This theme of conflict had its philosophical background in Solon's ideas, here to be repeated in brief. Solon says in his elegies that whoever by injustice (*hubris*) acquires wealth in the broadest sense of the word will become inflated (*koros*).[9] It arouses the displeasure of the gods and envy (*phthonos*), and it provokes nemesis and human ruin (*ate*), for everything will end as Zeus has determined. This thought process was also found in Anaximander: that retribution is proportional to the violation, since only in this way can the universe preserve its constancy and stability.

But as Solon, like everyone else, made the disturbing, unjust observation that some people get away with crimes, *hubris*, etc., without being punished, it implies, still with respect to the cosmic order, that not the guilty but the guilty party's family must bear the burden of these sins. They are inherited as a contamination (*miasma*)—"Yet it comes with dread certainty in later times: the innocent pay for their deeds,/either their children or the family line thereafter."[10] So it is no use to flee. For time itself, together with Fate, will always punish the guilty—"For the deeds of *hubris* do not prosper long for mortals:/ rather, Zeus oversees the end of all things."[11]

2

Just as Homer imagines his way towards Solon's *eunomia*, a utopia of social legislation and justice, Aeschylus works on the basis of Solon's doctrine of a universal order and shows how it is maintained. And where these fundamental ideas are linked to the great family myths and are connected with the notion of succession that Hesiod develops in the *Theogony*, there we have the supporting principle in his trilogies. For while Sophocles and Euripides seek a dramatic culmination, the point, in a psychological compression around the key figures of their works (an Oedipus or a Medea), Aeschylus can, with the epic foundation of his trilogy, produce a broader description of the combination of crime, curse and conciliation/ conversion—or culpability, punishment and penance, which is generated in the family's heritage.

The trilogy thereby becomes a clear demonstration of the family as a medium for a series of curses and its expiation; as is said in *Seven Against Thebes*, it generally takes three generations to play through this drama: "Old is the tale of sin I tell/ but swift in retribution: to the third generation it abides" (742-44). This causality of consummation apparently fascinated Aeschylus. If the description of it in the *Oresteia* has a greater range than the other trilogies, it is because he here shows how a family curse and its atonement at the individual level creates a collective change in the sexual as well as in political life in the shift from the maternal to the paternal system. On this basis and from the other tragedies surviving from the original trilogies, we can without more ado establish that the ideas and compositional development in the *Oresteia* are by no means unique but, on the contrary, are inherent to Aeschylus' drama.

However, each in their way, the tragedies prior to the *Oresteia* lead thematically to and are gathered together in this, the only completely preserved trilogy from Aeschylus' final years. So our discussion of these works will, on the one hand, illustrate this process of development in the earliest Greek tragedy and, on the other serve as preparation for an interpretation of the *Oresteia*, the tragedy above all tragedies and reveal Aeschylus' development and vision of life.

The Persians

1

The Persians, from 472 B.C., is the earliest tragedy we possess. And with respect to my general characterization of Aeschylus' use of myth and the trilogy, I must begin with the modification that *The Persians* is not part of a trilogy and, in the strict sense, is not based on myth. It is based upon a verifiable historical event: the Greeks' amazing victory over the many times larger Persian fleet in the battle of Salamis, 480 B.C.—a defeat for the Persian King Xerxes that was to be the beginning of the end for his wars of conquest, ultimately ending in defeat a year later at Plataia. For Athens, it was the starting gun for the establishment of a great power center.

If Aeschylus could make use of this historical material, the explanation must be that, during the intervening decade between the event and its fictionalization, it had become a mythical event for the city and for himself as, according to the same mythical tradition, he had participated in the battle. In a way, there is a deeper significance in the fact that, of the eighty-plus lost tragedies from Aeschylus' hand for which we have titles, it is *The Persians* and the *Oresteia* that have survived. *The Persians* opens this historic process, while the *Oresteia* is its culmination. In this context, Xerxes' bankrupt belligerency reflects a higher justice by which life is governed and wrongdoing punished and which implicitly made Athens into the chosen *polis* of the gods. *The Persians* is, at the same time, the Aeschylean tragedy that most explicitly reveals the notions of the *hubris* of arrogance and the *ate* of annihilation, which Hesiod and Solon before him had diagnosed.

Thus, Hesiod could exhort his pompous brother: "Follow right; control your pride. / For pride is evil in a common man. / Even a noble finds it hard to bear."[12] In Aeschylus' *Oresteia*, it is put this way: "for the very child / of vanity is violence."[13] This is to say that, by a law of nature, the arrogant person is tyrannical in his conduct and aims to get his way regardless—just like, for example, Agamemnon, when, in order to promote his ruthless and arrogant project of annihilating Troy, he heartlessly sacrifices his daughter.

2

The most dramatic surprise in *The Persians* is that Aeschylus views the defeat from the point of view of the losers and does so without gloating but, rather, empathetically. The reason for this narrative stance must be that through it he can directly present those who are to learn from the suffering that the catastrophe of the defeat is the Persian Empire's fall from greatness. And from this it is possible for the audience to deduce the universality of the tragedy, to learn from its causes and to turn them into self-understanding. In short, it is a "mobilization-text," a text that leads to soul-searching and *sophrosyne*.

It could in fact be said that it is this world of insight to which Xerxes' mother, Queen Atossa, gains access in a premonitory dream at the beginning of the work. Her son has been trying to chain two proud women to a chariot: one in a Persian gown who willingly finds herself in subjugation and the other, dressed in a Greek *peplos*, who rips the reins to pieces and, as happened at Salamis, leaves Xerxes sprawling in the dust.

In her anxiety, the distressed queen calls upon the gods and her dead husband Dareios from the realm of the dead. With this aesthetically bold step, Aeschylus is able to use the king's spirit as a soothsayer (*nekromanteia*) endowed with the gravity of insight that belongs to the dead and to which Homer had Odysseus gain access during his *katabasis*. Indeed, the dead king at once embodies *pathos*, suffering, and the lesson, *mathos*, that can be derived from it, along with the full authority of his position. He thereby confirms the truth of the bad omens that have surrounded the expedition and of his wife's nightmare. He confirms that the will of Zeus will be realized in the fullness of time—"Alas! That prophecy was quick to act!/ Zeus hurled against my son its lightning-end" (739-40).

Soothsaying and compositional consciousness meet in the fulfilled purpose of the god, his *telos*, which is behind Xerxes' unhappy fate. Its cause, the dead father states, is that in the arrogance of youth his son offended the gods and so has merely reaped what he has sown: "Mortal though he was,/ By folly thought to conquer all gods" (748-49). The father links ungodliness and *hubris*, noting that Xerxes acted against the will of the gods when he tried to build a bridge across the Hellespont. A disease of the soul[14] is what Dareios actually calls his arrogance; whereas, as said above, the job of tragedy by contrast is to promote a healthy soul. Aeschylus describes this in one of a series of metaphors that he may have learned from Homeric similes—and which made Euripides (in Aristophanes) mock his imagery: "Insolence, once blossoming, bears/ Its fruit, a tasseled field of doom, from which/ A weeping harvest's reaped, all tears" (821-23).

The word for "doom" here is *ate*, playing on the well-known register from delusion and self-deceit (*peitho*)—self-deceit is described as the child of *ate*—to the all-encompassing destruction in which *hubris* results. This occurs in a chain reaction of misfortunes that lie behind Xerxes' defeat and the destruction of his army. He has, as the chorus laments, filled "the house of death" with the youth and future of the country. That is to say that if a person with Xerxes' qualities is king, he will take his people with him into the catastrophes that are tied to his arrogant nature.

If we look at the morphology of arrogance in this context, one striking feature is that arrogance "inflates." The result is an inflation (*koros*) of the personal sense of having the right to do anything—in spite of everything. This produces in turn a greediness to acquire ever more property, but, as Dareios maintains, "Zeus is the chastener of overboastful/ Minds, a grievous corrector" (827-28).

3

If Dareios has so far indicated the reason for suffering to be his son's immense arrogance, his words take a change in direction, since his royal duty now—on behalf of Aeschylus—is to formulate the lesson to be drawn, the lesson of *sophrosyne*: "Therefore advise/ Him, admonished by reason, to be wise,/ And cease his overboastful temper from/ Sinning against the gods." (829-32). But at the same time, Dareios predicts the definitive defeat of the Persian army at Plataea, the year after Salamis. Then, Dareios disappears into the earth again, leaving the stage to Xerxes. Ragged, torn and broken, he enters as an image of what awaits anyone who in arrogance and greed incurs the wrath of the gods.

Completing the picture we can conclude that the Persians are broken, because Xerxes led the army with an irresponsible arrogance (519), while conversely the Athenians were victorious because they possessed the necessary *sophrosyne* and respect for the gods. Herodotus adopts fundamentally the same point of view in his history. This is seen both in his description of why the richest man on earth, King Croesus, was chastised—"because he thought he was of all mankind the most blessed"[15]—and in his discussion of Xerxes' arrogance and impiety.

Seven Against Thebes

1

Considering how few of Aeschylus' tragedies have survived, it is amazing that in *The Frogs* Aristophanes mentions both *The Persians* and *Seven Against Thebes*, from five years earlier, as examples of military bravado. Aeschylus replies that they were written in praise of Ares—that is to say as a sort of mobilization-text intended to arouse the spectators' "spirit of war" and the desire to fight the enemy by showing what true heroic courage is.[16]

As emerged from *The Persians*, the overall moral was to show moderation, while the enemy was destroyed by *hubris*. The theme is continued in an easily recognizable form in *Seven Against Thebes*, though in a more ambiguous manner since Eteokles, King of Thebes after Oedipus, must defend the city against his brother Polyneikes. It was determined that they should rule in turn, but Eteokles has refused to give up the throne. So his brother now stands with six allies from the Argive army before the seven gates of Thebes.

From the point of view of analysis, the simple fact that the tragedy is the last part of a trilogy increases the degree of complexity in relation to *The Persians*. The other plays bore the titles *Laios* and *Oedipus*, and it must be assumed that their plots had much in common with both Sophocles' dramas based on the same sequence of events and Euripides' *The Phoenician Women*. In brief, the battle between the brothers is part of a family feud whose source is in the conflicts about which the two lost tragedies dealt and whose more precise contents we can infer from the references we find in *Seven Against Thebes*.

2

If we sort out the prehistory, it is clear that Aeschylus used the trilogy to show how a family is struck down by a curse and how it wreaks havoc until final reconciliation in the third generation, which the brothers represent. We also understand that the curse on the family has come because he "by folly thought to conquer all the gods" (749) as it is formulaically put in *The Persians*. But arrogance as tyrannical egoism is also linked to an elemental disturbance of the instinctual drives.

King Laios was warned three times by the oracle at Delphi that he would save his kingdom if he died childless; but, driven by his sexual urge, "by loving folly" (750),[17] he conceived Oedipus and brought the curse on his family, making himself and his descendants deeply hated by the gods.

Oedipus inherits this guilt from his father and we must assume—as in Sophocles—that, in the tragedy bearing his name, he killed him and married his mother. As it emerges from *Seven Against Thebes*, he discovers the way of things and blinds himself. As we shall see, Sophocles presents this self-inflicted punishment as an expression of arrogance and anger in his being, an anger that also makes him curse his sons when they lock him up or banish him.[18] In any event, it is from him that the curse upon the family is carried on in such a fatal way that the sons are doomed to kill each other, as the last item in the reckoning with the gods, which has its cause in Laios' confused, godless desire, radicalized through Oedipus' patricide and marriage to his mother.

3

Whereas in the two subsequent tragedians, Eteokles and Polyneikes possess the same tyrannical, self-willed disposition, Aeschylus' point is to differentiate between the brothers: Eteokles is established in the first half of the tragedy as an ideal king (despite the fact that he has robbed his brother of the right to the throne), while Polyneikes is defined by the Greek meaning of his name—"he who seeks many conflicts"—as a troublemaker. Their different personalities are reflected in the warriors with whom they surround themselves.

In this context, the similarity to *The Persians* is striking. The Thebans correspond to the Athenians, as Eteokles is devoted to a higher cause—that of defending the city, its women and children, against aggressors, who in the parallelogram of forces correspond to the Persians. This is clearly underlined by their conduct. With one important exception, the Argive generals are governed by impious arrogance. As it is said of Kapaneus, he threatens violence and, though mortal he declares, "he'll sack/ our city with the Gods' good will or ill" (426). They all behave thus, while their arrogance is reflected in the boasting heraldry on their shields.

An exception among the attackers is the warrior and seer Amphiaraos. He has received such terrifying omens that he tries to hold the army back and calls for moderation, only to be told that it is out of cowardice that he seeks to avoid battle and death. He himself curses the contentious Polyneikes on his side, calling him: "Murderer,/ cause of confusion to the city" (570). And he is the only one who carries a shield without self-aggrandizing ornamentation.

It is in itself a sign of Eteokles' *sophrosyne* that he can recognize an honorable man in this enemy, calling him "wise, just, good, and holy" (610), a man who has fallen into bad company. Eteokles' warriors are of the same caliber as himself, pious and noble—for example, Melanippos, "Laggard in all things base he is wont to be/ but not a coward" (411–12). Nor do they carry shields with the heraldry of braggarts, but are supported by the gods themselves.

4

However, it is not for nothing that Eteokles is struck by a family curse, bearing it within him like a barb. The result is that, in the conflict with his brother, he himself changes—despite the chorus' prayers and warnings to avoid the guilt (*ate*) of fratricide and not to be hasty. For as the chorus says, directly translated: "Do not be borne away by the flood/ of blind spear-maddened rage, heart-swollen and wild./ Cast out this corrupting lust (*kakou erotos*) now and for good."[19]

But these admonitions have no effect, as the father's avenging spirit, the Eriny, strikes him, even though he has sought by prayer to exorcise it to remain quiet. This means that—after the brothers have killed each other and despite the self-control he displays in the first part of the tragedy—Eteokles is finally assessed on the same terms as his contentious brother. Both are "unclean"—"They have earned their name too well/ and 'men of strife' (*polyneikeis*) they have perished/ through impious intent" (829-30). And both are characterized as "misguided" (*dysphrones*, 875), impervious to good advice.

Generally speaking, this is clear evidence of the view that Aeschylus shares with Solon: that where a family member is seized by *hubris*—in this case, King Laios' uncontrollable sexuality—the family will ultimately be punished for his impiety. The tragic paradox is that Eteokles, the really moderate and god-fearing man, must be destroyed due to the sins of his forefathers. Liberation and expiation, meanwhile, lie in the fact that this is what he actually does and so saves his native city. If this destruction is Zeus' *telos*, it leads to atonement. The relieved chorus can declare that the quarrel ended "in frantic strife (*neikos*)" (935).[20]

So far, it has been the exposition of arrogance through a combination of sexuality and war frenzy. But it also appears from *Seven Against Thebes* that *hubris* can degenerate into a sort of hysteria or emotional over-reaction. There is just a hint of this theme in *The Persians*, where the chorus' cry of despair is interpreted as a barbaric lack of self-control under pressure. In *Seven Against Thebes*, the theme is developed into a stark contrast between the masculine form of *sophrosyne* displayed by Eteokles in the first half of the play and fear of the attackers on the part of the female chorus.

In fear of death, they cleave to the statues of the gods. When Eteokles at the same time tries to infuse the people with hope and courage, he harshly condemns the women's behavior, seeing a total lack of self-control in their emotional patterns—"an object of hatred for all temperate souls" (186) is his judgment, a judgment he extends to the female sex as such: "Neither in evils nor in fair good luck/ may I share a dwelling with the tribe of women!/ When she's triumphant, hers a confidence/ past converse with another, when afraid/ an evil greater both for home and city" (187-90) And an invocation to Zeus runs: "O Zeus, what a tribe you have given us in women" (256).

Regardless of the situation, woman is a trouble to man. For if she is powerful, like Klytemnestra, she offers men defiance; if she is a nervous type, she fills the house with her fear.[21] So Eteokles concludes that only a man can see to the interests of the city. Accordingly, he calls the chorus of women to order with harsh words, for their terror must not possess Thebes. But Aeschylus has here raised a complex problem that we first saw formulated in Hesiod's straightforward misogyny. And this tension between the sexes, which here is gathering momentum, is the main theme in the trilogy to which *The Suppliant Maidens* belongs.

The Suppliant Maidens

1

While arrogance as a phenomenon of desire and a violation of the gods was partially hidden in *Seven Against Thebes*, as it had to be traced back to Laios' instinctual drive, this link to sexuality, violence and *hubris* is plain to see in *The Suppliant Maidens*. The protagonist here is the chorus of fifty young girls, the Danaids, who must flee from their country on the Nile to avoid their fifty cousins' lascivious demand that they should marry them. Their flight takes them to Argos, whence, through their primordial mother, Io, they originally come. As we shall see in *Prometheus Bound*, Io's transformation into a cow and subsequent flight through Europe and Asia is due to Zeus' desire for her. Not until she reaches Egypt is she transformed once again into a human being and as the result of Zeus' loving caress gives birth to their son Epaphos, whose name is derived from the verb "to caress" (*epaphao*). In this sense, he symbolizes the transformation of desire into human *eros*, as "Epaphos, Caress" (48).

Both the Danaids and their cousins (or the Egyptians, as they are called), being dark-skinned, descend from Epaphos. The girls' resistance to sexual intercourse is due to their fear of impiety, *asebeia*, which is why they and their father, as leader and friend, have sought refuge at Argos with King Pelasges. And let it be said immediately that the cause of this fear is that the Danaids, without any explanation of how, have achieved an awareness of sexuality that until that point had been hidden as pure physical desire in the mythic fertility cults, serving fertilization and the primordial mother. It is this incestuous primordial stage they wish to renounce and consider unholy. We shall shortly return to this.

At the same time it must indicate that the Egyptians have not passed beyond this mental stage: they are at one with it and so see no offense in it. But from the higher level of consciousness in the text and from patriarchy's taboo on incest, they are guilty of *hubris* as a result of pursuing their fleeing cousins. Again and again, it is stressed that arrogance is based on a combination of violence and desire. They are compared to wild animals and robbers. Just as clear from this perspective is the fact that the Danaids' *sophrosyne* is primarily in the chastity, sexual self-control and abstinence impressed upon them by their father.

It might also be said that the king of Argos, Pelasges—like Dareios and Eteokles—exemplifies *sophrosyne* as a well-founded concern when it comes to royal matters. The girls' prayers at the altar for the protection to which they are entitled as refugees puts the king in a dilemma. On the one hand, he cannot reject the Danaids without acting against Zeus Hikesios, who protects the suppliants, and they and their father threaten him with Zeus' punishment if he neglects his sacred duty. On the other hand, he is reluctant to bring his country to war with the Egyptians on account of these errant girls. He says this explicitly and thereby expresses a view of women similar to that of Eteokles. He will not help them unless he has the consent of his people, and in this respect he is portrayed as anything but tyrannical. When he receives his people's consent, he can fulfill his duty to the gods.

2

In *The Suppliant Maidens*, Aeschylus has clearly and definably introduced a dichotomy between the *hubris* of violent desire and the *sophrosyne* of chastity. However, lacking the other parts of the trilogy of which *The Suppliant Maidens* was the first—the other titles of which seem to have been *The Egyptians* and *The Danaids*—problems of interpretation arise when we seek to make an in-depth study. On the basis of the general disposition of Aeschylus' trilogies, we must assume in this context that the potential conflict, apparently defused by the king's protection in the following tragedies, is fully developed through war and reconciliation (the latter because this is the condition for maintaining the cosmic justice that Aeschylus wanted to demonstrate with the theodicean content of his tragedies). But what was this sequence of events? The following reading must by its very nature be hypothetical as I am forced to rely on the myths he uses plus the Prometheus trilogy (of which two thirds are missing) and the *Oresteia*.

If we return to our starting point, the question (to which I have already given a preliminary answer) is raised as to why the Danaids view marriage with their cousins as unlawful and impious, while the Egyptians apparently see nothing illegitimate or unholy about it? And what role is played by their father and the flight to Argos, their old homeland?

As the Egyptian messenger maintains, he can propose his demand for marriage because the Egyptians worship other gods than those in Argos: "I do not fear these gods before me: they/ Did not nurse me, their nursing did not age me." (892-93). As we shall see in our interpretation of *Oedipus the King*, neither has the protagonist's mother, Iokaste, any objection to marrying her son, and she shows no particular respect for the Olympian gods. It is clear that incest is not something abominable to her, much less an unbearable thought. And her autonomy can only be explained by the fact that she ultimately belongs to a different reality, an atavistic world based on the mother's fertilization/marriage by/with the son/lover.

So if the Egyptians do not object to or even think about incest in their sexuality, we can only draw the conclusion that the gods the Egyptian men worship are different from the gods in Argos and belong to the fertility cults linked to the Great Mother. These Egyptian men are at the same level of consciousness as King Aiolos in the *Odyssey*, who with no concern about incest marries his six daughters to the same number of their brothers.

It must be from this mythical world the Danaids break out and flee because they have acquired insight into and an awareness of a sexuality that, in the mythical reality, remains in the subconscious as physical desire. Where their father rules, they have entered a higher level of consciousness. And it is he whom they follow in their escape and call father, counseling friend and guide. With him in the lead, they have become subject to the patriarchal principle and seek the protection of the Olympian gods in Argos. And the prohibition that the father and the world of laws to which he is linked lay down is the prohibition on incest. *The Suppliant Maidens* anticipates the patriarchy later constituted in the *Oresteia* by an oppression of: 1) the Erinyes of the mother cult. 2) blood revenge. 3) the latent incestuous relationship between mother and son.

The father in *The Suppliant Maidens* has quite simply stationed himself as guardian of his daughters' sexuality, inculcating the *sophrosyne* of chastity as though lashing them with a whip. His first word to them is: "Prudence" (*phronein*, 176). He stresses to them that they must conduct themselves modestly and humbly as refugees: "You are an exile, a needy stranger, / And rashness never suits the weaker" (202-03). They must be sexually abstemious since, he explains in general terms, men with their desire under Aphrodite's guidance in general will seek to rob them of their virtue, which, as the fresh flowers they are, men are ready to pluck: "you who have/ That bloom which draws men's eyes" (read: desire, 997-98). He concludes, "Only regard this command of your father:/ Honor modesty more than your life" (1010-11). And as evidence of their complete subjugation, the girls reply, "but, father,/ Be not anxious for our summer's blush" (1014-15).

Although the girls dare not renounce Aphrodite entirely, well aware that, along with Hera (who punished their ancestor, Io), she exercises the greatest power except for Zeus, their preferred goddess is nevertheless Artemis the pure. They pray to her to be spared the marriage bed (*gamos*, 1030). And it may be imagined that this contrast in the goddesses and their works anticipates what is to happen later in the lost portions of the trilogy.

That the flight to Argos under their father's guardianship is really a breach with the chthonic cult world of Egypt is made probable from the topographic symbols. The Olympian gods are not worshipped in Egypt but in Argos, which is also named Apia.[22] Apis, after whom Argos was called, was a prophet, a son of Apollo. And as it is related in *The Suppliant Maidens*, he received that honor of which the naming is an expression, because he cleared the land of deadly monsters that the Earth had generated, "deadly, monstrous/ Serpents" (262-63), just as his father had fought the Python at Delphi.

If this is linked to the description in the *Oresteia* of how Apollo struggles with chthonic serpentine creatures, the Erinyes, as a part of the transition from the blood revenge of the mother cult to paternal rule and its heavenly gods, it seems to refer to the same shift in ages as that originated by his son in *The Suppliant Maidens*. If this is correct, then it means in the larger context that the Egyptian world from which the Danaids flee corresponds to the earlier stage in which Argos found itself. It can also be noted in parenthesis that it was also from the swampy delta of the Nile that Helen brought her soothing palliatives (see p. 156).

At the same time it explains why the Egyptians are compared to snakes and wolves and is also the reason whey the Danaids seek refuge where consciousness has acquired the theological form of the Olympian gods. So the idea of a marriage with their primitive cousins is unthinkable. The girls do not share their faith and norms but are their father's daughters—and with him as administrator of their sexuality—arrive in a country whose reality and gods correspond to the stage of development they have reached.

3

We can get no further with *The Suppliant Maidens*, and it is quite difficult to imagine the continuation of the trilogy. Many suggestions have been made. However, it seems relatively certain that in *The Egyptians* Aeschylus found himself compelled to follow the well-known myth in which the Danaids are indeed forced to marry their violent cousins. On their wedding night, they plunge hairpins, with which their father has supplied them, through the hearts of their unwanted grooms, killing them. The sole exception is Hypermestra, who falls in love with Lynkeus—perhaps, because he does not deflower her.

Prometheus prophesied this course of events to Io in *Prometheus Bound*, and also the love that would grip Hypermestra. She chooses to be called a coward rather than a murderer and becomes the ancestral mother of Argos' new royal family. There is thus a sort of repetition in the family. As said above, Io was the object of Zeus' burning desire, which is only transformed in the loving caress from which Epaphos is born. A transformation of the same sort becomes the basis for the love between Hypermestra and the Egyptian Lynkeus, who become the founders of a new family.

The sisters' murder is the optimal and visible consequence of the inhibiting of the ability to love caused by the father's taboo on sexuality and his demand for absolute chastity. This is a form of frigidity that only finds fulfillment in death. This demonic and destructive aspect to their nature—fundamentally as great as their cousins' *hubristic* violence—is hinted at in *The Suppliant Maidens*, when they threaten to hang themselves by their belts from the statues of the gods if King Pelasges does not heed their prayers—the same sort of exaggerated emotion we found in the female chorus in *Seven Against Thebes*. Notably, then, at the same time as the girls fulfill their father's law by killing the suitors, they clearly regress in the killing to the reality from which they broke by transforming themselves into the vengeful, demonic virgin goddesses known from the female cults.

In contrast, Hypermestra represents a step forward by breaching her father's mandate. She integrates her act of love and the sexual fertility between which her father has interposed himself. It is possible that her defiance of her father's order led to a trial in which she was condemned to death by stoning. Reconciliation and liberation may be due to the intervention of Aphrodite, whom she has followed in her heart, the goddess of love acting as divine mediator and arbitrator just as Athene does for Orestes in the *Oresteia*.

One fragment may point in this direction. During the trial, Aphrodite is supposed to have spoken the words: "The holy Heaven yearns to wound the Earth, and yearning layeth hold on the Earth to join in wedlock; the rain, fallen from the amorous Heaven, impregnates the Earth, and it bringeth forth for mankind the food of flocks and herds and Demeter's gifts; and from that moist marriage-rite the woods put on their bloom. Of all these things I am the cause."[23]

The goddess speaks for universal, conciliatory love, which governs Heaven and Earth and which all people should follow.[24] The organizing principle is love itself. And it must be assumed that the other sisters in some way or other have accepted this notion of love. Perhaps they were liberated from the *miasma* of their blood guilt by ritual cleansing and ultimately married to confirm this cosmic love.

In the theories on the trilogy's story of reconciliation, it has been imagined, as is described by Apollodorus,[25] that the murdered Egyptians were honored at their funeral and later cleansed by Athene and Hermes, while in extension of Aphrodite's intervention and cleansing the Danaids were married to the winners of an athletics contest intended to point to the most suitable husbands. But after their death, they are punished for their murders by having to pour water into a bottomless vessel for ever.

Aeschylus seems to have had the same objective in this trilogy as later in the *Oresteia*: to show the shift from the maternal to the paternal system, its stages and its costs. The escape from Egypt is not only a sign of this (since the Danaids under their father's guidance flee this world and seek protection under the Olympian regime), but also the further development anticipated by Hypermestra's personalization of love. Together with Lynkeus, she becomes not only in general terms the source of a new royal family for the Argives, but simply the progenitor of the greatest heroes in the struggle against the primordial matriarchy: Perseus and Herakles, who both find their tutelary goddess in Athene and thus point towards the ultimate establishment of patriarchal reality in a democratic Athens. But the line from Hypermestra not only leads there but has its prehistory in her own ancestral mother, Io, whom we meet in *Prometheus Bound* at the dawn of mankind.

The Fire-Bringer—*Prometheus Bound*

1

Of all Aeschylus' tragedies, *Prometheus Bound* is surrounded by the greatest uncertainty. Not only do philologists doubt the extent to which he is the creator of the tragedy at all (since its language is claimed to be different than the others), but it is debatable where it fits in the trilogy.[26] As we have already discussed, it is related to the trilogy on the Danaids in that Prometheus' prophecy directly describes the story of their ancestral mother, Io. In addition, *Prometheus Bound* has clear thematic links with Aeschylus' other works by contributing its distinctive version of the *hubris-sophrosyne* motif and the doctrine of suffering, *pathei mathos*.

Moreover, we have in it an exemplary demonstration of how the succession motif is an underlying paradigm. Interestingly enough, in *Prometheus Bound*, this problem is transferred to the world of the gods and reveals that it is actually subject to a progression in which the developmental process of mankind is also dialectically enveloped. This is the theme of the *Oresteia* as well, though with the difference that in this work Zeus appears as virtually fully developed.

Be that as it may, the Prometheus trilogy presumably consisted of the following titles: the surviving *Prometheus Bound* (*Desmetes*), *Prometheus Liberated* (*Lyomenos*), and *Prometheus the Fire-Bringer* (*Pyrphoros*).[27] The last tragedy may have been the first, since it describes how, against Zeus' will, Prometheus brings fire to mankind and thereby gives them consciousness, the event that is the reason for his punishment in *Prometheus Bound*. Because Prometheus will not reveal how the supreme god might once again lose his power, Zeus casts him down to Tartaros. In *Prometheus Lyomenos*, Zeus must have undergone a transformation and become reconciled with Prometheus. He may in the final play be transformed into the merciful guiding force that forms the basis for the ordering of the universe. This marks a development from an immature god to a god of justice in his reconciliation with Prometheus, a process we can follow in the transition from the *Iliad* to the *Odyssey*.

If scientific truth has anything to do with simplicity, it seems most obvious to consider *Prometheus Desmetes* as the central play in the trilogy.

2

In the extant part, *Prometheus Bound*, Zeus seems to be a new god who rules with all the brutality of an upstart in his conflict with Prometheus the Titan, who has assisted him in the struggle with the Titans, the so-called *Titanomachy*. Later, Prometheus has had to save mankind, when Zeus in his lust for power wanted to destroy it. Not only has Prometheus saved mankind, but, to Zeus' great irritation, he has provided them with the fire of the gods—"the brightness of fire that devises all" (7). In short, he has given mankind the knowledge necessary to survive and to develop the skills that make it possible to calculate, navigate and force the Earth to yield its minerals.

This gift makes Hermes call him "subtle-spirit (*sophisten*), you/ bitterly overbitter" (944-45), using a term, sophist, that already has the same negative connotations it would have later but here also designates great knowledge. In other words, we find ourselves at the transition from an atavistic mythical world to a world of human inventiveness and consciousness. Men previously lived in a state of spiritual torpidity; of course they possessed prophetic abilities like the gods and could see into the future, but they mixed everything together like a dream—"Like the shapes of dreams they dragged/ through their long lives and handled/ all things in bewilderment and confusion" (448–50). They also lived in sunless caves, suggesting that, like the Kyklopes, they are still children of the Earth.

Okeanos and his daughters, the Okeanides, are still in this dream-like state, as Okeanos can move from place to place by the power and will of thought, just like the ships of the Phaiakians (see p. 220). Thus, the river god announces his arrival at the rock to which Prometheus is chained: "with the mind/ alone, no bridle needed, I direct/ my swift-winged bird" (286–89).

When Prometheus deprived men of their visionary capacity, he gave them not only fire but also hope and memory. Hope, on which they can live through hard times, and memory, which is the precondition for the creation of consciousness. By virtue of memory, individuals are capable of understanding themselves in context, creating an identity and thereby distinguishing themselves from their original unity with nature and the simultaneity of this state. So Prometheus also considers memory—"the combining of letters as a means of remembering all things" (461)—to be the prime source of civilization.

As compensation for the loss of the omnipotence that was part of the original mythical state of consciousness, mankind has received a surrounding objective world, and insight into the consistency in things and the connection between them, which they can exploit in the process of developing civilization. But it also shares in the pain that the process of separation also entails, always accompanied— as we saw in the *Odyssey*—by the regressive need again to go down into a completely undemanding and pleasurable state, to return to the womb, so to speak— or, as in Biblical mythology, a return to the time before the Fall. In this way, Prometheus becomes in the deepest sense the forefather of civilized man.[28]

3

So although Prometheus supported Zeus in the *Titanomachy*, he punishes his obstinacy and orders two violent bullies, Kratos and Bia (who, according to Hesiod, always accompany him[29])—i.e., elemental forces that act as a sort of emanation of Zeus's own violent nature—to chain Prometheus until he shows remorse and yields to the new divine law. Various well-meaning gods—among them, Hephaistos, who has received the thankless task of chaining Prometheus—try in vain to persuade Prometheus to compromise and to adapt to the new divine power to which Hephaistos himself has yielded, saying: "For the mind of Zeus is hard to soften with prayer,/ and every ruler is harsh whose rule is new" (34–35).

The very conflict in the trilogy consists of the fact that, despite his wisdom, Prometheus yields nothing to Zeus in obstinacy—at least, not in the eyes of the chorus: "You are stout of heart, unyielding/ to the bitterness of pain./ You are free of tongue, too free" (179–81). Hermes, too, asks him to show compliance, *sophrosyne* (982), and better judgment (1035)—"Look, you, and reflect/ and never think that obstinacy is better/ than prudent counsel" (1033–35). As also applies to Okeanos' terrified warning, this is, however, *sophrosyne* without pride or greatness—indeed, it almost has the character of opportunistic cowardice when Aeschylus, through Okeanos, lets it be understood that moderation is, after all, the premise for self-insight: "Know yourself and reform your ways to new ways,/ for new is he that rules among the Gods" (309-10).

Even though he is a god, Prometheus suffers organic pain, like Jesus on the Cross—or like a human being. However, since his name means "prescient," he can bear his suffering. He knows that Zeus' power, like that of his predecessors, is limited in time. So it is pure illusion for Kratos to claim that Zeus is the only one who is "free." No, he is also subject to Fate. Prometheus has the secret knowledge that Zeus himself will be overthrown, just as he overthrew Kronos, his father. If he impregnates Thetis, she will bear him a son he cannot resist. (This is the reason she is married to Peleus and conceives Achilleus).

This knowledge, which is not accessible to Zeus, reveals that Prometheus in his titanic might is a chthonic primordial power. For as he himself explains, his knowledge comes directly to him from the primordial mother, from Themis and Gaia (i.e., from the death-bound forces of the Earth, which constitute a unity)—"she that was my mother, Themis, Earth (. . .) had prophesied to me how it should be,/ even how the fates decreed it" (211-14). The depth of insight these goddesses possess comes from the fact that they have at their disposal the past and future of the very mystery of creation itself. It is from here Zeus will be struck, from the necessity that is mythologically incarnated in the form of "Fates and the remembering Furies" (515), as Prometheus warns. Against this power, all are powerless.

4

The nature and power of young Zeus, with which he defies and steamrolls his way through the world, are not only expressed in his assault on Prometheus, but can—as in the case of the Egyptians—be read in the violent nature of his desire. For the extent of Zeus' wildness and cruelty is illuminated through an erotic counterpart to Prometheus, the princess Io. This princess is herded about in the form of a cow because of the desire Zeus harbors for her and has inspired in her in dreams.

The transformation of Io into an animal may be intended to point out the animalistic nature of this instinctual world, while at the same time sexuality is described as madness when Io is driven off by the stings of a gadfly. For only a few moments during her conversation with Prometheus does she regain her normal consciousness, exclaiming in pain: "*Eleleu, eleleu*/ It creeps on me again, the twitching spasm,/ the mind-destroying madness, burning me up" (877-80). Prometheus does not doubt for a moment that her suffering must be ascribed to Zeus: "He was a God and sought to lie in love/ with this girl who was mortal" (737-38). And with the prescience that Prometheus, according to his name, possesses, he can see how things will end in the future.

"Do not hide from me what I must endure (*pathein*, 625)," Io begs, using a phrase that clearly points toward the theme of suffering in the trilogy and throughout Aeschylus' works generally. Prometheus reveals to her what pain is in her path but in a way that creates a clear parallel to his own situation and future. The two are thus profoundly connected: he may be seen as the father of mankind, while she will be the mother of the Egyptians and the Greek ruling families in Argos and Thebes.

As has already been said, this meanwhile presumes the complete transformation of Zeus: that his desire is transposed into true love demonstrating that his character of violence and desire has become a home in which divine *sophrosyne* can reside. Love arises—indeed, is born—from Io's pain. He transforms her again from an animal into a woman, whereupon the fertilization takes place that produces the previously mentioned Epaphos and actually constitutes the previous history to *The Suppliant Maidens*.

In order to be changed into a conciliatory god, even Zeus must yield to the code of suffering, as is indicated by Prometheus in a brief exchange with Hermes. For when Prometheus utters a mournful sigh (*omoi*) and Hermes claims that Zeus in his power knows nothing of the same pain and weakness, the Titan, who is the only one who knows the risk in which he lives and the fear that will strike the supreme god for the same reason, replies: "Time in its aging course teaches all things" (981). Thus, time and the suffering it brings is a teacher. And as a divinity that, like man, can feel physical pain, Prometheus, although knowing everything in advance, is himself to learn this lesson through the torments he suffers.

In other words, there is a form of family curse in the world of the gods. Only the chained Prometheus knows the answer of how to break the succession of violence that Zeus with his own punishment is in the process of continuing. Zeus can only receive the answer enlightening him if he releases Prometheus from his chains. But at the end of the play, he shows his worst side by casting Prometheus into the abyss of Hades. However, Prometheus knows that the day will come when Zeus will seek his advice:

> I know that he is savage: and his justice
> A thing he keeps by his own standard: still
> That will of his shall melt to softness yet
> When he is broken in the way I know,
> And though his temper now is oaken hard
> It shall be softened: hastily, he'll come
> To meet my haste, to join in amity
> And union with me—one day he shall come.
>
> (187-93)

The lost last part presumably deals with this prophetic transformation into a merciful god. In which case, this trilogy, along with the *Oresteia*, is evidence that succession takes place through revolt, the assertion of tyrannical power, and atonement.

THE *ORESTEIA*
Metaphorical Paraphrase
1

In the *Oresteia*, which he wrote in 458 B.C., a few years before his death at Gela, Sicily, Aeschylus provided the most extensive and aesthetically convincing example of his dramatic art in the form of a trilogy. Here, with unprecedented dramatic tension, he joins together the primary motifs of the other works. The tyrannical violation of the gods through arrogance is maintained as the curse, the guilt, the *daimon* or *alastor*, as it is also called, of the Atreid family.

This guilt is ultimately only resolved in a development of consciousness, in which the primordial, death-bound world of blood revenge in mother cults is replaced by the paternal rule of the Olympian gods. Aeschylus takes this theme, consisting of the opposition between female and male, up through the constitution of Athenian democracy linked to the Areopagus Council. The worlds of gods, men and state are linked together in a common life, the basis of which is sanctified *sophrosyne* and *eusebia*, piety. The source of law becomes: "wisdom/ comes alone through suffering" (Ag. 177-78). For as the chorus of Erinyes puts it: "There is/ advantage/ in the wisdom won from pain" (*Eum.* 519-21). And the Erinyes continue: "for the very child/ of vanity is violence (*hubris*);/ but out of health/ in the heart issues the beloved/ and the longed-for, prosperity" (*Eum.* 533-37). And as King Dareios saw a sick soul in his son Xerxes, the goal of Zeus (and Aeschylus) in the *Oresteia* is to promote a healthy soul (*hygieia phrenon, Eum.* 535).

My interpretation will also to a certain extent be a demonstration of Aeschylus' fabulous ability linguistically and metaphorically to structure his narrative universe so as to form a comprehensive whole. It is this ability that Aristophanes has Euripides mock in *The Frogs* as incomprehensible and as heavy as lead. Generally speaking, this technique is based on an accumulation of meanings. What is first read and experienced as separate words and images gradually, through repetition and linguistic similarities, becomes a metaphorical chain that creates the symbolic universe in which Aeschylus unfolds his conceptual world.

Since these symbols appear throughout the entire trilogy, they bind it together into a compositional whole. On the other hand, the imagery demonstrates how aesthetically aware Aeschylus is as a poet, as it is on this level that his intentions can most clearly be read in the overall text. He thereby creates an incredible tension between the strict order of form and the chaos on which it is built and which I will briefly paraphrase as a prelude to my analysis of the trilogy.

2

In the words of Aristotle, the event or the *mythos* of the trilogy is the load-bearing element in the drama. When the *Oresteia* begins, the darkness resting over the palace at Argos is rent asunder by the bonfire announcing that, after ten years, Troy has finally fallen. Agamemnon has been absent for all that time. The darkness is real, as it is night, but, as it will emerge, it has a symbolic meaning that extends right to the end of the trilogy. Along the way, darkness becomes an image of the anxiety and uncertainty that governs the land and in all souls affected. The king has sacrificed his daughter, the departed warriors are received as corpses, the queen has found a new lover; she murders her husband and is later herself killed by her son. It is difficult to bring the light of hope and resolution to this. Several times, the chorus thinks that it has returned. But it is an illusion, and it will only happen at the end.

As in Homer, Agamemnon has gone to Troy to take back Helen and avenge Paris' violation of guest friendship, a religious offence against Zeus in his attribute as the god of guest friendship. A herald confirms to the still doubting citizens that the torchlight speaks the truth. Agamemnon is just outside the door, and he is greeted as the light to cast off many years of darkness and despair. By his hand, victorious Zeus has finally cast his "binding net" (Ag. 358) over Troy.[30]

But Klytemnestra, his wife, who has ruled over Argos in his absence, has in the meantime cast her lot with the craven Aigisthos, Agamemnon's cousin. She merely makes a show of receiving her husband and king with pleasure. He brings with him, as the spoils of war and as his mistress, the visionary princess Kassandra—an additional provocation to Klytemnestra, who has already determined to kill Agamemnon in (blood) revenge because he sacrificed their daughter Iphigenia at the outset of his voyage. By doing so, he has reactivated the family curse and blood guilt for which his forefathers were to blame. The murder itself is carried out in robes that resemble a hunting net. As the net has already been used as an image of how Agamemnon captured Troy, this symbol establishes an underlying connection between the sacrifice of the daughter, clad in a robe, the conquest of Troy and the later murder of Agamemnon by Klytemnestra herself.

Kassandra, who prophesied this turn of events, including her own death, but whose prophetic abilities have been discredited by Apollo's intervention, is murdered at the same time. Nevertheless, she reveals that the cause of the curse resting upon that family is to be found in its earlier acts of cruelty.

In *The Libation Bearers*, the son Orestes returns home to avenge his murdered father, encouraged by Apollo himself, who has threatened him with catastrophic consequences if he does not do so. After his reunion with his sister Elektra, they jointly plan the murder of their mother and her lover. Like his mother, Orestes proceeds with cunning—in order to catch her with the same net of deceit (*Lib.* 557) that she used against his father. The net acquires the same significance as Penelope's weaving had when it was used as part of the *metis* of cunning. At the moment of the killing, he understandably enough hesitates at the thought of killing his mother. However, his friend Pylades reminds him that he is acting on Apollo's orders. He commits the murder but immediately begins to doubt whether he has acted correctly—at the same time as, internally, like an attack of madness, he is visited by his mother's Erinyes.

What is momentarily experienced at the beginning of the trilogy as a liberating light now turns, if possible, into an even deeper darkness that streams forth from the killings. From the night come the avenging Erinyes, awakened by the mother's blood, which has seeped into the ground, calling for recompense: a life for a life. The Erinyes pursue Orestes down the long path of suffering which in the final part of the trilogy, *The Eumenides*, leads him to the temple of Apollo at Delphi, where he is cleansed with blood of his so-called blood guilt. The mother's ghost awakens the Erinyes, who are taking a nap, and chastises them for letting Orestes slip through the net and goading them to exert themselves and chase him to his death.

On Apollo's advice, Orestes goes to the temple of Athene in Athens to be acquitted by a formal trial. After yet another long and painful odyssey, he reaches Athens and asks the goddess for help and justice. In the subsequent trial in which Apollo and the Erinyes contend, respectively, as defender and prosecutor, the Athenian Areopagus Council is instituted on the Hill of Ares, the Areopagus, consisting of the city's best citizens, which in the future is to determine all questions of criminal guilt.

Opposed to the Erinyes' maintenance of the principle of revenge, an eye for an eye, and their claim that the new gods are overruling their primordial right, Apollo in his defense of Orestes sets out a new order of the day. The blood revenge, which the Erinyes uphold as representatives of the original maternal rule, is to be replaced by an external court and at the same time this new order is to be internalized in a true awareness of justice by all. As Athene endorses and formulates the principles for such a legal system, when judgment is pronounced, she tips the scales of justice against the Erinyes and in favor of Orestes. The equal split in the voting thereby achieved means that he is acquitted. His path of suffering is at an end and he can return to his ancestral estate at Argos as the one who released his family from the curse. Full of gratitude, he enters into an alliance with Athens.

To put it mildly, the Erinyes are dissatisfied with the outcome of the case and take it as an example of how the new gods humiliate and tread on them and their function as avengers, and they threaten to lay waste to everything. That they have such power reveals their connection to the primal maternal, blood, fertility, etc. Athene has also realized this, which is why she dares not banish them from Athens. On the contrary. She tries to persuade them to let go of their anger and, as honored guests, settle down in a cave in the cliff of the Areopagus. Her attempt at persuasion is successful and the transformation that now takes place in the Erinyes is reinforced by the fact that they change their names and become the kindly Eumenides. In the future they will protect Athens and ensure the city's fertility. Then they are led with songs of joy in a torchlight procession—by young girls!—to their sacred spot beneath the earth from which they are to provide their eternal blessing—evidence that they have still preserved their affiliation with the earth.

Zeus Teleios

1

On the face of it we might assume that, as the supreme Olympian god, Zeus was an unchangeable, unshakable figure. We have already seen in Homer that this is far from the case. In the *Iliad*, he seems relatively young and untested, still insecure in his role as a ruler. In the *Odyssey*, he is to a certain extent metaphysically distant, virtually identical to cosmic justice, both punishing and ensuring that Odysseus arrives home at the right time. Hesiod described the succession in the world of the gods, including Zeus' path to power and his clash with Prometheus and how he later governed inscrutably but justly. The Presocratics made him more or less identical to the highest conceivable reason and world order—the only god— while Solon pointed out that no one escapes his watchful eye. Arrogance of one sort or another will always be punished, either by the criminal himself or a member of his family being struck. It is also important to notice how Zeus, as we have seen anticipated in *Prometheus Bound*, changes in the course of the trilogy, so that he appears as a different person at the end from what he was at the beginning.

Furthermore, we face the crucial interpretational problem that Zeus is one god, but gathers a large number of attributes within his figure, functions that, like radii, extend into and reflect the human world of action and motives. As in Xenophanes,[31] Zeus does not—as he did in the *Iliad*—have an anthropomorphic manifestation but acts only through the power of thought and will. It is here a great help, as I have suggested before, that some of his existential attributes are summarized with informative epithets.

In *The Persians*, we met him as a castigator of *hubris*, Zeus Kolastes. He appears as Zeus the Defender (Alexeterios[32]) in *Seven Against Thebes*. He is the god Zeus Hikesios to the suppliants and connected to the realm of the dead as Zeus Chthonios and, as Zeus Xenios, he is the protector of guest friendship. He is called "the third," as he is invoked in prayer as the third, identified with Zeus the Savior (Soter[33]), and finally he is apostrophized in *The Eumenides* as the divinity of assemblies or, rather, the social order under the name Zeus Agoraios (*Eum.* 973).

2

In the *Oresteia*, we encounter most of these aspects of Zeus' nature, actions and ways, amalgamated in Zeus Teleios, i.e. the strength of will through which—as in the Homeric epics—he achieves whatever his intention and plan is. In itself, this confirms that the universe functions in accordance with his plan as a cosmic order that in the final instance only he can control and have full insight into. The fullest description of this orderliness is found in *The Suppliant Maidens*, in which it is said: "But Zeus' desire is not easily traced/ for the paths of His mind/ maze through dusk and briers/ and my eyes cannot follow/ It falls surefooted, not on its back,/

whatever command Zeus shakes from His head/ And it flares in the dark/ and carries black portents/ that men cannot read."[34]

Just as Homer fundamentally connected his compositional awareness to Zeus Teleios as the divinity directing and fulfilling a sequence of events (for instance Odysseus' fate) Zeus the Accomplisher also becomes the deepest foundation for the *Oresteia*. In this activity, he forms the basis of the composition. And the insight that the trilogy wishes to convey ultimately consists of a coincidence between the creative authorial consciousness and the divine plan itself.

The interpretation of Zeus' multiplicity and accompanying *telos* is complicated by the fact that he is not an immutable entity but, despite his divinity, a phenomenon subject to succession, a sort of maturation process that reflects the formation of consciousness in which he participates and through which he is perceived. In the *Prometheus Trilogy*, we have been able to observe the new hierarchy of gods in embryo and, on this basis, stipulate the further development to the divine norm that Aeschylus in the *Oresteia* has made the guiding principle and result. In this sense, the description of Zeus' development in the *Prometheus Trilogy* may be viewed as a sort of prehistory to the *Oresteia*.

If we assume that Zeus is ultimately reconciled with Prometheus, if for nothing else then to avoid the fall that Prometheus has prophesied for him, then through this reconciliation and doctrine of suffering Zeus attains the level of consciousness that generally characterizes him in the *Oresteia*. Here, Zeus is no longer subject to Fate. His will governs everywhere. However, even though it is this transformed Zeus acting strictly and mercifully in the *Oresteia*, we are still faced with the fact that he also changes character during this trilogy. Indeed, from this point of view, his very transformation may be said to be part of the shift from blood revenge to the patriarchal legal system that is exercised by the Areopagus.

If the consistency and credibility of the *Odyssey*'s divine world were dependent on the protagonist's ability to endure pain and, with cunning, to retain his composure, then this fundamental step in human history from the maternal to the paternal system is made dramatically dependent in the *Oresteia* on Orestes' will to take responsibility for the worst imaginable crime—the murder of his mother. Or in other words, Zeus' over-riding project, his *telos*, over the course of the trilogy is to make himself into a purely patriarchal god—by distinguishing himself from the mother cult's world of blood revenge with which his omnipotence at the beginning of the tragedy is one and which opens the way through.

3

If it can be difficult to nail down such a radical change in Zeus' own nature, the primary reason is that he appears from the beginning of the tragedy as the cause of all things—"final loftiest Zeus" (*Eum.* 28). And it is emphasized several times that everything is fulfilled by his omnipotence. In the hope of gaining revenge on her husband, Klytemnestra calls upon Zeus Teleios with the words: "Zeus, Zeus accomplisher, accomplish these my prayers" (*Ag.* 973). "Accomplish" here is a synonym for *telos*.[35] This exclamation corresponds to the chorus' view of Zeus' omnipotence—"for what thing without Zeus is done among mortals?" (*Ag.* 1486). In Greek, reference is made directly to *Dios teleitai*. Ultimately, the "end will be destiny" (*Ag.* 67)—again, *teleitai* is used, meaning that something will be fulfilled.

Further evidence that everything that happens in life is linked to Zeus' will is that Apollo has never prophesied anything from his oracle "except/ that which Zeus, father of Olympians, might command" (*Eum.* 617-18). That is to say that Zeus' intention is enigmatically communicated through the Delphic Oracle in the Sybil's hexameters. When Apollo, and later Athene, intervenes to transform the curse of the Atreid family, this too does not fundamentally happen on its own but on behalf of Zeus and as a part of his overall goal. For the same reason, Athene does not herself take the honor for persuading the Erinyes to transform themselves but refers to the fulfillment of the underlying plan of the whole tragedy: "Zeus, who guides men's speech in councils, was too/ strong" (*Eum.* 973-74). The moment his will achieves final victory (once again, a variation of the word *telos* is used), he steps forth in a new figuration, with a new epithet indicating the nature of his achievement. He is called Zeus Agoraios, i.e. he who watches over the Athenian popular assembly and a *eunomia* of social stability.

4

The crucial thing to understand is that, until his final transformation, which is the purpose of the entire plot, Zeus acts through the *nomos* that has the effect everywhere of retribution: "It is but law that when the red drops have been spilled/ upon the ground they cry aloud for fresh/ blood" (*Lib.* 400-02). It is this law of retribution that Zeus in his wrath sends down *from above* upon mankind in collaboration with his daughter, the goddess of justice Dike, about whom it is said: "all things she steers to fulfillment" (*Ag.* 781). In other words, she is part of *telos* with its cosmic effect. But tied to the mother cults as blood revenge genealogically is, the powers of the underworld also take part in this form of punishment. *From below*, they carry out vengeance in the shape of the Erinyes, whom the victim's blood calls forth, acting at the behest of Gaia and Moira, the Earth and Fate.

That there really is an alliance of this sort between the Olympian and the much older gods of the underworld is verified by the fact that the ruler of the underworld is called the Zeus of the underworld (*Chthonios Dios, Ag.* 1386). Hesiod encouraged people to address prayers for a good harvest to this Zeus from the depths of the earth.[36] And insofar as Zeus rules all, this lower Zeus must in some way act as an attribute of the upper Zeus, as the coincidence of names makes clear. Or put another way, it reveals his chthonic dimension and origin, since Zeus, as it has been pointed out several times, grew up under Gaia's protection in a cave in Crete.

It is likewise to Zeus in this configuration that Klytemnestra presents her slain husband, saying that the third blow was struck as an offering to Zeus Chthonios, the savior of the dead: "I struck him the third blow, in thanks and reverence/ to Zeus the lord of dead men underneath the ground" (*Ag.* 1385-87). With bloody irony, she plays on Zeus' role as savior, since at mealtimes people gave Zeus Soter the third offering. The first went to Zeus (and Hera), the second to the heroes.[37] And Orestes repeats this formula before the matricide: "Our Fury who is never starved for blood shall drink/ for the third time a cupful of unwatered blood" (*Lib.* 577-78).

The close connection between the Olympian and the infernal powers in the first two tragedies of the trilogy is further emphasized by Orestes' invocation of both powers, the celestial and the infernal, on killing his mother. Moreover, the Erinyes clearly act on behalf of Zeus since, as Zeus Xenios, the protector of guest friendship, in his anger at Paris' violation of guest friendship, he unleashes "vengeance" (the Erinyes, *Ag.* 749) on Troy, while Agamemnon and Menelaos become the concrete executioners of this retribution.

5

In the *Agamemnon* and *The Libation Bearers*, Zeus is the supreme representative and guarantor of the principle of justice and retribution, *lex talionis*—"the truth stands ever beside God's throne/ eternal" (*Ag.* 1563-64)—a law requiring that "for the word of hatred spoken, let hate/ be a word fulfilled (. . .) blood stroke for the stroke of blood/ shall be paid" (*Lib.* 310-14). Life shall be paid with life, blood with blood. So the great leap in thought in *The Eumenides* is also that Zeus separates himself from the blood revenge of retribution. This primordial reality is now administered exclusively by the Erinyes, who appear as terrifying relics of the past from whom the Olympian gods, especially Apollo, turn in deep disgust.

The Erinyes themselves are aware of this repudiation. They complain that Zeus has banished them from the fine society of Olympus even at the same time as they apply the old law on his behalf. "Here we stand in our haste to wrench from all others/ these devisings" (*Eum.* 360-61), they complain and, by the "others" they can only mean Zeus. Therefore, they demand their right to kill the matricide Orestes and remain highly regarded as the true upholders of the law.

Parallel to the separation of the Olympian and chthonic worlds from each other after Orestes' murder, the Erinyes change character or, rather, they acquire character (see p. 398) and become demonic and monstrous, like the figures Odysseus meets on his voyage. This is a change that can only be understood in the context of Zeus' own transformation. If he appeared in anger in the *Agamemnon* as the offended protector of guest friendship, it is his intention through the killing done by Orestes to call forth the side of his nature that is full of *charis* (beneficence) towards mankind. All place their trust in this: "high the grace of God/ shall be exalted, that did this" (*Ag.* 580-81). And his display of mercy counterbalances human suffering—"the (gods') pleasure is not unworthy of the grief that gave it" (*Ag.* 354), chant the chorus upon Agamemnon's arrival, in the hope that things will come out for the best.

From this perspective, it may be said that, with Apollo as mediator, Zeus displays his mercy by making Orestes the savior of his family through the crime of killing his mother. For there is also the law that purification can only take place if someone from the family itself wields the knife: "Here in the house there lies/ the cure for this, not to be brought/ from outside, never from others/ but in themselves, through the fierce wreck and bloodshed" (*Lib.* 471-74). The interesting feature is also that, after the matricide, Orestes is directly described as "the savior. He came. Shall I call/ it that, or death" (*Lib.* 1073-74). This question is asked by the chorus, which has no earthly chance of divining the god's overarching plan. But the statement can only be related to Zeus as the divinity who will change and save the world—through Orestes.

By virtue of this purification and later judgment (*telos*) through which Zeus rules, the trial and acquittal of Orestes, in which everything goes according to Zeus' plan, allowing him to appear as "the all-ordaining god/ the Savior" (*Eum.* 759-60). Elektra and Orestes place their faith in him before the murder in the hope that everything will turn out well—"let Force (Kratos), and Right (Dike),/ and Zeus almighty, the third with them, be on your side" (*Lib.* 244-45), Elektra prays on behalf of Orestes.

6

After the acquittal, Orestes is no longer of significance to Zeus and he leaves the tragedy. By means of allurements and open threats, Athene then tries to persuade the Erinyes to become the peaceful, beneficent Eumenides. Only then can Zeus definitively appear in the fulfillment of his design that has been the subtext of the trilogy. And this happens when Athene praises him as the victor, as Zeus Agoraios. As said above, in this name Zeus is the protector of the popular assembly, which must be understood here in connection with the legal system in the form of the Areopagus Council that replaces blood revenge and the Erinyes, whose chthonic reality from now on becomes integrated into paternal rule.

Thus, in his omnipotence, Zeus, who guides and accomplishes, has had the intention of transforming his own legal order. This transformation is made concrete in Orestes' willingness to sacrifice, in that his purging of family guilt leads to the establishment of the new legal system of the Areopagus. And in this sense, Zeus is dependent on Orestes just as he was dependent on Odysseus' ability to endure the travails of his voyage—to return home, to purge and to establish peace. The justice (*dike*), peace (*eirene*) and *eunomia* of which Hesiod and Solon speak are also expressed in the *Oresteia* when the converted Erinyes announce that they will ensure the end of fraternal conflict ceases and the emergence of brotherly love—"let them render grace for grace./ Let love be their common will" (*koinophilei dianoia*, Eum. 984-85).

Zeus certainly guides the action in the *Oresteia*, but he is himself transformed from the wrathful deity who, in collaboration with the Erinyes, dispatched

Agamemnon on his expedition of vengeance to Troy into the god who, through suffering, has established a new world order. In sum, this means that the curse which the alternation of strife (*eris*) and love (*eros*) has been to the Greeks is annulled, but it has at the same time cleared the way for the formation of a new individual. The entire process is effectuated through the pathos of tragedy, its form of suffering, which changes from being predominantly physical in *Prometheus Bound* to take on an increasingly psychological character, constituting a precursor to a conscience-plagued intellect, the *pathei mathos*, that leads to *sophrosyne* in the requirement to know oneself.

Suffering and Learning

1

Early in the *Agamemnon*, the chorus of elders chants a hymn to Zeus. It contains the doctrine of *pathei mathos*: what is meaningful in suffering is its revelation of insight, a suffering that Zeus inflicts upon man, often for incomprehensible reasons:

Zeus: whatever he may be, if this name
Pleases him in invocation,
Thus I call upon him.
I have pondered everything
Yet I cannot find a way,
Only Zeus, to case this dead weight of ignorance
Finally from out my brain.

He who in time long ago was great,
Throbbing with gigantic strength,
Shall be as if he never were, unspoken.
He who followed him has found
His master, and is gone.
Cry aloud without fear the victory of Zeus,
You will not have failed the truth:
Zeus, who guided men to think,
Who has laid it down that wisdom
Comes alone through suffering.
Still there drips in sleep against the heart
Grief of memory; against
Our pleasure we are temperate
From the gods who sit in grandeur
Grace comes somehow violent.

(*Ag.* 160-83)

I want to begin with a brief digression on the credibility of the chorus. Since these strophes express the chorus' assessment, they must be subjected to closer analysis.

For the chorus is certainly qualified to be privy to the actual events, but they are only partially informed of them, and they rarely if ever understand them fully. The chorus often shifts opportunistically during the action, as is typical of popular sentiment, living so to speak from hand to mouth. Their great emotional shifts between fear and hope make their interpretations unreliable to some extent. However, the chorus in Aeschylus is more important for forming an opinion than is the case in Sophocles and Euripides. In the latter, the chorus is sometimes reduced to a mere evocative accompaniment. The chorus' prominent position in Aeschylus' tragedies may thus be an indication that he is still close to the origin of tragedy in the *dithyrambic* chorus—indeed, in *The Persians* and, to some extent, *The Suppliant Maidens*, the chorus are principal figures.

The chorus becomes at once participant and observer—particularly with respect to points of view determined by the action, but it can also present Aeschylus' own view of life. It is clear that, in the *Agamemnon*, the chorus has strong feelings both in its condemnation of the expedition against Troy, which it views as irresponsible, and in its anger over the soldiers who were returned home dead. Likewise, the chorus recoils in fear of the catastrophe on Agamemnon's return—which it correctly foresees. But significantly enough, the chorus refuses to become fully aware of its intuitions. On the contrary. In a sort of resignation, it seeks to know as little as possible and to take things in the order in which they occur. A typical declaration is: "the future/ you shall know when it has come; before then, forget it" (Ag. 251-52) or "Still I pray; may all this/ expectation fade as vanity/ into unfulfillment, and not be" (*Ag.* 998-1000).

In particular, this innocence appears when the chorus resists relating its knowledge of the *daimon* curse that has ravaged the Atreid family to Kassandra's prophesies in which she gathers together and presents the sins of the past and the horrific deeds to come. In short, the chorus refuses in its own present to couple the past and the future together. That this inevitable sequence of events occurs completely on its own means that the chorus' insight becomes its fate. It is gradually forced to look the facts in the face, which is why the hymn on the doctrine of suffering assumes a tone of tragic irony, because when it utters these words, the chorus has not yet learned this lesson.

Thus, on one hand, we can equate the intentions of the hymn with those of Aeschylus, but with the qualification that the chorus must learn by experience what, due to its ignorance, were only empty words. On the other hand, it is present in Aeschylus' artistic consciousness, since he is thoroughly familiar with the doctrine and has made it one with Zeus' *telos*, which is why the maxim *pathei mathos* can be applied to the entire trilogy.

In comparison with Homer, Aeschylus has taken this form of insight-creating suffering much further. In the *Iliad*, pain is known as a basis for knowledge only in the sense of learning from experience—"Once a thing has been done, the fool sees it" (XVII, 32). Quite a different matter is whether it is not possible in the *Odyssey* to see the first lesson on the path of suffering to self-insight in the hero's developmental process. It is certainly nowhere expressed directly, but just as Odysseus masters an early form of introspection, it may be asked whether his travels, travails and the cunning with which he learns to deal with his trials are a concrete demonstration of suffering as life's true teacher?

2

Returning to the hymn, we can establish that, through the chorus' chanting and partial unconsciousness, it expresses Aeschylus' vision of life. The fundamental formula—to suffer is to learn—is found throughout the entire trilogy and in so many different contexts that the formula can only refer to the implicit narrator's own view of life.

In the first strophe, Zeus' overall position of power is evoked. So elevated is it that doubts are sown as to whether he has a name at all. So elevated is he that his ways become inexplicable to humans but, according to the chorus' corresponding statements in *The Suppliant Maidens*, he is capable of comprehending everything, unshakably certain in his deeds and purposes. And it is in the awareness of resting in the hands of this inscrutable but also incorruptible, all-seeing power that the chorus finds consolation for the fear aroused by the trilogy's menacing action, a consolation that also includes the hope of redemption.

The second strophe in the quotation shows how there is an incessant drama of succession in the lives of men, where one form of law and consciousness is replaced by another, just as there have been several shifts of power in the divine hierarchy. Hesiod's theogony is clearly behind this highly stylized description of the various rulers and usurpers, including the violent changes to which the revolts contributed in the development of consciousness. Zeus is the most recent ruler and is himself part of the steady pace of development.

The *Oresteia* is thematically so permeated with the doctrine of suffering that even the Erinyes share the conviction that happiness lies in "the wisdom won from pain" (*Eum.* 520). And men may as well keep this lesson in mind, as no one is free from guilt: "There is no mortal man who shall turn/ unhurt his life's course to an end not marred./ There is trouble here. There is more to come" (*Lib.* 1018-20). Thus, the chorus laments at the sight of Orestes, when after killing his mother he is haunted by doubt, and the Erinyes "pain flowers for him" (*Lib.* 1009). And Orestes also adopts a position on this theme during his trial. He knows that the suffering he is experiencing is part of life's greater *telos*—"I have been beaten and been taught, I understand/ the many rules of absolution" (*Eum.* 276-77).

So seen overall, the process of succession and the related evolution for both gods and men are conditioned by suffering. Finding one's way in life presuppose that an individual can endure suffering, learn from life's pain and then act accordingly. This requires on the one hand a reflexive consciousness and, on the other, the ability to learn from experience, from the mistakes of which it is impossible to avoid being guilty. So the past intervenes in the present and the future as a never-resting reminder of yet unpunished crimes. As the Erinyes say of Hades: "Hades calls men to reckoning/ there under the ground,/ sees all, and cuts it deep in his recording mind" (*Eum.* 273-75). As said above, this debt to the gods is realized in time, since, as asserted by Solon, the guilt is passed down in the family until it is expiated.

In short, having suffering as a guide provides the individual with the opportunity to change his life. To begin with, this possibility can be considered a sort of grace (*charis*) from the gods' harsh reality. Second, the obvious consequence of this is that, if people behave properly, they will be redeemed by the god whose wrath they have aroused. This form of memory is, in part, retrospective remorse and, in part, progressive and fruitful in its forward-looking perspective, as it can guide and keep people on the right path. In the same way, the recalcitrant individual will be brought to his senses through the doctrine of suffering and thereby brought to moderation and salvation.

Not surprisingly, the Greek word used is *sophronein*, i.e. the *sophrosyne* that tells a person to choose the middle path of moderation. When the Eumenides bid farewell to the people of Athens, they include a salutation to this people who finally learned the way of wisdom, *sophrosyne* (*Eum.* 1000).

Hubris—The Sure Road to Perdition

1

On the basis of Aeschylus' other tragedies, we can immediately establish that the curse passed down in the Atreid family has its source in *hubris*, a *hubris* orchestrated in its full range as a blend of aristocratic arrogance, brutal violence, rampant sexuality and impious ways of thinking. It is the family's misfortune that this character is repeated in each new generation, which mirror each other in a true series of disasters which, if we include the myths, goes back to the origins of the family. Aeschylus displays only the three stages with which, as said above (see p. 348), he is operating, from offense to conciliation.

As quoted above, the basic tension between arrogance and impiousness, *asebeia*, and fortune as a consequence of a curing of the soul is expressed by the chorus of the Erinyes: "for the very child/ of vanity is violence;/ but out of health/ in the heart issues the beloved/ and the longed-for, prosperity" (*Eum.* 533-37). *Hubris* is contrasted with the healthy soul, *hygieia phrenon*.

To understand that the family's curse is not merely a symptom of the gods' random whims and metaphysical inscrutability but involves what Aristotle termed *hamartia* (error), it is necessary to see what it is in a person's character and in the actions deriving from it that is the true cause. Reckless arrogance violates the fundamental principles of life and calls down the wrath of the gods. The theme is so fundamental that we can observe its phenomenology in all the characters who have anything to say about this, including the chorus; but it appears most clearly and concretely in the character of Agamemnon.

2

At the sight of the murdered Agamemnon, the chorus chants: Who can now believe that this once so powerful and apparently blessed king had any portion of happiness? The extinction of his happiness was due to his "slakeless" thirst for fortune. In other words, he failed to control himself because much will always have more. The moral of the chorus—as with Solon—is that one cannot feel safe even at the height of one's health and ability because, metaphorically speaking, there will always be rocks upon which one's ship of fortune may founder. (The shipwreck metaphor is one of Aeschylus' favorites, often applied to a society in decline).[38] So, to stay with the image, instead of acquiring more wealth it is wiser to do the opposite and sacrifice some of one's "cargo" and come safely through the rocks.

Moderation arouses the understanding of the gods, who always keep a watchful eye on those who raise themselves highest and who, like the mountain, are the first to be struck by Zeus' lightning bolt (*Ag.* 462-74). Consequently, the members of the chorus pray that it will never be granted to them—as it was to Agamemnon—to sack a city. Happiness is an illusion, prized only by women, as it is put—implying that this is because they are so simple.

All in all, this means that no one can feel secure in his abundance (*ploutos*)—especially if it violates justice: "There is not any armor/ in gold against perdition/ for him who spurns the high altar/ of Justice down to the darkness" (*Ag.* 381-84). For the gods turn a deaf ear to those who, like Paris, invoke their protection after having committed an outrageous act. He is brought down on their command.

Likewise, Zeus hates any form of prodigality. As it is put in *The Persians*, "let no man hereafter,/ Despising what he has from heaven, turn lustful eyes/ To others, and spill a store of great prosperity" (824-26). Although Klytemnestra is wise and understands the wrath and envy of the gods, she reveals her inherent arrogance in her desire for splendor and magnificence, when she and Aigisthos have attained power—"they go proud/ in the high style and luxury of what you worked/ to win" (*Lib.* 135-37), says Elektra to her murdered father, praying that he will help Orestes to come home as an avenger. The new rulers, Aigisthos and Klytemnestra, govern as tyrants. The veneration previously shown to the king—Agamemnon did, after all, convene assemblies—is now replaced with a deep fear of the ruling couple; after the murder of Agamemnon, the country has sunk into endless darkness.

In the *Odyssey*, Kalypso reproached the gods for their envy (*phthonos*) because they would not let her keep Odysseus. In the *Oresteia*, it is too narrow to see only envy. It is a matter of a universal watchfulness for unjust arrogance that leads to the abuse of power and ultimately tyranny.

3

The family crime is defined in various terms. Kassandra describes how this *hamartia* (*Ag.* 1197) is displayed in her soul's inner mirror. From here, she summons up the images of the cruelties of the past that will reach into the imminent future when Klytemnestra murders her husband and Orestes his mother. Meanwhile, it is the chorus of elders that connects the family curse and *hubris* in the *Agamemnon*, chanting:

> But Pride (*hubris*) aging is made
> In men's dark actions
> Ripe with the young pride (*hubris*)
> Late or soon when the dawn of destiny
> Comes and birth is given
> To the spirit (*daimon*) none may fight or beat down
>
> (*Ag.* 763-71)

The guilt causes a chain reaction or a vicious circle without redemption. In this cycle, the *daimon* or *alastor*, at once evil spirit and executioner, wielding the sin and the stream of disasters following in its wake, wreaks havoc as one "offence" (*ate*) produces the next. The *daimon* assisted Klytemnestra in her murder of Agamemnon —"from his father's blood/ might swarm some fiend (*daimon*) to guide you" (*Ag.* 1506-07), the chorus laments. This must mean that she fundamentally acts as a tool for blood revenge, herself an Eriny, participating in an otherwise indeterminate divine punishment. There is also talk of a "divinity" (Ag. 1468) striking the house of the Atreids in the form of the two sisters, Klytemnestra and Helen, the first killing her husband, the second abandoning hers and being to blame for the death of many people.

To this, however, the chorus also expresses an opposing point of view, a far more optimistic belief that the vicious circle can be broken if the family can only find its way to the path of justice, i.e. a way out of arrogance. This attitude corresponds better to the work as a whole than the fatalistic elements in the compositional attitude. So it also contains a deeper truth that also points towards Aeschylus himself when the chorus says, using the first person singular:

> Far from others I hold my own
> Mind; only the act of evil
> Breeds others to follow,
> Young sins in its own likeness.
> Houses clear in their right are given
> Children in all loveliness.
>
> (*Ag.* 757-61)

The redeemer or savior the quotation implicitly points to is Orestes. As an ostracized, remorseful and self-sacrificing figure, he has the gods behind him in killing his mother. He is to become the righteous avenger with the future in front of him—as opposed to his murdered father.

4

How the family's inherited *hubris* is formed is given concrete expression through the fate of Agamemnon. However, as the tragedy starts *in medias res* on his homecoming, the revelation of his guilt and his psychological similarity to the family's earlier male members is only gradually revealed and first fully presented in Kassandra's prophetic visions. In the *Oresteia*, too, family guilt runs until the third generation. However, the *Agamemnon* contains suggestions that the arrogance associated with the family curse has far deeper roots. It is directly stated that the evil spirit has settled in "the blood of Tantalos" (*Ag.* 1469) and "this seed of the Pelopidae" (*Lib.* 503).

In other words, this inherited *miasma*, which still arouses new *hubris*, goes back to King Pelops and in the myths even further back to his father, Tantalos, which is why the family is called the Tantalids. As has already been said, the series of misdeeds has the same fundamental characteristics, which are repeated in a cycle of inevitability. Tantalos, the son of Zeus, served his son, Pelops, to the gods, whether to test their powers of observation or in shame that he did not have enough food—the explanations are divided. The gods discover it after Demeter has already eaten a shoulder. Pelops is then revived, but he remains without the devoured limb.

Meanwhile, the actual curse seems to come into the family via Pelops himself. In order to win his wife Hippodameia, he had to beat her father Oinomaos in a chariot race. Many had lost their lives, but Pelops persuades his driver Mytrilos to meddle with his wheel hub, and Oinomaos is dragged to his death. In order to hide his sabotage, Pelops is compelled to kill the driver but thereby calls down the curse on himself, and it is then passed on to the family.

5

In brief, this is a rough family even in its origins. And Agamemnon continues this pattern of *hubris* when he sacrifices his daughter Iphigenia to Artemis to safeguard his voyage to Troy after the goddess had provided breezes for the becalmed fleet back at Aulis and demanded a blood sacrifice from him. The sacrifice is the direct reason for Klytemnestra's murdering him. She says of the family *daimon* to the chorus: "Thus have you set the speech of your lips/ straight, calling by name/ the spirit (*daimon*) thrice glutted that lives in this face" (Ag. 1475-77).

At this time, Kassandra has already in her visions established the link between Agamemnon's sacrifice and earlier child sacrifices in the family. She reveals the earlier history: that Atreus, Agamemnon's father, avenged himself on his brother Thyestes for seducing his wife. Just like his ancestor Tantalos, Atreus served up the twins his wife had born to Thyestes. And Aigisthos points out that Atreus is behind the murder of Agamemnon: "it was I, in my right, who wrought this murder" (*Ag.* 1604). There are still repetitions in the family of infidelity, sacrifice and "cannibalism."

Aigisthos has seduced Klytemnestra, just as his father seduced Atreus' wife—i.e., the bloody sacrifices are woven together in sexual offenses and infidelity in a way that reveals the content of the family's *hubris* and shows that the family members do not yet have an individual fate but only the family fate they have inherited. They are predestined to it and obviously have no free will but proceed as though determined by some higher metaphysics. Orestes and Elektra assume the same fate in the matricide, but with the aim of liberating the family from its curse, as it is done on orders from Apollo, who for his part acts as a medium for Zeus and his own transformation into Agoraios, the protector of democracy.

6

This is the reason why it is always said that Aeschylus is not interested in the individual as a psychological character, as Sophocles and later Euripides are, but focuses solely on the concept of the family. Agamemnon's constitution is the result of an inherited family *hubris*, a sign that he still inhabits the same physical world of understanding as in the *Iliad*, lacking the more developed comprehension that Orestes' torments of conscience about the murder of his mother document. Agamemnon sacrifices his daughter without any subsequent feeling of guilt.

As the transitional text the *Oresteia* is, this difference between Agamemnon and his son illustrates that the trilogy contains greater spaciousness and is not merely linked to the family. Aeschylus actually seems to provide Agamemnon with a choice of options that shows that the poet has an understanding of human free will, as maintained by Zeus in the introduction to the *Odyssey*, where Aigisthos, it will be remembered, received an alternative from Zeus but chose to follow his *hubris*. The point here was that, according to Zeus, the guilt for misdeeds and misfortunes is projected back on to the gods instead of being fixed in man himself, where these mistakes rightly belong.

As Agamemnon is introduced in the *Oresteia*, he is encapsulated in the needs of the physical world and is oriented according to it in his self-realization so that he almost corresponds to the problematic hero we meet under his name in the *Iliad*. In Aeschylus, his obtuseness is conditioned precisely by the arrogant nature he shares with his forefathers. He is incapable of controlling it, much less of displaying *sophrosyne*, when his arrogance is tested. He is blind to his own motives and Klytemnestra exploits this blindness in her murderous arts of seduction when she tempts him to commit *hubris* against the gods—by stepping on to "the red carpet." He certainly fears the anger of the gods but is unable to see through her, although she has reason enough to seek revenge, just as he cannot resist the temptation to assert himself.

7

To characterize Agamemnon's violent nature Aeschylus has selected two nature metaphors, whose structural function will only be hinted at here. When he and his brother Menelaos go to Troy, they are described in an omen from Zeus as two eagles striking down and devouring a pregnant hare. One eagle is black, the other white. Although the image is not detailed, it can hardly be wrong to see Agamemnon as the black eagle, which is verified by the other wild animal metaphor. For in the conquest of Troy, Agamemnon is compared to the sanguineous ferocity of a lion. He uses the metaphor himself on his homecoming when he tells how—once the Wooden Horse gave the Greeks access to Troy—he and the army in a sort of metonymic unity went over the wall like a greedy (*homestes*) lion to "glut its hunger lapping at the blood of kings" (*Ag.* 828).

The eagle and the lion are familiar metaphors in the *Odyssey*. Odysseus is attributed with the nature of an eagle in dreams and omens in the slaughter of the arrogant suitors (20, 232), while he later walks among the corpses, soiled like a ferocious lion.

The importance (and originality) of the image in Aeschylus appears from the fact that he tells a brief independent animal parable about a man who raises a lion cub. When small, it is delightful, but it proves to have been sent to his estate by the gods to bring about devastation (*ate, Ag.* 717-26).

Judging by the context, this story refers to Helen and the destructive effect she has on Troy. Meanwhile, the metaphor can also apply to Agamemnon and the other characters who act within the same catalogue of sins. This is how Kassandra views both Aigisthos—"one that plots vengeance for this, the strengthless lion rolling in his master's bed" (*Ag.* 1224)—and Klytemnestra: as lions. Of the queen it is said: "This is the woman-lioness, who goes to bed/ with the wolf, when her proud lion ranges far away" (*Ag.* 1258-59). The wolf is Aigisthos, while Klytemnestra is later compared to a she-wolf; the lion, of course, is Agamemnon.[39]

In this way, these nature images of violence and *hubris*—eagle, wolf and lion— merge into each other and symbolically express the gory and *hubristic* reality that the characters share and in which they annihilate each other with guilty hands and blood on their lips.

Choice and Sacrifice

1

Thus is Agamemnon's *hubristic* nature. We shall look more closely at the choice he faces in sacrificing his daughter. For although he has assumed his *hubris* as a family curse and although he is sent to Troy as an instrument of punishment on behalf of Zeus Xenios, whom Paris offended in his attribute as protector of guest friendship, Agamemnon nevertheless faces a test in which he may *de facto* break with his presumption by setting his paternal love above arrogance and vanity. This would require a leap of consciousness, as it would release him from his subconscious state, which has vanity as its deepest motivation.

The problem that faces Agamemnon with this alternative is that Artemis has blocked the fleet in Aulis with a storm. To release it, Artemis requires Agamemnon to sacrifice Iphigenia. Portrayed in this way, Artemis appears as a cruel and blood-thirsty goddess. But according to the construction put on it by the seer Kalchas, the opposite is the case. In the omen portraying Agamemnon and his brother as birds of prey killing a pregnant hare, Artemis appears in her quality of a chthonic guardian (*potnia theron*) of the suckling offspring of wild animals. In the seer's interpretation, "Artemis the undefiled/ is angered with pity/ at the flying hounds of her father/ eating the unborn young in the hare and the shivering mother./ She is sick at the eagles' feasting" (*Ag.* 133-37).

On the one hand, Artemis' concern reveals the wrathful nature of her offended father. On the other, according to the *Iliad*, she is Troy's tutelary goddess, and in order to protect the city from destruction, she erects the worst conceivable obstacle in the way of Agamemnon: the sacrifice of his daughter. It is intended to put a stop to his plan of revenge. The implication is that by refusing the sacrifice, he can lift the curse from his family, which consists of the sacrifice of children. Artemis cannot give a harder twist to the screw. But Agamemnon's *hubris* is greater than his paternal feelings.

That it really is arrogance behind his decision to sacrifice his daughter is documented, if nothing else, by the fact that he never suggests that he feels forced to fulfill Zeus' vengeance. No, it is purely and simply for the sake of his honor, something that Euripides makes the primary motif in his *Iphigenia at Aulis*. For, as Agamemnon also says in Aeschylus, he cannot let down the army. He certainly feels the sacrifice of his daughter—the jewel of the house—as a heavy burden, but it apparently strikes him as even heavier to abandon his plan and lose prestige. As Ovid later puts it: Interests of state prevail over personal interests.[40]

Can I betray the fleet? he asks rhetorically, concluding: "It is right. May all be well yet" (*Ag.* 216). By this, he means to murder his daughter in order to still the wind. From that moment, he and the army are struck with the blood frenzy and passion for war, which also characterizes the massacre at Troy: "Her supplications and her cries of father/ were nothing, nor the child's lamentation/ to kings passioned for battle" (*Ag.* 227-30). And with a deeply moving empathy, Aeschylus describes Iphigenia's vain pleas for her young life. But the arrogance governing Agamemnon is heartless, only willing its own demonic self-fulfillment, where no look will any longer prevent murder.

2

As Artemis' obstruction and gruesome demand for blood sacrifice is retold through the seer Kalchas' prophetic speech, this passage is the densest and most difficult to interpret in the *Oresteia*. The rest of the text supports the view that Agamemnon is placed in a situation of choice and chooses the worst imaginable solution. While he—and, with him, the army—are drawn into a spiral of violence, those around him—i.e., the citizens who have stayed behind in Argos—have, remarkably, the opposite interpretation. They see no reasonable connection between wanting to bring his brother's runaway wife back by hook or by crook and killing his own daughter. The chorus of elders put it this way:

> When you marshaled this armament
> For Helen's sake, I will not hide it,
> In ugly style you were written in my heart
> For steering aslant the mind's course
> To bring home by blood
> Sacrifice and dead men that wild spirit
> (*Ag.* 799-804)

Yet, typical of the opportunistic nature of the chorus, it changes its tune and praises Agamemnon when he returns home victorious.

We understand meanwhile that, during the expedition, trouble has been brewing among the people. A veritable hatred of the rulers has arisen since, in order to bring back a seduced woman, they send the ashes of heroes back home from Troy in urns: "[the god of war] sent to their dearest the dust/ heavy and bitter with tears shed/ packing smooth the urns with ashes that once were men" (*Ag.* 441-44). Similarly, as a result of his arrogant expedition, Xerxes had filled Hades with Persians. Thus, the ordinary people come to feel greater pain than what Menelaos must have suffered over the loss of Helen—"the curse of the people must be paid for" (*Ag.* 457).

3

So we can establish first of all that (as God required of Abraham) Zeus demanded the sacrifice of the daughter and secondly that Agamemnon makes no reference to Zeus on making his decision. In short, this must mean that, on receiving Artemis' demand for blood, he had the option of making up his own mind and changing course, but instead he chooses to put the war and his own honor above his love for his daughter. Through the mouth of the chorus, a general judgment is pronounced on his choice and his delusion, which are due to rashness and must necessarily activate the family's evil *daimon*. For when, forced by necessity, he was faced with a choice:

> He changed, and from the heart the breath came bitter
> And sacrilegious, utterly infidel,
> To warp a will now to be stopped at nothing.
> The sickening in men's minds, tough,
> Reckless in fresh cruelty brings daring.
> (*Ag.* 220-24)

If possible, the Greek text describes his action even more clearly, as something of the utmost daring (*pantotolmos*, *Ag.* 221). The same word is used of Klytemnestra in connection with her revenge killing (*Ag.* 1237)—she dared anything. In this sense, the two are made of the same stuff. However, Klytemnestra distinguishes herself from Agamemnon in one crucial respect. In her appalling boldness, she has made herself conscious of something that remains unconscious to Agamemnon.

Blinded by arrogance, he has not understood the consequence of his sacrifice and does not see the account sketched by Kalchas. The seer calls the sacrifice demanded by Artemis "unholy, untasted,/ working bitterness in the blood/ and faith lost" (*Ag.* 151-53). With his gruesome sacrifice, Agamemnon has unleashed his wife's contempt for her husband. That is to say that Klytemnestra can no longer respect him but on the contrary must hate him. And he has thus called forth an anger that lurks there and will not forget, another expression of the family *daimon* that "returns like a sickness to lurk in the house;/ the secret anger remembers the child that shall be avenged" (*Ag.* 154-55).

4

Of course, on returning home, Agamemnon is enveloped in the belief or illusion that he has the gods on his side: "we hail you./ You have won, our labor is made gladness" (*Ag.* 806-07). So he sees as a victory the devastation he has caused like a bloodthirsty lion. And it shows his absolute unity with the physical world that he has no memory or awareness of the price: his daughter's life and thereby his own enrollment in the ranks of the family guilt and Hades' memory of spilt blood. For if we ask here what sort of reality it is to which he has subjected himself with the sacrifice, the answer must be: the bloody sacrifices of the primal mother's fertility cult.

So, like the other primal goddesses, Artemis has a latent dual meaning.[41] She is both a goddess caring for the young animals the eagles would kill; and the Great Mother, herself served by eunuch priests. Against this awesome reality, Apollo is invoked by the chorus—"Healer Apollo, I pray you" (*Ag.* 146), and it is he who finally takes up the battle against the Erinyes, who derive from the same reality.

This must indicate that, in order to accomplish what he has in mind, Agamemnon has also regressed with the sacrifice to the female primordial world, where spirit and blood are one. Two things verify this: 1) That upon his return, he is met by the same demand in the demand of blood for blood in that Klytemnestra is certainly Iphigenia's mother, but also the Erinyes of her blood. In relation to her two other children, she is an unnatural mother. 2) It is from this link to blood and tribe that Orestes ultimately redeems the family, at the same time that his own consciousness is activated as conscience.

Klytemnestra

1

It says everything about Klytemnestra's mental superiority that she not only punishes the *hubris* of which Agamemnon made himself guilty in the sacrifice of their daughter, but, with insight into his arrogant nature, she uses it to strike at him. Significantly, she sets her revenge in motion by insinuating herself into exactly where his subconscious and his muscular self-assertion are unrestrained—quite concretely in the way she greets him in the role of the longing, patient wife, as she pretends to honor him by rolling out the crimson runners or carpets on which he is to process in triumph. At the same time, she hints at what awaits him through her as the instrument of vengeance.

> Let there spring up into the house he never hoped
> To see, where Justice (Dike) leads him in, a crimson path.
> In all things else, my heart's unsleeping care shall act
> With the gods' aid to set aright what fate ordained.
>
> (*Ag.* 910-13)

Not only is this quotation remarkable in anticipating the murder but it is yet another example of how Aeschylus establishes the network of correlations in his work. For if Dike and the crimson carpet are linked, it is due to an association with an earlier point in the text. Here, in a passage reminiscent of Solon, the chorus speaks of the man who arrogantly "tramples down the delicacy of things/ inviolable" (*Ag.* 370-71) and in his quest for vast riches spurns the altar of justice (Dike) and for his *hubris* will be punished with ruin (see quotation p. 374).

This is an indirect description of Agamemnon's sacrifice and points forward to Klytemnestra's reception in which she entices him to step on to the blood-colored carpet and thereby in his *hubris* to tread upon the gods' unwritten rules, something that will inevitably unleash the punishment of Dike. These metaphorical connections are also used in *The Eumenides* when the Erinyes claim that the young gods trample upon their ancient and honorable business: blood revenge, an association that reveals the deeper context between them and Klytemnestra in her role as her daughter's Eriny.

2

At first, Agamemnon will not step on to the carpet, will not be hailed like a barbarian, since he well knows that one should fear "the wrath of heaven" (*phthonos*, *Ag.* 921). Only the gods have this supreme honor, he says, adding: "God's most lordly gift to man/ is decency of mind" (*Ag.* 927-28). But Klytemnestra knows how to stoke his vanity. She points out that King Priam would never have refused such an honor. She thereby activates the deepest layer in his consciousness, which is—as in the sacrifice—focused on the conquest of Troy. As the conversation is described here, he still lives in this past in which his violent nature revealed in the sacrifice of his daughter and his behavior towards the Trojans naturally leads to his offending the gods.

So as his arrogance prevents him from resisting the temptation, Agamemnon steps upon the crimson carpet in the vain hope that "no god's eyes of hatred" (*Ag.*

947) will strike him from afar. The fateful step is that he does it, and it shows clearly that Klytemnestra knows how to link her thirst for revenge to his deepest motivation. She moves with ease about his subconscious psychological life, whips up his arrogance, and thereby cuts him off from any possible protection from the gods as he arouses their envy with his haughty behavior, provoking their punitive anger and his own death.

3

Klytemnestra is the *Oresteia*'s most nuanced character. This is not least because she is described in two dimensions: realistically and mythically. In her realistic figuration, she even has contemporary relevance. For while women in Homer are generally not seen as oppressed, Klytemnestra becomes an exemplar of the subjugation of women, which began with Hesiod's misogyny and had a counterpart or anticipation in Odysseus' intimidation of Kirke in his fear of being "castrated." This theme will be examined in more detail in connection with Euripides and Plato, where it is described how women in democratic Athens were the object of unheard-of repression in the course of men's attempt to establish masculine sovereignty. It also seems to be an underlying theme for the systematic shift from maternal rule to paternal rule in the *Oresteia*.

Klytemnestra does not conceal that a tangible feeling of humiliation also plays a role in her revenge upon her husband. For she lists him as being guilty of the following offenses: first, he left her for many years on account of his brother's wife; then he killed their daughter to ensure the success of his expedition; whereupon (as it appears in the *Iliad*) he took lovers at Troy to satisfy his intense carnal desires. And it once again reveals Agamemnon's arrogance and fatal lack of understanding of her situation and character that he brings along Kassandra as the spoils of war—and his mistress.

4

From a "feminist" point of view, it may be said that Klytemnestra's unfortunate fate is to be born a woman. In a way, this makes it reasonable for those around her to interpret her nature and power through masculinity, as she is in every sense superior to the men with whom she is linked: her husband Agamemnon and her lover Aigisthos.

For the ten years of Agamemnon's absence during which she has controlled the throne, she has demonstrated that, in terms of intelligence and the ability to act, she is inferior to no man. She has "a lady's/ male strength of heart" (*Ag.* 10-11). The chorus praises her power—"I have come in reverence, Klytemnestra, of your power" (*kratos, Ag.* 258). She is actually a contrast to the timorous chorus in *Seven Against Thebes*. Their lamentations made Eteokles rebuke them though at the same time renouncing the powerful (*kratousa*) woman who can never be satisfied.

Klytemnestra, if anyone, is an incarnation of just such a *kratousa*.

Her speech has the grace of a man's (*Ag.* 351). With the cunning of Odysseus, she lures her husband into the trap and, afterwards when the chorus threatens her, she demonstrates a rare courage, raising herself up in all her female *kratousa*: "You try me out as if I were a woman and vain; / but my heart (*kardia*) is not fluttered as I speak before you" (*Ag.* 1401-03). And this courage she preserves to the end, when she meets her murderer in her son Orestes, shouting: "Bring me quick, somebody, an axe to kill a man" (*Lib.* 889). This is a woman who will defend herself like a lioness to her last drop of blood.

Cunning as she also is, meanwhile, she consistently tries to underplay her superiority and pretends that the man, in this case a particularly feminine and weak Aigisthos, is the leader. When she learns that Troy has fallen, she expresses the hope that it has happened without any of the gods being offended, for it requires fortune to return home. But, she adds, full of implicit meaning: it could also happen that the ghosts of the dead awoke, thinking of Iphigenia and her own blood revenge. Yet, she immediately plays down her role. When she seeks to stop Aigisthos and the avalanche of blood revenge after the slaying of Agamemnon, she says: "Thus a woman speaks among you. Shall men deign to understand?" (*Ag.* 1661). And later, she says to Orestes, whom she has not recognized but on the contrary believes to be dead, that he must take his message to Aigisthos: "if/ you have some higher business, more a matter of state,/ that is the men's concern" (*Lib.* 670-72).

As the tragedy reveals right from the start, Klytemnestra is the equal of any man—and better than most. On the one hand, this is undoubtedly due to her possessing masculine qualities such as the power of reason and action. But on the other hand, she also reveals her mythical femininity in this psychological constitution. For in her absolute power (*kratousa*) we find a strong reminder of the strength possessed by Antikleia and the Phaiakian queen Arete and which made them even mightier than their respective husbands, although they were kings. These men were still at a transitional stage to the independent man, just as Agamemnon in his warrior's brutality acts within the sphere of chthonic, primordial femininity and ends as the victim of a woman. In this respect, Klytemnestra is the demonic version of Arete and Antikleia, whether this is due to the factual circumstances or to her character.

In her unprecedented audacity, Klytemnestra is characterized as someone with the boldness to dare anything, even the worst deed (*pantotolmos*), an expression—as said before—that puts her in the same category as Agamemnon, when he pushes aside all doubt in sacrificing his daughter. This very species of *hubristic* audacity, termed "the high daring in the will/ of man" (*Lib.* 594-95), is contrasted with a corresponding audacity in the woman, but in her case linked to a no less ruthless sexuality—to which I will return shortly.

Furthermore, Klytemnestra is said to be of exactly the same disposition as her sister Helen, the personification of woman's blind desire (*Ag.* 1470-71). Hence, she must have both the masculine and the feminine at her command to the utmost extent. It explains her power, which is confirmed by the epithets with which she is attributed. She is called "the woman-lioness" (*Ag.* 1257), which shows her unobstructed and sanguineous ferocity in which she is not inferior to Agamemnon. Her daughter Elektra identifies her with a she-wolf and when she stands over the bodies of Agamemnon and Kassandra, she is called a "carrion crow" (*Ag.* 1472).

To these traits must be added a number of related characteristics that demonstrate her unprecedented audacity. After the murder, she breaks out in blasphemous jubilation at having given Agamemnon the third, fatal blow, like a sacrifice to Zeus Chthonios; she is sadistic in her treatment of Kassandra, and her language abounds with obscene connotations. But the strength of her intelligence, her indisputable *metis*, we see primarily during her seduction of Agamemnon. She uses a net in the actual murder, which may be seen as an image of her cunning, a cunning that in the *Odyssey* corresponds to Penelope's weaving, which belongs under the category of *metis*.

5

When Kassandra anticipates the course of events in her prophetic visions, she uses a surprising image: "Keep from his mate the bull" (*Ag.* 1125). The curious feature is that there seems to be no doubt that Klytemnestra is the bull, Agamemnon its mate. For the following lines run: "the folded web's/ entanglement she pinions him and with the black horn/ strikes" (*Ag.* 1126-28). Her horn is taken from the image of the bull, which is why Aeschylus must necessarily have imagined her as the bull.

But how should such an unnatural image be explained? The only interpretation that seems to elucidate the significance of the image relates to the chthonic primal mother. As said above, female revenge assumes a masculine character in the form of dragons or wild beasts. It is into this context that Klytemnestra as an avenging bull with black horns must be fitted, just as a vicious bull kills Hippolytos in *Hippolytos*. It is made quite clear when Euripides has the wronged Medea in her desire for revenge cast an ominous look at her sons—like a mad bull (*tauroumenen*, 92), a look filled with destructive, primordial female anger. Finally, the connotations of the bull with the chthonic are supported by the fact that in *The Bacchae* Dionysos appears as the bull-horned god (see p. 489) and by the Minoan bull cult.

In other words, when a woman is violated, as both Klytemnestra and Medea are by their men, or when the blood bond is broken, as when Agamemnon sacrifices his daughter, the primordial feminine rises up in its demonic, destructive forms. It is from this same reality that the snake-like Erinyes arise. That Klytemnestra is really seen as her daughter's Eriny emerges at several junctures. So Kassandra identifies her with a poisonous snake (*amphisbaina*, *Ag.* 1233), an identification that appears again in *The Libation Bearers* when Orestes has killed her, when she is compared to "water snake, some viper" (*Lib.* 995) and the chorus lauds the fact that he stepped on the snake's head.

It is also a sign that the family reproduces itself in each other that Orestes himself is described as a snake. Klytemnestra dreamed that she nourished a snake in her bosom. This is, in fact, the reason why she begins to make sacrifices to Agamemnon at the beginning of *The Libation Bearers* in the hope of being able to placate the dead. Confirmation that it is Orestes she has seen in her dreams and that he views himself as a snake comes just before the act of vengeance itself, when he says, "I turn snake to kill her" (*ekdrakontotheis*, *Lib.* 549) and in this form he will carry out the blood revenge on his mother.

Deep down, the snake must be linked with the blood of the murder victim who calls for revenge from the underworld, as it is apostrophized again and again in various versions: the chthonic, Gaia and the dead father. For example, Elektra prays: "Hear me, Earth. Hear me, grandeurs of Darkness" (*Lib.* 399). In this sense, the snake is also connected to the Erinyes. After the killing, Orestes sees in his inner eye a group of women with snakes twisted around their heads: "They come like Gorgons, they/ wear robes of black, and they are wreathed in a tangle/ of snakes" (*Lib.* 1048-50). And when Kassandra calls Klytemnestra a snake, she identifies her with none other than Skylla herself—"Viper double-fanged, or Skylla witch/ holed in the rocks and bane of men that range the sea" (*Ag.* 1233-36). In Greek, she is called "a Hades-mother" (*Haidou meter*, *Ag.* 1235), which even more strongly emphasizes her connection with the underworld.

6

The long and short of it is that, in Orestes' struggle with his mother, we are presented on the archetypal level with the basic mythical conflict between the primal mother and the wicked, rebellious son who wants to free himself from his maternal origin. Aeschylus has been perfectly aware of this, as is shown by the fact that Orestes is proclaimed to be Perseus—"Yours to raise high within/ your body the heart of Perseus" (*Lib.* 830-31), chants the chorus. He must identify himself with the descendant of Hypermestra and Lynkeus, whose task, guided by Athene, was to conquer the fearsome mother figure in the gorgon form of the Medusa. So when Orestes is compared to a snake and to Perseus, we see here a dual idea unfolded— that he has inherited his snake nature from his mother and, as his father's avenger, he liberates the male sex from the dominance of the primordial mother.

If we summarize Aeschylus' identification system, Klytemnestra appears as Skylla, a mother from Hades, Medusa herself, whom her son Orestes, in a configuration with Perseus (and Odysseus/Skylla), kills. He thereby once again brings light into the family and society—and liberates himself for a higher consciousness. The fact that as her daughter's avenger Klytemnestra is really conceived as an Eriny reveals the text's own latent identification. Orestes says that it was his mother "of the dark heart" (*Eum.* 460) who murdered Agamemnon. The Greek word used here (*kelainophron*) is applied directly to the Erinyes, when they are called "the black Furies" (*kelainia*, *Ag.* 462). Her identification with the Erinyes is also expressed when she calls on them during the murder (*Ag.* 1433), while the net she uses is said to be woven by the Erinyes (*Ag.* 1580-81).

Finally, because of the net, she is described as a spider—"Caught in this spider's web you lie" (*Ag.* 1492). Together with the images of her as a she-wolf, a lioness and a snake, this gives an indication of the extent of her nature, since the spider has a special meaning, suggesting the primordial conflict between the feminine and the masculine, as it is well known that the female spider consumes the male after coupling.

So throughout this range of imagery, Aeschylus shows that, in the act of revenge, she merges with the fateful, nature-determined and gory exercise of maternal power in the primeval world. For when she exultantly proclaims her murder of Agamemnon, it is in a series of images whose depth is incomprehensible unless interpreted on the basis of the primordial feminine:

> Thus he went down, and the life struggled out of him;
> And as he died he spattered me with the dark red
> And violent driven rain of bitter savored blood
> To make me glad, as gardens stand among the showers
> Of God in glory at the birthtime of the buds.
>
> (1388-92)

In this description, Klytemnestra must at the same time be viewed as the Earth drinking blood, a goddess of the Earth and vengeance, who has called forth the stream of blood that is nourishing like rain. The quotation confirms that, in her vengeance, she has so to speak been transformed into the violent, murderous primordial nature that she also was in the form of an attacking bull.

However, Klytemnestra defends herself against Orestes on the plane of reality by claiming that "Destiny had some part in that, my child" (*Lib.* 909). Agamemnon died as he deserved: "with the sword he struck,/ with the sword he paid for his own act" (*Ag.* 1528-29), she claims, alleging that throughout the killing she sought to expiate the family curse—possibly evidence that, through the suffering of catastrophic events, she has achieved insight. And on this basis, she declares herself ready to conclude a pact with the evil *daimon* and never to bear a fate so hard: "let him (the *daimon*) go forth to make bleed with death/ and guilt the houses of others" (Ag. 1573-76). But inofar as it can be said that Klytemnestra participates in the family's expiation of guilt, it happens in an awkward manner: she kills her husband and is killed by her son, a queen of the night and sister to Helen.

Helen—the dialectic between *eros* and *eris*

1

The curse in the family is due to *hubris*, a graceless arrogance, but, as in the Homeric epics, the source of the *daimon* that wreaks havoc with the family and sows discord is to be sought in the erotic, in sexuality. And more clearly than in Homer and in agreement with Hesiod, Aeschylus assigns the destructive nature of sexuality explicitly to women. The chorus in *The Libation Bearers*, consisting of Trojan women, claims that, just as excessive audacity (*hypertolmos*) characterizes men, women are controlled by "all-adventurous passions" (*pantolmous erotas*, *Lib.* 597).

Neither, of course, leads to any good. The audacity of men leads to *hubris*. Women's misguided desire, on the other hand, wrecks the relationship between the sexes, as sexuality has the same power over the woman as over the animal: "The female force, the desperate/ love crams its resisted way/ on marriage and the dark embrace/ of brute beasts, of mortal men" (*Lib.* 598-601). And as in the *Odyssey*, there is listed a whole gallery of women who in their wayward sexuality have been guilty of the ultimate crime. Reference may be made here simply to the fact that the Atreid family curse, as described in the *Oresteia*, arose when Atreus' wife Aerope deceived her husband with her brother-in-law Thyestes. This unleashed a fraternal conflict in which Atreus served up Thyestes' children to their father, something which, in turn, led to his son Aigisthos seducing Klytemnestra and participating in the murder of Agamemnon.

2

For Aeschylus as for Homer (and many other poets), Helen becomes the archetype of the danger of female desire. This emerges from the following verses, in which her sexual criminality and the element of strife are compared:

Alas, Helen, wild heart
For the multitudes, for the thousand lives
You killed under Troy's shadow,
You alone, to shine in man's memory
As blood flower never to be washed out. Surely a demon then
Of death walked in the house, men's agony.

(*Ag.* 1455-61)

In the Greek, the word for "demon of death" is *eris*. Thus, Helen, with her sexual violation of marriage, unleashed the bloody strife that led to her sister killing Agamemnon because he sacrificed Iphigenia—in order to bring Helen home. The circle is closed.

For, even though Paris is the seducer, the interpretation of sexuality as demonic is linked primarily to the female, to Helen, the bitch as she is repeatedly called by different poets—and by herself in the *Odyssey*. It is described how she stole away with her dowry and brought destruction to Troy (*Ag.* 403 ff.). In the same context, Aeschylus tells his fable of the lion cub that is fed and cared for but grows up to be a predator, laying waste to those around it.

3

There are at least two explanations for why Helen's sin, her violation of the marriage bed, is viewed as the worst crime imaginable. Of course, it diminishes a man's reputation that he has been unable to control his wife and—what in a family society is just as bad—it raises a fundamental doubt about the identity of the biological father of the offspring, who are to continue the family and its wealth. In the underlying myths, the Atreid clan is teeming with children of unclear paternity, a confusion of incestuous relationships and complications that clearly demonstrate the chaotic forces of sexuality.

A woman's danger lies in the fact that, in a very special way, she masters sexuality and has thereby a fatal, binding power over men. Although physically stronger, he is here the weaker party. It is said of Helen that she is "the blossom that breaks the heart with longing" (*Ag.* 741). And her erotic power weaves such a spell upon Menelaos' mind and senses that, after her disappearance, he completely loses the desire to live and dwindles to a shadow as he seeks her everywhere; he becomes a man "where in the emptiness of eyes/ all passion has faded" (*Ag.* 418-19). In this respect, she, if anyone, becomes an example of *eros thanatos*, sexuality as a death urge.

While with his sexual escapades, including his bringing Kassandra home as the spoils of war, Agamemnon demonstrates that it is obviously not a problem for men to have lovers, the opposite is not the case. So it is necessary to tie women to the *sophrosyne* that in *The Suppliant Maidens* comes from the father's view of reason as a sexual restriction. Klytemnestra's inclusion of Agamemnon's infidelity in her detailed catalogue of his sins is an interpretation that is not shared by the unfaithful husband. It costs him his life and is evidence that she is every bit as unwilling as a man to tolerate such humiliation.

4

Since Helen and Klytemnestra are claimed to be so similar in nature, we might say that the portrait of Helen as a femme fatale also paints a picture of Klytemnestra's dauntless sexuality. Just as Helen deceived Menelaos, so she deceives his brother Agamemnon with his cousin Aigisthos. Moreover, Klytemnestra claims that she has nothing to fear as long as Aigisthos "makes the fire shine on my hearth" (*Ag.* 1435), an expression that, along with similar statements, is intended to demonstrate her obscenity. Their relationship is based less on love than a mutual hatred of Agamemnon. For as Aigisthos is described, he is far from being a man equal to her or one who can measure up to Agamemnon; the chorus says of him: "So then you, like a woman, waited the war out/ here in the house, shaming the master's bed with lust,/ and planned against the lord of war this treacherous death?" (*Ag.* 1625-27).

To this must be added his vanity and, it almost goes without saying, boundless arrogance. He corresponds to the suitors who filled Odysseus' house and is a sort of caricature of Agamemnon. He allows Klytemnestra to carry out the murder, but when he wants to punish the chorus she stops him with the words: "There is pain enough already. Let us not be bloody now" (*Ag.* 1656). She hopes in this way to stop the blood vengeance that, in the shape of Orestes, is standing at the door.

However, the sagacity she presupposes in a ruler is limited. She and Aigisthos at all events rule as tyrants with an extravagance that brings down an ominous darkness over the country, pregnant with the fear of the people and the never-failing causality of blood revenge.

The Untrustworthy Seer

Of course, it seems to be as a consequence of personal insight that Klytemnestra is able to manipulate her way into Agamemnon's subconscious. At the same time, it is an insight that harks back to the special world of knowledge to which she has access as a woman—a knowledge that is fundamentally bound to the mystery of creation, to the fecundity of the Earth, conception and blood. This is discernible in the Delphic Oracle, which originally belonged to Gaia and other fertility goddesses. And the chthonic metaphors that surround Klytemnestra's character emphasize her relationship to this reality, a perspective thrown into even greater relief through Kassandra and the Erinyes.

When Agamemnon, full of himself, steps into the house on the crimson carpets, the drama shifts in a tension-building crosscut to Kassandra. Through her vision of horror, the impending murder and its prehistory in the family are laid out. If she has knowledge of all this—of which Agamemnon is unaware and which the chorus does its best to deflect—and is able to see into the future, it is because, according to her myth, Apollo has granted her prophetic powers. As punishment for refusing to surrender herself to the god, her soothsaying will never be believed, as was also the case when she predicted the fall of Troy.

Aeschylus, however, goes somewhat deeper by having her visions come from the same world as the Erinyes and the Moira, the goddesses of fate: the eternally remembering Earth. Thus, Kassandra proclaims that the guilt of the family is imprinted in her soul. The blood of those killed has seeped into the earth from which she draws her visions. "Through too much glut of blood drunk by our fostering ground/ the vengeful gore is caked and hard, will not drain through" (*Lib.* 66-67), as the chorus of Erinyes says. Her consciousness simply acts in congruence with the process of chthonic memory when she says the guilt of the family is written into her soul. Her visions arise directly from the earth into which the blood from those killed has seeped, just as in principle she draws on the same primordial consciousness from which the prescient Prometheus acquires his knowledge of Zeus' possible fate and the oracle its auguries: the Great Mother goddesses, Gaia and Themis.

By having this "inscription of blood" rise up as visions in her mind, Kassandra is able not only to foresee the murders of Agamemnon and herself but, with the memory of past sins contained in the vision, she can see and point to the premise for all this—the feast Atreus served to his brother. This means in short that Kassandra links Atreus' feast, Agamemnon's sacrifice, and the murder of him. But as part of the seer's ability, bound to the Earth and the realm of the dead, a gift which Teiresias also possessed (which of course is why Odysseus was to visit him), she can reach so far into the future that Orestes, too, is revealed and made visible in the mirror of her soul as the one who in time will atone and free the family from the succession of sacrifices for which, through her visions, she has created the inner cohesion:

> (. . .) We two
> Must die, yet die not vengeless by the gods. For there
> Shall come one to avenge us also, born to slay
> His mother, and to wreak death for his father's blood.
> Outlaw and wanderer, driven far from his own land,
> He will come back to cope these stones of inward hate.
> For this is a strong oath and sworn by the high gods,
> That he shall cast men headlong for his father felled.
>
> (*Ag.* 1280-85)

With her prophecy, she breaches the framework of the *Agamemnon* within which she herself is murdered and takes the story of atonement to the trilogy's middle play on Orestes' matricide.

The Matricide

1

Will Orestes return "to come to judge them (*dikasten*), or to give them punishment (*dikephoron*)?" (*Lib.* 120), asks Elektra. The chorus responds bluntly: "to kill them, for the life they took" (*Lib.* 121), i.e. as an avenger. In this way, he will inevitably enter into the family's series of revenge killings, as his father demands retribution and rages against the murderous couple—"under earth/ dead men held a grudge still/ and smoldered at their murderers" (*Lib.* 39-41).

But even if by virtue of his inheritance Orestes comes to act in obvious extension of Agamemnon's arrogance and his mother's snake-like nature, there is the crucial difference that Orestes acts both consciously and under compulsion from Apollo: "The big strength of Apollo's oracle will not/ forsake me. For he charged me to win through this hazard" (*Lib.* 269-70). While in Sophocles' tragedy *Elektra*, portraying the same sequence of events, Apollo only informs him how he must kill his mother—by employing cunning as she did— the god intervenes far more violently and willfully in Aeschylus' version. If Orestes does not do as he is told, the god will ensure that he is not only pursued by the Erinyes that arose from his father's blood but that he will be struck by madness and ultimately die— banished, despised, and friendless. On the other hand, if he kills his mother, he will be persecuted by her Erinyes. He is thus faced with a dual problem in that, regardless of what he does, he will do wrong.

Once again, Aeschylus uses a crosscut to achieve the dramatic effect in *The Libation Bearers*: Orestes is sent home by Apollo to murder his mother. At the same time, his mother dreams she has given birth to a snake, offering her breast to it (*Lib.*

527). As said above, the dream fills her with such fear that she sends the chorus of Trojan women to offer libations at Agamemnon's grave to take the sting out of the ominous dream.[42] The vengeful Elektra, who is longing for her brother's return, asks the chorus whether the offering may be turned against the queen herself, and this prayer is answered.

The Argos to which Orestes returns is shrouded in a heavy darkness into which it is his task to bring light. Of the palace, viewed as a collective metaphor for the country's situation, the chorus says: "Sunless and where men fear to walk/ the mists huddle upon this house/ where the high lords have perished" (*Lib.* 51-53). This darkness is the result of tyrannical rule, the still unavenged murder of Agamemnon, and the fact that Klytemnestra has not given her murdered husband a dignified burial. And while she herself lives in extravagant luxury, she has betrayed her children. The nurse Kilissa has been in her place, saying: "darling Orestes! I wore out my life/ for him" (*Lib.* 549-50).

Here, we once again encounter the doubling of the maternal role that we observed in the *Odyssey* between the nurse Eurykleia and the biological mother Antikleia. In relation to Orestes and Elektra, Klytemnestra reveals herself to be "the evil mother." Not only has she made her children fatherless, but the royal couple now hate and persecute them. This is confirmed by the scarcely concealed delight with which they receive the false news that Orestes, the potential avenger, is dead.

Orestes is guided in his vengeance by Apollo and consideration for his dead father, but he is also personally motivated on account of the misery he himself has had to endure—"the loss of my estates wears hard on me" (*Lib.* 301).

2

So although Apollo may be said to be the instigator of the blood revenge—ultimately, it is Zeus—the punishment comes from the underworld. For like Klytemnestra, Orestes and Elektra call at the same time upon the Olympian and the chthonic forces to avenge the blood that has been spilt. As Elektra says in her prayer: "Hear me, Earth. Hear me, grandeurs of Darkness" (*Lib.* 399). This must moreover mean that, since they repay evil with evil, Elektra and Orestes, like Klytemnestra, acquire the character of Erinyes and daimonic beings. And they acknowledge this heritage in their action of retribution.

Thus, Elektra identifies herself with her mother, calling herself a wolf—"born from the savage mother" (*Lib.* 422), while Orestes views himself as the snake with which the mother is also compared and which she has dreamt will kill her—"I turn snake to kill her" (*ekdrakontotheis, Lib.* 550), and he solemnly promises that the Erinyes shall not lack blood.

The act of vengeance itself takes place under the cover of deception: Orestes appears as a foreign messenger bringing the news that Orestes has met his end. His mother Klytemnestra feigns grief, but it is a relief for her that Agamemnon's potential avenger can no longer be counted among the living. In Homer's use of Orestes as the ideal mirror figure for Telemachos, he apparently only kills Aigisthos, but it is indirectly understood that he may also have killed his mother, as she and her lover are both buried on the return of Menelaos (see p. 65). What is still hidden in the *Odyssey* (perhaps, to make Orestes' ideal status as elevated as possible) becomes the primary theme in Aeschylus.

Yet, although the siblings see themselves as a she-wolf and a snake in their roles as avengers, bearers of the family's catalogue of sins, they appear very different from their parents. This is, of course, the condition for their gruesome deed leading to atonement. In their revenge, they are perpetually tormented by profound doubts: "If you know any better course than mine, tell me" (*Lib.* 105), Elektra implores the chorus, just as the brother and sister constantly seek help from the higher and lower gods and from their father. Elektra, for example, says: "Such is my prayer, my father. Hear me; hear" (*Lib.* 139).

3

Aeschylus actually presents an Elektra different from the one Sophocles and Euripides introduce later. There, she is devoid of *sophrosyne* and at one with blood revenge—"one cannot/ be moderate and restrained nor pious either,"[43] she proclaims directly in Sophocles. In *The Libation Bearers*, on the other hand, she asks, "for myself, grant that I be more temperate of heart than my mother; that I act with purer hand" (*Lib.* 140-41). Orestes displays the same reticence, wishing that he could escape the dual problem with which the god has faced him. As he puts it, echoing Telemachos (see p. 138): if only his father had been killed at Troy, then the Atreid family would have won a great reputation: "If only at Ilium,/ father, and by some Lycian's hands/ you had gone down at the spear's stroke,/ you would have left high fame in your house" (*Lib.* 345-49). This is a thought not shared by Elektra. She believes that his death would have pleased those who killed him and who themselves deserve death.

It is remarkable that Elektra and Orestes always use the term "they" about the guilty parties, i.e. their mother and Aigisthos. On the other hand, they constantly call their father—father. That is to say, they try to avoid using the explosive word: Mother. Not until the act of revenge does the word appear, when she directly addresses Orestes as her son and, with her exposed breast, reminds him who suckled him. His humanity is expressed at the moment of the killing. For while Agamemnon is deaf to the pleas of his daughter at the sacrifice, Orestes loses the initiative and names his mother for the first time, *mater.* "What shall I do, Pylades? Be shamed to kill my mother?" (*Lib.* 899). His friend replies with his only lines: "Count all men hateful to you rather than the gods" (*Lib.* 902).

4

In a dramatic parallel to Klytemnestra's gloating over the bodies of Agamemnon and Kassandra, Orestes stands over the bodies of Klytemnestra and Aigisthos, in witness to the deed, raising towards the sun the net in which his father was caught and killed. But he does not feel the same triumph as his mother. On the contrary, at the very moment when he provides evidence of the justice of his victory and revenge, his thoughts begin to go in the opposite direction. He begins quite simply to doubt whether his mother was guilty. Yes, she must have been, the bloodstain proves it!

On reflection, a light rises within him, not the light of liberation, but a light from inside at the thought that he has made himself a participant in the family curse, even in the worst imaginable way—as a matricide. This makes his mind flicker in the light of madness: "my rebellious senses/ bolt with me headlong" (*Lib.* 1023-24). With his inner eye, he sees his mother's Erinyes gather around him, a vengeful pack of hounds that only he can see: "You cannot see them, but I see them" (*Lib.* 1061), he says to the chorus—a way in which Aeschylus indicates that the Erinyes are not just an external phenomenon but something psychological, a preconscious stage of conscience. Euripides clearly stressed this endogenous trait in the tragedies of *Orestes* and *Iphigenia at Tauris* by having Orestes suffer from repeated attacks of madness, directly referring to his attacks as the mind's own acknowledgement of guilt (see p. 475)—that is to say as pangs of conscience.

The unity of blood and spirit has so far been the existential foundation of the family, a mythical and concrete reality to which Zeus and the Erinyes belonged as upholders of the law of retribution, *lex talionis*. This unity is now being broken. For whereas Agamemnon in his arrogance acted as a physical force of violence without any pangs of remorse, not even when he killed his daughter to promote his ambition, Orestes finds it nightmarish, and the murder of his mother haunts him with tormenting visions.

Whatever suffering he must endure in this state, however, means that he is in the process of developing thoughts of a more complex character. His spiritual life, understood as the guilt and pain of acknowledgement, is separated from his blood bond and is individualized in his dawning conscience. Indeed, it is this personally experienced pathos or form of suffering that Aeschylus in *The Eumenides* raises to the status of a universal drama. For through Orestes' murderous deed, Zeus similarly breaks away from his bloody, primordial coexistence with the Erinyes and the interpretation of blood revenge they maintain, while these hate-filled shadow figures, having arisen from the underworld by the victim's cry for retribution, are transformed into the charitable Eumenides.

5

Orestes himself says of his act of revenge that "my victory is soiled" (*Lib.* 1017), using the Greek term *miasma*—i.e., "blood guilt" or pollution by which the killer is contaminated by the victim and requires purification. He hastens to Delphi, so that Apollo can undertake the ritual purification—with blood.

The enormous significance that Aeschylus attributed to *miasma* shows how far he has moved away from Homer for whom *miasma* plays a very small role. As said above, Telemachos can without further ado take the prescient murderer Theoklymenos on board his ship. He is not unclean, just as Oedipus in Homer's account continues to rule even after the discovery of his marriage to his mother. In Homeric times, cleanness was mainly a physical question: washing one's hands before a sacrifice, for example. However, Odysseus has a true purification ritual carried out after the slaughter of the suitors: "Bring me brimstone, old dame, the cure of evils, and bring me/ fire, so I can sulphur the hall" (22, 480-81). Even in Hesiod around 700 B.C., it must be assumed that *miasma* is not yet a crucial phenomenon, as he makes no mention of the concept in *Works and Days*.

No unambiguous explanation can be given as to why the notion of *miasma*[44] becomes so important in the fifth and fourth centuries B.C., as is documented by the tragedians. It can be imagined that the intense awareness of *miasma* is linked to the shift from the prevailing physical and concrete collectivity to an increasingly spiritualized, individualized world in which the influence of external forces, as in the case of Orestes, now acts as a more or less internalized psychological reality. As the individual is thrown back on himself, his own reason and judgment, and his inner life, there is a shift in focus outward: the world becomes more difficult to take in and understand and human intentions are dark and dangerous—something that Euripides in particular specializes in describing with his "nihilism" of values.

In Aeschylus, this shift in focus is sensed in Zeus' distance and in the passages in which the chorus has no idea what to think or believe as Zeus is at once strict, merciful and inscrutable, as is implicit in the words of the hymn: "Zeus: whatever he may be, if this name/ pleases him in invocation,/ thus I call upon him" (*Ag.* 160-63). So bearers and creators of culture such as Odysseus, Orestes and Oedipus are forced to find themselves on the path of suffering, where everything depends on their own integrity, strength of will and ability to make judgments.

Without going into more depth, we can still ascertain that we are looking at a crucial development from a culture based on *shame* to one based on a true sense of *guilt*.[45] As we have seen, shame for Homeric men is generally connected to a sense of honor. The subject feels humiliated at being captured and observed in painful, degrading situations. Hence, Odysseus can shame the army when it retreats. That is to say, it is impossible to conceive of shame without a consensus between the individual and those around him. A sense of shame arises when a person in a given situation is conscious of the contempt he inspires by his action or lack thereof. Such awareness unleashes self-hatred and he has the choice of suicide or the hope of regaining his honor.

While this kind of shame still exists over time, a consciousness of guilt is also formed, which in Orestes' case presumes the gradual independence of the subject. The self is not only held to account before an external judgment but develops a sense of justice effective as an internal judge, regardless of whether or not the rest of the world knows of the violation. However, ever since Anaximander, people were of the opinion that the gods were compelled to impose punishment if the cosmos was to preserve its harmony.

And, as said above, Solon was the first in the transitional phase to make the fundamentally simple observation, or at least to use it existentially, that such punishment may skip a generation only to break out suddenly and savagely again, like a genetic disease, a *miasma* in full flower. It was an experience that called for rules and regulations, leading to a general furor for purification by fire and water to prevent plague from breaking out and striking at random.

6

In the brooding darkness that hangs over *The Libation Bearers*, there is after all a longing for atonement and the hope that Kassandra kindled with her prophetic presentiment of Orestes' revenge. The chorus links this hope to him after the matricide:

> Light is here to behold.
> The big bit that held our house is taken away.
> Rise up, you halls, arise; for time grown too long
> You lay tumbled along the ground.
>
> (*Lib.* 961-64)

But the chorus is too quick off the mark, subject as it is to the euphoria and delusion of the situation. Shortly after this, they have to admit: "Dismal the death that was your ending./ He is left alive; pain flowers for him" (*Lib.* 1007-08). Once again, the chorus changes its mind in parallel to what happens on the inner stage of the tragedy.

When the chorus concludes with the question: "Where shall the fury of Fate/ be stilled to sleep, be done with?", the answer is to be found in the last part of *The Eumenides*, in which, after his purification at Delphi, Orestes is acquitted by the court Athene establishes at the Areopagus. On an individual level, it is a path of suffering for Orestes, but it is a path he takes as the third savior, one where, in an identification with Zeus the Savior and Perseus, though a snake himself, he has saved his family by treading on the head of the snake and ending the family curse.

The *lex talionis* of Blood Vengeance

1

It is perceptive of Aeschylus on the one hand to connect the feud in Argos and its resolution with the establishment of Athenian law, and, on the other, to furnish the Erinyes with a physical appearance they had never had before, and finally have them merge with the Eumenides, or Semnai as they are properly called.

The Erinyes, depicted as vindictive, menacing forces in *The Eumenides*, reveal the dark side of the chthonic matriarchal cult. They know only one answer and that is blood for blood in a spiral of retaliation which they enforce along with the Fates, their sisters, and Dike. Even in Heraclitus, the Erinyes appear as an element in the divine justice needed to maintain the universe when he writes: "The sun will not transgress his measures. If he does, the Furies, ministers of justice (Dike), will find him out" (*CK* XLIV; *DK* 94).[46]

It is also clear in the *Agamemnon* that they act at the behest of Zeus and ensure that the guilty are suitably punished: "The spoiler is robbed; he killed, he has paid./ The truth stands ever beside God's throne/ eternal: he who has wrought shall pay; that is law" (*Ag.* 1562-64). *Lex talionis*, the law of retaliation. However, parallel with the fulfillment of blood revenge through the murders of Agamemnon (for sacrificing Iphigenia) and Klytemnestra (for the murder of Agamemnon), the unity of familial blood and spirit is sundered when the Olympian gods and the forces of the underworld ordained to take blood, the Erinyes, confront each other—with the transformation of the Erinyes into the Eumenides as a consequence.

2

In *The Eumenides*, we meet the Erinyes at the sacred stone *omphalos*, which stands at the center of the oracle. Orestes has sought refuge here to be purified by Apollo, a purification in which blood is cleansed by the blood of sacrificial animals. The Erinyes snore loudly, their breath has a poisonous stench, and tears of blood run from their eyes.

The very description of the appearance of the Erinyes signals their affiliation with the underworld—"black and utterly repulsive" (*Eum.* 51). Aeschylus' view of these beings has an impact on posterity. In Homer, they are not yet personalized but are goddesses of wrath who correct interference in the natural order, including breach of oath, and they punish wrongs against parents. For example, Telemachos feared that his mother's Erinyes would persecute him if he married her off against her will. It is also as a personification of wrath against breaches of the law that the Erinyes appear in the *Agamemnon* and, in part, *The Libation Bearers*.

Not until after the killing of Klytemnestra do they seriously begin to take shape as her Erinyes. In his mind's eye, Orestes sees them, arriving in a flock with blood dripping from their eyes (*Lib.* 1057-58). In his account, Aeschylus has clearly drawn on descriptions of the Gorgons—that is to say, Medusa and her two sisters— wreathed in a tangle of snakes.[47] Even the priestess of Delphi sees them at first as resembling the Gorgons but concludes that they are different after all. Aeschylus also draws on certain traits of the so-called Keres that we met in Homer as true goddesses of death, which Zeus uses as "weights" in the scales of Fate (see p. 107) and which Telemachos threatens to set on the suitors. The Erinyes and the Keres both appear in Hesiod, but merge to some extent.

According to Hesiod, the Erinyes are the children of the Earth, conceived by the blood from Uranos' severed member;[48] but in Aeschylus they are the progeny of the Night.[49] In the *Shield of Herakles* (which tradition has handed down in Hesiod's name), the Keres have an awesome appearance reminiscent of Aeschylus' vampire-like Erinyes. For as the Erinyes themselves say in *The Eumenides*, they follow the blood trail of Orestes, whipped up by the smell of his blood, and they lasciviously look forward to sucking the blood from his limbs, until finally, abandoned, cast out, joyless, he ends up "blood drained, chewed dry by the powers of death, a wraith, a shell" (*Eum.* 302). They also paralyze their victims with a song of enchantment (*Eum.* 306), just as Kirke and Medusa did.

In short, the chthonic origin and nature of the Erinyes is confirmed by many things: Night is their mother (*Eum.* 416), and they reside deep in the underworld. Apollo says they dwell in Tartaros (*Eum.* 72) whence they rise up to carry out their bloody handiwork. With bow taut, he commands them to depart to the barbaric world of Persia, where bodies are tortured; they belong in such a "bloodthirsty lion's den" (*Eum.* 193), it is said with yet another reference to the central lion metaphor. And in the same way as Agamemnon took Troy with blood on his lips, they are described as vampires.

<h1 style="text-align:center">3</h1>

If the Erinyes are described in such barbaric terms in *The Eumenides*, it must be evidence that not only has Zeus has distanced himself from their bloodthirsty reality but that Aeschylus himself has changed his view. The fact of the matter is that the Erinyes in the *Agamemnon* and *The Libation Bearers* merely enforce the law of the old world, which still holds sway. They are clearly frustrated that they are no longer supported and honored for their work and try to elicit understanding for the necessity of it. The Erinyes are only acting as they have always done and have been compelled to do.

They point desperately to the fact that they act as the protectors of the old order in cooperation with Zeus and Dike and they claim that, from the dawn of time, they have carried out a "privilege primeval" (*Eum.* 393), granted them by Fate, Moira, and that in fact they thereby spare Zeus the trouble of undertaking the necessary blood revenge himself. So the Erinyes feel violated by the young gods, whom they claim trample upon their honorable work (as the *hubristic* Agamemnon did on sacred custom and the crimson carpets): "We/ drive through our duties, spurned, outcast/ from gods, driven apart to stand in light/ not of the sun" (*Eum.* 385-88).

At the same time, our knowledge of their chthonic affiliation with blood and the (primal) maternal is deepened. For if the Erinyes did not persecute Klytemnestra for the murder of her husband, it is precisely because she did *not* murder a blood relative—"Such a murder would not be the shedding of kindred blood" (*Eum.* 212). This is in contrast to Orestes, the matricide. Her blood "drives me on [to vengeance]" (*Eum.* 230), as the chorus of Erinyes says.

In their blood-running eyes, the matricide is the most terrible of all crimes, as of course it is the very principle of blood that is violated, nature's biological bond between mother and child—"His mother's blood spilled on the ground/ can not come back again" (*Eum.* 261-62), and this loss of blood will never be forgotten, since the god of death himself keeps records. In that sense, it is a lawful and organic process:

> It is but law that when the red drops have been spilled
> Upon the ground they cry aloud for fresh Blood.
> For the death act calls out on Fury (Erinyes)
> To bring out of those who were slain before
> New ruin (*ate*) on ruin (*ate*) accomplished.
>
> (*Lib.* 400-04)

In condensed form, Aeschylus here describes the vicious circle of blood revenge, for the writing that blood draws on the earth can never be erased. Why? Because the violated soul of the murder victim is in the blood, and the blood is drunk by mother Earth, who bears within her the principle of fertility: reproduction and creation in the broadest meaning of the terms. This is fundamentally the essence of familial blood ties. When the blood of the murdered person sinks into the Earth, into Gaia, the goddess viewed as the origin of everything—"Earth, mother of all things" (*Lib.* 44)—then the sleeping Erinyes are awakened by the seeping, guilt-infested blood. And from the darkness of the maternal womb, they rise as an avenging, ever-mindful, primal feminine force that knows only one answer: blood for blood.

In this reality, blood and spirit are one; but when Orestes offends against this unity by murdering his mother, he cuts himself off from the family and makes himself, as it is put in *Oedipus the King*, an enemy of the family (see p. 432). At the same time, however, in his awareness of sin he forms the seeds of his subjective self. As it may be seen even more clearly in Sophocles, this takes place in the form of suffering, which Aeschylus considers to be the way to insight and *sophrosyne*.

The Principle of Father Power

1

For the same reason Apollo, the god who has imposed on Orestes the murder of his mother, is difficult to interpret. As said above, he acts as an extension of Zeus, whose will speaks through the oracle. We may thereby infer that both gods are working within the framework of the old chthonic system: blood revenge.

This link is all the more apparent as far as Apollo is concerned because Aeschylus allows himself a liberty in relation to the better known myths dealing with Apollo's takeover of the shrine at Delphi. It is here depicted as a perfectly bloodless succession in which the sacred spot is handed down from Gaia via Themis and the Titan Phoibe, a daughter of Uranos and Gaia, all mother goddesses, to Apollo, who receives the oracle at birth. In honor of Phoibe, he bears the epithet Phoibos, the Shining One.

The accepted succession story—which, for example, Euripides uses in *Iphigenia at Tauris*—tells the opposite story on in which Apollo came from Delos and took possession of the oracle by an act of violence in which with his bow he killed the sentinel Python (a counterpart to the Erechtheus serpent in the grotto of the Parthenon), described by Euripides as a "serpent with bright scales/ And blood-red eyes, a creature born of Earth."[50] And in the *Hymn to Apollo*, in which Apollo also arrives from Delos, the snake is called "the bloated, great she-dragon."[51] As a punishment for killing the serpent, Apollo was forced wander about Thessaly and later, as an act of atonement, established the Pythian games, corresponding to the Nemeian and Olympic games.

This version of the myth can doubtless be interpreed as showing how the descendant of the Olympian father god with patriarchal power at his disposal, symbolized by the bow and arrow, took possession of the original mother cult in killing the earth-snake, the Python. The bloody act demands a penalty to assuage the violated primordial forces, just as he appoints a priestess to pass on the cryptic knowledge that still rises from the depths of the earth. This sort of confrontation does not take place in the *Oresteia* or, rather, it takes place in the course of the tragedy. The original harmony between the chthonic and Olympian gods in which the Erinyes act together with Zeus—Orestes calls on both worlds in his revenge—shows the process of development. Harmony leads to conflict and, ultimately, to reconciliation.

2

As previously pointed out, Apollo has two origins: Crete and Delphi, the two poles in his development. As an infant, Zeus, it will be remembered, was taken care of by Gaia in a cave in Crete. Apollo has the same genesis, lost in primordial times. Both are a part of a matrilinear line, because both are born of mothers. So it must be in his Cretan guise that Apollo takes over the oracle in a peaceful succession.

It is first as a representative of the Olympian father god that he kills the serpent and breaks the mother cult's original right to the oracle. He then takes up his position in Delphi and is met by Dionysos, who similarly has a chthonic origin but has been brought in under the new patriarchal principle, so that the two gods together stretch from earth to heaven but still, to a greater or lesser extent, retain traces from their time as fertility gods—like, for example, Zeus Chthonios, who according to Hesiod was a part of the fertility rites. This origin must be behind Apollo's demand that Orestes should shed his mother's blood and his more than tense relationship and rivalry with the Erinyes.

This becomes if possible even clearer when we consider how Athene associates with these powers of the underworld. Paternally born, she represents their true antithesis and by virtue of her *metis* treats them with deference—and implied threats. Consequently, it is also clear evidence of Apollo's transformation that he is not linked to his blood sister, the mother goddess Artemis, but to Athene. Together, they constitute a unity, *phratriai*,[53] and, as such, belong under Zeus as the father god, just as the familial, fraternal relationships that constituted the original *phyles* after Cleisthenes' reforms ultimately included all the citizens of Athens. Even in the *Iliad*, this "fraternal" and patriarchal trinity of Father Zeus, Athene and Apollo (XVI, 97) is invoked.

That is to say that Apollo's developmental history originates in the fertility cults, but he ends up as the guarantor of the religion of Olympian paternal power. In the *Oresteia*, he does not fight this battle for transformation of the system and himself with the Python at Delphi but he fights instead with the Erinyes. Even though they call him a young god, his nature has much in common with them, including the requirement of blood revenge, which is why it is also up to Athene to undertake the true transformation of the underworld goddesses of revenge. Apollo also uses her birth from the head of Zeus as an argument that the father is the true progenitor, a point of view with which the god (and Aeschylus) releases the individual from the familial bond of blood and blood revenge, bringing the individual into the law and practice of paternal right.

3

Meanwhile, it is quite crucial that it is Athene who must resolve the conflict between Apollo and the Erinyes. Indeed, as said above, his struggle with the Erinyes becomes a parallel to the original myth of how he broke with the mother cult by killing the Python and establishing the oracle on the basis of his own radiant consciousness. This action is displaced by Aeschylus with the establishment of the Areopagus Council. That is to say that through blood revenge, Apollo has, so to speak, acted his way into the maternal world—in order to assert the new masculine awareness of right, whose highest exponent—paradoxically but logically enough according to the text's own consistency—becomes a woman, Athene, as she is the only one born of a man. She can thus do what Apollo cannot, because in his genealogical ambivalence he is too much a part of the old reality against which he is rebelling.

But when Orestes presents his case to Athene, it is not so as to be cleansed of his *miasma*—Apollo has already done that. He does so to be acquitted by gods and men. In this context, Athene really is one of the young gods against whom the Erinyes rage, as is stressed by her ignorance: she simply does not know them and asks who they are. They identify themselves as chthonic powers: "We are the gloomy children of the Night" (*Eum.* 416). But unlike Apollo, Athene immediately understands the importance of *not* quarrelling with these atavistic forces. It puts her in a dilemma. She neither can nor will judge Orestes. On the other hand, she cannot chase the Erinyes away since she realizes that they will then inflict an everlasting crop failure on her people, the Athenians—in which case, "the venom of their resolution will return/ to infect the soil, and sicken all my land to death" (*Eum.* 478-79).

Therefore, the solution is to do both: to acquit Orestes and to transform the Erinyes into the Eumenides, so they can be integrated into the new community governed by law as the forces for fertility they potentially are, for they belong to the earth. It is already a semi-victory for Athene, when she persuades them to allow her to pass a valid judgment by pointing out to them that they should rather seek justice than blindly pursue their goal. But since she herself is in great doubt, she does not wish to pronounce judgment but chooses the best among the men of the city, "to make clear where in this action the truth lies" (*Eum.* 489).

4

The legal arguments themselves, which take place before the Areopagus Council on the Hill of Ares in Athens, lead to a heated duel of words between Apollo and the Erinyes, as defense and prosecution respectively. The true theme of this argument is the relationship to the chthonic and the breakaway from it, as is confirmed when Apollo, opposed to the demand for blood revenge on a matricide, establishes a law for a new age in which the spiritual pact between two spouses is placed higher than the blood bond. Even at the first encounter with the Erinyes at Delphi, when they defended Klytemnestra's murder by arguing that she did not kill someone of the same blood, Apollo's reply anticipates the outcome of the trial with a reference to the marriage of Hera and Zeus: "for married love between/ man and woman is bigger than oaths, guarded by right of nature" (*Eum.* 217-18).

During the trial, he expands on this view, arguing that a woman like Klytemnestra has killed a heroic man in a humiliating fashion. And in his emphasis on the spiritual pact between man and woman, including the requirement that the wife should honor the marriage bed and her husband as a clear marker of the prerogative of paternal rule, Apollo plays his trump card. He simply redefines the laws of nature and the claim of maternal rights on the biological relationship between mother and child. His assertion is that the woman is to be viewed only as a sort of vessel; she is "only the nurse of the new-planted seed" (*Eum.* 649)—no, the progenitor is the man: "The parent is he who mounts" (*Eum.* 660). And as proof that the man, without a woman's help, can be a "mother," he points out that Athene was born from her father.

On this basis, that is to say in confirmation of paternal rule, Athene herself votes for Orestes' acquittal, making reference to her own origin:

> There is no mother anywhere who gave me birth,
> And, but for marriage, I am always for the male
> With all my heart, and strongly on my father's side.
> (*Eum.* 736-38)

Athene is the tutelary deity of the city—a position which, as said above (p. 133), she received in a conflict with Poseidon, an event that must also reflect how Athens chose paternal rule over the chthonic cults that Poseidon as god of the sea represented. Against this background, Athene does not hide the fact that, for her, the case against Orestes has a higher goal: to give the Athenians a court that can always judge in murder cases. She asks them all to be silent, so that everyone can "learn/ the measures I have laid down into the rest of time" (*Eum.* 571-72). However, it is not until after the trial, but before the verdict, that she provides more detail as to the contents of the new law, which by the nature of things must consist of a general liberation from maternal rule.

So it is no coincidence that the Areopagus Council takes its seat on the Hill of Ares. Here, Theseus defeated the Amazons, who sought to conquer the city. According to mythology, they wanted to retake their queen Hippolyte, whom Theseus took prisoner and made his wife during his expedition together with Herakles to capture her belt. In this respect, Theseus becomes a sort of heroic analogy to Perseus and his struggle against Medusa. For in Theseus' victory over the wild, barbarian female warriors, there is an anticipation of the victory over the Erinyes and what they symbolize, as paternal rule replaces maternal rule. In Athene's words: "I establish this tribunal. It shall be untouched/ by money-making, grave but quick to wrath, watchful/ to protect those who sleep, a sentry on the land" (*Eum.* 704-06).

The democratic element in the law, which from now on is to bring strength and growth, depends on whether tyranny or anarchy is to govern—"No anarchy (*anarchos*), no rule of a single master (*despotoumenos*). Thus/ I advise my citizens to govern and to grace" (*Eum.* 696-97). This institutionalizes a political way of thinking reflecting the contemporary political situation in which despotism flourished in Argos and Sparta, while at the same time Aeschylus warns against the consequences that may arise if the Areogapus Council's aristocratic dominance is too radically limited by the democratically-minded Ephialtes (462 B.C.). It was a political initiative that Aeschylus not unreasonably feared would lead to lawlessness, as indeed happened some thirty years later after Pericles' death, as will later be seen in our discussion of Thucydides' history.

5

It can be said that, at the prospect of such political chaos, Aeschylus makes a crucial concession to the Erinyes: the importance of citizens retaining their fear or awe of the gods and state institutions. During the trial, the Erinyes argue for the necessity of the very terror they arouse, which maintains the world order and ensures proper behavior: "Should the city, should the man/ rear a heart that nowhere goes/ in fear, how shall such a one/ any more respect the right?" (*Eum.* 522-25). With this, Aeschylus sought to oppose the impending anarchy and mob rule on the one hand and the possibility of tyranny on the other.

Athene also speaks of the necessity of fear as a central element in the new law. But fear is now to be the guiding principle invoked by respect for the elevated court of the Areopagus and a fear of acting impiously: "Here the reverence/ of citizens, their fear and kindred do-no-wrong shall hold" (*Eum.* 690-91). Just as crime is now subject to and determined by an external court, governed by men, there is also a consequential internalization of external law. From now on, each individual must stand to account before his own sense of justice.

As evidence that primordial law's union of blood and spirit via Orestes' process of development has led to a separation, the inner person himself thus becomes the setting for a trial. This occurs in the form of the conscience-like voice and sense of justice that all men should develop and by which Orestes himself is struck when after the matricide the Erinyes take possession of his consciousness with insane visions.

6

When Orestes is acquitted by an equal split of the votes, his significance for the radical shift from maternal to paternal rule is at an end. Together with Apollo, he leaves the stage to return, cleansed and acquitted, to Argos as savior and ruler. Nevertheless, the change in system has taken place as a result of his spirit of self-sacrifice to which is linked insight via the path of suffering. Not to put too fine a point on it, his biological parents have been replaced with new parents, connected to the strengthening of his will and his superior awareness: Athene has the role of mother, Apollo the role of father. That Aeschylus writes Orestes into the political situation of his day also explains that, as the ruler of Argos and in gratitude for his acquittal, he concludes a pact with Athens as a defense against Sparta.

In the context of the chronology in the *Agamemnon*, we have made a remarkable move forward in time—from a prehistoric mythical age to the current political world of reality. This is anticipated at an early stage of the trial when Orestes promises, if acquitted, "to stand [Athens'] staunch companion for the rest of time" (*Eum.* 291). From a political perspective, two things can be concluded on the basis of this: 1) Orestes has liberated Argos from the tyrannical rule that Aigisthos and Klytemnestra imposed on a people that in its need to rebel against this government heralded *demos-kratos*, the power of the people. 2) This is apparently already a reality in *The Eumenides*, as Athens obviously only has one ruler, Athene, and is otherwise led by a political council.

In this sense, the *Oresteia* works temporally in several dimensions. On the level of the action, the trilogy spans a relatively small number of years; on the political level it compresses a development taking several hundred years from monarchy to tyranny to popular government. And finally, the tragedy is inserted into an even greater and more indefinable period of time stretching from the start of maternal rule in primordial times to its replacement by the democratic court at Areopagus.

7

Although the trial is formally concluded, the dispute with the Erinyes and their form of life is not yet resolved. On the contrary, the forces of the underworld are furious at the decision, feeling that the primeval law of blood revenge, *lex talionis*, has been mocked by the young gods—and threatening to "breed/ cancer, the leafless, the barren/ to strike, for the right, their low lands" (*Eum.* 784-86). So the dramatic focus now shifts to Athene's attempt to persuade them to join the new order of existence that she has established with her court. Their acceptance and accompanying transformation are quite simply the condition for their continuing role. In an empathetic and cunning way different from Apollo, she approaches them, gentle and persuasive but with threatening undertones.

First, she flatters them by saying that her wisdom is far from comparable to theirs, as they descend from the dawn of time. On the other hand, she is—and here, she threatens in turn—the only one who knows the key to the room in which Zeus' devastating bolts of lightning are to be found. The implication is that if they do not behave, they will be forever cast into the primordial darkness of Tartaros below Hades whence they come.

Calling upon Peitho, the goddess of persuasion, Athene—like another Odysseus—manages with honeyed words, "in the sweet beguilement of my voice" (*Eum.* 886), to persuade the Erinyes finally to transform themselves. An anticipation of this change could be seen in the fact that they went along with the case being submitted to Athene. But even before this, their potential for such a conversion has been suggested, when they emphasize that they serve a higher law that not only includes blood vengeance but also punishes those who sin against "god or guest/ or hurt parents who were close and dear" (*Eum.* 270-71).

As a consequence of this latitude in their enforcement of justice, which also explains why they can even work with Zeus and Dike, they are also to serve the new legal system. Athene explains that their old honor as avenging goddesses is replaced by a new, no less honorable significance. In brief, they are to grant her city and its citizens fertility in the broadest sense of the word: with seeds in the field and in the mothers' wombs. Indeed, as the chthonic forces they are and remain, they must ward off any evil coming from the underworld. In the case of war, however, Athene herself will see to the protection of Athens.

These are obviously prospects for the future that attract the Erinyes, who must also realize that they have no choice. So their previous threat to lay waste to everything is exchanged for a promise to enrich everything in cooperation with the goddesses of fate. They promise that the sun's gentle rays will make the earth "break out wave/on wave of all the happiness life can give" (*Eum.* 924-25). In other words, they still derive their power from the earth. And they also retain their wrathful nature, still coming down hard on anyone who acts arrogantly without wanting or being able to free themselves from the sins of the fathers. This is consonant with Athene's own thought that awe must guide the citizens' sense of justice.

And just as Athene establishes a court from which patriarchal law is to govern, she creates a home for the Erinyes in their changed form: "In the primeval dark of earth-hollows/ held in high veneration with rights sacrificial" (*Eum.* 1036-37). The fact that the place is referred to as being in the underground emphasizes its chthonic significance. And here it is significant that, although they are now protecting spirits for all Athens' citizens, both men and women, it is torch-bearing girls dressed in purple robes like the women at the Panathenian festival, girls from Athene's own temple, headed by the goddess, who guide the Erinyes to their destination in the cave near the Areopagus or down in the chasm itself.

8

In the paean to them, the Erinyes are called in Greek Semnai (*Eum.* 1041), the most venerable, which shows that on this point as well Aeschylus has created his own personal myth, merging the Erinyes with the fertility cult and the goddesses who under the name of Semnai were worshipped in such a cave near the Areopagus.[53] The Eumenides are never mentioned in the text, so the title is undoubtedly a later invention. Indeed, as a matter of pure fact, the Eumenides were never worshipped in Athens but in Colonus, a small suburb of Athens, described in *Oedipus at Colonus* (see p. 446), and other places on the Peloponnesus.

Finally, it is a curious proof of the chthonic phenomenology of the Semnai that the prominent noble family, the Eupatridae, were forbidden access to the cult, because this family was known for its worship of the patriarchal Apollo.[54]

This might indicate that, despite the integration of the fertility gods, including Dionysos and Demeter, which the tyrant Peisistratos had orchestrated in the 6th century B.C., a strict demarcation was upheld between mother and father cults, respectively. And this is also noted by Aeschylus in *The Eumenides*; for, despite the reconciliation between the chthonic and the Olympian gods, there is still a clear acknowledgement of the upper and lower worlds, heaven and earth.

The idea of *telos* (which in the *Oresteia* has promoted insight, linked as it is to the doctrine of suffering), has been shown to have the aim of divesting itself of its original identification with the Erinyes and blood vengeance, of separating blood and spirit, the female from the male, but in an act of transformation in which a cosmic solidarity and division of labor arise. Under this patriarchal law, incest has become a more or less hidden taboo, since this form of sexuality predominates in sexual relations between mother and son/lover in the mother cult.

Athene does not form part of the original primordial femininity to which both Zeus and Apollo belonged. She is motherless and born of her father, whereas children at this earliest stage of development were born of their mothers and fatherless (see p. 92). That Athene has this dual role implies that she, if anyone, can act as a mediating figure between the old and the new reality and there develop a future harmony. As a theological (and teleological) phenomenon, she is, so to speak, the divine projection of this necessity.

9

The distribution of powers in itself is a result of Zeus' achieving his will. In Athene's words: "Zeus, who guides men's speech in councils, was too/ strong" (*Eum.* 973-74). In Greek, Zeus is now called Agoriaios, his epithet indicating his role as protector of the popular assembly on the square (*agora*). More specifically, it becomes a definition of how in his *telos* as a spiritual reality he has stepped out of the wrathful world of blood revenge and is now, as Agoraios, the supreme guarantor of a law-based social life among Athenian citizens. At the same time, with Athene's intervention, he has ensured that the city flourishes in both its crops and the lives of its mothers through the beneficence of the Eumenides.

This entire change in system is confirmed by the fact that Zeus as Agoraios assumes the role that previously belonged to Themis, whose link with the earth is emphasized in *Prometheus Bound*, where Themis is identified with Gaia (see p. 361). Likewise it is she who she rules over the assemblies in Homer and is invoked by Telemachos at the assembly—"I supplicate you, by Zeus the Olympian and by Themis/ who breaks up the assemblies of men and calls them in session" (2, 68-69). Even Zeus in the *Iliad* seems to have recourse to her when he wants to assemble the gods: "But Zeus, from the many-folded peak of Olympos,/ told Themis to summon all the gods into assembly" (XX, 4-5).

Meanwhile, Homer generally assumes that Themis, as the personification of this universal law, will ensure that popular assemblies take place in the right spirit. Exactly what she signifies is not specified until Hesiod, who lets her conceive Dike, Eirene (peace) and Eunomia (the social order) by Zeus.[55] If Zeus as Agoraios takes over after Themis, a clearer signal cannot be given that the city's life, its peace, its justice and social governance have been incorporated into a purely patriarchal sphere of power, as he is not a god of the earth but of the *polis* and politics.

This could also be put in another way: the victory means that good conflict takes the place of evil conflict. This leads to some sense of brotherly love in which everyone can be united, as the Erinyes have formulated it directly: "Let them render grace for grace./ Let love be their common will;/ let them hate with single heart" (*Eum.* 984-86).

Like the *Odyssey*, the *Oresteia* concludes with a utopia of the same character as Hesiod's and Solon's conception of a happy society based on *eunomia*. In both Homer and Aeschylus, it is Zeus and Athene who establish this order. And whereas Odysseus, subject to harsh necessity, was the first to walk the path of suffering and liberation, Orestes in the *Oresteia* also attributes to it manly courage and the spirit of sacrifice. He submits his fate to the will of the gods, as do the characters in Sophocles more than in any other poet. How and why we shall see in the following.

XVI
SOPHOCLES*

Metaphysical Indeterminacy
1

AS WAS THE CASE WITH THE OTHER TRAGEDIANS, BIOGRAPHICAL INFORMA-tion on Sophocles is sparse, mythologized and difficult to verify. Nevertheless, we do know with certainty that he lived to an old age of around 90 (496–406 B.C.). Tradition has it that he was a charming person, unusually harmonious in his way of life, a man of ideals who, among other things, acted several times as *strategos* (general).[1] He was the son of an affluent armorer, born at Colonus near Athens, where in his last tragedy he has Oedipus laid to rest in the grove of the Eumenides as the protector of Athens. Sophocles may himself have been revered as such a protector under the name of Dexion, serving for a period as a priest of Asclepios when he granted the latter's cult temporary abode in his house during its move from Epidauros to Athens.

If this data are compared with the theology in his works, there is no doubt that Sophocles was of a religious disposition, but it is difficult to ascertain the nature of his personal belief. On the other hand, it is possible to make clear the fundamental theological patterns in his tragedies. Although they were developed over a great number of years, they have a uniform expression that is revealed across a variety choruses, characters and times.

So, in pinning down the constituent elements in his works, I want first to describe his general view of the relationship between gods and men and then go into detail regarding his view of human psychological development through a close reading of his most important tragedies. I will also interpret the hidden contemporary criticism that clearly bears traces of a utopia in his tragedy, *Philoktetes*.

---

*Trans. note: Except as otherwise indicated, all quotations of Sophocles' plays are from English translations in *The Complete Greek Tragedies* (Univ. of Chicago Press).

2

Sophocles is known to posterity for having introduced the third actor in the dramatic repertoire. Along with this, however, it is more important that he abandoned the trilogy. Instead, Sophocles focuses his plays on a single protagonist, which in itself points towards a material shift in the tragic view of the world, just as the third actor becomes necessary as a part of the psychological analysis he is attempting since the actors now function as a mirror to each other.

When Aeschylus needed the trilogy, the reason was simple: his intention was to describe the gods' display of power in a family and its generations, but by this also to achieve reconciliation between gods and men with a view to establishing a new world order. So for him personally, it is less about character than about the collective, while in his tragedies, it is always possible in the causality of blood guilt and the implacable *lex talionis* of retaliation to follow the motives of the gods and to ask the question *why*. By way of contrast, the causal effect in Sophocles is shifted to the question of *how*.

3

As Sophocles generally speaking makes no use of inherited (blood) guilt as a cause and explanation, the true scene of the tragic consequently moves to the individual, placed at the centre of a tragedy. The tragic fate becomes visible in the dramatic sequence in which the tale of suffering unfolds, while a certain form of dramatic irony rests on this because only the gods know the plan for the life in which the hero, in the grip of his illusions, is enveloped. But for the acting subject, as can most clearly be seen in the case of Oedipus, suffering provides the opportunity for achieving self-insight.

At the same time, the hero's character is reflected in the contrast to the other characters. This can be a negative reflection, as Kreon is to Antigone, Odysseus to Philoktetes, or the opposite: Odysseus as a positive counterpoint to Ajax. But the family curse still haunts the Oedipus plays, the *Antigone* and the *Elektra*, as these tragedies are linked to the families in Thebes (the Labdakidae) and Mycenae/Argos (the Atreidae).

This is to say that, for better or worse, these heroic figures bind the narrative of the tragedy together. Their fates are inseparable from their character, just as their strength and powerful position paradoxically lead to their no less spectacular fall. So even though their characters are individually drawn, the actors nevertheless become archetypes of the suffering hero and the uncertainty of life as such—an uncertainty that is ultimately due to the fact that the distance between the gods and the human world has become insurmountably great and impossible to interpret.

4

As we have seen earlier, the reality of men became to a considerable degree separated from that of the gods in the transition from the *Iliad* to the *Odyssey*. The

Olympian forces were not present to anything like the same energetic extent in the *Odyssey* as in the Trojan War. The result of this was that prophecies, omens and visions came in as sources of information by which to interpret the intentions of the gods. The divine powers make their presence known through these channels. Indeed, as we shall see, from this point of view, *Oedipus the King* deals primarily with the truth of Apollo's oracle. Despite the gratitude the honorable citizens in the chorus feel for Oedipus as the savior of the city, they thereby indirectly pray for his destruction as king and human being in order to preserve the god's credibility.

The magnificent feature is that Sophocles has conceived Oedipus, for example, in the context of metaphysical indeterminacy. And the radical quality of such an interpretation is supported by the fact that the other tragedians who deal with the same material link the misfortunes to a chain of provable offences against the gods.

Thus, in Aeschylus' *Seven Against Thebes*, King Laios has been warned three times by Apollo not to have children if he wants to save his kingdom, but he cannot control his senseless desire and unleashes the devastating curse on the family. In *The Phoenician Women*, which has largely the same theme as Aeschylus' play, Euripides gives no fewer than two explanations of why things go desperately wrong for Oedipus and his family (see p. 464). Perhaps we can see in this an expression of the "realistic" author's need to establish a clear cause and effect. Both authors suggest why things happen, and the actual causes are defined. Sophocles, on the other hand, writes in an intangible metaphysical space, allowing the will of the gods to appear in the pattern of events and to set limits for human beings.

In Sophocles, there is the same uncertainty regarding the gods as in the hymn to Zeus in the *Oresteia*, though the chorus in the *Antigone* believes that no wonder in the world is greater than man—"many the wonders but nothing walks stranger than man" (*Ant.* 332). Man is great in having subjugated both the sea and the earth, since ships plough the seas as the plough turns the soil—an image of the enterprising appropriation of nature. But high above mankind are the gods in their sometimes inexplicable cruelty. Only true heroes can bear their misfortunes, because they can most often be traced back to their own psychological constitution, while at the sight of these catastrophes the choruses, who are on the general human level, pray: "May destiny ever find me/ pious in word and deed/ prescribed by the laws that live on high" (*Oed.* 862-66).

5

The god is everything, man nothing, in Sophocles' religious universe. Odysseus puts it this way explicitly in the *Ajax*: "We are dim shapes, no more, and weightless shadow" (*Aj.* 125). On the other hand, it is said countless times that the gods never age. Forever young, they live by their laws and actions—for example, Zeus: "unaged in time/ monarchy you rule of Olympus' gleaming light" (608-09), as the chorus exclaims in the *Antigone*. As in Aeschylus, here, too, Zeus is the supreme power, an omnipotent ruler who has created the laws and purposefully enforces his hidden intentions.

As Teleios, the accomplisher, Zeus "oversees all things in sovereign power" (*El.* 175). These words appear in the *Elektra*, which together with *Oedipus the King* most clearly illustrates the idea that Zeus unfolds the purposiveness of his nature through time, as we have touched on before (see p. 342). Indeed, it is said that time in itself is "a kindly God" (*El.*, 178). Thus, it was also time that ultimately caught up with Oedipus and brought his crimes into the light of day—"time who sees all has found you out/ against your will" (*Oed.* 1215).

It is in time that Zeus realizes Fate and builds bridges between gods and men, and in this resides its healing power. Or put another way: justice works in and with time as a medium through the laws, which always contain the highest consciousness and a universal memory, for "no forgetfulness shall lull them [the laws] to sleep" (*Oed.* 868), since the god lives "great in them and grows not old" (*Oed.* 870). The consequence is that any violation will sooner or later be revealed and avenged. However, a certain margin of uncertainty exists, for we can never know when it will happen—"no prophecy can deal with men's affairs." (*Ant.* 1160). All that is certain is that justice will be done, even though we cannot always say exactly why. What is the need, for instance, for Philoktetes to be punished?

The Greek notion of *miasma* is based on the conviction that a crime is always punished, as the gods never forget. But it is difficult to understand how the punishment can skip generations and strike apparently innocent people. So the question naturally arises in the case of a sudden misfortune whether the person concerned has been the victim of an as yet unatoned misdeed committed by an earlier member of the family.

It is crucial that the order of the universe, which has been disturbed by a crime, is restored and healed—an idea, as has been mentioned several times, that derives from Anaximander and Solon. And since Zeus, who controls everything, is ultimately the one to ensure the healing, we find here striking parallels to a monotheistic principle of a god, who keeps the cosmos in place through punishment and reward. Yet Sophocles' religious outlook is fundamentally the polytheistic theology characterising the idea of the Olympian gods, with a cohort of divine actors. Beside the high gods themselves, Fate—most often given the name of Moira or Tyche—determines the specific sequence of lives and events. It is to Moira that Oedipus surrenders when the truth about his guilty identity finally becomes clear to him.

6

This sort of unerringly exact principle of Fate means that no one can escape retribution or an even greater and, to man, completely inscrutable plan. Both King Laios and Oedipus try—Laios by having his newborn son killed, Oedipus by abandoning the king and queen in Corinth, believing them to be his true parents and not wishing to harm them, as has been prophesied for him. He flees, but only by doing so to meet and fulfill his inevitable fate.

There is talk of "a fruitless fight against the gods" (*Women of Trach.* 493), and many similar expressions in the tragedies cement this basic human experience: "what will be is in other hands than ours" (*Ant.* 1337). When Oedipus has finally learned his true identity—thanks to his reckless persistence—his piety is demonstrated by the fact that he accepts it with the words: "Well, let my fate (Moira)/ go where it will" (*Oed.* 1459), a goal he does not know, to be sure, until the very end.

For it is the fundamental condition of the solitary individual that the gods alone have full knowledge of the outcome of Fate—"Truly Zeus and Apollo are wise/ and in human things all knowing;/ but amongst men there is not distinct judgment" (*Oed.* 498-99). Not until the final day of our life do we really understand the reason for our fate and can see the unfolded plan and purpose of our lives. So no one can count himself fortunate until his last day of life. Life reveals that even the apparently most privileged person—Oedipus, for example—may suddenly be struck down by Fate, as Fate is most often associated with misfortune. "Count no mortal happy till/ he has passed the final limit of his life secure from pain" (1529-30) are the chorus' final word in *Oedipus the King*.

Nothing is permanent—"Luck sets it straight, and luck she overturns/the happy are unhappy day by day./ No prophecy can deal with men's affairs" (*Ant.* 1158-60). Most often, the outcome is manifested in a physical trauma with accompanying mental isolation: Oedipus in his blindness and Philoktetes on his desert island, exiled because of his evil-smelling wound.

7

That such high-minded, noble heroes are struck down so cruelly makes Sophocles in several contexts raise the theodicy problem, of whether the gods are in reality cruel? It is appropriate for them to punish Kreon in the *Antigone*, as by refusing Polyneikes a burial he has violated the gods' sacred laws. But why do they not they save Antigone, the only one who will uphold the laws? She obviously cannot herself understand that: "Why, in my misery, look to the gods for help?/ Can I call any of them my ally?" (922-23). In the fourth stasimon, the chorus also points out that Fate "has terrible power" (951) and in the exercise of its power spares nothing.

Likewise, in the tragedy *The Women of Trachis*, Herakles' son Hyllos is close to condemning the gods after his father's violent death. In order to regain Herakles' love, his wife, Deianeira, has sent him a magic shirt, which she does not know is poisoned and which burns into his skin and causes unendurable pain. The son pleads for the sympathy of those around him on account of the lack of kindness that the gods and Zeus, who are behind this, reveal in the monstrous event: "Recall the great cruelty of the gods in the deeds that are being done" (*Women of Trach.* 1265).

Every so often, the gods seem really to enjoy their power to inflict suffering. Athene, for example, invites Odysseus to witness the sight of the mad Ajax: "Is not the sweetest mockery the mockery of enemies?" (*Aj.* 79). And when Philoktetes hears that the best among the Greeks, Achilleus and Ajax, are dead, he claims that the gods always keep the worst men alive the longest: "They find their pleasure in turning back from Death/ the rogues and tricksters, but the just and good/ they are always sending out of the world./ How can I reckon the score, how can I praise,/ when praising Heaven I found the Gods are bad?" (*Phil.* 448-52).

The answer is not easy to see. For it appears that Philoktetes and Oedipus are part of a greater, hidden plan in which the gods elevate them after they have been tested in their incomprehensible sufferings. Once more, it is confirmed that it is not given to men to see the intention of the gods. They propose, but the gods dispose.

The *daimon* of the Tragic Hero

1

Against this background it is not surprising that, at the sight of Oedipus, the chorus of old men at Colonus see death as a liberator from the insufferable pain of existence: "Not to be born surpassed thought and speech" (*Oed. at Col.* 1223). The expression of such a defeatist desire by the chorus is—as in Aeschylus—vital to our understanding of the function of the chorus and of the degree to which we should lend credence to its interpretation. For the chorus seldom expresses Sophocles' own assessment. An exception, to judge from the context, is the hymn to *hubris* in *Oedipus the King* (871-94).

Otherwise, the chorus is characterized by a philistine common sense morality, as when it stresses to the charismatic hero Ajax: "My lord, no blustering words./ Your situation's desperate; can't you see?" (386-87). Yet, as we have heard several times, despite the shame into which he falls when, due to the blindness Athene inflicted upon him, he killed a flock of sheep instead of Odysseus, who he believed had unjustly robbed him of Achilleus' arms, Ajax shows his heroic greatness by maintaining his hatred of Odysseus: "Ah, if I could just once catch sight of him!/ Crushed as I am" (384-85). Thus does the true hero speak, utterly without compromise. He is like iron and fire. He preserves the integrity of his nature regardless, which in the case of Ajax breeds the *hubris* for which he is punished.

It can be said of the figures made of the right heroic stuff that their tragic center lies in their enterprise and action. They break the accepted rules, because all rules limit their need to develop, which makes them pathfinders for new worlds. They are probably victims of their own passions, i.e., the *hamartia* of which Aristotle speaks as characteristic of heroes. They are punished harshly if not brutally; but nevertheless the gods act with and through Oedipus, Philoktetes and Ajax. So the heroes are obviously subject to a link between fate and personal character. In this, they correspond to Heraclitus' saying: a man's fate is his *daimon*. The heroes' psychological makeup and the patterns of behavior that come with it are the fateful elements by which they fulfill their life potential.

2

When Oedipus blinds himself, the chorus asks him whether he did it himself or whether some *daimon* has been manipulating him (*Oed.* 1302). The question confirms that *daimon*, fate and personality merge together. It is not difficult to see that Oedipus' act of blinding himself, a deed so incomprehensible to those around him, is closely connected to his impetuous nature, his irresistible desire to act by imposing the punishment upon himself. Character and *daimon* harmonize with each other and he preserves to the end his hot-headed temperament, which has caused him such great problems but has also opened his way to self-insight and the understanding of self that comes with it.

In this sense, the dramatic irony in Sophocles arises by a paradigmatic contrast: heroes act almost blindly in a world completely separate from the radiant Olympian world from which the gods govern, one where the depth of their fall is proportional to their heroic caliber. Regardless of greatness, strength or beauty, these heroes are to be counted merely as shadows. This most clearly is the case with Oedipus. For this, the most erudite of men, who has solved the riddle of the sphinx, is crushed in an ironic *tour de force* when he tries to discover the truth about the cause of the plague and meets the vision of himself, a vision so unendurable that he gouges out the eyes that made him see that reality.

But although the contradiction in this irony feels unbearable, it is at the same time with this that Sophocles creates the strongest conceivable response—that is to say the sympathy pervading his works. It is occasionally expressed directly, as when, instead of rejoicing at the sight of the mad Ajax as Athene invites him to do, Odysseus is seized by a profound compassion, well aware that he himself could be struck at any moment in the same way—"Yet I pity/ His wretchedness, though he is my enemy,/ For the terrible yoke of blindness that is on him" (*Aj.* 121-24). Something similar applies to Neoptolemos, who at the sight of Philoktetes' terrible sufferings exclaims: "A kind of compassion,/ a terrible compassion, has come upon me" (*Phil.* 965). Through this very compassion, the as yet inexperienced Neoptolemos finds his true nature and extricates himself from the treachery he is in the process of committing. His soul is purified and, as spectators, we may ask: Is it not in compassion that we find the deepest explanation for what is to be understood by *katharsis*?

Ajax—The Steadfast Tragic Hero

1

For good reason, the *Ajax* is considered one of Sophocles' oldest surviving tragedies. It is the most reminiscent of Aeschylus and continues his obsession with conflict between human *hubris* and the accompanying requirement of *sophrosyne*. At the same time, it may be this play that best illuminates what a tragic hero is in his greatness and fall. Moreover, the tragedy also illustrates the way in which, by introducing a number of figures mirroring each other, Sophocles achieves the psychological effect of a relief.

The chorus speaks of Ajax as "inflexible Ajax whose name means anguish" (913-14) in that his name is here linked to the expression of distress: *aiai*—oh woe, oh woe. And insofar as fate and character cannot be separated, we can conclude from this that the pain which he bears in his name comes from the ruin he brings down on himself by his unwavering *megalomania*.

If we piece together Ajax's self-understanding, as it gradually emerges through his own words, we obtain a distillation of a character profile, whose *megalomania* or *megalopsychia* makes the gods fly into a rage. This was in no way the case in the *Iliad*. Here, the hero could brag as much as he liked about his own power without having the hammer fall—and so he did, because his reputation thus helped to consolidate his heroic *arete*. In the tragedians, however, the effect is exactly the opposite. This is a reversal that must fundamentally based on an understanding most clearly seen in the *Oresteia* that a human being who exalts (*hubris*) and expropriates (*koros*) calls down the "envious" (*phthonos*) gods' inexorable punishment (*ate/nemesis*). So *sophrosyne* should be shown in all acts and deeds.

2

This is the basic theme of the *Ajax*, but Sophocles has deep sympathy with and respect for his protagonist, whom in his fatal arrogance he places among the greatest for transgressive figures. We understand indirectly that Ajax has inherited this characteristic. His father, Telamon, now an old man, is likewise described as a defiant and wrathful man (1017), so we have a father/child constellation which we shall see repeated in the relationship between Oedipus and Antigone, and Oedipus and his father Laios. Even after his shameful *hamartia*, Ajax also wishes his son to inherit his own ruthlessness after his death: as Ajax commands, "Break in/ The colt straight off to his father's rugged ways;/ Train him to have a nature like his sire" (547-49).

There is no sign here of a resigned moderation. It is not because he does not know of *sophrosyne*, but he only invokes the need for *sophrosyne* with respect to his wife Tekmessa, when he prepares her for his suicide: "Self-restraint is a virtue" (586), he says to her. That he does not apply this point of view to himself emerges a few verses later, when he stubbornly maintains his arrogant stance, even though it has caused him such great harm: "Don't you know by now/ That I owe any the gods no service any more?" (589-90). However, this disrespect for the gods is nothing new in him. As he tells Athene to her face, he is proud—"I think I may boast as much. I don't deny it" (96). And to the chorus' dissatisfaction, he elevates himself at the cost of the other heroes: "You shall no longer see this man,/ such a man (let me now speak my boast)/ As Troy ne'er saw the like of, not in all/ The warlike host that hither came from Greece " (421-25).

The problem is obviously that he says this—that he so fiercely asserts himself through this idea. But as testified by a number of eyewitnesses, it is not just empty talk: single-handed, he defended the Greek army when the Trojans were about to achieve victory. And as a reason why, after his suicide, Ajax must have the funeral that the Atreids deny him, Odysseus, his enemy, says that he was the noblest, the bravest and the best in battle. That he was also his own master, subject to no other, appears from the fact that he participated in the war because he felt obliged by his oath, while Odysseus and Achilleus, each in his own way, tried to avoid fulfilling their oaths.

3

If this is the epitome of Ajax's heroic character and status, it is also in this personality structure that we find the cause of the flaw in his character (*hamartia*) and of his fall and shame. His arrogance and sense of honor leave no room for moderation when he is deprived of Achilleus' arms and wants to avenge himself on Odysseus. What is worse, in his autonomy he even wants to make himself free of the gods. But this is where the line is drawn. For as the prophet Kalchas makes clear, Ajax was too much of a braggart when, on his departure, his arrogant response to his father, who advised him always to seek the assistance of the gods, was: "Father, with God's help even a worthless man/ Could triumph. I propose, without that help,/ To win my prize of fame" (768-69).

No, he should never have said that, and not even have thought it. For it is as a general consequence of this contumely that Athene strikes him with the madness of delusion, for, as she portentously explains to Odysseus: "Know that the gods/ Love men of steady sense and hate the proud" (132-33). It is put the same way in the *Antigone*: "The bad becomes the good/ to him a god would doom" (621-22). Even the greatest heroes are brought down because they are ultimately only human beings.

4

Odysseus is the positive counterpart to Ajax. And on the basis of the fundamental idea of the tragedy it can be maintained that there is a deeper meaning to the fact that he is given Achilleus' arms and armor, as—along with Theseus in *Oedipus at Colonus*—he more than any other figure in Sophocles' dramatic universe is governed by the wisdom and self-control that makes him Athene's favorite. On the other hand, Odysseus does not have Ajax's tragic caliber; he is human, cautious, obedient and generous. This latter quality appears when he ensures that Ajax is laid to rest in the ground, which the Atreidae oppose.

In this respect, the Atreidae, Menelaos and Agamemnon, constitute the negative counterparts to Ajax and Odysseus, since they clearly exemplify what Sophocles formulates in *Oedipus the King*—that *hubris* is the father of tyranny (871). The Atreidae are made of the same despotic stuff as King Kreon in the *Antigone*. And thus does Menelaus explain the anatomy of power as a question of spreading fear: "Never can the laws maintain a prosperous course in a city where fear has no fixed place" (1073-74). In order to make an example of him, Ajax is refused a tomb, even though he has defended the army. Instead, the Atreidae mock him for not yielding to their judgment when they gave Achilleus' arms to Odysseus. In the same way, they besmirch his half-brother Teukros, calling him a bastard and demanding fealty and self-control without themselves being able to exercise self-control.

In this context, Odysseus and his *sophrosyne* show their effectiveness when he warns the Atreidae that they are on the verge of violating the sacred laws. And, as it appears in *Oedipus the King*, the premise for staying on a good footing with celestial powers is to keep oneself within the law, in word and deed—see the chorus' prayer to be "pious in word and deed/prescribed by the laws that live on high" (865-66). On the same basis, Odysseus admonishes Agamemnon: "Don't in the gods' name be so hard./Vindictiveness should not so govern you/ As to make you trample on the right" (1342-44). Odysseus succeeds in moving the Atreidae with his warning and his own magnanimity towards an enemy who has tried to kill him. They yield reluctantly. Ajax is given his funeral. However, though reconciled with Odysseus, Teukros dare not allow him to participate in the funeral, for it might make the dead man angry, while at the same time Teukros himself sees "a nobleman" in Odysseus (1399). So even in death, Ajax preserves his nature intact, as is confirmed in the *Odyssey* by his refusing to dignify Odysseus with a word on their meeting in Hades.

Antigone—The Tragic Heroine
1

It may be too much to speak of a happy ending in the *Ajax*. On the other hand, we see the gods and *sophrosyne* simultaneously triumph through Odysseus, which after all limits the extent of the tragedy. Compared to this, the *Antigone*, which seems to have been written at about the same time, around 440 B.C., is far blacker and more difficult to bear. Certainly, it is appropriate that Kreon should be punished for his *hubris*; but as this is achieved by his innocent wife and his level-headed son being dragged down along with Antigone, the tragedy in all its gruesomeness shows the chasm between the omnipotence of the gods and the powerlessness of men.

Like Odysseus, Antigone speaks on behalf of divine laws, as, like the Atreidae, Kreon refuses to allow Polyneikes to be buried in the proper fashion, because—as described by Aeschylus in *Seven against Thebes* and Euripides in *The Phoenician Women*—he tried to conquer Thebes after his brother Eteokles broke the agreement to rule in turn after Oedipus' abdication. Meanwhile, the tragedy is not about this conflict. Instead, Sophocles focuses on and expands the problem outlined in the last half of the *Ajax*: the refusal by the Atreidae to allow Ajax to be buried. Through this he obviously wanted to illustrate *hubris* in a negative contrast to Ajax's heroic arrogance and investigate the egoism of the hunger for power, which was also one of the Atreidae's motives.

For like the Atreidae, Kreon, who as Oedipus' brother-in-law has become king after his fall, now wants to demonstrate his strength by despotically denying the fallen Polyneikes a grave, even though he thereby violates unwritten laws. On the pretext of preserving the welfare of the state, Kreon has put his own laws in their stead. But gradually as his intentions are revealed, it becomes clear that he only serves himself and his despotic desires. *Hubris* is demonstrated once again to be the father of tyranny. For as he maintains, no one knows a man before he has seen "his practice of the government and law" (177).

He reveals his spiritual meanness in the way he interprets the many warnings he receives, accusing the chorus as well as the prophet Teiresias of acting only for the sake of profit—in short, of having been bribed. In the same way, he dismisses Antigone's protests on behalf of the sacred laws. For she does not understand how he, a mortal, dare "over-run/ the gods' unwritten and unfailing laws" (454-55). She herself fears no one and nothing, provided she does not, for "neglect [of] these laws,/ drawn myself to the gods' sure punishment" (458-59). Her objections and the burial of her brother, Kreon interprets as intolerable impudence, since, by placing the laws of the gods above his, the king's, she blocks his attempt to make himself a tyrant: "I am no man and she the man instead /if she can have this conquest without pain" (484-85). And he reveals his selfishness and his power-hungry nature by condemning her to death: "She is my sister's child, but were she child/of closer kin than any at my hearth,/ she and her sister should not so escape/ their death and doom" (486-88).

In other words, to promote his power, Kreon not only imagines himself beyond a relationship with the gods but beyond any family considerations—just like Agamemnon in the *Oresteia* with the sacrifice of his daughter. In short, Kreon acts in a directly opposite way to Antigone, who devotes her life to fulfilling her duty to the gods and family. As it similarly appears from the quotation, he is also driven by a latent misogyny. For in condemning Antigone, he wants to show to those around him that he will not be dominated by a woman, but is a man with hair on his chest: "No woman rules me while I live" (525). So deep does his contempt or fear of women reach that he believes his son Haimon, who it betrothed to Antigone, can simply find himself another field to plough, a metaphor already described as reeking of patriarchal self-assertion (see p. 92).

Kreon understands no more of what love is than of family feeling, as Haimon loves Antigone and cannot simply choose another woman. Nor, it appears, does the father respect his son's integrity, for when Haimon makes it clear to him that yielding is no shame but a sign of wisdom and points out that Thebes does not share Kreon's view of what is just, it only increases his father's fury. As the puppy he is, the son must obey his father's will and not, from desire, make himself the slave of a woman.

Moreover, it now emerges that his lawgiving is in no way intended to benefit the city but is only to serve as an exercise of his right to private property. Is Thebes to dictate my laws? he asks. "No city is property of a single man," Haimon points out; to which Kreon replies, "But custom gives possession to the ruler" (737-38).

2

To prevent Thebes from being struck by *miasma*, Kreon has ordered Antigone to be buried alive in a cave outside the city. However, as the final person to try to bring Kreon to think better, Teiresias can relate that the anger of the gods is revealed in omens that will make Thebes groan with pain. Kreon can still change his mind and show respect to the dead. But so trapped is Kreon in his circle of egoistic motives that he cannot undertake this maneuver. Instead, he claims that Teiresias is motivated by a desire for financial gain. However, Kreon thereby only reveals how infected his own ideological world is with this sort of thinking, since, as he says, he would not change his decision for gold, not even for fear of offending the gods.

The accusation that he could have been bribed enrages Teiresias, and it makes him reveal his secret knowledge of what awaits Kreon: because he has robbed Polyneikes of his right to a burial ceremony, the Erinyes of the realm of the dead will come after him—"So the pursuing horrors lie in wait/ to track you down." (1075-76). The seer's words so fill Kreon with terror that at last he changes his mind. Yet he does so only to save his own skin, even though his arrogance and vanity make it difficult for him: "To yield is dreadful. But to stand against him./ Dreadful to strike my spirit to destruction" (1096-97).

However, the process he has set in motion shows itself now to be irreversible. The gods have initiated their punishment: Antigone has hanged herself and, when Haimon fails to kill his father, he and later his mother Eurydike, Kreon's wife, likewise commit suicide. Of course, Kreon is still breathing, but from now on he can only be deemed one of the living dead, stripped of everything, even though he now assumes the blame for all the misery he has caused: "This is my guilt, all mine. I killed you, I say it clear" (1319).

3

As long as Antigone is only viewed as a contrast to Kreon, she is unambiguously positive in her defense of her dead brother and divine laws. But can it be true that Sophocles deliberately created such a one-dimensional character? Does she not have any flaws (*hamartia*)? The tragedy reveals that she possesses a far more spacious and problematic character, something, however, that only by its ambiguity makes her greater as a tragic heroine. In order to put these character traits into perspective, we must turn to the chorus' view of her. As said above, it is problematic to interpret the chorus as a spokesman for the poet, as the chorus most often expresses the same general mood of the people. I believe in this case, however, that we can place a good deal of trust in the chorus of old men from Thebes because their view of Antigone corresponds to the tragedy's revelation of her conduct and psychology.

Two things are crucial in determining Antigone's fate: on the one hand, the inherited family curse that strikes her through her father Oedipus and, on the other, the "defiant spirit" (471) she has from him according to the chorus. That is, in terms of categories she is possessed by a *megalopsychia* that in many ways corresponds to Ajax's arrogance.

Understanding Antigone is more complex because she has coupled her family curse and obstinacy with her heroic self-sacrifice on behalf of the divine laws, which inevitably reveals her inner drive. There is no doubt that her goal is to achieve a splendid reputation by accepting the curse in its utmost consequences, in death, so that from this point of view piety actually becomes a vehicle for her own self-promotion. One of her motives is to secure for herself an immortal reputation in the style of the great heroes: "And yet what greater glory (*kleos*) could I find/than giving my own brother funeral?" (502-03).

4

In this sense, Antigone's life is defined by death from the beginning of the play. It is no pain for her to die, but on the contrary is a victory when such great suffering torments one as it does in her case, and at the same time it provides her with an identity to meet her dead family. "For you chose to live when I chose death" (555), she says in her second conversation with her sister Ismene. And it is in this contrast and conversation with Ismene that we find the most precise diagnosis of Antigone's arrogance in her effort to achieve what for a woman is an unusual reputation.

When, in the introductory scene, Ismene tries to talk sense into her sister, pointing out that they are the last remaining members of their family and that, as women, they are in a weak position vis-à-vis the new king, their uncle Kreon, the objections have the opposite effect of what was intended—they strengthen Antigone's desire to rebel. This stirs in her, if it were not present before, a radicality deeply rooted in the honor she expects to win by her sacrificial death. That it really is a matter of honor emerges clearly from the fact that, when Ismene recommends that she should keep her project secret, Antigone replies: "Denounce me. I shall hate you more/ if silent, not proclaiming this to all" (86-87). She wants at any price to make her action visible, for if there are no witnesses to it, there will be no honor to be won. In the same breath, she adds: "But let me and my own ill-counseling/ suffer this terror" (95-96). In Greek, the term used is *dysboulia*—that is to say, folly or rashness, although she realizes she is crossing the bounds of reason, for which reason Ismene also characterizes her as demented (*anous*, 98).

Antigone is well under way with a project from which there can be no return, but only a single path leading to certain death. However, since death is for her synonymous with fame and reunion with her beloved dead relatives, this is the path she seeks—irreversible as the process set in motion now is. And as a sign that she is absolute in her striving for honor, she doggedly rejects her sister when, after Antigone's death sentence, she says she wishes to go with her. She relentlessly cuts off Ismene, as she does not want her or others to diminish the reputation she expects from her heroic death. She wants her death and her reputation for herself: "You did not/ wish for a part, nor did I give you one" (538-39), she says, rejecting Ismene, so that she can achieve even greater visibility.

5

Ismene is certainly Antigone's sister, but she also represents an inner boundary in Antigone herself, which she quite deliberately crosses in order to realize herself through death. This means, paradoxically enough, that on one level she defends divine laws and declares her fear of breaking them; but, on another level, of which she herself is unconscious, she is guilty of *hubris*, as she uses piety to rise to fame and glory. That she has lost her sound judgment in this process is revealed when she compares her sacrifice to fate to what Niobe had to suffer with the loss of her children. The chorus leader hastens to respond: "God's child and god she was" (832).

That this is actually a condemnation is shown by the chorus' following assessment: Antigone is undoubtedly a victim of her family's curse, but as the chorus maintains: "Your self-sufficiency has brought you down" (875). For in this state of mind, she went to fatal extremes: "You went to the furthest verge/ of daring, but there you found/ the high foundation of justice (Dike), and fell" (853-54). The chorus here speaks from a much larger context, as Sophocles seems to draw on the words in the *Oresteia* to the effect that riches will not protect anyone who strikes against the altar of Dike, for such a person is ungodly, struck by *ate*.

Antigone's actions and the strength of her motivation and her crossing the line (*dysboulia*) seem to confirm the truth of the chorus' words. And that she herself realizes that she has landed in this minefield seems apparent from her closing line. For although she has defended divine laws, she obviously no longer has contact with the gods. They do not respond to her as "I stand convicted of impiety,/ the evidence my pious duty done" (923-24). Yet, she is ready to take her punishment if it occurs in accordance with the will of the gods: "But if it is the others who are wrong/ I wish them no greater punishment than mine" (927-28).

6

It is significant that, even in the hour of her death, Antigone maintains her heroic self-perception: she will take her punishment but she declares at the same time that it is unjust (*ekdikos*, 928). This must indicate that she does not understand her own motivation, the vain assertion of her own worth for which she uses the gods, since she defends their laws. She can only see the defense, not the reason, just as she has no understanding of the psychological change that has taken place in her since her ability to love has at the same time been transformed into a death urge and a lust for glory.

For if from this angle we approach the driving force in her intention—to win *kleos* through her association with the fate of her family—the enterprise that leads her to the gallows is linked to this exaggeration in her psyche: that she allows love to find its fulfilment in death. If this is not taken into consideration, it is incomprehensible why she must be betrothed to Kreon's son Haimon. Long ago, as she herself points out, she renounced life to serve the dead. She has dedicated her love to them, not to the living Haimon. Significantly, she practically describes her brother as a dead lover—"Friend shall I lie with him, yes friend with friend,/ when I have dared the crime of piety" (73-74). So she characterizes her approaching death as "best" (originally " beautiful": *kalos*, 72). Thus, when she says to Kreon that, "I cannot share in hatred, but in love" (523), the love she is talking about is not linked to anything in this world, since in her own words she may serve the dead much longer than the living.

This association with death has such weight that, as a final proof of her *dysboulia*, her folly, Antigone hangs herself, just as a reprieve is on its way, spurred by Kreon's misgivings. Love and death, *eros thanatos*, are also combined as a common gravitational field in Antigone's own mind, when she calls the cave in which she is enclosed her bridal chamber (*to nympheion*, 891). The cave here takes the place of the awaiting bridal bed, while, now in death's embrace, she will meet her beloved relatives: brother, mother and father. On the other hand, Haimon dies by his own hand for love of the girl—and life.

7

The lesson from suffering that can be derived from the tragedies by Sophocles discussed above can be summarized in the chorus' final lines:

> Our happiness depends
> On wisdom all the way.
> The gods must have their due.
> Great words by men of pride'
> Bring greater blows upon them.
> So wisdom comes to the old.
> (1348-53)

These words hold good for the *Ajax* and the *Antigone*. Wisdom—the prerequisite for moderation—is represented by an Odysseus or an Ismene. They may well be *personae dramatis* in their own right, but they also constitute a boundary mark for the characters whom they face and which these characters cross in the desire for the grandiose—proud individuals who in word and deed, each in their own way, cross the line.

We meet their negation in the Atreidae and especially in King Kreon. Of course, he ends by acknowledging his guilt, but it is not an insight he has gained through personal development or experience. It is brought to him from outside in that his yielding is forced upon him partly through fear and partly by the sight of the tragedy he has called down upon his closest family. His *hubris* is transformed into blind submission in the hope of appeasing the gods in this way lest they drag him along into death.

Whether we are dealing with heroic or unheroic characters, it appears that in their egotism and self-assertion they find themselves at odds with the gods, but at the same time insist on themselves and thereby the individual as a developing psychological entity, as was also the case in Homer. Thus, heroism's limit as a form of consciousness is that it liberates the subject but does not in itself provide a means of understanding what being a subject implies. The characters who live within this form of understanding are consequently preconscious and merely early forms of a true individual.

In the case of Antigone, this means that she realizes her life purely on the premises of heroism—as a heroine. It is significant that she seeks the self-realization of her human potential in the heroic view of reputation, *kleos*, as the most important prize for a human being to acquire—at least if one wants to be a hero or heroine. Thus, Antigone's reputation, like Penelope's, has reached the heavens and become famous throughout all time.

In addition, the object of Antigone's world of longing demonstrates the sort of reality to which she ultimately belongs—that of the family. It is this with which she wants to unite her ability to love. And so, in contrast to the *Oresteia*, no real separation of blood and spirit has taken place within her. In this respect, she is atavistic. Ultimately, this means that although she knows she is going too far, she is unable to develop this understanding further into insight. On the contrary, it forces her into death, in that her inability to accept advice only accelerates, so that her thinking never becomes deliberation.

What such deliberation formed by suffering is, we will now examine in Sophocles' two tragedies on Oedipus. They deal with how an individual comes into existence. This is achieved by clinging to pain, since in contrast to Ajax and Antigone, Oedipus does not commit suicide but accepts his suffering, thereby destroying his own reputation and his association with his family and its curse. This occurs by penetrating the very mystery of gender and by separating the bonds of blood and spiritual reality. The Oedipal tragedies here show from within what the *Oresteia* views from without, but both groups of texts relate to the same world of consciousness: suffering as the path to insight and to the self.

Oedipus the King—Riddle and Prehistory

1

How central a figure Oedipus was for Sophocles can be shown simply by the fact that he wrote his two tragedies about the Theban king at a space of twenty-five years. Just as Aeschylus before his death summarized his view of life in the *Oresteia*, it seems as though shortly before his death at the age of ninety Sophocles was unable to let go of the tragedy of Oedipus, wanting to demonstrate explicitly that it was meaningful and, above all, an example of how grandly the gods can view a man's destiny, since they finally sanctify Oedipus.

In the *Odyssey's* portrayal of him, Oedipus continues to rule (11, 271 ff.) even after the nature of his marriage has been revealed, including the murder of his father. Iokaste certainly hangs herself, but Oedipus remains on the throne.

However, even Aeschylus has him acknowledge his guilt by gouging out his eyes and cursing his sons. This is related in *Seven Against Thebes*, where we do not learn about his subsequent fate—which is presumably dealt with in the lost middle portion, *Oedipus*. In Sophocles, he also blinds himself and is driven into exile by his family, helped only by his two daughters; this is an exile that only ends with his death at Colonus. In Euripides' *The Phoenician Women*, Kreon and his sons lock him up in the hope that the world will forget him. But even here his curse leads to his sons murdering each other, while Iokaste commits suicide.

2

As we have heard above, in his *Poetics* Aristotle uses *Oedipus the King* as the paradigm of the optimal tragedy, which understands how dramatically to unite action and the spoken word. Here, too, Sophocles differs from Aeschylus. The latter primarily looks at things from the outside and, as shown, uses his characters to illustrate steps in the tragedy's chain of consciousness. In principle, Orestes does not develop but remains a fixed character, whereas Oedipus' psychology and passionate nature is the fundamental driving force behind the tragic sequence of events in his royal destruction.

Oedipus is such a singular psychological drama that we must go all the way to Henrik Ibsen in order to find a corresponding method: a gradual, retrospective revelation of a previous history and its catastrophic effect and consequence when a crisis arises at the play's beginning—in *Oedipus*, a devastating plague.

While the compositional consciousness in the *Oresteia* is one with Zeus' overall fateful plan, the riddle of the protagonist's identity and the solution of this riddle are buried in the composition of *Oedipus* and only gradually appear. The riddle remains in the subconscious and is solved the moment the knot (*desis*) of the subconscious is illuminated (*lysis*). Therefore, as interpreters, we are forced to unravel the compositional plan as Oedipus' own detective work penetrates it. External events and psychological truth merge at the point when his identity stands fully illuminated in all its horror and, by blinding himself, he chooses to accept this fateful identity.

In modern terms, it could be claimed that *Oedipus* is presented in the form of a whodunit. At the beginning of the play, Thebes is being ravaged by the plague, which makes everything wither and die. The oracle at Delphi divines that its cause is that the previous king's murderer was never been found and suitably punished.

So who is the murderer? This question and its explanation raise *Oedipus* from a mythical tragedy to something approaching a psychoanalytical thriller. As king and the person who previously saved the city from the sphinx by solving its riddle, Oedipus must now again move into action as the investigator and detective— bitterly opposed by the figures around him who know the truth. But with his uncompromising character, no one can stop him. On the contrary. The stronger the evidence becomes against him, the more diligently he presses on to discover his identity, even if it should cost him his life and royal dignity. And it will!

The play thus deals with a man who, without knowing it, is looking for his hidden identity and who, the moment he discovers the murderer and the fateful truth, stands fully revealed in the tragedy's *anagnorisis* and is cut off from his earlier life, stripped of all former power, blind and totally isolated. On the other hand, he now knows who he is.

3

If we remove the earlier events from the composition in which it is also deconstructed and successively made visible, it can be retold chronologically as follows:

The oracle at Delphi prophesied to Laios and Iokaste, the rulers of Thebes, that the son they would bring into the world would kill his father and marry his mother. So, when Oedipus is born, the mother gives him to a shepherd with the instruction that he is to be exposed on Mount Kithairon, near Thebes. His feet are bound together and pierced; from this event, Fate has given him his name (1033), claims the messenger from Corinth, to whom Oedipus was passed when the shepherd could not bring himself to kill him. The name is supposed to mean "he with the swollen foot."

The messenger passed the infant Oedipus to Polybos and Merope, the childless royal couple in Corinth, who pass him off as their own son. As a young man, Oedipus is mocked by a drunk who questions his biological legitimacy. His parents deny it when he asks them whether he was adopted. But Oedipus is nagged by doubt. He secretly seeks enlightenment from Apollo at Delphi and is told that he will murder his father and marry his mother.

Terrified at such a gruesome prospect, he determines not to return to Corinth. At a crossroads between Delphi and Thebes, he runs into King Laios, on his way with his entourage to Delphi.[2] Irascible as they both are, neither will yield to the other. There is a brief battle in which Laios first strikes Oedipus in the head with a spiked stick. However, Oedipus grabs the cudgel and with it kills his father and the rest of the company with the exception of the shepherd who once had the task of putting him to death.

Oedipus travels towards Thebes, which is plagued by a sphinx.[3] Travelers must solve its riddle or be killed. Oedipus solves the riddle and thereby kills the sphinx, thanks to his power of interpretation. On his arrival at Thebes, he is hailed as a savior, proclaimed king and married to his mother Iokaste. No one investigates the killing of King Laios, but the shepherd, who survived, immediately asks to be allowed to leave the city when he sees Oedipus as king. Oedipus and Iokaste now live together for approximately fifteen years and have four children, two of each sex, when the plague breaks out.

Oedipus sends his brother-in-law Kreon to Delphi to discover the reason for the blight on the crops. This is the situation as the play opens *in medias res*, when a group of older reputable citizens, the chorus, seek out Oedipus to ask him to intervene in their troubles, since he once had the fortune of solving the riddle of the sphinx.

4

The plague is described as "fire-bearing divinity" (28), but the indeterminacy that generally governs in *Oedipus the King* makes it impossible to name this divinity with certainty. In the *Iliad*, it is explicitly Apollo who sends the plague on the Greek encampment, and he is also deeply involved here. It is from him that the prophecy of being cleansed of the murderer derives. Teiresias says specifically that Oedipus will be brought down by Apollo himself (376); in addition, Oedipus ultimately confirms that everything comes by and from him—"It was Apollo, friends, Apollo, that brought this bitterness" (1330)—just as the god is the dominant force in *Oedipus at Colonus*.

Yet the chorus seems to believe that Ares is the originator of the plague and prays that Zeus may kill him with a thunderbolt, just as the chorus seeks protection from Athene, Artemis and Dionysos, the latter because his mother was the Theban princess and moon goddess Semele. That the plague is attributed to Ares may be due to his name, which means wrath and destruction, or perhaps it reflects an old grudge from the god: Oedipus' forefather Kadmos killed his son, which Euripides makes the primary cause of the family curse in *The Phoenician Women*.

All we can establish with certainty is that the plague derives from the *miasma* that has struck the country through Oedipus' patricide and his incestuous marriage to his mother, though this is not directly stated. Through the oracle on which Kreon reports on arriving home from Delphi, Apollo has: "Commanded us/to drive out a pollution from our land,/ pollution grown ingrained within the land" (98-99). The guilty person must be punished by death or driven from the country.

The infection is usually only linked to the guilty party, his family, and those with whom he comes into contact. If the whole country must suffer here for Oedipus' crime, it must be because, as king, he embodies its soul. A sick king makes his kingdom sick, as Euripides says King Laios did with his untameable desire. As Teiresias says to Kreon in *The Phoenician Women*: "The land has long been sick,/ since Laios made a child against heaven's will/ and begot poor Oedipus" (866-68).

That it is the blood bond that is violated by the murder, as in the *Oresteia*, is confirmed by the chorus when it says that the murderer is pursued by the Erinyes of darkness (470). In the Greek text, however, Sophocles does not use the word Erinyes but the related death spirits, Keres. The effect is the same. For just as after losing their case in the *Oresteia* the Erinyes threatened to visit a blight on the Athenian crops, the plague has a similar effect. The very source of fertility is hit, everything alive withers in the fields and in the wombs of the women.

The figure behind these events, Apollo as the god of vengeance, has something of the same ambiguity he had in Aeschylus. He points back towards the primordial mother and thereby becomes the mainspring for the development that in the *Oresteia* leads to the establishment of the court at Areopagus and in *Oedipus the King* to the constitution of the self which the god is ultimately magnanimous enough to sanctify in *Oedipus at Colonus*.

The Riddle Solver

1

As detective, Oedipus has the worst conceivable task because it is the riddle of himself that he is to solve. For even though he has solved the riddle of the sphinx, it continues to pursue him in a new form. Ignorant as he is about his own origin, the plague faces him with the question of who he really is.

In this sense, the riddle of the sphinx coincides compositionally with Oedipus' subconscious and constitutes its subtext. For when he answered its question the first time, he gained access to his biological mother and thereby an even deeper riddle, that is to say his identity as his father's murderer and his link to the primordial feminine as his mother's son and husband.

Moreover, the sphinx forms part of the composition in a topographical sense, insofar as its riddle coincides geographically with the cities through which Oedipus passes as the stages on life's way. For when the sphinx asks "Who is it who first goes on all fours?", the answer is a crawling baby, which as far as Oedipus is concerned means the little boy in Corinth with his foster parents. Who walks on two legs? An adult does, who in the shape of Oedipus—by killing his father and solving the riddle of the sphinx—comes to Thebes, where he is married to his mother. To walk on three legs is ultimately an anticipation of how, blind and later as an old man, he must wander about the world supported by a stick or his daughters until he reaches Colonus, where he dies.

Thus, the riddle about his self and his ages merges with these cities in a concrete symbolic unity in which each individual city represents different forms of consciousness. Corinth is associated with being cared for and growing up, Thebes with the maternal, the family and the blood, while Colonus constitutes the forward-directed spiritual reality of which Athens is the primary exponent.

Mythologically, the sphinx comes from Egypt and is a composite of a woman's head and a winged lion's body. In *The Phoenician Women*, Euripides makes its chthonic affinity entirely clear by pointing out that it is the daughter of the Earth: "You winged thing, earth's offspring."[4] It thus represents a stage of consciousness that corresponds to its duality: half animal, half human—or in other words, the primordial maternal nature and the preconscious, dreamlike human state. In principle, Oedipus brings men out of this atavistic stage, since, with his idea and his answer, he places the individual in the world as a conscious being, personified by Oedipus himself.

The topographical evidence of the final stage of this transformation is Oedipus' arrival at Colonus. But he must first endure much suffering without understanding why but very conscious of how.

2

So the plague becomes the driving force in this process. When Zeus' high priest turns to Oedipus on behalf of the people and asks him to solve the riddle of the plague, he emphasizes that he could only answer the sphinx's question by taking counsel of the gods, as he is not himself the equal of the gods. However, the aura that rests upon Oedipus reveals that he is raised high above his subjects—so high indeed that they hardly know him—not, at any rate, as a public person. For when he finally appears before the citizenry, after having ruled in Thebes for many years, he must introduce himself by his reputation as the riddle solver: "I Oedipus whom all men call the Great" (8).

Oedipus thus seems to be known in daily life more in name than in actual fact. In all these years, he has not shown himself in public but has remained hidden or at an "intermediate stage" between gods and men. It appears later that his brother-in-law Kreon carries out the practical tasks concerned with the exercise of the royal power. In keeping with his grand self-esteem as riddle solver, Oedipus feels that he belongs to a supra-individual sphere for, as he says: while all others suffer alone during the plague, he suffers collectively—"I know you are all sick,/ yet there is not one of you, sick though you are,/ that is as sick as myself (. . .) my spirit groans/for city and myself and you at once" (60-64).

The underlying idea here—as in Homer—is that the king is the head of the country. A good king makes his land flourish and grow rich, a poor and sick king is the cause of its decline. As the chorus in *The Suppliant Maidens* says to the king: "You the people, you the government."[5] Therefore, the king, as the representative of the gods on earth (see p. 264), must take care not to act unjustly and bring down a *miasma* that might desolate his kingdom, just as the *miasma* of the plague now threatens to destroy Thebes.

Curiously enough, no one has previously tried to solve the murder of King Laios. Kreon excuses himself by saying that the problems with the sphinx got in the way. This might imply that Sophocles imagines the sphinx only showed up as a result of the murder—a sort of Eriny for the unavenged blood. Nor did Oedipus do anything about it. When he now puts all of his efforts into finding the murderer, it happens in a dual identification. At the same time, he seeks to appropriate the power both of the gods and of his predecessors in the answer of the oracle. It is a deadly irony of fate, when he says that Laios' son, if he had had one, would have been his own through marriage with Iokaste—"I fight in his defence as for my father,/ and I shall try all means to take the murderer/ of Laios" (263-64). He also binds himself with his determination to the will of Apollo: "So I stand forth a champion of the God/ and of the man who died" (243-44).

This, of course, is a truth the consequence and extent of which he is ignorant, but which in a greater perspective shows Apollo's inscrutable and long-term plans. For what could be viewed here as an expression of Oedipus' *hubristic* image of himself, persuades the god in *Oedipus at Colonus* to give him the god-like protective function that casts a meaningful light back over his whole uncompromising life of suffering.

3

Yet Oedipus is not merely a distant, elevated and sanctified royal figure. He has a spiritual trait or flaw (*hamartia*) that links him to earthly life in a highly tangible fashion—his wrathful nature, the irascibility that constantly brings him on a collision course with his surroundings. The mythical tradition around Oedipus has also placed enormous weight on this characteristic. Even the chorus in *Seven Against*

Thebes warned Eteokles against letting himself be carried along by his father's nature—"Do not become, in your anger, like the man whose name makes the sound of a most evil omen."[6] Even Antigone's obstinacy, it will be remembered, was deemed an inheritance from her father (see p. 420). The extent to which Oedipus suffered from a character defect has been intensely debated, and the idea has been rejected that some *hamartia* is to be found in his irascibility.[7] Instead, emphasis is placed on his ignorance of his own origin.

But if this were to be accepted as correct, it would mean that he was without a flaw, because his sin is inherited. To begin with, it would become inexplicable as to why so much is made of describing his anger. Secondly, the link between his psychology and the development he undergoes would be incomprehensible. The two things cannot be kept apart. It is precisely his anger and irascibility that are behind the killing of his father, which opens the way to his mother, just as it is through his anger that he forces his way into the riddle of his own identity, solves it, blinds himself and is ultimately redeemed as a holy man.

If anything, it is this attribute that, for good or ill, makes Oedipus the person he is—and remains. Time and again, those around him point out that his anger makes him act rashly and insanely. "Let your temper rage/ as wildly as you will" (343-44), says Teiresias, for example, who knows that the king will be caught by retribution. And even though Oedipus is old and decrepit in *Oedipus at Colonus*, notwithstanding the patience he has learned, his is still the same choleric nature.

Thymos is the Greek word used to describe his temperament. Insofar as *thymos* is developing towards a true ego-controlled arbiter of consciousness, whose purpose is to create psychological harmony between the world of desires and the superego, the use of the word in this context shows the character of Oedipus' innermost nature, which in its irascibility is always in danger of meltdown. No ordinary *sophrosyne* governs here. On the contrary, anger makes him transcend the limits with which those around him seek to clip his wings. They all ask him to show compliance; even Antigone in *Oedipus at Colonus* makes reference to his "terrible wrath" (*kakos thymos*, *Oed. at Col.* 1199), which can be traced back to the dragon seed and is the cause of all evil in the family. As she says: "how terrible an end/ terrible wrath may have" (*Oed. at Col.* 1199-1200; "swift to anger," 1193). And when Oedipus accuses Kreon of high treason, the chorus pleads: "Be gracious, be merciful" (649). Once he is seized by his emotion, it is impossible to stop him. "Natures like yours/ are justly heaviest for themselves to bear" (673-74), Kreon points out. In other words, they are their own worst enemies.

Paradoxically, his anger stands in the way of solving the riddle, although it is at the same time the very thing that makes him press on when Teiresias, Iokaste and the shepherd try to put themselves between him and the truth, well knowing that the explanation will lead to catastrophe.

To the morphology of irascibility there also belongs a form of impulsive suddenness. Oedipus is thus inclined to hurry with his decisions in order always to be at the forefront of developments and to ensure that the plot he suspects is underway does not rob him of his power—"When he that plots against me secretly/ moves quickly, I must quickly counterplot" (618-20). And when he blinds himself, he fundamentally acts on the basis of the same suddenness, rashly, as he also regrets in *Oedipus at Colonus*—"I had begun to think my rage excessive,/ my punishment too great for what I had done" (437-38). And in this context, he makes reference to his misguided *thymos*.

All things considered, rage or irascibility is the primary cause of the plague. For King Laios and Oedipus share the evil nature to which Antigone referred and which has its source in the dragon seed. The mythological story that is clearly behind the misfortunes in *The Phoenician Women* is in brief that, when King Kadmos came to Thebes, Athene gave him the task of killing Ares' dragon, which guarded the spring of Castalia. Next, he was to sow its teeth in the ground. This he did. And from the teeth grew armed warriors who immediately began to fight each other until only five were left, the so-called *spartoi* or "seed men," the forefathers of the Theban noble families.

Laios descends from Kadmos, Iokaste from the warrior called Echion, which means dragon or serpent. All these warriors have purely chthonic names, one actually being called Chthonios. In other words, they are not only sowed men but snake-men and *autochthonoi*, brought forth by the Earth without fertilization. In *The Bacchae*, Dionysos punishes Kadmos by changing his sick family, along with his wife, into snakes. In this form, he is to be the leader of a great army of barbarians, until in an attack on Delphi he is killed by Apollo but saved by Ares for the land of the blessed.[8]

The myth is a cryptogram. But interpreted in the present context, it may be understood first of all that the Theban family has a chthonic origin; secondly that, developmentally, this disposition requires a transformation. The general task—as in the *Oresteia*—is to break away from the uniform world of the family and blood. Kadmos and his family do not succeed. So they are doomed to disaster, incapable metaphorically speaking of killing the serpent in themselves, as Apollo killed the Python serpent at Delphi.

But the anger from the dragon seed is also the ferment that explains why Oedipus is the first to find and maintain his fatal identity as the family's enemy. It is in extension of this that, in *Oedipus at Colonus*, he renounces the heritage of his biological family by anathematizing the Theban dragon seed in his sons. Instead, he settles down at Athens as a spiritual father to that city's king. Thus, the transformation from blood to spirit, from maternal rule to paternal rule, is brought about, and on this new foundation he becomes a protective hero—against his native city of Thebes—for the people of Athens. To get so far, however, he is forced to take upon himself the chthonic reality of his family and his blood in marriage to his own mother, to penetrate this reality as Odysseus did on his voyage home.

4

The crucial thing is that rage, the legacy of the dragon seed from which Oedipus springs, and his own aggressive refusal to compromise lead him down the long road of development and suffering. With this and without trembling hands, he maintains his determined and unswerving need and quest for the truth. With his *thymos*, he does everything in his power to reveal what others try to conceal, skip over or separate off. If anything, the tendency of other people to repress or leave in the subconscious increases his anger and paranoia. As he points out, this is presaged by the fact that he and he alone solved the riddle of the sphinx through the power of his thought. So there is a deeper significance to the fact that, in his confrontation with Teiresias, he so fiercely insists that the prophet was no match for the monster. For, Oedipus claims, it required true prophetic gifts:

> Plainly you had no such gift of prophecy
> From birds nor otherwise from any God
> To glean a word of knowledge. But I came,
> Oedipus, who knew nothing, and I stopped her.
> I solved the riddle by my wit alone.
>
> (394-98)

Here, the tragic irony radiates towards all the corners of the world: the blind man sees, the sighted man is blind.

Oedipus himself called for the blind prophet to interpret the curse of the plague by his inner clairvoyance. But when, with his knowledge of how things really hang together, Teiresias refuses to say anything, Oedipus' irascibility is aroused, and he forces the prophet, whose own anger Oedipus has aroused, to name him as the source of the infection: "Had you had eyes/ I would have said alone you murdered him" (345-46). In the subsequent increasingly heated discussion, Teiresias stamps him as "an enemy to kith and kin" (416). This is at once a curse and a redemption.

It is impossible to decide whether Teiresias himself understands the full implication of his prophecy, though it is most likely that he does not. He is thinking here only that, by killing his father and marrying his mother, Oedipus has become a pestilence to the country, the family and himself. The broader perspective, on the other hand, must be said to be reserved exclusively for the gods—and the compositional consciousness: that Oedipus is to be transformed into the spiritual identity that is the aim in *Oedipus at Colonus*. And there, as in the *Oresteia*, blood and spirit are separated. Or in other words: When he penetrates the biological world of his first ancestress, the primal core of the family, and again breaks away from it, it is now as an autonomous individual for whom the family surrounding him is an enemy on whom he places a curse.

No, not even Teiresias can obviously see so far, which is why he only outlines the fatal consequences of Oedipus' investigation: "You are the land's pollution" (352). He will be driven from the kingdom, robbed of daylight as a blind man: "Misery shall grind no man as it will you" (427), threatens the angry prophet. This does not suggest that he has any knowledge of the *apotheosis* awaiting Oedipus at Colonus.

As a reaction to this prophecy, Oedipus goes into a raging interpretative counter-storm, accusing Teiresias not only of being the perpetrator of the murder in con-spiracy with Kreon, but also of being incompetent, as he was unable to answer the sphinx. And as Oedipus insists on his own intellectual ability, he from now on forces out one interpretation after another. This takes him straight into the tragedy of which, knowingly unknowing, he has not the faintest idea, but which nevertheless ends by granting him knowledge of things about which he is at present ignorant.

Kreon—The Pragmatic Politician

The paranoid idea of being the victim of a conspiracy is at its height during his clash with his brother-in-law Kreon, who according to Oedipus was supposedly using Teiresias in his power game to win the throne. There are clear differences of nuance in the way in which Sophocles uses the figure of Kreon in the *Antigone* and in the later *Oedipus at Colonus*, but there are also many common features in the image of him as a more or less cynical practitioner of *realpolitik*. The light is least negative in *Oedipus the King*, although even here he is pragmatically inclined and describes himself as a "reasonable man" (*sophronein*, 589). He is circumspect and takes precautions by consulting with the god (1440), i.e., Apollo, and generally wants no problems in his official capacity.

Likewise, he rejects the accusations of being hungry for power by asserting that he lives in the best of all possible worlds, since he gets everything from Oedipus and lives in safety—"But if I were the king myself, I must/ do much that went against the grain" (590-91). In addition, he already has power in the sense that everything dealing with the day-to-day administration goes through him. So why want more?: "I am not so besotted yet that I/ want other honors than those that come with profit" (594-95).

In other words, he defines himself by reason, though here a rather pallid, circum-scribed kind. He is unheroic in every sense, a spokesman for small-mindedness. No tragedy can be made out of this character. This stands in glaring contrast to Oedipus' view that the king has made the fate and suffering of the people his own. In this sense, Kreon is bereft of any higher intent or spiritual dimension. He is in a corridor of power where only personal gain counts and, caught up in the momentary fulfill-ment of power, is thus, in contrast to the riddle-solving Oedipus, devoid of visions.

Wife—Mother

1

Iokaste is Oedipus' mother and wife. In order to grasp how these two roles encroach upon one another and, not least, on the history of his development, let us first look at her significance as spouse. There is apparently the same *homophrosyne*, spiritual unity between them as between Odysseus and Penelope, despite their age difference, to which no reference is made. Oedipus addresses her as "Dearest Iokaste" (950), revealing his passion and respect and similarly claiming: "I honour you more than I honour" all others (701). Because of the equality he assumes between them, he has given her broad authority—at least Kreon says to Oedipus: "You rule/this country giving her an equal share/ in the government?" (578-79). And Oedipus himself puts it in simple terms, but in such a way that it strikes sparks in the light of the tragedy as a whole: "Everything she wants/ she has from me" (580-01). But when she seeks to stop his investigation, he finally breaks her will.

That their love is mutual is partly revealed by the way in which she tries to calm Oedipus when things turn against him. She displays here a radical quality that can not only be founded on her wifely care but reaches deep into her femininity, not to say her primordial femininity.

The justification for this view is confirmed by her showing contempt, like Polyphemos, for the oracles and prophetic mediator of the gods—that is to say, a religious reality based on the patriarchal world of the Olympian gods. So she rejects Teiresias' prophecy, saying: "Human beings/ have no part in the craft of prophecy" (709-10). And as an example she points out that Apollo's oracle indicating that Laios would be killed by his son was not fulfilled. No, she says, struck by the irony that always strikes those who are deluded; that was what came out that oracle.

As Oedipus' fear grows, Iokaste denies and indeed goes so far as to question "the outcome of the holy oracles of the Gods" (951). That she is here close to blaspheming can be seen from the violent reaction of the chorus, which makes the logical but also fatal demand that the oracle should demonstrate that it speaks the truth, for what would otherwise happen with faith? —"Apollo is nowhere clear in honour; God's service perishes" (910). This is a fateful prayer and desire, because it can only be fulfilled with the death of the man and the king on whom their hope of salvation depends.

2

When the messenger from Corinth announces to Oedipus that his father is dead, for a brief moment apparently annulling the prophecy, Iokaste takes it both as evidence that prophecies cannot be counted on and as an opportunity for inspiring strength in Oedipus, when he asks whether he should not fear his mother's bed? No, she replies. Since human beings in any case cannot divine the paths of Fate, one should be relaxed about life. And she continues:

> Before this, in dreams too, as well as oracles,
> Many a man has lain with his own mother.
> But he to whom such things are nothing bears
> His life most easily.

> (981-84)

The fantastic thing about this quotation is less the use to which Freud put it than that here for the first and only time in world literature we hear with our own ears how a mother goddess actually thinks and speaks to her son and lover.

Of course, it is about dreaming, but the words nevertheless show that, if it is to be, Iokaste is ready to undertake the dual role of wife and mother to the same man. It is evidence that deep down she has nothing against incest, which is as natural a thing to her as it was for primordial mothers. She does not attach weight to incest as a patriarchal morality would do, but at the same time she knows that in his dreams a man harbors this primordial history in which he is his mother's spouse. It is these dreams from which civilized man has intellectually separated himself but is caught by in his dream life, if we are to believe Iokaste—and Freud.

This is actually a very sensitive area among the Greeks, as we have already seen in *The Suppliant Maidens*, where their father orders the Danaids to flee from incestuous marriages to their cousins. The motif can also be found in Plato. In the *Republic*, it seems to be a well-known secret that dreams can have an incestuous content of this kind—"[A dream] does not shrink from attempting to lie with a mother in fancy."⁹ In the most rabid and shameless way, the dream raises itself above the regime of laws and reason. Partly by reference to Oedipus, Plato makes it plain in *The Laws* that incestuous relationships are "all unhallowed, abominations to God, deeds of black shame."¹⁰

Insofar as these laws and these gods have a patriarchal origin and provide the basis for Athens' legal system, Iokaste's indifferent view of the seriousness of incest becomes in itself an indication of the atavistic and feminine primordial stage in which she in reality finds herself and on the basis of which she acts. In other words, by solving the riddle of the sphinx with his answer, Oedipus has opened the way to this mother's embrace and thereby penetrated the mystery of femininity. Iokaste certainly becomes his wife, but she is at the same time his biological mother.

Although little is told about King Laios, from an archetypal perspective we can say that as he agrees to murder his newborn son, he must be subjected to Iokaste in the role of the evil mother. And in order to stress that she has this primordial character of an evil mother who sacrifices her sons, it is emphasized that the planned murder of Oedipus is at her behest (1166 ff.). Like the kings Laertes and Alkinoos, in the *Odyssey*, Laios is for better or for worse dominated by his wife. They are all only half liberated in their masculinity and still fixated at the primordial maternal stage.

At the same time, the father as lawgiver stands in the way of the son and will do anything to preserve the inertia of his power, which is why Laios must be removed, as happens in the crossroads at Delphi. However, as a result Oedipus makes his way directly into the maternal reality, which remains as an unknown territory in his pre-consciousness until the plague appears from outside as a sign of what is wrong within.

3

That behind her roles as woman, wife and queen, Iokaste has roots in this layer of the (sub)conscious (as do also, for instance, the Erinyes), is confirmed by the way in which she both deals with the gods' oracle and seeks to keep Oedipus in ignorance when she realizes who he is, ready herself to maintain their marriage in a forbidden incestuous relationship.

Like Klytemnestra in the *Oresteia*, she is identified or synonymized with the mythical primordial mother, who produces the seeds of the earth and uses them in her self-breeding. In the *Oresteia*, the primordial mother Gaia is called she "who brings all things to birth, who gives them strength, then gathers their big yield into herself at last" (*Lib.* 127). She has herself been impregnated by her own sons. Not until the son can separate himself from this *perpetuum mobile* is culture a possibility in that as a man he can now form and act on the basis of his liberated masculine subject.

The text's own imagery establishes the presence of such a complex. In smooth metaphorical transitions, Iokaste and Gaia are coupled together so that they are ultimately united in the primordial mother. In his prophecy Teiresias already touches on the fact that Oedipus in his marriage has sailed before a favorable wind into a dangerous harbor—"when you shall learn the secret of your marriage,/ which steered you to a haven in this house,—/ haven no haven, after lucky voyage?" (421-23). And the very same image appears again towards the end, when their relationship stands fully illuminated and the chorus plaintively chants that the wife opened her "harbor" to both husband and son.[11] Oedipus is indeed several times compared to an oarsman standing at the helm of state: "you who steered the country I love safely" (693), as it is put, for example, using an expression that Sophocles frequently employs in his tragedies and is also found in Aeschylus: the state viewed as a ship.[12] But if ship and harbor are linked to Oedipus as helmsman, this explains why the country is struck by the plague.

The image is extended even further when it is taken directly into organic imagery of the actual fertilization and breeding. For the question is now raised of how it could be that the same maternal womb, like a field, could be sowed by the son as well as the father. Again, the image of the ploughed field appears in the chorus' words: "How, O how, have the furrows ploughed/[13] by your father endured to bear you, poor wretch,/ and hold their peace so long?" (1210-12). And in an extension of what has already been said, it could be claimed that this silence actually comes from the fact that Iokaste, as a mother, has nothing to object to; she is ready, if it can be put this way, to allow herself to be ploughed further.

That there is a violation of patriarchy's prohibition of incest is something of which the tragedy itself provides evidence in that the image anticipates the servants' description of how, standing before his mother's body, Oedipus has called upon his wife: "This mother's womb, this field of double sowing whence I sprang/ and where I sowed my children" (1256-57). It is this coincidence of imagery that leads to the identification that Oedipus in the pain of self-recognition undertakes when he ascribes to Iokaste her hidden emblematic meaning as Gaia, Mother Earth, who from the same womb bred fathers and sons:

You bred me and again when you had bred
Bred children of your child and showed to men
Brides, wives and mothers and the foulest deeds
That can be in this world of ours.

(1405-09)

Behind the image of Iokaste as a Gaia figure there is further embedded in the text's own iconography a hugely magnified mother figuration linked to the sur-roundings—namely, the mountainous landscape around Thebes: Kithairon as par-turient nature. For as the messenger from Corinth relates, it was from this (mater-nal) landscape (or symbolical womb) that Oedipus, consecrated and doomed to death, was born: "On Kithairon's slopes/in the twisting thickets you were found" (1026-27).

And when, in the belief that he was born of unknown, poor parents, Oedipus makes Fate (Tyche) herself his mother[14] with the words: "If I am your prophet and wise of heart/you shall not fail, Kithairon" (1089-90), the chorus immediately assigns his conception to Kithairon, which, as the chorus says, acted as "native to him and mother and nurse at once" (1092). Finally, even in the hour of his fate, Oedipus himself anthropomorphizes Kithairon as a maternal mountain: "Kithairon, why did you receive me? Why/ having received me did you not kill me straight?" (1393-94).

Becoming Your Own Self

1

From being an isolated question about the identity of the murderer whose blood guilt has brought the plague to Thebes, things move very quickly. Now it is a question of who Oedipus is. And as in the moment of truth, the drama's *anagnori-sis*, it emerges that the two questions cannot be kept apart; the worst possible con-sequences are unleashed. Even during the encounter with Teiresias, things begin to go wrong. For the prophet succeeds in sowing doubt in the mind of Oedipus when he says that Oedipus' parents will find him wise. "What parents? Stop! Who are they of all the world?" (428), Oedipus asks. Teiresias mocks him now because he who believes himself created for solving riddles cannot interpret the message: that his birth will be his death.

Stubbornly, Oedipus nevertheless maintains his search for the truth when those around him who hold the answer to his identity refuse to give it to him. When, to her horror, his mother makes the connection between things, she tries to stop Oedipus, who replies: "I will not be persuaded to let be/ the chance of finding out the whole thing clearly" (1062-63). And when his mother replies: "God keep you from the knowledge of who you are" (1069), he insists on continuing: "Break out what will! I at least shall be/ willing to see my ancestry, though humble" (1077-78). He says this when he learns that he was found on Mount Kithairon. Only a person who is determined to discover his own identity regardless of the cost will speak in this way.

When the herdsman who was to have exposed him and was later present at the killing of King Laios is finally called as state evidence, he, too, attempts to keep silent about the true facts. When the shepherd declares that he is on the point of saying frightful things, Oedipus exclaims in fury: "And I of frightful hearing. But I must hear" (1165). Regardless of what fear Oedipus may have, he forces the true answer out of him by his own violence.

2

In the meantime, after a final vain attempt to stop her son's detective work, Iokaste flees to her bedchamber, to the marriage bed, the place of sexuality and fertility, where, calling upon Laios, she hangs herself. Since it may be said that the cause of her suicide was Oedipus' solving the riddle of himself and thereby the reality of their marriage, a sort of parallel arises to his solving the riddle of the sphinx, which also led to the death of that female monster. The sphinx plunged into the abyss, just as in certain myths it is told that Iokaste threw herself into an abyss.

If we try to maintain this mythical symbolism for a moment, the sphinx and Iokaste are mirrored in each other in the same way as we earlier saw in the relationship between Kirke and Skylla, the same duality as the sphinx's of woman and monster, a day side and a night side. Oedipus has opened his way into this reality in his investigation of his hidden identity. And this involvement in the secret of gender in the son's differentiation from it makes incest into a taboo and creates a masculine awareness.

As was the case with Odysseus, what Oedipus experiences is typologically speaking his second birth in his encounter with the primordial feminine as both personal and a collective subconscious. This riddle existing in the surrounding world is confronted, endured, decoded and integrated as the self is made truly independent.

At this intersection, as we also have already seen, there are only two possibilities in the hero's life: regression or progression. Iokaste clearly seeks to persuade Oedipus to a regression into the Great Mother, into subjection, by keeping him in ignorance of who he is and to whom he is married. It is this form of castration to which Odysseus feared Kirke would expose him, the self-castration to which the priests subjected themselves in various fertility cults.

But the plague with which Apollo as the divinity of consciousness reveals the untenability in the marital relationship between mother and son forces Oedipus via his anger to free himself from his mother's embrace. Fundamentally, he "brings her down" just as Odysseus brought down the wild boar. Both are marked by a trauma as evidence of the individuating experience, a mark by which they can always be recognized later: Odysseus by his scar, Oedipus by his unseeing eyes.

In short, in Oedipus' previous history a doubling, or perhaps rather a split, has taken place in the actual parental constellation, as we saw in the case of Odysseus. Thus his adoptive parents in Corinth represent what we usually understand by normal, caring parents, who look after and raise their children. When, in his misunderstanding, Oedipus flees from Corinth to avoid the terrible oracle, it is only as part of his painful process of gaining insight to be led into the mythical mystery of creation, linked to family, blood, birth and what is beneath the earth, as it is called in tragedies.

3

Only when he recognizes who he is does Oedipus release himself from the dark knowledge and power of the maternal womb that holds the family together. He has become himself, a self, in utter negation. A plague, hated by the gods. "To this guilt I bore witness against myself" (1386), he says, ready to allow his fate to be sealed: "Let my fate /go where it will" (1459). And as prophesied by Teiresias, he remains "an enemy to kith and kin" (416).

When he blinds himself, an action he later regrets in *Oedipus at Colonus*, he follows his impulsive irascibility and need to act. At the present moment, he feels the necessity of making himself his own judge and executioner, since with the fate he has met he can no longer face the world with open eyes. They shall never again see what he has suffered and brought about. And he stabs them, not only once, but again and again with his mother's golden pins, which held together the hanged woman's costume, from which he has taken them.

In this self-blinding, the gory paradox of suffering is realized. For as he stabs out his eyes, with which he has been hitherto been unable to discern the cohesion in his existence, he receives the gift of internal sight in exchange and can now—like the blind Teiresias—see the unity of his life and accept this unity as consciousness and the unifying structure of memory. Oedipus has thereby once again shown himself to be a riddle solver and has here done what he promised to do at the beginning of the tragedy: to find the murderer and to punish him properly; he has removed the mark of shame—"a champion of my country and the God" (136). Once again, he saves his native city, Thebes, but this time by taking the punishment upon himself as the guilty party hated by the gods, and the plague releases its hold on the city.

4

Even in his fall, Oedipus maintains his link with Fate. He shows piety in his anger when he yields to Fate, because it is one with his identity, his *daimon*. And it is done voluntarily, that is to say as an expression of his own freedom to choose and to act, which he characterizes in this way:

> It was Apollo, friends, Apollo,
> That brought this bitterness, my sorrows to completion.
> But the hand that struck me
> Was none but my own.
> (1329-33)

So he calculates with some sort of division of labor. Apollo is certainly the origin of everything, but when it comes to the point, he took his own fate into his hands when he stabbed out his eyes. He did it of his own free will and as his own idea. That by the radical nature of his action he has also made himself incomprehensible to those around him can be seen quite clearly from the chorus' conventional reaction: has he been driven to this by a *daimon*, an evil spirit, he was unable to control? The chorus also expresses the pious wish that it had never heard his name and believes that it would have been much better for him, if he were rather "dead than blind and living" (1369). These words infuriate him, yet another piece of evidence that he has retained his integrity, as he simply tells the chorus to be silent: "Do not give me further counsel" (1371).

The blood flows freely from his punctured eyes, down over his cheeks, coloring his beard red as a sign that the power with which he has been one in his sexuality, the power of blood, is now broken. The transformation commences when he peels away all external power and blinds himself as evidence of that transformation: as father and brother he now stretches out to his daughters "a brother's hands" (1482). In his love for his daughters, sexuality, so far linked together with power to Iokaste, is thereby transformed. The lust for possession has now become a deeply felt spiritual *eros*.

He leaves Thebes, as predicted by the riddle of the sphinx, on three legs, with his daughters supporting him as crutches. However, it is difficult from the course of this fateful suffering to discover for certain whether Oedipus really thereby achieves complete selfhood, separated from the maternally-determined nature and blood of the family.

For several reasons, this interpretation may be doubted. In part, because he blinds himself with his mother's decorative broaches; in part, because he finally disappears into the symbolic maternal mountain range, Kithairon, where he originally should have been put to death. Here, Aktaion was killed by Artemis and, here, the Bacchae remain to tear King Pentheus apart in *The Bacchae*. So it may seem as if Oedipus regresses, that is to say that he has lost the battle to liberate himself from the nature of the primordial mother. But judging from the context, this cannot be Sophocles' intention. There is on the contrary a progression in which, through his traumatization, he is made into a free man, a subject, and a human being who, with this long and painful "rebirth," is ultimately part of Apollo's much greater plan. This is, however, only revealed at the end of his life. For if we extend his life into *Oedipus at Colonus*, we can no longer doubt that Sophocles' overall intention was to show the way to a free self and a psychological reality in which the primordial feminine is no longer dominant. Uncertain of the path assigned to him by fate, he begins his long journey of suffering towards death at Colonus. If the question in *Oedipus the King* was: Who am I? - then in *Oedipus at Colonus* he is confronted with the final riddle: What did the gods want of me?

Oedipus at Colonus— A Gift to Mankind

1

When we once again meet Oedipus in *Oedipus at Colonus*—as said above written approximately twenty-five years after *Oedipus the King* and the last tragedy

Sophocles created— so much time has gone by that, like the poet himself, he has become old and is facing death. But with this, the uncertainty that *Oedipus the King* could raise is also gone. Oedipus, having arrived at the grove of the Eumenides in Colonus, a village near Athens, is at the end of his road. Through the oracle of Apollo, which is passed to him by his daughter Ismene, he now knows with certainty that he is acting in accordance with the heavy-handed plans for his life allotted to him by the god before he was born and the extent of which he has to hitherto not known. When the hour of death arrives, there will be an omen for him in the form of a peal of thunder.

To the chorus, consisting of citizens from Colonus who want to drive him away from the sacred place, he says that they shall not force him to leave because he is there with the understanding of the gods:

> Therefore be mindful of me and of Apollo,
> for when he gave me oracles of evil,
> he also spoke of this a resting place,
> after long years, in the last country, where
> I should find home among the sacred Furies.
>
> (85-89)

The chorus calls him willful and impious because he will not leave. And when they realise who he really is, they are seized with panic at the idea that Oedipus with his guilt will be a source of infection for the country: "Our country is not for you!/ Wind no further/ your clinging evil upon us" (233-35).

2

During this entire intermezzo, we are witnesses to the fact that, despite his claim of having learned patience—"suffering and time,/ vast time, have been instructors in contentment" (5-6)—Oedipus has not lost his contentious nature. So his daughter Antigone must ask him several times to moderate himself, at one point referring, as previously mentioned, to the family's "terrible wrath" (*kakos thymos*, 1195). To the chorus' amazement, this wreck of a man claims not only that the god Apollo has led him there but that "all I shall say will be clear-sighted indeed" (74). And he warns the chorus against acting contrary to the will of the gods, for, all-seeing, they punish anyone who defies them, and Oedipus is in their eyes a holy man.

Haggard, with unshorn hair, covered in filthy rags that have rubbed into his skin—a portrait reminiscent of Odysseus as a beggar—his external appearance corresponds to the sufferings he has endured on his wanderings, accompanied only by his daughters since falling from power in Thebes, but it does not reflect his inner reality. He has preserved all his regal authority as inner dignity and still speaks like a ruler. He has put his life in the hands of the god and will "confer benefit on those who receive me" (92), but "a curse on those who have driven me away" (93), like Thebes. And so this pile of rags can give himself as a sacred gift to the King of

Athens, Theseus: "For I come here as one endowed with grace/ by those who are over Nature; and I bring/ advantage to this race" (286-288).

Indeed, after his death, in connection with the cult[15] that will arise around him, he will be a force that protects against any threat coming from outside. And here he is thinking especially of his own family in Thebes, the dragon seed, who, as will be seen, want to get their hands on him for the same reason. To Theseus, he says:

> I come to give you something, and the gift
> Is my own beaten self: No feast for the eyes;
> Yet in me is a more lasting grace than beauty.
>
> (575-77)

The way in which Oedipus has presented himself here corresponds to his appearance before the people in *Oedipus the King* as an elevated monarch, one suffering on their behalf. Looking back on this, he speaks with words given weight by the suffering he took upon himself when he solved the mystery of his own life: "One soul, I think, often can make atonement/ for many others, if it be sincere" (498-99).

Guilt-Free and Sacred

1

It is not without reason that Oedipus believes no other human being has had so heavy a burden as he. At the same time, he declares himself now free of guilt. This interpretation is clearly different from what he had in *Oedipus the King*, where it is precisely the recognition of his own guilt that makes him gouge out his eyes. Now, he understands: "For I suffered those deeds more than I acted them" (266).

To the curious chorus, who interrogate him about his crime, he explains that it is true he killed his father, but that it happened without his realizing it. He did not know who it was. And so he can now declare: "Before the law, before God, I am innocent" (547). Indeed, even if he murdered his father knowing who he was, he would still, according to law, be free of guilt, since it happened in self-defense. He came ignorant to the scene of his crime—"But those who wronged me knew, and ruined me" (274). With these words, he is thinking of his parents, who were fully conscious of what they were doing when they attempted to kill him.

When, during their violent confrontation, Kreon later forces him to retell in even more detail the story of his suffering and thereby further torments him, Oedipus declares himself guiltless. And he puts forward the hypothesis that his misfortune must be due to an inherited curse in the family, as he cannot connect what happened with anything criminal in himself:

> In me myself you could not find such evil
> As would have made me sin against my own.
> And tell me this: If there were prophecies
> Repeated by the oracles of the gods,

That father's death should come through his own son,
How could you justly blame it upon me?
On me, who was yet unborn, yet unconceived,
Not yet existent for my father and mother?
If then I came into the world—as I did come—
In wretchedness, and met my father in fight,
And knocked him down, not knowing that I had killed him
Nor whom I killed—again, how could you find
Guilt in that unmeditated act?

(966-78)

On the other hand, he knows for certain that he acted from a much greater will, that of the gods: "*Forced into it by the gods*" (998).

2

Through his trauma, Oedipus—and with him Sophocles—has also arrived at a different view of justice than what applied in *Oedipus the King*. For, remarkably enough, no one there took up a position on the fact that he had no earthly idea or awareness of the fate in which he was involved. His actions alone spoke for him. In the intervening years, a crucial development seems to have taken place, so that *Oedipus at Colonus* comes to represent a higher sense of justice. There is now a clear distinction between motive and action. Not only has a sense of justice become an internal matter, as has already been described in the *Oresteia*, but by shouldering his fate, Oedipus has also brought the law so far that the court must now take up a position on intention in every crime.

He has done nothing on purpose, but was brought by the gods to the fate he bears. Consequently, he also assesses his self-blinding differently from what he did at that time. He believes now that he judged himself too harshly when he gouged out his eyes, the consequence of his obdurate mind: "It was only later, when my madness cooled,/ and I had begun to think my rage excessive" (436-37). But when, as he likewise explains in *Oedipus at Colonus*, he finally achieved this insight and his gloom was made light, he was driven away by the people and Kreon.

Feeling that the gods see in him a pious man, Oedipus has kept himself going on his doddering legs until, in the grove of the Eumenides, he finds the place to which he is destined. Through his daughter Ismene, Apollo reveals what has always been the purpose of his suffering: after his death, he will become a force of supreme value for the people with whom he finds rest. His daughter Ismene sums up the result of his life in these words: "For the gods who threw you down sustain you now" (394). The royal power he lost in Thebes is replaced by a supra-individual, spiritual power which, as the future protector of Athens, he receives directly from the gods.

The Tempters

1

The immediate drama in *Oedipus at Colonus* is this: the family in Thebes, learning of the prophecy of Oedipus'.power as protector, seeks him out in order to lure him back even though the family also drove him away just when he had come to an understanding of his fate. This potential temptation meets him in two forms: King Kreon and his son Polyneikes, in that order.

Pretending to act out of love for him, Kreon demands of Oedipus: "You should have more reverence for Thebes,/ since long ago she was your kindly nurse" (759-60). Oedipus sees through him and furiously calls him a deceiver, who is once again trying to catch him in his net (764). And when Kreon sets himself up as judge of Odysseus' fate, he is revealed as the one who is really breaking the law. Not only, as in the *Antigone*, does he seek his own advantage, but he uses violence in an attempt to kidnap Oedipus and to blackmail him by taking his daughters.

With his intervention, Theseus also stamps Kreon as a person who does not observe the laws of the country—"You cast aside her authority,/ take what you please, and worse, by violence" (915-16). Despite the white hair he claims to have, Kreon is a man without insight—"A long life/seems to have left you witless as you are old" (929-30), says Theseus. On the other hand, Theseus appears as a king who thinks of others rather than himself and opposes the tyrannical Kreon with the words:"The whole city/ must not seem overpowered by one man" (1032-33).This supra-individual self-understanding puts Theseus in the same category as Oedipus.

2

Upon meeting Theseus, Oedipus can by a spiritual congruence with him recognize his own mirror image and greets him: "I thank you with these words./ All that I have I owe to your courtesy" (1129-30). The chorus also views Theseus as a savior, without stating precisely how. Sophocles has assumed here that the audience knew Theseus as the mythical hero who, through Herculean trials, unified Attica, made Athens its capital and became its lawgiver. That is to say that he is ascribed many of the same functions as, in the *Oresteia*, are attributed to Athene, namely the formation of democracy and the establishment of a man-made court and legal practice.

As said during the analysis of the *Oresteia*, Theseus also represents a revolt against the feminine, as he defeats the Amazons (see p. 404) who wish to reconquer their queen, the wife of Theseus—and the mother of Hippolytos. To the same scheme of things belongs the fact that, coming from the outside, he breaks with the chthonic family system that, in the form of snake kings such as Kekrops and Erechtheus, has previously ruled Athens, and he thereby opens the way for democracy. It is also this democratic law that Kreon cunningly asserts in order to have Oedipus delivered to him: "Such at least was my estimate of the wisdom/ native to the Areopagus; I thought/ Athens was not a home for such exiles" (946-49). However, Theseus is not deceived by Kreon's attempt to tie him to a view of law that Kreon himself does not follow.

3

In order to get Thebes and the Theban family finally separated from Oedipus and in a further spiritual sense to make Athens his new native city and Theseus his heir and "son," Sophocles adds the reckoning with his biological son and brother, Polyneikes. Like Kreon, Oedipus' sons put power first and so are in a state of mutual conflict. This also applies to their relationship with their father, who complains that they "would not give up the throne to have me back" (418).

Polyneikes tries to persuade his father to join his side in a military expedition, after he has been driven away from the city by Kreon and his brother, Eteokles, with whom he is to take it in turn to rule. As said above, this war and the brothers' killing of each other is the background to *Seven Against Thebes*, *Antigone* and Euripides' *The Phoenician Women*. As in these works, according to *Oedipus at Colonus*, the mutual fratricide will also be a direct consequence of the curse Oedipus has called down upon his sons.

When Polyneikes tries to obtain his father's support, Oedipus has such difficulty restraining his temper that Antigone is forced to intercede and again asks her father to control himself and listen to his son, which he then does. Yet, even though Polyneikes tries to justify his earlier actions and desires forgiveness, Oedipus sends him away, because he will not acknowledge his sons as his children:

> Now go! For I abominate and disown you!
> You utter scoundrel! Go with the malediction,
> I here pronounce for you: that you shall never
> Master your native land by force of arms,
> Nor ever see your home again in Argos,
> The land below the hills; but you shall die
> By your own brother's hand (. . .).
>
> (1383-87)

Oedipus desires and prophesies, as indeed happens, that the brothers will destroy each other with the quarrelsome disposition they have inherited through Oedipus from the Kadmos family and the dragon seed, against which he himself will now protect the Athenians. For he predicts, as was historically the case in Sophocles' time, that Thebes would attack Athens and that he, Oedipus, would come up from his grave to "drink hot blood of theirs" (622).

Antigone fails to persuade Polyneikes not to let hatred rule and thus once again bring misfortune upon Thebes. Making reference to her father's curse, she begs: "See how you fulfil his prophesies!/ Did he not cry that you should kill each other?" (1424-25). Not for nothing is Polyneikes his father's son. As the eldest, he cannot tolerate being dishonored by his brother. Since he goes to his fate cursed by Oedipus, who populates his road with "his avenging Furies" (1434), he makes Antigone promise that she will take care of his burial, when his father's curse is fulfilled.

By thus cutting off all connection with this family and his sons and seeing in them now only strangers and enemies, Oedipus has settled his account and finally separated himself from the mythical reality that the world of Thebes constitutes. He has thus consummated the family curse. The power he possesses now no longer consists of the bond of blood, but as a spiritual reality has moved from Thebes to Athens and to its ruler Theseus. And the family ties that Oedipus now establishes with Theseus are based on a community of fate, whereas his biological sons have refused him protection. Theseus has shown magnanimity by immediately receiving and protecting Oedipus despite his earlier history because in Oedipus he is reminded of his own fate as a child: "I/ too was an exile. I grew up abroad,/ and in strange lands I fought as few men have/ with danger and with death" (561-64).

Apotheosis
1

When Polyneikes—the last character from Thebes—has left the stage, it begins to thunder, the sign that Oedipus is about to reach his goal; the time has come. Only the "pure" remain. The chorus first fears that the gods are thundering in anger, since they have had dealings with the sinful Oedipus. However, he lets Theseus understand that he will now redeem his promise in gratitude for his goodness and give himself to him and Athens as protector. At the same time, he will initiate Theseus into the secret words or things that he alone may know and must pass on to his descendants. Thus will they for ever be able to protect themselves against the dragon brood from Thebes.

The subsequent heroization of Oedipus is shrouded in mystery. As in *Oedipus the King*, a messenger describes what he calls a "thing that seems so marvellous" (1587). No man before him has passed away in such an astounding manner. Perhaps a god fetched him or Hades benevolently opened its depths. The inconsolable Antigone likewise believes that he received a death that anyone would wish for but neither words nor ideas can comprehend—"Something invisible and strange/ caught him up—or down—into a space unseen" (1681-82).

From the moment he crosses the copper threshold into the ravine, where the Eumenides' sacred spot is located, the events come under and are coloured by chthonic iconography. So far, he has been led in his blindness by his daughters, but as the sanctified person he now is, no one may touch him any longer. Now it is he who leads, as he calls upon Persephone and Hermes in their function as *psychopomps* guiding souls to the underworld. With water taken from Demeter's hill, he washes himself, sacrifices and dresses festively, ready for his *apotheosis*.

The ruler of the underworld, Zeus Chthonios (1605), answers with a roll of thunder, corresponding to the thunder that is due to Zeus Teleios (1079), the accomplisher, who from first to last has made his mark on Oedipus' fate—and on the compositional consciousness. Thus the upper and the lower Zeus are united in his death. A unity of the Olympian and the chthonic, which is further emphasized by the fact that, after the *epiphany*, Theseus sacrifices to both Gaia and the gods of Olympus: "We saw him do reverence/ to Earth and to the powers of the air" (1653).

A peal of thunder impatiently calls on Oedipus by the name that has identified his fate from birth, the pierced heels: "Oedipus! Oedipus! Why are we waiting?/ You delay too long; you delay too long to go" (1627-28). He must say farewell to his daughters, since the rest is forbidden knowledge in which only Theseus is entitled to participate. He remains behind as a witness, but at a distance he can be seen shading his eyes with his hand, dazzled by the resplendence that appears as Oedipus disappears into the sacred space.[16]

<h2 style="text-align:center">2</h2>

Since Oedipus finds rest in death with the Eumenides, the question again emerges of whether he returns to the world of the primordial mothers, which he has just chosen to leave by renouncing Thebes and, if so, whether this is a regression so that his liberation and independence have gone awry? This can hardly be the intention, nor is it.

The Eumenides are certainly attributed with the same characteristics as the Erinyes—"most dreadful are its divinities, most feared,/ daughters of darkness and mysterious earth" (39-40). Right from the start, an underlying connection is established between them and Oedipus as of course the chorus also sees him as terrifying. But the Eumenides are also mentioned in passing as "powers holy and awful" (*semnai theai*, 458), i.e., in the same way as the awesome goddesses with whom the Erinyes merge after their transformation in the *Oresteia*. It is also in this transformed shape that Oedipus meets the divine powers of the underworld, who, as their peaceful nature reveals, are subject to the will of Apollo as yet another proof of the peaceful covenant between the chthonic, the Olympian, and the human sense of justice.

By making himself into an enemy of the family and accepting his guilt, Oedipus creates a reality of the same character as arose when the Erinyes in the *Oresteia* were transformed into the Eumenides. So it makes sense that he should end his days with them since together with them he is to ensure for the city state of Athens the strength to resist its enemies, a role corresponding to that which Athene herself assumed in the *Oresteia*.

The Eumenides in Aeschylus certainly guaranteed fertility for Athens, but they kept their original fearful appearance and were still supposed to punish the sinful. In his heroization, Oedipus comes to possess the same duality. In relation to his family in Thebes, he is described as an Eriny who will drink the warm blood of his family if they attack Athens. From now on, he is the worst enemy of his family and his enemies, but at the same time he is a loyal and caring protector to his friends. To put this in the context of the underlying political reality, it can be said that Oedipus becomes the ideal protector of Athenian democracy and its new legal order or perhaps the supreme incarnation of the free citizen, who is clear-sighted enough to make the right moral choices. In this sense, he is a descendant of Odysseus and a precursor to Socrates.

3

Oedipus has achieved the power he possesses by refashioning the nature of power itself. The earthly power which he had as king in Thebes is replaced by spiritual power from the gods. As said above, a similar change takes place in his ability to love. The sexuality of his marriage to Iokaste is transformed into the concern he feels for his daughters and in a supra-individual sense shows to Athens, the symbolical contrast to his bloodstained maternal and familial world in Thebes, which he has rejected in his impetuous search for the truth.

And as a consequence of their belligerent behavior and betrayal of him, Oedipus has at the same time taken revenge on his sons. On the other hand, he shows gratitude for his daughters' self-sacrifice and blesses them at the moment of his departure: "I know it was hard, my children.—And yet one word/ makes all those difficulties disappear: that word is love" (1614-16). That the daughters have felt this love is revealed by their inconsolate sorrow at their father's departure.

Theseus has promised Oedipus that he will take care of them—as though they were sisters or daughters and he himself a spiritual father or brother. However, Antigone does not wish to remain in Athens. Together with her sister, she will return to Thebes in the hope of in time being able to mediate between her brothers and ward off their father's curse on them and the city—"Send us back, then, to ancient Thebes/ and we may stop the bloody war/ from coming between our brothers" (1770-73), says Antigone to Theseus. It remains a pious wish. As we saw in the *Antigone*, written many years before, the brothers murder each other and fulfill the curse the father has called down upon them. Antigone, on the other hand, by burying her brother in defiance of the king's decree, places her ability to love above earthly law and, like Oedipus, honors the gods, thereby raising a lasting monument to herself.

Philoktetes—A Moral Mobilization Tract

1

Keeping in mind the huge crisis in which Athens found itself politically and morally at the time when Sophocles was writing *Oedipus at Colonus*, we can view the tragedy as a sort of mobilization tract: Oedipus and Theseus represent the elevated and partly heroic values that contemporary society had lost. That this thought was extremely important to Sophocles, as it also was to Euripides, can be documented by the tragedy *Philoktetes* (409 B.C.), also written a few years before his death. In this sense, the play may be considered as a sort of subtext to and visualization of the contemporary perspective implicit in *Oedipus at Colonus*, which is why my analysis of *Philoktetes* will also aim at retrospectively making the hidden meaning clear.

In other words, as tragedy, *Philoktetes* only becomes fully comprehensible if we view it as a parable of the contemporary crisis of values in spiritual life and politics. That is to say, the *Philoktetes* is a text which, dressed up as myth, interprets the collective breakdown and, in a counter-move deriving from the power unleashed by the noble heroes in the course of the tragedy, tries to construct a utopia on a view of life going back to the *arete* of earlier times.

So the purpose of this reading is to reveal this side of Sophocles' thought and to create a transition to Euripides and Plato, where we shall see this thematic world displayed in its entirety. This will be done partly by bringing in Thucydides' history to throw light on Athenian degeneration during the Peloponnesian War, and partly by investigating of the role of the Sophists. Sophocles may have found inspiration for his work in his younger colleague Euripides in the way in which he uses myth to interpret contemporary conflicts. Sophocles is methodical in his use of the mirroring technique; he sets off his characters against each other just as the environment has an evident role as a symbolical marker.

2

The latter is not least true in the *Philoktetes*, because the play is set on a deserted island, which is intended to mirror the total isolation from humankind in which Philoktetes lives, having been left there by the Greeks on the advice of Odysseus on their way to Troy because of the suppurating and evil-smelling snake bite on his foot, from which he still suffers terribly. The Greek army has made a vain attempt to conquer Troy when the Trojan prince and prophet, Helenos, whom Odysseus has taken prisoner, reveals under torture that the city can only be taken by Philoktetes with the bow he inherited from Herakles, because he was the only one who is willing to light his funeral pyre.

This is the situation at the beginning of the tragedy. Odysseus has been given the task of bringing the suffering hero back. However, it will be impossible for him. Philoktetes hates him as Odysseus recommended he should be marooned and because he harbors the same hatred towards his cunning type of mind that Achilleus expressed in the *Iliad*. So it is dramatically alarming that it is Achilleus' innocent young son, Neoptolemos, whom Odysseus decides to use for his purpose. In contrast to his description in the *Ajax*, Sophocles has made Odysseus into a pragmatic and cynical power broker, who has more in common with Kreon in the *Antigone* and *Oedipus at Colonus*, and the negative portraits in Euripides modeling Odysseus on an image of the Sophistic politician.

It is amazing that Sophocles could create such divergent interpretations of Odysseus. We can simply marvel at the psychological span of this character. Sophocles has simply forced apart the positive and negative sides in his nature which in the *Odyssey* exist side by side and in the *Philoktetes* concentrated on those features pointing towards his grandfather, whether he is identified as Autolykos or in this case as Sisyphos. By absolutizing these tainted characteristics, his interpretation has so detached itself from Homer that it primarily reflects his own purpose.

3

We may wonder why a single man should be able to make such a great difference for the Greek army and what specific characteristics Philoktetes must be in possession of. It is here the contemporary context offers a helpful explanatory key. For just as the Greeks were unable to take Troy, it can be seen as a sign that Athenian state power was being undermined by the city's inability to go the distance in the war against Sparta.

The moral decay of the Greek army in the Trojan War is illustrated by all the best heroes having fallen, as Neoptolemos explains to Philoktetes, who even though a super-hero has been put out of action. His father Achilleus, the greatest of the great, is dead, as are Patroklos, Antilochos and Ajax. All that are left in addition to Odysseus are the tarnished figures of the Atreidae and, a veritable example of how catastrophic things are, Thersites, a man of ugly appearance and speech, who in the *Iliad* symbolized unheroic conduct and was seen as the lowest of the low. This provokes Philoktetes to utter the previously quoted, almost blasphemous, rejection of the gods (p. 413), which is particularly aimed at Odysseus.

From the contemporary perspective, Sophocles' idea must be that an army or state whose leaders are not in possession of true virtues is doomed. Due to poor leadership, Athens was about to be destroyed and, five years later in 404 B.C., it had to capitulate to Sparta. Pericles' death in 429 B.C. was also a turning point, after which all values gradually became radically transformed in a negative, not to say nihilistic, direction by the Sophists among others; meanwhile the political system was undermined from within by party struggles, as Thucydides describes (see p. 457).

By reading the manifest and the latent text of the *Philoktetes* together, it can be ascertained that the premise for the conquest of Troy in mythical times and the salvation of Athens in contemporary times must be the same: that it was possible to call in someone with the necessary character, that is to say heroic *arete*, moral fiber, bravery and decency, such as Achilleus and Pericles. Against this background, it must be possible to understand Philoktetes' symbolical meaning, which at first sight is strangely ambiguous, by appreciating that he is saddled with an evil-smelling wound like someone struck by the plague and is at the same time in possession of the golden bow which destroys everything that its owner captures within its sights.

The Wound, the Bow and the Weapon of the Tongue

1

It is necessary to discern a deeper meaning in such remarkable signalling. The stigmata of the wound keeps him out of any human community and puts him back in a pre-social state, where like some Robinson Crusoe he, must rediscover life and endure the utmost privation. He lives in a rough stone cave and lights his fire by striking stones against each other, while the only witnesses to his screams of pain are barren mountains and birds.

He seems to have ended in this situation quite undeservedly, as he is described as the noblest of the noble. Like Oedipus, he is yet another example of the gods striking down the best, but also a sign that some greater plan, to which no human being is privy, will ultimately appear as a signature of divine providence: Oedipus as a protective hero, and now Philoktetes as the man who, after ten years of trial, is to conquer Troy because, like Homer's Odysseus, he has learned to endure suffering: "Necessity (*anangke*) has taught me, /little by little, to suffer and be patient" (539-40).

That is to say that his strength and ennobling are the deeper reason why only he can conquer the city. He has borne the suffering inflicted on him by the gods without losing his heroic integrity. On the contrary, the play itself becomes proof of his personal steadfastness, supported by a fiery temperament and a self-esteem that is not far from Oedipus' psychological profile. This is to be seen not least in his hatred of Odysseus and the Atreidae, described in a context in which Philoktetes' thoughts during the manipulation to which he is subjected have focused on a hope of returning safely home to his country and his aged father.

When he realizes the deception, he is unyielding in his anger and impervious to any argument. He will not go to Troy either to win immortal honor or to be cured, as he will not for any price enter into the reality to which his despised enemies belong. He would rather bear the trauma of loneliness and his wound. His autonomy is further emphasized by the fact that, unlike Odysseus, he went to Troy voluntarily because, like Ajax, he felt bound by the common oath. Nor would he yield his freedom to choose now, even if he is to meet his end in unbearable pain on the island: "I would rather suffer anything than this./ There is still my steep and rugged precipice here" (1000-01).

In this, his self-validation, hardened by suffering inflicted by the gods, resides all the authenticity that is no longer to be found in the Greek army. And as in the *Odyssey*, the image of his *menos* is the bow. This is partly a symbol of the power with which he has maintained his life on the island, and partly an image of the power of the continuity of Greek civilization, as he has taken it over from Herakles, who received it from Apollo. With this bow, Herakles himself took Troy. In short, the power of the bow is linked to human integrity, which the army lacks and which Odysseus on its behalf tries to obtain by tricking Philoktetes out of his weapon.

Man, wound and bow thus constitute an unbreakable unity. And it is evidence that the Greeks have lost this quality and the insight accompanying it when Odysseus imagines that it is enough to get hold of the bow, as there are other great archers among the Greeks able to use it, himself included (1061). At the same time, it reveals that Odysseus is certainly in possession of some good sense, but that this good sense lacks insight in the same way as Sophist philosophy, viewed negatively, was without depth. Knowledge and wisdom have become mere cleverness.

Neoptolemos, on the other hand, shows that despite his youthful inexperience, as the son of Achilleus, he belongs to the same sphere as Philoktetes, as he instinctively knows that man and bow form an inseparable whole: "I see we have hunted in vain,/ vainly have captured our quarry the bow, if we sail without him" (839-40).

2

Just as the bow is the symbol of nobility and coherence, a mark of nobility borne by Philoktetes, so the tongue is the organ by which Odysseus is characterized—both by himself and Sophocles. The author must here build on an association with Achilleus' answer in the *Iliad*—a hidden address to Odysseus: "For as I detest the doorways of Death, I detest that man, who/ hides one thing in the depths of his heart, and speaks forth another" (IX, 312-13). Sophocles exploits this statement elegantly, allowing Achilleus' son Neoptolemos together with Philoktetes to represent the reality in which your word is your bond, while making Odysseus the son of Sisyphos, the master of deception *par excellence*.

When Neoptolemos regrets his action and gives back to Philoktetes the bow which on the advice of Odysseus he has used treachery to take from him, Philoktetes replies: "You have shown your nature and true breeding,/ son of Achilles and not Sisyphos" (1310-11). Hence, two traditions meet in the tragedy, one deriving from Sisyphos, the tongue of deception, and one deriving from Achilleus, the noble action symbolized by the bow (in other words, the bow has no negative connotations of cowardice as it has, for example, in the *Iliad*; see p. 51).

Odysseus, too, has made his tongue his most important weapon. Taught by experience, he has realized, as he puts it, that: "It is the tongue that wins and not the deed" (100). The sort of indoctrination to which Odysseus subjects Neoptolemos shows that Sophocles does not regard him as a Homeric hero but rather a Sophist teacher insofar as Sophist teaching, which will be examined in more detail as we proceed, assumes that there are no absolute values. Consequently, it is simply a matter of using the best rhetorical devices to make a weak cause victorious, just as the strongest is always right regardless of whether he has right on his side.

In such a context it is, of course, impossible to maintain any heroic or human morality. This leads to a breakdown of interpretation, a relativization and leveling off of values—in other words, all those things of which the Sophists have been made exponents and which they have tried to support with their philosophy. In the *Philoktetes*, Odysseus is the messenger of this new world of thought. When he persuades Neoptolemos to deceive Philoktetes, he refers repeatedly to the tongue as the greatest tool: "Ensnare/ the soul of Philoktetes with your words" (56-57). When Neoptolemos reflects his own true nature by asking whether it is not shameful to lie, Odysseus responds: "When one does something for gain, one need not blush" (110).

Yet Odysseus knows perfectly well what Neoptolemos himself points out—that his heritage is not such that he is made for "treachery" (89). Odysseus agrees, but entices him with the prospect of the rewards of victory and plays down the aspect of lying: Neoptolemos is only briefly to indulge in "deception." Later, he will be named among the noblest of men.

There can hardly be any clearer demonstration that Odysseus completely suspends the code of honor in which a man is his word. He operates on the same duality of external and internal of which Achilles accused him in the *Iliad*. For Odysseus, it is a matter of victory and gain. The manner in which it is done, stealing the weapon on which Philoktetes depends on the desert island, is subordinate. In short, Odysseus has no sense of honor, conscience or sympathy. This is the crucial difference between him and Neoptolemos.

3

However, Odysseus only succeeds by playing on Neoptolemos' sense of duty to the Greek army, when Neoptolemos realizes that the necessary victory is to be won via the deception of Philoktetes. In this sense, Neoptolemos becomes a victim of the power of the tongue and, in the contemporary context, an example of how, in order to gain the greatest benefit for themselves, the Sophists manipulate younger and weaker brethren with their rhetoric. Neoptolemos must suppress his fundamental aristocratic feelings with the view that he is acting together with Fate (192), which first inflicted a wound on Philoktetes and will later allow Troy to fall to his arrows. He is himself merely one part of this noble plan.

As Neoptolemos is presented psychologically, he is at first not to be considered as more than a youth with promise, placed between extreme existential possibilities: Philoktetes and Odysseus. On the other hand, he is by no means an unknown quantity in that he bears his father's noble nature within himself. This explains why he resists Odysseus' deception and why, after the revelation of the deception, even Philoktetes can maintain that Neoptolemos did not act out of ill will but as the instrument of evil people. Indeed, Philoktetes even goes so far as to say to Odysseus that Neoptolemos does not resemble him but is more like Philoktetes himself— "one/ that is no mate for you but worthy of me" (1009-10).

This surprising identification is significant as it documents that, in Neoptolemos, his immediate adversary, Philoktetes can nevertheless re-discover the deeper aristocratic stratum in his nature, the heritage of his fathers. Furthermore, it explains why Neoptolemos immediately feels such a liking for Philoktetes, as he resembles his own dead father. Of course, he must keep his liking at bay as long as he still believes he is acting correctly on behalf of Odysseus, the army and Fate.

An attack of pain from his wound that suddenly strikes Philoktetes has such a violent emotional effect that it evokes in Neoptolemos a feeling that is stronger than the "Sophist" indoctrination he has for a time received and which functions purely as a superego. He has profound doubts about his actions, just as he fundamentally feels that he has betrayed the originally human and subsequently friendly contact with Philoktetes, who believes that he is to be saved and taken home from this desolate place. This fundamentally once again brings Neoptolemos into contact with the true nature of his being.

All these things make him return the bow to Philoktetes in order to "undo the wrong" (1221) and to prove that he now wants to help him in all honesty. His action is meant to convince Philoktetes who, understandably enough, no longer has any confidence in his word. Nor can Neoptolemos persuade him to come with him to Troy, to take the city and to be healed. This is a vain attempt because Philoktetes places his integrity higher and will not serve the corrupt leaders of the Greek army.

4

The decisive change takes place at the end, when, as in a play by Euripides, Herakles intervenes as a *deus ex machina* and sets out the divinely determined guidelines for the characters: Philoktetes is to take Troy with his bow and be cured of his wound. Herakles here makes reference to the path of suffering which he himself had to follow to achieve his divinity. But the conquest of Troy assumes that Philoktetes acts together with Neoptolemos. They must, Herakles stresses, fight together "like twin lions hunting together" (1438). Sophocles plays here on the same imagery in the *Oresteia*, where, as we saw, it nevertheless has the opposite meaning by being applied to Agamemnon's blood-thirst and *hubris*, which cost him his life.

With Herakles' prophetic preamble, the underlying plan and *telos* of Philoktetes' life has finally been revealed, and as in the case of Oedipus it occurs far later in the path through life and after endless suffering. Philoktetes submits on the spot, which not even Odysseus' claim that he, Odysseus, is acting from Zeus' will (989-90), has been able to persuade him to do. In this instance, he fastened on to Odysseus' deceptive character, corresponding to the general moral decay in the army. Things are completely different with Herakles. As the bow's original owner, he constitutes the authentic starting point for the *arete* personified by Philoktetes himself.

Seen in this way, we find a pattern in the text through which Sophocles can expose the political situation of his own time with its corruption of state and values. At the same time, with the description of Philoktetes' steadfastness, he looks back to what has been lost, a loss that, in contemporary times, is a contributory cause to the imminent defeat of Athens in the war against Sparta and to the moral dissolution. In the myth's recalling of the sufferings that Philoktetes and, before him, Herakles, have borne, Sophocles can likewise testify to the power they possessed as the owners of the bow.

5

If this past can be connected to the future, there is hope for the Athenian city-state. Neoptolemos becomes the bearer of this utopia, born of a noble father and so in possession of the same qualities that appear in the insight and sympathy to which he personally gains access after having been "wrongly coded" by Odysseus. This, too, is the requirement for Athens, its citizens and politicians, that they can be reawakened in the current crisis to the memory of this honorable past. A new type of human being must be developed that does not make use of deception but of truth.

Similarly, as was demonstrated in the analysis of his final work *Oedipus at Colonus*, the now ancient poet wanted in his writing to create a protector for beleaguered Athens in its struggle against Thebes, the city of the dragon seed and the ally of Sparta. And as is the case with Philoktetes, Oedipus' spiritual strength is gained by suffering, endurance and self-insight.

We shall trace how similar moral scruples are presented in Euripides, whose critical analysis does not have the same utopian impact but, on the contrary, is almost dystopian. Socrates, on the other hand, does possess moral courage—the conduct of his life may be seen from this point of view as a revolt against the type of Sophist represented by Odysseus. At the same time, Socrates has a far more positive attitude to Homer's Odysseus, viewing him as an ideal which Plato made into a prefiguration of Socrates himself.

XVII

EURIPIDES

Poet of Crisis

1

E URIPIDES' BIRTHPLACE WAS SALAMIS, AND ACCORDING TO THE SYMBOLICAL historical ideas of antiquity he was born at the very place and on the very day in September 480 B.C. that the Greeks defeated the Persians. In his own lifetime, however, Euripides was no vanquisher. Unlike Aeschylus and Sophocles, he only won a few first prizes because he was viewed disapprovingly as a social rebel who portrayed man in a temporal world characterised by fortuitous and conflicting actions and motives.

And although his dramas, like those of the other tragedians, are based upon the legacy of Greek myths, he gives them content that reflects the political, social and psychological crisis of the time more than was previously the case. His main characters display hitherto unseen passions, and dramatically peripheral or useless figures such as peasants appear on stage and are credited with a noble quality that the traditional heroic types lack in their arrogance. In addition, the gods seem to be deranged and Fate irresistible and unavoidable, while love leads to destruction. Women seem to be hated and men pathetic in their oppression.

If all this indicates a process of dissolution, then in this analysis of decay and dystopia there is at the same time embedded a contrary implication in the form of a moral mobilization and piety, stirred by the sense of catastrophe itself and along with it the dream of a new human integrity. On the one hand, the contours of the actual breakdown in cultural and religious values are laid out, the very values that were the basis of the flowering and culmination of Greek civilization after the Persian wars. On the other hand, this state of dissolution is to be seen as an epochal transitional phase containing signs of the transformation and spiritual wealth that are accomplished philosophically by Socrates.

2

Socrates attended the performances of Euripides' tragedies. And it can be seen as evidence that they both formed part of the intellectual quality of the new age with its focus on the individual and on psychological life that they were both attacked and ridiculed by the conservative castigator of society, Aristophanes. As said above, he pits Euripides against Aeschylus in *The Frogs*. Aristophanes hits below the belt when he lets Aeschylus say that Euripides writes on the basis of the bankruptcy of his own marriage: "You wrote those things about other people's wives, and then you were struck with the same affliction yourself!"[1] Forced on to the defensive, Euripides asks what is improbable about what he has written of Phaedra. To this Aeschylus replies that, "It's the duty of a poet, of all people, to conceal what is wicked (. . .) I set a good example that you utterly perverted."[2] The same holds true of the heroic, which Euripides similarly offends—"by dressing men of kingly station in rags, so as to make people see them as objects of pity."[3]

It was this rejection of the heroic and especially the mythical that more than two thousand years later persuaded Nietzsche to attack Euripides. As already said, his argument is that Euripides destroyed tragedy by removing it from its primordial Dionysian roots. That is to say that he uses the chorus as more of a lyrical accompaniment, something that Aristotle maintains Agathon was the first to do.[4] Like Aristophanes, Nietzsche[5] believes at the same time that all the lubricity in his plays means that they fail to convey any metaphysical comfort. The metaphysical content is reduced to a *deus ex machina*. *Pathos* has become melodramatic sentimentality in which reflection on the metaphysical finally very largely turns into a meta-reflection on the aesthetic shock devices of tragedy.

3

By portraying the mythical prehistory of Athens, it can be said that Aeschylus and Sophocles identified themselves with its glory as a divine state. They were the poets of the newly created democracy and the power that radiated from it in the form of self-confidence and optimism, reaching its political zenith after the Persian wars and under Pericles' government and reforms. Euripides, on the other hand, writes most of his tragedies during the period of Athenian decline.

The reversal came with the long-lasting Peloponnesian War, which broke out in 431 B.C., while a few years later the plague began to lay waste to Athens. In *Oedipus the King*, the plague was the concrete and psychological manifestation of a kingdom that was fundamentally rotten because the ruler—in this case unconsciously—was guilty of a series of crimes. Thucydides also uses the plague to describe a state in dissolution. To a greater extent than Herodotus, he was the founder of historical writing, because in contrast to his predecessor he sticks close to the facts and in his works provides a chronological description of the Peloponnesian War, though without completing it. And while Herodotus saw the defeat of the Persians as punishment from the gods because of their barbaric *hubris*, Thucydides—like Euripides—finds the primary causes of the crisis in human motives and blemishes of character, particularly among the rulers. Since the gods have now been dismissed in people's minds as driving forces, there is no longer any power to modify the free play of forces, which is why the ruthless dominate the weak, as Plato lets those hungry for power say themselves (see p. 501).

So the plague, by which Thucydides himself was struck and which he describes with disquieting personal experience, gives him the opportunity to discuss the moral laxity of every conceivable kind that followed in the wake of the epidemic. The corpses were not treated with the reverence accorded by prevailing laws and customs but were simply thrown on to whatever pyres there were within reach, and he continues:

> In other respects also Athens owed to the plague the beginnings of a state of unprecedented lawlessness. Seeing how quick and abrupt were the changes of fortune, which came to the rich who suddenly died and to those who had previously been penniless but now inherited their wealth, people now began openly to venture on acts of self-indulgence which before then they used to keep dark. Thus they resolved to spend their money quickly and to spend it on pleasure, since money and life alike seemed equally ephemeral. As for what is called honor, no one showed himself willing to abide by its laws, so doubtful was it whether one would survive to enjoy the name for it (. . .) no fear of god or law of man had a restraining influence. As for the gods, it seemed to be the same thing whether one worshiped them or not, when one saw the good and the bad dying indiscriminately. As for offences against human law, no-one expected to live long enough to be brought to trial and punished: instead everyone felt that already a far heavier sentence had been passed on him and was hanging over him (. . .).[6]

According to Thucydides, Pericles had been incorruptible while in office, and it was said that: "the state was wisely led and firmly guarded."[7] Thucydides' portrait of Pericles is somewhat hagiographic. For although, judging by his speeches, he was certainly democratically minded, his rule was virtually absolute, and he was equally jealous of his own honor and that of Athens. He was a thoroughgoing exponent of practical politics and warned against the expansion that would later cost the Greeks much in the expedition to Sicily. There, under the command of Alcibiades, their losses included that of the fleet in the Bay of Syracuse, 415-13 B.C., a loss from which the Athenians never recovered. After the death of Pericles from the plague in 429 B.C., political control collapsed in a welter of corruption. Brutality held sway among politicians, regardless of whether they belonged to the oligarchs or democrats. Thucydides provides a thorough analysis of how party strife led to a complete transformation of all values hitherto:

> "To fit in with the change of events, words, too, had to change their usual meanings. What used to be described as a thoughtless act of aggression was now regarded as the courage one would expect to find in a party member; to think of the future and wait was merely another way of saying one was a coward; any idea of moderation was just an attempt to disguise one's unmanly character; ability to understand the question from all sides meant that one was totally unfitted for action. Fanatical enthusiasm was the mark of a real man, and to plot against an enemy behind his back was perfectly legitimate self-defence."[8]

Thucydides continues his catalogue of decadence in the political apparatus, a dissolution the cause of which, when it comes to it, he can summarize quite precisely:

"Love of power, operating through greed and through personal ambition, was the cause of all these evils."[9] In addition, there was the relativization of values in the general view of the world, which followed from the activities of the Sophists. Against this background, it is quite understandable that people experienced life as pure chaos and attributed the confusion arising from a breakdown in the foundation of their lives to the gods, who now appeared arbitrary and untrustworthy.

4

As a result, the myths reflecting such an anarchic reality in Euripides' tragedies are infused with rootless "modernity." The world order is threatened, if not simply dissolved, by confusion and moral decay: "Confused is the world in which we live" (*El.* 368), as one phrase has it, or, to quote another:

> Even the Gods, with all Their name for wisdom,
> Have only dreams and lies and lose Their course,
> Blinded, confused, and ignorant as we—
> > (*Iph. T.* 571-74)

In the *Elektra*, this confusion, the sign of a lack of insight, is traced back to the god of wisdom, to Apollo himself, who is sspecifically called unwise. How catastrophic this must have been appears from Apollo's significance for a society that was without a state religion but placed its religious conviction in Delphi's omphalos and place of truth—"For this god surely is in such matters for all mankind the interpreter of the religion of their fathers who from his seat in the middle and at the very naval of the earth delivers his interpretation,"[10] as Socrates puts it.

The phenomenon might perhaps also be called a religious defocusing. Zeus appears—as in the *Oresteia*'s hymn (p. 371)—as an unknown, indeterminate god. As Hekuba complains in *The Trojan Women*:

> Oh power, who mount the world, wheel where the world rides,
> Oh mystery of man's knowledge, whosoever you be,
> Zeus named, nature's necessity or mortal mind—
> > (885-88)

Herakles expresses a similar uncertainty in the tragedy about his raging insanity: "and Zeus, whoever this Zeus may be" (*Her.* 1263). The same indeterminacy may ultimately be expressed in this way:

> O Zeus, what can I say?
> That you look on man and care?
> Or do we, holding that the gods exist,
> Deceive ourselves with unsubstantial dreams
> And lies, while random careless chance and change
> Alone control the world?
> > (*Her.* 484-87)

Placed in this fundamental doubt about the existence of Zeus and the trust-worthiness of the gods, men in Euripides do not bow to their power, as in Sophocles' tragedies. As it is put in one passage, they feel like the slaves of the gods (*Or.* 418). So his characters rage and despair, since suffering does not—as in Aeschylus' hymn to Zeus—become a path to knowledge. But as we shall see in his tragedies on Orestes, even in the confusion, it is possible to find an order that can be traced back to a hidden divine control. In general, however, it must be said that, as subjectivity in its all too human desire moves into the foreground, confidence in the gods disappears. So chaos arises, raising the question of what meaning at all there can be in life.

5

It is difficult to determine how the political crisis and the new philosophical currents influence each other. There was presumably some sort of interaction. The chaotic external situation has acted together with the Sophists' subjectivization of values in such a way that the individual tries to create a coherence in his inner life as the norms of the external world were crumbling, while at the same time it has further relativized the fundamental notions of society. This struggle to compensate for the loss of the external may also be one of the explanations for why Socrates sought to develop "the inner man" as a counterweight to the moral demise.

As an exponent of this whole process, Euripides, consciously or unconsciously, continues the tradition from Xenophanes who, it will be remembered, claimed that the gods were nothing but projections. Aristophanes links Euripides to this doctrine, when in *Thesmophoriazusae* he writes of the poet: "this wretch had persuaded the spectators by his tragedies that there were no gods."[11]

The same view may be responsible for the tradition that the Sophist Protagoras read aloud his essay "On Gods" in Euripides' home. It begins: "About the gods I have no means of knowing either that they exist or that they do not exist or what they are like to look at; many things prevent my knowing—among others, the fact that they are never seen and the shortness of human life."[12] These words correspond to Plato's claim that Protagoras left the gods out of any discussion because he based his knowledge solely on the senses—"You drag in the gods, whose existence or nonexistence I expressly refuse to discuss in my speeches and writings,"[13] is his rea-soning. This means for instance that the Sophists suspended Heraclitus' idea that there is a correspondence between reason and cosmos, a uniformity that makes it possible for men to acknowledge a divine order.

Instead, the Sophists operated with a rational understanding of life that was cou-pled with the necessity of arguing one's case in a democratic society. Thus, rhetoric became a decisive power factor. It now became much more important to speak convincingly than truly. Belief in *a priori* truth was thus broken down from within by subjective relativism. It was first and foremost a matter of seeming, not being. And it is this liberation from any absolute truth we find in Protagoras' so-called *homo mensura* theorem: that man is the measure of all things.

The written laws passed down from Solon no longer possessed an absolute truth that Heraclitus assumed in his formulation: "For all human laws are nourished by a divine one"[14] We already witnessed an incipient relativization of the laws in Sophocles' *Antigone*, when Kreon in his lust for power wanted to place his own laws above those of the gods. And that is exactly what the Sophists do as they exploit the increasing complexity in society to formulate new rules of human conduct.

The Sophists presumed the laws, which had otherwise been viewed as true and inviolable, given by the gods as protection against the chaos of nature, to be a product of social consensus. The laws could now be changed by argument. The power of rhetoric ultimately became the measure and truth.[15] As a Sophist says in Plato: "the just is the same thing everywhere, the advantage of the stronger."[16] This development necessarily led to a form of nihilism and subjectivity in which the individual is thrown back on himself and bound by the pallid projection of his own motives.

6

If man, not the gods, is made into the object of everything, the metaphysical loses its significance as the basis for orientation, and spiritual life becomes a more or less pathological stage for passions, although rationality has pride of place. The demand for self-control and reason is, of course, still prominent in Euripides, the straw through which everyone vainly tries to control the chaos of the unleashed instinctual world.

But, in all its human frailness and fragility, as may be seen in tragedies such as the *Hippolytos* and *The Bacchae*, this is a strategy that has the exactly opposite effect. On the contrary, logic and sagacity fail before the merciless forces of existence in such a way as to show that the irrational must be assimilated if emotional life is not to be demonized and annihilate both the individual and civilization. This also means that, although he had in his nature the dissonances of the time as polar tensions, Euripides allows space in his tragedies for a latent longing for the metaphysical, which reaches beyond the contemporary assessment of him.

With his nineteen plays, he is the tragedian who left the greatest number of dramas. It is not possible to examine them all in depth, and so I have made a virtue of necessity and decided to concentrate on the tragedies in which we can most clearly see the duality on the basis of which he wrote: his reflection of the crisis of the time and his dream of a new reality. I will take my starting point in his plays about the fall of Troy, where in the figure of Odysseus we meet an analogy to the contemporary cynical and pragmatic politician whom Sophocles—perhaps, under the influence of Euripides—described in the tragedy of *Philoktetes*. This will moreover illustrate in concrete terms how Euripides uses myth in his analysis of the lust for political power in his own time.

Odysseus' Cynicism
1

If the external and the internal no longer correspond to one another and everything is viewed as chance, the subject is thrown upon his own judgment. And if at the same time a person should renounce any moral or religious demand, that person could seize power through sheer cynicism. Euripides makes Odysseus the exponent of this process.[17] He is presented as a cynic, a Sophist politician who seeks to promote his objective no matter what the cost to others. He is crafty and malevolent. That is to say that Euripides isolates and exploits his negative side, his heritage from Autolykos. However, he also presents the other Homeric heroes as limited, selfish people, as according to the heroic moral code everyone looks after himself and his own honor.

So neither Agamemnon nor Menelaos, as they are portrayed in *Iphigenia at Aulis*, has anything like the same inner power as Odysseus, determined as he is by his pragmatic cynicism. His shadow also rests heavily upon *The Trojan Women* (415 B.C.), even though he does not appear there. After the conquest of Troy he is behind the advice to murder Hektor's little son Astyanax in order to eliminate a potential avenger; Kassandra predicts in general terms his long voyage home and all its dangers; and Queen Hekuba breaks down when she is given to Odysseus as war booty:

> Must I?
> To be given as slave to serve that vile, that slippery man,
> Right's enemy, brute, murderous beast,
> That mouth of lies and treachery, that makes void
> Faith in things promised
> And that which was beloved turns to hate.
>
> (282-88)

The tragedy ends with her being led down to Odysseus' ship.

2

In the encounter between the old Trojan queen and Odysseus, described in *Hekuba* (424 B.C.), the character traits just discussed are most prominent. Odysseus arrives in person to seize her daughter Polyxena and to sacrifice her—in honor of Achilleus, as he has demanded from his tomb. Euripides has here created a scene with the greatest conceivable contrast in order to present Odysseus in as negative a light as possible. Just before he steps on to the stage, we have witnessed the mother's inconsolable grief at the thought of her daughter's willingness to sacrifice herself, as Polyxena's life is in any case transformed into thraldom and shame. Death will only be a liberation for her. Odysseus enters this world of grief and elevated self-sacrifice with his brutal command that the queen must not compel him to take the girl by force.

In terms of motif, Euripides introduces a problem here. For he (re)uses the situation in the *Odyssey* in which Odysseus comes in disguise to Troy and is helped by Helen (see p. 157), but Euripides lets Hekuba save him. This is contrary to all reason, as she would then be a traitor. The crucial element for Euripides, however, was to put Odysseus into the impossible situation of having to take life from someone who has given him life. And when he carries out his order, it shows how callous he is in the pursuit of his goal. As Hekuba says, he is like other men who merely strive for the honor of their own power: "these politicians/ who cringe for favors from a screaming mob/ and do not care what harm they do their friends" (256-58).

In a long tirade, he disclaims any responsibility—like Agamemnon at the sacrifice of his daughter. Hekuba has saved his life, and so he wants to save her, but at the same time he admits that he has supported the sacrifice of Polyxena. And as justification, he says he is only doing what the people, i.e., the army, want. Without an honorable sacrifice, it will be difficult to assemble the army on another occasion, as honor is the only reward a dead warrior can attain. Odysseus ends by mercilessly dragging the blameless girl to the sacrificial pyre. She is radiant in her willingness to be sacrificed, while more than anywhere else in the entire world of ancient Greek tragedy, he is devalued to a mere seeker of power.

<h1 style="text-align:center">3</h1>

Meanwhile, the best developed, most catastrophic portrait of a power-hungry character is to be found in the analysis of King Eteokles in *The Phoenician Women* (ca. 410 B.C.). Euripides certainly takes the same theme as Aeschylus in *Seven Against Thebes* and to some extent Sophocles in *Antigone* and *Oedipus at Colonus*, but his personal objective is made clear by the fact that Eteokles possesses no heroic virtues and argues like a politician of the Sophist school.

As in Aeschylus, the plot's turning point is the siege of Thebes by Polyneikes and his six companions to assert his rights against his brother Eteokles. The latter, as we have already heard, held on to the throne despite the brothers' agreement to take it in turn to rule. Although this personal conflict is a cause of the war, there is another reason—the curse that the blind Oedipus has called down upon his sons for locking him up in the hope that the world would forget his existence: "They shall divide this house with sharpened steel" (69).

It is Iokaste who provides this information, implying that she has not committed suicide, as she does in Sophocles. This she does over her sons' bodies at the end of *The Phoenician Women*. However, there seems to be an even deeper reason for the curse: Ares' anger that Kadmos, the founder of the city, killed his son, the monster serpent, and sowed the teeth from which a race of dragon warriors grew out of the ground. During the course of the drama, Kreon's son attempts to atone for this curse by vainly sacrificing his young life.

Euripides is actually working with a family curse, the cause of which is not King Laios' sex drive as it is in *Seven Against Thebes*, for, as Teiresias declares, Ares demands a victim from the family, "He must, in that chamber where the earth-born dragon/ was born, the watcher over Dirke's streams,/ be slaughtered, and so give libation blood" (931-33). At its deepest level, all misfortunes are centered on the family at Thebes in this atavistic world. However, Euripides does not follow through on this clash between an old and a new reality, as he does in others of his tragedies. The dramatic course of events is generally connected to the egocentric motives of the contending parties, which with seemingly crushing inevitability actually become their fate but which could be changed, if they could become reconciled through self-control.

In a desperate attempt to save her sons and Thebes, Iokaste has prevailed upon them to meet for a possible reconciliation, though given their desire for power, this is doomed to failure. Polyneikes does not hide the fact that his true motive for regaining royal power is materialistic—. "'Men honor property above all else;/ it has the greatest power in human life.'/ And so I seek it with ten thousand spears" (440-42), he says, driving a wedge into the heroic self-understanding in which the most important thing was a fine name. That wealth played its part in increasing fame is another matter.

The two brothers are made of the same dreadful stuff. Eteokles' refusal to compromise shows how materialism and a Sophist relativization of values have broken down former absolute values: "If all men saw the fair and wise the same/ men would not have debaters' double strife" (500-01). And he goes on: "I'll speak to you, Mother, without concealment:/ I'd go to the stars beyond the eastern sky/ I'd go to the stars beyond the eastern sky/ or under earth, if I could do one thing/ seize tyranny, the greatest of the gods (. . .) If one must do a wrong, it's best to do it/ pursuing power—otherwise, let's have virtue" (503-25). So, too, say the Sophist power theorists we shall meet in Plato.

Against this background, it is clear that Iokaste cannot effect a reconciliation between the brothers, although she replies to Eteokles' torrent of words by trying to get him to understand that he craves the most evil of the goddesses, ambition: "Why do you honor so much tyrannic power/ and think that unjust happiness is great?/ It's fine to be looked up to? But it's empty" (548-50).

Of course, her words fall on deaf ears, and the brothers draw their mother Iokaste into the bloody consequences of their striving for power when she commits suicide. One last time, the blind Oedipus touches his mother and wife. Then, on the advice of Teiresias, he is driven from Thebes and begins his long journey to Colonus, where, as in Sophocles' version, he knows he will be well received and end his days. And it is hinted that Antigone will bury her dead brother, contrary to the orders of King Kreon.

This interpretation could indicate that, despite his skeptical nature, Euripides does not only possess insight into a family curse but is also aware of its possible path towards reconciliation. It can be difficult to prove, since, unlike Aeschylus, he does not work with a view to reconciliation. We shall nevertheless make the attempt by following his personal interpretation of the fateful story of the Tantalids as it is told in the *Orestes*. However, it requires certain interpretative modifications (see below) to show how Euripides is able at the same time to interpret the trauma of his own times and to incorporate them into the original structure of consciousness in the myth.

Iphigenia at Aulis—The Sacrifice

1

It will hardly be a surprise that Euripides' tragedies on the curse of the Tantalid family and ultimate redemption through Orestes' matricide must inevitably carry echoes of the *Oresteia* and often almost take over passages from Aeschylus. Nevertheless, he maintains his own interpretative purpose and understanding. And as in Sophocles' tragedies, we should not seek Euripides' conclusion in the lines of the protagonists, as they are expressions of their own characters. We find him rather him in the compositional whole.

So my analysis of these works based on the Mycenaean saga will follow the progress of the plot, although I will breach the chronological order in which the works were written. The very fact that I can make use of this analytical apparatus confirms that Euripides' interpretation remained more or less fixed throughout his life. Shortly before his death in 406 B.C., he wrote *The Bacchae* and *Iphigenia at Aulis*, which in its description of the sacrifice of the daughter constitutes the background to the family's ultimate crisis. We can only speculate about this. But it looks as though—like Sophocles in *Oedipus the King*—Euripides felt that he had been unable to furnish his tragedies on Orestes with the story of what had gone before. For Orestes is present at his sister's sacrifice as a small boy (1241) and thus witnesses the event that is to form his life as a young man.

2

The epic background is that Agamemnon has offended Artemis—perhaps, as is related elsewhere, by shooting a sacred hind,[18] which is why, at the beginning of the play, the goddess has refused to provide the expedition with a fair wind to sail to Troy. As penance, she demands that Agamemnon should sacrifice his daughter.

Since the tragedy deals with the agonies through which Agamemnon must go before he lays his daughter on the altar and the sacrificial knife is taken to her throat, we have the psychological situation unfolded dramatically, which in the *Oresteia* was recounted in such condensed fashion that we only had a very narrow basis from which to wrest the meaning out of the text. Euripides inserts a psychological pattern of reaction that was not present in Aeschylus in the same way. In order better to understand Euripides' version, it is necessary to provide a paraphrased reading, which has the advantage of further illuminating the compositional structure.

3

At the beginning of the tragedy, Agamemnon regrets agreeing to sacrifice his daughter, as the priest and the prophet on behalf of Artemis have demanded. Paternal sentiments have taken the upper hand, and he feels pressured by the priest as well as his brother Menelaos whose interest the expedition actually serves. As his brother later claims, however, Agamemnon sent for Iphigenia "not by compulsion" (361) but on the pretext of marrying her to the glorious hero Achilleus, with whose reputation Euripides does not meddle. This is a splendid choice for her and one she longs to have fulfilled. But Agamemnon now feels that, by co-operating in this deception, "his mind is crazed" (136) and he writes a letter to prevent her journey to Aulis.

As I said in the introduction to my analysis of Euripides and his times, people felt cast adrift in a permanent state of confusion, because the gods' intentions are incomprehensible. Agamemnon is no exception:

> At one time, it is an enterprise
> Of the gods which failing,
> Overturns a man's life. At another,
> The wills of men, many and malignant,
> Ruin life utterly.

> (23-27)

Agamemnon is thinking here of a peculiar duality of metaphysical fate and the multiplicity of human motives. However, it is only the first half of his reasoning that has validity for him, as he has subconsciously already decided on the sacrifice. Or rather, the king denies any personal responsibility at the same time as Euripides shows that, as in Aeschylus, he has a real alternative. He can abstain from the sacrifice but reveals when he chooses to carry it out that he is governed by his lust for power without taking responsibility for it. Instead, as in the *Iliad* and the *Oresteia*, he seems to be a person lacking in self-awareness, who pursues the tyrannical *hubris* of his desire, the deepest motivation in his nature.

4

Euripides undertakes a remarkable revelation of Agamemnon's true nature. For when through a series of complications in which Menelaos intercepts the letter to Iphigenia and—after putting severe pressure on Agamemnon to keep his word—Menelaos suddenly changes his mind and suggests that he should not sacrifice his innocent daughter, his fatherly love disappears at that moment, and a lust for power emerges as the absolute governing force in his psychology: "A compulsion absolute/ Now works the slaughter of the child" (510-11).

Agamemnon thereby involuntarily reveals that his fatherly sentiments do not have the same psychological hold and gravity as the egoism of his ambition, which he defends as being determined by fate. Without being able to fathom the weight of his own words, he claims that "fate chains me" (443—the same metaphor used in the *Oresteia*) and that he is caught in a trap. A divinity more wily than he has outwitted him—though only a few lines later, he admits: "Decorum rules our lives" (449).

Yet he neither can nor will bring this into his own self-understanding but as said above, he pushes the responsibility away from himself. He calls his need to assert himself in others' eyes an absolute necessity to him. He claims that under the leadership of Odysseus, the son of Sisyphos, the army will wipe him and his family out—"with these words/ Will he [Odysseus] arouse and seize the very soul/ Of the army, order them to kill you/ And me—and sacrifice the girl" (531-33). So he rejects any attempt on the part of Menelaos to talk him out of his error with the words: "Now in my despair I am/ Quite helpless, and it is God's will" (537). The obstruction is his own arrogance, which makes him unreceptive to Menelaos' attempts to arouse his paternal love. Later, Klytemnestra asks, "Is your thought/ And need only to brandish scepters and/ lead armies?" (1194-95) to which he replies, "Terrible it is to me, my wife, to dare/ This thing. Terrible not to dare it./ Here is my compulsion absolute" (1257-58). We hear the echo from Agamemnon's similar decision in the *Oresteia*.

5

Like Polyxena, Iphigenia also finally declares herself ready to be sacrificed, comforted by the fact that it will immortalize her. So Achilleus, who after having seen her spiritual greatness wants her for his wife, is not to defend her. She is then led to the altar in Artemis' grove.

At the actual sacrifice, Agamemnon walks around the altar praying: "O child of Zeus, O slayer of wild beasts,/ You who turn your disk of shining light" (1570-71). He prays for a fair wind and for victory over Troy. He has already said that the mock wedding was scheduled for the day when "the full moon comes" (717), which means that the sacrifice takes place at full moon.

With his reference to the sacrificial rite and Artemis as moon goddess, Euripides moves the center of gravity in a way that is more or less repeated in his other tragedies. He gradually but methodically shifts the predominantly psychological text from its manifest plot, where in this case Agamemnon's grab for power is explained, to the subtext: the latent, archetypal and symbolical plane on which the cultic chain of events in which the characters are enmeshed is played out.

For although it looks as though through the sacrifice of his daughter Agamemnon achieves enormous strength with which he obliterates Troy, it is a brief respite and a victory with a fatal price. In reality, he only achieves all this by submitting to Artemis as a mother goddess who demands human blood sacrifice. As in the *Oresteia*, it may be said that, on the symbolical level, he undertakes a sort of self-castration to attain the beneficence of the goddess—like the priests mentioned earlier, who castrated themselves and handed over their genitals to the Great Mother as a part of the fertility cult.

It is in this incestuous scenario that Agamemnon places himself in order to obtain the power he wants. And as a result of his sacrifice, Klytemnestra is transformed into the evil primal mother. She has already forgiven him for slaying her first husband and their child, but she will not do it again this time, she says several times, threatening him not to give her "provocation so that upon your/ Homecoming we give you the welcome that/ Is wholly due" (1182-83). This is no longer a wife speaking but the mother goddess or her daughter's Eriny.

The tragedy ends in this bloody future for the family at the same time as reconciliation is indirectly suggested. For at the moment the priest is about to drive the knife into Iphigenia's throat, Artemis replaces her with a hind and—we learn in *Iphigenia at Tauris*—whisks her to Tauris, a barbaric place near the Black Sea, to be her priestess. Orestes is to bring her back and thus atone for the family's blood guilt. But before we get that far, Klytemnestra has murdered Agamemnon with a double axe and hunting net, an event of which Euripides has left no account, but which nevertheless forms the background to the three tragedies belonging to the same cycle and introduced by the matricide.

Elektra—The Matricide

1

As emerged in the *Oresteia*, the need for revenge aimed at the mother and her lover, Aigisthos, seems to be most strongly rooted in Elektra. Indeed, she seems to be almost a counterpart to her mother, an Eriny who wants to avenge her father. Orestes returns home, having spent his childhood with his uncle to whom he was brought by a faithful slave, so that Aigisthos could not kill him. He is in a weaker position than his sister by being faced by a double problem: on the one hand, there is Apollo's demand that he should kill his mother; on the other, there is a blood bond between them. This makes him so hesitant that he must be helped by Elektra and Pylades, his cousin and friend.

The influence of Aeschylus can of course be pointed out in many places.[19] The portrait of Elektra, however, is far more carefully prepared by virtue of the psychological treatment Sophocles gives the figure. For he adds a social dimension to her in that she has been driven from the palace by Aigisthos and must clean like a slave, ageing and unmarried. Only the idea of vengeance keeps her going. Sophocles dramatically contrasts her with her more cautious sister Chrysothemis (a parallel to Ismene in the *Antigone*). Together with the chorus, she encourages Elektra not to follow the path of self-destruction, from which there is no return—"To destruction (*ate*) self-inflicted/ you fall so shamefully,"[20] are the words uttered by many terrified lips. But, like Antigone, she is unreceptive to "good" advice and refuses to be intimidated by Aigisthos' threat to have her buried alive. On the contrary, when she believes that Orestes is no longer among the living, she declares that she herself will carry out the killing, even though she is not a man. Nor does it make any impression on her when the chorus says that she would win greater respect by showing deference for the laws of the gods. And when she and Orestes finally carry out the matricide, it happens in triumph, without the torments that Aeschylus provided for Orestes and which are continued by Euripides.

2

Nevertheless, Euripides has taken over Elektra's character profile from Sophocles, and he radicalizes it to boot by stressing her social fall, which is without parallel in Greek tragedy. In order to prevent her from giving birth to a potential avenger, her mother and stepfather have married her off to a peasant. And, although Euripides describes the peasant as a man of integrity, "an honest, decent and god-fearing man" (*Or.* 921), Elektra, who has much of the same self-aggrandizing nature as her father, considers this marriage to be the worst dishonor that could befall her, as Kastor, one of the two glorious Dioscuri, had been selected to be her spouse.

When Klytemnestra defends the murder of Agamemnon as vengeance for the murder of her daughter Iphigenia, Elektra replies that her fate—that Aigisthos has excluded her from the palace and married her, a princess, off to a peasant—is worse than what befell her sister: "why has *he* not gone in exile for your son/ or died to pay for me who still alive have died/ my sister's death twice over" (1091-93). Indeed, she several times emphasises the fatal significance of the wedding—"a wedding much like death" (*thanasimon gamon*, 247). Yet, she has kind words to say of her husband as she is still a virgin, but everyone can see the social degradation she has suffered by having now to carry out the tasks of a peasant's wife.

3

Elektra does nothing to hide her feelings of shame. She seems rather to take an almost masochistic pleasure in displaying her physical misery: she is thin, dressed in ragged clothes, with dried skin and hair cut short (108) in the manner of the Scythians (241)—like a barbarian. Elektra's appearance may be the best example of what Aristophanes attacked Euripides for: presenting royal figures in rags and tatters.

Elektra's conscious renunciation of sexuality must be understood against the background of her betrothal to Kastor, which came to nothing. It also creates a special connection between father and daughter since it was Agamemnon who planned the erotic alliance. Orestes seems to sense all this when he sees her down-and-out exterior as a sign of the deep mourning she wears for her father.

The simultaneous loss of her prospective husband and her father, and the interdependence of the two, endows the general description of Elektra's sorrow and vengeance with a powerful undertone of the erotic nature that is repressed beneath the surface. Fundamentally, her sexuality is linked to her dead father. Thus, shortly before the murder Klytemnestra claims in self-defense that her daughter always loved her father more than her:

> My child, from birth you always have adored your father.
> This is part of life. Some children always love
> The male, some turn more closely to their mother than him.
>
> (1102-04)

When Elektra on several occasions (693; 982) strongly challenges Orestes to show manly courage, it is not merely a question of firing her irresolute brother with courage, but, in the hour of revenge, of his entering into an existential configuration with her beloved father, whom she also invokes: "Come now and bring as army all the dead below" (680). In Sophocles, she actually identifies her brother and father with an astonishing greeting to Orestes: "Bless you!/ for in you I think I see my father."[21]

Full of foreboding, Elektra sees her father's image in the man she herself wants to marry in the future. He must not be handsome like Aigisthos, a seducer and a fool—"let me have a husband/ not girlish-faced like you but graceful in male courage" (948-49). Real men dedicate their lives to the god of war, whereas the handsome take delight in dancing. Elektra looks passionately forward to her brother stepping into character as a man on a level with her father—by carrying out the vengeance with the very same axe that murdered Agamemnon.

Elektra's fervent wait for her brother to avenge her father must be understood in combination with the general skepticism that the characters in Euripides harbor with respect to divine justice. Here, as elsewhere, men fail to fathom the will and the ways of the gods. In Elektra's words: "Gods? Not one god has heard/ my helpless cry or watched of old/ over my murdered father" (198-200). And just as Sophocles considered time as an avenger because everything will ultimately be revealed and punished by the gods, Elektra also directs her prayer to time and asks it to hasten a little more: "Quicken the foot's rush—time has struck—O/ walk now, walk now weeping aloud,/ O for my grief?" (112-13).

That the punishment is just within reach is evidence that, despite his distrust of the gods, which he apparently has in common with his characters, Euripides still attributes to them unfathomable long-term plans, insofar as Orestes ultimately redeems himself and his family. And to underline this, a compositional reversal takes place in the *Elektra*, when she bemoans the deafness of the gods. Orestes arrives on orders from Apollo, who in the same spirit as Elektra has demanded "to counterchange my father's death for death to his killers" (89). This is the moment of truth and the turning point, which is the beginning of atonement for the family curse.

4

In the earlier dramatists, Orestes steps forward strongly and boldly. He hesitates only briefly in Aeschylus before killing his mother. In Sophocles, he acts of his own volition. Apollo is merely an adviser as to how to carry out the killing. By contrast, however, Euripides first has Orestes prowl about at the country's borders, ready to flee at the first sign of danger. In other words, he is presented as a young man almost devoid of energy and determination. And in the first instance his confusion is due to a lack of guidance from Apollo. He does not know that, through the matricide, he is to extricate himself and his family from the cycle of blood guilt that his father continued from his forefathers with his sacrifice of Iphigenia. He finds himself in a transitional stage in which he has difficulty liberating himself from the son's original bond with his mother. Dedicated to her bloody purpose, however, Elektra talks him out of this ineffectiveness and into the murder.

Furthermore, Orestes is struck by the crisis of the times exposed by the tragedy as a whole and reflected in Orestes' words: "Alas, we look for good on earth and cannot recognize it/ when met, since all our human heritage runs mongrel (. . .). We can only toss our judgments random on the wind" (367-68; 379). In other words, his mental confusion is not only due to his uncertainty concerning Apollo but corresponds to what Thucydides said: all values are turned upside down. External and internal do not correspond to each other: "Inside the souls of wealthy men bleak famine lives/ while minds of stature struggle trapped in starving bodies" (371-72) is Orestes' comment. The only way you can find out who is good or bad is by looking at their choice of friends.

"Apollo's oracles/ are strong, though human prophecy is best ignored" (398-99), Orestes continues. But even the instances of reason and the word of the gods, if not annulled, are at least problematized during the course of the tragedy. For by using his reason, Orestes comes to doubt Apollo's inhuman demand on him that he should kill the person who gave birth to him: "How can I kill her when she brought me up and bore me?" (969). On the one hand he interprets Apollo's oracle as decidedly evil, as something that can only lead to madness: "O Phoibos, your holy word was brute and ignorant" (971). And on the other, in his disoriented state, he actually airs the possibility that it is not a god at all but that a "polluted demon (*alastor*) spoke it in the shape of a god" (979). According to this interpretation, the *daimon* is in harmony with the insane fortuitousness of the world, and the murder that is to serve a loftier justice is proof that the world order is in chaos.

To counter his doubt, Elektra identifies herself with Apollo's orders and commands Orestes to show he is a man and a son worthy of his father. Elektra thus inserts her bloody motive of revenge into a doubt that might have led the way to a far more humane view, and a judgment on the mother by the court at Areopagus, and so, as her mother's daughter, she looks almost like the Erinyes that belong to the maternal rule.

5

Reluctantly, Orestes takes it upon himself to murder his mother—"I walk a cliff-edge in a sea/ of evil, and evil I will do" (985-86), he says. He fulfills his sister's demand that he should act like a man and submit to the answer from the oracle, which he finds evil. Meanwhile, his conduct during the murder itself reveals that Orestes is powerless because he can no longer connect reason and action. He must literally carry out his murder blindfolded. When Klytemnestra begs him to show mercy and seizes him about the neck, he drops his sword. He must hide his eyes behind his cloak as he drives the sword into his mother's throat, supported and guided by Elektra's hand.

Elektra sees in her mother the counterpart of her sister Helen. In their murderous sexuality, they are like two peas in a pod. For, as Elektra says accusingly, Agamemnon was hardly out the door before the mother began to make herself up: "Now any woman who works on her beauty when her man/ is gone from home indicts herself as being a whore" (1072-73). Klytemnestra defends herself by saying that her sexuality as a woman was violated by Agamemnon. For although he sacrificed their daughter, Iphigenia, she would not have murdered him if he had not brought a woman, Kassandra, home from Troy to the marriage bed: "He came home to me with a mad, god-filled girl/ and introduced her to our bed" (1032-33). She points out that a woman's blood is hot but that the same laws do not apply to a man as to a woman. If women take a friend, all hell breaks loose; whereas if men are the cause, they "are never blamed at all" (1040).

The leader of the chorus responds that according to the law of the time she is correct but in a disgraceful way: "A wife should give way to her husband in all things" (1052). The statement—like countless other passages in Euripides—speaks out strongly in favor of keeping women down.

6

As in the *Oresteia*, however, Klytemnestra and Aigisthos are punished because of *hubris*, expressed in concrete terms in their ostentatious extravagance—in glaring contrast to the haggard and destitute daughter and vagabonding son: "My mother in the glory of her Phrygian rugs/ sits on the throne, while circled at her feet the girls/ of Asia stoop, whom Father won at the sack of Troy" (314-16), says Elektra. Moreover, Aigisthos drives around in Agamemnon's chariot, with his hands stained by his blood. In the vengeful speech she makes to Aigisthos' decapitated head, Elektra mocks him for foolishly letting himself be seduced by riches and not realizing that "wealth which lives with us on terms of crime/ wings swiftly from the house after brief blossoming" (943-44).

Klytemnestra is enticed into visiting Elektra on the pretext of attending the "baptism" of her grandchild. When the daughter attacks her for having killed Agamemnon, she speaks of the crime with regret: "I am not so happy/ either, child, with what I have done or with myself (. . .). Perhaps I drove my hate too hard against my husband" (1105-10). But even with this regret, she cannot arouse her daughter's pity. And she is killed.

Logically enough, at the moment of the killing itself, the tragedy's gradually accumulating energy is drained. Orestes is almost mad with despair, turning to the Earth and Zeus and exclaiming: "Look at this work of blood/ and corruption" (1178-79). This is an outburst that brings in Elektra, who must remorsefully acknowledge that as the guilty party she has been driven by her blind hatred: "I am guilty./ A girl flaming in hurt I marched against/ the mother who bore me" (1182-83).

As Orestes well knows, his future is now blocked by the *miasma* he has incurred. He will be compelled to go into exile and will have difficulty finding a friend or a city that would dare look him in the eyes for fear of being infected (1192-95). Euripides confirms Orestes' interpretation of his situation as "polluted"—in the *Orestes*, where his grandfather King Tyndareios, filled with disgust, refuses to speak to him, a snake that has killed his mother. In the same tragedy, however, it is revealed that Orestes has a friend in Pylades, who will not shun him. On the contrary, when Orestes warns him against the danger of infection, he insists on standing by him: "Fear in friendship is an ugly trait" (794).[22]

7

After the killing, the situation becomes, if possible, even more unbearable for Elektra and Orestes, as from their heaven the Dioscuri support Orestes in his distrust of the oracle and Apollo's word. Kastor, the spokesman, says directly that Klytemnestra may well have been justly punished, but Orestes' murder of her was still wrong. Although Apollo is Kastor's superior and the one who ordered the killing, the oracles were "lies" (1246). Orestes himself must bear the guilt and, in words that partially paraphrase the corresponding event in *The Eumenides*, is instructed to go to the court at the Areopagus, "where the gods/ first took their seats to judge murder by public vote" (1263).

The question is whether the Dioscuri, who help distressed sailors, here represent the "humane" view of life and death, which is linked to the Areopagus Council where judgment lies in human hands. This interpretation could be supported by the tragedy *Orestes*, as King Tyndareios suggests an alternative to the killing—that Orestes should have brought his mother before the just court that bases its judgment on the law saying that murderers must leave the country and atone for their guilt. In this way, new blood revenge could be avoided.

Finally, the Dioscuri reveal how Orestes is to found a city in Arcadia when the Erinyes have been exorcized. But the people must bury Aigisthos first, while Menelaos, who has just returned home, is to bury Klytemnestra. He brings Helen with him since Euripides applies the interpretation he also uses in *Helen*, which is based on the myth that it was not she but only an image of her that was sent to Troy, while she herself was in Egypt.

Euripides' use of this myth means that the Trojan War—the countless dead, the destruction of the city, the sorrow and gnashing of teeth—was a vain sacrifice—for the benefit of whom? Well, for Zeus, the father of all things, since the blood bath was determined by him with the single purpose: "so men might die in hate (*eris*) and blood" (1283). We are given no explanation of Zeus' intentions and so must draw the conclusion that human life is subject to the evil principle of strife, incarnated in the god from whom men otherwise seek to derive wisdom and justice.

In other words, it is impossible to count on the gods. From them come all human flaws. This makes the human world an absurdity in which reason can do nothing, insignificant and powerless as the individual is against the confusion, blindness and fortuitousness that Orestes claims governs existence.

8

As interpreters, we run into a dilemma. If we read *Elektra* on the premises of the play alone, we must agree with the Dioscuri when they claim that Apollo's lies have drawn Orestes into a disastrous sequence of events. However, this interpretation leads to a different result if the tragedy is placed within the context of the other tragedies on the curse of the Tantalid family and Orestes' role as conciliator. For in that case we are no longer dependent upon the protagonists' more or less fallible understanding of life and the gods.

For it appears that to no less an extent than in Aeschylus, Orestes is part of a larger archetypal drama: With the matricide, he not only liberates himself in his subjective history from the primal mother, but he contributes to the transformation in the world of the gods from maternal to paternal rule. This confirms that his tragedy has a nuanced and latent narrative level. There are two planes. The first, linked to the subjective story of the characters, reflects their psychology and crisis. The second level is embodied in a mythological, fateful perspective which is played out both individually and collectively.

Since Klytemnestra is presented with such clear and moving characteristics in her remorse at the murder of her husband, it is primarily evidence of the increasing psychological insight featuring in Euripides' drama, not least his sympathetic understanding of her situation and that of women in general. Agamemnon has not only murdered her daughter, but has brought home a mistress as if it were the most natural thing in the world. On the other hand, this does not mean that she has lost the mythical character of avenging mother goddess into which she is transformed in *Iphigenia at Aulis* when her husband with his knife sacrifices their daughter to ensure he has wind in his sails.

And it is in this figuration that Orestes as her son must use the knife on his mother. In the context of the mother cult, he is quite simply compelled to kill his mother in order to achieve an independent existence and break the chain of misfortunes linked to the world of blood.

That Euripides really conceived of Klytemnestra in this context is supported by the fact that she is identified with her sister Helen, who with her almost anonymous sexuality is an Aphrodite-like nature goddess. And on this basis, it is a perfectly understandable artistic ploy on the part of Euripides to let him kill Helen in the *Orestes* as the cultic figure she fundamentally is. Then, on Apollo's orders, he can marry her daughter Hermione, released from her maternal bonds—as Orestes himself is from his mother. His knife is a liberating force.

The sign that Orestes has won himself and brought his family into a new reality is that, according to Apollo's orders in the *Orestes*, he must first be acquitted by the court at the Areopagus, but then return to his native city Argos as ruler. The Dioscuri, on the other hand, promised he would found a city in Arcadia—after first having visited the Areopagus. If the two are put together, we may be tempted to claim that the Dioscuri are secondary to Apollo's superior, hidden intention. For when Kastor speaks of the god's "lies," he does not actually know what he is saying, since these "lies" bring Orestes back as a liberator of his family's native city of Mycenae. However, the premise is that he should carry out the matricide and accept the suffering that follows from it, as is portrayed in the tragedy that bears his name.

Orestes—The Erinyes of Conscience

1

Aeschylus clearly saw it as his primary task to describe the establishment of the Areopagus Council as a transition from maternal to paternal rule and thereby the foundation of Athenian democracy. Because of his psychological focus, it is in the case of Euripides imperative to further explore Orestes' conflict of conscience, which Aeschylus hints at in *The Libation Bearers*: his inner visions of his mother's

Erinyes (see p. 395). As said above, Kastor predicted in the *Elektra* that after the matricide Orestes would be pursued by the avenging spirits of the dead woman— "The dreadful beast-faced goddesses of destiny/ will roll you like a wheel through maddened wandering" (1252-53).

In the *Orestes* and *Iphigenia at Tauris*, we (and those around Orestes) witness how in epileptic-like fits he is beset by terrifying visions of the Erinyes, which are visible to him only and not to the world around him. When Menelaos asks about the nature of his disease, he responds: "I call it conscience./ The certain knowledge of wrong, the conviction of crime" (395-96).[23] As proof of the radical nature of this statement, Menelaos repeats, in amazement: "You speak somewhat obscurely. What do you mean?" (397).

From this answer, we must infer that Menelaos is not familiar with this form of consciousness, *syneidesis*, of which Orestes speaks, whereas Orestes himself arrives at a true knowledge of the difference between external and internal reality. To the question of what sort of visions horrify him, he must acknowledge that they forced their way into his consciousness six days before, that is to say when he buried his mother and her curse called forth three avenging goddesses, here called Semnai (408), the highly honored, while these furies in the *Elektra* are called Keres (1252) and in *Iphigenia at Tauris* are referred to as Erinyes (292). Euripides apparently does not distinguish among these avenging goddesses, whether as emissaries from the blood of the murdered person they walk the earth the earth or whether they are internal visions of terror.

The important thing is that, with his pangs of conscience, Orestes has come to an awareness of himself as a subject, as something essentially different from his surroundings. He has appropriated a purely personal subjectivity, as he says in his own words—he has attained self-knowledge. And as it emerges in the herdsman's description in *Iphigenia at Tauris*, he seems to be an incarnation of the Erinyes to the extent to which they have taken possession of his inner self: "by the way he jerked his head/ Whenever a dog barked or a cow mooed,/ That if a Fury wasn't chasing him/ He thought there was in every sound he heard" (292-94). As in the tragedies on Oedipus, the description shows what travails a person is forced to suffer—the harsh necessity of which Odysseus spoke—to become a self.

2

In vain, Orestes tries to move Menelaos to help him when Apollo still hesitates to come to his relief. As he says with the same uncertainty that characterized him in the *Elektra*: "Gods are slow by nature" (420). But the practical politician Menelaos, a man of the same stuff as King Kreon, will not provide Orestes with support as with Orestes' and Elektra's death sentence he will inherit their kingdom.

As has been told above, on the advice of the faithful Pylades, Orestes kills Helen in order to have the honor of killing the woman who was the cause of the misery and death of so many young warriors and has cast shame upon the female sex. As Zeus' daughter, Helen cannot die but appears in an airy vision above the palace roof; she has been taken among the gods on Olympos to which Apollo has led her. And Apollo, the *deus ex machina*, now demands that Orestes should seek atonement from the Areopagus Council and later marry Hermione (the daughter of Helen and Menelaos),[24] while Pylades is to marry Elektra. Thus, Elektra ends by getting a husband who answers to her demand to be married to a real man.

Iphigenia at Tauris—The Reconciliation

1

While it was understandable that, in the *Elektra*, Orestes could feel at a loss about Apollo's intentions for him, particularly after Kastor's critique of his lies, the god's concluding speech gives him the clear hope of a way out of his existential crisis. In his cry at the end, he says: "Hail, Apollo,/ for your prophetic oracles! True prophet,/ not false!/ And yet, when I heard you speak,/ I thought I heard the whispers of some fiend/ speaking through your mouth" (*Or.* 1666-69). The quotation plays on his doubt in the *Elektra* about the extent to which he was under the influence of Apollo or a *daimon* that had taken the form the god.

It is still, however, only a matter of whether Orestes should seek his individual liberation at the court at the Areopagus. Unlike Aeschylus, Euripides apparently does not let this court arise as a collective event in the world of gods and humans.

Nevertheless, this sort of thinking is not alien to Euripides. On the contrary, it is part of the underlying stratum in his Orestes tragedies, as evidenced by the quite personal version he provides in *Iphigenia at Tauris* (approx. 415 B.C.). Here, the story continues, describing how Orestes flees his mother's army of snake-like Erinyes. For although he is acquitted by the court in Athens and, as described in the *Oresteia*, a large group of Erinyes is transformed into the Eumenides, those who did not go along and are not exorcized and transformed into fertility goddesses are still on his trail and conjure up his conscience-plagued nightmare. So Apollo has given him a mission, which is to be his last: he is to take Artemis' idol to Brauron on the coast of Attica coast near Athens. This idol has fallen from heaven and is worshipped with blood sacrifices by the barbaric people of Tauris.

What Orestes does not know is that his sister Iphigenia acts as priestess at the temple of Artemis. Artemis herself has brought her here after saving her from her father's sacrifice by putting a hind in her place. Iphigenia's task, according to the country's ancient custom, is to initiate all recently arrived Hellenes to the blood sacrifice carried out in the very shrine of Artemis in her attribute as the country's fertility goddess and as a demand she herself has made, clearly revealing her chthonic character.

It is a fabulous artistic gambit Euripides employs here. He simply creates a mirror image or identification between Apollo and Orestes. As an "agent" for Apollo, Orestes is to save his sister from the cultic world of the primal mother to which she still belongs and which also made her demand a blood sacrifice in *Iphigenia in Aulis*. He is to kidnap her as a part of the change in system from maternal to paternal power, so that she undergoes the same transformation as the Erinyes underwent in becoming the Eumenides.

But not only that. Unwittingly, Orestes is at the same time also to save his sister from this cultic world she serves. And his thereby being able to liberate himself from the pursuing Erinyes must simply be because by finding and saving his sister, he is atoning for the murder of the mother they have in common.

To sum up: One divine brother sends the other off to bring home their sisters. The hidden purpose known only to the Olympian god is that Orestes is to liberate them from the gory maternal world and, instead, constitute a sister world with a form of love that is liberated from the possessive and propagating sexuality that dominates the Great Mother. Oedipus went through the same psychological evolution, when after the marriage to his mother he wandered the world accompanied and protected by his daughters, his sisters.

<h1 style="text-align:center">2</h1>

The change of fortune in *Iphigenia at Tauris* is connected to the recognition between brother and sister, the tragedy's *anagnorisis*. When Iphigenia is about to sacrifice her brother and discovers who he is, she realizes that the dream she had of him and interpreted as proof that her family was dead was wrong. This sudden insight may be described as an awakening from the dream-like world with which she has been one—and helped to maintain as the priestess of Artemis and which, in her conscious state, she is now ready to leave.

Put another way: in the split second of recognition, she becomes conscious of herself as an acting individual. In her brother and the love she feels for him, she can see a fellow human being, whom she is about to sacrifice for the mother cult, which in her waking state she can now observe from the outside. Horrified, she sees herself with the knife, poised to continue the murderous curse of the family and she cries: "But I came so near,/ my hand so nearly set the final seal,/ That I still shake as though you lay here dead" (867-69).

Only with this exclamation of self-possession does the mother cult release its grip upon Iphigenia. Only now can she define herself in a humanized dissimilarity. For his part, Orestes has reached his sister via the murder of his mother who in this perspective is a counterpart to Artemis, since she has "sacrificed" Agamemnon to the mother cult and the Erinyes.

Together, the siblings can accomplish Apollo's task of carrying away Artemis' idol. Orestes finally acts without the uncertainty that has dogged his path hitherto. He has had revealed the inner meaning and plan in his grievous fate. But the premise for this has been that, despite his chronic uncertainty with respect to the gods' intentions and his tormented conscience, he has had sufficient courage to attain the answer to the riddle, which—as in *Oedipus*—proved to be embedded in the world around him.

The final proof, parallel to the *Oresteia*, is that it is not Apollo but Athene—as tutelary goddess for the sacred city of Athens—who as a *deus ex machina* prevents the barbarian king from seizing the brother and sister and re-taking the idol. She proclaims that the idol must be placed in a temple dedicated to Artemis and called after the land of Tauris. Here, Iphigenia is to serve as priestess; but the former blood sacrifice will take the form of a symbolic slit in the throat. So blood vengeance is once and for all replaced by the same law as in the *Oresteia*: "An evenly divided verdict wins" (1473). Finally, the blood guilt of the family is atoned, stressed by the simultaneous change in the world of the gods linked to Artemis' transformation into a kind of Eumenide.

Medea—Uncontrolled Passion

1

If, as it is claimed, Euripides was a rationalist, he was so in a very inclusive way, in that he analyzes the crisis of his times through tragedy, emphasizing rationality's vain attempt to limit irrational forces. Thus, in three of his most significant tragedies written over the course of a generation: *Medea* (431 B.C.), *Hippolytos* (428 B.C.) and *The Bacchae* (406 B.C.), he demonstrates how the world of nature and instinct possesses a strength and a compass in the face of which mankind comes to grief with the control of its thought.

Against this background, it may be appropriate to quote something on Euripides from his enemy Nietzsche's *Midnight Song*: "Die Welt is tief, und tiefer als der Tag gedacht." For in connection with nocturnal divinities such as Aphrodite and Dionysos, there comes a wisdom that far surpasses—indeed, explodes—the reason to which figures such as Hippolytos and King Pentheus in *The Bacchae* cling with their restrictive *sophrosyne*, which really seems like arrogance towards the cosmic powers of nature. And these powers, which they reject, punish them with death. The tragedies bespeak an insight on the part of Euripides to the effect that in order to be whole the human world must absorb these primal forces.

2

In the *Medea*, we are confronted with a fatal interplay of erotic passion, woman's social abandonment and the stereotype of a cynical dominant male. The passionate, barbaric Medea is put in contrast to her pragmatic Hellenic husband Iason. At the beginning of the play, Medea, acting out of love has helped him to gain the Golden Fleece, thereby bringing about the death of her brother and the loss of her family. Iason, however, tired of wandering around aimlessly without social power or prestige, has decided out of pure calculation to marry into the royal family of Corinth.

In short, he simply ignores the fact that he is violating the woman who has dedicated her whole existence to their love. But, as Klytemnestra said in the *Elektra*, a woman's blood is hot. Inverting her love to hate, Medea wipes out all life around her: the children they have together and his new bride. There is thus every reason for the nurse in speaking of Medea to refer to: "the wildness and bitter nature/ of that proud mind" (103-04). Medea also maintains that she is not made of the same stuff as other women, who, according to the convention at that time in Athens, were supposed to be tractable. She, on the other hand, says she is "one who can hurt my enemies and help my friends" (809), an attribute that Aphrodite likewise claims for herself in *Hippolytos*, where she spares no means to avenge herself.

Meanwhile, the nurse considers Medea's passion to be delusion inflicted on her by a *daimon* (14) and recommends moderation to her. But as a contemporary piece of evidence that Euripides lets human beings govern their own actions, he has Medea make a conscious choice. On the one hand, at the thought of murdering her children, she says: "Do not, O my heart, do these things!/ Poor heart, let them go, have pity upon the children" (1057-58). On the other, she must admit that she is so in the grip of her passions that she cannot act differently: "I know indeed what evil I intend to do,/ But stronger than all my afterthoughts is my fury,/ Fury that brings upon mortals the greatest evils" (1078-80). While Iason is devoid of the ability to love, Medea conversely has no reason to calm her passions, summed up by the term *thymos*.

3

Her name is associated with wiliness and the sex organ,[25] Medea is allegedly one of those women who according to Hippolytos are the most dangerous, because by virtue of their intelligence they know how to devise a special form of evil. Iason's future father-in-law, King Kreon (who must not be confused with the king of Thebes by the same name) is of the same view, which is why he wants to banish her. Kreon believes with good reason that she intends evil and bases this on the fact that she is "versed in evil arts" (285). It will be the ruin of him and his family that he does not maintain this interpretation but yields to Medea's prayer to remain just one more day during which to plan her future.

At the same time, Medea expresses the oppression of women as reflected in contemporary Athens: "We women are the most unfortunate creatures" (231). And she recites how a woman is forced with her dowry to buy a husband, who then has free use of her. He can divorce her, deny her sexual intercourse, and go out when he is bored at home. The man is free, whereas he is the only thing the woman can cling to. At the same time, giving birth is far more painful and dangerous than going to war. In the section on Socrates, we shall look further into the actual status of women and merely conclude here with Medea that woman may well be weak, but "when once she is wronged in the matter of love,/ No other soul can hold so many thoughts of blood" (265-66).

If this description of woman as a beast of prey is applied to Medea and is linked to her hatching her schemes in the night, she becomes a frightening example of what happens when a mother in the real world undergoes an archetypal metamorphosis. She becomes, in short, the chastising mother figure in the same category as the Erinyes, whose work also takes place under cover of darkness.

4

So there are two sides to Medea. On the immediate level of the plot she is an ordinary woman, deserted by her husband. And in this role, she calls upon Zeus and Themis, so that these gods, as the guardians of the oath of the marriage pact, must punish Iason (209). But at the same time she has a mythical dimension, emphasized by the fact that—like Kirke—she is skilled in the art of producing the deadly potions of the witch and moon goddess Hekate (396), whom she invokes, clearly signalling her chthonic affiliation. If we look at Medea's mythological emblematic significance, it is further confirmed that she belongs in this context. Kirke and Pasiphae, King Minos' wife, who mated with the Minotaur, are her aunts—sisters of her father, King Aietes and Phaedra, the daughter of Pasiphae, her cousin.[26] These women have so many features in common that they can easily be identified with each other as original mother goddesses. Medea also acts as an offended maternal power. From being an unconditional supporter of Iason, she becomes a no less uncompromising avenger.

This interpretation is not only documented by her connection to Hekate, but also by a number of basic metaphorical personifications. She is on several occasions compared to a lioness (186; 1342; 1359) in order to express her predatory wildness. As Iason puts it after her murder of his bride and children, she is even more murderous than Skylla (1344). And this latent connection to the animal and the primordial feminine is confirmed by the fact that she accepts this characterization, explaining that he himself called forth these attributes when he betrayed her. As we saw, Aeschylus used the same metaphorical links: lioness and Skylla to illustrate the dark side of Klytemnestra's nature as female avenger.

5

One particular feature of this heritage stresses Medea's dangerous femininity, in that she is attributed with a barbaric origin. Not only does she come from a place far from Greece, Colchis, but through her father King Aietes, a son of Helios and the nymph Perse, she is closely related to Kirke and Phaedra. By following her *thymos* and in its possession killing her children, she regresses to this barbaric world from which Iason has led her. Before her murders, he describes Medea as a woman who was spoken of throughout Hellas for her wisdom (*sophen*, 539), a wisdom she significantly enough only attained after he had taken her away from "living among barbarians" (537) and she had learned what "law and justice" meant. After the murders, he characterizes her directly as a barbarian—"There is no Greek woman who would have dared such deeds" (1339).

Euripides draws here upon the general Greek attitude that foreigners, for instance the Persians, were to be seen as barbarians. And this foreignness, this barbarism, is applied to the female together with the animal with the aim of showing that she is a creature of nature, governed by sexuality, wild and animal, and so a great danger to man. Hesiod had been the first to formulate a corresponding misogyny. Iason expresses an archetypal fear of the woman's nature, as the barbaric quality in Medea is attributed to women who break man's monopoly of power.

6

Like Hippolytos, Iason wishes for that same reason that men could give birth, because if women could be made superfluous in this way, "then life would have been good" (575), as he says. True humanity—as in Hesiod (see p. 290)—is identical with the male, while the non-human is attributed to woman as uncontrolled emotion and nature. That is to say that Iason finds himself virtually on the same level of development as obtained in the *Iliad*, where the heroes lived in an isolated world of heroic masculine ideals that repressed the female, after which, in the *Odyssey*, it appeared in the shape of the monsters of the *Apologoi*, demanding confrontation and integration. When, in his pragmatic calculations, Iason suspends this side of life, its demony is inevitably turned against him: Medea kills that life of which she, as a mother, is the guarantor. The primal mother takes back what she gave.

As a hero, Iason is said to be is characterized by self-love. He vehemently insists that his new marriage is not based on passion but on practical social considerations that he himself calls "wise" (548) and claims will benefit Medea and their children. The nurse, however, expresses the view that his actions reveal a ruthless arrogance when she talks of the tyranny arising from *hubris*: "Great people's tempers are terrible, always/ Having their own way, seldom checked" (119-20). And she points to the price: the angry divinity or *daimon* will crack down all the harder on the arrogant who place their faith in riches (*koros*). In the *Hippolytos*, it is similarly stated: "The ways of life that are most fanatical/ trip us up more, they say, than bring us joy" (261-62). So the most important motto in life is: Be moderate in all things.

Since similar Solonian sayings appear in other works by Euripides, we must take them as evidence that he shares the Greeks' general view of *hubris* and *sophrosyne*. But only to a certain extent. For where an obsession with *sophrosyne* becomes a blunting of the feelings, it leads to self-destruction, as will be seen in *Hippolytos* and *The Bacchae*.

7

It is an artistic master stroke on the part of Euripides that, in the form of Medea, he presents woman as man fears her but at the same time shows how the oppression women suffer has for the same reason led to a stunting and demonization of emotional life, while the man has become a cynical pragmatist. Euripides does disparage a woman's connection with the elemental primal forces and untamed nature, but he concedes the rights of love and the irrational as necessary in life if it is not to atrophy. This presupposes a balance between masculine and feminine values, although Plato is the first to express this directly in his utopian state.

It was thus to limit the woman's Aphrodite-like nature that men in ancient Athens allocated a place to women in the home. But even though Medea herself is a poisoner, she is herself poisoned by Aphrodite: burning love for a man is turned into a no less a burning hatred. The chorus nevertheless wishes to give Aphrodite a place in social life and must on this point agree with Euripides, for if Aphrodite comes cautiously, "there is no other power at all so gracious" (630). And they pray urgently that she will never strike them with her arrows, dipped "in the poison of desire" (633). They hope that self-control, *sophrosyne*, will accompany them as "the god's best gift" (636).

We here see Aphrodite as a mortally dangerous natural force that disturbs the mind through desire. If you are struck by it, you are at its mercy. As Euripides' plays on Medea, Phaedra, and the Bacchae show, women in particular are subject to such danger. But he obviously also believes that the ability to love can be a blessing, if it can only work together with *sophrosyne*, where self-control does not recoil in fear but stands open to the fundamental forces in life. This is one of the primary themes in the *Hippolytos*.

Hippolytos—Sexual Purism

1

Euripides' critical consciousness leads to an otherwise completely blameless hero such as Iason being turned into an anti-hero. This is if possible even clearer in the *Hippolytos*, in which the man's fear of and hatred for the woman takes on a phobic dimension, the ultimate source of which is in sexuality's link with the primal maternal.

The conflict arises when King Theseus' son Hippolytos repudiates Aphrodite by refusing to sacrifice to her in order to avoid his erotic fate. The lowest of the gods, he calls her. At the same time, to preserve his purity, strengthen his young masculinity and elevate his intelligence as a counterweight to the Great Mother figure, he has attached himself to the virgin goddess Artemis, who supports him as a sisterly friend—as Athene helped Odysseus.

Euripides gives no explanation for Hippolytos' choice of Artemis and renunciation of sexuality as personified by Aphrodite. He may possibly have taken for granted the audience's knowledge of the deeper reason for his affinity to the goddess of chastity. As said above, Hippolytos' mother was the Amazon queen Hippolyte, whom Theseus had captured on an expedition with Herakles, who on his ninth labor was to take her belt. The legends vary, but it is a recurrent feature that Hippolyte falls in love with Theseus and helps him put the Amazons to flight when they attack Athens to retrieve their queen. In the *Oresteia*, this expulsion was an omen of the final victory of paternal rule over the maternal world.

Meanwhile, Hippolytos shares this worship of Artemis with the Amazons. But there is one crucial difference in that the Amazons did not repudiate sexuality but on the contrary cultivated it in the same amorphous and anonymous way as Aphrodite in her attribute as goddess of desire. They simply refused to submit to men and so came to represent the same barbaric ferocity as a Medea. As early as in *The Suppliant Maidens* we met this contrast between Aphrodite and Artemis when the Danaids pray to Artemis the chaste to be spared the marriage bed, which is the domain of the goddess of love Kypris. So it is in the spirit of Artemis that with the exception of Hypermestra they all murder their Egyptian husbands and so reveal that in her fundamental mythical manifestation Artemis really belongs to the same level of consciousness as Aphrodite: absolute chastity as opposed to senseless, nature-bound sexual frenzy.[27]

In this mythical subtext, it seems as though Queen Hippolyte, like Hypermestra, has allowed love in a superior, binding form to penetrate her being in her encounter with Theseus, whereas the Amazons remain in their archaic primal form. They have not achieved the level of civilization that appears with the growing of crops in which Demeter becomes more developed as a cultic earth goddess for organized agriculture.

So despite the worship of Artemis as mother goddess and protector of animals on Crete, for example, Artemis must in the *Hippolytos* be placed at a higher level of consciousness. In her opposition to Aphrodite, she acts—in her relationship with Telemachos—on a par with Athene as a spiritual force to liberate Hippolytos' incipient manhood from the cultic mother's engulfing demand for love. But for Hippolytos, it becomes fatal, as by rejecting love he blocks his emotional life and cuts himself off from the universality that Aphrodite's power of creation incarnates. What we fail to assimilate turns against us, and this repudiation and rejection achieve a fateful significance for him.

2

Once again, Euripides demonstrates his ability to see through the paradox of existence. For although he is a poet of *sophrosyne*,[28] that is to say that just like Plato, for instance, he sees self-control as a cardinal virtue, he can also see that as an emotionally limiting instrument of control, *sophrosyne* can counteract the great forces of life. Indeed, in the case of Hippolytos it can degenerate into a *hubris*-like arrogance. He clearly sees himself as a purer person than anyone else—"You see the earth and air about you, father?/ In all of that there lives no man more chaste/ than I" (993-95). In a purity of this kind lurks absolutism's annihilation of everything experienced as impure—in the present context sexuality and women.

Aphrodite avenges his contemptuous rejection by having Phaedra, Hippolytos' step-mother, seized of an uncontrollable desire for him, which ends up taking both their lives. It may be said that as she is a tool of Aphrodite and is overwhelmed by the nature of her desire, Phaedra herself becomes a victim of the primal female.

Here, too, the underlying kinships are important. Not only is she a cousin of Medea, but her mother is King Minos' queen, Pasiphae, whom Poseidon—because Minos neglected to sacrifice to him—fired with an unhappy love for the bull Minotauros, who lived in the Cretan labyrinth (of death). Theseus killed this monster with the help of Phaedra's sister, Ariadne, an act that once again symbolizes how young masculine heroes conquer the chthonic powers.

Phaedra herself knows that she is demonized: "It was the madness sent from some God/ that caused my fall" (241-42), she says. No more than Medea is she able to keep her passion in check "with discretion and good sense" (398), but she must acknowledge that, when it comes down to it, people will always be controlled by their lust:

I think that our lives are worse than the mind's quality
Would warrant. There are many who know virtue.
We know the good, we apprehend it clearly.
But we can't bring it to achievement. Some
Are betrayed by their own laziness, and others
Value some pleasure above virtue.

(377-83)

With this acknowledgement of the nature of lust, the chorus cannot be blamed for its fear of the erotic and sexual, which are primarily traced to Aphrodite. In the *Medea*, she unleashes the "poison of desire" (637) and the chorus prays "On me let mighty Kypris/ Inflict no wordy wars or restless anger/ to urge my passion to a different love" (638). The goddess' effect is also, characteristically enough, linked to other mother goddesses. Thus, the chorus believes that Phaedra's fatal passion and the madness of her desire is due to Kybele, Rhea or Hekate, with whom Medea is also connected.

3

Since Phaedra despises infidelity, she wants to commit suicide, while her nurse tries to convince her of Aphrodite's cosmic nature and irresistibility. She says:

> (…) the tide of love,
> at its full surge, is not withstandable.
> Upon the yielding spirit she comes gently,
> But to the proud and the fanatic heart
> She is a torturer with the brand of shame
> She wings her way through the air; she is in the sea,
> In its foaming billows; from her everything,
> That is, is born. For she engenders us
> And sows the seed of desire whereof we're born,
> All we her children, living on the earth.
>
> (442-49)

In this way, Aphrodite is represented as a cosmic creative power with clear similarities to the view of *eros* expressed by Hesiod in the *Theogony* and by Aeschylus in the trilogy on the Danaids. Sophocles makes the same admission in the *Women of Trachis*, where the chorus says: "Great and mighty is the victory which the Cyprian queen always bears away."[29] In the *Hippolytos*, the nurse states that love is both sweet and painful, painful because even good people love although it is sinful. And this means that Aphrodite is not merely a god: "You are something stronger than God if that can be./ You have ruined her and me and all this house" (361-62).

In Aphrodite's dual attributes—gentle and good to her proselytes, formidable and castigating toward those who, like Hippolytos, reject her—she takes on not only the same identity as the Great Mother but points toward Dionysos. In *The Bacchae*, he also avenges himself, pointing out that he is a god at once fearsome and infinitely gentle with people (p. 491).

Sexuality is such an immense, unmanageable force that marriage as a defense against it seems a highly fragile institution. The sexual instinct is radical in that it wants only its own fulfilment irrespective of and in spite of all reasonable words and arrangements. The instinct is a fixation and delusion and admits of nothing but itself, just as Aphrodite in the work's symbolism cannot endure Hippolytos doing without her in his desire for purity.

When, contrary to Phaedra's wishes, the nurse suggests to Hippolytos that he should start a sexual relationship with her—in order to free her from the plague Aphrodite has inflicted on her—he reacts with dismay at the thought of the impurity (*miasma*) that her words evoke in him. Indeed, the mere fact that this unmentionable thing is mentioned to him, the pure one, causes an idiosyncratic sense of being soiled. He rushes out of the palace and in a rage forbids the nurse with her supplicant gesture to touch his clothes. "I'll go to a running stream and pour its waters/ into my ear to purge away the filth" (652-53), he cries in the monologue in which he renounces the female sex in general.

4

Against this background, it is understandable if the women of Athens, as Aristophanes presents them in the *Thesmophoriazusae* (411 B.C.), despised Euripides and in the comedy have only one point on their progam at the festival of Thesmophoria, which is to have Euripides condemned to death, because, as they say, he "mishandles them" by making them sex-crazy, drunken and faithless.[30] He "loads us with every kind of indignity" and has destroyed family life.[31]

Without embarking on a deeper analysis of the *Andromache*, this tragedy contains a plethora of statements showing how dependent and forsaken women were. It is said, among other things, that a woman's virtue is a man's delight (208) and that if she is robbed of her husband, she loses her life (372). So she is forced to endure his poor treatment (213), even when he is a bad person. Yet, women are also described as so cunning that they always find a way out (845). They are thus a pestilence on this earth (273) and a wise man refuses women access to his house (921).

However, this is a hidden critique of the situation of women in democratic Athens, where they were not enfranchised, could not own land, were kept out of all aspects of public life and tied to running the home, as I shall describe in more detail in connection with Socrates. For the same reason, it is also more correct to say that with the nuanced descriptions of his female characters Euripides provided an insight into their complex nature and the oppression to which they are subjected. He lets Phaedra—like Medea—relate how unfortunate women are, because they must, so to speak, buy a husband with the dowries they bring to a marriage, after which men dominate them as they think fit. The repetition of this criticism in itself stresses its seriousness and authenticity.

Hippolytos, on the other hand, makes the dowry a proof of women's evil: "we have a proof how great a curse is woman./ For the father who begets her, rears her up,/ must add a dowry gift to pack her off" (627-29). And like Iason, he wishes that children could be conceived in another way, so that men could avoid the curse that lies in women's fertility. Once again there is this fear of the maternal containing the hope of being definitively liberated from it and fundamentally explaining his fanaticism with regard to purity. It particularly frightens him to think of the harm that a wise woman can cause, for which reason a man should prefer a nonentity.

On these grounds Hippolytos formulates what he himself calls a hatred of women (*mison gynaikas*, 664), even though others criticize him for it. That those around him try to curb his hatred can be taken as a sign that he actually creates a dangerous imbalance by denying Aphrodite and the female sex. Hence, the old servant tries to persuade him to display piety before the statue of Aphrodite. He refuses, giving as a reason his wish to distance himself from Aphrodite's chthonic nature and saying that he will not honor a divinity who is worshipped at night. The servant then tries in vain to persuade the goddess to be patient with Hippolytos—making reference to the rashness of youth.

5

Considering that Aphrodite is described as a cosmic force, it may be said that on the one hand Hippolytos is punished by the primordial forces he repudiates in her cult and, on the other hand, is brought down as the result of a repression that sees Phaedra as "impure." In her despair at this, combined with his rejection of her, she drags him down with her in her own fall, acting as an extension of the goddess.

The mutual misunderstanding between Phaedra and Hippolytos is based upon a misinterpretation—he thinks the nurse is doing her bidding, while she believes he wants to expose her passion and thereby bring an unbearable shame upon her. So she drags him into her suicide by speaking in a letter to her husband Theseus, the father of Hippolytos, of a consummated sexual relationship.

With the accusation contained in her letter of improper behavior on the part of Hippolytos, Phaedra also wants to teach him a lesson—to teach him *sophrosyne* in the sense of respect for women—a process strongly reminiscent of the way in which Dionysos punishes King Pentheus in his self-righteousness by dressing him in women's clothes and having him killed by his mother's all-consuming madness.

6

After Phaedra's death and accusations, the well-known question of *miasma* is raised for Theseus and Hippolytos, the latter explicitly addressing whether the misfortunes by which the family is now being struck is inherited guilt that has skipped several generations:

> Father, your deadly curse!
> This evil comes from some manslaying of old,
> Some ancient tale of murder among my kin.
> But why should it strike me, who am clear of guilt?
>
> (1376-79)

Theseus has several times mentioned the reverse side of his son's piety: that he enjoys his own purity and suffers from a hypocritical smugness: "Yes, in self-worship you are certainly practiced./You are more at home there than in the other virtues,/ justice, for instance, and duty toward a father" (1080-83). The paradox is that, by his denial of sexuality and its goddess, Hippolytos has linked himself negatively to what he is consciously trying to repress with all his strength. He has thereby brought himself into conflict with a greater and older reality than he can handle and is struck down by what he denies. It happens quite simply: his father Theseus tells Poseidon, who has promised to fulfil three wishes, to kill his son.

We know from Homer that Poseidon represents a masculine form of the chthonic, that is to say that in practice Theseus conjures up the primal force of the sea against his son. However, Poseidon acts first and foremost on behalf of Aphrodite as the offended mother goddess. From the sea, he sends an enormous bull, which makes Hippolytos' team of horses, which he believed he could control like his own urges, bolt. He becomes entangled in the reins and is dragged to his death by the stampeding mares, which significantly disappear with the disturbing bull into an abyss in the mountains.

7

The oath Hippolytos swears to the nurse not to reveal her plea on Phaedra's behalf that he should give himself to her has prevented him from telling his father the true story. His father, on the other hand, refuses to believe his assurances of innocence and purity, but on the contrary mocks him for being smug. So in the final tableau Artemis appears and informs Theseus of the truth, when Hippolytos is already dying and beyond help: "Miserable man, what joy have you in this?/ You have murdered a son, you have broken nature's laws" (1286-87).

Artemis has been unable to stop Aphrodite on the basis of the fundamental rule that the gods do not interfere in each other's projects. But she promises that, when the occasion arises, she will exact payment and strike down the favorite of the goddess of love (1419). Euripides must be thinking of Adonis, Aphrodite's young lover, who was killed by a wild boar.[32] For whereas Artemis acts almost as a spiritual mirror of Hippolytos, in this act of retribution she activates her *figura* as the evil mother. And in contrast to Odysseus, who on being initiated from puberty into manhood succeeds in killing the charging wild boar, Adonis is unable to do the same and, like Hippolytos, he finds death in an obvious regression to the Great Mother.

The Bacchae—A Vision

1

Interestingly enough, there are almost 25 years between the *Hippolytos* and *The Bacchae*, which was posthumously performed after Euripides' death in 406 B.C. It may be that he left the play incomplete and that his son prepared it for performance—at any rate, the conclusion as it has come down to us is fragmentary. The remarkable thing, however, is that these two works resemble each other so very much in theme, despite their distance in time, which again seems to document a high degree of consistency in Euripides' thinking.

Both dramas have at their center a young man who in his *hubris*-like self-control tries to repress a cosmic natural power: Hippolytos in the form of Aphrodite, while Pentheus, the very young king of Thebes, wants to prevent the ecstatic divinity Dionysos from gaining a foothold in the city from which he comes on his mother's side and to which he has just returned from a victorious expedition through Asia, accompanied by a chorus of Bacchantic women. So we see that for almost a generation Euripides was attentive to these groundbreaking divine forces that, in all their irrational might, challenged the rationality with which, as a poet inspired by the Sophists, he himself was identified.

Not only does he register a fascination but, as our interpretation of the *Hippolytos* has shown, he has also understood with analytic clarity that psychological control and repression can lead to self-destruction. So it is vital that these powers should be experienced, endured and integrated into both the personal and the collective mentality. At the same time, he has interpreted this conflict as a part of the archetypal process by which a young man is to liberate himself from his source in the primordial mother. Neither young man succeeds, though it could be said that by admitting these forces into his drama Euripides himself endows them with the *katharsis* of tragedy.

2

As a sign of their common nature, Aphrodite and Dionysos belong to the night and its form of consciousness, which the two young men loathe. As Hippolytos says in dissociating himself from the goddess of love: "God of nocturnal prowess is not my God" (106). And to a question from Pentheus on when one celebrates his cult, Dionysos replies: "Mostly by night./ The darkness is well suited to devotion" (485-86). Then, when Pentheus unsuccessfully tries to imprison the god, he makes the following ironical and deluded remark: "Since he desires the darkness, give him what he wants./ Let him dance down there in the dark" (510-11). If he naively thinks he can lay a god in chains, it is because Dionysos appears in human form—as his own prophet. He and Pentheus are also the same age, even cousins, as Dionysos' mother Semele is the sister of the king's mother Agave.

So King Pentheus, who has succeeded his grandfather Kadmos, the founder of Thebes, tries to oppose Dionysos with his logical reason. Pentheus sees him as an effeminate, decadent being with his free-flowing, light, long hair: "scour the city/ for that effeminate stranger, the man who infects our women/ with this strange disease and pollutes our beds" (351-54). The Bacchae also dance with loose hair, which they cast back and forth. He himself has his hair plaited and wrapped around his head, tightly bound as a sign that he controls his sexuality. And he can be heard at a great distance, because as another proof of his manhood he tramps off dressed in his soldier's boots. To his eye, Dionysos is primarily a dreamer and a charlatan (233).

To his great annoyance, Pentheus meets the prophet Teiresias and his grandfather, dressed in deerskin and holding each other's hand, on their way to participate in the celebration of the new divinity. One is old, the other blind, so they must support each other, but to the Bacchantic procession they must go, as the god does not distinguish between young and old. They are "foolish" (252), rages Pentheus. Teiresias' unambiguous answer is a clear explanation of the fact that, with Dionysos, they are looking at a new form of knowledge which ordinary reason cannot reach: "We do not trifle with divinity (. . .) whatever subtleties this clever age invents" (200-03). And the chorus of Asian women that follows Dionysos states explicitly that wisdom (*sophia*) is not knowledge or rational cleverness: "what passes for wisdom is not" (394). That is to say that this cleverness, which seeks more than what human limitations allow, is doomed.

In a brilliant ironic exchange, Pentheus claims that Dionysos may well be wise but not when he should be: "You are clever—very—/ but not where it counts" (655-56). To this, the god answers, "Where it counts the most/ there I *am* clever" (656). Both use the Greek word *sophos*, but with the crucial difference resting in the fact that Pentheus is talking about reason, while Dionysos answers on the basis of his divine *Sophia*.

3

As Dionysos is described in *The Bacchae*, he comes to Greece from the north, from Thrace, representing an epoch.[33] His being accompanied solely by women is not the same as saying that he is only a god for women. As the tragedy and the later worship of him shows, he is the divinity for everyone. But because of their openness towards nature and the mystery of sexuality, the women are the first to surrender to him. For these women, he comes as though in answer to their feelings and oppressed position, which Pentheus desperately tries to maintain in a defense of paternal rule.

The women go off into the countryside, away from social life, and like Medea and Phaedra they surrender to the barbaric frenzy that Greek men ascribe to them and which may be said to be a natural consequence of their inability to have their irrationality incorporated into the masculine world of the city-state. As implied by Teiresias' statement that a new wisdom has arrived with Dionysos, it is a matter of creating a larger frame of understanding that also includes the emotional life—and that seems also to be Euripides' message.

The chorus of Bacchantic women is dressed in animal skins with snakes as belts. They copulate indiscriminately like the primal mothers and suckle young animals while shouting wildly in invocation to the god. All nature is drawn into the whirlwind as they dance with the *thyrsos* and chant: "Unarmed, they swooped down upon the herds of cattle" (735) and "scraps smeared with blood hung from the fir trees" (741). The biggest beasts are the bulls—"bulls, their raging fury gathered in their horns" (742). Through their communion when they tear the bull to pieces (*sparagmos*) and consume (*omophagia*) it, the chorus derives a share of its primordial power, as it is said that Dionysos was born as a bull and is called "the bull-horned god" (102). And when Pentheus follows Dionysos through Thebes on the path to his death, he also notices how his companion transforms himself from human form into a bull: "And you—you are a bull/ who walks before me there. Horns have sprouted/ from your head" (920-22).

When Teiresias implores Pentheus to accept Dionysos into the religious life of Thebes, it must be because the god comes as a call from a deep, atavistic longing for a religious life that looks back to the original fertility cults, a longing for nature that the Olympian gods in their anthropomorphic elevation and rational constructivism have not been able to accommodate. Dionysos, on the other hand, answers this need for a mental, "totemic" communion with the god, with which Euripides must have been familiar, to judge from the sympathetic insight in his description of the Bacchantic *mania*.

No wonder male rulers could react in the way of King Pentheus. A radical new departure was on the way, giving a higher priority to the fertility rites. When Heraclitus writes that Hades and Dionysos are one and the same, he is referring to this fact. For, like the witch Medea, Dionysos is linked to the mother goddess Rhea and the earth cults on Crete,[34] where the child Zeus was protected from his father. Later, Orphism modified the Dionysian cult to a worship of Dionysos Zagreus.[35]

4

Pentheus' name means torment,[36] which is certainly to be associated with the punishment that awaits him from Dionysos because of his denial of the god, an association referred to several times—for example, when Teiresias prophesies that his refusal will inflict "sufferings" (368) on his grandfather. The prophet has not only warned Pentheus in abstract terms of the danger into which he is placing himself and his family through his blasphemous denial of the god, but he tries to reveal this knowledge to him by referring to Aktaion's insult to Artemis. As a mirror figure, Aktaion was torn apart by Artemis' dogs when he boasted of being a greater hunter.[37] And it ends with Pentheus up being torn to pieces by the Bacchae at the very spot on Kithairon, where Aktaion was done to death (1291).

The infant Oedipus was exposed in the same mountains and he returned to them as a blind man. In other words, Kithairon's iconographic links to the primal mother are maintained by Euripides when he, too, lets Pentheus meet his fate on this symbol-laden spot where the Bacchae assemble. It takes place as the result of a sequence of events in which, as in Euripides' other tragedies, there is a psychological progression into archetypal consciousness.

Dionysos is able to awaken a desire in Pentheus to spy on the Bacchae's wild sport. The condition is that he must dress in women's garments or rather the costume of the Bacchae, so they will not discover him. However, the clothing symbolizes that the reality Pentheus has tried to control through his intellect now usurps his being and so to speak takes possession of him from within. He is facing annihilation resulting from his own repressed inner life, the demonization of which is first revealed in his transvestism and voyeurism.

Like the hero in the *Hippolytos*, he is destroyed by the natural forces he denies. He regresses to the stage of the primal mother, from which he vainly tried to liberate himself with his reason and macho behavior. The young king's intention is of course to wage war on the Bacchic women, which is why he does not accept an offer from Dionysos to lead them to him peacefully. When from the top of a pine tree—with its obvious phallic connotations—he spies on the Bacchae, Dionysos obscures his vision so that he can only see them engaged in peaceful pursuits.

But just as Hippolytos is dragged to his death by runaway mares, Pentheus is ripped apart. The terrible irony is that maternal power strikes him in the form of his own mother. She tears him to death in the mistaken belief that she has killed a lion, the head of which she carries in triumph to the palace.

His mother Agave is herself a victim of Dionysos, because, like her sisters, she refused to acknowledge that his mother Semele bore him as Zeus' son, but claims that she simply had him with some random mortal man. At the same time, it is a revelation of the duality that characterizes both the god of wine and the goddess of love in the *Hippolytos*: their care is infinite, their revenge fearful, as Dionysos states on his own account, when he emphasizes that the king must learn to understand that he, Dionysos, is a son of Zeus, "most terrible, and yet most gentle, to mankind" (861). When Dionysos appears in all his glory at the end,[38] it is to announce the various forms of punishment he will visit on the city and his mother's family. Finally, he asserts that the fate now befalling them was determined by Zeus: "Long ago my father Zeus ordained these things" (1349).

5

It is surprising, to put it mildly, that Dionysos as the leader of his wild entourage of Bacchae—"He is Bromios who leads us" (140)—finally argues that the punishment he is imposing on Thebes, its king Kadmos and its citizens is due to Zeus and to the fact that he himself is Zeus' son. Shortly before this, in announcing the sentence, he further emphasized the significance of this relationship: "If then, when you would not, you had muzzled your madness,/ you should have an ally now in the son of Zeus" (1343-45). He here uses the expression *sophronein* about the wisdom he has brought with him, but which has been rejected—a wisdom that is not rationality but is linked to the most fundamental human happiness.

As he is hardly thinking of Bacchantian madness we must, in order to find an explanation, look again at his double birth, to which I referred when describing the birth of tragedy in the Dionysian *dithramb* (see p. 334). From this it was seen that—after having killed his mother Semele with a thunderbolt—Zeus took Dionysos into his own thigh, which acted as a womb, and from it gave birth to him as Dithyrambos.

As in the other tragedies in which we have seen the transformation of the gods, *The Bacchae* deals with the possibility of such a transformation. As the young god he is, Dionysos is in a transitional phase. He may be compared to the boy god Zeus, who, as we have heard, grew up in the care of Gaia in a cave in Crete before becoming the ruler of Olympos as an adult. This comparison is by no means far-fetched, as the chorus of Bacchae refers to this event in juxtaposition with Dionysos' own upbringing. In this form, he is still his mother's son and is also invoked as

"Bromios, son of Semele" (363). Zeus' mother Rhea has given them the tambourine from the Kouretes, who attended the child Zeus on Crete and drowned out his cries with their noise.

So in the cult of the Bacchae, Dionysos is still linked to the maternal. *The Bacchae* evidently constitutes a watershed in his development in that—as his father's son—he has returned to Thebes to be received by the *polis* and patriarchs, an event that ideologically heralds the change in system—from a matriarchal to a patriarchal principle and organization.

The prophetic Teiresias must have understood this, since he wants to associate himself with the new divinity and is accompanied by Kadmos. The paradoxical thing is that these two older gentlemen have the emotional openness that the obstinate young king lacks. And his form of intelligence is itself evidence of the rigorous form of government he has imposed on the city with his intellect and of the extent to which, for the same reason, it needs to be re-fertilized by the sphere of feelings that Dionysos has to offer.

Consequently, it becomes the curse of Thebes that as a ruler Pentheus refuses to admit the new life because in his human form the god looks foppish in his flowing, golden locks. And at the same time, it becomes the young king's personal fate to have his head separated from his body, as with his reason he represses this reality, which then becomes part of his subconscious and to which, dressed in women's garments, he regresses. He is ripped apart by his (primal) mother and the blind forces of nature to which she has surrendered herself. For as Pentheus has refused to receive Dionysos into the city, he has been unable to subdue these wild powers and receive them in the blessing that Dionysos himself maintains he would have given—as a gift of wisdom from Zeus himself.

6

In contrast to Pentheus, Peisistratos had in a historical perspective incorporated Dionysos into Athenian religious life (see p. 118) and honored him with the great Dionysia and tragedy competitions. He thereby indulged the enormous popular appeal that the god had and harnessed his natural force as a control measure for the state and for the enrichment of religious life. Meanwhile, as it emerges from the *Medea* and *Hippolytos*, Euripides must have felt that the rationality of the Sophists, with whom he has been identified, led to the atrophy of emotional life. In his dystopian experience of this, he is able as a negation to demonstrate the kind of forces Athens must once again share in: forces of nature and emotion that can make the state fertile and lift it out of the value vacuum into which it had sunk. In this context, of course, Thebes is nothing but a symbolical topos for Athens.

And in this sense, we can say that in his final great tragedy Euripides merges his composition with the will or plan of Zeus in the same way as happens in Homer, Aeschylus and Sophocles. It becomes a testamentary message expressing his insight into and longing for a link with these primeval religious forces. This insight can be traced back to the *Hippolytos*, the point of which is that there is a much deeper wisdom than that of the Sophists, which dominated Athens at the time.

To prevent the subconscious from rising up in all its destructive force, it is vital to meet and integrate this psychological reality into the subject—as a part of its becoming independent. This was what Odysseus and Oedipus, each in his own way, had been able to do, and what Socrates at the same time attempted to achieve in his dialectical development of the inner person.

The End of Tragedy

1

When Aristotle wrote his *Poetics* in the middle of the 5th century B.C., he could from time to time list tragedians and titles—for example, Timotheos and Philoxenos, who had written works with titles such as *The Persians* and *The Kyklops*. These, however, are names and works that have been lost, presumably because the harsh judge of time did not find them worth preserving. And Aristotle finds his primary paradigms in tragedies created more than one hundred years earlier. Why? It is impossible to give a clear answer, yet it is nevertheless surprising that only these three great dramatists have survived for posterity.

The simple explanation may be, as it appears in Aristophanes' *The Frogs*, that there were no longer any good tragedians after the deaths of Sophocles and Euripides—"those that live are bad,"[39] as Dionysos says in despair that no plays are being put on that honor him. So he feels compelled to go to the realm of the dead to bring Euripides back. Instead, it becomes Aeschylus and his tragedies—contrary to the tradition of single performances—that are once again on the playbill.

This must mean that tragedy in its great, trail-blazing form died with Sophocles and Euripides in the same year, 406 B.C., when they wrote their major testamentary works, *Oedipus at Colonus* and *The Bacchae*. In reality, tragedy only had a great age of about 65 years, going back to *The Persians*. A number of tragic poets are mentioned in *The Frogs*, among them Iophon, the son of Sophocles, of whom it is ironically said that it will be seen whether he can do anything on his own now that his father is dead. A younger Euripides also stood behind the performance of the older man's plays. The long and short of it is that one is inclined to draw the same conclusion as Dionysos—that only the bad ones are left. And so they have disappeared.

2

In consideration of the fact that, after the death of the three great tragedians, tragedies were produced almost on an assembly line for the annual Dionysia, we cannot help but ask why were they so bad if they had such a strong tradition to support them. Any answer must necessarily be hypothetical and based on an extrapolation from the works we have analyzed and on the development of tragedy. Of course, we could just say that the great writers were geniuses, but we then enter the endless discussion as to how a given age is capable of evoking and unleashing the potential genius of a generation, as the Renaissance and Romanticism created something approaching a chain reaction of incredible artistic achievements. As Aristophanes maintains—with Dionysos as his spokesman—regarding the successors of the great ones:

> Those are left-overs, mere chatterboxes, 'quires of swallows', debauchers of their art, who, if they so much as get a chorus, disappear again pretty rapidly after pissing over Tragedy just once. If you looked for a really potent poet, one who can give voice to a pedigree phrase, you couldn't find one any more.[40]

If we take this satire at its word, it means quite simply that after Aeschylus, Sophocles and Euripides there were only powerless echoes of the poets. The real dramatic foundation was washed away, leaving only the dross. No wonder history has not preserved them.

3

Placed in this context, the great tragedies came into existence in the conflict between men, gods and Fate, in which suffering became a doctrine of life and created a fundamentally new basis for existence. For, as described above, Aeschylus appeared from the embryonic stage of tragedy at the same time as the need for a new interpretation was being felt after the battle of Salamis and the final manifestation of the Athenian city-state as a Greek power center. Tragedy became the genre of this age.

Tragedy developed gradually. It is psychologized in Sophocles, who renounces the trilogy as, unlike Aeschylus, he does not segmentalize in dealing with dramatic events in the life of the family. With Euripides, the mythical life of tragedy has penetrated even more deeply into everyday life or has become permeated by experiences from it, and the significance of the chorus is weakened even further. But splendid dramatic figures still arise from the mythical primordial ground in the misguided *hamartia* of their minds, and the gods still act, not as abstract, allegorical concepts, but as violent, intervening and inscrutable forces. Aristotle may well think that Euripides is the most effective in terms of drama, but—as a symptom of decadence—he alleges that he is not always as assured in his composition[41] and is far inferior when compared to Aeschylus.[42]

If this line of development is extended into the later tragic universe of which we know nothing, I do not think that it is difficult to imagine that tragedy in its supreme form loses ground in the turbulent years of crisis during the war against Sparta with its philosophical relativism and general depravity. It can simply no longer function with the same necessity as a unifying organ of interpretation, since values have become more diffuse. The need for theatrical effects had taken the place of an interpretation of life. Even in Agathon, the choral poems are transformed into free-floating lyrical effects only to disappear in the new genre of comedy (Menander), and the heroes who put their own lives and those of others at risk with their magnificent blunders are replaced by everyday people and troubles—as in middle-class drama a couple of thousand years later.

All in all, such a process would inevitably reduce tragedy from an interpretation of life, experienced by the audience with horror and pity, to entertainment without having a cathartic effect. This is why Dionysos feels compelled to bring the great older tragedians back from Hades, Aristophanes to caricature and satirize (lament) the tragedians of his day—while Aristotle had difficulty in finding other qualified models for the exemplary aesthetics in his *Poetics*.

That the fate drama had become anti-tragedy would also be a natural consequence of the much-discussed homogenization of values in philosophy and political pragmatism, where pallid deliberation, caution, and philistine *sophrosyne* were victorious and made the confrontation between the metaphysical and the heroic ideal implode in its tragic grandiosity. But where tragedy had so far fulfilled a role by providing an interpretation of life through the 5th century B.C., philosophy stepped in to fill the vacuum after the great age of tragedy. It happened in a search for lost truth and divinity, concentrated in the inner man, on spiritual life. This philosophical and existential initiative was primarily linked to one man—Socrates —and one author, who wrote and established him in this sense—Plato.

XVIII

SOCRATES*

I WOULD LIKE FIRST TO OUTLINE MY MAIN POINTS IN ORDER TO CREATE AN overview of the content and composition of this section.

I interpret Plato's dialogues as a single, cohesive work with a common thematic universe and Socrates as the principal protagonist. Through his figure and death, the work is directed toward a utopia of the good and the "inner human being". I view Socrates as the incarnation of this interpretation, while the principle of personal development is described as an erotic process. Development of the self requires a method such as is presented through Socrates' interlocutory technique and philosophical dialectic. His conviction and death is the turning point in Plato's writings, prompting him to set up the norms for a utopian state based on the philosophical person and human self-development in general, which is why Odysseus is incorporated into his work as Socrates' most important prefiguration.

The Unity of Plato's Work
1

The relationship between Socrates and Plato is a special problem for an analysis of Plato's writings, which has absorbed scholars since antiquity. Both were real people. Plato followed Socrates for six to seven years from about 407 B.C. and subsequently

---

* All quotations from Plato are from *The Collected Dialogues of Plato*, ed. by Edith Hamilton and Huntington Cairns (1978), including the following translations: *Apology, Crito, Phaedo*—Hugh Tredennick, *Charmides, Laches, Menexenus, Cratylus*—Benjamin Jowett, *Euthyphro*—Lane Cooper, *Gorgias*—W. D. Woodhead, *Protagoras, Meno*—W. K. C. Guthrie, *Phaedrus*—R. Hackforth, *Lysis*—J. Wright, *Symposium*—Michael Joyce, *Republic*—Paul Shorey, *Theatetus*—F. M. Cornford, *Critias, Laws*—A. E. Taylor, *Letters*—L. A. Post. Citations from the *Alcibiades I* are from the Loeb Class. Lib., vol. XII (trans. by W. R. M. Lamb).

There is a particular translation problem with respect to the word God or the god (*ho theos*). Various translations of Plato interchange these two. I can accept use of the word God with a capital G in certain instances based upon my interpretation of the sun metaphor in the *Republic* (p. 552) in which the good is said to be identical to the force of creation, i.e., a synonym for God. On the other hand, the god is always Apollo, whose significance—along with the other gods—is part of the theological world view of Plato/Socrates. This divine principle has a fundamental monotheistic character and has its source in Xenophanes. So I want to stress with my differentiation of God, the god and the gods the more or less hidden presence of this crucial aspect of meaning.

dedicated his life and his philosophy to him—indeed, in his second letter to Dionysios, the tyrant of Syracuse, Plato is able to write expressly that "there is not and will not be any written work of Plato's own. What are now called his are the work of a Socrates embellished and modernized" (*Letters* 314c).[1] Just as Odysseus was Homer's supreme consciousness, so Socrates becomes the supreme view for Plato.

As Kierkegaard writes, this interweaving means, that it is "impossible to decide what belongs to each, since the one constantly has nothing because he possesses everything in the 'other'."[2] So it is impossible to draw a clear boundary between where one stops and the other starts. Nevertheless, like many others, Kierkegaard tries to separate out the genuine Socratic dialogues, which are traditionally assumed to be among Plato's early writings and primarily describe Socrates' art of dialectics, based according to Kierkegaard on irony, which ends in the negation of pure nothingness. On the other hand, Plato was supposed to have used Socrates to represent his own views or, to use another Kierkegaardian expression, to have given him the Idea.[3]

In general, however, it must be said that the various attempts to establish a chronology and stages in the development of Plato's writings have not borne much fruit.[4] Two theories may be advanced: 1) Plato develops. 2) Plato does not develop. The results are consequently quite divergent, a fact which in itself helps stress the indissoluble linkage between Socrates and Plato. A dialogue like the *Protagoras* may be an early work, because it is clearly more dialectical than the *Republic*. In it, the political theory is placed in the mouth of Socrates but presumably reflects Plato's own thoughts, which correspond to the work of his old age, *The Laws*, in which Socrates does not figure. On the other hand, we could respond that, even though Plato presents his ideas more in the form of an edifying monologue, he nevertheless does so as a result of the potential in Socrates' view of life. And so we are back where we started.

2

Analytically, the most amenable point of view strikes me as the hypothesis that Plato simply gathers the whole corpus of his writings around the character of Socrates and makes of it a drama of fate with his death as the crucial turning point. From this angle, we can—as in the case of Homer—see Plato's dialogues as an organic whole, governed by a *utopian* goal, towards which Socrates points with his dialectical irony and dissolution of the norms of the time and personifies with his integrity: The *Republic* is a philosophical masterpiece in which Plato sets out his utopia as a countermeasure to the prevailing political and human confusion—through an analogy between the formation of a new state and spiritual development.

The sense of unity is supported by the fact that virtually all the dialogues deal with the same fundamental themes: the good, the cardinal virtues, the nature and immortality of the soul, etc. And whatever differences there may be in the interpretations, the dialogues nevertheless correspond to each other and with their many small changes in view produce a prism of the thematic refractions surrounding the figure of Socrates. Or we could say that they are contrapuntally linked by common guiding themes that create cohesion and context. Philosophy takes the place of tragedy, the role of which as an interpretative organ for the democratic state seems to have been played out with Euripides.

Against this background, the methodical consequence will be—again as in the reading of Homer—that Socrates will be interpreted as a *metaphorical* figure, a third alternative to the Socrates who actually existed in Athens four hundred years before Christ, and the Socrates based on the biographical person who is nevertheless primarily Plato's interpretation. Although we try to find a mean based on all the existing sources, it is not possible to claim a final, historically authentic portrait of Socrates. Conversely, we can claim that like the other myths Plato uses—despite his criticism of poetry—Socrates simply becomes his philosophy's myth par excellence.

Since Plato thus draws on the figure of Socrates and his life and uses it for his own purposes, he distorts Socrates' biographical reality to some indeterminate extent. He becomes an interpretation, a symbol and a fictive metaphorical figuration for a comprehensive philosophy in which Plato can give substance to his world of ideas in the form of Socrates. And he sees him die as a witness to the truth of the divine laws upon which the state was originally based but which its guardians betray in their desire for power when they condemn Socrates to death. In this sense, Socrates becomes an example to follow.

3

Like the tragedies, the aesthetic effect of the dialogue genre lies in the fact that, as readers, we experience the event as if we were contemporaries. Narrative time and narrated time virtually merge together, so we experience in the present the vitality of the disagreements between the contending parties. We are inside, even a part of, the controversy between the interlocutors, while the actors become a metaphorical expression of their respective views of life.

Thus, various Sophists—Protagoras, Gorgias and others—represent the various forms of the rhetorical nihilism that lead directly to hunger for power and a world of deeds without justice. This is a world in which only the power of the strong counts, as personified by the figures of Callicles in the *Gorgias*, Thrasymachus in the *Republic*, and Alcibiades. The latter figure is particularly enveloped by charismatic ambiguity, as Socrates is in love with him even though his desire for power is proof of the decay of the state.

That is to say that Plato uses these figures as kinds of metaphorical markers and reflections, the same compositional principle Homer used, for example, in his contrast between Achilleus and Odysseus. As the unifying figure, Socrates is elevated in the comprehensive Platonic project to the epiphany of myth. For it is evident in many passages that, when he can no longer present the complexity of his thoughts through the path of discursiveness and abstraction, Plato seizes upon the symbolism of myth: the image of the cave in the *Republic*, the charioteer and his horses in the *Phaedrus*, Diotima in the *Symposium*—not to mention "Socrates."

On one hand, this metaphorical and mythical function is attributed to Socrates *from within* with the help of authentic material. On the other hand, he absorbs energy *from without*—that is to say from the more or less covert mythical configurations he enters into. As indicated, the most important is Odysseus, his endurance, self-possession and discursiveness, to which Socrates often refers. That Plato engages in this interpretative practice is only surprising insofar as he rejects the poets, not least Homer. For the allegorical interpretation of Homer had already been made earlier by Theagenes (see p. 67) and was carried on by others including the Cynics, whose founder Antisthenes, like Plato, was a student of Socrates but interpreted him differently.

For although there are many consistencies in the various accounts of Socrates—his poverty, ugliness, bare feet, dialectical method and contemplative reveries—these interpretations primarily reflect their originators. On the other hand, they also reveal Socrates' enormous span, since he can encompass huge differences in meaning. And on this basis, we can assert that, in Plato's work, Socrates is a constitutional, metaphorical figure who by virtue of his personal characteristics—like Odysseus in Homer—is to create the precondition for Plato's philosophical utopia and support it in its entirety.

Utopia and *telos*

1

If I do not find it rash to draw a parallel between Homer and Plato, this is because the works of both men came into existence during a period of crisis and strife. Both contain a critique of the status quo—most explicitly in Plato—and a utopian description of a different and better world which we can define on the basis of Solon's terminology as a *eunomia*: justice and peace. In the writings of both men, we have at the center of the narrative a subject who has been through a long, difficult process of self-development making their lives exemplary and establishing themselves as epic points of co-ordination: Odysseus and Socrates.

In short, it is my claim that the psychologically self-possessed character being formed in Odysseus is realized by Socrates as he is seen in Plato's version. Moreover, Odysseus clearly functions as a prefiguration. Odysseus' debates with his *thymos* and his mastery of his inner spiritual life are an ideal for Socrates' *sophrosyne* indeed, in a way—a foundation for his entire dialectical method.

For Homer, the *telos*, the utopian goal, was the peace that Zeus Teleios, the Accomplisher, finally institionalized in the *Odyssey* as the conclusion of the Trojan War and the crimes that were its cause. What defines the telos in Plato's work, if we view it as a single unified whole, is Socrates and the *arete* he personifies. He is the starting point and finishing point, as he is the nearest it is possible to come to an individual fulfilling the ideal of philosopher and ruler that Plato establishes in the *Republic* as a counterweight to the decline of the status quo. Socrates thereby becomes elevated into metaphor and myth, reaching beyond his historical existence and into the future philosophical thinking of the West.

2

In Homer's two epics, we had to uncover a utopian dimension and a longing for social stability on the basis of the compositional subtext and the explicit narrator's renunciation of the heroic ethos: the mistreatment of corpses, the sacrifice of human beings, etc. In Plato's seventh letter, on the other hand, we have his own words for the existential necessity in his life and work: dizziness (*iliggos*). It was in such physically concrete terms that he experienced his contemporary political world. That he first felt a strong urge to participate in political life was not surprising in consideration of the fact that, as a citizen of Athens, he had rights and duties in the state. A man's identity was determined by his patronymic—who his father was and from what state/city he came. Socrates came from Alopeke, a suburb of Athens, and his father was Sophroniscus.

Moreover, Plato's family was deeply involved in political life and encouraged him to take an active part. For example, Critias, the most important of the thirty tyrants, was his mother's cousin. At the sight of the "abuses" (*Letters* 325a) during the reign of terror of the thirty tyrants in 404-03 B.C., however, Plato withdrew. After the fall of the tyrants, he again hesitantly entered politics, but only to face the event constituting the ultimate turning point in his life and writings: the death sentence on Socrates, "the justest man of his time" (*Letters* 324 e).

Shocked, he had to acknowledge that the state was no longer being governed in accordance with the thinking of its forefathers and, ultimately, the divine origin of the laws, and he "felt dizzy" (*Letters* 325 e). He now turned definitively from politics to philosophy: "Hence I was forced to say in praise of the correct philosophy that it affords a vantage point from which we can discern in all cases what is just for communities and for individuals, and that accordingly the human race will not see better days until either the stock of those who rightly and genuinely follow philosophy acquire political authority, or else the class who have political control be led by some dispensation of providence to become real philosophers" (*Letters* 326 b).

3

This quotation contains Plato's entire motivational world and thought in condensed form. His thoughts turn outwards when he later establishes the philosophical Academy, which was to educate Aristotle and other important successors and continue for nine hundred years until the Christian emperor Justinian closed it in A.D. 529. The quotation also provides an insight into the aim behind his writings: to develop the self and a philosophical awareness that can bring justice and truth to the world and thereby wipe out evil. For it is Socrates' and Plato's bold (naïve?) belief that evil is simply due to lack of insight: those who through personal development have acquired insight into goodness will act on that basis and thereby find happiness, which makes it impossible for them in the future to act in bad faith, as they would then make themselves unhappy. On the other hand, evil men act out of a fundamental lack of wisdom, as they believe themselves omniscient, driven by the *tyranny* of their subconscious and atheistic *hubris*.

The unifying purpose in all of Plato's writings is the idea of a new form of state, which is described in the *Republic* and will be discussed later. We can say in brief here that, through their personal development, citizens are to seek the good, by which the state is, so to speak, restored from within. The selflessness required here is guaranteed by the most highly developed person, the philosopher king. And Socrates becomes the guiding star.

4

That goodness (*arete*) is the ultimate arbiter can be shown in countless passages. Let me just adduce a couple of statements from the *Gorgias* in which Socrates, conversing with the Sophist and power-seeker Callicles, persuades him to assent to the following rhetorical question: "Do you too share our opinion, that the good is the end of all actions and that everything else should be done for its sake, not for the sake of everything else?" (499 e). As Socrates suggests at the end, the point is "not to seem but to be good, whether in private or in public life" (527 b).

But in this apparently respectable objective—of guiding citizens toward the good—we presumably also find the deeper reason why Socrates was accused and executed. For as he sees it as his job to urge the citizens of the state to seek the good in themselves, the state is actually transformed from an external social matter to internal "political life." He turns the demand made by the state on its citizens into a subjective matter, as a new state can only arise under the aegis of philosophy.

In the *Apology*, Socrates claims that Apollo himself, the divinity of wisdom and consciousness, has given him this mission. He assumes a peculiar duality in the city of Athens, since he is a gift of the gods and a gadfly to the state, which is like a large, beautiful horse that because of its large body is somewhat lazy and must be kept moving by constant stings (*Ap.* 30 e–31 a). Indeed, in the *Gorgias*, he is so ironical as to push things to extremes by turning them on their head. He claims that great statesmen such as Pericles and Themistocles were poor leaders. For they did not make their citizens good, but were on the contrary a cause of the current decay: greediness and laziness. Therefore, logically enough, as one who seeks to draw citizens toward the good, Socrates believes himself to be the only true statesman—"I think that I am one of very few Athenians, not to say the only one, engaged in the true political art, and that of the men of today I alone practice statesmanship" (*Gorg.* 521 d), he claims provocatively.

From this claim, we can draw one or, rather, two lines through Plato's works. One to Socrates' condemnation and death, since in the long run it must have been difficult for those in power to ignore his attacks; the other to Plato's outline of a new state, founded on justice and the cosmic soul of the inner man, in which cosmos means order purely and simply. Time and time again, Socrates attacks the Sophists because they have destroyed this order—for instance, the Sophist Protagoras makes man the measure of all things. The authority of divine laws has been lost as a result and all values have been relativized, while justice has become a question of rhetoric and the right of the strong.

5

This is most clearly seen in his conversation with the militant Callicles in the *Gorgias*, when, with a candidness for which Socrates praises him, he openly defends this view (like Thrasymachus in the *Republic*). His claim is that the laws are created by the weak who, out of shame, dare not follow their desires at the cost of others. So they have made moderation, *sophrosyne*, and justice into mechanisms for control and oppression. Conversely, the strong find their happiness in the fulfilment of lust and desire, which are effected no matter what. For the same reason, he recommends that Socrates should join those who have strength and power as he considers philosophers to be children who need a spanking if they refuse to participate actively in the life of the state—i.e. in the struggle of all against all. It is an early, vulgarized form of the ideas of Darwin and Nietzsche. He also claims that Socrates would never pull through if he were subjected to false charges.

In this way, Plato anticipates the unjust basis of the trial against Socrates and at the same time lets him respond to Callicles with the opposite point of view, that it is better to suffer than to commit injustice—"Of these two then, inflicting and suffering wrong, we say it is a greater evil to inflict it, a lesser to suffer it" (*Gorg.* 509 c). As Socrates' condemnation shows, he does not here put forward a view without implications, as he pays for his views with his life. Nor is it surprising that, unlike Callicles, he believes it necessary to suppress desire to promote virtue.

As already said, it is a matter of finding the plan in the soul that makes it cosmic. Socrates actually uses the Greek word *kosmos* about the plan, thereby recalling the idea of order that appeared in Anaximander's conception of universal justice (p. 315), an immanent order in the world of man and nature, just as Heraklitus also assumes an epistemological connection between the *logos* of the subject and the *logos* governing all things. As Socrates asks rhetorically: "It is then the presence in each thing of the order (*kosmos*) appropriate to it that makes everything good?" (506 e).

6

In extension of this, Socrates establishes what could be characterized as the morphology of goodness, not only in the *Gorgias* but throughout his works, although the content may change a little from dialogue to dialogue. We can say in general that *arete* as an attribute of the divine is made up of the so-called cardinal virtues, through which the cosmos of the soul is organized and guided: wisdom, courage, moderation and justice. Certain passages include piety, which in other passages is viewed as a phenomenon distributed among the others. Furthermore, goodness, which is a synthesis and development of all the virtues, is synonymous with beauty and justice.

For the reader, a dilemma quickly arises in that we feel compelled to account for how these concepts relate to and affect each other. But as I have chosen to view the dialogues as a prism-like unity, I do not see it as my task to make these graduated comparisons. This seems even less important as they have an almost metonymic interchangeability. For whether Socrates is talking about moderation (*Charmides*), justice (*Gorgias* and *Republic*) or courage (*Laches*), it is ultimately about the same thing: letting the searching soul recall the good and act in accordance with it so that the various virtues support each other.

In the utopian state, consequently, the task for philosophy—described in the *Republic's* most important image—is to come out of the cave of illusion and look at the truth in the sunlight, emanating directly from the underlying goodness, that is to say God. However reluctantly, the philosopher is *compelled* again to descend into the cave to save those who, chained to their false conceptions, continue in the belief that this is the true reality. But he knows at the same time that the person who brings them true insight risks his life: "Now if he should be required to contend with these perpetual prisoners in 'evaluating' these shadows (. . .) would they not kill him?" (517 a).

When Plato lets him ask this, Socrates has been dead for a long time. He was Plato's answer to the crisis of values and a personification of the inner cosmic man, whom Plato had made the focal point in his work. On this basis, we will now concentrate directly on Socrates as a person and a myth.

"Socrates"

1

As Socrates himself declared, he was above all a philosopher, that is to say a person whose *eros* urged him to seek wisdom, since *philo-sophia* quite simply means love, or lover, of wisdom. This must also indicate that *eros* is to the highest degree identical with the striving for knowledge, while wisdom itself becomes identical with goodness (*arete*).

Compared with Homer's view of *arete*, there has in the intervening period been a significant shift in opinion regarding this concept. But not until Socrates does it achieve its culmination as the epitome of human and social moral integrity. In the *Iliad*, the term *arete* designated purely external qualities such as excellence on the battlefield, courage and physical beauty; whereas for Socrates, *arete* is something spiritual, whose origin can be found in the divine but can still be observed as an incarnation (*hypostasis*) in the beauty of the body. In this sense, a link with the past is retained, although the concept has become much expanded and finds its true center in the spiritual.

Like no one else, Socrates gives concrete expression to this process of development. He quite simply embodies the inner man in whom the psyche is a completely developed psychological reality, placed in sharp contrast to the life of the body and its desires. That inner beauty should quite literally be far superior to the external variety is substantiated by his own ugliness, which is almost a denial of the Homeric hero's flamboyant appearance.

2

In order to give an account of Socrates as a man who lives according to these inner values, Plato makes brilliant use of compositional mirroring in the *Symposium*.

For just as Socrates acquires a profile and character through his ironic conversations with, for example, the Sophists, Plato creates real ambiguity by contrasting Socrates and Alcibiades. In their forms of desire, they are diametrical opposites. Socrates is a philosopher, Alcibiades an opportunistic power-seeker. Socrates is master of his soul's inner lines, Alcibiades of the political and military battlefield. Socrates is the ugliest person in his exterior but the most beautiful inside; Alcibiades, by contrast, is the most beautiful young man in Athens, but he has a worm-eaten interior. Moreover, there is the piquant element that Socrates admitted he was in love with this beautiful young man who unsuccessfully tried to seduce Socrates in the hope of acquiring a shortcut to knowledge.

Plato's greatest coup, however, is letting the drunken Alcibiades, bursting in on the symposium late at night, describe Socrates as the incarnation of the erotic in the sense of the highest striving, which he has just described in his speech on Eros—in an interpretation of Diotima's doctrine on this. At the same time as Socrates thus emerges in Alicibiades' speech as an erotic man, Alcibiades sets himself apart from the ensouled reality he describes in Socrates. In his drunken state, he is allowed to describe the spiritual reality to which he himself is denied access. In this way, Plato presents Socrates as a truth-seeker in contrast with Alcibiades, whose internal being does not correspond to his outer beauty.

As will be remembered, Odysseus had already asserted that a beautiful exterior does not necessarily correspond to a corresponding interior, and conversely a lack of external beauty may be accompanied by a spiritual beauty that evokes the admiration of all (see p. 82). As Plato's mythical protagonist, Socrates shows the truth of this claim that external ugliness means nothing in relation to internal beauty.

Alcibiades exemplifies this duality by comparing Socrates to a Silenus, known from sculpture. In its exterior, the Silenus is characterized by a strikingly grotesque quality, half man, half animal, often equipped with horse's ears and legs; but, says Alcibiades, if you open these statues in which there is a kind of cupboard door, there is an image of divine beauty within. Socrates is most reminiscent in his exterior of the satyr Marsyas, who played the flute so beautifully that he challenged Apollo. That was going too far. The god flayed his skin off as punishment. But, continues Alcibiades, Socrates' words are just as wonderfully seductive as Marsyas' music and with his words he reveals a current of inner beauty. In the comparison with Alcibiades' uncle, the famous orator and statesman Pericles, he intervenes in a far more radical way in the life of the individual, because he speaks from the heart—to the heart. However, a deeper understanding requires one to be ready to submit to the Socratic dialectic.

3

If we are to judge from the written sources and statues, Socrates had bulging eyes, a pug nose and thick lips that looked as if they were swollen after a fight; in addition, he had a short neck and pot-belly, and was thickset with enormous flat feet. He did nothing to improve his looks. On the contrary. For while a famous Sophist like Gorgias paraded dressed in purple and wearing gold sandals, Socrates wore a threadbare cloak. In the *Symposium*, it is made into something of an event that he is wearing sandals for the festive occasion. As a rule, he walked bare-foot and stayed outdoors where he could meet people and conduct conversations. Most of all he resembled a beggar, an outcast, while he "taught" free of charge. The Sophists charged sky-high fees for their instruction, which took place indoors—hence, the Sophists' nickname of "paleface."

In Xenophon's description of a symposium, there is an episode that shows that Socrates was quite aware of his appearance and could be ironic about it.[5] In brief, he asks a beautiful young man, Critobulus, whether it is not true that something can be called beautiful if, like a sword, it serves its purpose well, meaning its *arete*. The young man has to admit this, after which Socrates is able to conclude that there is beauty in his own grotesque appearance: His bulging eyes must clearly be the most beautiful, since they can see by far the most. His pug nose is beautiful, because it does not—as does the young man's high bridge—hinder his vision. The Naiads are mothers of the Silenuses, who like him have thick lips. Summa summarum—he who is the ugliest becomes the most beautiful.

4

That Socrates can joke in this way—and indeed in a virtually exhibitionist manner put his ugliness on display—must be due to his making his appearance and tramp-like dress a sign of inner strength, of his detachment from state and home and everything that hampers the work of the spirit. And just as Odysseus resisted the basic necessities of life—for example, the demands of the stomach—and could withstand pressure from those around him, a series of examples is listed demonstrating that Socrates similarly places himself above instincts. He is also without any fear of death and is veritably bursting with *menos*, the life force that the Homeric gods breathe into their heroes.

So as an eye witness, Alcibiades can tell from the war against Potidaia in northern Greece in 432 B.C. (a city that had been allied to Athens but rebelled) that, although it was bitterly cold and the others who were dressed in all their clothes still had their teeth chattering, Socrates was dressed in his usual cloak and walked barefoot over the ice. Nor was he tormented by thirst and hunger like all the others. During the battle itself, he displayed unusual courage. He saved Alcibiades from death but allowed him to be awarded the prize for bravery, since, in the nature of things, he himself attached no importance to such external signs of honor (*Symp*. 219 e-220 e).

During the Peloponnesian War, when the Athenians suffered defeat at the hands of the Boetians at Delium in 424 B.C., Alcibiades relates in the *Symposium* (221 a-b) how, as a hoplite during the retreat, Socrates calmly wandered around with the critical eye that Aristophanes ridicules in *The Clouds*.[6] In this way, he forced the enemy to respect his spiritual strength, so to speak, since they let him go in peace, well aware that he would defend himself tooth and nail.

In another way, too, Socrates reveals the unique courage that comes from the fact that he had taken possession of his self and therefore did not fear for his life. For example, during his trial, he tells how, in 406 B.C., he was a member of the state council, which contrary to his wishes was filled with citizens appointed in turn by drawing lots in order to spread the democratic form of government. He found it hard to believe that everyone was equally qualified. However, he would not oppose the laws of the state and so took his turn. But when they wanted to force him as a member of the *prytaneis* to condemn to death the strategists who on account of high seas after victory in a battle at sea at Arginussae in 406 B.C. had failed to rescue the Athenians who had fallen or been shipwrecked, he dug his heels in and refused to contribute to condemning them collectively. Similarly, he opposed the order of the thirty tyrants that a man from Salamis should be brought to Athens for execution. The others complied with the order, but Socrates went home—to Xanthippe.[7]

But if we think of Socrates as an ascetic, an idea that can perhaps be derived from the fact that Antisthenes, one of his closest disciples, created the fanatical abstentionist philosophy, cynicism, we must think again. He denied himself no pleasure. (This pleasurable aspect is emphasized by the philosophical hedonism of another of his students, Aristippus). That such divergent philosophers can start out from Socrates is itself evidence of the breadth of his personality. Socrates himself had total control over his physical needs. It is impossible to make him drink too much and when Alcibiades tries to seduce him, he rejects him and stays alert while Alcibiades sleeps beside him. And when all the participants in the *Symposium* fall asleep at dawn, Socrates goes to the baths and spends the day in conversation, returning home in the evening.

Eros—The Path to Self-Development

1

With Plato's contrast of Socrates and Alcibiades, we cannot help thinking back on the spectacular contrast between Odysseus transformed into a beggar and the boastful, degenerate suitors. For it is a world turned upside down: those who on the outside look like a beggar actually have a royal personality and are highly conscious; whereas the arrogant suitors are in the thrall of the idle tyranny of the desires and of the subconscious. It is a contrast that provides Plato with the opportunity to show that the path of self-development is in reality an erotic process on the spiritual plane, a striving for knowledge.

In this context, the description of Alcibiades and his speech for Socrates in the *Symposium* is a study of subtext. Through Alcibiades' own narrative voice, Plato is able to represent him as a vain, undeveloped power seeker, the ultimate result of the moral decay of the time, a spokesman for the philosophy of injustice. His political career is a lesson in the opportunistic striving for power, power as a sort of erotic dementia. He constantly shifts his political position and enters into alliances with conflicting parties. One moment, he is a general for the Athenians against Sparta, the next moment the reverse, until he is liquidated in Asia Minor. By accepting the prize of honor that rightly belonged to Socrates, he is presented indirectly as a person whose sense of honor is venal. Seen in the context of Greek poetry, he is reminiscent of

Agamemnon, a man without inner substance, capricious in his tyrannical self-esteem. With his presentation of Alcibiades as a contrast to Socrates, Plato succeeds in separating the latter definitively from the corridors of brute power and liberating him for a spiritual power that Plato, like a son, undertakes to continue.

2

It is significant that Socrates was the person who acquired the most power over the military commander Alcibiades, by which Plato can show the superiority of the spirit over even a depraved man. Of this, Alcibiades says: "I've been bitten in the heart, or the mind, or whatever you like to call it, by Socrates' philosophy, which clings like an adder to any young and gifted mind it can get hold of, and does exactly what it likes with it." (*Symp.* 218 a).

Despite all his victories, Alcibiades does not feel life is worth living, since he must admit to having neglected his inner development. Instead, he has pursued external goals, such as honors, but such things are unable to meet the true need Socrates has aroused in him. His behavior up to that point makes him feel such shame that, as he admits in his drunken state, he actually tries to flee from Socrates and the dilemma in which—as if Socrates were the Sirens—he places him.

Socrates confesses in the *Gorgias* that he is in love with Alcibiades (481 d). But when, as the conqueror he is, Alcibiades tries through this love to acquire the deeper self he lacks by seducing Socrates, he does not succeed—"I used to flatter myself that he was smitten with me and (...) . I'd only got to be a bit accommodating and I'd hear everything he had to say" (*Symp.* 217 a). As narrator, Alcibiades knows that Socrates is in control of his senses and in possession of "temperance and sobriety" (*sophrosynes*, 216 d). For when Alcibiades crawls over to him, Socrates mocks what is Alcibiades' greatest asset, his beauty, since he claims that Alcibiades is "driving a very hard bargain" (218 e), like Glaukos who in the *Iliad* gave Diomedes his gold armor for one of copper. This event is interpreted by Homer as delusion, but Socrates is not prey to delusion.[8]

Even though the driving force in Socrates' dialogues is *eros*, it can at any time be liberated from the specific object of his passion. When in the *Gorgias* he speaks of his love, he adds (481 d) that he is also in love with philosophy, in the love of wisdom itself. In this way, the inner is victorious over the outer and at the same time Socrates with his irony enables Alcibiades to objectify and understand his beauty as something purely external and subordinate to personal development, which at the same time he feels such a powerful urge to participate in, but lacks the strength of will to maintain.

3

In his imaginary pride, Alcibiades believes that he is possessed of so many excellent qualities, including his appearance, that he can match anyone. His illusion is described in a painful way in the dialogue *Alcibiades I.* The situation is that Socrates, who was his first lover, is also his last, as everyone else has abandoned Alcibiades now that he has grown older. So the time has come to introduce Alcibiades to true insight, since that is the precondition for his becoming wise as a statesman. Opposed to what Alcibiades believes, it is not his external advantages Socrates loves, not his body, but his soul: "I was the only lover of *you*, whereas the rest were lovers of what is yours" (131 e).

The dialogue does not develop the idea obvious in the greater context that Socrates may have first fallen in love with Alcibiades' physical beauty. For as is to be understood in Diotima's teaching in the *Symposium*, the ability to love is aroused by physical beauty, which is then gradually spiritualized. This could mean that Socrates fell in love with young Alcibiades in the hope that he would be able to develop in him a desire for inner beauty corresponding to his fair appearance, a project in which he did not succeed.

As it also appears in the *Symposium*, one finds one's true essence through self-knowledge and development. But how? In the reflective objectification for which love opens a possibility. As Socrates asks Alcibiades: "And have you observed that the face of the person who looks into another's eye is shown in the optic confronting him, as in a mirror, and we call this the pupil, for in a sort it is an image of the person look-ing?" (*Alc.* 132 e–133 a). Just as we can be reflected in each other's pupils,[9] so we can reflect our soul in the soul of the beloved and thereby learn to know ourselves.

Socrates' words obviously penetrate into Alcibiades and transform him. He declares that their roles are now switched. Whereas he previously enjoyed being a sex object for Socrates' love, the situation has now been reversed, and it is now he who will always follow Socrates, understood as his spiritual love in whom he can be reflected and, through this reflection, care for the development of his soul. But since the dialogue was written after Alcibiades' death, it ends with a denial by Socrates in which he certainly admits that Alcibiades had potential but adds that he was far too much of a man under the influence of power.

4

As he describes it in the *Symposium*, when Alcibiades tried to seduce Socrates by crawling in under his cloak and wrapping his arms around him, he called Socrates the truly "daimonic" man (*daimonios*, 219 c). That Plato uses this expression deliber-ately is obvious from the context that is hereby established throughout the *Symposium*. Diotima, from whom Socrates claims to have received his knowledge about the nature of *eros*, earlier pointed out that the person with insight into the mysteries of love is a "daimonic man" (*daimonios aner*, *Symp.* 203 a). This corresponds to the fact that Socrates welcomes the proposal to pay tribute to Eros in speeches, "when I claim that love is the one thing in the world I understand" (177 e).

As a *daimonic* man, Socrates has the same longing for the divine as Eros, who is himself a *daimon*. In other words, Socrates is not only an expert on *eros*, but quite simply through these linguistic identifications he becomes the earthly incarnation of *eros* as a quest. Before I go into this theme in more detail, I would like to open up the retrospective perspective, so to speak, as the *daimonic* creates a surprising intertextual link to Odysseus, whom the crew calls *daimonic* when with Kirke he has evidently forgotten everything about his journey home (10, 472).[10]

Even though the *daimonic* in Odysseus' case is primarily associated with being possessed by a *daimon*, the concept contains the same latent meaning as in the description of Socrates. It refers to a human being who, touched by the divine (as Odysseus was by Athene), becomes incomprehensible to those around him. And it is very much the case for Socrates that the *daimonic* aspect applies to his doctrine, works and life. With a reference to Hesiod's Golden Age and the subsequent fall, Socrates identifies *daimones* in the *Cratylus* with the wise and noble people of the age and concludes: "I have the most entire conviction that he called them daemons, because they were *daimones* (knowing or wise), and in our older Attic dialect the word itself occurs" (*Cr.* 398 c).

He takes yet another step in the dialogue's etymological explanation of the content of the words *heros* and *eros*, which he believes have the same roots. His point is that heroes are demigods (either on the paternal or maternal side), who know how to ask questions (*erotan, Cr.* 398 d) and thus constitute a class of seekers of wisdom. A syllogism connecting these statements might be: Socrates is a good man, so he is a *daimon*. This goodness he has achieved by questioning, that is to say by virtue of *eros*, which makes him into a *heros*, a demigod, placed as a *daimonic* mediator between heaven and earth.

5

We have touched on the fact that *daimones* populate the area of consciousness that arises between gods and men after the gods in the transition from the *Iliad* to the *Odyssey* became more distant and elevated. The *daimones* appear as more or less anonymous forms of explanation for the metaphysical indeterminacy that especially Sophocles captured in his writings. At the same time, they can also be seen as an expression of a person's character formation, as Heraclitus claimed: "Man's character is his *daimon*."[11] And Socrates must imagine something similar. In the *Phaedo*, he explains that every single individual has his own *daimon*, which follows him from birth to death. As such, the *daimon* constitutes the person's fate, character or perhaps his quest.

According to Diotima, the truth about Eros is that he is not, as claimed by Phaedrus, a god but a *daimon*, a messenger between gods and men: "They are the envoys and interpreters that ply between heaven and earth, flying upward with our worship and our prayers, and descending with the heavenly answers and commandments, and since they are between the two estates they weld both sides together and merge them into one great whole" (*Symp.* 202 e). And as we heard above, the person who has achieved insight into the mystery of love becomes *daimonic* himself, a *heros* and demigod, who acts as a mediator between heaven and earth.

The description of Eros as barefoot and homeless, sinewy and sun-burned also leads inevitably to the idea of Socrates himself, confirming the interpretation of him as an *eros* figure, just as Eros can conversely be said to be a philosophical figure by, like Socrates, longing for the good. For while the gods are divinely beautiful, lack nothing and are happy, wise and so statically in balance, Eros is, metaphorically speaking, a hunter. He is defined by an eternal deficiency that makes him crave the beautiful and the good that he himself does not possess; and he thereby fills the vacuum between the now invisible gods and the inhabitants of earth.

6

In Hesiod, Eros was identical with the force of creation, while love is the mainspring in creative knowledge for Socrates. Love has many blind alleys but only one true path. The ingenious composition of the *Symposium* is such that the five speakers who precede Socrates and praise Eros each in their own way come to represent the aberrations. They point toward Socrates as the one who formulates the right path; after which, in Alcibiades' description of him, he actually comes to appear as the embodiment of true love.

When Socrates' turn comes as the last speaker, he starts with apparent modesty, saying that what he has feared most has come to pass. The others have spoken in such a way about Eros that they far surpass his abilities. This is even more embarrassing to him as he has already claimed that love is the one thing in the world he understands (177 e). Now he is embarrassed, he says—ironically, of course.

With an image borrowed from the *Odyssey*, he reduces the previous speakers to versions of Sophists. Agathon, whose victory in the dramatic competition in 416 B.C. they are celebrating, is simply compared by Socrates to Gorgias. He says, during Agathon's encomium he felt like Odysseus in Hades, fleeing for fear of being petrified by Medusa, who has been sent by the Queen of the Dead, Persephone. In other words, he manages to reverse the implication so that the symposium and panegyric to Eros placed in the mouths of the speakers is transformed into a voyage of death—with himself in the role of Odysseus.

For if the speeches made for Eros are compared by Socrates to a journey to the realm of the dead, it is because, by praising the god of love, they have in Socrates' estimation adorned their panegyric with Sophist lies: "I don't mind telling you the truth about Love, if you're interested; only, if I do, I must tell it in my own way, for I'm not going to make a fool of myself, at my age, trying to imitate the grand manner that sits so well on the rest of you" (199 b).

7

As he declares himself fundamentally ignorant about the divine, Socrates creates a new figure, Diotima, in his speech on Eros. She has explained to him that Eros' dual nature of lack and longing is derived from his parentage. At the feast in celebration of Aphrodite's birth, Eros' mother, Penia (poverty), was a beggar who was able to copulate with Metis' drunken son, Poros (plenty), a lover of all things beautiful. So Eros has inherited his sense of deficiency from his mother and his longing from his father. In this way, Eros embraces everything, since his goal, physical as well as psychological, is to bring good into the world through beauty. But just as poetry is reduced to a single genre and is not seen as a comprehensive expression for art as a whole, Eros is also particularized, so his elevated intention is lost.

Likewise, we find here the reason for Eros' many forms and, as the other speakers have focussed on, earthly and heavenly love. According to Diotima, Eros as a creative force aims at immortality. But he will enter into the personal development of different individuals in different ways according to disposition or *daimonic* inclination. Thus, "those whose procreancy is of the body" (208 e) try to remain eternally alive through their children; whereas "those whose procreancy is of the spirit" (209 a) conceive with the soul. That is to say that they find eternal life through an insight in which old knowledge is transformed and lost in new knowledge but lives on as a hidden precondition. Here, it is possible to give birth without the beloved actually being present and, as for a Homer or a Hesiod, the "children" can become works (209 d) whose knowledge forms the basis for the education Socrates continues in his development.

8

Diotima places the actual erotic longing for insight into beauty in an individuated series of steps extending from physical sexuality to pure revelation, direct glimpses of eternal beauty and the immutable forms of ideas. That is to say that love as a source of insight starts out in the corporal, in physical love for another individual when the sense of beauty is aroused at the sight of physical beauty in the beloved (boy). On the next level, love is transformed beyond the individual to embrace all beautiful bodies, which is an indirect explanation for the fact that Socrates feels no jealousy.

When burning love and enthrallment with the physical appearance of the beloved are no longer crucial but give way to spiritually-aroused *eros*, we are capable of loving without real physical attraction. This is the underlying reason why Socrates can continue to love Alcibiades even when his glamorous exterior has begun to fade. At this level of consciousness comes the final but most important erotic guide, which consists of bursting "chains of bondage" and moving from the beauty of appearance and action to a beauty in knowledge, described in concrete terms as a movement from *eros* for boys to an epiphany of "the open sea of beauty" (210 d)—an insight, however, that cannot be maintained, as one will always be on the move and as it is only given to God to have this form of appearance always available. So Diotima refers to the Eleusinian Mysteries to clarify the character of this supreme insight, which is reminiscent of the mystical experience of unity of which Christian mystics also speak.

9

In other words, the goal for Socrates becomes a beauty that does not, as in literature or art, reside in the external but in the internal, in a recall of the divine form of ideas which the human soul possesses from an earlier existence and which, in the dialogues, he wishes to re-awaken in himself and his interlocutors. And in this context, *eros* can be viewed as a ferment in the philosophical quest for the self and inseparable from the personal self-development that Alcibiades lacks.

As Socrates explains in the *Phaedo*, we are able to cognize, because we already bear in our soul (72 e–73 b) an image of the ideal world we want to understand. Consequently, understanding, development and knowledge are a reawakening of what we knew before we were born into actual reality. Personal development, therefore, is ultimately an erotically conditioned quest for the image of the divine in the self. And this was just what Alcibiades was unable to do, because he only knew love in the lowest form of desire as self-reflection and a striving for power.

On the other hand, Socrates uses the *eros* of his dialectics to lead others out of the misinterpretations of their lives and to give them back to themselves through their own psychological work—as an aid to self-help. For as his friend Cebes says in a repetition of ideas for which Socrates has obviously made himself a spokesman: "What we call learning is really just recollection. If that is true, then surely what we recollect now we must have learned at some time before, which is impossible unless our souls existed somewhere before they entered this human shape. So in that way too it seems likely that the soul is immortal" (72 e).

10

However, it is in the *Phaedrus* that Socrates uses a mythical image to provide the deepest insight into the heavenly pre-existence of the soul: souls originally moved as winged phenomena among the immortals. But unlike the gods, who by virtue of their divine purity can remain up in celestial space, souls are drawn towards the earth and the world of the body. Only the best souls can momentarily gain access to this highest reality, this pure vision. But the soul that is subject to earthly gravity will fall and in incarnation itself lose its wings.

Yet, these wings, which remain behind in embryonic form, will grow again in cooperation with *eros*, i.e. as a quest and longing. This can happen in the erotic form of madness and revelation with which poets are also familiar or the very moment when an individual sees in his beloved the beauty that evokes the memory of this lost beauty. For this warmth of feeling that beauty evokes through the eyes acts upon the original wing embryos like rain upon plants. They sprout once again from their roots, a process during which the soul is shot through and tormented "even as a teething child feels an aching and pain in its gums" (251 c).

It seems as though Plato bases his conception of the true world of ideas on Parmenides, who likewise had a female guide. But whereas Parmenides saw only sources of error in the senses as opposed to the true world of being, Socrates there points out the connection with concrete, sensuous reality. For, as has been said above, he starts out in his erotic quest from the beautiful form of the body and finds in it a reflection of the ideal world of beauty. "To love is to bring forth upon the beautiful (*kalos*), both in body (*soma*) and in soul (*psyche*)" (*Symp.* 206 b), just as goodness is due to health in body and soul. As the classic motto goes: a healthy soul in a healthy body—a way of thinking that Socrates echoes in the *Gorgias* (501 b).

Not only did Alcibiades deem Socrates a *daimonic* person, Socrates did so himself and found divine guidance in his life, as we shall now see in his discussion of his *daimonic* voice. At the same time, we must be aware of the fact that this *daimony* was one of the charges that led to his death.

Daimonion

1

The *Apology* demonstrates that Socrates really does view himself as a *daimonic* messenger—like Eros. One primary point in his defense is that the god Apollo has named him the wisest of all human beings, and his job is *de facto* to communicate what this god is primarily identified with—knowledge of one's self, echoing the Delphic apothegm—know thyself. Self-insight is the precondition for being able to take care of oneself. And it is characteristic that self-knowledge is made synonymous with temperance, *sophrosyne*, because as Critias says in the *Charmides* with explicit reference to the Delphic admonition—"temperance is self-knowledge" (165 b). It was precisely Socrates' temperance that made it impossible for Alcibiades to seduce him.

In this context, the charge against Socrates of blasphemy (*asebeia*)—"of believing in deities of his own invention instead of the gods recognized by the state" (*Ap.* 24 b)—is shown to be nonsense. If there is a *daimonic* function, it is on account of the god's bidding—"This, I do assure you, is what my God commands" (*Ap.* 30 a). The god has sent him to the city as a gadfly (*Ap.* 30 e), so that through his dialectical activity he is to arouse, prompt, and admonish. Like Eros, he wants to instigate in every citizen a psychological progression leading from the sensuous world of desire to inner goodness—and ultimately to the realm of ideas.

According to his own assessment, the basis for the charges is that he has revealed the pillars of society to be victims of *hubristic* illusion that they are omniscient. What conversely makes Socrates the wisest in Apollo's eyes is that he is the only human being to know that he knows nothing. His ignorance of course does not relate to the purely factual, for he had knowledge few possessed, but to the divine truth that he seeks to understand but which will ultimately always be unattainable.

2

Nevertheless, Socrates claims that he is chosen by the gods. Since childhood, he has been guided by something *daimonic*, his so-called *daimonion,* of which he often speaks in the dialogues and which is thus the basis for the charge that he wants to introduce new *daimonic* doctrines. He himself introduces the *daimonion* in the *Apology* as "a divine and supernatural experience" (31 d). The divine and the *daimonic* are linked so closely that, seen through his eyes, it is exactly what he is accused of that makes him a pious person. In the *Republic*, he says, not without some self-esteem, "it has happened to few or none before me" (496 c).

As a basis for further discussion of the phenomenon, we can refer to a description by Xenophon. He makes the divine voice into an actual guide for Socrates, since according to Xenophon it informs him of "what he must do and what he must not do."[12] In Plato, on the other hand, Socrates explains the psychological effect of the *daimonion* as a sort of negation, since the voice provides a warning when a choice is to be made. He describes the phenomenon unambiguously in this way: "It began in my early childhood—a sort of voice which comes to me, and when it comes it always dissuades me from what I am proposing to do, and never urges me on" (31 d). In other words, it is not an absolutely preventative entity but appears more like an interlocutor in the dialogues, able to steer him to the right path. It is most clearly described in the *Phaedrus*, where Socrates has first spoken critically of the erotic, identifying it with physical desire, but is reprimanded by his *daimonion*. He says to Phaedrus:

> At the moment when I was about to cross the river, dear friend, there came to me my familiar divine sign (*daimonion*)—which always checks me when on the point of doing something or other—and all at once I seemed to hear a voice forbidding me to leave the spot until I had made atonement for some offense to heaven. Now, you must know, I am a seer—not a very good one, it's true, but, like a poor scholar, good enough for my own purposes—hence I understand already well enough what my office was. The fact is, you know, Phaedrus, the mind itself has a kind of *divining power*" (242 c, my italics).

This same voice kept him out of political life, as he also says in the *Apology*, emphasizing the subjective character of the *daimonion*. As his "customary prophetic voice" (40 a) has not appeared during the trial and later judgment, not even when he is condemned to death, as it otherwise would do, "if I was going to take the wrong course" (40 a), then he can interpret it as confirming that he is acting in agreement with the truth to which his life has led him. However unjustly the trial may end, therefore, it will be seen as good, "because my accustomed sign (*daimonion*) could not have failed to oppose me if what I was doing had not been sure to bring some good result" (40 c).

3

The question of whether Socrates heard voices from the outside or from within has been the source of intense debate. But as the *daimonion* makes itself felt as a voice inside him and as he speaks of the soul as having a "divining power" (*Phaedrus*, 242 c), the latter seems most probable—that is to say, it comes from within. If this is really the case, we can with modern psychological terminology perhaps say that the voice constitutes a sort of superego function, the voice of conscience, an internal judge who watches over the deeds of a human being and only works in his or her consciousness. This was the case when we heard how Orestes in Euripides experienced the Erinyes as internal phenomena of his conscience (see p. 475). This process could be traced back to the internalization of the law, which took place in Aeschylus'

Eumenides—by the split between external law, attributed to the Areopagus Council, and the inner fear of committing sacrilege (see p. 404). In such a sense of awe, the individual human being must himself be accountable for his actions.

However, although—in an extension of the introduction to the *Odyssey*—the tragedies assume free human responsibility, the individual is still subject to the decision of the gods, Moira, who allows Zeus to do with human beings as he likes. On the other hand, subjects in Plato's view are generally responsible for their own lives and are not punished according to their deserts until after death. Nevertheless, Socrates expresses a form of fatalism, claiming after his death sentence that this cannot be "a matter of indifference to the gods" (*Ap.* 41 d).

However this may be, it is beyond any doubt that Socrates himself views the voice as numinous, as God's voice speaking to him. As such, he adapts himself to it and acts on the basis of it in his efforts to lead others one by one to the good, like Eros acting here as a *daimonic* mediator.

In other words, he not only renounces the state in his subjectivity but, in a radical personification, he adopts the religious belief that the Greeks otherwise associated with collective cultic acts. Out of regard for his own spiritual life, Socrates becomes politically provocative. The negation of political life makes him into a political actor, which at this time, shortly after the fall of the tyranny, may have been seen as a threat to efforts to achieve a political coalition, especially, it is claimed, by turning the heads of its young people, the future of democracy.

But he unhesitatingly allows himself to be guided by his *daimonion*. And that this voice was to him an absolutely divine authority is confirmed by the fact that he never questions, *never* makes this voice an object of his critical and ironical dialectic. Thus, he refutes all other statements in life, since as a dialectician he is subject to a fundamental uncertainty that appears in doubt and in human insufficiency in relation to the gods. And so we will go deeper into the Socratic method of inquiry.

The Dialectical Method—The Paradox of the Oral Tradition

1

In terms of method, conversation for Socrates becomes erotic in the sense that it must act as a trigger for human self-development, as a midwife, in that dialogue aims at a systematic breakdown of false consciousness. Let us try to imagine this intention on the basis of his biological source. His father, Sophroniscus, mentioned in the *Laches* (180 d) and elsewhere, was a sculptor; his mother, Phainarete, a midwife. Metaphorically speaking, we can say that Socrates carries on their functions in society through his conversational practice. He tried to create, not beautiful forms in stone like his father, but beautiful souls, and for this he used his mother's skills as a midwife, the maieutic method: "But this midwife's art is a gift from heaven; my mother had it for women, and I for young men of a generous spirit and for all in whom beauty dwells" (*Th.* 210 c).

Not only does Socrates use the positive analogy of the midwife to characterize his dialectical method but in his surgical treatment of the Sophists' arguments he also often invokes the medical arts. In the doctor's art he clearly sees a professional competence that he wants to transfer to his dialectical method, and on a no less empirical basis he wants to make himself a doctor of the soul.

The analogy between a doctor for body and soul is made possible by the fact that both presuppose the same cosmic balance and harmony that ensure health. This is the case, for example, when Charmides (in the dialogue of the same name) asks Socrates to help him with a headache. However, Socrates will only do so if he may cure his soul at the same time. For, as he has had explained by a Thracian field doctor, only a "holistic" thinking can effect a cure. This Thracian doctor said to him, "The reason why the cure of many diseases is unknown to the physicians of Hellas, [is] because they disregard the whole, which ought to be studied also, for the part can never be well unless the whole is well" (*Charm.* 156 e).

Just as the goal for the doctor—taking account of the whole person—is to cure diseases of the body with his professional expertise, so it is Socrates' intention to do the same in the spiritual area. In the psychological world, he sees himself as a healer removing delusions, which like an inflammation obscure the truth. Through conversation, the individual learns to take care of his soul in a steady process of development and amplification.

2

So as Socrates makes clear in his apology, it is his task on behalf of the god to reveal stupidities in order to lead people to the moral awareness with which they were born but which is hidden and unconscious because the individual is striving for external rewards in the form of money and fame: "That is why I still go about seeking and searching in obedience to the divine command, if I think that anyone is wise, whether citizen or stranger, and when I think that any person is not wise, I try to help the cause of God by proving that he is not" (*Ap.* 23 b).

He later explains his mission in greater depth: "This, I do assure you, is what my god commands, and it is my belief that no greater good has ever befallen you in this city than my service to my God. For I spend all my time going about trying to persuade you, young and old, to make your first and chief concern not for your bodies nor for your possessions, but for the highest welfare of your souls" (*Ap.* 30 a-b).

Just as at a birth, the sleeping consciousness is awakened and it is raised up into a transfigured everyday world as conversation dissolves the usual conceptions. So in contrast to the Sophists, Socrates does not supply fixed keys to comprehension, but constantly protests his ignorance. As said above, he is not without factual knowledge, but as only the gods have perfect insight, he must declare himself ignorant and taunt those people who by virtue of their profession believe themselves to be in possession of absolute knowledge. This ignorance also explains why he so often ends his inquiry aporetically, i.e. in deep doubt as to whether the conversation has led to a dead end, even though it has proceeded logically: there came "from what quarter I cannot tell, the strangest sort of suspicion. It was that the conclusions to which we had arrived were not true" (*Lys.* 218 c).

3

The conversation is in principle endless, a factor that further substantiates why Plato's works as a whole can be viewed as a continuum, built up around the contradictions and paradoxes of the dialogues that both force the listeners to make their own choices and reveal that the very process of gaining knowledge can in principle never be concluded. Which is also the reason why Socrates is guilty of so many contradictions, able to believe one thing in one dialogue and the opposite in another. New questions are constantly being raised which show humanity in its fundamental ignorance—and quest.

Consequently, the dialogues have primarily the character of hypotheses that can be adjusted or disproved by new information. This stands in direct contrast to conclusions based upon a closed system of syllogisms. On the other hand, this is not the same thing as saying that Socrates regards his method as subjective and superficial. On the contrary, in his critique of the Sophists' rhetorical proficiency in the *Phaedrus*, he makes a great show of pointing to its scientific nature. For as his dialectic unfolds in an attempt to establish valid definitions, analyses of individual words and concepts, it becomes analytical and logical. Things are broken down into their component parts only to be put back together in a common form, type by type— or in his words: "unless the aspirant to oratory can on the one hand list the various natures among his prospective audiences, and on the other divide things into their kinds and embrace each individual thing under a single form, he will never attain such success as I within the grasp of mankind" (*Phaedrus* 273 d-e).

4

If Socrates fights a particularly formidable battle against the Sophists (even though there may be similarities in their rhetorical method), it is ultimately related to the concept of truth. He presupposes here that there is such a thing as objectively valid truth, since the concepts actually exist as ideas. So the concept of a horse has not only an abstract but also an ontological status. The idea has the highest reality of which, for instance, all tangible horses are only more or less imperfect derivatives. For the Sophists on the other hand, truth is a relative matter, created through rhetorical argument—as testimony the individual orator's power to convince. In this context, the weaker case can suddenly be turned around to become the stronger, a manipulation that Socrates is unjustly accused of committing.

In the actual vacuum of values in which the Sophists thrive, they seek to argue their way to a purely subjective truth. Ethical values are not attributed with an objective *a priori* existence as immutable and eternal, but appear instead as fortuitous, created by the relevant situation and skill of the speaker. Consequently, it is for Socrates a matter of showing that they have no idea what they are talking about. And precisely because the truth is absent from their rhetoric, neither is the good present, which is why according to Socrates the Sophists do not really exist at all. And—with due reference to the *Odyssey*—he places them in Hades as shades, as emerges from his description of the Sophist Protagoras and his circle, to which we shall return.

No, it is not the *truth* to which the Sophists relate, but the *probable*. And here lies the entire difference, for in the probable lies the power to convince the many by virtue of the fact that it looks probable. From this, it follows that the Sophists can remove the truth from a trial for instance simply because it apparently conflicts with what it probable. So the rhetorical is set free in the fabric (*Phaedrus* 268 a), as the Sophists do not know or are not interested in the whole truth but only in the convincing or striking details: "In law courts nobody cares a rap for the truth about these matters, but only about what is *plausible*. And that is the same as what is probable, and is what must occupy the attention of the would-be master of the art of speech" (*Phaedrus* 273 d-e, my italics).

This is an observation that again on the part of Plato anticipates the unjust trial of Socrates in which the law is obviously adapted to what the mob deems probable. For where the probable is defined in advance (*Phaedrus* 273 d), the truth is by the nature of things unknown. It must be acquired through the blind alleys of dialectic maneuvers.

5

So the maieutic method consists of creating conscious confusion (*aporia*) in order by this means to track down the truth. And the question is whether the powerful ironical element in Socrates' form of conversation does not arise in the discrepancy between being totally ignorant as a human being about those things on which only the gods are fully informed? And insofar as irony has contrast as its categorial basis, we could go on to ask whether we have the first sign of it in the description of Odysseus? I am thinking once again of Achilleus' statement that no person is more disgusting to him than he who says one thing and believes another (see p. 22), a characterization corresponding to irony in its most basic form.

In any event, there is no denying that Socrates is ironical in the way in which he separates the subject from the phenomenal world and the interpretations that are linked to it. In this way, he puts mankind face to face with the impermanence of life. And since, because of this impermanence, he does not believe that the truth is something that can be communicated, he must also deny in the *Apology* that—in contrast to the Sophists—he has ever acted as a teacher (*Ap.* 33 a).

He did not accept payment but allowed everyone, regardless of means, to enter into a dialogue with him. The protreptic method by which he prompts and investigates in the form of questions assumes on the other hand that his interlocutor is ready to give up any notion of being omniscient. Socrates himself is only distinguished by an illusionless and so acute knowledge of his lack of knowledge—"Then, said I [Socrates], is not dialectic the only process of inquiry that advances in this manner, doing away with hypotheses, up to the first principle itself in order to find confirmation there? And it is literally true that when the eye of the soul is sunk in the barbaric slough of the Orphic myth, dialectic gently draws it forth and leads it up" (533 d), as he says in the *Republic*.

6

If, on this basis, we analyze the forces that form part of the protreptic method, they seem remarkably enough to correspond to the forces we met in the understanding of the world in Homer and Hesiod: *eros* and *eris*—or *philotes* and *neikos* as Empedokles called them. Thus, in the space of the conversation itself, a disintegrative, eristic activity takes place, the intention of which is to split apart the logic of the argument and thus continuously reveal its false premises, at the same time as the process of cognition, as described above, is erotically transcendent. In the Sophists, this sort of dialectic leads to pure hair-splitting, because—by way of contrast to Socrates—they make the questionable or polemical a goal in itself.

Yet Socrates did not merely conduct conversations with others but also to a great extent with himself. Here, I am thinking of his *daimonion*. No, judging from all the evidence he seems to have developed a meditation technique in which he could contemplatively immerse his consciousness in the spiritual depths from which he obtained his insight in the form of a spiritual liberating force that was visionary in nature. During the campaign against Potidaia, he fell into a meditative state that lasted no less than twenty-four hours, during which he remained absorbed in himself and lost to the outside world (*Symp.* 220 c-d). Something similar happens on the way to the symposium at the home of Agathon. He fails to appear because he suddenly becomes lost in a trance in the middle of a doorway in a neighboring house. No one is to disturb him, says one of his friends, for he does this often. And when he almost dies within himself in this way, no one can follow him; but when he opens up his ugly, lost exterior, his inner is radiant like an aura.

7

What characterizes the dialogue genre as a form of consciousness? If my earlier claim that, with Plato's dialogues, philosophy filled a vacuum left after tragedy is correct, it can be maintained that it certainly carried on the dialogue form of dramatic poetry. At the same time, however, it acquired an epic character through Socrates as a person who assembles all the dialogues into one great oeuvre. On the face of it, he is the direct opposite of a tragic hero. An ugly man who does not speak in the elevated style that is a distinctive feature of tragedy. As Aristotle notes: "The perfection of diction is for it to be at once clear and not mean. (. . .) the diction becomes distinguished and non-prosaic by the use of unfamiliar terms, i.e. strange words, metaphors, lengthened forms, and everything that deviates from the ordinary modes of speech."[13]

In this respect, we may say that Plato's dialogues are everything a tragedy is not and should not be. Not only is Socrates, the hero, ugly in the ordinary sense, but he makes a virtue of it just as Alcibiades criticizes his primitive and banal illustrations: "He talks about pack assess and blacksmiths and shoemakers and tanners, and he always *seems* to be saying the same old thing in just the same old way, so that anyone who wasn't used to his style and wasn't very quick on the uptake would naturally take it for the most utter nonsense" (*Symp.* 221 e, my italics). The word "seems" indicates that this language, like his character, contains a duality; for "if you open up his arguments, and really get into the skin of them, you'll find that (. . .) nobody else's are so godlike, so rich in images of virtue, or so peculiarly, so pertinent to those inquiries that help the seeker on his way to the goal of true nobility" (222 a).

So the paradox is that Socrates starts out from the lowest in order to illustrate the highest, a conscious tactic in which the everyday is used to puncture the pompous, spectacular rhetoric of the Sophists. Here, matter-of-fact, everyday truths act as a corrective. We find clear proof that there is a conscious strategy on the part of Socrates at the end of the *Symposium*. For when everyone except Aristophanes and Agathon has passed out from exhaustion and inebriation, Socrates makes these two poets admit the following: "that the same man might be capable of writing both comedy and tragedy—that the tragic poet, *who is truly an artist*, might be a comedian as well" (223 d, my italics).

It is significant that a tragic poet and a writer of comedies must acknowledge this, i.e. be forced to take over the other's form of consciousness with a view to a higher unity and insight, if they want to claim to be artists. But since we cannot imagine such a strange fusion in the repertoire of genres known before that time, Socrates indirectly establishes a *tertium quid* uniting tragedy and comedy, and answering the challenge is the genre of his own dialogues, which combine the high moral demands of tragedy with the everyday use of the language of comedy.

The *Symposium* is in itself the best conceivable example of this sort of innovation and expansion of genre insofar as it spans these genres, which until now have been separate. Not to put too fine a point on it, Agathon and Aristophanes must become one artist. That the highest and the lowest are really combined in the dialogue is demonstrated when the dead-drunk Alcibiades, who is incapable of developing his own subject, describes Socrates with a profundity the extent of which he does not himself understand, as Plato in this combination and at an ironic distance forces these polar opposites together. And as a whole, the work encompasses an insight into Eros that extends from Aristophanes to Diotima and her initiation of Socrates.

As Aristotle defined it, comedy seeks to make "its personages worse" and tragedy makes them "better than the men of the present day."[14] Since the dialogue assembles these two expressions of life and strikes a balance by creating this sort of fusion of the elevated and the low, it is able to show how the divine is emanated in everyday things. It is only a matter of catching sight of this beauty; that is to say it must be "opened" in the same way as Socrates' words and character. In this way, things are not kept apart as in the idealization of tragedy and parody of comedy, which from this perspective distort the truth, but existence is concentrated on one and the same focal point, which is the precondition for being able to speak the truth.

In conclusion, it can be said that Plato's Socrates can be used as a central epic figure by this kind of combination of the tragic and the comic. His appearance and speech tend toward the comic, as Aristophanes used him in *The Clouds*. On the other hand, he is the greatest hero of all—called by God, suffering a tragic death and, if anyone does, becoming an example of the doctrine of suffering.

8

In order to place himself as near as possible to the Socratic form of speech, Plato has, of course, selected the dialogue for his philosophical work. It is more surprising that he ensnares not only himself but also his protagonist in an ambiguous form of irony.

Socrates, who did not himself leave any written work, has only come down to posterity through the writings of others. There is nothing wrong with that in itself. The problem is that, if we are to believe Plato, Socrates viewed writing as a sign of degeneration. In his discussion of oratory in the *Phaedrus*, he makes the art of writing and the world of books problematic (275 d-e). The written word, he claims, is just as dead as the figures in a painting. Written down, the words circulate freely among both ignorant and wise, which inevitably results in a catastrophic forgetfulness in people, "because they rely on that which is written, calling things to remembrance no longer from within themselves" (275 a).

In short, writing stands in the way of conversation, the living word. For the written image is a closed external manifestation that short-circuits the inner growth otherwise instigated by the direct energy of speech. As I have already suggested (see p. 279), the long, gradual transition from an oral tradition to a written medium will entail the gradual weakening of the ability to remember, which otherwise creates continuity in identity.[15] For the self-development at which Socrates aims cannot be conceived without the memory of the ideal images embedded in the soul.

If we maintain this interpretation, it means that—by locking Socrates behind the amnesiac bars of writing—Plato betrays the person to whom he owes everything and wishes to establish as a future (philosophical) ideal figure. Not only that. To this must be added the fact that, in contrast to his model—although it is expressed through his mouth (whereby Socrates is forced into a logical conflict with himself)—Plato renounces the oral form that is the foundation of his philosophy. In the *Republic*, he contrasts philosophy and poetry as hostile to each other despite the fact that he himself uses a dramatic form of representation and even creates his own myths when the ability to reflect deserts him.

Plato is very ambiguous in his attitude to poetry. In the *Phaedrus*, it is described as a sacred madness on a level with *eros*. This is meant positively; for he who dares to knock at the gate of poetry "without the madness of the Muses, persuaded that skill alone will make him a good poet, then shall he and his works of sanity with him be brought to nought by the poetry of madness" (245 a).

In the *Symposium*, works of poetry are spoken of as a sort of "progeny" (209 d), conceived by a union between beauty and the *eros* of the soul. And the same inspirational idea seems to lie behind Socrates' description of the poets in the *Apology*. Like the prophets, they have a kind of "instinct or inspiration" (22 c), he claims. They "deliver all their sublime messages without knowing in the least what they mean;" yet, this "made them think that they had a perfect understanding of all other subjects, of which they were totally ignorant" (22 c).[16]

9

Like the Sophists, Socrates—and thereby Plato—draws on the heritage of classical literature in his conversations but nevertheless ends up banishing the poets from his future state. As is described in Book 3 of the *Republic*, it may well be that the guardians still have the pleasure of poetry during their training, on the condition that it is purged of all negative information about the gods, etc. In Book 10, the poets are turned out, and poetry and philosophy are confronted as deadly enemies. Plato is clearly following a line of thought begun by Heraclitus and Xenophanes, who, as described above, each in their own way denounce the great names of epic poetry—Homer and Hesiod.

As Eric A. Havelock demonstrates, Plato fundamentally settles accounts with the oral tradition in which patriotic poetry formed part of the (private) education of boys and young men as an encyclopedic basic knowledge, founded on passive learning and memorizing. Consequently, the student was not able to undertake an intellectual, critical study of the material. This was due partly to the manifest character of memory itself and partly to the subject thereby becoming embedded in traditional history, which he unconsciously continued to memorize. As a result, this form of rote oral learning was not only conservative but it also stood directly in the way of personal development.

It is also important for me to emphasize that this passive process of memorization stands in sharp contrast to the form of memory that in the course of my analysis was linked to awakening. For here, memory acts as a selective category of experience in which the individual concentrates on the crucial, fateful choices that form a human life.

Furthermore, it is interesting that Plato is critical of precisely the aesthetic effect most highly valued in Homer—seduction (*thelgein*, see p. 83), because it makes people forget temporal sorrows—by raising them into the world of beauty. Plato attacks the act of seduction that captures the listener's subconscious like a narcotic—"So mighty is the spell that these adornments naturally exercise" (*Rep.* 601 b), he says, making reference to the peculiar way in which poetry expresses itself in, for example, the rhythmic, bliss-inducing melodiousness of the verse.

Finally, in Plato's view, the fatal flaw of poetry is its imitative character, its *mimesis*, in which the poet knows nothing of what he is talking about: "The imitator will neither know nor opine rightly concerning the beauty nor opine rightly concerning the beauty or the badness of his imitations" (*Rep.* 602 a). And since poetry is endowed with this air of seduction and an illusory world, it can neither convey the truth nor hold the passions in check. On the contrary, it stimulates all the impulses of desire—"it waters and fosters these feelings when what we ought to do is to dry them up, and it establishes them as our rulers when they ought to be ruled, to the end that we may be better and happier men instead of worse and more miserable" (*Rep.* 606 d).

As Socrates further emphasizes to Glaucon, Plato's brother, he must show respect to those who see in Homer the greatest poet and master and have shaped their lives according to him. But the only poetry that belongs in a future republic is that which praises the gods and particularly distinguished men. Socrates continues: "For if you grant admission to the honeyed Muse in lyric or epic, pleasure and pain will be lords in your city instead of law and that which shall from time to time have approved itself to the general reason as best" (*Rep.* 607 a). So, in short, it is necessary to throw the poets out of the utopian republic, so that reason can step into the governing role required of it, as the *logos* of philosophy is confronted with the *mythos* of poetry.

Sex and State—Xanthippe and the Role of Women in Democracy

1

The democracy we meet in Athens through Plato's dialogues is a social institution afflicted with an inflationary greed for power. The philosophical background is the nihilism of values that, according to Plato's interpretation, the Sophists promoted and of which they themselves were an expression: the individual or rather the power of the individual was the goal, even if it had to be attained by injustice. But as we have at the same time been able to observe in tragedy, if it is viewed as mythical reflections of contemporary political life, there is hidden in this reality another reality which is more specifically related to the division of power between the sexes.[17]

Meanwhile, this theme apparently plays a subordinate role in Plato, but it is implicitly present if only for the reason that his protagonist Socrates was both a husband and a lover. Once again, we face a paradox, for in this free, democratic system, the individual male citizen was of great significance, while women in Athens were downtrodden. This is a curious situation that calls for analysis and a possible answer. We will take our analytical starting point in the most famous of all women of the time—Socrates' own tough and neglected wife, Xanthippe.

2

Let us be fair. The awful reputation Xanthippe has acquired in a later age is due to neither Socrates nor Plato. In the *Phaedo*, she weeps because her husband is soon to be executed and displays such great sorrow that he is forced to send her home with their smallest child which is sitting on her lap (60 a). This indicates concern on his part, a concern that can be found in Xenophon as well. He describes an episode in which Xanthippe has apparently been bickering with her eldest son Lamprokles, to whom Socrates, defends her in a lengthy dialogue. For when the son claims that the brutality of a wild animal is less than that of his mother, Socrates demands that he should show his mother respect. Not only has she born him but she has taken care of him during illness, prayed to the gods to bless him, etc., and she loves him more than anything in the world—"if you can't endure a mother like her, you can't endure a good thing,"[18] he asserts. So he must pray to the gods for forgiveness for the contempt he has shown his mother, for otherwise no one will believe that he can ever feel gratitude for any kindness shown to him.

In Xenophon's *Symposium*, Socrates argues—as in the *Republic*—that women are not lesser creatures than men, except when it comes to physical strength and judgment. For this reason, a husband must instruct his wife in everything, a radical point of view in consideration of the oppressed position of women. However, this makes the Cynic philosopher Antisthenes raise objections; for, as he says, if this is Socrates' opinion, why has be not himself practiced the doctrine in training Xanthippe? Instead, he "has the world's most difficult wife—in fact, I believe she's the most difficult woman that ever has lived or will live."[19]

Socrates does not deny this but instead pays oblique homage to Xanthippe through a parable: The man who really wishes to become expert in horses does not choose a gentle, easy one, but a horse with spirit; for if he can control it, then he can manage all others. In the same way, Socrates claims that, if he can manage his wife, he will not have problems with the rest of mankind whose welfare he has so much in mind. That is to say that his compliment to Xanthippe is that he compares her to a racehorse.

It is probably from Antisthenes' characterization that Xanthippe will always stand as the paradigm of a bad-tempered shrew, the archetype of the battle-axe. It is a female stereotype that is still given credence, a sign that in Xanthippe we find the first *modern* woman, as we nowadays hardly meet a Klytemnestra or a Penelope in the same way. She is new also in the sense that her like is not to be found in Greek poetry.

If we were to provide an explanation for Xanthippe's alleged rage, an obvious conclusion is that she expresses the primeval fury of female frustration, as did Klytemnestra in the *Oresteia*. If we only look at her on her home front, this is not so incomprehensible. She had three sons with Socrates; the oldest, Lamprokles, was in puberty, the two younger ones, Sophroniscus (named after his grandfather) and Menexenos were still small, the youngest apparently an infant. In other words, this must mean that Socrates was not a young man when he married Xanthippe. While she was of childbearing age, he must have been about fifty-five years old when he married, as he was seventy when he died.

Be that as it may. It must have been a greater problem that, in the *Apology*, Socrates actually makes a virtue of the fact that, as a philosopher, he could not provide for his family: "If you doubt whether I am really the sort of person who would have been sent to this city as a gift from God, you can convince yourselves by looking at it in this way. Does it seem natural that I should have neglected my own affairs and endured the humiliations of allowing my family to be neglected for all these years, while I busied myself all the time on your behalf, going like a father or an elder brother to see each one of you privately, and urging you to set your thoughts on goodness?" (31 b). He had previously maintained that: "In fact, my service to God has reduced me to extreme poverty" (23 b-c).

In this way, he freed himself of all practical responsibilities and political connections in order solely to serve this mission that he had been given by the gods. He set aside his duty as head of the family in order to become a father for everyone who was interested. He was never at home, always on the square or with company at symposia, in the baths or the sports arena and only came home when the thought struck him. In addition, there was his predilection for young boys. All this makes it understandable why Xanthippe became, well, a Xanthippe.

But apart from the fact that Socrates apparently neglected his family duties, he took the same liberties that male citizens generally possessed. So we can also see in Xanthippe an exemplary representative of the latent anger that housewives must have felt at their husbands' more or less conscious neglect of them and their needs.

<h1 style="text-align:center">3</h1>

We shall look more closely at the status of women at the time of Athens' greatness in order further to establish the kind of successive oppression of the female sex that followed in the wake of the independence of masculine self-awareness. About 600 B.C., Solon drew up the first laws for female citizens. If they wanted to be deemed chaste, they should only leave their homes with the permission of their husbands; they should wear a veil, and they could only be allowed to participate in funerals and religious ceremonies and could, as mentioned above, be present at the performances of tragedies.

That women in Athens were still allowed to celebrate their female divinities, especially Demeter and Athene, at cultic festivals such as the Thesmophoria to which men were denied access, can be regarded as a form of repressive tolerance, while at the same time the festivals were intended to ensure female fertility. The cultivation of the soil, fertility and the gods of the underworld in a week-long cultic festival clearly hearkens back to before the Olympian mythology and reveals a continuity with the primal goddesses, but now incorporated into the life of the state and thus subject to its control. And as said above (see p. 92), tradition has it that marriage arose as such a measure during the mythical King Kekrops—as a patriarchal measure to ensure that fathers could identify their children and subdue women's original barbaric and animal nature which, among other things, revealed itself in women mating promiscuously. Instead, they were to be kept within the four walls of the house.

Solon's laws were in effect for several centuries. In an extension of them, Pericles, in his famous funeral oration for those who had fallen in the Peloponnesian War, made reference to the widows: "Your great glory is not to be inferior to what God has made you, and the greatest glory of a woman is to be least talked about by men, whether they are praising you or criticizing you."[20]

We find what is probably the clearest evidence of the precarious position of women and wives in a somewhat more recent text from around 340 B.C., an indictment against the prostitute Neaera. Here, the male prosecutor states: "Mistresses [hetairai] we keep for the sake of pleasure, concubines for the daily care of our persons, but wives to bear us legitimate children and to be faithful guardians of our households."[21]

The paradox is that in Athenian democracy, where we would immediately expect to encounter the highest conceivable freedom, women were on the contrary oppressed. As it clearly emerges from the above quotation, the woman's role was in the home, in the *oikos*, where under her husband's dominion she attended to the legitimacy of reproduction and everyday domestic chores. Her field of action was in all important respects indoors, while that of her husband was outside the home. In short, respectable housewives did not actively participate in democratic rights. They were not allowed to express themselves in public assemblies and were not allowed to vote or purchase or own land, the most important way in which an Athenian citizen could accumulate wealth—as a landowner. Women in Athens were thus on the same social level as immigrants (*metoics*) and slaves, who were also denied democratic rights.

4

The emotional contact between the spouses was as a rule slender. They did not get married for emotional reasons but through arrangements and contract by the father to ensure advantageous financial connections. For the same reason, the wedding was relatively informal. The girl moved in with her future husband and sought through corn rituals to ensure fertility, her primary justification for existence.

The marriageable age for a girl was fourteen to fifteen years old, when she became sexually mature. The husband, on the other hand, tended to be around thirty, as he first had to do his military service and achieve financial independence. From birth to death, the girl—and, later, the adult woman—was thus subject to male guardianship, the so-called *kyrios*, her father or a close relative, a function the husband took over. Her most important civil right was that she was financially assured of the dowry she brought into the marriage, which her husband administered but which remained her property in the event of a divorce.

A divorce was as simple as a wedding—at least for the husband. If she did not meet his expectations, he could simply return her. For the woman, it was more difficult. It presumed the acceptance of the highest authority (the archons), something of which we have evidence from when Hipparte tried to divorce Alcibiades. A special set of circumstances applied if there were no sons to inherit. In that case, the fortune went to the daughter eligible to inherit (*epikleros*). In such a situation, a male member of the family could be forced to marry her, if necessary divorcing his present wife, in order to keep the fortune in the family's hands.

5

We found the first example of an angst-laden devaluation of women in Hesiod. In his advice to his dissolute brother, it will be remembered, he went on that his brother should stay away from showy girls—they would dissipate his sexuality. Instead, he should find a young virgin whom he could educate according to his own mind and for his own purposes. It is a necessary evil to have the house looked after and to procure offspring who could ensure one's maintenance in old age. In the *Oresteia*, the role of the woman in reproduction was reduced to being a container for the breeding man.

In Sophocles, the husband is the active party, the plow, while the woman is merely his furrow. In Euripides, Iason and Hippolytos agree that the world would be happier without women if you could only breed without them. But even though Euripides may for this reason have been hated by the women of Athens, we have seen that he has a deep understanding of their situation, whether they were victims such as Medea, Iphigenia or Polyxena, while in *The Bacchae* he showed the necessity of absorbing the Dionysian into the masculine world.

That educational principles were decisive for a future wife in democratic Athens appears quite clearly in a dialogue by Xenophon between the newly married Ischomachos and Socrates. The writing is significantly enough called *Oikonomikos*, household administration, and it describes virtually the only learning a girl received during her upbringing. The argument from Hesiod is repeated here—that reproduction is important as a provision for old age, while Ischomachos instructs his young wife with a metaphor on how she is to behave in the home and manage and divide work among the slaves, as a queen bee does with her bees.

But the queen bee function of the wife in the *oikos* was not the same as absolute power. On the contrary. As Elektra, for example, says in Euripides: "O what perversion, when the woman in the house/ stands out as master, not the man."[22] The man's position of power and the repression of women can even be read in the architectural design of the house. Together with the other women in the house, the wife lived furthest away from the outside world, at the back or in the uppermost part of the house. She had no access to world around her, in which the husband on the other hand was very much at home.[23]

At the same time, he was the only one to have what might be called a comfortable living space, *andron*, a sort of living room in which the floor might be inlaid with mosaics, while the floors in the rest of the house were of clay. In this room, he could extend his outdoor activities—with friends, conversations and symposia. Women were excluded in the nature of things from this legal universe of pleasure—in itself something that could create frustration à la Xanthippe when the man left the house in the morning to live his free life—as a man.

6

In the *Symposium*, we get an indirect insight into the literally repressed life female citizens had to live with each other. The dialogue also illustrates men's sexual freedom. For when the male participants in the party agree not to get drunk but instead to hold speeches in honor of Eros, the female flute player who had been summoned is sent away. The text says she may play for herself or for the ladies in the adjoining room.

With this, two contradictory female models are laid side by side: the free woman as opposed to the bondwoman. The ladies mentioned in the adjoining apartments were not allowed to participate in the men's festivities, whereas the men were clearly within their rights to summon a so-called free woman to play for them and—if the desire arose—to provide more intimate services. The woman flautist is free to choose. Being in possession of artistic skills makes it possible for her to maintain a life for herself.

These free women might be hetaerae or *pornai*, i.e. prostitutes. The transition here has been a gray zone, but in the clear external points, hetaerae were well-educated (like Japanese geishas) and prostitutes were merely there to satisfy the male sexual urges.[24] From Solon's time, as a privilege of democratic custom men had free access to state bordellos, which were adorned with the image of a phallos; services cost an *obol*. In addition, slave girls within the four walls of the house were available for the man ad libitum. Girls who lost their innocence could be sold as slaves. An unfaithful wife was punished by divorce.

Through this amorous practice, men were able in the anonymization and forms of sexuality to diffuse the erotic power of women, to make it controllable and the expression of pure lust. So sexuality was not entirely separated from the relationship with women, as Hippolytos dreamed, something that was in any case impossible with respect to the maintenance of the man's *oikos*. He showed his sense of duty to his wife by fulfilling his marital sexual duty three times a month, and after her death he might well raise a sepulchral stele in grateful memory. But since the emotional relationship to one's wife was weak or entirely absent, love faded into anonymity. Love as a subjective form of passion and suffering was, as we shall see, displaced by pedophilic relationships.[25]

7

As demonstrated in my analysis of Euripides' tragedies, the oppression of women had its source in the view of her nature as barbaric and animalistic, especially on account of her alleged uninhibited sexuality. This view must also lie behind the myth of how Zeus and Hera call upon the prophet Teiresias—who had been both man and woman—to decide their dispute as to which sex got the most out of the act of love. The answer is that a woman's sexual enjoyment is nine times greater than a man's.[26]

Women's sexual nature is also a recurring theme in Aristophanes' three comedies focusing on women: *Thesmophoriazusae* (411 B.C.), *Lysistrata* (411 B.C.) and *The Assembly of Women* (*Ecclesiazusae*, 391 B.C.). On one level a demonstration of Aristotle's view that the comedy genre turns things on their heads, these comedies reflect two things: 1) The demonization of women resulting from their oppression. 2) The fear of women Aristophanes shared. He continues in caricature the misogyny or fear of women first expressed by Hesiod: women's sexuality is naturally stronger than men's. So a woman is emotional and greedy in all of life's demands, which is why she should not participate in the business of the state but on principle be enclosed in her husband's home.

So this means that although through the women's condemnation of Euripides in

Thesmophorizusae Aristophanes expresses his own disgust at tragedies such as *Medea* and *Hippolytos*, he nevertheless seems to maintain the general view of women. As said above, the accusation the women direct against Euripides is concerned with his slander: Has he not "slandered us, calling us whore-wives, man-chasers, wine-bibbers, betrayers, chatterboxes, no-goods, men's great curse?"[27] In order to save his life, Euripides promises to improve his ways—he will never again speak evil of women.

We may infer that Aristophanes probably had the same assessment as that attributed to Euripides from the fact that in *Lysistrata*—in connection with the sex strike she initiates to stop the war against Sparta—the female title character expresses exactly the same point of view: "What an absolute race of nymphomaniacs we are, the lot of us! No wonder the tragedies get written round us: we're nothing but Poseidon and a tub."[28] What Aristophanes parodies through the magical mirror of comedy is the rebellious frustrations and lasciviousness of women. To Lysistrata's despair, they break their oath time and time again, unable to keep away from men, driven as they are by their sexual appetites.

And yet Aristophanes indicates that there may be a connection between the women's oppressed circumstances and their conduct, for at the same time he attacks the male politicians who are unable to put a stop to the war. So, from this angle, *Lysistrata* illuminates his longing for peace. Alongside the woman motif, he also shows in *The Assembly of Women* that he does not have a generally high opinion of the capabilities of politicians. It is at once a presentation of the nature of women and the incompetence of politicians. For when the women, dressed in men's clothing, take power and establish a new constitution, it happens in direct protest against poor political leadership. As the main character Praxagora says, "I grieve to note/ The sad condition of the State's affairs/ I see the State employing evermore/ Unworthy ministers; if one do well/ A single day, he'll act amiss for ten."[29]

The women's law in *The Assembly of Women* is extremely radical. It requires communal property, collectives and free sexuality—and also introduces a special law that old women have first choice in sexual partners. This law must presumably be seen against the background of the experience Lysistrata had—namely, that old men can go to the bridal bed with young girls, while a woman's time of opportunity, as she says, is short-lived.[30] This law provides scope for great fun when a young man on his way to his lover is accosted by first a 70-year-old, then an 80-year-old and finally a 90-year-old woman, all of whom demand that he should fulfill the new law.

This example illustrates the ambiguity in Aristophanes insofar as he is correct in his analysis of sexual inequality, but the description of the randy old women is yet another example of women's lack of restraint. As the leader of the chorus of old men in *Lysistrata* says, "No beast, nor yet fire, is harder to get the better of than a woman is, nor is any leopard so ruthless."[31] And, therefore, "I shall never give over hating women."[32]

This unresolved dilemma between the sexes becomes the axis around which Aristophanes' comedies on women revolve. On the one hand, men hate women and on the other they cannot do without them. A paradox that the female chorus leader notes in *Thesmophoriazusae* as she fails to understand why, since they view women as "a curse,"[33] men nevertheless want to marry: "Why do you want to keep and guard your 'curse' with all this great determination?/ And if the little woman does go out somewhere, and then you find her out of the house, you go absolutely insane."[34]

The answer is naturally once again the same as in Hesiod: men cannot do without women for reproduction and to take care of their *oikos*, but women must be kept down because of their sexual instability. Consequently, men must control women's education. And it is also typical that Lysistrata, who is no fool, acknowledges that she has all her knowledge from her father's world: "I am not badly educated either, having heard a great deal of the talk of/ my father and of other older men."[35]

The remarkable feature about the women's new laws is that they actually attempt to repeal patriarchal law. This law will no longer be valid, the argument goes, because it is no longer necessary when everything is common. This means that the matriarchy, about which the women in reality have some vague notion if they come to power, corresponds to and depends on regression to the amorphous, natural promiscuity of the original primal maternal world. It is fundamentally this anxiety-inducing reality against which the men react—in order to defend their masculinity, supported by the strict rules of paternal rule prescribing the conduct of women. In such a women's regime no man would know who his father was. When one of the men timidly asks how a man could recognize his own son, he receives the answer: "They will never be known: it can never be told;/ All youths will in common be sons of old."[36]

This is to say: the women in *The Assembly of Women* are trying to take their old privileges back by reducing the man to a subordinate breeder. And the very scenario of the comedy reveals in a manner that at once gives rise to laughter and anxiety how such a female authority would look. For in *The Assembly of Women*, the women are played by men dressed up as women playing men, while the men themselves are also played by men, but dressed in women's clothes. All gender relations are thus in principle suspended in a swamp of pure estrogen.

8

It is a surprising fact that the collectivism of the women corresponds to Plato's utopian state. For chronological reasons, Aristophanes cannot have been parodying the *Republic*, which was written much later. Nevertheless, Plato's idea is that the guardians of the state must have common property, so that in the exercise of their elevated political purpose they do not become fixated on the need to enrich themselves at the cost of others. In addition, the law of joint property must also apply to women and children in order to ensure that the family is not placed above respect for the governance of the state.

We shall shortly return to Plato's theory of the state. In the present context, we can merely observe in anticipation that there is a fundamental difference between

Aristophanes and Plato. For although Aristophanes apparently has an eye to the wretched position of women in society, he shares the general masculine view of their dangerous qualities. Socrates and Plato, on the other hand, wish to give women equal status with men.

As said above, according to Xenophon, Socrates spoke in the cause of women when he claimed that it is only in their physical strength that they are inferior to men. There is something authentic about the statement, since Plato makes him repeat it in the *Republic*. Here, she is attributed with an equality that means that, after receiving the necessary training and schooling, she will be able to take the post of head of state in line with the philosopher kings. He thus says to Glaucon: "You must not suppose that my words apply to the men more than to all women who arise among them endowed with the requisite qualities" (*Rep.* 540 c).

Against the background of the oppression of women described, this is a radical idea with almost incalculable perspectives for which Socrates makes himself a spokesman: that women in principle have the same potential for development as men. Of course, his view is not elaborated—unfortunately, we might say. But what is groundbreaking is that the process of consciousness which we have witnessed and which culminates in Athenian democracy is based on the oppression of women and the development and emancipation of men. It is a feature in the origin of democracy, which our culture has since carried as a more or less hidden trauma.

But as the description of Diotima implies, Socrates and Plato can imagine a future in which the antagonism between the sexes has ceased and in which women as well as men can attain the wisdom that can make her head of state—to remain with Plato's terminology. This presumes a non-gender-specific but *human* self-development to which the formal skills that are part of practical schooling are connected. How this will look, taking into consideration the physical differences between men and women, is something we are not told. But although Plato does not elaborate on this, we can say that in this way he overcomes the hostile dichotomy constituting the gender-determined poles of tension. As guardians of the state, women will thereby achieve an inner liberation of their spiritual potential, ensuring against the dangers of the sexual urge, which Plato also sees as one of the greatest hindrances to human cognition. What is crucial is that a form of *homophrosyne* is achieved between the sexes, a mutual empathy in which sexual identity is retained without tearing off each other's heads because of it.

9

The fact that Socrates' wife is given an unflattering role may be explained by the contrast that is thereby created in men's minds. As something approaching pure spirit, Socrates has liberated himself from the feminine, which is offended and furious. So the question is whether, in a democracy reserved for men, we can see the victory of the male sex over women as awe-inspiring creatures of nature and fertility. If this victory were displayed in social and political life, the significance of the great welfare and freedom provided to the individual citizen—if he were a man, that is—would be hidden.

In this process of development we have followed, the gradual assumption of power by men and the establishment of paternal rule consisted of a rising consciousness and separation from nature, where the actual liberation from nature and the maternal lets loose a form of sublimation. The spiritual *eros* aroused by the desire of the body is gradually transferred to a cosmic world of beauty, a movement that must be understood as an ever deeper penetration into the subconscious.

The Free Man and the Lover of Boys

1

The husband left the *oikos* early in the morning, leaving the women to be women, and sought the freedom of the regular masculine social life. As head of the family, he did the shopping and had the goods taken home by accompanying slaves. He took part in the hectic conversations in the city square and participated in the popular assemblies every ninth day at the Pnyx, southwest of the Agora, with seating for 6000 men. He could do this from the time he turned 20, but was only eligible for office from the age of 30. Then, he could be elected by lottery to the governing organs of the state, to a superior or more humble position, for shorter or longer periods, depending on the nature of the post.

Democracy was exclusively a masculine affair, a parallel to the *Iliad*'s heroic male identity and world, which also had as its goal the establishment of a purely masculine universe, liberated from mythical femininity. So it is not so strange that the ideals from this epoch through Homer's heroic language and code came to act as the ideal educational paradigm for bringing up boys, even though there now existed a significantly greater consciousness of the independent worth of the subject.

The similarity can be demonstrated by the fact that the masculine realm in the active outside world had closed in on itself—in the sports arena, in the baths, the male clubs (*thiasoi*), bordellos—all those places to which women had no access and where men could mutually build up their own self-confidence—in a common, more or less unconscious fear of women. This was most strongly manifested in the idealization of pederastic love between a man and a boy.[37] So at the same time as women are kept in the home—as a compulsory measure and a prophylactic against her nature—male social life created a self-validating space for the emotional life, its desires and its spirituality.

2

As the word implies, pederasty consists of loving (*eran*) boys (*pais*). The older man is the lover (*erastes*), the young man or boy the beloved (*eromenos*). Socrates can be teased about his burning love for Alcibiades. And in Xenophon's version of the symposium, Critobolus describes his fondness for Cleinias with a passion that recalls Sappho's bitter-sweet love poems or Phaedra's hunger for love: "Looking at Cleinias gives me more pleasure than looking at any other human beauty; I'd gladly be blind to everything else if I would just see one man, Cleinias."[38]

So in the circle around Socrates, love in the sense we associated with this phenomenon is exclusively limited to pedophilia. As Socrates himself pointed out, his maieutic art is aimed at "young men of a generous spirit" (*Th*. 210 e). And several of the speeches in Plato's *Symposium* contain such explicit misogyny that we might infer that pederasty is related to the great difficulty men had in differentiating themselves from the maternal world.

Historically speaking, it is interesting that pedophilia is not yet found in Homer, even though the relationship between Achilleus and Patroklos is interpreted this way in the *Symposium*—nor is it found in Hesiod, despite his characteristic fear and hatred of women. The explanation for the rise of homosexuality is sometimes traced back to the time before Homer—among other things in the speculation that its genesis must be in immigrant warrior tribes that had no access to women, but this view cannot be confirmed from the sources.

Chronologically, this behavior dates from later than both Homer and Hesiod, which is why in other contexts it is linked to the aristocratic hedonism which arose in the wake of the great colonization from around 750 B.C. with the introduction of luxury goods, symposia, etc.

Homosexuality was an open practice in the region around Athens for only a relatively short time. Pericles' democratic reforms around 450 B.C., which reduced the political influence of the aristocracy, hearkened back ideologically to the Homeric ideals and thus to the heterosexual heroes.[39] His reforms brought homosexual conduct into discredit. It was subsequently cultivated in closed intellectual circles, such as those which formed around Socrates, and where pedophilia moved to an indeterminate extent from the physical to a form of spiritual transcendence. This was a transformation that may perhaps be explained by the fact that, in his late work *The Laws*, Plato surprisingly enough renounces this form of *eros*, since, as he writes, "there should be (. . .) no sterile and *unnatural* intercourse with males" (841 d, my italics).

3

Pederasty in classical Athens was a form of love connected in an intimate way with a boy's initiation into citizenship and his life as a free man, free from the feeling of women's power, we might say. The ambivalence towards women, which we meet for instance in Euripides' tragedies, presumably has its psychological cause in the conditions under which a boy was raised. He lived with his mother in the women's part of the house until his seventh year. And if her marital situation is seen in relation to the father's absence from the home, the extent to which a man participated in his son's life during these early years must have been quite limited. Indeed, we may cautiously infer that the more frustrated and emotionally unfulfilled the mother was, the stronger the passion she bestowed on her son.[40] So he became psychologically entangled in a fundamental conflict, such as we saw develop in Telemachos' relationship with his mother, the bond from which he could free himself only with great difficulty and with help from Athene by going away and finding himself along the way.

So when a boy of seven is removed from his mother and is first sent to a pedagogue and later introduced into a pederastic relationship with an older man and his education, it in reality serves a dual purpose and has the character of an initiation. In part, it is to liberate him from the emotional suffocation of his mother; in part, it is to guide him towards democratic masculinity with its inherent demand for high intellectual and physical development and moral integrity.

The pederastic relationship was introduced when the boy's intelligence began to awaken, as referenced, for instance, in Phaedrus' statement that the lover of males does not love boys "for no boy can please him until he has shown the first signs of dawning intelligence, signs which generally appear with the first growth of beard" (*Symp.* 181 d). The relationship lasted through puberty, from when the boy was around twelve until he was about eighteen, when he was registered as a citizen—the period during which sexuality appears as a reality and an entry into an exclusive male world with all its freedoms in practical as well as sexual arenas.

4

In the *Symposium*, this sexual problem is most clearly expressed by Pausanias. He distinguishes between a heavenly love (*Urania*) and a love for the mob (*Pandemos*), linked to physical sexuality. The difference arises in the origin of these forms of love. The inferior *eros* was the progeny of Zeus and Dione, while the heavenly was born of Zeus alone, without a mother. Just as Athene was born of her father. In other words, it has "nothing of the female, but [is] altogether male" (*Symp.* 181 c). It cannot be documented more clearly that this process, including "democratization," has to do with liberating oneself from woman and all her works.

Consequently, only the latter form of love, the purely masculine, has a higher moral goal. Since the older man only loves clever boys, this confirms first of all that the purpose of pederasty is to control sexual energy during the process of the boy's intellectual awakening, to develop and elevate his spiritual potential as a whole, as indicated in the quotation from Socrates about redeeming young men of generous spirit. And, secondly, this pedophiliac form of education contributes to perfecting the lover himself, since as an ideal he must strive to act as beautifully and nobly as he can.

Just as in dialectics, this mutuality is presented as an exchange of *eros* and *eris*, though strife here is exclusively viewed in positive terms, as prompting noble behavior (*Symp.* 179 a), where both parties, the lover and the beloved, in mutual competition try to promote virtue and avoid anything that might bring shame: "If only, then, a city or an army could be composed of none but lover and beloved, how could they deserve better of their country than by shunning all that is base, in mutual emulation?" (*Symp.* 178 e).

This moral view clearly mimics the conceptions of *arete* and shame that characterized the heroes of the *Iliad*, while the notion of noble competition has its origin in Hesiod's speech about the good, competitive *eris* (see p. 294). Finally, it implies that this form of homosexuality has nothing to do with female softness. On the contrary, the "effeminate" man is mocked. The whole idea of achievement is concerned with the opposite, with equipping the boy to become a man who can control his wife and his house and speak with authority when men are assembled.

Diotima

1

Considering the expulsion of women from the sphere of men, it is something of a mystery why Socrates uses a woman to express the highest insight into the mystery of love. As the person who initiated Socrates into the secrets of *eros*, however, Diotima is a many-layered metaphor—or another of Plato's subtle myths. Of course, this does not exclude the possibility that she really existed, although opinions on this have been strongly divided.[41] In Socrates' description, she has distinct individual features; she can laugh and be ironical with him. He uses her pseudonymously to avoid speaking in the form of a monologue without the dialectics with which he otherwise always seeks to achieve knowledge through conversation. So she is attributed with an initiatory function such as the Muses have in Homer and Hesiod, or like that of the goddess in Parmenides' didactic poem. This is underlined by the meaning of her name—"honored by Zeus" or "she who honors Zeus."

That she is actually his mouthpiece is revealed discreetly by the fact that her monologue passes directly into a discussion about the nature of Eros. So she directly refers to and answers Aristophanes' preceding speech. She rejects his account of how lovers seek their lost halves (*Symp.* 205 e). This is in reality Socrates' answer. In this sense, he and Diotima reflect each other, so they cannot ultimately be separated.

Clearly, her femininity must nevertheless have another purpose. It may be expressed most briefly in the way in which she brings him spiritually into the world, "gives birth" to him. From his own mother he had transferred the maieutic function into a philosophical dialectic, insofar as she herself is only to be considered as his biological source. Her name, Phainarete means, symbolically, "She who gives birth to goodness"—by implication, in the form of her son Socrates. However, it is Diotima who initiates him directly in the nature of the good and teaches him how it is acquired through erotic sublimation. She "gives birth" to him for a second time in a purely spiritual sense, just as in the story of Odysseus' development it was a crucial feature that he was "born" twice (see p. 214).

2

This interpretation of Diotima's symbolic meaning is further supported by the fact that her speech deals with conception, pregnancy and birth. Indeed, the entire metaphor she uses to describe the genesis, maturation and ways of the soul is taken from this area of life. As we have heard before, she distinguishes between the "procre-

ancy of the flesh," which applies to women, and that which has to do with boys—
"those whose procreancy is of the spirit rather than of the flesh—and they are not
unknown, Socrates—conceive and bear the things of the spirit. And what are they?
you ask. Wisdom (*phronesin*) and all her sister virtues (*areten*)" (208 e-209 a).

At this level of understanding, we face the no longer unnatural fact that a man
can be fertile and long to give birth, but this requires something beautiful to
redeem him. The logic of this thought process is guided by the soul-*eros* of pederasty: that the beautiful can only be a young, beautiful boy, since women by their
nature are part of the physical world from which one should completely liberate
onself—"And hence his procreant nature is attracted by a comely body rather than
an ill-favored one, and if, besides, he happens on a soul which is at once beautiful,
distinguished and agreeable (. . .) by constant association with so much beauty, and
by thinking of his friend when he is present and when he is away, he will be delivered of the burden he has labored under all these years" (209 b-c).

With corporal beauty as its outset, boy-*eros* provides a psychological starting
point for an erotic elevation into the realm of beauty. This form of *eros* consists of
the restraining of desire and a self-control that both liberates and channels erotic
forces as the pure energy of sublimation. Thus, the lover and the beloved are
released from the original natural connection with maternal power, and the liberated male subject can then invest his wisdom in the life of the state.

3

The female figure of which Diotima is most reminiscent is Athene. This goddess
had the same meaning for Odysseus as Diotima has for Socrates—elevating the
subconscious into the clarity of consciousness. The comparison with Athene is
made reasonable by the religious aura that Diotima radiates. Not only is she a
priestess but she originates from Mantinea, a word associated with the Greek word
mantis, i.e. "seer" and similar connotations. She also links herself to insight, "the
beholder," with what occurs in the "visionary" mysteries of Eleusis. Here, one receives
the highest insight (*epoptika*, 210 a), which she doubts Socrates will be able to achieve.
However, she will try her best to initiate him into the secrets of the cult. And insofar as this cult was linked to Demeter and contained secret knowledge about the
mystery of fertility, we find in other words a hidden connection with the chthonic,
the cycle of the seasons, etc. This could be a deeper explanation for the fact that
Diotima has been able to ward off the plague for ten years: "It was she who brought
about a ten years' postponement of the great plague of Athens on the occasion of
a certain sacrifice" (201 d). If we ask who else had such a capacity, the answer is—
the Erinyes or, rather, the Eumenides, who as chthonic forces could ensure fecundity as well as unleash crop failure if they were offended.

In other words, taken to its extreme, Diotima ultimately derives the authority of
her insight regarding the pregnancy and birth of the soul from this configuration.
And this means that Socrates—and Plato—in this remarkable way can certainly

renounce the feminine as a lower form of existence determined by nature, but as the projection Diotima is for Socrates at the same time, he integrates her as a Sophia figure. Elevated as she now is in the world of consciousness, she no longer consti- tutes a threat to men. On the contrary, she has become a spiritual redeemer and guide just as Penelope became the embodiment of Odysseus' self-development when he liberated her from the suitors' world of desire.

Odysseus' integration and redemption of the feminine is fulfilled in the arms of his beloved wife. Socrates, on the other hand, adopts Diotima as an internal visuali- zation of the soul's path and knowledge, at the same time as his own wife, Xanthippe, if we are to believe Antisthenes, henpecked him like the frustrated housewife she may have been. At any rate, this interpretation became her fate in posterity.

4

As said above, Socrates is also a spokesman for the women's cause as he claims that women are not inferior to men except physically, which is why women may become the leaders of a state if they "are endowed with the requisite qualities" (*Rep.* 540 c). If this view is further combined with Plato's statement that homosexuality is contrary to nature, we have a perspective on the future in which the rivalry between male and female finally comes to an end. Men no longer oppress women out of fear. Nor are women any longer solely determined by biology and blood, seeking to destroy their sons who wish to become free in order to constitute their own masculine identity.

Several things connect Socrates to such a process: 1) As a philosopher, he describes himself as a midwife. 2) From Diotima's account of the philosopher's erotic quest, he may be said to have a feminine dimension, as he is pregnant with his soul and wants to give birth to the highest *arete*. 3) In his description of him, Alcibiades refers to the fact that—being pregnant—he bears the most beautiful images within his ugly exterior. 4) The path to immortality is paved for him by an elevated female figure with a strong resemblance to Diotima.

Immediately before his execution, he dreams of a radiant female figure (p. 557), who acts as an agent from the bright world of the beholder to which he will be taken after his death. It is this world into which Diotima, as the prefiguration of this dream woman, has initiated him and to which he now longs to return as a lost homeland. But first, in democratic Athens, he must be accused and condemned to death.

Accusation, Judgment, and Death

1

Socrates shows the same contempt he has for the Sophists in his treatment of politicians who corrupt the state; moreover, in the *Gorgias*, he claimed to be the only true statesman himself because he was concerned for the citizens' souls (see p. 501). So what he turned against was inevitably to be turned against him as a false charge, as is also anticipated in the *Gorgias*. It contains several factors, but can be summed up in brief by the word impiety, *asebeia*. The fact that impiety could be made into a capital charge must be seen in light of the fact that the life of the state was deeply interwoven with the religious. Or vice versa. Cultic events permeated the everyday life of Athenians. And even though there was no official state religion, but relatively wide religious freedom, the gods were nevertheless viewed as providential to society, which is why religion and its rituals were a social matter.

Other *asebeia* cases were conducted before his; and in consideration of the fact that even in the comedy *The Clouds* from 423 B.C., Aristophanes had represented Socrates as a blaspheming aerial spirit, some time passed before he was finally charged in 399 B.C. in the following terms: "This indictment and affidavit is sworn by Meletus, the son of Meletus of Pitthos, against Socrates, son of Sophroniscus of Alopece: Socrates is guilty of refusing to recognize the gods recognized by the state, and of introducing other new divinities [*daimonia*]. He is also guilty of corrupting the youth. The penalty demanded is death."[42]

Plato's reproduction of the indictment is evidence that his defense speech is close to the actual events. Socrates' more or less paraphrased recapitulation of the indictment in the *Apology*, which he formulates twice, reads in combined form as follows: "Socrates is guilty of criminal meddling, in that he inquires into things below the earth and in the sky, and makes the weaker argument defeat the stronger, and teaches others to follow his example" (19 b-c); "Socrates is guilty of corrupting the minds of the young, and of believing in deities of his own invention instead of the gods recognized by the state" (24 b-c).

2

There were three prosecutors in the trial against Socrates. Only Meletus is described in detail. In the *Euthyphro*, Socrates says that he does not know with certainty who he is but that he is probably from the village of Pitthos, a young "hook-nosed man with long straight hair, and not much beard" (1 b). Euthyphro believes that the accusation of impiety must be due to Socrates' *daimonion* and hopes that the case will come to nothing.

In the *Apology*, Socrates himself divides up the prosecutors in this way: "Meletus being aggrieved on behalf of the poets, Anytus on behalf of the professional men and politicians, and Lycon on behalf of the orators" (23 e-24 a). Lycon is not known to posterity, but it is known that Anytus was a prominent democratic politician and a tanner by profession. In his abbreviated version of the defense speech, Xenophon tells of a clash between Anytus and Socrates, which turned on the fact that Anytus' son had belonged to the circle around Socrates.[43] He warned the father against apprenticing his son as a tanner. Because of his weak character and lack of upbringing, the son became a drunkard and—as predicted by Socrates—brought great disgrace to his father because, despite warnings, the father apprenticed his unsuitable son as a tanner.

Behind these allegedly religious grounds for dragging Socrates into court, there is a sense that there were hidden personal motives. Young Meletus could use the sensational court case as a springboard for his career. And it might be that Anytus wanted to avenge their dispute and at the same time make use of the case as a cunning politician. For the trial could act as a focal point for the Athenians during the political restoration. This was taking place after the long war against Sparta and the terror regime of the tyrants and constituted a countermeasure against the general skepticism that natural philosophy and the Sophists had brought about.

The interesting feature in the process of dissolution was an internal connection between natural philosophy and the Sophists. Just as the Sophists used natural philosophy to provide information on religious values, so at the same time they undermined their own doctrine with claims that natural philosophy did not contain ideas capable of forming the basis for a new social morality. The Sophists viewed the laws as man-made, practical measures for life in society. As its logical conclusion, this view led to the arbitrary subjectivity in which the person won who knew best how to put his case. The art of rhetoric was all decisive, power a goal in itself, as appears in the statement that the just is nothing but "the advantage of the stronger" (*Rep.* 339 a).

Remarkably enough, several of Socrates' proselytes were among the representatives of such an egocentric exercise of power—first and foremost, Alcibiades and Critias. Xenophon cites this as a strong contributory reason for his being accused.[44] At the same time, as said above, Socrates had also questioned democratic practice, i.e. its random elections by lottery of the members of the popular assembly, as he did not believe that everyone was equally suited to assume such a position. He himself was very reluctant to participate in political life but shouldered the civil responsibilities as required.

In addition, Xenophon implies that Socrates was envied because he was more favored by the god than anyone else.[45] This is a view that is confirmed by Socrates himself as he points to the hatred he provoked after Apollo nominated him the wisest man on earth when, in order to test and understand what the god meant, he sought enlightenment from various groups—politicians, poets and craftsmen. Through this questioning, it quickly became clear to him, as he says, that he must be the wisest. He, at least, realized that he knew nothing, while everyone he questioned made himself out to be wise in others' and especially their own eyes, while this was not really the case. Consequently, he conceded the oracle was correct: "It was best for me to be as I was" (22 e).

In his inquiries, Socrates thus reveals a form of illusion that arises, when, because of power or education, people establish an interpretation and self-understanding from which they uncritically derive their view of life in the belief that they are good and wise, an illusion that no one questions with impunity. In Socrates' eyes, this attitude was an expression of intellectual arrogance and *hubris*—"It is the greatest evil, and this ignorance, which thinks that it knows what it does not" (29 b). By probing on behalf of himself and the god, he attracted resentment for which, as we have heard, Meletus represented the infuriated poets, Lycon the irate orators, and Anytus the provoked politicians and craftsmen.

3

If we delve a little more deeply into the phrasing of the indictment, it clearly tries to hit Socrates via the connection between natural philosophy and Sophism: that he ponders things beneath the earth and up in heaven and, with his dialectics, makes the weaker case into the stronger. Implicit in this is that he is both a Sophist and a natural philosopher, Protagoras and Anaxagoras at the same time. They were incidentally both prosecuted for activities hostile to the state.

Socrates distinguishes among the charges in a surprising way in his dialogue with his opponents, a legal institution we saw Aeschylus use in the battle of words between Apollo and the Erinyes at the Areopagus. Socrates both explicitly distances himself from the natural philosopher Anaxagoras and makes the prosecutors themselves into Sophists. That he, like Anaxagoras, should merely consider the sun and the moon as earth and rock, he calls pure nonsense (26 b-e). He regards the planets as animated—as emanations of God (*theos*) or the gods. In the *Phaedo*, he elaborates on his relationship with Anaxagoras. He tells how he visited him as a young man to get an explanation of causal laws but was bitterly disappointed, as "the fellow made no use of mind and assigned to it no causality for the order of the world, but adduced causes like air and æther and water and many other absurdities" (98 b-c).

In discussing the most important charge—that he believes in "*daimonic* voices" (*Ap.* 24 c), i.e. his *daimonion*—he draws the conclusion that the person who believes in *daimones* must necessarily believe in the gods, since *daimones* are of divine origin. In addition, his *daimonion* originates from Apollo, who has chosen him for a mission as a "gadfly" for the state. This means that he, Socrates, speaks the truth, whereas Meletus with the absurdity of his accusations speaks falsely and impiously. So it is not he, Socrates, but his accusers who, like the Sophists, make the weaker case the stronger and commit criminal acts by teaching others to act likewise.

4

As in the *Symposium* in which Socrates admonishes the other speakers for their stilted, untruthful description of Eros, he also uses his ironical interpretative tactic in his *Apology*. When he says of his accusers that "their arguments were so convincing" (17 a), it really means that they were nothing but lies. On the other hand, he himself will speak the pure and unadorned truth.

So the trial is turned on its head: he, the accused, must not only defend himself and his life but society itself against its own representatives. With his truth, Socrates distinguishes the laws and the state from the accusers, since it is they who, with their lies and the consequential travesty of justice, bring down the state and the laws to which he ascribes absolute goodness. The accused makes himself into the accusers' accuser. He claims, "you shall hear from me the whole truth" (17 b), since his speech will be without the mendacity of rhetorical flourish.

Socrates feels that he is called by and rests in God, and so he does not fear death, which puts his judges in the predicament of actuallly having to condemn him to death as the indictment demands. For as a witness for the truth, he will in this way bring down a punishment on them, so that their wrong will become an awful warning to others. In the words of Aeschylus, it might be said that he thereby places the trial under the veneration that Athenian citizens should display to the gods and the state.

Time and time again, with his superior dialectics, Socrates makes Meletus guilty of contradicting himself, as when he claims for instance that Socrates believes in *daimones* and not gods, even though *daimones* are children of gods. Consequently, Socrates claims that the charge was drawn up "out of sheer wanton aggressiveness and self-assertion" (26 e), which reveals the accuser's youthful folly. So regardless of the outcome, the case will do no harm to him, Socrates, but only to his accusers and judges, because "I do not believe that the law of God permits a better man to be harmed by a worse" (39 d).

As he also claims in the *Gorgias*, it is better to suffer than to do wrong. And we can say that he can safely adopt this attitude in view of the fact that—rooted back in Anaximander's concept of *dike* (p. 315)—he calculates on a universal conception of justice. This is most clearly expressed in the *Theatetus*, in which he says, "In the divine there is no shadow of unrighteousness, only the perfection of righteousness, and nothing is more like the divine than any one of us who becomes as righteous as possible. It is here that a man shows his true spirit and power or lack of spirit and nothingness. For to know this is wisdom and excellence of the genuine sort; not to know it is to be manifestly blind and base" (176 c).

The punishment that will be imposed upon him, which is a "gift from God" (31 a), will consequently rebound on the judges: "I tell you, my executioners, that as soon as I am dead, vengeance shall fall upon you with a punishment far more painful than your killing of me" (39 c). If the judges imagine that they can kill people without standing to account for their actions, they must think again in this case. For in reality, they have accomplished the opposite. They will be accused by younger and stronger forces, since the most honorable thing is not to stop the mouths of others. On the contrary, "the best and easiest way is not to stop the mouths of others, but to make yourselves as good men as you can" (39 d). In short, Socrates sets his conception of self-development against the injustice of which the judges are guilty and maintains here, as in many other passages, that only through the good can a person become himself—and thereby a just citizen.

The quandary in which Socrates places the judges on his own behalf and that of the laws is further emphasized by the fact that he refuses to help them with the case by entering into a compromise. He will not be banished, accept a fine or—like otherwise brave people who, in order to obtain clemency, make themselves pathetic at the hour of judgment—whine about his age or the need to provide for his children. This is not a possibility for him. On the contrary. In his calling by God, he demands that the judges should not break their oath to the laws—"If I tried to persuade you and prevail upon you by my entreaties to go against your solemn oath, I should be teaching you contempt for religion, and by my very defense I should be accusing myself of having no religious belief" (35 d).

Socrates has created for himself such a supreme standpoint in the *Apology* that he can say ironically and teasingly that he is not displaying "deliberate perversity" (37 a), when instead of the death sentence he demands that, for all the good he has done for the state on behalf of the god, he should receive what is appropriate for him as a poor man and benefactor of the state—to be fed at public expense at the Prytaneion. Indeed, he deserves this even more than Olympic winners, as the honor they have provided for Athens is only the external semblance of success, while he provides "the reality" (36 d)—*eudaimonia*—which is the goal and result of the justice he has just been denied.

5

So right up to the hour of judgment and death, Socrates remains the wasp or gadfly he claims that the gods have set upon the horse of the state. As in life, he will to the end follow the god's demand on him that he should be an example of goodness, as he connects Apollo's oracle—that he is the wisest—with the idea that goodness (*arete*, 20 b) and wisdom (*sophia*, 20 d) are one: "virtue is knowledge" (87 c), as it is correspondingly put in the *Meno*. In this way, he is able to disclaim any connection between the charge and the defense. He invalidates both the charge and the sentence through his connection with God, raising himself above the reality from which he is accused and condemned.

In general, it can be maintained that, as Plato presents it, the trial is a concretization of Socrates' calling and personal qualities and a demonstration of the accusers'—and subsequently the judges'—lack of the same morality and reason. By sacrificing his life in the service of the god, he becomes a witness to the truth, who unmasks the injustice of which state officials are guilty. Through this, the philosopher is raised up as an example of one who is persecuted for his love of truth. And around this interpretation, linked to Socrates' death, Plato has fundamentally crystallized his entire oeuvre, as he tries in the *Republic* to translate his ideas into a political utopia based on the self-development of the individual.

With his life and death, Socrates made himself an example of the view that insight is only acquired by *personal* effort. Against this background, his claim that no one does ill against his own will becomes more understandable, for as he says in the *Protagoras*: "For myself I am fairly certain that no wise man believes anyone sins willingly or willingly perpetrates any evil or base act. They know very well that all evil or base action is involuntary" (345 d-e). If we have gained access to the good through our development, we will experience our sense of belonging to it as the supreme happiness. And as this existential state constitutes our identity from then on, it will naturally not be in our own interest to act against it. On the contrary, we will experience the good as a special form of desire, well knowing that "to do wrong and to disobey my superior, whether God or man, is wicked and dishonorable" (*Ap.* 29 b).

This is also his answer to Callicles who, in the *Gorgias*, claimed that happiness consists of the fulfillment of desire—yet another example of how through widely interwoven references the dialogues constitute a unity—with Socrates' death as the pinnacle and focal point.

6

Just as Socrates displayed uncompromising courage while fighting during war, he denies during the trial that it will be possible to silence him. Like Odysseus on his storm-tossed journey, he had to endure many tribulations in his labors on behalf of the god. With direct reference to this, Socrates says, "I want you to think of my adventures as a sort of pilgrimage undertaken to establish the truth of the oracle once for all" (22 a). Hard work is part of his business, and he does not budge an inch.

So neither is it possible for his friends, shortly before the death sentence is carried out, to persuade him to flee, as is described in the *Crito*. His friends feel guilty for not having done more for Socrates, and believe that he will be letting down his family by being executed. Everything is made ready for his escape—and the state, it may be imagined, was prepared to look the other way, as they want both to condemn him and to avoid carrying out the sentence, which could cause unrest among his influential adherents.

But—like Christ in the desert—Socrates resists the temptation, relying on the clarity and peace that he has at the prospect of death, just as his *daimonion* neither protests nor, like his friends, demands that he should flee. He cannot, simply because he is going to die, betray the greater goal he was put into the world to achieve. If he fled, he would descend to the level of his accusers and repay wrong with wrong. The act of fleeing would veil the fact that his judges broke the laws when they condemned him. With his death, on the other hand, he will provide a defense of the laws and save them from their practitioners.

In order to prove that the laws are derived from life, he quite surprisingly personifies them—indeed, he gives them, so to speak, a *daimonic* voice with which he can enter into a dialogue: if he ran away now, the laws would take him to task and among other things justifiably claim that they ensured that his father gave him an education. And as one ought to treat one's parents fairly, so should one treat one's fatherland and its laws in the same way. The state is based on law. Law-breaking would mean the dissolution of the state, one's sacred fatherland. If, on the other hand, they are dissatisfied with the state, everyone is free to settle somewhere else (51 d).

Socrates refers to the fact that he has had seventy years in which to make his considerations and he has been extremely content with the laws and the state. He has brought up his children in this city and he has only left Athens during a military campaign—to preserve the state—and on one other occasion. By fleeing, he would be acting like "the lowest type of menial" (*Cri.* 52 d) who runs away. So he will not and cannot break the laws in accordance with which he has promised to act. Escape would bring no good. On the contrary, it would leave his friends in trouble and expose them to the risk of banishment. At the same time, he would confirm his accusers' claims, violate the laws and corrupt the young, as it has been claimed that he does.

Crito has no answer to these objections. And it may be seen that, even in the shadow of death, Socrates shows that he has internalized the laws as part of his personal faith and piety. As we have already heard in Aeschylus and Sophocles, the laws are an act on the part of the gods—"Olympus only/ is their father,"[46] the chorus says in *Oedipus the King*. And it is in honorable respect for the laws—"the gods' unwritten and unfailing laws"[47] that Antigone sacrifices her young life when she buries her brother in defiance of the king's order. And like Antigone, Socrates has affirmed their divine status by giving his life to maintain the laws. He is able to die happily in the knowledge that, inwardly, he has secured a pact between the state and the laws, which through his reputation can have a retrospective cleansing effect on the punishment he predicts will be inflicted on his judges.

7

On the morning before his execution, Socrates was surrounded by a circle of his friends, as it is described in the *Phaedo*. Plato himself was ill and thus absent. Socrates sends the weeping Xanthippe home. He rubs his bent leg, where the chains have chaffed his skin and concludes that the pain they have inflicted will be replaced by pleasure: "I had a pain in my leg from the fetter, and now I feel the pleasure coming that follows it" (60 c).

He has been in prison for a relatively long time, because the sacred ship must first be sent to Delos and return to Athens before he can be executed. In the interim, he has used the time to translate Aesop's fables into verse, as a dream has prompted him to practice the arts and he believes that philosophy "is the greatest of the arts" (61 a). But as he cannot invent like a real poet, he tackles Aesop instead. He calls himself happy and says that sensible men should follow him soon, though not by suicide, which is forbidden, since they are in the keeping of the gods.

It is also on the basis of his longing to die that Socrates reinterprets the requiem of the swan. The originators of the view that the song sung by swans as they are dying was a song of lament were men who feared death, he claims (85 a-b). In reality, they sing from the happiness and joy of going away to be united with the god in whose service they have been. And this interpretation corresponds to the way in which he himself views his death as a meaningful part of his life's mission, imposed upon him by the gods.

8

Even in his defense speech, Socrates explained why death was no threat to him, but rather a liberation, an ultimate good, which is why fear of death is a deluded concept. Men know nothing of death, which may well be a blessing, "but people dread it as though they were certain that it is the greatest evil, and this is ignorance" (*Ap.* 29 a-b).

He provides a good-humored, even humorous elaboration of this view in the *Phaedo* in conversation with his despairing friends. He tries to comfort them in his last hours by proving the existence of the power that conquers the impending death he faces—the immortality of the soul. He makes use of a dichotomy that quite simply states that contradictions cannot absorb and contain each other: "The opposites themselves do not admit one another, but it also looks as though any things which, though not themselves opposites, always have opposites in them, similarly do not admit the opposite form to that which is in them, but on its approach either cease to exist or retire before it" (104 b–c).

If one then asks what must be added to the body so it can have life, the answer is the soul. And since life and death are opposites, it must necessarily follow that the soul as life cannot be united with death. Therefore, it is immortal. This is a notion that is also linked to a cyclical idea as the soul and life must arise from death just as death arises from the living: "So if they are opposites, they come from one another, and have their two processes of generation between the two of them?" (71 c). And so on ad infinitum.

And just as the soul forms a contrast to death, so does the soul to the body to which it gives life but which, as a body, falls within the domain of death. In death, the body returns in its dissolution, while on the other hand the soul, as a life that moves in itself, is liberated from the prison house or sepulchre of the body, as it is put in the *Phaedrus* (250 c). The expression reveals that, in his interpretation of immortal life, Plato had derived inspiration from the Orphics (he mentions the Orphic poet Musaios, *Rep.* 363 c) and the Pythagoreans, in that they had established a metaphorical link between *soma* = body and *sema* = grave (*Gorg.* 493 a). Characteristically, Socrates himself takes this link as an etymological fact in the *Cratylus* (400 b–c).

So if death is so coveted by the philosopher and the reasonable person, the explanation must be found primarily in the fact that the soul is liberated from the world of the senses and the body in which it is of necessity incorporated as an organ of knowledge, but the impulses and desires of which disturb the soul in its erotically-determined quest. Socrates expresses his view in this way: "We are in fact convinced that if we are ever to have pure knowledge of anything, we must get rid of the body and contemplate things by themselves with the soul by itself. It seems, to judge from the argument, that the wisdom which we desire and upon which we profess to have set our hearts will be attainable only when we are dead, and not in our lifetime" (66 d–e).

If the soul is thus liberated from the body in death, it will move of its own volition towards that which always exists. This corresponds to the knowledge that the philosopher seeks in life by recalling or awakening images lodged in memory from this earlier life, which is the basis for the immortality and autonomy of the soul.

9

As it is the individual's greatest task in life to care for himself as a consequence of the immortality of the soul, death cannot be definitive. This means that death for "the wicked" (107 c) will simply be a boon, as in this case they will be liberated not only from their bodies but also from their spiritual wickedness. After death, there must logically be a judgment on the life we have lived, and after this we are taken to the place assigned in the judgment by the *daimon* of our life, as Socrates explains in the *Phaedo*. In the *Republic*, on the other hand, we must ourselves choose our *daimon* after death.

The *daimon* that is assigned to everyone as a protector in life does not immediately correspond to Socrates' own *daimonic* voice—or does it? In any event, Plato's view of a person's *daimon* seems to correspond to Heraclitus' assertion that our character is our *daimon*. The *daimon* thus becomes the sum of the choices in life that the individual has made and now after death must stand to account for. Thus, this *daimon* has the status of a *psychopomp* like Hermes: "When any man dies, his own guardian spirit, which was given charge over him in his life, tries to bring him to a certain place where all must assemble, and from which, after submitting their several cases to judgment, they must set out for the next world, under the guidance of one who has the office of escorting souls from this world to the other" (107 d-e).

After a judgment on their life is pronounced, souls are led to the places due to them. The soul "that has lived throughout its life in purity and soberness enjoys divine company and guidance" (108 c), while impure souls, that is to say those who have been guided by their body and desire in all sense of the words, are led back to cave-like places beneath the earth, and the greatest criminals are taken to Tartaros. Plato's description of the *katabasis* is clearly inspired by Odysseus' journey to Hades, to which he also refers in the *Gorgias* (526 d), where, among other things, there is mention of the punishment of Sisyphos (525 e).[48]

10

Yet, with a little smile, Socrates must acknowledge that his friends have probably derived little from his speech on caring for their souls—for their own sakes and for his. For Crito now asks him how he wants to be buried. But just as Socrates did not fundamentally love Alcibiades in his physical shape but loved his soul (or, rather, his soul's potential to be as beautiful as his exterior), then it is not Socrates who will die but only his body—his soul will continue in immortal life. They can bury his body as they will and in conformity with custom. His true self will "depart to a state of heavenly happiness" (115 d) after he has drunk the deadly poison.

His longing is now so directed towards the life beyond that he rejects his friends' attempts to persuade him—like other condemned men—to drag out the time. He will not be made a fool of by hanging on to a life in which nothing remains: "Whether I was right in this ambition, and whether we have achieved anything, we shall know for certain, if God wills, when we reach the other world, and that, I imagine will be fairly soon" (69 d). But first he wants to take a bath in order to save the women the inconvenience of washing his corpse.

After the bath, he takes leave of his three sons and female relatives, which must mean that Xanthippe has returned from their home to the prison. They are sent away, and a slave summons the executioner with the cup of poison. Socrates is not allowed to sacrifice to the gods from the drink as the fatal dose is measured precisely. However, he is allowed to pray for a smooth passage to the other side and calmly empties the cup. In order to spread the poison throughout his body, he walks around until he feels heavy; then, he lies down on the bench with a cloth over his face. When the lower part of his body has become stiff and cold, he moves the cloth to one side and exclaims to Crito: "We ought to offer a cock to Asclepius. See to it, and don't forget" (118 a). These are his final words. He makes no reply when Crito asks whether anything else should be done. Spasms go through his body. Crito closes his eyes and mouth.

But why Asclepios? That question has been asked almost ever since. It is obviously not enough to say that Asclepios, the god of healing, was the son of Apollo. One possible solution to the puzzle could be this: from the way in which Socrates thinks about life and death, body and soul, his idea at the moment of death seems to be simply that, just as Asclepios with his healing potions can provide cures in life, he can—as in Socrates' case—provide a cure for life with his deadly potion. In death, he will finally achieve the clarity of vision that life inevitably blocks by virtue of the distractions deriving from the life of the senses. As an immortal soul, he will be reunited with the world of pure knowledge in which he existed prior to his incarnation in this difficult life on earth.

As the poison spreads, it kills the body, limb by limb, so to speak, thereby successively liberating the soul. With the help of the poison and Asclepios, the final barrier is removed to the liberation of the soul, and Socrates can go over into the absolute, coveted existence—and die into Plato's writings with all the significance he has had ever since.

His character at the end of the *Phaedo* is summarized in this way: "of all those whom we knew in our time, the bravest and also the wisest and most upright man" (118 a). In the *Apology*, he himself said, "This present experience of mine has not come about mechanically" (41 d). This must have been partly to comfort those of his judges who voted to acquit him, but also in order to place his death within an overall purpose that gives it a higher meaning. He has now definitively put his life in the hands of the god who called him, Apollo, and he knows that the gods will not let him down any more than they did in life (41 d).

This clarity speaking and radiating from Socrates is very reminiscent of the strength and certainty with which Oedipus met his death at Colonus, convinced that he knew Apollo's intention in his story of sufferings: that, sanctified, he should become a protector of Athens. Similarly, it can be said that, with his death, Socrates fulfills what he saw as his mission: to show the path towards truth and knowledge. Thus, like Oedipus, he can become the exponent of the more just state he imagines and which Plato outlines in utopian form in the *Republic*.

The Utopian State

1

On the basis of the story of Socrates' fate, Plato—by putting the words into Socrates' mouth—can establish his utopian state, which does not put the just to death but on the contrary appoints wisdom-loving philosophers as rulers. But let it be said immediately that this concept of the state is to be seen primarily as a framework around the development of the soul. The state is ultimately an analogy, yet another of Plato's myths. Admittedly, it is indicated along the way in the *Republic* that such a state has a future—"It is not a thing impossible to happen, nor are we speaking of impossibilities" (499 d). But at the same time, it is made clear that a new state can arise in a very different way, as it cannot be proved that something must "be realized in deed as it is spoken in word" (473 a).

When all comes to all, Plato does not hide the fact that this state is primarily a beautiful fantasy. For when Glaucon expresses his skepticism, arguing that a state of this sort is inconceivable on earth, Socrates answers, "Perhaps there is a pattern of it laid up in heaven for him who wishes to contemplate it and so beholding to constitute himself its citizen. But it makes no difference whether it exists now or ever will come into being" (592 b).

Perhaps Socrates can be so nonchalant about the utopian state he has just established because he is not really talking about an external but an internal constitution, something that is emphasized by his speaking, as in the *Gorgias*, of the cosmic order of the soul. It is quite a different matter that the existing state could be saved if its citizens were to put themselves in order through dialectic self-development. This would re-create the justice that is the starting point of the dialogue, with Socrates' unjust death as its implicit background. At the same time, it would refute Thrasymachus' tyrannical statement that the just is "the advantage of the stronger" (339 a).

2

An interpretation of the utopian state will throw light on Plato's political ideas, his criticism of the existing constitution and the connection between the life of the soul and the morality (*arete*) he believes it is necessary to re-establish, taking Socrates as his example. And as he assumes an analogy between state and soul, he is able to place Athenian democracy analytically within a historical succession that—with the corruption of the changing political forms of government as its parameter—is reminiscent of Hesiod's different ages. It can be paraphrased briefly as follows:

The oldest, and a good and just regime, was aristocracy or kingship, insofar as a single person was at the head. This was a social order that, as the name implies, was looked after by "the best" (*aristoi*).

What in Plato's eyes was an ideal form of state going far back in time was lost when a conflict among the rulers and a certain laxness in observing the laws gradually arose. Community of property was dissolved and the military took over, as was known in Sparta and on Crete. Goodness and wisdom were no longer given the highest priority, being replaced by honor, which is why this form of government is known as timocracy, derived from *time*, honor.

According to Socrates/Plato, conflict was automatically embedded in this form of government as the quest for wealth became an obsession. This led to a new constitution of the state, oligarchy, which is characterized by the fact that the rulers were taken from the propertied class—something that by the nature of things led to class division, an upper class and an underclass, in which the rich are made even richer at the cost of the poor. The poor reacted partly with criminality and partly by provoking war and revolution with help from outside. And when they had conquered the propertied class, confiscated their property and driven them out of the country, they introduced democracy, the free constitution, the rights of the people.

Ironically, however, the tyrant arises in the course of this, a figure who exploits the prevailing freedom to usurp power and wealth. The political reality is that democracy risks turning straight into tyranny, which in Plato's opinion has already happened. For it is actually on the basis of such a tyrannical form of government that Callicles and Thrasymachus argue in making the law of the strong the supreme justice.

3

There are psychological parallels to these stages in the process of political development: the aristocratic and just type is based on reason, while the extreme contrast—the tyrant—follows his instinctive life of the subconscious known as "the beastly and savage part" (571 c) of the soul. This world of desire reveals its tyranny by making the person a slave. The interesting thing is that Plato has by analogy identified the instinctive life with dream visions that are communicated in sleep, when daytime consciousness is switched off. This whole oceanic, criminal world of desires erupts with the dream and demands fulfillment. For as Socrates says to Glaucon: "You are aware that in such case there is nothing it will not venture to undertake as being released from all sense of shame and all reason. It does not shrink from attempting to lie with a mother in fancy or with anyone else, man, god, or brute. It is ready for any foul deed of blood; it abstains from no food, and, in a word, falls short of no extreme of folly and shamelessness" (571 c-d).

It is this subconscious world of dreams that is played out and adapted in the tragedies in order to gain insight and empathetic *katharsis*. In a corrupt political system, on the other hand, where justice no longer rules, the tyrannical soul will force through its desires, the manifestation of the superman, in favor of which Callicles argues in the mistaken belief that in this way he will find supreme happiness. This makes Socrates state: "The son of Ariston pronounced the best man and the most righteous to be the happiest, and that he is the one who is the most kingly and a king over himself, and declared that the most evil and most unjust is the most unhappy, who again is the man who, having the most of the tyrannical temper in himself, becomes most of a tyrant over himself and over the state" (580 b-c).

It goes without saying that the replacement of such a tyrannical form of government and consciousness cannot come from outside but must, as Socrates' whole endeavor illustrates, come from within. As it is put directly: "It is better for everyone to be governed by the divine and the intelligent, preferably indwelling and his own, but in default of that imposed from without, in order that we all so far as possible may be akin and friendly because our governance and guidance are the same" (590 d). We can trace this idea back to the conclusion of the *Odyssey* in which Odysseus must live amicably with the families of the suitors and in the eunomia that Solon makes the program for his state and which is found again in the final words of the *Oresteia* about loving one another.[49]

It is here that philosopher is to enter as the supreme guardian of the state. He is to lead souls back to the cosmic order they have lost but still possess as potential memory and which is presupposed in the interaction between state, soul and universality. The condition is that both become like a *tabula rasa*, cleansed of earlier blemishes, a process headed by the philosophers but which Socrates acknowledges is not easy to manage.

In a contrary approach to the political agenda, its peculiar blend of democracy and tyranny, the basis is sketched out for the way in which the state can undergo this transformation. A graduated plan is established for the education of the future guardians of the state. I will not go into the contents and duration of this education in detail but instead concentrate on describing the required form of knowledge and its constant combination of polity and psychological reality.

4

The idea is that a future state must be governed by three social classes. At the head must be the philosophers, kings, who in their quest for knowledge and renunciation of earthly goods are to govern the realm with the help of the next class, the warriors. Together, these two classes constitute the guardians. To ensure that they watch over the interests of the state unselfishly, they must undergo a long process of education. Among other things this includes gymnastics on the basis of the idea we have already touched on that a healthy society demands a healthy soul in a healthy body. Poetry and music contribute to the edification of the soul, though, as said above, Plato is very restrictive concerning poetry as a source of education. Any frivolity to gods and men must be avoided. And in Book 10 this ends with the banishment of poets from the future ideal state.

The process of selection of the guardians will be too complicated to explore. But although Plato regards war as an unnecessary evil created by an unjust state, he nevertheless incorporates the militant training in (self)discipline through which the guardians must go between the ages of 35 and 50. Everything must be done in common in order to prevent private considerations from replacing considerations of state and the general welfare. Not until they reach the age of 50 can they be selected as leaders who during this long process have proved themselves to be true lovers of wisdom, that is to say philosophers, who from their inner enlightenment govern the state in the period during which they are compelled to participate in social life. This compulsion is a necessary and bitter duty, as at heart they want to dedicate themselves to the philosophical life. Finally, there is the third social class of the craftsmen, whose job is to take care of the state's practical and economical life.

Analogically, it is possible to view the state and its strucure as images of the soul's own function and constitution. The social classes and their functions can quite simply be compared with the topography of the body: the craftsmen correspond to the lower part of the body (and the desires), the warriors to the breast and the courage of the heart, while the leaders, the philosopher kings, are placed in the center behind the forehead.

We have already observed this tripartite division of the soul in the *Phaedrus*, where the soul is described as a chariot. Here in the *Republic*, it is described as a sphinx-like creature, consisting of a person, a lion and a many-headed beast (588 d–589 b). The interpretation is that with the aid of the lion's physical strength human beings are to secure themselves against becoming victim to the ignoble nature of the many-headed beast. Plato's psychological definition of the soul's tripartite structure—reason, will and desire—is perhaps reminiscent of Freud's model of the structure of the psyche with the conscience-determined superego, the mediating ego and the amorphous, libidinous id. In Plato, the idea is that the will comes to the aid of reason when the world of desire threatens to take over, just as the lion with its strength tries to support the human being.

5

Throughout the Platonic texts, Socrates' life and work are the ultimate testament to the development of consciousness and soul that is required to become a leader. If we look more closely at this process, it is best exemplified by the famous image of the cave at the beginning of Book 7. Socrates relates that human beings find themselves prisoners in the darkness of the cave, bound hand and foot, incapable of distinguishing the ideal from the phenomenal world. Caught in the illusions of the elementary senses, they apprehend the shadows of things that are projected from behind them on to the cave wall before them as the true reality. Insight into this deception requires them to turn around and, in the sun's own light, shift their sense of sight away from this delusion.

Genetically, the reason why men find themselves in this state of bondage, as described in the *Phaedrus*, is that, at the dawn of time, the soul tried to find its bearings in its surroundings. As a result, it was captured by material, fell and lost the wings supporting the soul and also its original clarity of vision. In this sense, the cave represents the psychological reality into which the soul has sunk: a sensual world of body and desire, sightless and devoid of any sense of the highest things and the truth. That some individuals can even happen on the idea of turning toward the light is because, like Socrates himself, they have a powerful impulse or actual calling that makes them seek the good. Such people must more strongly than others have retained the feeling of the inner spark from divine creation that makes them recall the knowledge that then raises them up towards the light of the inner vision.

6

In order to explain further the conversion of vision that is a prerequisite for dawning cognition, Plato has to introduce the image of the sun—as a contrast to the cave. It takes power to turn imprisoned souls away from the shadows which they view as real and relinquish only reluctantly, as it at first hurts the eyes to stare into the sun's insight-providing source of light. Indeed, it is so strong that people must become accustomed to it by looking at things as reflections, for example, in water, before they can endure catching glimpses of the sun itself.

If it is at all possible to look at the sun and, by its light, see and come to recognise sensible phenomena as they really are, it is because the sun by hypostatization has created the concrete world, including the human eye. And because of this similarity with the sun, the eye can truly see and observe things in their true essence. But the sun is not only the creator of the world. It is itself created—by goodness, which gives "birth in the visible world to light, and the author of light and itself in the intelligible world" (517 c).[50]

On the one hand, this must imply that the good as a force of creation is simply identical with God and on the other hand that even the world of the senses, conceived as it is by the sun and thus also by the goodness of God, is an emanation of this divinity. This is really confirmed by Diotima when she describes how the appreciation of the highest *arete* is awakened by the sight of a beautiful (boy's) body. In other words, Plato is not a dualist like Parmenides. Rather the opposite. He assumes that the world of the senses is derived from and bears traces of the divine. To regain this lost vision will, of course, require a dialectical process that, with a starting point in the veiled world of things, moves consciously toward the highest stage, the "beholding" as it was called in the *Symposium*. So the philosophical quest must really be a form of re-emanation via the upward-striving force of *eros*. And in their love of knowledge, "philosophy", philosophers become the designated leaders of the new state.

7

Like Socrates, these philosopher kings must live without external luster, so they do not, like tyrants, fall into the temptation of seizing property by virtue of their great power. Another feature is that those who have seen the light will desire to remain permanently in that elevated state, as the philosophical life is a purely inner matter. So this is where their responsibility to the state comes in. As a sort of national duty, they must be motivated—not to say forced—back into the instinctual darkness of the cave and educate people to seek the true light, now that they themselves can understand the difference between the illusory image and the reality of which it is a shadow. In this way, it is said, "Our city will be governed by us and you with waking minds, and not as most cities now which are inhabited and ruled darkly as in a dream by men who fight one another for shadows and wrangle for office as if that were a great good" (520 c-d).

Yet, Socrates does not conceal what awaits the philosopher in his more or less forced return to the darkness of the cave. He who now prophesies the truth of the light will be received with laughter and mocked by the prisoners in the cave, who in their delusory sagacity claim that he has had his eyes ruined by all that sunlight. And if he attempts to liberate them from their spiritual prison, they will not hesitate to kill him—"If it were possible to lay hands on and to kill the man who tried to release them and lead them up, would they not kill him?" (517 a).

The question is rhetorical and, from Socrates' narrative position, prophetic, as Plato anticipates what Socrates himself will be subjected to in his attempt to turn the citizens of Athens towards the light. Properly speaking, he is sentenced to death because he ascended from the cave in its comprehensive metaphoric meaning, became a "beholder" and later took it upon himself as his life's work to proclaim it—as a *daimonic* emissary from the god of light and consciousness, Apollo. Socrates tried to bring the sunlight down into the darkness of illusions and enlighten the arrogant self-perception of the ruling classes in Athens during a period of decadence. And so he himself appears as a solar hero, but in contrast to Odysseus, he is sacrificed on the altar of darkness.

8

With the philosopher king, Plato tries to hearken back to the aristocratic form of government and *arete*, but in such a radically different way that what is external at that time—courage and beauty—has now become something internal. A new state must be governed by these inner values—insight, justice, etc.—in short, the cardinal virtues. That this was a *utopian* project in political terms, however, is emphasized by the fact that Plato wrote *The Laws* shortly before his death, a work far more pragmatic in conception and containing concrete proposals on wealth, state administration, marriage, education, punishment, etc. However, I want to concentrate on pursuing further the line of thought that after all ultimately derives from the *Republic*, showing that Plato's utopian goal had much in common with those of Homer and Solon—of projecting a state *eunomia* on the basis of peace and toleration among law-abiding citizens.

The person who, in a form almost of the monologue, presents the work's main points is no longer Socrates but an anonymous Athenian. This Athenian is staying on Crete, conversing with a man from Crete and one from Sparta. However, his ideas are so closely related to those with which we are already familiar from the other dialogues they both reveal Plato to be their true originator and demonstrate the uniformity of his writings. The three classes from the *Republic* have certainly been abandoned; but to ensure the laws a group of so-called guardians of the laws is introduced instead, a self-supplementing secret society, which possesses the right way of thinking and meets at dawn, "the time above all others when a man is always freest from all other business, private or public" (961 b).

It is also the task of the guardians of the laws through the laws to ensure the goodness which is still the general aim of the state—"all the gold on earth or under earth is no equal exchange for goodness" (728 a). And as happened in the presumably early dialogue *Protagoras*, the content of goodness is also discussed here with reference to the cardinal virtues. As before, the long and the short of it is that it is a case of understanding the unity of the manifold nature of the virtues, since what creates the unity is the underlying goodness, which ultimately must be God, the objective of all things. For as it is stated explicitly, "It is God who is, for you and me, of a truth the 'measure of all things', much more truly than, as they say, 'man.'" (716 c). Of course, this contains a hidden reference to and protest against Protagoras' slogan, cited directly by Socrates in the *Theatetus*: "Man is the measure of all things" (152 a). And just as he pointed out the divine origin of the laws in the *Crito*, it is also a fundamental idea here that the gods are served by the laws, since the laws derive from the gods.

9

It might be said that the laws actually represent a sort of process of recall of a happy past that should be imitated when laws are drafted. This hearkens back to the epoch in which Kronos (as is also related in *The Statesman*) governed and placed good *daimones* as shepherds to watch over mankind. He did this in recognition of the fact that people cannot tolerate power without being struck by arrogance. The peace and order created by the *daimones* constitute divine happiness, which is to be imitated in and through legislation. So the rulers must be servants of the laws in their original divinity. They must not promulgate new laws that trample those of the gods underfoot for their own power and profit.

At the same time, it is Plato's view that arrogance will be punished by God. This means that here, like Socrates in the *Apology*, he assumes an immanent divine justice: "Where the law is overruled or obsolete, I see destruction hanging over the community; where it is sovereign over the authorities and they its humble servants, I discern the presence of salvation and every blessing heaven sends on a society" (715 d).

That for Plato, as for Homer and Solon, it is ultimately a matter of allowing peace to take the place of war is apparent from the very premise of *The Laws*. Here, the Athenian turns to his interlocutors, who as a Spartan and Cretan respectively represent a political system with a military-based constitution. The objective here is to acquire skills in war, where a poet such as Tyrtaeus, as we heard (see p. 302), set bravery in battle, man against man, above all other human qualities.

The point of the Athenian's speech about peace—on the basis of the analogy between state and soul that is continued from the *Republic*—is that it is not a matter of promoting bravery at the cost of the other virtues, but balancing it with justice and temperance (*sophrosyne*). For the overall utopian goal is that war—as in the *Odyssey*—can be concluded in peaceful reconciliation, which makes everything blossom in happiness and friendship.

10

One interesting aspect of *The Laws* is the Athenian's account of how a state achieves such a *eunomia*. Here, Dionysos is attributed with central importance.

In *The Bacchae*, Teiresias had recommended that the young king should incorporate Dionysos into the life of the state, because so much new vitality and wisdom accompanied this divinity. The king's misfortune was that he did not listen to this advice. At the same time, Euripides himself indirectly recommended that the irrational should be revitalized in Athenian public life in order to overcome its crisis in values. What Euripides did not say explicitly, Plato puts into words. Not only does he give women equal rights in his utopian state, but in *The Laws* he also stresses how necessary it is for Dionysos to function in society along with Apollo.

Thus, he envisions how people after the day's "hardships" (653 d) can rest and regain their strength through dancing and singing in honor of these two gods—"with all the spiritual sustenance these deities bring to the feast" (653 d). Dance and the magic of choral songs are part of the formation of "a just and religious life" (663 b), it is further stated, which implies that these artistic forms of expression help ensure the order and stability of the state.

However, in Plato's experience, it appears that people become both more reticent with age and less inclined to appear in choruses. It is here that Dionysos and wine can inspire spiritual life. On the other hand, young people must not enjoy wine because they are weaker and in their natural enthusiasm have no need of such stimulants. Not until people approach forty should wine be drunk, invoking Dionysos, as "a comfortable medicine against the dryness of old age, that we might renew our youth, and our harsher mood be melted to softness" (666 b).

A state that is thus pervaded with song and dance, performed in festive fellowship by young and old alike in this way, will by the nature of things become peaceful and musical in contrast to the militant state of Sparta. We shall not go further into this except to say that, like Euripides, Plato sees the well-being of the state linked to the activation of the Dionysian life-force. On the basis of this same way of thinking, Plato tries to abolish the animosity towards women, with whom the figure of Dionysos is so closely associated, and to see them as equal, spiritual beings. It is also on this basis explicable that he condemns homosexuality as contrary to nature, as it defines women as a corporally bound negation, exactly as we heard in the *Symposium*.

11

In a spectacular historical retrospective, Plato (as in the *Timaeus*) provides an account of how existing civilization and its laws have arisen. Possibly inspired by the myth of how Zeus launched a flood on the world to punish the wicked people of the Bronze Age, in which, as in the case of Noah, only Prometheus' son Deukalion and his wife were saved on an ark, Plato imagines that there existed a highly developed human world which was destroyed in a catastrophe reminiscent of the Fall of Man. Only mountain shepherds survived, and they lived long without hostility. But gradually larger social groups were formed, requiring rulers and laws, and they began to make war upon each other, each with their own view of the law.

Plato saw the Trojan War as a part of this catastrophic series of events: "Now during this period of ten years while Ilium was under investment, occurred the various domestic misfortunes of the different besiegers, occasioned by the insurrectionary movements of the younger generation. Moreover, when the warriors returned to their cities and families, the reception they met at the hands of these young men was neither honorable nor equitable, but attended with numerous instances of homicide, massacre, and expulsion" (682 d–e).

In this condensed historical perspective, it could be claimed that, in developing the figure of Odysseus and his victory over the forces of chaos in the shape of the suitors, Homer tried to create a cessation in the dynamic of war, sanctioned by the highest gods, Zeus and Athene. Partly on the basis of the death of Socrates, brought about by unjust and tyrannical powerful figures, Plato can conclude that strife will remain a chronic condition unless a new being emerges, developed from within in pious obedience to the gods, the laws and its own inner self. Socrates was always his image of such a person, while at the same time Odysseus is the hidden ideal behind his figure, just as Homer is that behind Plato himself.

The Fulfillment of the Prefiguration

1

It seems an undeniably ironical paradox that, on the one hand, Plato renounces Homer's poetry, because it fosters an illusory reality but, on the other hand, uses the Homeric epics himself to provide ever greater perspective for the interpretation of character, creating a comprehensive totality in the dialogues through which to achieve an exemplary amplification of his own thought. There was a tradition for this sort of interpretative practice, as the Sophists largely incorporated the heroes of the past into their teaching, but as part of a superficial, pedantic instruction.

In Plato's interpretation, Socrates clearly does things entirely differently. For just as he understood how to internalize the laws, he appropriates the earlier mythical figures in a form of imitation, which he can recollect, and through which he can identify his own situation in life. This of course corresponds to the ability of knowledge to reawaken the memory of the lost world of the gods. Indeed, it can even be said that the doctrine of immortality itself promotes the idea of prefiguration by creating a lasting sense of the potential presence of the dead.

So Socrates looks forward after his death not only to meeting the wise gods but also people who preceded him and who are better than those living now (*Phaedo* 63 b). He does not indicate in the *Phaedo* whom he has in mind but in his defense speech he mentions the just judges of an earlier age, those who in contrast to his own judges adjudicated in the name of truth, including King Minos. But he also longed to meet the great poets Homer and Hesiod and, among the heroes, Odysseus (*Ap.* 41 c). In addition, he invokes Achilleus as an example of his own steadfastness. That is to say that in his self-understanding he surreptitiously uses the opposition in the Homeric poems between the representative of force, *bia*, represented by Achilleus, and spiritual strength, *metis*, embodied by Odysseus. In collaboration with his *daimonion*, these configurations come to constitute examples to be followed, taking them over not passively but in a synergetic interaction.

2

If he were to flee from death and thereby the task the god had laid upon him, it would be like saying that the heroes who had fought and fallen at Troy were merely to be considered losers, claims Socrates. And he points to Achilleus, who was unable to act dishonourably. He therefore chose death when his mother informed him that it would be the certain consequence if he killed Hektor to avenge Patroklos' death: "He made light of his death and danger, being much more afraid of an ignoble life and of failing to avenge his friends" (*Ap.* 28 c–d). Diotima also uses Achilleus' vengeance as an example of the immortal reputation as a lover that he thereby wished to attain (*Symp.* 208 d).

In this sense, Achilleus is made into an ideal figure and a role model for a courage accepting death for the cause he defends. Socrates himself had done this in his defense of Athens during the war, and he does it now as Apollo's champion. And during his trial Socrates makes direct reference to Achilleus and his own steadfastness in the war: "The truth of the matter is this, gentlemen. Where a man has once taken up his stand, either because it seems best to him or in obedience to his orders, there I believe he is bound to remain and face the danger, taking no account of death or anything else before dishonor" (*Ap.* 28 d).

Socrates even brings in Achilleus with regard to the journey to the realm of the dead he faces. The night before Crito attempts to persuade him to escape from prison—that is, three days before his execution—he dreams, as described above, that a beautiful, stately woman in white robes says to him: "'To the pleasant land of Phthia on the third day thou shalt come'" (*Crito* 44 b).

Surprisingly, the woman in the dream alludes to the line in the *Iliad* (IX, 363) in which Achilleus threatens in anger to leave Troy, thinking that with a good wind he can reach his beloved native land on the third day. The dream is associated with the fact that in a few days Socrates will reach his homeland—in this case, the place in the realm of the dead where he belongs after his battle, not against Troy, but against the Athenian authorities who have treated him so badly—as the Greeks did Achilleus. After sacrificing his life in the service of the god, it is Phthia that awaits him, a "pure abode" (*Phaedo* 114 c).

The mythology of the scenario acts here as a topos for the spiritual homeland, a heavenly Athens, perhaps, which, in contrast to the earthly Athens, will accept him. Consequently, the woman of whom he dreams must be a messenger from that place in which goodness and wisdom rule through an incarnation of Metis or Sophia. She thereby also becomes the honoring of female insight of which Diotima is a prefiguration, just as the moon-like Penelope had been as the goal for Odysseus' longing for home as Athene of course the divine configuration of his supreme consciousness.

3

Odysseus is without doubt the mythical heroic figure with whose sufferings on his voyage home, personal development and great ability of understanding Socrates most often identifies himself in the dialogues.

For Socrates' disciple Antisthenes and his school of Cynics, Odysseus (together with Herakles) also became an ideal for endurance, wisdom and the humility that lay in his transformation into a beggar among the suitors. However, Antisthenes' use of Odysseus is different from that of Socrates, as Antisthenes advocated a purely voluntaristic form of life—that is to say that like the Sophists he used the mythical models for the formation of will without true reflection. In contrast, Socrates meditatively appropriated Odysseus as a paradigm of knowledge he was able to encounter as a divine power and demand within himself.

As said above, it is difficult to determine where Socrates ends and Plato begins, but Socrates may be at his clearest in his use of the Odysseus figure. For that it is certainly Socrates himself, not Plato, who finds his spiritual reflection and forefather in Odysseus can be inferred from the fact that Xenophon also says that Socrates incorporated Odysseus into his dialogues and self-understanding. Thus, for example, Socrates depicts Odysseus "a sure speaker" (*asphale retora*),[51] as capable as himself of conducting a logical discourse from truth to truth.

The remarkable feature is that this quotation actually comes from the scene in the *Odyssey* in which the Phaiakian king mocks Odysseus, who then brusquely points out that outer and inner far from always correspond to each other. One person may be divinely beautiful but foolish; another unimpressive, yet "the god puts comeliness on his words, and they who look toward *him/* are filled with joy at the sight" (8, 170-71). Socrates is himself just such a figure. And from this perspective, it can actually be claimed that Odysseus not only anticipates the idea of spiritual beauty, independent of the external, but from his own experience, later symbolized by his transformation into a beggar, he points out that the crucial thing is what a human being possesses by way of truth and value. Like Odysseus, Socrates is a royal self in rags, guided and enlightened by his search for truth and the overall goal of his life, while his accusers and judges, like the suitors, harbor darkness deep within their souls.

4

In our reading of Homer, a central point was that Odysseus had insight into and, thus, control over the demands of his instincts, raised above hunger and thirst. So he alone from his ship's crew returned home. Consequently, his homecoming could be read as an image of the power of the spirit over the body, just as Socrates demonstrates his spiritual strength by controlling the physical. According to Xenophon, Socrates claimed that—with a little help from Hermes—Odysseus was able to resist Kirke and was not transformed into a pig because he did not fall for the temptation to over-eat.[52] Socrates himself never crossed the line, although he did not shrink from drinking or eating. We have heard that he could drink everyone under the table without himself becoming drunk, that he could walk bare-footed over ice and resist Alcibiades' attempts at seduction. Self-control, of course, requires that the soul should be made as independent of the life of the body as possible.

When, face to face with death, Socrates explains to his friends why the soul is a force independent of the body, Simmias, filled with skepticism, asks whether body and soul do not belong together and are tuned in the same way as a lyre and its strings (*Phaedo* 85 e-86 d). Socrates says no and refers to how, in Book 20, Odysseus experiences a rush of anger at the sight of his faithless maidservants and is on the verge of murdering them. Instead, he calms himself with a psychological effort I have described as possibly the first expression of an introspective spiritual instance in Homer—and Odysseus: "He struck himself on the chest and spoke to his heart and scolded it:/ 'Bear up, my heart. You have had worse to endure before this'" (20, 17-18).

With specific reference to this passage, Socrates proves that the soul is something entirely on its own and not the companion of "physical feelings" (*Phaedo* 94 e). The soul is simply of a far superior nature than the harmony that must exist between the lyre and its strings. And he uses the same quotation in the *Republic* (390 d) as an illustration of the reason that is an indispensable necessity if the state is to become an orderly, fertile place, an external manifestation of goodness.

5

As quoted above, as proof that he has seen a model human being in Odysseus, Socrates during the trial summarizes the sufferings and development to which he has been subjected on his journey towards knowledge. There is a clear allusion here to Odysseus who, hard tested by his mission, went in great torment (see quotation, p. 543). Throughout the dialogues' intricately ramified network of references, the words correspond to Alcibiades' direct comparison between Socrates and Odysseus, when he describes Socrates' courage and endurance during the war. What "our valiant hero [endured] and did" (*Symp.* 220 c, trans. note: diverging from Joyce's trans. to echo Lattimore's), he says, quoting from Book 4 of the *Odyssey* (242). That is to say that Socrates was not only able to derive his view of self-control from Odysseus, but could also, in his sufferings, mirror his own status as an outcast, as he himself strongly emphasized that a life without trials is no life.[53]

Socrates also identified himself with Odysseus on his journey to Hades when his friends in the *Symposium* made their speeches for Eros (see p. 510). As said there, the purpose of this metaphor was to show that his friends' thoughts were an expression of pure illusion, as a result of which they only possessed a sort of dead soul without a share in the true mystery of love, to which Socrates then initiates them through Diotima.

How important this conception was for Socrates/Plato appears from the fact that we actually find a parallel situation in the *Protagoras*. The situation here, as retold by Socrates, is that, while he was at the home of the wealthy Callias, who provided accommodation for the Sophists (and was said to have been ruined as a result), he met the greatest of them, Protagoras, and his circle of disciples, including two other well-known Sophists, Hippias of Elis and Prodikos of Ceos. Once again, Socrates describes the encounter within the framework of Book 11 of the *Odyssey*, the descent into Hades, in which he sees himself directly as Odysseus and uses his formulations as more or less obscure references to the Sophists. Thus, Protagoras is compared to Sisyphos, the greatest of all liars, and Prodikos to Tantalos. Addressing the latter, Socrates speaks Odysseus' words: "And I saw Tantalos, also" (11, 582).

That is to say that the leading Sophists are not only reduced in this way to liars and criminals but also, like the speakers in the *Symposium*, despite all their knowledge, to mere shadows of the dead. They have no real insight and so exist in the cave world of the realm of the dead, which Socrates dedicated his life to enlightening with his search for wisdom (see the image of the cave in the *Republic*). Similarly, we can draw the inference that Socrates can only use Odysseus as his reflected image because he attributes the life of wisdom to him.

And precisely at the conclusion of the *Republic*, we have the strongest evidence that Odysseus in Socrates'—and Plato's—interpretation attained possession of his insight and consequently constitutes an exemplary image. Socrates describes here how Odysseus makes choices after his death and arrival in the realm of the dead. Whereas the *Phaedo* maintained that souls at their birth receive a *daimon* distributed by the gods, it is now said that the souls themselves after death must choose a new *daimon*, which, according to the doctrine of reincarnation, they must take with them in their next life. Far more *daimones* are available than there are dead souls. In short, there are plenty to choose from, so everyone should be able to be satisfied with their choice, regardless of their choice number. For they choose by lottery— that is, on the basis of an overarching principle of fate, guided by necessity's goddesses of fate. Nevertheless, the individual's choice as such is free.

However, this situation of free choice is risky, as it is a matter of choosing the good. And already the first to draw a lot has greedily chosen "the greatest tyranny" (*Rep.* 619 b), just as all those who follow choose from greed based on the predilections of their former lives. These choices demonstrate that things are not going well for human self-development. The only exception is Odysseus, who draws the last lot. Let us hear what Socrates has to say: "The soul of Odysseus drew the last lot of all and came to make its choice, and, from memory of its former toils having flung away ambition, went about for a long time in quest of the life of an ordinary citizen who minded his own business, and with difficulty found it lying in some corner disregarded by the others, and upon seeing it said that it would have done the same had it drawn the first lot, and chose it gladly" (620 c-d).

Based on self-development, compelled by necessity, Odysseus thus chooses his future destiny as a private citizen or, put in another way, like Socrates. Unlike his predecessor, Socrates was to pay for his endeavors with nothing less than his life. As both a man and a myth, he becomes by virtue of his clear-sightedness the incarnation of good and of the sun—a solar hero who in a mythological sense enlightens the cave world and kingdom of death of his time.

And in this respect, Socrates becomes a completely developed model for the internalization and spiritualization that Odysseus anticipates—even in Socrates' own account. This, which despite everything was still external in Homer, finally becomes completely internal in Socrates. And as the body for Socrates is an external shell around inner truth, so the Wooden Horse was for Odysseus only a hiding place, shaped by his intelligence, which brought an end to the heroic world and opened the way to the long (though in a historical sense, incredibly compressed) development of consciousness, which we can trace through Greek art and culture. And so it should be seen here that just as Odysseus was inside the Wooden Horse, so we find Socrates inside Odysseus.

NOTES

I: THE WOODEN HORSE—THE MYTH OF DISCURSIVITY

1. Interestingly enough, by joining together the many and varied epithets Homer applies to Troy, it is possible to form a good impression of how he conceived the city, whether he had seen it himself or had only heard about it. That Troy is a magnificent city only makes the Greeks' achievement greater and more honorable than if it had only been a small town. Several times, he calls Troy "holy" (XIII, 657) as a sign that it is protected by the gods. Before the war, Athene had her Palladium there, which Odysseus carries off in order that the Greeks may take Troy, protected as it is during the war by, among others, Aphrodite and Ares. Troy is "extensive" (XXIV, 256) and "mighty" (XIII, 433), "towering" (or well fortified, I, 129); it is "lovely" (V, 210) with "sheer walls" (IX, 685) and "wide ways" (IX, 27). Surrounded by "rich soil" (III, 74; VI, 315), it is situated where the rivers Skamandros and Simios collide (V, 774) and, from the Hellespont, there still blows a fresh north wind, which made Homer speak of Troy as "windy" (XII, 115; XIII, 724).

The most accurate dating of Troy's fall can be calculated from a marble tablet (*parium*) from Paros, which states that the city was taken on the seventh from the last day in the month of *Thargelion* during the 22nd year of the reign of King Menestheus. This king appears several times in the *Iliad* (among other places, II, 552; IV, 327; XII, 331). A recalculation provides the date 5 June 1209 B.C. (*Troia*, p. 174). Herodotus (born c. 485 B.C.) says (2.145) that it was supposed to have been about 800 years before his time—that is, c. 1285 B.C. In antiquity, Eratosthenes of Cyrene (c. 285-194 B.C.), the most important librarian of the day at the library in Alexandria, puts the date 100 years later at 1184 B.C. Excavations of the Hisarlik mound on the west coast of Asia Minor have shown that Troy was hit by an earthquake around 1300 B.C. and burned down around 1250 B.C. So, all the datings with respect to Homer's Troy fall within a relatively short timeframe. In the many layers of which the city consists, Homer's Troy is Troy VI-VII (results of recent research on Troy are described in *Troia*, 2001).

Even though the *Iliad* is conceived in and around the mythology of the Olympian gods, just as the heroes have mythic status and divine origin, there is much to indicate that there is a concrete event that is the basis for the myth of the Trojan War. Homer's literalness made it possible for Henrich Schliemann in the last century to excavate Troy—based more or less on the *Iliad*'s topographic references. However, the general location of Troy had been known since antiquity and, even then, it was an excursion spot. In the mid-19th century, it was believed that Troy was situated on the Pinarbasi heights, which seemed logical, given its strategic location approximately 8 kilometres south of Hisarlik. As Schliemann relates, even as a child, he had a dream of excavating Troy. On his way to Turkey, he was fortunate enough on the boat across the Dardanelles on 1 August 1868 to run into the Englishman Frank Calvert, who, ignorant of Schliemann's intentions, presented his theory that Troy was located at Hisarlik. Schliemann took over the theory and, in 1870, by virtue of the fortune he had accumulated as, among other things, a grain dealer, was able to commence his excavations. At intervals, Troy has been excavated since 1988 under the leadership of the German Manfred Korfmann, who writes that what particularly fascinates him is Homer's precision: Dass ich von Jahr zu Jahr immer mehr entdeckte, wie glaubwürdig Homer zumindest als Zeitzeuge ist" (*Troia*, pp. 26ff. and 64ff.). In the same work there is a description of the construction and development of Troy (ibid., pp. 347ff.), while soil sampling has demonstrated that the sea went in toward

Hisarlik, forming a great bay, so that the Greek fleet lay close to Troy and the battles were fought on the relatively narrow piece of ground between the city and the sea.

2. It is difficult to define mythical thinking; for, as G. S. Kirk puts it, there is no one definition of myth, no Platonic form. Moreover, myths are too differentiated, both morphologically and in their social function. Nevertheless, Kirk concludes that no Western culture has been governed by a developed mythical tradition to the same degree as the Greek (*Myth*, p. 250). A presentation and a critique of the most important theories of myths from Frazer to Lévy-Strauss may also be found in Kirk, including Jung's conception of archetypal mythologems. Kirk has himself tried to systematize the thematic world of the Greek myths (*ibid.*, p. 187 ff.).

Myth is an open word, which derives from the Greek word *mythos*, simply meaning tale or the content of a tale. It does not constitute, as such, a categorization or clear genre determination. Myths deal with gods and heroes, their origin, development and trials and include features from the imaginative world of folktales as well as legends and sagas, which are based upon historical reality. Even though Kirk believes that it is difficult to draw a line between folktale and myth since they encroach upon one another as genres, he nevertheless tries to show some constituent differences (ibid., p. 36 ff.) He uses social affiliations as the predominant criterion. The folktale comes primarily from poor peasants. The heroes are humble, do not have distinctive names and do not recount their heritage. In their trials, they meet fantastic trolls, giants, etc., with a view to fulfilling a social dream—gaining half a kingdom and a princess. As opposed to this, myths are about heroes who arise from the aristocracy. The heroes have long genealogies, are individualized, and do not strive in the same way as in the folktale for financial gain (wealth, however, may be said to be a desirable goal, but mostly because it increases the honor of the hero to possess many valuables). In opposition to the folktale, heroic myths take place in prehistoric times. This means that folktales are taken less seriously, in general—they are viewed more as entertainment than are the heroic myths. Kirk takes no position on the fact that it is also possible to show archetypal patterns in folktales.

The prerequisite for a myth to achieve status as a mythic tale is, in my view, its character as an experience of and adaptation of reality—that a myth is established by and can, at all events, attain collective assent. In its origin, this mythopoetic process must have been pre-intellectual in the sense of non-abstract, as humankind has only had the mythos of the tale through which to understand and order life—by so to speak making a tale of the world. These embryonic myths were brief, simple tales—anonymous and autonomous speech acts that did not, as such, contain any need for interpretation or seek any causal explanations. However, as far as the Greek myths are concerned, we only know of this stage from powerful adaptations and elaborations in written sources for oral narrative traditions—such as, for example, Homer and Hesiod. This confirms that myth is not a static phenomenon but undergoes constant transformations, corresponding to changing epochs and their interpretive needs. Any material that can expand and enrich it is brought within its narrative and interpretive capacity, just as this material evokes new sides in its given conceptual potential.

In this sense, myth reveals its durability as a general statement about life through its iterativity—that it is relevant enough to be retold from generation to generation. Its general validity can only be conceived as the result of a collective interpretive effort and consensus. This also applies to socio-psychological interactions: the relationship between parents and children, mothers and sons, initiation myths and rituals in the transition from child to adult, life and death, and gender relations. In relation to the outside world, it is a matter of telling about and making sense of otherwise incomprehensible natural events, to ensure fertility with seasonal rituals, such as those celebrated, for example, by the Elusinian Mysteries.

Another question is the extent to which myth and ritual constitute a unity. This cannot be answered clearly. For example, in *Themis*, Jane E. Harrison is of the opinion that ritual and myth in the original cult activity, *dromenon*, were an inseparable unit. The ritual is here the things that are done, *ergon*, while the things that are recited thereunder are *mythos* or *legomena* (p. 43)—"Ritual is the utterance of an emotion, a thing felt, in action, myth in words and thoughts. They arise pari passu" (p. 16). Myth is not conceived as explanation. Only when the feeling created by the ritual has died away does myth achieve a true etiological character. Prytz Johansen believes that a distinction should be made between cult myths, which reproduce the cult's inner meaning, and myths that have no closer connection to the cult (*Illustreret Religionshistorie* I, p. 63). I.e., myths do not necessarily need to have a connection to rituals or fall under the religious–theological. The myth of the Wooden Horse, for example, is a "new" myth, without ritual meaning.

The understanding of myth requires the interpreter to be capable of inferring the underlying meaning from the tale's concrete manifestation—an interpretation that has great similarity to dream interpretation in which one must infer from the manifest dream sequence its latent text. Therefore, a thorough process of interpretation can only be done by amplification, i.e., by a continuous accumulation of data in the context that provides an opportunity to determine precisely the type of content in the myth, text or dream. This also means that, even though the myths may seem to have a uniform meaning, it is necessary to determine in each individual case the actual content of meaning from the context. Since the myths undergo constant adaptation, expansion and transformation, we cannot trust that individual mythic elements will remain static and always articulate the same thing.

As Mircea Eliade has described in *Cosmos and History: The Myth of the Eternal Return*, the feeling of life's depth is in an original mythic understanding of the "beginning," as it is viewed in creation myths, where the beginning of all things is the focal point. It is also from such a beginning, ex arches, that Hesiod seeks enlightenment from the Muses—"tell/ from the beginning, which first came to be" (*Theogony*, v. 115). Therefore, there was a sense of eternity behind all events in life—among them, the cycle of seasons—and it provided an "archetypal" experience of the presence of the eternal in every moment. In a mythic form of consciousness, life was not merely a segment, linearly organized, but a comprehensive space that stretched beyond the purely subjective in that the individual was to stand in for and carry on what was given at the beginning. If the ability to maintain this cyclical space in consciousness and being was lost, the individual would be lost. By contrast, modern men experience the beginning as a purely chronological, clearly delimited temporal springboard that divides existence into an infinite series of beginnings.

In daily life, myths were, as it was mentioned, supposed to ensure concrete knowledge and continuity in an otherwise incomprehensible and dangerous world. Lightning, thunder, floods, disease, wild animals, etc. were gathered within a sort of narrative formula that could then be taken over by and absorbed into consciousness. And as such fundamental tales about the riddles of the world, myth becomes a sort of practical science. In its imagery and adaptation of experience, it borders on poetry and has subsequent moral significance in codifying social and religious/ritual values.

If it is at all possible for individuals to recognize themselves and their experiences of life and its problems in the great mythic tales, it is ultimately due, in my view and that of many others, to a fundamental condition in the development of every individual: the phylo-ontogenetic determination. By this, I mean that every person from embryo to adult goes through the development of the entire species and human race. Archetypal patterns date from this process, embedded as closed codes in our normal everyday consciousness. Myths reach down into the undersea, collective structures of (sub)consciousness. Thus, as concrete manifestations of imagery, myths become symbolically representative. And their interpretation is governed by a dual goal. Just as, through a sort of recollection, we penetrate the world of myths analytically in order to interpret past forms of experience, however alien they may seem, we also penetrate into the psychological mechanisms that are in our own subconscious and thereby form us with inevitable psychological necessity. Here, too, we have the explanation for the fact that Odysseus has become a key figure in Western literature and self-understanding—for example, in Joyce's *Ulysses*, even though that novel interprets a modernist view of existence.

To the development of consciousness from a mythically closed world to a more realistic, social reality belongs an internalization in which the individual pulls conceptions that are projected onto the outside world in the form of gods, *daimons*, etc., into oneself and acknowledges these figures as endogenous. When projections are incorporated in this way, the individual comes to appear as something essentially different from nature. Odysseus is the harbinger of this sort of process with his invention of the Wooden Horse.

The art of understanding and interpreting myths is far from a new phenomenon reserved for depth psychology. It is a form of interpretation that arises as a necessity from the exemplary nature of myth. This is already the case in the interpretive practice of Homer and Hesiod. However, the first known example of a true interpretation is from Theagenes of Rhegion, who around 500 B.C. is to have undertaken an allegorical reading of the Homeric epics. Odysseus has a similar meaning as an exemplar for Socrates and his students—for example, the Cynics, for whom the Odysseus figure was a model of the virtue of patience. This confirms that myth is based on a metaphorical-symbolic form of mediation. A subtext is embedded in the concrete and manifest tale, which it means or has the possibility of meaning, when its mythic narrative space is passed on to posterity with all the experience and knowledge it has accumulated in its ordering-imposing recollection (cf., note 1 to "III The Dual Religiosity").

3. Quintus Smyrnaeus, *The Fall of Troy*, Book 12, v. 1920. As it is in Homer, *metis* is connected here with *dolos* (craftiness).

4. Quintus Smyrnaeus 12, 67.

5. Apollodorus, *Epitome* V. 8-13.

6. The description of the Wooden Horse and the conquest of Troy is based upon information from the *Odyssey*, Book 12 of Quintus Smyrnaeus' cyclical poem *The Little Iliad* (*Ilias Mikra*), Apollodorus' *Epitome* V. 14-20 and Book 2 of Virgil's *Aeneid*. Reference is also made to Øivind Andersen, "Odysseus and the Wooden Horse," and B.A. Sparkes, "The Trojan Horse in Classical Art."

7. *Aeneid*, Book 2, v. 15.

8. Apollodorus, *Epitome* V. 17.

9. *Aeneid*, Book 2, v. 52-53 (Robert Fitzgerald, trans.) (New York 1983, p. 35).

10. Apollodorus, *Epitome* V. 17.

11. Quintus Smyrnaeus 12, 530 ff.

12. *Ibid.*, 12, 360 ff.

13. *The Little Iliad*, 13 in *Hesiod, Homeric Hymns, Epic Cycle, Homerica* (Loeb Class. Lib. 57), p. 518.

14. This question gave the title to Gregory Nagy's book *The Best of the Achaeans*.

15. Max Horkheimer and Theodor W. Adorno in *The Dialectic of Enlightenment* have no doubt in naming the *Odyssey* as "the basic text of European civilization" (p. 46), while Odysseus himself comes to stand as "a prototype of the bourgeois individual, a notion originating in the consistent self-affirmation which has its ancient pattern in the figure of the protagonist compelled to wander" (*ibid.*, p. 43.). This characterization, which is not positively meant, corresponds in many ways to Herbert Marcuse's use of the Prometheus figure in *Eros and Civilization*, which had a similar ideological errand. See note 28 to "XV. Aeschylus."

16. For example, in *The Ulysses Theme*, W. B. Stanford has traced Odysseus' metamorphoses to the present.

17. On the basis of Indian mythology, P. Radin has in *The Trickster* provided the following description of the trickster figure, known throughout the world: "Trickster is at one and the same time creator and destroyer, giver and negator, he who dupes others and who is always duped himself. He wills nothing consciously" (p. IX). Odysseus may be recognized in this characterization as both a creator and a destroyer, as his name implies (cf. 176). However, as the conscious individual he is, he seems fundamentally different from the archaic trickster of legend, who undergoes no personal development. According to Kerényi, the trickster has as his task "to add disorder to order and so make a whole, to render possible, within the fixed bounds of what is permitted, an experience of what is not permitted" (*ibid.*, p. 185). As he also makes Hermes, Odysseus' "grandfather," such a trickster, one senses that the material from which Odysseus developed has its origin here.

II: THE HOMERIC PROJECT

1. *Hymn to Apollo* v. 174-75.

2. Gilbert Murray, *The Rise of the Greek Epic*, p. 261 ff.

3. Herodotus, *The History* 2.53.

4. G. S. Kirk maintains that both Homeric epics were known throughout Greece around 650 B.C., see *The Iliad: A Commentary*, vol. 1, p. 4.

Homer's place in the oral tradition and the question of the written tradition of his works is discussed by Minna Skafte Jensen in *The Homeric Question and the Oral-Formulais Theory* (1980). She argues that Homer's works were written down by a scribe named Onomakritos at the bidding of the tyrant Pisistratos (c. 525 B.C.) as dictated by a rhapsode. However, as with other poetry based on an oral tradition, it is difficult—if not impossible—to date this version definitively. Meanwhile, it is probably not entirely wrong to make a conjecture of 700 B.C. as the probable date—around the same time as Hesiod, see note 14.

5. *On the Origin of Homer and Hesiod and Their Contest* in Hesiod, *Homeric Hymns and Homerica* (Loeb Class. Lib. 57), p. 569.

6. C. M. Bowra, *Heroic Poetry*, p. 406.

7. G. Nagy, *The Best of the Achaeans*, p. 296 ff.

8. 2 *Nemean Ode* v. 1 ff.

9. Remarkably enough, we find exactly the same wording in the cyclical poem *Cypria*, see *Cypria* 3 in Hesiod, *Homeric Hymns and Homerica* (Loeb Class. Lib. 57), p. 496.

10. *Poetics*, chap. 5 (1460a5–10).

11. *Theogony* v. 52–53.

12. J. Clay, "The Plaktai and Moly: Divine Naming and Knowing in Homer."

13. In *Homeric Modifications of Formulaic Prototypes*, A. Hoekstra describes how Homer has modified an older oral prototype of formulas for his own use and the flexibility it has given his works. See J.B. Hainsworth, *Flexibility of the Homeric Formula*.

14. In *Homer and the Origin of the Greek Alphabet*, Barry B. Powell, examining shorter and longer inscriptions, has investigated the origin of the Greek alphabet from around 800 B.C., the date of the earliest inscriptions. On this basis, he has concluded that the *Iliad* and the *Odyssey* may have been composed between 800 and 750 B.C., p. 219. See note 4.

15. M. I. Finley, *The World of Odysseus*, p. 38.

16. With respect to the oral tradition, general reference is made to the following works: Walther J. Ong, *Orality and Literacy*, A. B. Lord, *The Singer of Tales*, and, particularly, Erich A. Havelock's books.

17. *Poetics*, chap. 4 (1448b27).

18. As an example of this, mention should be made of the eminent philologist Denys Page's *The Homeric Odyssey*.

19. From a highly stylized perspective, Jean-Pierre Vernant has demonstrated in *The Origins of Greek Thought* this process of restructuring from the god-king (*wanax*) of Mycenaean times to oligarchic aristocracy to the democracy of the city-state, *polis*, formed in the dialectic between *eros* and *eris* (p. 45 ff.).

20. A comprehensive archaeological documentation with respect to "the dark ages" may be found in A. M. Snodgrass, *The Dark Ages of Greece*, an empirical investigation on the basis of pottery shards, burial customs, metallurgy, etc.

21. G. Murray, *The Rise of the Greek Epic*, pp. 127–34.

22. See the commentary to the *Odyssey* 20, 194 in *A Commentary to Homer's Odyssey*.

23. In many instances, heroes were worshipped after their death by so-called hero cults—Herakles and Oedipus are such examples. Perhaps there were deceased relatives with extraordinary abilities to which fertilizing characteristics were attributed, like fertility gods. This is Jane E Harrison's claim in *Themis*, where she argues that the heroes are collective projections (p. 260). Yet, this unction is much reduced in Homer, where the heroes behave as "gentlemen" (p. 335), without magic and without any connection to a cult of death and growth. They are characterized by the individualization they seek to claim through the slaughter of battle. A development that, according to Harrison, occurred with the emigration to Asia Minor (p. 336).

24. See Arthur W. H. Adkins, *Merit and Responsibility* to which reference is generally made for a more thorough description of the content and development of Greek moral concepts.

25. In *The Gift*, Marcel Mauss has provided on a broad ethnographic foundation—taking its starting point with the *Edda* poem "Hávamál"—a description of the morphology and social function of the gift: to establish friendships and political alliances, since gifts were closely related to the person of the giver. The significance of a gift was an expression of generosity and social solidarity.

26. In *Sophrosyne*, Helen North uses this concept (p. 2) in opposition to sober-mindedness (*sophrosyne*). She traces *sophrosyne* from its origin in Homer throughout Greek literature.

27. *Ibid.*, p. 3.

28. *Ibid.*, pp. 6-7.

29. See W. B. Standford, *The Ulysses Theme*. The meaning of the name was originally determined by Willamovitz. Another possibility might be that the father fought far from home.

30. Plato, *The Laws* 706a; 934b.

31. Jane E. Harrison, *Themis*, p. 473 ff.

32. *The Birth of Tragedy*, chap. 16. Insofar as Apollo embodies this principle, Niestzche's purpose is to go beyond his state of consciousness in order to be reunited with the wisdom of Dionysian nature. See the analysis of *The Bacchae*.

33. For the conception of Homeric psychology and world view, this analysis has been influenced—beyond the works themselves—by the following authors, among others: Bruno Snell, *The Discovery of the Mind*; E. R. Dodds, *The Greeks and the Irrational*; R. B. Onians, *The Origins of European Thought*; Jan Bremmer, *The Early Concept of the Soul*; B. Williams, *Shame and Necessity*. The latter work is particularly interesting for Williams' corrective critique of Snell's view of Homeric men as "automatons," see note 40.

34. The linguistic aspect is analyzed in *The Discovery of the Mind: The Greek Origins to European Thought*, chapter 1.

35. M. Eliade, *The Myth of the Eternal Return*.

36. B. Snell describes this development as a precondition for the development of scientific thought, see chap 10.

37. In *Odysseus Polytropos*, P. Pucci provides a number of examples of such intertextuality between the *Iliad* and the *Odyssey*.

38. Magdalene Stoevesandt has calculated the chronology of events in the *Iliad* as having a duration of exactly 51 days, see *Troia*, p. 92.

39. According to this view, a "fixed" character stamps the heroic figure in the tradition of oral poetry. For example, W. J. Ong speaks of "heavy" or "flat" character and mentions as examples the wrathful Achilleus and the wise Odysseus (*Orality and Literacy*, p. 70). This method of characterization was to serve as a mnemonic aid for the narrator. With writing, the psychological portrait, "the round character," is developed (*ibid.*, p. 151 ff.).

40. E. R. Dodds claims in *The Ancient Concept of Progress* that, even though the word for development (progress) does not appear in the most ancient Greek poetry in our sense of the word, this experience is present latently from the beginning, linked to a figure such as Prometheus—and one may also add, Odysseus. B. Williams has demonstrated in the same way in *Shame and Necessity* that the Homeric man has no word for "deciding," which is not synonymous with the notion that they could never make a decision (p. 35 ff.). This view is opposed to Bruno Snell, see note 33. It is Snell's claim that neither body nor soul belong together in Homer but are, as in contemporary vase paintings a form a disjecta membra. I share Williams' criticism, since the alleged split is an absurdity. It would, at any rate, make it impossible for individuals to act or think—and for Homer to describe such a world of motivation. In short, this means that, despite the fact that no concepts are found for certain aspects of human conduct in early Greek poetry, the experience can certainly be present in the very pattern of the action.

41. In *The Greeks and the Irrational*, E.R. Dodds has dedicated the whole of chapter 5 to the shamanistic tradition in Greek spiritual life. In addition, reference is made to M. Eliade, *Archaic Techniques of Ecstasy*.

42. Ragnar Höistad has demonstrated Odysseus' significance as a subsequent and ideal figure in *Cynic Hero and Cynic King*, pp. 94–192.

43. Medieval biblical exegesis is based on analogical figural thinking in which portentous events in the Old Testament are brought to fulfillment in the New Testament—an interpretive practice that can, for example, be found in Dante's *Divine Comedy*, in which Virgil is Dante's own precursor.

44. *Poetics,* chap. 24 (1459b31).

45. See A. Hoekstra, *Homeric Modifications of Formulaic Prototypes*, p. 101 ff.

46. *Poetics*, chap. 24 (1459b26-29).

47. The expression solar hero, which will be employed in several contexts, is used for the lack of another phrase to designate a manifold psychic reality: 1. The solar hero is reborn like the sun through the realm of the dead. 2. This birth relates to the higher, masculine consciousness and becoming conscious that is linked to the sun and the god of light Apollo as its divine incarnation. 3. The solar aspect is evidence that the subject has found himself (the treasure of gold) and meets his feminine counterpart, his "redeemed anima" in the form of his beloved, sometimes viewed as a lunar goddess, see note 26 to Part VII: The Trials of Homecoming.

48. H. Fränkel, *Early Greek Poetry and Philosophy*, p. 14 ff. I have made great use of this work, as is the case with Werner Jaeger's *Paideia*.

49. Plato, *The Apology* 22 c.

50. Plato, *Phaedrus*, where Socrates speaks of "the form of possession or madness (*mania*), of which the Muses are the source" (245 a), see *The Laws*: "when a poet takes his seat on the Muse's tripod, his judgment takes leave of him. He is like a fountain which gives free course to the rush of its waters" (719 c).

51. *Theogony* v. 27.

52. G. Nagy, *The Best of the Achaeans*, p. 27.

53. In *The Wound and the Bow*, Edmund Wilson has discussed the wounded hero as the archetype of the artist based on Sophocles' tragedy *Philoktetes* (chap. 7).

54. Apollodorus describes how Teiresias was transformed into a woman at the sight of two copulating snakes and was transformed into a man once again, when he saw another such pair. A number of explanations have been given for Teiresias' blindness and psychic abilities. One version relates that Athene blinded him after he saw her naked. However, his mother, a nymph of whom the goddess was fond, contrived it so that, even though Athene could not restore his sight, she could give him the ability to understand the songs of birds. Another version says that Zeus made him a "seer," when Hera blinded him, because he claimed that the sexual enjoyment of women was nine times that of men, something he knew from being transformed into a woman. (*Bibl.* III. 6.5-7).

55. See G. Nagy, *The Best of the Achaeans*, p. 17; P. Pucci, *Odysseus Polytropos*, p. 196.

56. This "inspirational" irresolution reaches into later poetry, as when, for example, Euripides' Elektra says to Aigisthos' decapitated head: "Which of our sufferings shall I speak in prelude,/ which shall I make finale, or marshal in the center?" (v. 907-08).

57. In chapter 6 of *The Origins of European Thought*, R. B. Onians describes *aion* as a life-source.

58. *Poetics*, chap. 24. Longinus in his later lengthy treatise on the sublime, *Peri hypsous*, maintained this conception, writing: "beautiful words are in very truth the peculiar light of thought" (30.1) (W. Rhys Roberts, trans.) (Cambridge 1899). He also views the *Odyssey* as an epilogue to the *Iliad* (9.12), written by an elderly Homer in that the narrative dominates and, therefore, lacks the sublime energy and intensity of the *Iliad* (see the comparison of the Homeric epics 9.11-15).

59. *Agamemnon* v. 182-83.

60. *Theogony* v. 102.

III. DUAL RELIGIOSITY

1. Plato, *The Laws* 886 a.

2. *Cratylus* 397 c–d.

3. Herodotus, *The History* 1. 131.

4. One source for my understanding the relationship between archetypical mythology and its psychological implications has been Erich Neumann's work *The Origins and History of Consciousness* (*Ursprungsgeschichte des Bewusstseins*, Zurich 1949). Neumann's basic conception is phylo-ontogenesis (see note 2 in "I. The Wooden Horse—The Myth of Discursivity"). We gain insight into the psychic primal tales that are in our unconscious through myth.

The starting point is the mystery of creation. First, there was Chaos, a formless void. From this arose the earth, personified in the goddess Gaia, who from herself breeds heaven, Uranos. This couple make up the first World Parents and exist at this primeval stage in an amalgamation, symbolically compared to egg of the world and the self-breeding snake Uroboros, which, biting itself in the tail, forms a complete whole and the cyclic rhythm of life. Since the parents are not separated, the children created remain in this closed circle, invisible. They are cradled by a caring Magna Mater, who sees to all needs and protects from all danger and suffering. In terms of consciousness, the state is defined by a drowsy, dreamlike basal unconsciousness. Neumann calls this earliest stage of consciousness "uroboric incest."

The next evolutionary step takes place in violence, when the son—among the Greeks, Kronos—assisted by his mother Gaia castrates his father. The castration, the symbolic rebellion against the father, leads to the separation of the parents: heaven and earth are separated as male and female and evil enters into the world. The son steps visibly forth between his parents. This story is repeated as a part of a consecutive series, through which experience says the development is shaped, as Zeus "castrates" his father, again helped by his mother, in a generational rebellion against the dominant father figure, who represents law, restrictions and stagnation. In short, the son wants to be his own father (see note 2 to V. "The Wanderings").

Parallel, on a psychological plane, the consciousness that was previously absorbed by maternal nature, now gradually becomes separate. The surrounding world thus appears to the subject in the form of unhappiness and suffering. Therefore, men begin—in order to understand and control this hostile reality—to tell myths and beseech the powers that be in rites that still presume a magical unity between people and the world (see note 2 to "I. The Wooden Horse—The Myth of Discursivity"). The paradoxic is that fear itself is an engine in the evolution and formation of consciousness.

Insofar as the subject, i.e. the male ego, attempts to separate from the Great Mother, for whom he has not only been a son but a lover with whom she has been able to propagate, a split occurs in the mother figure. She divides and meets the "rebellious" son in his emancipation as the evil, vengeful and smothering mother, known in fairy-tales, transformed into a dragon, a witch or a wild animal. The "weak" son in a confrontation with this dangerous world will regress, slide back into the peace and pleasure of uroboric incest. "Strong" individuals, who bear the future culture and a true ego consciousness in themselves, on the other hand, will as heroes (kings, chiefs, princes, etc.) take up the struggle against the dragon. The killing of the primeval maternal force itself is evidence that they have temporarily overcome the maternal connection, have developed their masculine selves, which they take into their possession as "a treasure of gold," at the same time that the now redeemed maternal image meets them in the form of the "princess."

With victory over the destructive maternal figure, the path is also clear to constitute a paternal universe, a system of patriarchal rights, to replace mother right—to use an expression from Bachofen's great work *Mutterrecht*, which with its elucidation of the significance of the Great Mother forms the basis of Neumann's analysis to a great degree. In addition, a corresponding shift in power takes place in the religious universe, among the gods. In the Greek context, an example is the fact that Zeus, the lightning-slinging god of the clouds, steps into the place of fertility goddesses and cults through which people worshipped the Earth and tried to maintain the eternal, cyclical rhythm of growth. With Zeus, as father of the gods situated on Olympus, an elevated patriarchal power is installed.

5. According to Apollodorus' *Bibl.* III. 12.1, Iasion was the son of Zeus and Atlas' daughter Elektra. When he attempted to rape Demeter, Zeus killed him with a bolt of lightning.

6. *Theogony* v. 971.

7. See E. O. James, *The Cult of the Mother-Goddess*, in which James argues that (De)metér derives from *mater*, while *De* is not dialect for earth but, rather, linked with her connection to grain.

8. *Hymn to Demeter* v. 123.

9. M. Eliade, *A History of Religious Ideas*, vol. 1, p. 120 and E. O. James, op. cit., chap. 5.

10. E. O. James, *The Cult of the Mother-Goddess*, p. 14.

11. Plato, *Menexenus* 237 e.

12. Sophocles, *Antigone* v. 569.

13. Sophocles, *Oedipus the King* v. 1213-15.

14. *Ibid.*, v. 1259.

15. See the analysis of this metaphorical development in Page duBois, *Sowing the Body*, p. 65 ff.

16. This view is based on Jane E. Harrison, *Themis*, p. 262 ff. The work as a whole is an analysis or demonstration of the relationship between the caring mythic maternal figure (*kourotrophos*) and the son (*kouros*). Harrison does not problematize this relationship as, for example, Erich Neumann does, see note 4. To the contrary, she sympathizes powerfully in *Themis* and *Prolegomena* with the chthonic primeval forces and has less to spare for the patriarchal gods of Olympos. She extends G. Murray's research in her description of the Year-*Daimon* (*Eniautos Daimon*). In *Themis*, Harrison attempts to show that, behind many of the most important gods—Zeus, Apollo and Dionysos—is the worship of the young kouros in the form of the Year-*Daimon*.

17. *Works and Days* v. 458-70.

18. *Hymn of the Kouretes* it is called by J. E. Harrison in *Themis*, chap. 1. The discovery of this hymn forms the foundation for her study of the *kourotrophos kouros* theory.

19. *Hymn to Demeter* v. 479-81 (trans. by Hugh G. Evelyn-White) in *The Homeric Hymns and Homerica*. Cambridge, 1914), p. 323.

20. See M. Eliade, *The History of Religious Ideas*, vol. 1, chaps. 97-99, pp. 256-63. A central figure in the Eleusinian Mysteries is Triptolemos, the young boy to whom Demeter entrusts the ear of corn in order that he may bring agriculture to the world. Elsewhere, he is viewed as a lover who has been sacrificed to serve vegetation and its queen and, as such, he also merges with Plutos, since his name remarkably enough means "thrice-plowed field".

21. *Hymn to Demeter* v. 268-69 (*Homeric Hymns*, p. 309).

22. *Ibid.*, v. 308-10 (p. 311).

23. *Ibid.*, v. 471 (p. 323).

24. As the goddess of cultivated earth and grain, Demeter represents a higher principle of development than Aphrodite, see note 21 to "V. The Telemachy."

25. See M. L. West's note to the *Theogony* v. 969.

26. *Hymn to Demeter* v. 487-88.

27. See Erich Neumann, note 1.

28. M. Eliade, *The History of Religious Ideas*, vol. 1, chaps. 83-84, p. 219.

29. *Theogony*, v. 857-58.

30. Erich Neumann names this psychic movement "heroic incest," see note 2 to "VII. The 'Wanderings.'"

31. Herodotus, *The History* 2.53 (trans. by David Grene, Chicago 1987. p. 155).

32 G. S. Kirk and J. E. Raven, *The Philosophers*, p. 498 f.

33. W. K. C. Guthrie, *Essays on the Odyssey*, especially p. 8.

34. See Jane E. Harrison, *Themis*, chap. 11.

35. *Works and Days* v. 260.

36. *Elektra* v. 1247-48.

37. *The Eumenides* v. 1046–47.

38. In *Prolegomena*, Jane E. Harrison provides an exhaustive account of the relationship between Keres, Erinyes and Eumenides.

39. *Theogony,* v. 211.

40. *The Libation Bearers* v. 66–67.

41. *The Eumenides* v.649–50.

42. E. R. Dodds, *The Ancient Concept of Progress*, p. 70.

43. Bruno Snell in particular is the originator of this view, which was later refuted by B. Williams. See note 32 to "II. The Homeric Project."

44. *Prometheus Bound* v. 34–35.

45. The most influential interpretation of the theme of blindness (*ate*) is provided by E. R. Dodds in *The Greeks and the Irrational*, chap. 1.

46. *Ajax* v. 123, 195, 307.

47. *Hippolytos* v. 379–81.

48. J. Jaynes, *The Origin of Consciousness in the Breakdown of the Bicameral Mind*, p. 273.

49. Jane Harrison writes: "Though the several festivals are ostensibly consecrated to various Olympians, and though there is in each an element of prayer and praises and sacrificial feasting such as is familiar to us in Homer, yet, when the ritual is closely examined, the main part of the ceremonies will be seen to be magical rather than what we should term religious. Further, this ritual is addressed, in so far as it is addressed to any one, not to the Olympians of the upper air, but to snakes and ghosts and underworld beings" (*Prolegomena*, p. 28).

The deepest amalgamation of Dionysos and Apollo took place in Orphism. Here, the Apollonian demand for spiritual purity explicitly encounters an ecstatic religiosity. Moreover, the more or less hidden conceptions of immortal life that define the chthonic religion of fertility are expressed in the eternal cycle of repetition directly in Orphism's doctrine of reincarnation, linked to the victim Dionysos Zagreus. Death does not imply the same definitive conclusion as in Homer's kingdom of shadows.

50. Thucydides, *The Peloponnesian War* 2.38 (Rex Warner, trans., p. 146).

IV: ATHENE AND THE APPLE OF DISCORD—ON *EROS, ERIS* AND *METIS*

1. See the cyclical poem *Cypria* 1, in Hesiod, *Homeric Hymns and Homerica* (Loeb Class. Lib. 57), p. 488 ff.

2. Apollodorus' *Epitome* III. 10.8.

3. *Ibid., Bibl.* III. 10.8.

4. *Theogony* v. 120.

5. Plato, *Symposium* 186a.

6. *Theogony* v. 224.

7. *Works and Days* v. 14.

8. Kirk and Raven, *The Philosophers* (Cambridge, 1980), fr. 423, p. 327.

9. Homer uses the expressions *philoteta* (24, 476) and *phileonton* (24, 485).

10. M. Detienne and J.-P. Vernant, *Cunning Intelligence*, p. 179. It is to Detienne's and Vernant's credit that they have shown the whole register of meaning that is entwined in *metis*—"a type of intelligence and of thought, a way of knowing; it implies a complex but very coherent body of mental attitudes and intellectual behaviour which combine flair, wisdom, forethought, subtlety of mind, deception, resourcefulness, vigilance, opportunism, various skills, and experience acquired over the years. It applied to situations which are transient, shifting, disconcerting and ambiguous, situations which do not lend themselves to precise measurement, exact calculation or rigorous logic" (p. 3 ff.).

11. Apollodorus' *Bibl.* II. 1.

12. *Theogony* v. 887.

13. *Works and Days* v. 267.

14. See Jane E. Harrison, *Themis*, ch. 11.

15. *Theogony* v. 896.

16. *Cunning Intelligence*, p. 180.

17. M. Grant, *Myths of the Greeks and Romans*, p. 180.

18. E. O. James writes in *The Cult of the Mother-Goddess*: "She was a tutelary goddess of the Cretan and Mycenaean princes, subsequently raised to the dignity of the goddess of the republican state, the important Attic city named after her" (p. 146).

19. Apollodorus' *Bibl.* III 14.6.

20. The *aegis* was made by Hephaistos for Zeus (XV, 308 ff.) and is really a shield he loans to Apollo as well as Athene, who also has access to his lightning. With his right hand, Zeus throws bolts of lightning, while with his other hand, he shakes the *aegis*, so the air is filled with thunder. If Medusa, who is depicted on the *aegis*, is said to be "Zeus' emblem" (*teras*, XV, 742), it may as a trophy symbolize his victory over chthonic maternal power, since it is his daughter Athene who, according to the myths, received it from Perseus.

21. Erich Neumann, *The Origins and History of Consciousness*, p. 217.

22. By leaping over all traces of the ancient reality that links Athene to the primal mother, M. Detienne and J.-P. Vernant in *Cunning Intelligence* can answer negatively to the question of her character as a goddess of fertility.

23. It feels like an inconsistency in the *Odyssey* when Hermes claims to Kalypso that, on the way home, Odysseus offended Athene: "on the voyage home they offended Athene,/ who let loose an evil tempest and tall waves against them" (5, 108-09). Here, various versions of the hero's difficult voyage home must have been confused. It is correct that Athene was furious with the Greeks, because Ajax, the son of Oileus, raped Kassandra at her alter during the taking of Troy, while the other Greeks stood by passively watching. She has him suffer shipwreck as well, "hated by Athene" (4, 502), but Poseidon would have saved him if he had not boasted of his rescue as though it had been the result of his own efforts.

A conflict, with characteristics of delusion from the gods (Odysseus speaks of a god scattering the people), arose between Agamemnon and Menelaos, when they were to sail from the destroyed city of Troy. Agamemnon wanted to stay and sacrifice. As Nestor tells Telemachos, Agamemnon was foolish enough to believe that, by sacrificing, he could dampen Athene's "deadly anger" (3, 146), but she was not to be reconciled—"The will of the everlasting gods is not turned suddenly" (3, 147), concludes Nestor. Menelaos wishes to set sail immediately, but his voyage home is almost as difficult and dangerous as Odysseus', because, as he himself says, he "had not tendered complete hecatombs" to the gods (4, 352). Athene is not designated as a particular enemy, but the gods as such, and Zeus carries out their punishment by killing his steersman off Cape Sounion and sending him on a seven-year voyage. Odysseus at first followed Menelaos, but returned and sacrificed with Agamemnon. That Odysseus does not feel that he has any conflict with Athene also emerges clearly in the fact that, in Book 13, he reproaches her for not having supported him since Troy.

24. The myth of how women—as a consequence of the competition between Athene and Poseidon to become god of Athens—lost the right to vote and should belong to only one man is clearly an example of the transition from matriarchy to patriarchy. See Jane E. Harrison, *Prolegomena*, p. 301 ff; *Themis*, p. 262.

25. According to M. Detienne and J.-P. Vernant, not only are the talented hunter or fisher related in their abilities to *metis*, but so are animals such as the fox and the octopus with their sophisticated methods of hunting associated (*Cunning Intelligence*, ch. 2). Moreover, this can work in the opposite direction, since the craftiness of the octopus becomes a metaphor for a crafty human being, which is why Odysseus is called "octopus" by Eustathius, *op. cit.*, p. 39.

V: THE *TELEMACHY*

1. The chronology in Homer—and other Greek poets—is very largely determined by the context, which can create some confusion in the reader. Thus, there is some confusion in the

Iliad about Achilleus' age. When he is forced to go on the expedition against Troy, the reason has to be that he must have been among Helen's suitors, even though he is not mentioned by Apollodorus (*Bibl.* III. 9.8). He has sworn an oath to support Menelaos, if he is troubled in his marriage. According to what she says (XXIV, 765-66), Helen has resided in Troy for 20 years. In which case, Achilleus is the same age as Odysseus, approaching 40, which is also consistent with his having a son Neoptolemos ("the very young warrior"); on the other hand, this does not agree with the statement in the *Iliad* that he is much younger—for example, when Odysseus refers to his being older and having far more experience (XIX, 219).

2. In *The Origins and History of Consciousness*, Erich Neumann has characterized this process in the following way: "The reborn is reborn through the father principle with which he identified himself in the initiation. Then he becomes the father's son without a mother, and, inasmuch as he is identical with the father, he is also the father of himself," p. 408.

3. In "Initiation Motifs in the Story of Telemachus," C. W. Eckert has tried to demonstrate the presence of this sort of mythical initiation paradigm in Telemachos' journey. It is a bit strained, because he wants the result "to work out." Although the *Telemachy* in its psychologization has moved away from the mythical pattern, remnants of it may still be sensed. For a deeper analysis of this initiation process, see M. Eliade, *Rites and Symbols of Initiation*. Jane E. Harrison states in *Themis* that in certain ritual contexts, before undergoing the initiation ritual to become men, young boys were viewed as girls, a claim she bases, among other things, on a reference to the fact that for instance Achilleus and Dionysos were dressed in girl's clothing (506 ff.).

4. See the commentary on 15, 86 in *A Commentary on Homer's Odyssey*, where the epithet's possible association with *nous* and *phrenes* is discussed.

5. Euripides uses a reverse mirroring in the *Orestes*, as Orestes refers to the fact that Telemachos would hardly kill his chaste mother (v. 600).

6. One Gunlaugr Ormstungu, for example, cannot make his way home to his betrothed by the appointed time, and so she marries his friend instead, and the two former friends end up killing each other.

7. Hesiod, *Homeric Hymns and Homerica* (Loeb Class. Lib. 57), in which the description is found in the so-called catalogue of women, attributed to Hesiod, fr. 12, p. 162.

8. This marriage is mentioned in the cyclical poems, for example, *Nostoi* 3 in *Homeric Hymns and, Homerica* (Loeb Class. Lib. 57, p. 528).

9. For example, in Plato's *Symposium*, where Phaedrus emphasizes in his speech on Eros that a homosexual relationship existed between Achilleus and Patroklos (Patroklos is directly referred to as his *erastes*), as Phaedrus refers to a lost tragedy of Aeschylus, *The Myrmidons*, which had this as a theme (Symp. 179e-180a).

10. M. Suzuki provides perspective in an analysis of Helen's various manifestations in *Metamorphoses of Helen*.

11. *The Trojan Women* v. 952 ff.

12. Aeschylos, *Agamemnon* v. 742.

13. This could be a quantity designation, see my account on p. 71.

14. *Andromache* v. 629-31.

15. *Lysistrata* v. 155-56.

16. Euripides, *The Trojan Women* v. 1042 ff.

17. *Ibid.*, v. 935-37.

18. *Ibid.*, v. 865 ff.

19. *Ibid*, v. 991 ff.

20. *Agamemnon* v. 1470.

21. Whereas Athene was born from the head of a god and, as such, is pure *metis*, Aphrodite was born from the testicles of another god, Uranos, whom Zeus castrated and whose genitalia fell into the ocean, creating the foam from which Aphrodite arose. Aphrodite thus represents a primeval chthonic stage. Demeter is on a higher level, since she organizes life in the form of agriculture and marriage. For Aphrodite, desire stands alone and is the only absolute power in the

world; anarchic, anonymous and hetaera-like, desire evokes enormous lust and infinite pain, of which Helen's story, if anything, is evidence. This significant process is a recurrent theme in J. J. Bachofen's *Mutterrecht*, in which he writes, among other things, that the lowest stage of development, linked to the earth, is "a stage of formless, orderless freedom, and the only bond between creatures is that of Aphroditean desire (like hetaerism) ... With agriculture, motherhood takes a new significance, a higher form. The wild swamp generation (linked with Aphrodite), which eternally rejuvenates matter in everlasting self-embrace, which brings forth only reeds and rushes or the 'swampy offspring of the sources,' and which springs up uselessly *without regard to man*, is replaced by the act of the tiller of the soil, who opens the womb of the earth with his plow" (*Myth, Religion and Mother Right*, p. 190 f.) This stage is represented by Demeter's *jus naturale*, which also seems to correspond to the reality that Demeter represents in Homer.

22. *Little Iliad* in Hesiod, *Homeric Hymns and Homerica* (Loeb Class. Lib. 57) p. 511.

VI: ODYSSEUS

1. In his book *Odysseus Polytropos*, Pietro Pucci has named his analysis of the *Odyssey* after this epithet, which he focuses on specifically, p. 18 ff., p. 24, p. 149. See also N. Austin, *Archery at the Dark of the Moon*, p. 140, and W. B. Stanford, *The Ulysses Theme*, p. 99 and p. 260 ff. In *Cunning Intelligence*, M. Detienne and J.-P. Vernant characterize the polytropic person in this way: "The polytropos one (...) is distinguished by the control he possesses: supple and shifting as he is, he is always master of himself and is only unstable in appearance. His volte-faces are a trap—the net in which his adversary becomes entangled. He is not the plaything of movement but its master" (p. 40). See the commentary to 1, 1 in *A Commentary to Homer's Odyssey*.

2. [Translator's note: Zeruneith's original text cites two Danish translations of the *Odyssey* by Christian Wilster (1837) and Otto Steen Due (2002). The Fagles quotation from his translation of *The Odyssey* (New York 1996), p. 77.] A. T. Murray in Loeb Class. Lib. uses the expression "the man of many devices."

3. Reference is made to mention of this verse in *A Commentary to Homer's Odyssey*.

4. The Autolykos side of the Odysseus figure and its reception is thoroughly described by W. B. Stanford in *The Ulysses Theme*, p. 10 ff.; p. 37 ff. Autolykos is otherwise a strange figure of "origin," since, according to Apollodorus' *Bibl.* I.9.16, he was not only Odysseus' grandfather but also Iason's through his daughter Polymede, even as he, along with Laertes, sails with the Argonauts. All these coincidences in the *Odyssey* mean that Odysseus and Iason are not only cousins but almost merge as figures.

5. The uncertain etymology of the name is discussed in the comment on 1, 62 in *A Commentary to Homer's Odyssey*.

6. One should, for the sake of completeness, mention that all the great heroes seem to possess this sort of duality, encompassing both good and evil, a day and a night side. Think of Herakles who killed his wife and children; Theseus, who caused his son's death; Agamemnon, who sacrificed his daughter—the examples are legion.

7. As Athene says to Odysseus in Sophocles' tragedy *Ajax* in recognition of these traits: "Know that the gods/ Love men of steady sense and hate the proud" (v. 132-33).

8. Pietro Pucci in *Odysseus Polytropos* has analyzed the meaning of the stomach (*gaster*) in a somewhat different way in chap. 17.

9. *Kyklops* v. 334-35.

10. *Agamemnon* v. 176-77.

11. Achilleus' mother is the sea goddess Thetis, his father the mortal king, Peleus.

12. Erich Auerbach's analysis may be found in chap. 1 of *Mimesis*. Homer is contrasted with the minimalist narrative form of the Bible. And on this basis, the broadly told story seems to appear superficial. "Delight in physical existence is everything to them (the Greeks), and their highest aim is to make that delight perceptible to us" (p. 13), claims Auerbach; whereas, the Bible shakes people to their foundation. Consequently, Auerbach abandons the interpretation

of Homer's every meaning, since, according to Auerbach, Homer is without secrets, contains no doctrine of life, interpretations are "forced and foreign, they do not crystallize into a unified doctrine" (pp. 13-14). Auerbach overlooks or does not see the aesthetic beauty that originates from a deeper form of religious feeling among the Greeks. Thus, his reference to the hunt during which Odysseus gets his scar becomes *eo ipso* an example of the interpreter's limits with the text. As he reads the episode, it is only an idyllic surface story and is unable to open "the darkness of an unilluminated past" (p. 6). On the contrary, as I show in my analysis, this so-called idyll contains the deepest imaginable biological and psychological identification of the protagonist, based on the fact that his maternal grandfather Autolykos in the light or shadow of his own fate names his grandchild (19, 409).

13. Apollodorus' *Bibl.* I. 9.16.

14. *Hymn to Hermes* v. 13, where the epithet *polytropos* indicates the ability of the gods to transform.

15. Sophocles, *Ajax* v. 189; Ovid, *Metamophoses*, Book 13, v. 32. In addition, Sophocles uses the same designation in the tragedy *Philoktetes* v. 413 and v. 1316.

16. Fr. 80 of *The Catalogue of Women* in Hesiod, *Homeric Hymns and Homerica* (Loeb Class. Lib. 57), p. 209.

17. Homer does not explain Sisyphos' punishment, but there were reasons enough. As the audience must have known, he fooled Hades, for example, and had him put in handcuffs, so that he had to annul death on earth, but, in fury, the gods forced Sisyphos to free death.

18. Emblematics means the register of signs and figures that, through the mythic tradition handed down, is available to the narrator, containing the adaptation of experiences from earlier times into fixed pictorial images (iconography).

19. Adonis is killed by Artemis, who in this context appears as the terrible mother, in vengeance for Aphrodite's killing of Hippolytos, as it is also indicated in Euripides' *Hippolytos* v. 1419-20.

20. The wild boar helmet that Odysseus puts on derives from the 16th-12th centuries B.C. See the illustrations in *Gods and Heroes of the Bronze Age*, p. 52 and p. 88. Semi-cylindrical shields and bronze mail are also known from these centuries.

21. It is also characteristic of this dual perspective that Parnassos and Delphi are places associated with both chthonic and Apollonian powers—in a myth Pausanias recounts, Lykoreia takes its name from a son of Apollo: Lykoros (Pausanias X.6.2).

22. See Peter Rose, *Sons of the Gods*, p. 129.

23. On these dual parents, Erich Neumann writes: "The fact that the hero has two fathers or two mothers is a central feature in the canon of the hero myth. Besides his personal father there is a 'higher', that is to say an archetypal, father figure, and similarly an archetypal mother appears beside the personal mother. This double descent, with its contrasted personal and suprapersonal parental figures, constellates the drama of the hero's life" (*The Origins and History of Consciousness*, p. 132).

24. If Antikleia is the biological mother, linked by bond of blood to her son, Eurykleia represents the good, attentive mother figure. We shall see this duality in the function of the mother in corresponding examples in tragic poetry. Iokaste is Oedipus' biological mother, while Merope, his mother in Corinth, attentively cares for him and corresponds, in this way, to Eurykleia. We meet the same contrast in Aeschylus' *Oresteia*, where Klytemnestra is Orestes' mother by blood, while he grew up under the protection of his nurse Kilissa.

VII: THE *WANDERINGS*

1. *Apologoi* derives from the Greek word *apologos*: tale. In Homeric scholarship, they are often traced back to Boeotia on account of their comparability and explicit references to the *Argonautica*. Undeniably, there are so many overlaps between the figures that it seems probable that the *Odyssey* either has the *Argonautica* as a source of inspiration or that these works draw upon a common original source. Iason is, like Odysseus, the maternal grandson of Autolykos.

Iason marries Medea, who is Kirke's niece, and these two resemble each other so much that they merge—just as do Iason and Odysseus (see note 4 in "VI. Odysseus").

2. With reference to Jung, E. Neumann defines this re-integration as "heroic incest"—a struggle with the primal mother in her destructive form as dragon or wild animal—which he characterizes in this way: "victory over the mother, frequently taking the form of actual entry into her, i.e. incest, brings absolutely a rebirth. The incest produces a transformation of personality which alone makes a hero a hero, that is, at higher and ideal representative of mankind (....) The struggle is variously represented as the entry into the cave, the descent to the underworld. That is shown most clearly in the hero myths which take the form of sun myths; here the swallowing of the hero by the dragon-night, sea, underworld corresponds to the sun's nocturnal journey, from which it emerges victoriously after having conquered the darkness." (p. 154 ff.; see also p. 318 f.)

3. During his long voyage home, Menelaos is also blown off course at Cape Maleia, see 3, 287.

4. See *Essays on the* Odyssey, p. 79.

5. The Roman grammarian Servius (circa A.D. 400) is the source of this myth in his commentary on Virgil's *Aeneid* III, v. 420.

6. Ovid, *Metamorphoses*, Book 14, v. 41-74.

7. In the *Helen*, Euripides describes the Sirens as "winged maidens, virgin daughters of Earth" (v. 168).

8. See Jane Harrison, *Prolegomena*, p. 139.

9. *Theogony* v. 483.

10. The caves of Kalypso and Skylla are designated as *speos*; of those of he Kyklopes' the word *antron* is used.

11. Like E. Neumann in note 2, M. Eliade also describes in *Rites and Symbols of Initiation* the liberation from the mother as a return to "the womb," where the hero must enter into caves, corresponding to the underworld (p. 62), and he sees in the cave a counterpart to the labyrinth and refers to Theseus' struggle with the Minotaur in the labyrinth of Knossos (p. 121). See note 3 to "VIII. The Trials of Homecoming."

12. An account of the dissemination of this myth may be found in Apollodorus vol. II (Loeb Class. Lib. 122): "Ulysses and Polyphemes," p. 404 ff. Here, it is stated that the adventure is found in 220 variants.

13. According to the *Theogony* (Th. 139), brought into the world by Gaia and the oldest monsters, who are named Kyklopes because of their ring-formed eyes (Th. 145). Plato (*The Laws* 680b) was of the opinion that the Kyklopes were a first primitive patriarchy after the flooding of the earth.

14. It is a significant sign that the wine, which has the power to drug the Kyklopes, comes from a priest of Apollo. Experimentally, this could be interpreted in such a way that in the wine is the same form of force as that with which Apollo killed the Python dragon at Delphi.

15. See commentary to 19, 25 in *A Commentary to Homer's Odyssey*.

16. *Theogony* v. 453.

17. See commentary to 13, 142 in *A Commentary to Homer's Odyssey*.

18. See M. Detienne and J.-P. Vernant, *Cunning Intelligence*, chap. 7.

19. Erich Neumann sets up "the terrible male/father" as a counterpart to "the terrible mother" (*The Origins and History of Consciousness*, p. 185 ff.). Charles H. Taylor also stresses the chthonic features of the figure of Poseidon in his essay, "The Obstacles to Odysseus' Return," when he writes: "The evidence now strongly suggests that he was chthonic in his origins" (p. 575). Taylor exemplifies this with the epithets that connect him to the earth—"Earth Encircler" and "Earthshaker"—as well as the fact that he was married to Demeter. And he compares Poseidon to Kalypso and Kirke: "Like Poseidon, Calypso in her cave and Kirke keeping men as domesticated animals are indeed chthonic personalities" (*ibid.*) This point of view is supported by E. O. James in *The Cult of the Mother-Goddess*, which similarly calls Poseidon a "male god of fertility" (p. 248).

20. According to the myths, it was Odysseus (Pausanias VIII, 14.4/5) who brought Poseidon

to Arkadia—perhaps in connection with his own departure from Boeotia (see J.A.K.Thomson, *Studies in the Odyssey*, p. 42f.). See also note 30 to "VIII. The Trials of Homecoming".

21. Hermes—like Athene—has access to Hades' helmet of invisibility; his winged wand is entwined by snakes, which like Athene's aegis, shows that the want receives its power of transformation from the chthonic.

22. Jane E. Harrison, *Prolegomena*, p. 45.

23. The question is whether *moly* corresponds to the golden bough in the *Aeneid* (VI, v. 136 ff.), which provides access to the realm of the dead and may only be taken by those chosen by fate, who thereby achieve insight into the mysteries of death?

24. As E. Neumann writes, the Great Mother is ruler of wild animals (see Artemis' epithet— ruler of animals, *potnia theron*). And he continues with respect to the swine as an accompanying animal for Demeter: Her attribute is the pig, a highly prolific animal; and upon it, or upon a basket—a female symbol like the cornucopia—the goddess sits with splayed legs, even in the supreme mystery of Eleusis" (*The Origins and History of Consciousness*, p. 84). Pigs were often sacrificed at the Eleusinian festivals and the Thesmophoria in honor of Demeter. This cult may also provide an explanation for why the pig was considered unclean in patriarchal Judaism, since Isaiah (66, 17), for example, says that the Lord condemns those who hold cult festivals and eat pigs and mice.

25. See E. Neumann's description of the sacred act, *op. cit.*, p. 53–61.

26. In the *Hymn to Aphrodite*, the Greek word *biothalmios*, life-force, is used (v. 189–90). Hesiod, *The Homeric Hymns and Homerica* (Loeb Class. Lib. 57), p. 219.

27. A parallel is Hesiod's *Catalogue of Women* in Hesiod, *Homeric Hymns and Homerica* (Loeb Class. Lib. 57).

28. See G. Nagy, *The Best of the Achaeans*, pp. 26–30.

29. Nestor and Menelaos also make it home, but are not counted as belonging to the highest echelon of heroes.

30. The background event is mentioned, *inter alia*, in *The Little Iliad* and Sophocles, *Ajax*. His suicide put a mark of shame on his honor, which is why he cannot by definition be the best of the Greek warriors.

31. See Ragnar Höistad, *Cynic Hero and Cynic King*.

32. In the *Iliad*, Homer addresses the Muses in almost the same manner (II, 485). The juxtaposition of the Muses and the Sirens is not in itself surprising, since in other sources the Sirens are the daughters of the Muses (Apollodorus' *Epitome* VII. 18).

33. Apollodorus relates (*Bibl.* I. 9.22) that, after Iason's passage, the rocks stood still in accordance with the determination of Fate. That they are also mobile—just like King Aiolos' island— may be another piece of evidence of material gathered from the icebergs of the far north.

34. In *Rites and Symbols*, M. Eliade mentions, for example, "the crab woman" as an example of a similarly castrating being (vagina dentata), p. 51 ff.

35. *Metamorphoses*, Book 14, v. 60.

36. See the astronomical calculation in the commentary to 5, 272 in *A Commentary to Homer's Odyssey*.

37. E. Neumann, *The Origins and History of Consciousness*, p. 212.

38. Gilbert Murray, *The Rise of the Greek Epic*, p. 212.

39. *Works and Days* v. 112–13.

40. *Catalogue of Women*, fr. 49 in Hesiod, *Homeric Hymns and Homerica* (Loeb Class. Lib. 57), p. 183.

VIII: THE TRIALS OF HOMECOMING

1. *Theogony* v. 212. That this interpretation was common in antiquity appears from the fact that Ovid in his *Metamorphoses* even gave sleep a place of residence in the realm of the dead. In the land of the Kimmerians, he claims there is a deep cave, which is "the house and sanctuary of drowsy Sleep" (*Metamorphoses*, XI, v. 593).

2. *Works and Days* v. 116.

3. In *Rites and Symbols of Initiation*, M. Eliade writes: "Access to the sacred and to the spirit is always figured as an embryonic gestation and a new birth" (p. 58). It is not strange that Odysseus is described several times in the death/birth context, since this form of birth can take place various times (*ibid.*, p. 59).

4. M. Eliade: "In all these contexts, the return to the mother signifies return to the chthonian Great Mother. The initiand is born again from the womb of Mother Earth (…) the chthonian Great Mother shows herself pre-eminently as Goddess of Death" (*Rites and Symbols of Initiation*, pp. 61 f.) See also note 11 in "VII. The 'Wanderings.'" The initiation of girls is not nearly so dramatic—she simply takes up residence in a hut or a cave to be initiated into the mysteries of conception and birth (*ibid.*, p. 51).

5. The vision has similarities with Njal's visions before his death at Bergthorsvoll: "Wondrously now it seems to me. Methinks I see all round the room, and it seems as though the gable wall were thrown down, but the whole board and the meat on it is one gore of blood" (chap. 127)(trans. by George W. Dasent).

6. See J. A. Russo, "The Inner Man in Archilochus and the Odyssey," p. 147.

7. A description of the number and names of the suitors is found in *A Commentary to Homer's* Odyssey, see commentary to 22, 241-329.

8. M. Eliade, *Rites and Symbols of Initiation*, p. 127.

9. This may be the explanation of Penelope's name. Etymologically, it should mean shelduck (*A Commentary to Homer's* Odyssey for 1, 222), which has been interpreted as a symbol of her fidelity, since ducks are monogamous. Penelope's name may be derived from thread, and this would then mean: she who weaves and unravels (*ibid.*, to 19, 130).

10. Apollodorus' *Epitome* VII. 38 and next note.

11. Pausanias VIII. 12.5.

12. Note 1 to Apollodorus' *Epitome* VII. 38

13. Euripides, *Orestes* v. 590.

14. Horn corresponds to the word *kraino* = fulfill—ivory (*elephas*) to *elephairomai*, which means to deceive. See commentary to 19, 562-63 in *A Commentary to Homer's* Odyssey.

15. *The Little Iliad* 1 (Hesiod, *Homeric Hymns and Homerica*, Loeb. Class. Lib. 57), pp. 508-10.

16. That, according to the *Odyssey*, Herakles killed Iphitos (21, 27) causes a slight chronological confusion that Herakles and Odysseus must be contemporaries, even though in Book 11 Odysseus indicates that Herakles, like other great heroes, goes back to earlier times (11, 630).

17. See the introduction to Book 22 in *A Commentary to Homer's* Odyssey in which the appearance and structure of types of bows and axes is discussed.

18. The fr. 100, p. 69. [Heraclitus, Kahn trans., LXXVIII (DK 51)].

19. The bow's enormous concentration of power is illustrated by the fact that the Greeks use the arrow shot as a metaphor for the most intense events in life. Thus, Penelope prays that Artemis' arrow might kill her before the wedding (20, 61), just as Apollo in the *Iliad* sends death upon the Greek army with his arrow shots. It is also with a shot from his bow that he, Apollo, takes down the serpent of Delphi and moves the cult from the primordial darkness of the maternal to the conscious world of light.

20. *Menos* is also a form of energy that can be infused into other beings than human, as when Athene—in a wager connected to Patroklos' death—infuses Diomedes' horse with a dose of *menos* (XXIII, 400). Otherwise, reference is made to analyses of *menos* in J. Bremer, *The Early Greek Concept of the Soul*, pp. 59 f. and R. B. Onians, *The Origins of European Thought*, pp. 52 f.

21. The many coincidences between the slaughter of the suitors and war in the *Iliad* may be observed in the commentary to Book 21 in *A Commentary to Homer's* Odyssey.

22. See the description of the zen of archery in Eugen Herrigel, *Zen in the Art of Archery*.

23. See *The Odyssey* (A. T. Murray edition in Loeb Class. Lib. 105): "The recurved, 'composite' bow, familiar from Mycenaean times, was made of wood, sinew, and pieces of horn, the latter, bound to the wood with sinew, acting in effect as a powerful spring" (p. 339).

24. Homer does not himself mention a new year; but, to judge from the context, he seems to view the winter solstice as the beginning of the new year. In that case, he is in alignment with the Norsemen (Yule) and the Anglo-Saxons (Geol). On the other hand, in the Attic calendar, the first month of the year, hekatombaion, was some time in June/July. See N. Austin, *Archery at the Dark of the Moon*, p. 251.

25. The epithet seems related to the word for light/lamp, *lynchnos*, but may also indicate that Apollo came from Lycia. See the comment to 19, 306 in *A Commentary to Homer's* Odyssey.

26. In *Quellen der Odyssee*, Otto Seech has collected the many features in the Odyssey that point to Odysseus' origin as a sun god or solar hero. However, Seech does not provide an overall interpretation (pp. 267-76). Even J. J. Bachofen nods to the significance to solar mythology, when he writes: "The moon governs the night as the sun governs the day. Mother right may be identified with the moon and the night, father right with the sun and the day. (…) The matriarchal system is reflected in the time reckoning that begins from midnight, the patriarchal system in the time reckoning that starts with the day. The lunar month corresponds to matriarchy, the solar year to patriarchy. (…) All the great heroes who triumphed over matriarchy take their place in the heavens as solar powers. In this solar myth there is no mother but only a father. The father is followed by a son who everlastingly regenerates himself" (*Myth, Religion and Mother Right*, pp. 148 f.). See also N. Austin's interpretation in *Archery at the Dark of the Moon*, pp. 237-53.

27. This connectedness between the sun and Odysseus is also indicated in several other instances. The Sun has 350 head of cattle on Thrinakia, corresponding roughly to the number of days in the year. In the same way, it is related that Odysseus has 360 head of cattle, which the suitors consume, which is why they are punished with death (see Seech, *op cit.* p. 267). In the *Iliad*, Apollo is indignant that the Greeks have captured the daughter of his priest and casts death-bringing arrows into the Greek army. If he is considered the god of light, the bow is an image of the sun, sending its rays like arrow shots into the world. Were this image to be transferred to Odysseus, it might be interpreted in this way:, with his bow and *menos*, he shoots, so to speak, his strength with the arrow like a sunray through the 12 axes, representing the 12 lunar cycles into which the year is divided and is itself a magic number.

28. See note 38 to "VII. The 'Wanderings.'"

29 M. Eliade, *The Myth of the Eternal Return*, p. 71.

30. Jane E. Harrison, among others, calls these cult gods and heroes, who ensure fertility, *Eniautos Daimon*. *Eniautos* means something like *etos*: year. Whereas *etos* is the designation for the year as a whole, *eniautos* defines a determinate cut off point in the year, namely, the arrival of the new year, at a point when the winter months move into the summer months (*Themis*, p. 182). The *Eniautos Daimon* phenomenon is so prominent in her *Prolegomena* and *Themis*, that these works are cited generally here.

According to J. A. K. Thomson, *Studies in the* Odyssey, Odysseus was worshipped as such a divinity in agrarian Boeotia. He bases his interpretation on Odysseus' journey to Hades, which he takes as evidence that Odysseus is defined by his solar myth (p. 95). His Boeotian origin is deduced from the fact that he meets the Boeotian seer Teiresias and because the parade of dead women whom Odysseus sees in Hades comprehends figures from the same area. Odysseus was to have gone thereafter to the Peloponnesus, as Pausanias locates him in various contexts in Arkadia and Mantineia (see note 20 to "VII. The 'Wanderings'"). Here, he meets the local fertility and moon goddess Penelope. The third and final stage in Odysseus' secularized transformation is his move to Ithaka, where he rules together with Penelope as the couple with which we are familiar in the Odyssey, though still preserving a trace of their genesis as original deities.

31. *Hymn to Apollo* v. 132.

32. See M. Eliade's description in *The History of Religious Ideas*, vol. I. sec. 125, pp. 328 ff.

33. The authenticity of this dialogue has been questioned.

34. Plato, *The Laws* 319c.

35. J. A. K. Thomson, *Studies in the* Odyssey, p. 58 and p. 102.

36. Pausanias III. 12.1-2.

37. *Ibid.* III. 20.10.11.

38. Many myths confirm this sort of mythical pattern among the Greeks. Gilbert Murray has ingeniously calculated that an encounter between sun and moon could only take place in the nineteenth year, a synod between sun and moon (*syonodos helios kai selenes, The Rise of Greek Religion*, p. 211). Correspondingly, it has been put this way: "If Odysseus is the Young King and the Sun Bridegroom, Penelopeia must be the Moon Bride" (J. A. K. Thomson, *Studies in the Odyssey*, p. 58). This retrograde cult in which the bridegroom is to capture and take home the bride is especially well-known from the tale about how Pelops won Hippodameia in a horse race with her father Oinomaos (see p. 377). Peleus drives his bride in a chariot of the sun (Jane E. Harrison, *Themis*, p. 200), in which the woman is represented as a moon. And Euripides has the sun and moon travel together in the tragedy *The Suppliant Maidens* (v. 990). The same references do not exist for Penelope as moon goddess as they do for Odysseus as a sun king. However, in her mythology, she has features that endow her with a lunar, primordial feminine sexuality, when she claims to be mother to Pan by by all the suitors (or Pan), an Aphrodite-like promiscuity that made Odyseus send her to Mantineia, see Apollodorus' *Epitome* VII. 38.

IX: THE HOMERIC UTOPIA

1. Plato, *Republic* 363 b–c.

2. *Theogony* v. 96.

2. *Works and Days* v. 225–27.

3. *Republic* 363 b.

5. See Peter W. Rose, *Sons of the Gods*, p. 83.

6. *Theogony* v. 902.

7. See Oswyn Murray, *Early Greece*, pp. 186 f.

8. Fr. 1 in *Greek Elegiac Poetry* (ed. by Douglas E. Gerber, Loeb Class. Lib. 258), p. 108 (Testimonium vitae).

9. Thus, it is no coincidence that Solon wrote in Ionian verse, because, as Werner Jaeger (*Paideia* II, p. 136) relates, Solon was able to forge a symbiosis between the centrifugal outward movement of the Ionian enlightenment, which liberated the individual citizen's potential energy, with Athen's centripetal limitation of individual development with regard to the state.

10. Fr. 4 in *Greek Elegiac Poetry*, p. 158.

11. For information on the phenomenon of *miasma*, its content and development, I refer generally to Robert Parker's book, *Miasma: Pollution and Purification in Early Greek Religion*.

12. Quoted in Aristotle's *The Constitution of Athens, in Aristotle and Xenophon on Democracy and Oligarchy* (trans. with commentary by J.M. Moore) Berkeley/Los Angeles 1975), p. 156.

13. *Ibid.*, fr. 6, p. 122.

14. The description of the evolution—devolution, if you will—of the aristocracy is treated with great precision by J.-P. Vernant, *The Origins of Greek Thought*, pp. 72 ff. and Oswyn Murray, *op cit.*, chap. 12.

15. Quoted in Aristotle's *The Constitution of Athens, in Aristotle and Xenophon on Democracy and Oligarchy, op. cit.*, p. 155.

16. See, for example, Minna Skafte Jensen's discussion in *The Homeric Question and the Oral-Formulaic Theory*, chap. 9, "The 'Pisistratean Recension'."

17. Herodotus, *History* 5. 65.

XI. HESIOD AS TRANSITIONAL POET

1. *On the Origin of Homer and Hesiod and Their Competition* in Hesiod, *Homeric Hymns and Homerica* (Loeb Class. Lib. 57), p. 587.

2. See E. R. Dodds, *The Ancient Concept of Progress*, pp. 1 ff., and note 38 in "II. The Homeric Project."

3. See G. S. Kirk and J. E. Raven, *The Presocratic Philosophers*, pp. 32 ff. Erich Neumann has thoroughly interpreted the psychological significance of this separation, which according to myth takes place between the heavenly parents, in *The Origins and History of Consciousness*, pp. 102-27, see Note 4 to "III. The Dual Religiosity."

4. See Helen North, *Sophrosyne*, p. 9.

5. Fr. 7, 93-94 in *Greek Elegy and Jambus II* (Loeb Class. Lib. 259), p. 222.

6. Jane E. Harrison writes, "Pandora is in ritual and matriarchal theology the earth as Kore, but in the patriarchal mythology of Hesiod her great figure is strangely changed and diminished" (*Prolegomena*, p. 284).

7. Pietro Pucci, *Hesiod and the Language of Poetry*, p. 89.

8. Kahn, *The Art and Thought of Heraclitus* (1979), LXXXIII (DK 53).

9. W. K. C. Guthrie, *Essays on the Odyssey*, pp. 7 ff.

10. For evidence that Hesiod bases his analogy of ages and metals on a common tradition, see the Biblical account of the Colossus with the feet of clay in the Book of Daniel, 2:41-45. The head is made of gold, the chest and arms of silver, belly and loins of copper, feet of iron and clay. It appears in Nebuchadnezzar's dream and is interpreted as the image of the kingdoms that follow one another, all to be crushed by the Kingdom of God.

XII. THE LYRICAL SENSE OF SELF

1. Translation from Loeb Class. Lib. 259, p. 99. Other dates are 5 April 647 B.C. and 27 June 660 B.C. (see *Greek Elegy and Jambus II*, p. 135, note 5).

2. *Greek Elegy and Jambus II*, p. 90 (*Testimonia vitae*).

3. *The Birth of Tragedy*, chap. 5 (Kaufmann ed., p. 48).

4. *Greek Elegy and Jambus II*, p. 84 (*Testimonia vitae*).

5. *Ibid.*, p. 97 (*Testimonia vitae*).

6. *Ibid.*, p. 86 (*Testimonia vitae*).

7. Unpubl. translation by William Blake Tyrell.

8. Translation from Loeb Class. Lib. 259, p. 101.

9. *Greek Elegy and Jambus II*, p. 57 (*Testimonia vitae*).

10. *Ibid.*, p. 57. (Davenport trans. 262, p. 87).

11. *Ibid.*, p. 84 and p. 86 (*Testimonia vitae*).

12. *Greek Lyric I*, fr. 32, p. 32 (*Testimonia vitae*).

13. *Ibid.*, fr. 8, p. 10 (*Testimonia vitae*).

14. *Ibid.*, fr. 8, p. 2 (*Testimonia vitae*).

15. Plato, *Phaedrus* 235c: *Sapphous tes kales*.

16. *Greek Lyric I*, fr. 60, p. 48 (*Testimonia vitae*).

17. *Ibid.*, fr. 57, p. 46 (*Testimonia vitae*).

18. *Ibid.* fr. 2, p. 6 (*Testimonia vitae*). Here, it is also pointed out, among other things, that she was married to the wealthy Keryklas. She was supposed to have written nine books of lyric poetry and one of elegies, see Fr. 1 (*Testimonia vitae*). In *Sappho's Sweet Bitter* Songs, Lyn H. Wilson has tried to form a comprehensive view, interpreting Sappho's person and works in combination with feminist and psychoanalytic theories.

19. *Ibid.*, fr. 38, p. 34 (*Testimonia vitae*).

20. *Ibid.*, fr. 1, p. 2 (*Testimonia vitae*).

21. *Ibid.*, fr. 2, p. 6 (*Testimonia vitae*).

22. *Ibid.*, fr. 2, p. 6 (*Testimonia vitae*).

23. Holger Friis Johansen, *Arkaisk græsk lyrik*, p. 33.

24. K. J. Dover, *Greek Homosexuality*, p. 174 ff.

25. *Greek Lyric I*, f. 20, (*Testimonia vitae*).

26. See Page du Bois, *Sowing the Body*, p. 27.

XIII. PRESOCRATIC THOUGHT

1. *Theogony* v. 115.

2. See generally Karsten Friis Johansen, *A History of Ancient Philosophy from the Beginnings to Augustine*. Moreover, among those to whom I am indebted are G. S. Kirk and J. E. Raven, *The Presocratic Philosophers*.

3. See *The Presocratic Philosophers*, p. 77.

4. Jane E. Harrison, for example, believes that the elemental philosophy with fire, water, derives from Persian nature gods, see *Themis*, p. 461 ff.

5. See *The Presocratic Philosophers*, p. 102.

6. Arthur Fairbanks, trans., in *The First Philosophers of Greece* (1898), p. 14.

7. See Werner Jaeger, *Paideia* I, p. 159 ff.

8. J.-P. Vernant, *The Origins of Greek Thought*, p. 130.

9. *Ibid.*, p. 121 and p. 126.

10. Kirk and Raven, *The Presocratic Philosophers*, fr. 169 and 170, p. 168.

11. *Ibid.*, fr. 174, p. 169.

12. *Ibid.*, fr. 173, p. 169.

13. *Ibid.*, fr. 189, p. 179.

14. Charles H. Kahn provides a thorough analysis of each fragment in *The Art and Thought of Heraclitus*.

15. *Theogony* v. 749.

16. Quotation from Aristotle, *Metaphysics* (W.D. Ross, trans.) 986a.

17. Arthur Fairbanks, trans., *op. cit.* p. 160.

18. *Ibid.*, p. 182.

19. Trans. note: the translation is from Kirk & Raven, except for the last clause, which is from Fairbanks' translation.

XIV. THE LIFE AND FORM OF TRAGEDY

1. Athenaios VIII, 39 (347), cited in Jane E. Harrison, *Themis*, p. 334.

2. Plato, *Republic* 595c.

3. An example of the many interpretations of the origin of tragedy—due primarily to a fundamental lack of knowledge hereof—is Gerald F. Else, *The Origin and Early Form of Greek Tragedy*. He rejects the idea that tragedy has anything to do with the Dionysian *dithramb* or a ritual *dromenon* in connection with a Year God, *Eniautos Daimon*, as Gilbert Murray and Jane E. Harrison have alleged (pp. 11 ff.) He does not find in the song of the chorus (p. 71) traces of Dionysos' wildness and madness, just as the dialogue in itself is anti-Dionysian (p. 69). In short, he rejects both Aristotle's and Nietzsche's views of the origin. The choral song, he believes, is derived from laments, *threnoi*, sung at funerals, for example.

However, Else acknowledges, honestly enough, that Dionysos always appears in this context (p. 27 and p. 30). Yet, this has no influence on his argument. And, surprisingly, he provides no explanation for why Dionysos becomes god of the tragedy competitions in his honor at the Great Dionysia. Nor does he take a position on Aristophanes' *The Frogs*, in which Dionysos appears as the god of tragedy, or Euripides' *The Bacchae*, whose plot deals with the god's desire to be brought into the life of the city-state—as Zeus' son, Dithrambos. By ignoring this, he can sharpen and establish his own hypothesis, which has two primary elements: 1. The creators of tragedy are Thespis and Aeschylus. 2. It belongs only to Athens. Thespis was supposed to have been the originator of tragedy—almost from nothing. According to Else, he creates it on the basis of Solon's philosophy of justice and by having the hero to step out in front of the chorus. This hero was taken primarily from the *Iliad* and displays his heroism and limitations. This first form Else calls *tragoidia* and its actors (and poets) *tragoidios*, because the first prize was a goat. The account the hero provides of his fate, his mistakes and death was to have been recited in iambic speech, echoing the chorus' lament, *threnos*, which was older than Homer. The lament expresses sorrow over the hero's suffering and, in this way, suffering (*pathos*) became placed in the center. This beginning, created by Thespis, leads Aeschylus to true tragedy. On the other hand, Else does not discuss the *Prometheus* due to the lack of dating of the piece.

4. *Poetics*, chap. 4 (1449a11-15).

5. Plato, *The Laws* 700).

6. *The Bacchae* v. 513-14.

7. *Ibid.* v. 515-16.

8. *Poetics*, ch. 4 (1449a 20-22).

9. Herodotus, *The History* 1.23.

10. *Ibid.* 5. 67.

11. *The Birth of Tragedy*, ch. 11 (Kaufmann, p. 63).

12. *Ibid.*, ch. 11 (Kaufmann, p. 62)

13. *Ibid.*, ch. 11 (Kaufmann, p. 77)

14. *Ibid.*, ch. 12 (Kaufmann, p. 83)

15. *Ibid.*, ch. 14 (Kaufmann, p. 92)

16. Jane E. Harrison's hypothesis, *Themis.* p. 339.

17. In *The Theatre of Dionysos in Athens*, A. Picard-Cambridge argued that the first theater in the early fifth century B.C. was located at the public square in Athens, where the seats were made of wood (pp. 12 ff.). The theater at the Acropolis also had wooden benches, while the stone seats as we know them today were not introduced until the fourth century B.C. (p. 138).

18. A. Picard-Cambridge, *The Dramatic Festivals of Athens*, p. 339.

19. *Poetics*, ch. 14 (1453b26).

20. *Ibid.*, ch. 20 (1451b26).

21. Aeschylus, *The Persians* v. 419-20 (Podlecki, trans.).

22. Aeschylus, *Agamemnon* v. 178.

23. Aeschylus, *The Eumenides* v. 535.

24. *Poetics*, ch. 6 (1450b1).

25. *Ibid.* (1450b5).

26. *Ibid.* (1449b20-25).

27. Plato, *Republic* 394b.

28. *Poetics*, ch. 9 (1451b5).

29. *Ibid.* (1451b5-7).

30. *Ibid.* (1451b7-8).

31. *Ibid.* (1453b25).

32. *Ibid.* (1449b27).

33. *The Eumenides* v. 520-21.

34. *The Frogs* v. 1009-10.

35. *Poetics*, ch. 15 (1454b9).

36. *Ibid.*, ch. 13 (1453a15).

37. *Ibid.* (1453a13).

38. *Ibid.* (1451a16).

39. *Ibid.* (1455b16).

40. *Ibid.* (1462b2).

41. *Oedipus the King* v. 1213.

42. *Poetics*, chap. 13 (1453a30).

XV. AESCHYLUS

1. *The Frogs* v. 884-85 (ed. and trans. by Alan H. Sommerstein, Aris & Phillipps Ltd, 1996).

2. Herbert W. Smyth's introduction to Aeschylus' *Tragedies* I (Loeb Class. Lib. 145), p. xv ff.

3. *Poetics*, chap. 4, 1449a15.

4. Gerald F. Else, *The Origin and Early Form of Greek Tragedy*, p. 57; p. 98.

5. Herbert W. Smyth's introduction to Aeschylus' *Tragedies* I (Loeb Class. Lib. 145), p. xxvi.

6. *The Frogs* v. 1004–05.

7. *Ibid.*, v. 940.

8. *Ibid.*, v. 1298.

9. The accumulation of money after the introduction of the monetary system in the 6th century B.C. became an end in itself. As Theognis writes in warning: "Those who own much today want double the amount. Wealth makes people crazy" (J.-P. Vernant, *The Origins of Greek Thought*, p. 83).

10. Trans. by John Porter, Univ. of Saskatchewan (www. uke.usask.ca/~porterj /DeptTransls/Solon.html).

11. *Ibid.*

12. *Works and Days* v. 213–15.

13. *The Eumenides* v. 533–34.

14. *"nosos phrenon,"* v. 750.

15. Herodotus, *The History* 1.34.

16. Aristophanes, *The Frogs* v. 1022.

17. *"philon aboulian".*

18. In Sophocles, Oedipus is banished, while in Euripides' *The Phoenician Women* he is locked up.

19. *Seven Against Thebes* v. 686–88.

20. The council of Thebes imposes an injunction against burying Polyneikes, but Antigone determines to do it anyway, which corresponds to the theme in Sophocles' *Antigone* and may be a later interpolation, unless Sophocles took the theme from Aeschylus.

21. The powerful woman is designated *kratousa*, v. 189, the fearsome *deisasa*, v. 190.

22. According to Pausanias II.5, before King Pelops, the Peloponnesus was called Apia after Apis, whom Aeschylus makes the son of Apollo. In the *Agamemnon*, as well, he uses the designation Apia for the Peloponnesus, Ag. 256–57.

23. Fr. 25 in Aeschylus, *Tragedies* II (Loeb Class. Lib. 146), p. 395.

24. See R. P. Winnington-Ingram, *Studies in Aeschylus*, p. 58 ff.

25. Apollodorus' *Bibl.* II. 1.5, which contains a complete description of the mythology surrounding the Danaids.

26. With *The Authenticity of Prometheus Bound*, M. Griffith has written what he himself says is "an unreadable book" (p. xii), by which through his analysis of the meter, style, vocabulary and syntax he believes he can show that *Prometheus Bound* cannot have been written by Aeschylus—so different is this tragedy from his other works. In that case, Griffith acknowledges that the unknown author must have known Aeschylus' texts extremely well (p. 253), but also Sophocles and Euripides. He then lists a series of possible authors whose works we know, which, it must be admitted, makes his conjecture of the author's identity quite arbitrary. Various hypotheses on the trilogy assume that it may have only been a dilogy consisting of *Prometheus Bound* and *Prometheus Liberated* (H. Lloyd-Jones, *The Justice of Zeus*, p. 98 ff), possibly because, as E. R. Dodds suggests, Aeschylus died before completing the last part (*The Ancient Concept of Progress*, p. 38). *Prometheus the Fire-Bringer* is mentioned only in a few places and may have been a satyr play, performed in connection with *The Persians*.

27. See, for example, H. W. Smith's discussion in Aeschylus' *Tragedies* II, (Loeb Class. Lib. 146), p. 445 ff. and R. P. Winnington-Ingram, *Studies in Aeschylus*, chap. 9.

28. In *Eros and Civilization*, H. Marcuse has made Prometheus into the archetype of the Western performance principle and he attributed to this figure much of the same significance that Adorno and Horkeimer attribute to Odysseus. See note 15 to "I. The Wooden Horse."

29. *Theogony* v. 385.

30. Among the passages in which the net (and associated connotations, including the *peplos* in which Agamemnon is captured) is used are: Ag. 867; Ag. 1115; Ag. 1381; Ag. 1516; Lib.

493; Lib. 554-87; Lib. 983-84; Eum. 634-35. Aeschylus' unparalleled use of such metaphorical chains, which gather together the three works in a common composition can be followed in Anne Lebech's study, *The Oresteia: A Study in Language and Structure.*

31. G. S. Kirk and J. E. Raven, *The Presocratic Philosophers,* p. 171.

32. "*Alexeterios,*" *Seven Against Thebes* v. 8.

33. "*Zeus soter tritos,*" *The Suppliant Maidens* v. 26.

34. *The Suppliant Maidens* v. 80-86.

35. "*Zeu, Zeu, telei, tas emas enchas telei!/ meloi de toi soi tonper an melles telein*" (v. 773-74).

36. *Works and Days* v. 465.

37. Aeschylus himself mentions in a fragment this sense of the tripartite offering, see Aeschylus' *Tragedies* II (Loeb Class. Lib. 146), p. 397.

38. The metaphor is used for example in *Seven Against Thebes* v. 777-78. This metaphor goes all the way back to Alkaeus, see for instance fr. 208 in *Greek Lyric* I (ed. by David N. Campbell, Loeb Class. Lib. 142), p. 320.

39. The metaphor is continued in Euripides. Orestes and Pylades are called two lions (*Orestes* v. 298), Klytemnestra is a "lioness" (*Elektra* v. 1163). Medea, too, is mentioned as a "lioness" (*Medea* v. 187).

40. *Metamorphoses,* Book 12 v. 29.

41. See E. O. James, *The Cult of the Mother-Goddess,* pp. 150-52.

42. The Greek title *Coephoroi* = *choe-phoros* means to bring a (death)offering.

43. *Elektra* v. 307.

44. See R. Parker, *Miasma, Pollution and Purification.*

45. See E. R. Dodds, *The Greeks and the Irrational,* ch. 2, "From Shame-Culture to Guilt-Culture."

46. C. Kahn, *The Art and Thought of Heraclitus,* p. 49.

47. Jane E. Harrison, *Prolegomena,* p. 223 f.

48. *Theogony* v. 180-85.

49. In the *Theogony,* v. 217, the merciless Keres are also children of the Night.

50. *Iphigenia at Tauris* v. 1245-46.

51. *Hymn to* Apollo v. 301 (Hugh G. Evelyn-White, trans.)

52. Jane E. Harrison, *Themis,* p. 502 f.

53. *Pausanias* I. 28.6.

54. Jane E. Harrison, *Prolegomena,* p. 246. This family's overwhelming political influence was to have been the basis for Solon's elegies in which he warns against hoarding power and prestige. See G. F. Else, *The Origin and Early Form of Greek Tragedy,* p. 34.

55. *Theogony* v. 902

XVI. SOPHOCLES

1. Socrates relates that Sophocles welcomed his old age because he was liberated from the scourge of sexuality. When asked whether he could still sleep with a girl, he was supposed to have answered, "Hush, man, most gladly have I escaped this thing you talk of, as if I had run away from a raging and savage beast of a master" (*The Republic* 329c).

2. Because of the indeterminacy that generally characterizes the tragedies, we shall never know what Laios wanted at Delphi. The myths give two different explanations: 1. To hear how he could get rid of the sphinx. 2. To learn what happened to his son.

3. In mythology, the reason is stated as being that King Laios had raped the young Chrysippos, the son of King Pelops, and Hera then sent the sphinx as punishment..

4. Euripides, *The Phoenician Women* v. 1014.

5. Aeschylus, *The Suppliant Maidens* v. 357.

6. Aeschylus, *Seven Against Thebes* vv. 659-60.

7. E. R. Dodds, *The Ancient Concept of Progress,* p. 67 ff.

8. Euripides, *The Bacchae* v. 1330–39.

9. Plato, *The Republic* 571 e–d.

10. Plato, *The Laws* 838 c.

11. The English translation reads: "O Oedipus, the famous prince/ for whom a great haven (*megas limen*)/ the same both as father and son/ sufficed for generation" (1206–09). The Greek text stresses the harbor metaphor.

12. See note 37 to "XV. Aeschylus."

13. "Furrows ploughed" strengthens the association with a field sown with seed.

14. In a certain sense, Oedipus has suddenly become an orphan, which brings Oedipus to a new interpretative stage—that Fate or chance, Tyche, is his mother. The chorus embraces this idea euphorically and speculates as to who his father might then be: is it Pan, Apollo or Dionysos) (1095–1106)

15. See note 22 to "II. The Homeric Project."

16. According to Homer, Oedipus is buried in Thebes (XXIII, 679), while Pausanias (I. 28.6–7) relates that, with his own eyes, he had seen his bones conveyed from Thebes to a temple for the sacred Semnai near the Areopagus. That is, in this context, Oedipus merges with the Eumenides in their transformation from the Erinyes at the end of the *Oresteia*, just as the Eumenides did not belong to Athens but Colonus and had a role there identical to the Semnai of this place (see J. E. Harrison, *Prolegomena*, p. 253 ff.

XVII. EURIPIDES

1. Aristophanes, *The Frogs* v. 1047–48 (trans. by Alan H. Sommerstein, *The Comedies of Aristophanes*, vol. 9, 1996).

2. *Ibid.* v. 1053 and 1064.

3. *Ibid.* v. 1066–67.

4. *The Poetics*, ch. 18, 1456a28–31.

5. *The Birth of Tragedy*, ch. 17 (Kaufmann, trans., *Basic Writings of Nietzsche*, pp. 106–07).

6. Thucydides, *The Peloponnesian War* II.52 (trans. by Rex Warner, Penguin Classics 1979). Despite the great difference in his methodology from Herodotus, Thucydides saw him as a predecessor, since he himself provides a rather detailed description of circumstances in Greece between the end of the Persian Wars in 479 B.C. and the outbreak of the Peloponnesian War. Thucydides tries to fill in the lacunae between the two works.

7. *Ibid.*, II.65.

8. *Ibid.*, III.82.

9. *Ibid.*

10. Plato, *The Republic* 427c.

11. Aristophanes, *Thesmophoriazusae*, vv. 449–51.

12. Cited in E.R. Dodds, *The Ancient Concept of Progress*, p. 96.

13. Plato, *Theatetus* 162d.

14. Heraclitus, CK XXX; DK 114.

15. P.W. Rose sees three stages in the Sophists' doctrine of society, *Sons of the Gods*, p. 274 ff.

16. Plato, *The Republic* 339a.

17. Of the three great tragedians, Euripides is the one who, in an extension of Homer, has most elaborately described the Trojan War and the story of the Tantalids. The fall of Troy is described in *The Trojan Women, Hekuba, Rhesos* (possibly, "not genuine"), the satyr plays *Helen* and *The Kyklops*—Odysseus' encounter with and victory over Polyphemos. The fateful story of the Tantalids is told in *Iphigenia at Aulis* on Agamemnon's sacrifice of his daughter, *Elektra* on the matricide, *Orestes* on the killing of Helen and, finally, *Iphigenia at Tauris*, in which Orestes liberates himself from his own and his family's curse.

In Euripides' exploitation of Book X of the *Iliad* in the *Rhesos*, the so-called Dolonia, in which Odysseus and Diomedes scout the Trojan army, Odysseus is called a "treacherous fighter" (709). In the play, Odysseus and Diomedes kill the scout Dolon and, furthermore, at Athene's request, the Thracian king Rhesos, as well. Hektor designates Odysseus the perpetrator: "What man else among the Argives could have planned and done it" (861-62).

18. See, the cyclic poem *Cypria* in Hesiod, *Homeric Hymns and Homerica* (Loeb Class. Lib. 57), p. 492.

19. Euripides' *Elektra* has many features in common with Sophocles' play of the same name. Moreover, the tragedy corresponds in many places to *The Libation Bearers*—there are several direct loans, sometimes in a slightly caricatured form: for example, the identification of Orestes by his footprint and the lock of hair he has used as a sacrifice at the tomb of Agamemnon.

20. Sophocles, *Elektra* v. 214-15) (David Grene, trans., in *Greek Tragedies* II, U of Chicago Press, 1958)

21. *Ibid.* v. 1361.

22. Correspondingly, in the *Herakles*, Theseus states that contagion cannot be conveyed from friend to friend, which he says after Herakles, blinded by Hera, has killed his children. He says, "for now you are in need of friends. But when the gods honor a man, he has no need of friends; for the god's aid, when he chooses to give it, is enough" (1337-39) (E. P. Coleridge, trans.). See R. Parker, *Miasma*, p. 309.

23. The phrasing in Greek is: "*he synesis, hoti synoida dein eirgasmenos*" (395). This passage is the first example of a direct articulation of a judging human conscience (p. 14). However, as in other cases, we must acknowledge that something can be experienced concretely before the concept has been formulated as such. Thus, it may be said that Orestes' inner vision of his mother's Erinyes in the *Oresteia* is an example of being plagued by conscience, see p. 395.

24. In the *Andromache*, Hermione is married to Neoptolemos, Achilleus' son. However, she cannot bear children. On the other hand, his war booty and mistress Andromache has born him a son. Together with her father Menelaos, Hermione wants, out of jealousy, to kill mother and child. They are prevented by King Peleus, while Orestes takes Hermione away and marries her, as he was previously "betrothed" to her.

25. See P. duBois, *Sowing the Body* (p. 114).

26. I do not think there has been sufficient emphasis laid by scholars on these familial relationships. They must have had great significance for the Greeks in their identification of special character traits, such as Klytemnestra and Helen being of one mind in contrast to their cousin Penelope, whereas there are uniform characteristics in Phaedra, Medea, Pasiphae and Kirke.

27. R. Just, *Women in Athenian Law and Life*, p. 240.

28. H. North, *Sophrosyne*, p. 69 ff.

29. Sophocles, *Women of Thracis* v. 497.

30. Aristophanes, *Thesmophoriazusae* v. 85.

31. *Ibid.*, v. 376.

32. Apollodorus, *Bibl.* III. 14.4.

33. The late dating is supported by the fact that, although Dionysos became the object of a widespread cult among a broad cross-section of the population, he hardly appears in Homer and then almost in the form of a divine hero. However, he already figures in Linear B tablets and so goes back into Mycenaean times.

34. Illustrations exist from antiquity that clearly show that Dionysos' mother Semele was viewed as an earth goddess, so that, in certain myths, Dionysos was not born from Zeus' thigh but from the earth itself—or, in Jane E. Harrison's formulation: "Semele, mother is the Earth," mother to "Earth-Dionysos" (*Prolegomena*, p. 404). The similarity between Dionysos and Zeus as *kouroi* is emphasized by the chorus' song about the Zeus child from Crete: "And I praise the holies of Crete,/ the caves of the dancing Curetes,/ there where Zeus was born" (120-23).

35. In short, Dionysos is torn apart by the Titans at the behest of the jealous Hera. But Rhea puts him together again—as Isis did with Osiris. It is significant that, according to the mythification, Zeus has the Dionysos child with Persephone, which places the myth in the fertility cult that is played out around Demeter and Kore/Persephone, as a part of the eternal cycle of

growth in which Dionysos becomes a symbol of reincarnation.

36. Pentheus is derived from *penthos*, see v. 368 and v. 1244 of the Greek text in which this etymological connection is played upon.

37. The myth that Aktaion had seen the goddess bathing naked is later.

38. The ending is very fragmentary. People have tried to fill the "lacunae" with additions and Greek fragments that seem to belong in this context.

39. Aristophanes, *The Frogs* v. 71.

40. *Ibid.*, vv. 92–97.

41. *Poetics*, ch. 13 (1453b24–30).

42. *Ibid.*, chap. 22 (1458b17–30).

XVIII. SOCRATES

1. The authenticity of Plato's letters is fiercely debated. In *Plato's Thought in the Making*, J. E. Raven refers to Lewis Campbell's detailed linguistic study of the similarities between the letters and Plato's later works, including *The Laws*, in which Campbell reaches the conclusion that there are so many agreements that the letters must be deemed genuine (p. 24 f.). With respect to the seventh letter, Raven concludes, acknowledging that he is no less subjective than others: "It is too discursive and digressive, and at the same time too characteristic of Plato, to be the work of anybody else" (p. 26).

2. S. Kierkegaard, *The Concept of Irony* (Lee Capel, trans., p. 67)

3. *Ibid.*, p. 181. Kierkegaard believes that Xenophon reduces Socrates to an absurdity by "cutting away all that was dangerous" (*ibid.*, p. 54), while Aristophanes' ridicule in *The Clouds*, according to Kierkegaard, was closer to the truth. The fact is that Aristophanes supplies a number of character traits that are rediscovered elsewhere. Thus, in Aristophanes, Socrates speaks of learning to know oneself, uses everyday parables and is described in all his ugliness; like the Sophists, he dissolves the old ideas with his airy arguments, which is why he floats in the air in a basket.

4. Like many before him, J. E. Raven tentatively divides the dialogues into three groups (*op. cit.* p. 32 ff.), a grouping that goes back to the Romantics.

5. *Symposium* V.

6. *The Clouds* v. 361.

7. In the *Apology*, Socrates himself describes these events in which he served as *prytanis*, i.e. selected as a member of the popular assembly that administered the daily business of Athens (32 a–e). Xenophon mentions the case against the commanders in his *Hellenica* I.7.3, where it is also said that the council members yielded to the lynching mood of the mob, but not Socrates. In the *Gorgias*, he also ironically describes himself as a terrible council chairman (*epistates*): "When I became a member of the Council and my tribe was presiding and it was my duty to put the question to the vote, I raised a laugh because I did not know how to" (474 a).

8. In his criticism of Socratic irony, the "enormous *daimon* [*sic*]" (*op. cit.*, p. 155), Kierkegaard makes his treatment of Alcibiades into an example of how Socrates, instead of being the one who loves, makes himself into the beloved—"a vampire who has sucked the blood out of her lover" (*ibid.* p. 86).

9. In Greek, a pupil is called *kore*, i.e. a girl, thereby indicating the small image of oneself that can be seen in the eyes of others. The word pupil comes from Latin, derived from a diminutive of pupa, pupilla.

10. Odysseus addresses Penelope in this way, when after the slaughter of the suitors she still refuses to acknowledge him, to which she responds that so he is, too (23, 166; 23, 174). Aphrodite (III, 399) and Hera (IV, 30) are also called *daimonie*.

11. Kirk and Raven, *The Presocratic Philosophers*, fr. 250 (DK 119), p. 213.

12. *Memorabilia* II.2.1–13.

13. Aristotle, *Poetics*, ch. 22 (1458a18–24).

14. *Ibid.*, ch. 2 (1448a18-19).

15. Eric A. Havelock has developed this view in, i.a., *Preface to Plato* and *The Muse Learns to Write*, see note 15 to "II. The Homeric Project."

16. There is a similar attack on the poets in the *Medea*—"Both stupid and lacking in foresight/ Those poets of old who wrote songs/ For revels and dinners and banquets " (191-93).

17. My analysis of gender relations and the position of women especially in democratic Athens is based, among others, on R. Just, *Women in Athenian Law and Life*, W. K. Lacey, *The Family in Classical Greece* and S. B. Pomeroy, *Goddesses, Whores, Wives and Slaves.*

18. *Memorabilia* II. 2.11 (Loeb Class. Lib., p. 111).

19. Xenophon, *Symposium*, II.9-10 (Raymond Larson, trans., p. 81). Diogenes Laertius (2.36-37) also makes use of Socrates' reply but relates further that Xanthippe sprayed water on Socrates and, in the square, ripped his mantle off him in a rage, but he tolerated this because she was the mother of his children.

20. Thucydides, *The Peloponnesian War* II.46 (Rex Warner, trans.).

21. Demosthenes, *Against Neaera*, 59.122 (trans. by Norman W. DeWitt and Norman J. DeWitt, 1949).

22. Euripides, *Elektra* v. 932-33.

23. What life was like in the women's apartments is difficult to say. However, as it appears in the Icelandic sagas, it can be imagined that there was a power struggle and friction between the husband's mother and the young, weaker girl who had married into the family.

24. That *hetairai* did not necessarily offer sexual services seems to be affirmed by the concept itself, derived from the Greek word for friend, *hetairos.*

25. This is said with the reservations that must be made individually when speaking of a general tendency. For example, Pericles had such an intense love for the highly gifted Aspasia that he divorced his distinguished wife, even though Aspasia was a *metoic*, i.e. an immigrant (from Miletus) and thus could not be married to him, according to Pericles' own law, which forbade marriage with non-Athenians.

26. Apollodorus' *Bibl.* III.6.7, see note 53 to "II. The Homeric Project."

27. *Thesmophorizausae* v. 390-92.

28. *Lysistrata* v. 137-39.

29. *The Assembly of Women* v. 177-81.

30. *Lysistrata* v. 595-601.

31. *Ibid.*, v. 1014.

32. *Ibid.*, v. 1018.

33. *Thesmophoriazusae* v. 788.

34. *Ibid.*, v. 793-94.

35. *Lysistrata* v. 1124-25.

36. *The Assembly of Women* v. 636-37.

37. Beyond those listed in note 17, important sources illuminating pederasty have been K. J. Dover, *Greek Homosexuality* and D. Halperin, *One Hundred Years of Homosexuality.*

38. *Symposium* IV.13-14. Cleinias was a younger cousin of Alcibiades. Critobulus appears in other Platonic dialogues and is present, for example, at the trial.

39. In *Early Greece*, Oswyn Murray writes about the causes of the sudden change in attitude towards homosexuality: "The first is that by the mid-fifth century the attitudes of the aristocracy no longer shaped culture, which under state patronage had become democratic and therefore more heterosexual in its attitudes and assumptions; homosexuality retreated into the closed world of the intellectual right and the philosophical circles of Socrates and Plato. The second factor is the resurgence of the themes of the Homeric and heroic ages both in art and in such public literary forms as tragedy—for this too involved a return to a heterosexual age" (p. 217).

The most extensive cultivation of homosexuality took place in the Spartan warrior society, where the physical closeness of older and younger men helped build and strengthen martial virtues such as self-control as well as developing social integrity (G. Murray, *The Rise of the*

Greek Epic, p. 174 f.). Young girls in Sparta, however, received an education which gave them greater freedom than elsewhere. They had their hair shaved for their wedding and had to wait for the betrothed dressed in men's clothing. As social symbolism, this must be an expression of the fact that the girls were now subject to patriarchal power, which in a combination of freedom and violent subjugation reveals features going back to the origin of patriarchy and testifies to the great difficulty it had in differentiating itself from the world of mothers.

40. Sarah B. Pomeroy argues for a similar point of view, stating: "The relationship between mother and son was marked by ambiguity and contradiction. The secluded woman nursed a repressed hostility against her elderly, inconsiderate, and mobile husband. In the absence of her husband, the mother substituted the son, alternately pouring forth her venom and doting on him. She demanded that he be successful and lived vicariously through. The emotionally powerful mother impressed herself upon the imagination of the young boy, becoming the seed, as it were, which developed into the dominant female characters of the mature playwright's mind" (*op. cit.* p. 95). The quotation is actually a socio-psychological illustration of the original relation between the primal mother and her son(s).

41. In Mantineia, a relief has been found that presumably depicts Diotima, a woman who served as a priestess in the temple of Apollo. She could interpret omens and could prophesy.

42. Diogenes Laertius II.40 (Loeb Class. Lib. 184, p. 171).

43. *Apology* 30–31.

44. *Memorabilia* I.2.12.

45. *Apology* 14, where Xenophon uses the word *phthonos*.

46. Sophocles, *Oedipus the King* v. 869.

47. Sophocles, *Antigone* v. 455.

48. In a sort of vision, Socrates also depicts the realm of the dead in levels in the *Phaedo* (110–14) and in the *Republic*, Book X.

49. *The Eumenides* v. 985.

50. To the images of the cave and the sun is added the so-called line metaphor at the end of Book 6, which leads to the image of the cave at the beginning of Book 7. It is a very complicated metaphor, the primary idea of which is that the line, considered vertically, can be divided into a number of segments. These move from the shadow images of visible phenomena to intelligible ideas, which can only be known through the dialectical process of knowledge. J. E. Raven has provided a thorough interpretation of the content and the connection between these three ideas in the chapter entitled "Sun, Divided Line and Cave" (*op. cit.* p. 131–87) to which you are referred. A variant of the sun/eye theme is found in the *Phaedo* 99 d-e.

51. *Memorabilia* IV.6.15.

52. *Ibid.* I.3.7.

53. Antiquity seems to have noticed the similarity between Odysseus and Socrates. In any event, the former was caricatured with a pot-belly and a pug nose—that is, in a figuration with clear similarities to Socrates. See W. B. Stanford, *The Ulysses Theme*, p. 254.

BIBLIOGRAPHY

1. Greek texts

In general, the Greek texts consulted have been those provided in the Loeb Classical Library (Harvard University and William Heinemann). Where particular philological concerns are applicable, they are provided in the notes.

DIEHLS, HERMAN AND WALTHER KRANZ, *Die Fragmente der Vorsokratiker*, vol. 1-3 (Zurich and Berlin), 11th ed. 1964.

KIRK, G.S. AND J.E. RAVEN, *The Presocratic Philosophers: A Critical History with a Selection of Texts* (1957) (Cambridge 1980).

2. Greek texts in English translation

Unless otherwise indicated, quotations from Greek tragedies are taken from the English translations found in The Complete Greek Tragedies (Univ. of Chicago Press), as specified below.

AESCHYLUS, *The Persians* (trans. by S. G. Benardete) Chicago 1956.

—— *Prometheus Bound* (trans. by David Grene) Chicago 1942.

—— *Oresteia* (trans. by Richmond Lattimore) Chicago 1953.

—— *Seven Against Thebes* (trans. by David Grene) Chicago 1956

—— *The Suppliant Maidens* (trans. by S. G. Benardete) Chicago 1956.

ARCHILOCHUS, *Carmina Archilochi: The Fragments of Archilochos* (trans. by Guy Davenport) Berkeley/Los Angeles 1964.

ARISTOPHANES, *Ecclesiazusae (The Assembly of Women)* (trans. by Eugene O'Neill, Jr.), New York 1938.

—— *The Frogs* (trans. by Alan H. Sommerstein) Warminster 1996.

—— *Lysistrata* (trans. by Alan H. Sommerstein), Warminster 1990.

—— *Thesmophoriazusae* (trans. by Alan H. Sommerstein), Warminster 1994.

ARISTOTLE, *The Basic Works of Aristotle* (ed. by Richard McKeon) New York 1941.

EURIPIDES, *The Bacchae* (trans. by William Arrowsmith) Chicago 1959.

—— *Electra* (trans. by Emily Townsend Vermeule) Chicago 1959.

—— *Hippolytus* (trans. by David Grene) Chicago 1942.

—— *Iphigenia in Aulis* (trans. by Charles R. Walker) Chicago 1958.

—— *Iphigenia in Tauris* (trans. by Witter Bynner) Chicago 1956.

—— *Medea*

—— *Orestes* (trans. by William Arrowsmith) Chicago 1958.

—— *The Phoenician Women* (trans. by Elizabeth Wyckoff) Chicago 1959.

—— *The Trojan Women* (trans. by Richmond Lattimore) Chicago 1958.

HERODOTUS, *The History* (trans. by David Grene), Chicago/London 1987.

HESIOD, *The Homeric Hymns and Homerica* (Loeb Class Lib. 57) (trans. by Hugh G. Evelyn-White) Cambridge and Heinemann 1974.

—— *Theogony and Works and Days* (trans. by Dorothea Wender) Harmondsworth 1973.

HOMER, *The Iliad* (trans. by Richmond Lattimore) Chicago 1951.

—— *The Odyssey* (trans. by Richmond Lattimore) Chicago 1965.

PLATO, *Alcibiades I* (Loeb Class. Lib. 201) (trans. by W.R.M. Lamb) Cambridge and Heinemann 1927.

—— *The Collected Dialogues of Plato* (ed. by Edith Hamilton and Huntington Cairns) Princeton 1961.

THE PRESOCRATICS

—— *The First Philosophers of Greece* (trans. by Arthur Fairbanks), London 1898.

—— *The Art and Thought of Heraclitus* (trans. by Charles H. Kahn), Cambridge 1995.

SAPPHO, *Sappho: A New Translation* (trans. by Mary Barnard) Berkeley 1975.

SOPHOCLES, *Ajax* (trans. by John Moore) Chicago 1957.

—— *Ajax* (trans. by Richard Jebb) Amsterdam 1967 (rep. 1907).

—— *Antigone* (trans. by Elizabeth Wyckoff) Chicago 1954.

—— *Electra* (trans. by David Grene) Chicago 1959.

—— *Oedipus at Colonus* (trans. by Robert Fitzgerald) Chicago 1941.

—— *Oedipus the King* (trans. by David Grene) Chicago 1942.

—— *Philoctetes* (trans. by David Grene) Chicago 1957.

THUCYDIDES, *The Peloponnesian War* (trans. by Rex Warner) Middlesex/New York 1954.

XENOPHON, *Apology and Symposium* (trans. by Raymond Larson) Kansas 1980.

—— *Memorabilia and Oeconomicus* (Loeb Class. Lib. 168) (trans. by E. C. Marchant) Cambridge and Heinemann 1968.

3. Secondary literature, including other Greek editions and commentaries

A Commentary on Homer's Odyssey, ed. by Alfred Heubeck *et. al.*, vol. 1-3, Oxford 1990-92.

ADKINS, ARTHUR W. H., *Merit and Responsibility: A Study in Greek Values*, Oxford 1960.

After Ovid: New Metamorphoses, ed. by Michael Hofmann and James Lasdum, New York 1994.

ANDERSEN, ØVIND, "Odysseus and The Wooden Horse," in *Symbolae Osloenses* 52, 1977.

AUERBACH, ERICH, *Mimesis: The Representation of Reality in Western Literature* (1946), Princeton 1953.

AUSTIN, N., *Archery at the Dark of the Moon. Poetic Problems in Homer's Odyssey*, Berkeley 1975.

BACHOFEN, JOHANN J., *Myth, Religion and Mother Right: Selected Writings*, Princeton 1967.

BARRETT, W.S., *Euripides: Hippolytos*, with commentary (1964), Oxford 1992.

BOITANI, PIERO, *Ulysses: Figures of a Myth*, Oxford 1994.

BORNEMANN, ERNST, *Das Patriarchat. Ursprung und Geschichte unseres Gesellschaft-systems*, Frankfurt 1975.

BOWRA, C.M., *Heroic Poetry*, London 1966.

—— *Sophoclean Tragedy* (1945), Oxford 1967.

BREMMER, JAN, *The Early Greek Concept and the Soul*, Princeton 1983.

BURNET, JOHN, *Plato: Euthyphro, Apology of Socrates, Crito*. Greek ed. with commentary (1924), Oxford 1977.

CASSIRER, ERNST, *An Essay on Man*, 1965.

CLAY, J., "The Planktai and Moly; Divine Naming and Knowing in Homer," *Hermes* 100, 1972.

CROPP, M.J., *Euripides: Electra*, Greek ed. with commentary, Wiltshire 1988.

DAWE, R.D., *Sophocles: Oedipus Rex*. Greek ed. with commentary, Cambridge 1982/95

DETIENNE, MARCEL, *L'invention de la mythologie*, Paris 1981.

—— and Jean-Pierre Vernant, *Cunning Intelligence in Greek Culture and Society* (1974), Chicago/London 1991.

DODDS, E.R., *The Ancient Concept of Progress and other Essays on Greek Literature and Belief*, Oxford 1973.

—— *The Greeks and the Irrational* (1951), Berkeley 1984.

DOVER, K.J., *Greek Homosexuality*, Cambridge 1978.

—— *Greek Popular Morality in the Time of Plato and Aristotle*, Oxford 1974.

DOVER, KENNETH, *Plato: Symposium*, Greek ed. with commentary, Cambridge 1980/95

DUBOIS, PAGE, *Centaurs and Amazons: Women and the Pre-History of the Great Chain of Being*, Ann Arbor 1982.

—— *Sowing the Body: Psychoanalysis and Ancient Representations of Women*, Chicago 1988.

DUNBAR, H. AND B. MARZULLO, *A Complete Concordance to the Odyssey on Homer*, Olms 1962.

ECKERT, C.W., "Initiation Motifs in the Story of Telemachus," in *Classical Journal* 59, 1963.

EDWARDS, ANTHONY T., "Achilles in the Odyssey: Ideologies of Heroism in the Homeric Epic," *Beiträge zur klassischen Philologie* 171, Königsheim 1985.

ELIADE, MIRCEA, *Archaic Techniques of Ecstasy*, London 1964.

—— *The History of Religious Ideas: From the Stone Age to the Eleusinian Mysteries,* vol. 1, 1984.

—— *The Myth of the Eternal Return* (1949), 2nd. rev. ed. 1997.

—— *Rites and Symbols of Initiation. The Mysteries of Birth and Rebirth*, (1958), Connecticut 1995.

ELSE, GERALD F., *The Origin and Early Form of Greek Tragedy*, Cambridge 1965.

Essays on the Odyssey, ed. by Charles H. Taylor Jr., Bloomington/ London 1962.

FINLEY, M.I., *The World of Odysseus* (1954), Penguin Books 1986.

FRAME, DOUGLAS, *The Myth of Return in Early Greek Epic*, New Haven 1978.

FRAZER, J.G., *The Golden Bough*, IV, New York/ London 1919.

FRIIS JOHANSEN, HOLGER, *Arkaisk græsk lyrik*, Copenhagen 1995.

FRIIS JOHANSEN, KARSTEN, *A History of Ancient Philosophy From the Beginnings to Augustine* (1991), Routledge 1999.

FRÄNKEL, HERMANN, *Early Greek Poetry and Philosophy*, New York/London 1975.

FRYE, NORTHROP, *The Great Code: The Bible and Literature* (1981), 1992.

GAGARIN, MICHAEl, *Aeschylean Drama*, Berkeley 1976.

GELLIE, G.H., *Sophocles: A Reading*, Melbourne 1972.

Gods and Heroes of the Bronze Age. Europe at the Time of Ulysses, Copenhagen 1998.

GOLDHILL, S.D., *Language, Sexuality, Narrative: The Oresteia*, Cambridge 1984.

GRANT, MICHAEL, *Myths of the Greeks and Romans* (1962), Meridian Book 1995.

GRIFFITH, MARK, *The Authenticity of "Prometheus Bound"*, Cambridge 1977.

GUHL, E. AND W. KORNER, *The Greeks: Their Life and Customs*, London 1994.

HAINSWORTH, J.B., *The Flexibility of the Homeric Formula*, Oxford 1968.

HALPERIN, DAVID D., *One Hundred Years of Homosexuality*, New York/London 1990.

HAMPE, R. AND E. SIMON, *Tausend Jahre frühgriechische Kunst*, Berlin 1980.

HARRISON, JANE E., *Prolegomena to the Study of Greek Religion* (1901), Cambridge, 3rd ed.1922.

—— *Themis: A Study or the Social Origins of Greek Religion* (1912), Cambridge, 2nd ed. 1927

HAVELOCK, ERIC A., *The Greek Concept of Justice: From Its Shadow in Homer to Its Substance in Plato*, Cambridge 1978.

—— *The Muse Learns to Write. Reflections on Orality and Literacy from Antiquity to the Present*, New Haven 1986.

—— *Preface to Plato*, Oxford 1963.

HERRIGEL, EUGEN, *Zen in the Art of Archery*, 1987.

HOEKSTRA, A., *Homeric Modifications of Formulaic Prototypes*, Amsterdam 1964.

HOGAN, JAMES C., *Aeschylos. A Commentary on the Complete Greek Tragedies*, Chicago/London 1984.

—— *The Plays of Sophocles*, Bristol 1991.

HORKHEIMER, MAX AND TH. W. ADORNO, *The Dialectic of Enlightenment*, London 1972.

HÖISTAD, RAGNAR, *Cynic Hero and Cynic King. Studies in the Cynic Conception of Man*, Lund 1948.

JAEGER, WERNER, *Paideia: The Ideals of Greek Culture*, vol. 1-3, New York 1943-45.

JAMES, E.O., *The Cult of the Mother-Goddess: An Archaelogical and Documentary Study*, London 1959.

JANKO, RICHARD, *Homer, Hesiod and the Hymns*, Cambridge 1982.

JAYNES, JULIAN, *The Origin of Consciousness in the Breakdown of the Bicameral Mind*, Boston 1977.

JUST, ROGER, *Women in Athenian Law and Life*, New York/London 1989.

KAHN, CHARLES H., *The Art and Thought of Heraclitus* (1979), ed. with commentary, Cambridge 1995.

KERÉNYI, KARL, *Hermes—Guide of Souls*, Zurich 1976.

KIERKEGAARD, SØREN: *The Concept of Irony With Constant Reference to Socrates* (trans. by Lee M. Capel), Bloomington/London 1965.

KIRK, G.S. (ed.), *The Iliad. A Commentary*, vol. 1-6, Cambridge 1995-96.

—— *Myth: Its Meaning and Functions in Ancient and Other Cultures*, Berkeley 1970.

—— *The Songs of Homer*, Cambridge 1962.

KITTO, H.D., *Greek Tragedy: A Literary Study* (1939), London 1973.

LACEY, W.K., *The Family in Classical Greece*, London 1968.

LANGER, SUSANNE K., *Philosophy in a New Key: A Study in the Symbolism of Reason, Rite, and Art*, Harvard Univ. Press 1974.

LEBECK, ANNE, *The Oresteia: A Study in Language and Structure*, Cambridge 1971.

LINDSAY, JACK, *The Clashing Rocks: A Study of Early Greek Religion and Culture and the Origins of Drama*, London 1965.

LLOYD-JONES, HUGH, *The Justice of Zeus*, Berkeley 1971.

LORD, ALBERT B., *The Singers of Tales*, Cambridge 1964.

MARCUSE, HERBERT, *Eros and Civilization: A Philosophical Inquiry into Freud* (1955), London 1970.

MAUSS, MARCEL, *The Gift: The Form and Reason for Exchange in Archaic Societies* (1924) London 2001.

MUMFORD, LEWIS, *The Story of Utopias*, New York 1962.

MURRAY, GILBERT, *The Rise of the Greek Epic*, Oxford 1934.

MURRAY, OSWYN, *Early Greece* (1978), 2nd. ed. 1993.

MÜLLER, HERMANN, *Odysseus: Mann, Seele und Schicksal, Chemnitz*, 2nd. ed. 1932.

Myth: A Symposium, ed. by Thomas A. Sebeok, Bloomington/London, 5th ed. 1972.

NAGY, GREGORY, *The Best of the Achaeans: Concepts of the Hero in Archaic Greek Poetry*, Baltimore 1979.

NEUMANN, ERICH, *The Origins and History of Consciousness* (1949), Princeton 1973.

NIETZSCHE, FR., *The Birth of Tragedy* in *The Basic Writings of Nietzsche* (ed. and trans. by Walter Kaufmann), New York 1966.

NILSSON, MARTIN P., *Primitive Time Reckoning*, Lund 1920.

Njal's Saga (*The Story of Burnt Njal*, trans. by George Dasent), London 1861.

NORTH, HELEN, *Sophrosyne: Self-Knowledge and Self-Restraint in Greek Literature*, Ithaca/New York 1966.

ONG, WALTER J., *Orality and Literacy. The Technologizing of the World* (1982), New York/London 1991.

ONIANS, R.B., *The Origins of European Thought: About the Body, the Mind, the Soul, the World, Time and Fate* (1951), Cambridge 1988.

PAGE DENYS, *The Homeric Odyssey*, Oxford 1955.

PARKER, ROBERT, *Miasma: Pollution and Purification in Early Greek Religion*, Oxford 1983.

PICARD-CAMBRIDGE, ARTHUR, *The Dramatic Festivals of Athens*, Oxford 1968.

—— *The Theatre of Dionysos in Athens*, Oxford (1946) 1976.

POMERY, SARAH B., *Goddesses, Whores, Wives and Slaves*, New York 1975.

POWELL, BARRY B., *Homer and the Origin of the Greek Alphabet*, Cambridge 1991.

PRENDERGAST, G. L. AND B. MARZULLO, *A Complete Concordance to the* Iliad *of Homer*, Olms 1962.

PRYTZ JOHANSEN, J., "Primitive Religion," in *Illustreret Religionshistorie*, vol. 1, Copenhagen 1968.

PUCCI, PIETRO, *Hesiod and the Language of Poetry*, London 1977.

—— *Odysseus Polytropos: Intertextual Readings in the Odyssey and the Iliad*, Ithaca/London 1987.

RADIN, PAUL, *The Trickster: A Study in American Indian Mythology*. With Commentaries by Karl Kerény and C.G. Jung, London 1956.

RAVEN, J.E., *Plato's Thought in the Making*, Cambridge 1965.

REEVE, C.D.C., *Socrates in the Apology: An Essay on Plato's Apology of Socrates*, Indianapolis/Cambridge 1989.

REYNOLDS, MARY T., *Joyce and Dante: The Shaping Imagination*, Princeton 1981.

RICHARDSON, SCOTT, *The Homeric Narrator*, Tennessee 1990.

ROHDE, E., *Psyche: The Cult of Souls and Belief in Immortality Among the Greeks*, New York/London 1925.

Rose, Peter W., *Sons of the Gods, Children of Earth: Ideology and Literary Form in Ancient Greece*, Ithaca/London 1992.

Rowe, C.J., *Plato: Phaedo*. Greek ed. with commentary, Cambridge 1993.

Russo, Joseph A., "The Inner Man in Archilochus and the Odyssey," in *Greek, Roman and Byzantine Studies* 15, Texas 1974.

Schadewaldt, Wolfgang, *Von Homers Welt und Werk*, Stuttgart 1965.

Schefold, K., *Götter—und Heldensagen der Griechen in der früh—und hocharchaischen Kunst*, Frankfurt 1993.

Seeck, Otto, *Quellen der Odyssee*, Berlin 1887.

Segal, Charles P., "The Phaeacians and the Symbolism of Odysseus' Return," in *Arion* vol. 1, no. 4, Texas 1962.

Skafte Jensen, Minna: *The Homeric Question and the Oral-Formulaic Theory*, Copenhagen 1980.

Snell, Bruno, *The Discovery of the Mind: The Greek Origins of European Thought* (1953), New York 1960.

Snodgrass, Anthony M., *The Dark Age of Greece: An Archaelogical Survey of the Eleventh to the Eighth Centuries BC*, Edinburgh 1971.

Sommerstein, Alan H., *Aeschylus: Eumenides*, Greek ed. with commentary, Cambridge 1989.

Sparkes, B.A., "The Trojan Horse in Classical Art," in *Greece and Rome*, London 1969-80, no. 18.

Stanford, W.B., *The Ulysses Theme: A Study in the Adaptability of a Traditional Hero*, 2nd ed. Oxford 1968.

Stelzenberger, Johann, *Syneidesis, Conscientia, Gewissen*. Paderborn 1963.

Stenius, Erik, *Tankens gryning*, 2nd ed. Helsinki 1975.

Suzuki, Mikoho, *Metamorphoses of Helen: Authority, Difference and the Epic*, Ithaca 1989.

Taylor, Charles H., "The Obstacles to Odysseus' Return: Identity and Consciousness in the Odyssey," in *Yale Review* Autumn 1960, New York 1961.

Thomson, J.A.K., *Studies in the Odyssey*, Oxford 1914.

Thornton, Agathe, *People and Themes in Homer's Odyssey*, London 1970.

—— *Troia. Traum und Wirklichkeit*, Stuttgart 2001.

—— *Ulysse. Il mito e la memoria*, Rome 1996.

Vernant, Jean-Pierre, *Mythe et pensée chez les Grecs*, Paris 1965. *The Origins of Greek Thought*, Ithaca 1982.

Virgil, *The Aeneid*. Trans. by Robert Fitzgerald, New York 1981.

West, M.L., *Hesiod: Theogony*, Oxford 1966.

Williams, Bernard, *Shame and Necessity*, Berkeley 1993.

Wilson Edmund, *The Wound and the Bow: Seven Studies in Literature* (1941), London 1961.

Wilson, Lyn H., *Sappho's Sweet Bitter Songs: Configuration of Female and Male in Ancient Greek Lyric*, New York/London 1996.

Winnington-Ingram, R.P., *Sophocles: An Interpretation*, Cambridge 1980.

—— *Studies in Aeschylus*, Cambridge 1983.

INDEX

The index, especially the part relating to the first main section of the book, is selective. Homer, his two epics and Odysseus appear so often in that section that only the most significant references are noted. The names of scholars appearing in the main text and in important contexts in the notes are included.